The Developing Structure of Temperament and Personality from Infancy to Adulthood

The Developing Structure of Temperament and Personality from Infancy to Adulthood

Edited by:

Charles F. Halverson, Jr.
University of Georgia

Geldolph A. Kohnstamm
Leiden University

Roy P. Martin
University of Georgia

LEA LAWRENCE ERLBAUM ASSOCIATES, PUBLISHERS
1994 Hillsdale, New Jersey   Hove, UK

Copyright © 1994 by Lawrence Erlbaum Associates, Inc.
All rights reserved. No part of this book may be reproduced in any form, by photostat, microfilm, retrieval system, or any other means, without the prior written permission of the publisher.

Lawrence Erlbaum Associates, Inc., Publishers
365 Broadway
Hillsdale, New Jersey 07642

Library of Congress Cataloging-in-Publication Data

The Developing structure of temperament and personality from infancy to adulthood / edited by Charles F. Halverson, Jr., Geldolph A. Kohnstamm, Roy P. Martin.
    p.   cm.
Includes bibliographical references and index.
ISBN 0-8058-1252-0 (c)   ISBN 0-8058-1669-0 (p)
1. Temperament. 2. Personality. 3. Individual differences. 4. Developmental psychology. I. Halverson, Charles F., 1938– . II. Kohnstamm, Geldolph A., 1937– . III. Martin, Roy P., 1943– .
BF811.D48 1994
155.2'5—dc20   93-50639
                                                                             CIP

Books published by Lawrence Erlbaum Associates are printed on acid-free paper, and their bindings are chosen for strength and durability.

Printed in the United States of America
10 9 8 7 6 5 4 3 2 1

CONTENTS

Preface ix

PART I CURRENT CONCEPTIONS OF THE STRUCTURE OF ADULT PERSONALITY 1

1 The Big Five Factor Structure as an Integrative Framework: An Empirical Comparison with Eysenck's P-E-N Model 7
 Lewis R. Goldberg and Tina K. Rosolack

2 The Big Five or Giant Three: Criteria for a Paradigm 37
 H. J. Eysenck

3 An Alternative Five-Factor Model for Personality 53
 Marvin Zuckerman

4 Temperament and the Big Five Factors of Personality 69
 Alois Angleitner and Fritz Ostendorf

5 The Big Five: A Tip of the Iceberg of Individual Differences 91
 Boele De Raad, A. A. Jolijn Hendriks, and Willem K. B. Hofstee

6	Structural Models for Multimode Designs in Personality and Temperament Research *A. T. Panter, J. S. Tanaka, and Rick H. Hoyle*	111
7	Stability and Change in Personality From Adolescence Through Adulthood *Paul T. Costa, Jr. and Robert R. McCrae*	139

PART II	EMERGING CONCEPTIONS OF THE CHILDHOOD PRECURSORS OF PERSONALITY STRUCTURE	151
8	Review of Factor Analytic Studies of Temperament Measures Based on the Thomas–Chess Structural Model: Implications for the Big Five *Roy P. Martin, Joseph Wisenbaker, and Matti Huttunen*	157
9	Temperament, Development, and the Five-Factor Model: Lessons from Activity Level *Warren O. Eaton*	173
10	Temperament, Development, and the Big Five *Stephan A. Ahadi and Mary K. Rothbart*	189
11	Fit, Context, and the Transition Between Temperament and Personality *Theodore D. Wachs*	209

PART III	DERIVING THE FIVE-FACTOR MODEL FROM PARENTAL RATINGS OF CHILDREN AND ADOLESCENTS	221
12	Infant Temperament and Early Childhood Functioning: Possible Relations to the Five-Factor Model *Berit Hagekull*	227
13	Genetics of Personality: A Twin Study of the Five-Factor Model and Parent–Offspring Analyses *H. H. Goldsmith, Sandra H. Losoya, Donna L. Bradshaw, and J. J. Campos*	241
14	Major Dimensions of Personality in Early Adolescence: The Big Five and Beyond *Richard W. Robins, Oliver P. John, and Avshalom Caspi*	267

15	The Big Five Personality Factors in Q-Sort Descriptions of Children and Adolescents *Cornelis F. M. van Lieshout and Gerbert J. T. Haselager*	293

PART IV DERIVING THE FIVE-FACTOR MODEL FROM TEACHER RATINGS OF CHILDREN AND ADOLESCENTS 319

16	Child Personality and Temperament: Does the Five-Factor Model Embrace Both Domains? *John M. Digman*	323
17	The Development of Agreeableness as a Dimension of Personality *William G. Graziano*	339
18	The Five-Factor Model Applied to Individual Differences in School Behavior *James B. Victor*	355

PART V A RESEARCH AGENDA FOR THE STUDY OF PERSONALITY AND TEMPERAMENT IN CHILDHOOD BASED ON FREE DESCRIPTION 367

19	Parents' Use of Big Five Categories in Their Natural Language Descriptions of Children *Valerie L. Havill, Kathryn Allen, Charles F. Halverson, and Geldolph A. Kohnstamm*	371
20	A Five-Factor Model Classification of Teachers' Constructs on Individual Differences Among Children Ages 4 to 12 *Ivan Mervielde*	387
21	The Five-Factor Model in Child Psychiatry: Parents' Free Personality Descriptions of Their Children *A. W. Goedhart, Ph. D. A. Treffers, and Geldolph A. Kohnstamm*	399
	Author Index	413
	Subject Index	425

PREFACE

This book had its beginnings as far back as a meeting of the "Occasional Conference" of temperament researchers in Athens, Georgia, a number of years ago. At that conference, the senior editor became acquainted with the research of the other two editors of this volume. Through a series of discussions, one of us (Halverson) was invited to visit Holland (Kohnstamm), where much important research on individual differences was taking place. Both Kohnstamm and Halverson spent a productive year as fellows at the Netherlands Institute of Advanced Study in Humanities and Social Sciences (NIAS), where much of the intellectual work for this volume was accomplished. Together with Roy Martin, we planned a workshop at NIAS to bring together researchers in individual differences in personality and temperament to explore whether there was any unity possible between the temperament researchers of infancy and childhood and the major researchers in adult personality.

During the NIAS year, we explored the literature that seemed to be documenting a growing consensus on the part of the adult personality researchers that five major personality dimensions may be sufficient to account for most of the important variance in adult individual differences in personality. This growing consensus was in marked contrast to the apparent disarray of the literature on child and infant individual differences, where there seemed to be a wide variety of opinions regarding the basic dimensions of difference in personality or temperament.

We believed we could encourage researchers from both the adult and child areas to consider the importance of a life-span conceptualization of individual differences if we could get them to discuss their research in terms of continuity in conceptualization of personality research across the life span. The conference was held at NIAS in Wassenaar, Holland, in 1991, where many of the preliminary papers for this volume were first presented. The chapters presented in this book are written by some of the most distinguished scholars in both the adult personality area and the area of temperament in infancy and childhood, and capture the excitement and stimulation we all felt at the original conference.

By sharing their recent data, techniques, and theoretical speculations, these authors have communicated the enthusiasm engendered by the growing consensus about the adult Big Five, as well as the exciting prospects of an integrative program of research from infancy to adulthood that will clarify and consolidate what is now a disparate set of methods, theory, and findings across the life span. We expect this volume will have considerable heuristic value in stimulating researchers to conceptualize their research in developmental, life-span approaches that will lead to a consolidation of individual differences research at every age.

We have organized the volume into five sections and have prepared an introduction to each section to help the reader with the issues raised by the authors. Some might perceive the order of the chapters as perverse. We begin with those contributed by researchers who have focused almost exclusively on adult personality. Some would want us, as developmentalists, to start at the beginning, with infancy. We did not, because it was the exciting research on the adult Big Five that originally led us to ask why there was no comparable consensus among infant and child researchers, and to ask why the adult and child researchers did not acknowledge each other at all. We believe it best to start with the convincing research on adults that shows there really may be a set of dimensions worthy of developmental investigation. This initial section on adult personality is followed by others documenting the emerging conceptions of childhood precursors of adult personality structure from infancy through adolescence. We conclude the volume with chapters outlining a research agenda for exploring the issues of personality structure in infancy and childhood.

We sincerely hope these chapters will raise new questions about the unity of personality over the life span. If we can work toward a common taxonomy, we can ask more interesting questions. For example, temperament approaches may map onto the Big Five dimensions at different times during childhood. Such links could provide important clues at to how personality develops and changes, and how and when certain personality traits emerge. Such research would help integrate the research on infant and child temperament and adult personality— domains that have until now remained separate areas of interest and scholarship.

The editors of this volume have many people to thank for their generous support in making this volume. We are deeply indebted to the Netherlands Institute of Advanced Study in Humanities and Social Science (NIAS) for providing the freedom to write and think during Halverson's and Kohnstamm's fellowship year. In addition, they provided much support for the conference that spawned the volume. Support also has come from our universities, Leiden University and the University of Georgia. We have also been supported by funds from the National Institute of Mental Health in the United States and the Royal Netherlands Academy of Arts and Science. We would also like to thank our research teams in both countries, who have provided much enthusiasm and hard work toward the realization of this project, especially Val Havill, Kathy Allen, Hallie Duke, Qiying Zhou, Hilary Rose, Eric Elphick, and Anne Marie Slotboom.

—Charles F. Halverson, Jr.
—Geldolph A. Kohnstamm
—Roy P. Martin

PART

I

CURRENT CONCEPTIONS OF THE STRUCTURE OF ADULT PERSONALITY

In this first section of the book, we have collected a set of chapters that fairly accurately mirrors the current conceptions, strategies and, to some extent, the controversies surrounding the development of taxonomies of adult personality. We do not recount here the long and complex history of the search for "the taxonomy" of adult personality, but simply say that the number of personality dimensions proposed, and the number of instruments created to measure them, is nothing short of remarkable (see for example, Goldberg, 1971; John, 1990; Wiggins & Trapnell, in press, for the detailed history of the search for personality structure).

Although such theoretical and methodological diversity may make the history of personality psychology exciting and challenging, it can, at the same time, make progress nearly impossible. In recent years there has been much emphasis on the search for a common set of personality descriptors that would identify a common dimensional structure. Such a common dimensional structure would facilitate an orderly accumulation of knowledge and stimulate more scholarly exchange of research findings.

Among personality psychologists there is a rapidly growing consensus that the domain of individual differences in adulthood, as measured by rating scales and questionnaire items, is almost completely described by five broad factors (e.g., Digman, 1989, 1990; Goldberg, 1981, 1990; McCrae & Costa, 1985, 1987;

McCrae, Costa, & Busch, 1986). This five-factor model of personality has proved robust across different groups of subjects, item pools, instruments, and methods of analysis, as well as across different languages and cultures. Major replications of the five factors obtained with English-speaking Americans have also been obtained in Holland (e.g., Hofstee & Van Heck, 1990) and Germany (e.g., Ostendorf, 1990).

Although theoretical explanations for these remarkable empirical regularities have begun to emerge (Buss, 1991; Costa, McCrae, & Dembroski, 1988; Hogan, 1983; John, 1990; Wiggins & Trapnell, in press), the Big Five model in adulthood owes its power more to the replicability of empirical results than to a set of generally accepted theoretical axioms about human personality structure. These models have not, however, obtained monolithic status. There is still serious debate about the generality of each of the dimensions, as well as the need for fewer or more dimensions in a "basic" personality taxonomy. The chapters in this section give the reader an excellent overview of the status of the major personality taxonomies and some of the continuing controversies in the field.

In chapter 1, Goldberg and Rosolack provide a convincing illustration of the power of the Big Five model to serve as a framework for comparison to other taxonomies such as Eysenck's well-known three-factor P-E-N model. By having Eysenck judge where each of the Goldberg Big Five clusters was located in his P-E-N model, Goldberg and Rosolak demonstrated that, contrary to Eysenck's assertions, the P-E-N model is not at a higher order level than the Big Five taxonomy; rather, E and N map onto the Extraversion and Neuroticism Big Five dimensions and Psychoticism appears to be a blend of Agreeableness and Conscientiousness (low), not a higher order dimension.

Eysenck, in chapter 2, remains unconvinced, arguing that his P-E-N system is more viable, being related to a wide nomological net of relations that have been theoretically predicted. The argument is mainly about what dimensions there may be beyond E and N (because the two major paradigms agree on those two dimensions). Eysenck discusses an extensive and impressive set of studies that he believes fills in much of the theoretically predicted nomological net with empirical findings ranging from biological causes to social consequences of P. The reader must judge the evidence provided by Eysenck as to whether P is more than "A" (Agreeableness) and "C" (Conscientiousness) from the Big Five. Clearly, the empirical work on the nomological nets of A and C remains to be done, but it could turn out to confirm any one of a variety of possibilities, from Eysenck's independent P notion to Goldberg and Rosolak's assertion that P is just a blend of A and C.

Adding to the previous discussion on taxonomy is Zuckerman's presentation of an alternative five-factor model, outlined in chapter 3. Zuckerman begins with factor analyses of personality and temperament questionnaire scales that show both established empirical validity and evidence of biological correlates. Like Eysenck, Zuckerman believes the determination of "basic factors" lies not in the lexicon, but in the nomological nets of constructs predicted from psychobiological theories. Further, he is suspicious of personality constructs based on single words or short phrases (as opposed to theoretically derived items describing a particular behavior or set of behaviors). Zuckerman goes on to reprise his steps in deriving his alternative five-factor model. It is based on several analyses of scales from a wide variety of questionnaires that meet his biological–nomological net criteria. Through several iterations and replications, Zuckerman describes three to six factors recovered from his analyses. With a final instrument in hand, he then compares his model to Eysenck's P-E-N and the Big Five model. Zuckerman clearly shows that Eysenck's P shares much variance with his own "impulsive sensation-seeking" variable and the Big Five construct of Conscientiousness, even though the labels sound quite different. Even though Zuckerman's, Eysenck's, and Costa and McCrae's models clearly stem from different assumptions, there is an impressive amount of overlap. The editors would like to see, however, some of Zuckerman's analyses done at the *item* level rather than the *scale* level. Scale-level factors analyses are biased heavily by the inclusiveness of the scales, whereas item factor analyses are not. It would be interesting to see if his constructs survived item-level factor analyses.

Following directly from the previous consideration is chapter 4 by Angleitner and Ostendorf, who also searched for a common structure among a group of temperament and personality instruments. Angleitner and Ostendorf had a group of adults respond to four widely used temperament inventories and two measures of the five-factor model of personality. Through a series of analyses, these authors clearly derived the Big Five personality structure, plus a sixth factor defined by Rhythmicity scales of the Dimensions of Temperament Scale. Given these diverse inventories, the confirmation of a single five-factor model subsuming both temperament and personality measures is impressive.

Chapter 5 by De Raad, Hendriks, and Hofstee extends the basic Big Five lexical model in important ways. These authors point out that taking measurement of personality structure one trait at a time is a problematic procedure because many trait descriptors have factor loadings on more than one of the Big Five. If one stays with the best descriptors (those with high loadings on only one trait) much of importance for person description is left out. Their solution is to combine the Big Five approach with the circumplex model, which has also a long, distinguished history in personality measurement (Trapnell & Wiggins, 1990; Wiggins, 1980).

De Raad and his colleagues show nicely how personality descriptions in the Dutch language are best represented by their intersection with two of the Big Five dimensions. In fact, the 10 two-dimensional spaces generated by the Big Five model can map nearly all personality words! The empirical finding that most words almost always load on *only* two dimensions means that this Abridged Big Five Circumplex (AB5C) model can represent the subtleties of person description. It may be that humans' mental structures for describing the nuances of individual differences are realized by a five-dimensional module that is tremendously generative yet relatively simple!

Chapter 6 by Panter, Tanaka, and Hoyle presents researchers with some old and new techniques to compare findings across test batteries. We believe it very important to acquaint personality researchers with improved and less biased ways to estimate a structure from two or more personality batteries. The chapter contains some needed precautions in interpreting the robustness of a particular model like the Big Five from the shared covariation across instruments, time, and/or informants. Using both exploratory and confirmatory models they give us important guidelines to test models for congruence and invariance.

Finally, Costa and McCrae examine the stability of the Big Five structure from age 12 to 63 years. That the Big Five is very stable in adulthood has been increasingly apparent to the authors from their earlier studies on the stability of personality (based on the Baltimore Longitudinal Study). They sought new data to determine in a more precise way when the major dimensions of personality reach maturity. Through a series of analyses, Costa and McCrae convincingly demonstrate both stability and change during late adolescence and early adulthood. There continue to be important developmental changes until about age 30, which the authors examine very carefully.

These seven chapters provide the reader with much data, theory, and different conceptualizations around the theme of the importance of some variant of the Big Five structure in adulthood. Subsequent portions of the book take up developmental themes in infancy and childhood in more detail. We need to move beyond adulthood and ask whether the Big Five model may be applied to earlier developmental periods. Further, we need research linking early temperament in infancy with the emergence of such personality concepts like Conscientiousness and Openness to Experience. These are the topics discussed in the remainder of the book.

REFERENCES

Buss, D. M. (1991). Evolutionary personality psychology. *Annual Review of Psychology, 42*, 459–491.

Costa, P. T., Jr., McCrae, R. R., & Dembroski, T. M. (1988). Agreeableness versus antagonism: Explication of a potential risk factor for children. In A. Siegman & T. M. Dembroski (Eds.), *In search of coronary-prone behavior* (pp. 41–63). Hillsdale, NJ: Lawrence Erlbaum Associates.

Digman, J. M. (1989). Five robust trait dimensions: Development, stability and utility. *Journal of Personality, 57*, 195–214.

Digman, J. M. (1990). Personality structure: Emergence of the five factor model. *Annual Review of Psychology, 41*, 417–440.

Goldberg, L. R. (1971). A historical survey of personality scales and surveys. In P. McReynolds (Ed.), *Advances in psychological assessment* (Vol. 2, pp. 293–336). Palo Alto, CA: Science and Behavior Books.

Goldberg, L. R. (1981). Language and individual differences: The search for universals in personality lexicons. In L. Wheeler (Ed.), *Review of personality and social psychology* (Vol. 2, pp. 141–165). Beverly Hills, CA: Sage.

Goldberg, L. R. (1990). An alternative "description of personality": The Big-Five factor structure. *Journal of Personality and Social Psychology, 59*, 1216–1229.

Hofstee, W. K. B., & Van Heck, G. L. (1990). Personality language [Special issue]. *European Journal of Personality, 4*.

Hogan, R. (1983). Socioanalytic theory of personality. In M. Page (Ed.), *1982 Nebraska symposium on motivation: Personality—current theory and research* (pp. 55–89). Lincoln, NE: University of Nebraska Press.

John, O. P. (1990). The "Big Five" factor taxonomy: Dimensions of personality in the natural language and in questionnaires. In L. A. Pervin (Ed.), *Handbook of personality: Theory and research* (pp. 66–100). New York: Guilford.

McCrae, R. R., & Costa, P. T. (1985). Updating Norman's "Adequate Taxonomy": In natural language and in questionnaires. *Journal of Personality and Social Psychology, 49*, 710–727.

McCrae, R. R., & Costa, P. T. (1987). Validation of the five factor model across instruments and observers. *Journal of Personality and Social Psychology, 52*, 81–90.

McCrae, R. R., Costa, P. T., & Busch, C. M. (1986). Evaluating comprehensiveness in personality systems: The California Q-set and the five-factor model. *Journal of Personality, 54*, 430–446.

Ostendorf, F. (1990). *Sprache und Persönlichkeitstruktur: Zur Validität des Fünf-Faktoren-Modells der Persönlichkeit* [Language and personality structure: Toward the validation of the five-factor model of personality]. Regensburg, Germany: S. Roderer Verlag.

Trapnell, P. D., & Wiggins, J. S. (1990). Extension of the interpersonal adjective scales to include the Big Five dimensions of personality. *Journal of Personality and Social Psychology, 59*, 781–790.

Wiggins, J. S. (1980). Circumplex models of interpersonal behavior. In L. Wheeler (Ed.), *Review of personality and social psychology* (Vol. 1, pp. 265–294). Beverly Hills, CA: Sage.

Wiggins, J. S., & Trapnell, P. D. (in press). Personality structure: The return of the Big Five. In R. Hogan, J. Johnson, & S. Briggs (Eds.), *Handbook of personality psychology*. San Diego, CA: Academic Press.

CHAPTER

1

THE BIG FIVE FACTOR STRUCTURE AS AN INTEGRATIVE FRAMEWORK: AN EMPIRICAL COMPARISON WITH EYSENCK'S P-E-N MODEL

Lewis R. Goldberg
Tina K. Rosolack
University of Oregon and Oregon Research Institute

The past decade has witnessed an electrifying burst of interest by scientists studying personality traits in the most fundamental problem of the field—the search for a scientifically compelling taxonomy of individual differences. More importantly, a consensus is emerging about the general framework of such a taxonomic representation. As a consequence, the scientific study of personality dispositions, which had been in the doldrums in the 1970s, is again an intellectually vigorous enterprise poised on the brink of a solution to a scientific problem whose roots extend back at least to Aristotle.

Specifically, across a wide variety of trait-descriptive terms, five orthogonal dimensions have consistently been found to be both necessary and sufficient to account for the interrelations among those terms. Moreover, this Big Five model has been shown to be a generalization of previous circumplex models of personality, such as the Interpersonal Circle (Hofstee, de Raad, & Goldberg, 1992; Peabody & Goldberg, 1989; Saucier, 1992). The longitudinal stability of the five factors has been demonstrated both in children (e.g., Digman & Inouye, 1986) and in adults (e.g., Costa & McCrae, 1988), and the structure has been shown to be virtually identical in self and observer ratings (e.g., Goldberg, 1990; McCrae & Costa, 1985b, 1987). Markers of the Big Five factors are now available using both trait-descriptive terms (Goldberg, 1990, 1992; Trapnell & Wiggins, 1990) and questionnaire statements (Costa & McCrae, 1985); see Briggs (1992) for a comparison among these alternative factor markers.

The present chapter has two major aims: to illustrate a general procedure for comparing alternative models of personality traits within the comprehensive representation provided by the Big Five factor structure, and to illustrate the power of such a comparative approach through a detailed examination of one particular personality model, Eysenck's three-factor Psychoticism-Extraversion-Neuroticism (P-E-N) representation, which is probably the most popular current competitor to the Big Five structure. More specifically, the chapter provides a first attempt to examine three prominent and influential current personality theories within the framework of the five-factor model. By providing theorists with a common language for describing their theories, we show how these theories can be contrasted and compared. In addition, we are able to compare the *explicit* relations postulated by a theorist in his writings with the *implicit* relations revealed when the theorist actually maps the facets of the Big Five model into his own theoretical structure. And, finally, we examine the relations between three important individual differences—intelligence, self-esteem, and sociopolitical attitudes—within this same five-factor framework.

THE BIG FIVE FACTOR STRUCTURE

The current five-factor representation was initially stimulated by Tupes and Christal (1961), who reanalyzed previous data sets using bipolar variables originally constructed by Cattell (1943, 1947). The Big Five factors are typically numbered and labeled: (I) Surgency (or Extraversion); (II) Agreeableness; (III) Conscientiousness; (IV) Emotional Stability; and (V) either Intellect or Openness to Experience. Given the strong consensus that has been emerging about the general nature of the Big Five domains, the disagreement about the specific nature of factor V is somewhat of a scientific embarrassment. The history of this controversy is included in several recent reviews of the Big Five model (e.g., Digman, 1990; John, 1990; McCrae & John, 1992; Wiggins & Pincus, 1992; Wiggins & Trapnell, in press).

Building on the earlier work of Allport and Odbert (1936) and Cattell (1947), Norman (1967) and Goldberg (1982, 1990) have been able to analyze a far larger and more representative pool of English trait terms than has been studied in the past, thereby providing more compelling evidence for the five-factor structure of the personality lexicon. For example, to establish the across-method generality of trait factor structures, Goldberg (1990) used 1,431 trait adjectives grouped into 75 clusters, and found virtually identical Big Five representations in 10 analyses, each based on a different factor analytic procedure. In a second study of 479 common trait adjectives grouped into 133 synonym clusters, Goldberg (1990) found the same five-factor structure in each of two samples of self ratings and each of two samples of peer ratings. None of the factors beyond the fifth generalized across the samples, thus establishing the generality of this structural representation across both targets and samples. In a third study, these synonym clusters were further refined by internal-consistency analyses, culminating in a set of 100 clusters derived from 339 trait adjectives.

Table 1.1 lists the terms in each of these clusters, as well as two indices of internal consistency—Coefficient Alpha and the mean interitem correlation. These values are based on a pooled sample from Goldberg (1990) that included 320 self descriptions plus 316 descriptions by the same subjects of others of their own age and sex whom they knew well and liked. For both subsets of the 636 targets, 587 trait adjectives were rated on nine-step scales. The tabled values are based on the standardized (z) scores of each subject across the 587 terms; on average, both estimates of homogeneity are about .06 higher when based on the original response values.

The average cluster includes three or four reasonably synonymous trait adjectives. Its mean item intercorrelation in this sample is .32, which is quite high for personality items. The average cluster has a Coefficient Alpha reliability of .57, which although low by absolute standards is extremely high for such short scales. The 100 clusters have now been analyzed in a variety of subject samples (e.g., Goldberg, 1990), where they have been shown to provide a structure that is virtually identical to those derived from much larger sets of trait terms. Moreover, the 100 clusters provide essentially the same factor structure for self and for peer descriptions.

A COMMON LANGUAGE FOR COMPARING PERSONALITY THEORIES

These 100 synonym clusters should be particularly useful as a framework for examining the structural dimensions proposed by personality theorists. Because the clusters were derived from studies of large and representative samples of common English trait-descriptive adjectives, they provide a broad-bandwidth assessment of the personality-trait domain. In addition, the 339 terms are part of the active vocabulary of most English speakers, and thus they are relatively easy to understand and to use. Moreover, in contrast to the few other sets of stimuli that have been used to compare theories, such as Block's (1961) California Q-Set, each of the clusters includes two or more terms, thus permitting an assessment of cluster reliability.

As an initial test of the utility of the 100 clusters as a framework for comparing alternative structural representations, we have begun with the theories of Eysenck, Cattell, and Tellegen. The locations of the clusters within the Psychoticism-Extraversion-Neuroticism (P-E-N) factors were provided by H. J. Eysenck, and are presented in Table 1.2. The locations of each of the 100 clusters within the 16 primary and 8 second-order factors in Cattell's system were provided by Eber, and are presented in Appendix A. And, finally, the locations of the 100 clusters within the 11 primary and 3 second-order factors from the Multidimensional Personality Questionnaire (MPQ) were provided by Tellegen, and are listed in Appendix B.

TABLE 1.1
The 100 Revised Synonym Clusters

Factor Pole	Cluster	Terms Included	Number of Terms	Reliability α	Mean r
I+					
	Gregariousness	Extroverted, gregarious, sociable	3	.59	.32
	Spirit	Enthusiastic, spirited, vivacious, zestful	4	.71	.38
	Expressiveness	Communicative, expressive, verbal	3	.65	.39
	Playfulness	Adventurous, mischievous, playful, rambunctious	4	.62	.30
	Energy Level	Active, energetic, vigorous	3	.69	.42
	Unrestraint	Impetuous, uninhibited, unrestrained	3	.36	.14
	Self-esteem	Assured, confident, proud	3	.58	.30
	Spontaneity	Carefree, happy-go-lucky, spontaneous	3	.58	.30
	Talkativeness	Talkative, verbose, wordy	3	.49	.24
	Assertion	Assertive, dominant, forceful	3	.65	.38
	Courage	Brave, courageous, daring	3	.71	.47
	Animation	Demonstrative, exhibitionistic, flamboyant	3	.40	.18
	Candor	Direct, frank, straightforward	3	.76	.51
	Ambition	Ambitious, enterprising, opportunistic	3	.54	.29
	Humor	Humorous, witty	2	.58	.41
	Optimism	Cheerful, jovial, merry, optimistic	4	.71	.38
I−					
	Silence	Quiet, silent, untalkative	3	.82	.61
	Aloofness	Seclusive, unsociable, withdrawn	3	.67	.40
	Shyness	Bashful, shy, timid	3	.83	.62
	Inhibition	Inhibited, restrained	2	.48	.32
	Unaggressiveness	Unadventurous, unaggressive, uncompetitive	3	.55	.29
	Reserve	Detached, reserved, secretive	3	.39	.18
	Insecurity	Defensive, fretful, insecure, negativistic, self-critical, self-pitying	6	.64	.23
	Passivity	Docile, passive, submissive	3	.57	.31
	Lethargy	Lethargic, sluggish	2	.43	.28
	Pessimism	Bitter, joyless, melancholic, moody, morose, pessimistic, somber	7	.61	.18
II+					
	Cooperation	Accommodating, agreeable, cooperative, helpful, patient, peaceful, reasonable	7	.71	.27
	Empathy	Considerate, kind, sympathetic, trustful, understanding	5	.73	.25
	Amiability	Amiable, cordial, friendly, genial, pleasant	5	.65	.27
	Leniency	Lenient, uncritical, undemanding	3	.48	.23
	Flexibility	Adaptable, flexible, obliging	3	.46	.22
	Courtesy	Courteous, diplomatic, polite, respectful, tactful	5	.63	.27
	Generosity	Benevolent, charitable, generous	3	.49	.23
	Modesty	Humble, modest, selfless, unassuming	4	.40	.14
	Warmth	Affectionate, compassionate, sentimental, warm	4	.75	.43
	Morality	Ethical, honest, moral, principled, sincere, truthful	6	.70	.28
	Earthiness	Down-to-earth, earthy, folksy, homespun, simple	5	.66	.28
	Naturalness	Casual, easygoing, informal, natural, relaxed	5	.63	.26

(Continued)

TABLE 1.1
(Continued)

Factor Pole	Cluster	Terms Included	Number of Terms	Reliability α	Mean r
II −					
	Overcriticalness	Faultfinding, harsh, unforgiving, unsympathetic	4	.45	.18
	Belligerence	Antagonistic, argumentative, combative, quarrelsome	4	.63	.29
	Bossiness	Bossy, demanding, domineering, manipulative	4	.64	.31
	Rudeness	Abusive, disrespectful, impolite, impudent, rude, scornful	6	.59	.19
	Conceit	Boastful, conceited, egocentric, egotistical, vain	5	.77	.41
	Cruelty	Cruel, ruthless, vindictive	3	.38	.17
	Pomposity	Condescending, pompous, smug, snobbish	4	.37	.12
	Irritability	Crabby, cranky, irritable, grumpy	4	.78	.47
	Distrust	Cynical, distrustful, skeptical, suspicious	4	.55	.23
	Callousness	Cold, impersonal, insensitive	3	.58	.31
	Selfishness	Greedy, selfish, self-indulgent	3	.46	.22
	Stubbornness	Bullheaded, obstinate, stubborn	3	.65	.38
	Thoughtlessness	Inconsiderate, tactless, thoughtless	3	.48	.24
	Surliness	Caustic, curt, flippant, gruff, surly	5	.47	.15
	Unfriendliness	Unfriendly, ungracious, unkind	3	.48	.24
	Prejudice	Bigoted, prejudiced	2	.69	.53
	Cunning	Crafty, cunning, devious, sly	4	.63	.30
	Deceit	Deceitful, dishonest, underhanded, unscrupulous	4	.47	.18
	Volatility	Explosive, tempestuous, volatile	3	.34	.16
	Stinginess	Miserly, stingy	2	.47	.31
III +					
	Efficiency	Concise, exacting, efficient, fastidious, self-disciplined	5	.61	.23
	Organization	Orderly, organized, systematic	3	.78	.54
	Dependability	Dependable, reliable, responsible	3	.86	.67
	Precision	Meticulous, perfectionistic, precise	3	.65	.39
	Decisiveness	Decisive, deliberate, firm, purposeful	4	.50	.20
	Persistence	Industrious, persistent, tenacious, thorough	4	.38	.13
	Dignity	Dignified, formal, mannerly	3	.48	.24
	Caution	Careful, cautious	2	.74	.59
	Punctuality	Prompt, punctual	2	.85	.74
	Predictability	Consistent, predictable, steady	3	.53	.28
	Thrift	Economical, thrifty	2	.72	.56
	Logic	Analytical, logical	2	.49	.33
	Conventionality	Conventional, traditional	2	.61	.45
III −					
	Disorganization	Disorganized, haphazard, inefficient, scatterbrained, sloppy, unsystematic	6	.73	.31
	Negligence	Careless, negligent, undependable, unconscientious, unreliable	5	.67	.28
	Inconsistency	Erratic, inconsistent, unpredictable	3	.44	.21
	Recklessness	Foolhardy, rash, reckless	3	.51	.25
	Forgetfulness	Forgetful, absent-minded	2	.73	.58
	Indecisiveness	Indecisive, wishy-washy	2	.51	.34
	Frivolity	Extravagant, frivolous, impractical	3	.47	.23
	Aimlessness	Aimless, unambitious	2	.52	.36
	Sloth	Lazy, slothful	2	.24	.14

(Continued)

TABLE 1.1
(Continued)

Factor Pole	Cluster	Terms Included	Number of Terms	Reliability α	Mean r
IV +					
	Placidity	Passionless, unexcitable, unemotional	3	.63	.36
IV −					
	Emotionality	Emotional, excitable	2	.40	.25
	Fear	Anxious, fearful, nervous	3	.48	.24
	Instability	Temperamental, touchy, unstable	3	.46	.22
	Envy	Envious, jealous	2	.62	.45
	Gullibility	Gullible, naive, suggestible	3	.47	.21
	Intrusiveness	Intrusive, meddlesome, nosy	3	.41	.18
V +					
	Intellectuality	Contemplative, intellectual, introspective, meditative, philosophical	5	.64	.27
	Depth	Complex, deep	2	.54	.37
	Creativity	Artistic, creative, imaginative, innovative, inventive	5	.76	.40
	Intelligence	Bright, intelligent, smart	3	.82	.60
	Foresight	Foresighted, insightful, perceptive	3	.46	.22
	Nonconformity	Nonconforming, rebellious, unconventional	3	.57	.31
	Sophistication	Cosmopolitan, cultured, refined, sophisticated, worldly	5	.67	.29
	Curiosity	Curious, inquisitive	2	.44	.29
	Independence	Autonomous, independent, individualistic	3	.43	.19
V −					
	Shallowness	Shallow, unintellectual, unreflective	3	.39	.18
	Unimaginativeness	Uncreative, unimaginative	2	.67	.51
	Imperceptiveness	Imperceptive, unobservant	2	.38	.24
	Stupidity	Dull, ignorant, unintelligent	3	.38	.18
		Mean	3.4	.57	.32

Note. The two estimates of internal consistency—Coefficient Alpha (α) and the mean interitem correlation (r)—were based on subject-standardized (z) responses across 587 trait terms, rated on nine-step scales. The values are based on a combined sample of 636 targets, 320 self descriptions and 316 peer descriptions.

To obtain these judgments from each of the three theorists, we used a three-stage procedure. First, the theorists were sent a copy of Table 1.1, and were asked to indicate for each cluster the dimension in their system with which it was most highly associated: "Specifically, for each of the clusters, would you please indicate on which of your dimensions it should load most highly. For clusters that you see as dimensionally complex in your system, please list the secondary dimension(s) with which you would expect a high association." After theorists had indicated the locations of each of the clusters, an initial version of Table 1.2 or its analogue was provided to them, with a request for another round

TABLE 1.2
Presumed Concordance Between Goldberg's 100 Synonym Clusters
and Eysenck's P-E-N Model

	Goldberg Cluster	Terms Included in Each Cluster	Presumed P-E-N Factor
I+			
	Gregariousness	Extroverted, gregarious, sociable	N−/E+
	Spirit	Enthusiastic, spirited, vivacious, zestful	E+
	Expressiveness	Communicative, expressive, verbal	E+
	Playfulness	Adventurous, mischievous, playful, rambunctious	E+
	Energy Level	Active, energetic, vigorous	E+
	Unrestraint	Impetuous, uninhibited, unrestrained	E+
	Self-esteem	Assured, confident, proud	E+/N−
	Spontaneity	Carefree, happy-go-lucky, spontaneous	N−/E+
	Talkativeness	Talkative, verbose, wordy	E+
	Assertion	Assertive, dominant, forceful	E+
	Courage	Brave, courageous, daring	E+/P+
	Animation	Demonstrative, exhibitionistic, flamboyant	E+
	Candor	Direct, frank, straightforward	E+
	Ambition	Ambitious, enterprising, opportunistic	E+
	Humor	Humorous, witty	E+/N−
	Optimism	Cheerful, jovial, merry, optimistic	E+
I−			
	Silence	Quiet, silent, untalkative	E−
	Aloofness	Seclusive, unsociable, withdrawn	E−/N+
	Shyness	Bashful, shy, timid	E−/N+
	Inhibition	Inhibited, restrained	E−/N+
	Unaggressiveness	Unadventurous, unaggressive, uncompetitive	E−
	Reserve	Detached, reserved, secretive	E−
	Insecurity	Defensive, fretful, insecure, negativistic, self-critical, self-pitying	N+
	Passivity	Docile, passive, submissive	E−/P−/N+
	Lethargy	Lethargic, sluggish	N+
	Pessimism	Bitter, joyless, melancholic, moody, morose, pessimistic, somber	E−/N+
II+			
	Cooperation	Accommodating, agreeable, cooperative, helpful, patient, peaceful, reasonable	P−
	Empathy	Considerate, kind, sympathetic, trustful, understanding	P−
	Amiability	Amiable, cordial, friendly, genial, pleasant	P−
	Leniency	Lenient, uncritical, undemanding	P−
	Flexibility	Adaptable, flexible, obliging	P−
	Courtesy	Courteous, diplomatic, polite, respectful, tactful	P−
	Generosity	Benevolent, charitable, generous	P−
	Modesty	Humble, modest, selfless, unassuming	P−
	Warmth	Affectionate, compassionate, sentimental, warm	P−
	Morality	Ethical, honest, moral, principled, sincere, truthful	P−
	Earthiness	Down-to-earth, earthy, folksy, homespun, simple	E+
	Naturalness	Casual, easygoing, informal, natural, relaxed	E+/N−

(Continued)

TABLE 1.2
(Continued)

	Goldberg Cluster	Terms Included in Each Cluster	Presumed P-E-N Factor
II –			
	Overcriticalness	Faultfinding, harsh, unforgiving, unsympathetic	P+
	Belligerence	Antagonistic, argumentative, combative, quarrelsome	P+
	Bossiness	Bossy, demanding, domineering, manipulative	P+
	Rudeness	Abusive, disrespectful, impolite, impudent, rude, scornful	P+
	Conceit	Boastful, conceited, egocentric, egotistical, vain	P+
	Cruelty	Cruel, ruthless, vindictive	P+
	Pomposity	Condescending, pompous, smug, snobbish	P+
	Irritability	Crabby, cranky, irritable, grumpy	P+/N+
	Distrust	Cynical, distrustful, skeptical, suspicious	P+
	Callousness	Cold, impersonal, insensitive	P+
	Selfishness	Greedy, selfish, self-indulgent	P+
	Stubbornness	Bullheaded, obstinate, stubborn	P+
	Thoughtlessness	Inconsiderate, tactless, thoughtless	P+
	Surliness	Caustic, curt, flippant, gruff, surly	P+
	Unfriendliness	Unfriendly, ungracious, unkind	P+
	Prejudice	Bigoted, prejudiced	P+
	Cunning	Crafty, cunning, devious, sly	P+
	Deceit	Deceitful, dishonest, underhanded, unscrupulous	P+
	Volatility	Explosive, tempestuous, volatile	P+/N+
	Stinginess	Miserly, stingy	N+
III +			
	Efficiency	Concise, exacting, efficient, fastidious, self-disciplined	E–
	Organization	Orderly, organized, systematic	E–
	Dependability	Dependable, reliable, responsible	E–
	Precision	Meticulous, perfectionistic, precise	N+
	Decisiveness	Decisive, deliberate, firm, purposeful	E–
	Persistence	Industrious, persistent, tenacious, thorough	E–/N–
	Dignity	Dignified, formal, mannerly	P–
	Caution	Careful, cautious	E–
	Punctuality	Prompt, punctual	E–
	Predictability	Consistent, predictable, steady	E–
	Thrift	Economical, thrifty	E–
	Logic	Analytical, logical	P–
	Conventionality	Conventional, traditional	P–
III –			
	Disorganization	Disorganized, haphazard, inefficient, scatter-brained, sloppy, unsystematic	E+/N+
	Negligence	Careless, negligent, undependable, unconscientious, unreliable	E+/N+
	Inconsistency	Erratic, inconsistent, unpredictable	E+/N+/P+
	Recklessness	Foolhardy, rash, reckless	E+/P+
	Forgetfulness	Forgetful, absent-minded	N+
	Indecisiveness	Indecisive, wishy-washy	P–
	Frivolity	Extravagant, frivolous, impractical	E+
	Aimlessness	Aimless, unambitious	P–
	Sloth	Lazy, slothful	N+/P–

(Continued)

TABLE 1.2
(Continued)

Goldberg Cluster		Terms Included in Each Cluster	Presumed P-E-N Factor
IV+			
	Placidity	Passionless, unexcitable, unemotional	N−
IV−			
	Emotionality	Emotional, excitable	N+
	Fear	Anxious, fearful, nervous	N+
	Instability	Temperamental, touchy, unstable	N+
	Envy	Envious, jealous	N+
	Gullibility	Gullible, naive, suggestible	N+
	Intrusiveness	Intrusive, meddlesome, nosy	N+
V+			
	Intellectuality	Contemplative, intellectual, introspective, meditative, philosophical	E−
	Depth	Complex, deep	E−
	Creativity	Artistic, creative, imaginative, innovative, inventive	P+/N+
	Intelligence	Bright, intelligent, smart	E+
	Foresight	Foresighted, insightful, perceptive	E−
	Nonconformity	Nonconforming, rebellious, unconventional	P+/E+
	Sophistication	Cosmopolitan, cultured, refined, sophisticated, worldly	E+
	Curiosity	Curious, inquisitive	E+
	Independence	Autonomous, independent, individualistic	N−/P+
V−			
	Shallowness	Shallow, unintellectual, unreflective	(?)
	Unimaginativeness	Uncreative, unimaginative	P−
	Imperceptiveness	Imperceptive, unobservant	(?)
	Stupidity	Dull, ignorant, unintelligent	(?)

Note. Locations of the clusters within the P-E-N system were provided by Eysenck. P = Psychoticism, E = Extraversion, and N = Neuroticism.

of assistance: "Specifically, would you please examine the table carefully to see whether every entry is exactly as it should be. Please pay special attention to the + and − signs." And then at the third stage, the revised table was again returned to the theorists with a request for any further thoughts or fine tuning.

These tables now provide examples of the ways that the constructs from diverse personality theories can be mapped within the same overarching framework. Indeed, because each table provides a concrete specification of the ideas of a theorist, they permit a variety of comparisons that would not be possible solely from the original publications of the theorists. For example, investigators interested in a particular construct can immediately obtain the equivalent concepts in each of the three other theories. And, as is shown later in this chapter, we can even compare a theorist's explicit and implicit representations.

EYSENCK'S P-E-N MODEL

To illustrate the power of this type of analysis, consider the concordance between the Big Five factors and those in Eysenck's model of Psychoticism, Extraversion, and Neuroticism. These three dimensions are presently measured by the 90-item Eysenck Personality Questionnaire (EPQ), which has been employed in a wide variety of studies and in numerous countries and settings. Before considering Eysenck's views about the place of the Big Five factors in his P-E-N model, let us examine the empirical evidence on the relations between the two representations.

Empirical Studies of Big Five versus P-E-N Concordance

McCrae and Costa (1985a). The first report of the relations between explicit markers of the two systems was provided by McCrae and Costa (1985a). Included in their study were the Eysenck Personality Inventory (EPI), which included measures of Extraversion and Neuroticism; a preliminary 53-item version of the Psychoticism scale from the Eysenck Personality Questionnaire (EPQ); the original NEO inventory, which included measures of Neuroticism, Extraversion, and Openness to Experience; preliminary versions of the NEO-PI scales for Agreeableness and Conscientiousness; and Big Five factor scores derived from 80 bipolar rating scales. The subjects were adult volunteers, and the sample sizes for various analyses of these self-report measures varied from 451 to 586.

As would be expected from prior theoretical analyses of the relations between the two models (e.g., Goldberg, 1981), there was a strong one-to-one concordance between the EPI Extraversion (E) scale and markers of Big Five Factor I ($r = .61$ and .69 with the bipolar factor scores and the NEO scale, respectively), as well as between the EPI Neuroticism (N) scale and markers of Factor IV ($r = .62$ and .75). Of more interest, however, are the Big Five correlates of the Psychoticism (P) scale; unfortunately, the internal consistency of the P scale was substantially lower than that of either E or N, thereby attenuating the size of its correlations with other measures. The most reliable version of the P scale included in this study ($\alpha = .68$) correlated roughly equally with Big Five Factors II and III; the correlations were $-.20$ (Factor II) and $-.29$ (Factor III) with the factor scores derived from the bipolar scales, and $-.45$ (Factor II) and $-.31$ (Factor III) with the corresponding NEO-PI scales. Seemingly, then, the P scale is a blend of the two orthogonal dimensions of Disagreeableness and Unconscientiousness.

Adjectival Correlates of the EPQ Scales. Because McCrae and Costa (1985a) included only preliminary (and therefore only modestly reliable) measures of Eysenck's P scale and of Big Five Factors II and III, their findings clearly need to be replicated. In the first of a series of such studies, we administered the EPQ and Goldberg's (1982) inventory of 566 trait-descriptive adjectives to a small ($N = 84$) sample of law-school students, who were paid for completing these and other measures. The trait adjectives most highly associated with each of the three major EPQ scales are listed in Table 1.3. Note the exquisite correspondence of EPQ

TABLE 1.3
Trait Adjectives Most Highly Associated with Scales in the Eysenck
Personality Questionnaire: Self Descriptions from Law Students ($N = 84$)

Extraversion

−.63	Quiet	.62	Social
−.61	Untalkative	.61	Sociable
−.60	Unsociable	.56	Extroverted
−.55	Uncommunicative	.54	Gregarious
−.55	Restrained	.53	Jovial
−.53	Silent	.52	Talkative
−.51	Introverted	.52	Flamboyant
−.48	Withdrawn	.49	Exuberant
−.48	Unfriendly	.48	Spontaneous
−.45	Reserved	.47	Rambunctious
−.43	Timid	.46	Communicative
−.42	Bashful	.45	Dominant

Neuroticism

−.50	Optimistic	.50	Melancholic
−.48	Assured	.49	Doleful
−.46	Steady	.49	Self-pitying
−.41	Confident	.48	Lonely
		.46	Envious
		.46	Obsessive
		.45	Unstable
		.45	Pessimistic
		.45	Temperamental
		.44	Anxious
		.43	Moody
		.43	Fretful
		.43	Morose
		.39	Nervous
		.38	Insecure

Psychoticism

−.38	Organized	.46	Disorganized
−.38	Punctual	.44	Devil-may-care
−.37	Prompt	.38	Foolhardy
−.37	Neat	.37	Reckless
−.35	Orderly	.37	Lazy
−.33	Strict	.33	Impulsive
−.32	Systematic	.33	Wishy-washy
−.31	Foresighted	.31	Inconsistent
		.31	Undependable
		.30	Unsystematic

Extraversion with Big Five Factor I (Surgency), Neuroticism with the negative pole of Factor IV (Emotional Stability), and Psychoticism with the negative pole of Factor III (Conscientiousness).

Big Five Factor Markers and the EPQ Scales. The evidence regarding the Big Five concordance of two of the factors in the P-E-N model—Extraversion with Factor I and Neuroticism with Factor IV—is persuasive. On the other hand, the location of Psychoticism in the Big Five structure is less clear. The study by McCrae and Costa (1985a) involved a large and heterogeneous sample of subjects, but included only preliminary markers of the relevant factors. And, the findings displayed here in Table 1.3 were based on a small and relatively homogeneous sample. What is needed is a large-sample replication with clear markers of Psychoticism and the Big Five factors. Fortunately, recent efforts to develop markers for the Big Five factors have led to the development of a set of 100 unipolar markers, 20 marking each of the Big Five factors, and these 100 markers have proved to be univocal factor definers in a variety of samples of self and peer descriptions (Goldberg, 1992).

An inventory including these 100 markers was administered to a sample of college students ($N = 503$), along with the EPQ and other measures; included in the latter set were two measures of sociopolitical attitudes (Altemeyer's, 1981, 24-item Right-Wing Authoritarianism scale and a 24-item version of Wilson's, 1973, Conservatism scale), a measure of self-esteem (Rosenberg's, 1965, classic 10-item scale), and a measure of verbal ability (the new 80-item revision of the Quick Word Test; Borgatta & Corsini, 1990).

Appendix C presents the varimax-rotated factor loadings for the 100 unipolar Big Five factor markers in this sample; all 100 variables had their highest loadings on the factor for which they had been selected as markers. Moreover, in the sample of 636 self and peer ratings described earlier, the correlations between the factor scores from these 100 unipolar markers and the 100 synonym clusters were .94, .82, .92, .83, and .89 for Factors I to V, respectively, attesting to the substantial convergent validities of these markers against those based on representative sets of trait adjectives.

The responses to the 90 EPQ items were factored, and four components were rotated by varimax; factor scores from these four factors correlated .97, .96, and .93 with scores on the EPQ Extraversion (E), Neuroticism (N), and Lie (L) scales, respectively, as compared to .83 with the Psychoticism (P) scale. Although these findings attest to the general factorial clarity of the EPQ, they also demonstrate the contrast between the psychometric properties of Psychoticism and the other three EPQ scales. The root of the problem with the Psychoticism scale is its low internal consistency; the mean item intercorrelations were .19 for both the Extraversion and Neuroticism scales ($\alpha = .83$ and .85), as compared to .09 for the Lie scale ($\alpha = .69$) and .07 ($\alpha = .63$) for the P scale.

1. THE BIG FIVE AND EYSENCK'S P-E-N MODEL

The 100 unipolar Big Five markers were scored from the subject-standardized responses to an inventory of 235 trait adjectives. When the factor scores derived from a varimax rotation of five principal components were compared with the scores from the five a priori scales, the correlations across the 503 subjects ranged from .95 to .97. For the scales, the mean item intercorrelations ranged from .18 to .29, and the Alpha coefficients ranged from .81 to .89 (the corresponding values based on original responses average about .04 higher than those based on these z scores).

The correlations between the Big Five markers and all of the other variables included in this study are presented in Table 1.4. The correlations with the EPQ scales provide a clear replication of the findings from McCrae and Costa (1985a). The Extraversion scale was correlated around .75 with Factor I (.88 when corrected for the unreliability of the scales), and the Neuroticism scale was correlated around −.70 with Factor IV (−.84 when corrected). The Psychoticism scale again turned out to be a mixture of Factors II and III, correlating in the range from −.40 to −.45 with each of them. The multiple correlation of Psychoticism with both Factors II and III is around .62, a value that rises to .85 when corrected for unreliability, due primarily to the low internal consistency of the P scale.

The additional variables included in this study also provide some important findings. The two measures of sociopolitical attitudes (which correlated .79 with each other) were negatively related to Factor V and positively related to Factor III; authoritarian and conservative college students describe themselves as relatively high in Conscientiousness and relatively low in Intellect. As would be expected, the measure of self-esteem correlated about .40 with Factor IV (Emotional Stability) and about .30 with Factor I (Surgency or Extraversion). And, finally, verbal aptitude test scores were related to Factor V, and to a lesser extent to Factor IV, and were completely independent of Factors I, II, and III in this sample of college undergraduates.

Are the P-E-N Factors at a Higher Order Than the Big Five?

Eysenck (1991) recently argued that his "Giant Three" factors are located at a hierarchical level above that of the Big Five, and specifically that Big Five Factors II (Agreeableness) and III (Conscientiousness) are each facets of Psychoticism: "Agreeableness and Conscientiousness are in fact traits in part defining P, and constituting two of the many first-order factors making up that super-order factor concept" (p. 782). This *explicit* statement of the relations between the Big Five and P-E-N models can be contrasted with the *implicit* relations that are reflected in Table 1.2: When Eysenck actually mapped the 100 clusters onto his P-E-N factors, he equated Psychoticism solely with Factor II (reflected) and incorporated most of the facets of Factor III into Extraversion. Consequently, there are now

TABLE 1.4
Correlations Between the EPQ Scales (and Factors) and Goldberg's 100 Unipolar Big Five Markers ($N = 503$)

		Goldberg Big Five Markers									
		I		II		III		IV		V	
		Scale	Factor	Scale	Factor	Scale	Factor	Scale	Factor	Scale	Factor
EPQ scales	E	**.76***	**.75***	.18	.17	-.02	-.05	.18	.03	.16	.09
	N	-.34	-.28	-.16	-.10	-.06	-.02	**-.71***	**-.67***	-.08	-.06
	P	.01	.01	**-.43**	**-.39***	**-.45***	**-.37**	-.09	-.07	.08	.10
	L	-.13	-.14	.21	.17	.26*	.23*	.17	.07	-.05	-.03
EPQ factors	E	**.73***	**.73***	.21	.21	.04	.00	.11	.10	.15	.07
	N	-.23	-.17	-.06	-.01	.02	.04	**-.68***	**-.67***	-.06	-.06
	P	-.02	.00	**-.47***	**-.46***	**-.32**	-.23	-.14	-.02	.02	.04
	L	-.16	-.16	.23	.19	**.31***	.27*	.10	.14	-.09	-.08
Additional Measures											
R-W-A scale		.14	.23	.04	.03	.23	.27	.03	-.06	**-.30***	**-.30***
Conservatism		.07	.13	.03	.02	.22	.25	.02	-.05	**-.25***	**-.25***
Self-esteem		**.32**	.29	.09	.05	.18	.17	**.40***	**.37***	.10	.09
Quick Word Test		-.01	-.10	.01	-.05	.06	.02	.15	.22	**.32***	**.32***

Note. The correlations between the EPQ scales and factors were .97, .96, .83, and .93 for the Extraversion (E), Neuroticism (N), Psychoticism (P), and Lie (L) scales, respectively. Goldberg's 100 unipolar factor markers were scored from the standardized (z) responses of each subject across 235 trait adjectives. The correlations between the Big Five marker scales and factors were .96, .95, .96, .95, and .97 for Factors I to V, respectively. R-W-A = Altemeyer's Right-Wing Authoritarianism scale; other measures include Wilson's Conservatism scale, Rosenberg's Self-esteem scale, and the Quick Word Test. All values greater than or equal to .30 are listed in boldface.

*The highest correlation for each variable.

1. THE BIG FIVE AND EYSENCK'S P-E-N MODEL

three alternative models of the relations between the Big Five and P-E-N factors: (a) Eysenck's explicit mapping in which Factors II and III are facets of Psychoticism, (b) Eysenck's implicit mapping in which Factor II corresponds to Psychoticism and Factors I and III (reflected) correspond to Extraversion, and (c) the mapping that has consistently emerged from the empirical studies of the EPQ by McCrae and Costa (1985a) and the present investigators in which Psychoticism is a blend of the orthogonal Factors II and III.

To test Eysenck's explicit and implicit hypotheses, we employed three strategies using the data sets already described in this chapter: (a) We carried out a series of hierarchical cluster analyses, using a number of different cluster algorithms, and examined the composition of the three most inclusive clusters at the top of each hierarchy; (b) we extracted three factors, rotated them to simple structure via the varimax algorithm, and examined the variables loading most highly on each factor; and, finally, (c) we extracted five, six, and seven factors, rotated each set of factors obliquely by the promax algorithm, factored the resulting oblique factors, always extracting and rotating three factors, and again examined the variables loading most highly on these highest-level factors.

To save space in this chapter, we do not provide the detailed findings from each of these procedures, but the results of our analyses are available from the first author. Our findings are easy to summarize: In no case were we able to recover either the explicit or the implicit versions of the P-E-N dimensions as highest-order superfactors. For example, using the second procedure described, when three factors were rotated, only Big Five Factors I, II, and III were recovered, and the clusters associated with Factor IV (which correspond to Factor N in the P-E-N system) were not related to any of the three factors. That is, contrary to Eysenck's explicit and implicit hypotheses, neither cluster analyses nor factor analyses of the 100 revised synonym clusters ever revealed the P-E-N dimensions as superfactors.

The Structure of the EPQ P Scale

Our previous analyses have shown that scores from the P scale are related to both Factors II and III in the Big Five structure. Logically, three types of scales could be so related: (a) a scale with all its items clustered around the midline or bisectrix of the two factors; (b) a scale composed of two clusters of items, one cluster associated with each of the two factors; and (c) a scale whose items are scattered throughout the interstitial region between the two factors. Because we already know that the P scale has low internal consistency, we can eliminate scale type (a) as a possibility. To discover the locations of the 25 P-scale items in Big Five space, we first factored the item responses, extracted two components, and then rotated them by varimax. Figure 1.1 shows the locations of each of the 25 P-scale items, with their EPQ item numbers and keying direction, in this two-dimensional space. In the figure, each item is presented twice—once within the circle as defined by its

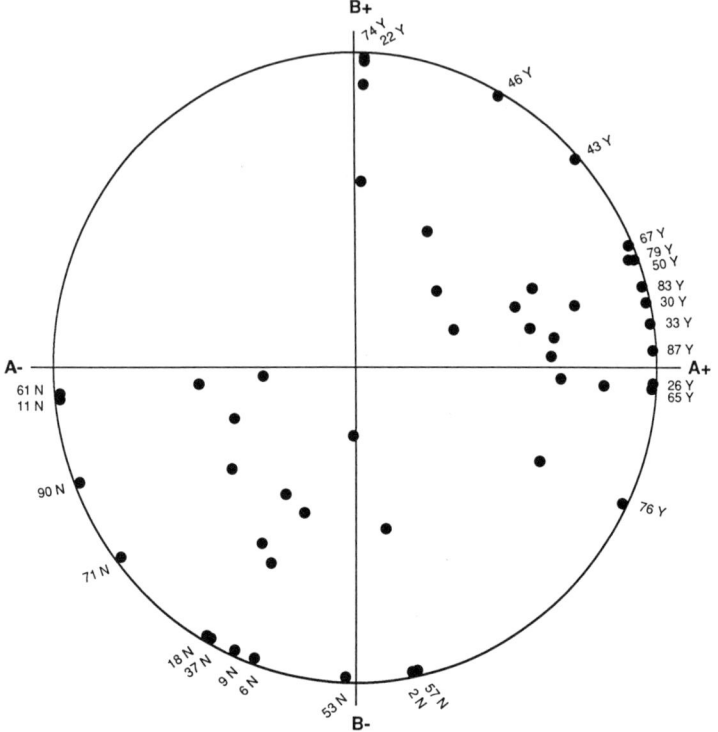

FIG. 1.1. The locations of each of the 25 P-scale items in the space defined by two varimax-rotated components (Factors A and B).

angular position and its distance from the origin, and again when projected to unit length onto the circumference of the circle. The reason for the low internal consistency of the P scale now becomes quite clear: The items are scattered in arcs of about 125 degrees in the space defined by the two orthogonal components, labeled A+ versus A− and B+ versus B− in the figure.

To locate each of the 25 P-scale items within the Big Five factor structure, responses to these items (and factor scores on Factors A and B within the P-scale item pool) were correlated with the factor scores based on the Big Five factor markers. Of the 25 P-scale items, eight were most highly associated with Big Five Factor II, eight with Factor III, five with Factor IV, and two each with Factors I and V. Factor A from the P-scale analysis correlated −.35 with Big Five Factor II and −.22 with Factor IV, whereas Factor B correlated −.40 with Big Five Factor III and +.22 with Factor V. The location of each of the 25 P-scale items in the space defined by Big Five Factors II and III is provided in Fig. 1.2; also included in that figure are the locations of Factors A and B. Again, the location of each item (and each of the two factors) is presented twice, once inside the circle, and once when projected onto its circumference. As would be expected,

1. THE BIG FIVE AND EYSENCK'S P-E-N MODEL

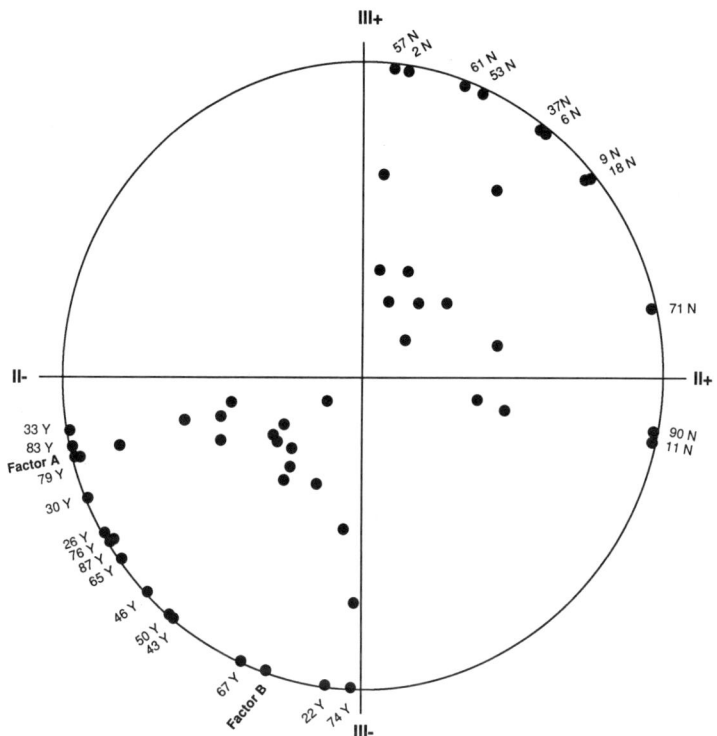

FIG. 1.2. Locations of the 25 P-scale items in the space defined by Big Five Factors II and III.

the locations of most of the 25 items (and both Factors A and B) fall either in the II+/III+ or northeast quadrant (false-keyed items) or in the II−/III− or southwest quadrant (true-keyed items), where they are distributed rather evenly across the two arcs of the circle. Surprisingly, however, two items (90N and 11N) are located in the II+/III− or southeast quadrant. Given the widespread distribution of the P-scale items in the space defined by Big Five Factors II and III, the reason for the low internal consistency of the scale is now clear.

SOME CONCLUSIONS AND IMPLICATIONS

Our long-term studies of the natural language of personality have culminated in the development of two sets of Big Five factor markers, the 100 synonym clusters (Goldberg, 1990) and the 100 unipolar terms (Goldberg, 1992), each useful for different purposes. The 100 synonym clusters, because they are based on a rather large and representative sample of common English trait adjectives, provide a relatively comprehensive framework for integrating the Big Five factor structure with other models. We have begun this effort at theory integration with Eysenck's P-E-N factors. Eysenck generously provided his own judgments about the locations of each of the 100 clusters in his P-E-N model (see Table 1.2), and suggested that the three P-E-N factors are located at a higher order than the Big Five.

In the present chapter, we have provided evidence that the P-E-N factors do not emerge in a wide variety of analyses of the 100 clusters, and therefore they should not be considered higher order constructs than the Big Five. Instead, it is now quite clear from the findings of McCrae and Costa (1985a) and those reported here that two of the P-E-N factors are nearly isomorphic with two of the Big Five factors, and the Psychoticism factor is a blend of Big Five Factors II and III. That is, a large-sample study using the 100 unipolar Big Five factor markers confirmed the association of Extraversion with Factor I, Neuroticism with Factor IV (reflected), and Psychoticism with Factors II and III.

Eysenck (chap. 2 in this volume) argues that Psychoticism is a more viable construct than either Agreeableness or Conscientiousness because scores on his P scale are significantly related to a wide variety of other variables. This argument is a logical non sequitur: Any variable, A, that is a blend of two others, B and C, will inevitably relate to all variables associated with B, with C, or with both. Because the Psychoticism scale includes items associated with the two orthogonal dimensions of Agreeableness and Conscientiousness, then all variables related to either Agreeableness or Conscientiousness will necessarily relate to the P scale. Indeed, we assume that some types of psychotics display behaviors that would be characterized as Disagreeable, other types of psychotics behave in ways that would be viewed as Unconscientious, and some types of psychotics may be characterized by both traits.

In summary, then, given the low internal consistency of the Psychoticism scale in this and other studies (e.g., McCrae & Costa, 1985a) and its now-replicated association with two of the orthogonal Big Five factors, it seems reasonable to conclude that Eysenck's three-factor model needs modification and expansion. At the very least, it would seem prudent to include distinct measures of Big Five Factors II, III, and V in all future investigations using the EPQ or other measures of the P-E-N model.

ACKNOWLEDGMENTS

This project was supported by grant MH-49227 from the National Institute of Mental Health. The authors are indebted to Herbert W. Eber, Hans J. Eysenck, and Auke Tellegen for their careful efforts to link the 100 clusters with the factors in the Cattell, Eysenck, and Tellegen models. In addition, we wish to thank William F. Chaplin, John M. Digman, Sarah E. Hampson, Willem K. B. Hofstee, Warren T. Norman, and Gerard Saucier for their thoughtful editorial suggestions.

APPENDIX A
Presumed Concordance Between Goldberg's 100 Synonym Clusters and Cattell's Oblique Factors

	Goldberg Cluster	Terms Included in Each Cluster	Presumed Cattell Factor Primary	Second-Order
I+				
	Gregariousness	Extroverted, gregarious, sociable	A+	E+
	Spirit	Enthusiastic, spirited, vivacious, zestful	F+	E+
	Expressiveness	Communicative, expressive, verbal	A+/I+	E+
	Playfulness	Adventurous, mischievous, playful, rambunctious	H+/F+	E+
	Energy Level	Active, energetic, vigorous	F+/H+	E+
	Unrestraint	Impetuous, uninhibited, unrestrained	D+/F+	E+/I+
	Self-esteem	Assured, confident, proud	C+/H+	I+/A−
	Spontaneity	Carefree, happy-go-lucky, spontaneous	F+	E+
	Talkativeness	Talkative, verbose, wordy	A+/F+	C−
	Assertion	Assertive, dominant, forceful	E+	E+/I+
	Courage	Brave, courageous, daring	H+/E+	I+
	Animation	Demonstrative, exhibitionistic, flamboyant	E+/Q_1+	I+
	Candor	Direct, frank, straightforward	N−	D−
	Ambition	Ambitious, enterprising, opportunistic	E+	I+/U−
	Humor	Humorous, witty	F+	E+
	Optimism	Cheerful, jovial, merry, optimistic	F+	E+
I−				
	Silence	Quiet, silent, untalkative	A−/F−	E−
	Aloofness	Seclusive, unsociable, withdrawn	A−	E−
	Shyness	Bashful, shy, timid	H−	E−
	Inhibition	Inhibited, restrained	H−/Q_3+	E−/U+
	Unaggressiveness	Unadventurous, unaggressive, uncompetitive	E−	E−
	Reserve	Detached, reserved, secretive	A−	E−
	Insecurity	Defensive, fretful, insecure, negativistic, self-critical, self-pitying	O+	A+
	Passivity	Docile, passive, submissive	E−	E−/I−
	Lethargy	Lethargic, sluggish	F−	E−/I−
	Pessimism	Bitter, joyless, melancholic, moody, morose, pessimistic, somber	F−	E−/A+
II+				
	Cooperation	Accommodating, agreeable, cooperative, helpful, patient, peaceful, reasonable	A+/G+	I−
	Empathy	Considerate, kind, sympathetic, trustful, understanding	I+	C−/A−
	Amiability	Amiable, cordial, friendly, genial, pleasant	A+/C+	E+/I−
	Leniency	Lenient, uncritical, undemanding	G−	U−
	Flexibility	Adaptable, flexible, obliging	G−/Q_3−	I−
	Courtesy	Courteous, diplomatic, polite, respectful, tactful	N+	D+
	Generosity	Benevolent, charitable, generous	A+	(?)

(Continued)

APPENDIX A
(Continued)

	Goldberg Cluster	Terms Included in Each Cluster	Presumed Cattell Factor Primary	Second-Order
II−	Modesty	Humble, modest, selfless, unassuming	H−	I−
	Warmth	Affectionate, compassionate, sentimental, warm	A+/I+	C−
	Morality	Ethical, honest, moral, principled, sincere, truthful	G+/Q$_3$+	U+
	Earthiness	Down-to-earth, earthy, folksy, homespun, simple	N−	C−/D−
	Naturalness	Casual, easygoing, informal, natural, relaxed	N−/Q$_3$−/Q$_4$−	D−/A−
	Overcriticalness	Faultfinding, harsh, unforgiving, unsympathetic	Q$_3$+/N+	C+
	Belligerence	Antagonistic, argumentative, combative, quarrelsome	E+/Q$_2$+	I+
	Bossiness	Bossy, demanding, domineering, manipulative	E+	I+
	Rudeness	Abusive, disrespectful, impolite, impudent, rude, scornful	H+/E+/I−	C+/I+
	Conceit	Boastful, conceited, egocentric, egotistical, vain	Q$_2$+/Q$_3$+	I+
	Cruelty	Cruel, ruthless, vindictive	E+/L+	(?)
	Pomposity	Condescending, pompous, smug, snobbish	Q$_2$+	(?)
	Irritability	Crabby, cranky, irritable, grumpy	Q$_4$+	A+
	Distrust	Cynical, distrustful, skeptical, suspicious	L+	A+
	Callousness	Cold, impersonal, insensitive	I−	C+
	Selfishness	Greedy, selfish, self-indulgent	Q$_2$+	I+
	Stubbornness	Bullheaded, obstinate, stubborn	E+/G+	I+/U+
	Thoughtlessness	Inconsiderate, tactless, thoughtless	I−	C+
	Surliness	Caustic, curt, flippant, gruff, surly	Q$_4$+	A+
	Unfriendliness	Unfriendly, ungracious, unkind	A−	E−/C+
	Prejudice	Bigoted, prejudiced	(?)	(?)
	Cunning	Crafty, cunning, devious, sly	N+	D+
	Deceit	Deceitful, dishonest, underhanded, unscrupulous	G−	U−
	Volatility	Explosive, tempestuous, volatile	D+/Q$_3$−	E+/I+
	Stinginess	Miserly, stingy	(?)	(?)
III+	Efficiency	Concise, exacting, efficient, fastidious, self-disciplined	Q$_3$+	U+
	Organization	Orderly, organized, systematic	Q$_3$+	U+
	Dependability	Dependable, reliable, responsible	G+/Q$_3$+	U+
	Precision	Meticulous, perfectionistic, precise	G+	U+
	Decisiveness	Decisive, deliberate, firm, purposeful	Q$_3$+	U+/I+
	Persistence	Industrious, persistent, tenacious, thorough	G+/Q$_3$+	U+
	Dignity	Dignified, formal, mannerly	Q$_2$+/Q$_3$+	U+/E−
	Caution	Careful, cautious	F−/H−/Q$_3$+	U+/E−/I−
	Punctuality	Prompt, punctual	Q$_3$+/G+	U+
	Predictability	Consistent, predictable, steady	Q$_3$+	U+

(Continued)

APPENDIX A
(Continued)

	Goldberg Cluster	Terms Included in Each Cluster	Presumed Cattell Factor Primary	Presumed Cattell Factor Second-Order
	Thrift	Economical, thrifty	(?)	(?)
	Logic	Analytical, logical	$I-/Q_2+/Q_3+$	$C+/U+$
	Conventionality	Conventional, traditional	Q_1-	$S-$
III−				
	Disorganization	Disorganized, haphazard, inefficient, scatterbrained, sloppy, unsystematic	Q_3-	$U-$
	Negligence	Careless, negligent, undependable, unconscientious, unreliable	$Q_3-/G-$	$U-$
	Inconsistency	Erratic, inconsistent, unpredictable	Q_3-	$U-$
	Recklessness	Foolhardy, rash, reckless	$D+/F+$	$I+$
	Forgetfulness	Forgetful, absent-minded	$Q_3-/M+$	$U-/S+$
	Indecisiveness	Indecisive, wishy-washy	Q_2+	$U-$
	Frivolity	Extravagant, frivolous, impractical	$F+/M+$	$S+/U-$
	Aimlessness	Aimless, unambitious	$G-/C-$	$I-/U-$
	Sloth	Lazy, slothful	Q_3-	$U-$
IV+				
	Placidity	Passionless, unexcitable, unemotional	$I-/H-/Q_4-$	$C+/A-$
IV−				
	Emotionality	Emotional, excitable	$C-$	$A+$
	Fear	Anxious, fearful, nervous	Q_4+	$A+$
	Instability	Temperamental, touchy, unstable	$C-$	$A+$
	Envy	Envious, jealous	$L+$	$A+$
	Gullibility	Gullible, naive, suggestible	$N-$	$D-$
	Intrusiveness	Intrusive, meddlesome, nosy	$E+$	$I+$
V+				
	Intellectuality	Contemplative, intellectual, introspective, meditative, philosophical	$B+/A-/M+$	$E-/IQ+$
	Depth	Complex, deep	$M+$	$S+$
	Creativity	Artistic, creative, imaginative, innovative, inventive	$M+/A-/H+$	$S+$
	Intelligence	Bright, intelligent, smart	$B+$	$C+/IQ+$
	Foresight	Foresighted, insightful, perceptive	$Q_3+/I+$	$IQ+$
	Nonconformity	Nonconforming, rebellious, unconventional	Q_1+	$I+$
	Sophistication	Cosmopolitan, cultured, refined, sophisticated, worldly	$N+$	$D+$
	Curiosity	Curious, inquisitive	$Q_1+/M+$	$I+/S+/C+$
	Independence	Autonomous, independent, individualistic	$E+/Q_2+$	$I+$
V−				
	Shallowness	Shallow, unintellectual, unreflective	$F+$	$D-$
	Unimaginativeness	Uncreative, unimaginative	$M-$	$S-$
	Imperceptiveness	Imperceptive, unobservant	$I-$	$C-$
	Stupidity	Dull, ignorant, unintelligent	$B-$	$IQ-$

Note. Locations of the clusters within the Cattell system were provided by Eber. At the second-order: E = Exvia, A = Anxiety, C = Cortertia, I = Independence, D = Discreetness, S = Subjectivism, U = Superego, and IQ = Intelligence.

APPENDIX B
Presumed Concordance Between Goldberg's 100 Synonym Clusters and Tellegen's M.P.Q. Factors

			Presumed Tellegen Factor	
	Goldberg Cluster	Terms Included in Each Cluster	Primary	Second-Order
I+				
	Gregariousness	Extroverted, gregarious, sociable	Sc+/Sp+	PE+[C+]
	Spirit	Enthusiastic, spirited, vivacious, zestful	Wb+	PE+
	Expressiveness	Communicative, expressive, verbal	Sc+/Sp+	PE+[C+]
	Playfulness	Adventurous, mischievous, playful, rambunctious	Cn−/Wb+/Ha−	−
	Energy Level	Active, energetic, vigorous	Ac+/Wb+	PE+[A+]
	Unrestraint	Impetuous, uninhibited, unrestrained	Cn−	CO−
	Self-esteem	Assured, confident, proud	Sr−/Sp+	−
	Spontaneity	Carefree, happy-go-lucky, spontaneous	Cn−	CO−
	Talkativeness	Talkative, verbose, wordy	Sp+	PE+
	Assertion	Assertive, dominant, forceful	Sp+	PE+
	Courage	Brave, courageous, daring	Ha−/Sp+	−
	Animation	Demonstrative, exhibitionistic, flamboyant	Sp+	PE+
	Candor	Direct, frank, straightforward	Sp+	PE+
	Ambition	Ambitious, enterprising, opportunistic	Ac+/Sp+	PE+[A+]
	Humor	Humorous, witty	Sc+/Sp+	PE+[C+]
	Optimism	Cheerful, jovial, merry, optimistic	Wb+/Sp+/Sc+	PE+[C+]
I−				
	Silence	Quiet, silent, untalkative	Sc−	PE−[C−]
	Aloofness	Seclusive, unsociable, withdrawn	Sc−	PE−[C−]
	Shyness	Bashful, shy, timid	Sp−/Sr+	−
	Inhibition	Inhibited, restrained	Cn+	CO+
	Unaggressiveness	Unadventurous, unaggressive, uncompetitive	Sp−/Ha+	−
	Reserve	Detached, reserved, secretive	Sc−	PE−[C−]
	Insecurity	Defensive, fretful, insecure, negativistic, self-critical, self-pitying	Sr+/Ag+	NE+
	Passivity	Docile, passive, submissive	Sp−	PE−
	Lethargy	Lethargic, sluggish	Wb−	PE−
	Pessimism	Bitter, joyless, melancholic, moody, morose, pessimistic, somber	Wb−/Al+	−
II+				
	Cooperation	Accommodating, agreeable, cooperative, helpful, patient, peaceful, reasonable	Ag−/Sc+	−
	Empathy	Considerate, kind, sympathetic, trustful, understanding	Sc+/Ag−/Al−	−
	Amiability	Amiable, cordial, friendly, genial, pleasant	Sc+/Ag−	−
	Leniency	Lenient, uncritical, undemanding	Ag−/Sp−	−
	Flexibility	Adaptable, flexible, obliging	Ag−/Sc+	−
	Courtesy	Courteous, diplomatic, polite, respectful, tactful	Ag−/Tr+	−

(Continued)

APPENDIX B
(Continued)

	Goldberg Cluster	Terms Included in Each Cluster	Presumed Tellegen Factor Primary	Second-Order
	Generosity	Benevolent, charitable, generous	Ag−/Sp+	−
	Modesty	Humble, modest, selfless, unassuming	Sp−/Ag−	−
	Warmth	Affectionate, compassionate, sentimental, warm	Sc+/Ag−	−
	Morality	Ethical, honest, moral, principled, sincere, truthful	Tr+/Cn+	CO+
	Earthiness	Down-to-earth, earthy, folksy, homespun, simple	Cn+/Ab−	−
	Naturalness	Casual, easygoing, informal, natural, relaxed	Cn−/Sr−	−
II−				
	Overcriticalness	Faultfinding, harsh, unforgiving, unsympathetic	Ag+	NE+
	Belligerence	Antagonistic, argumentative, combative, quarrelsome	Ag+/Sp+	−
	Bossiness	Bossy, demanding, domineering, manipulative	Sp+/Ag+	−
	Rudeness	Abusive, disrespectful, impolite, impudent, rude, scornful	Ag+/Tr−/Sp+	−
	Conceit	Boastful, conceited, egocentric, egotistical, vain	Sp+/Ag+	−
	Cruelty	Cruel, ruthless, vindictive	Ag+	NE+
	Pomposity	Condescending, pompous, smug, snobbish	Sp+/Sc−	−
	Irritability	Crabby, cranky, irritable, grumpy	Ag+/Sr+	NE+
	Distrust	Cynical, distrustful, skeptical, suspicious	Ag+/Al+	NE+
	Callousness	Cold, impersonal, insensitive	Sc−/Ag+	−
	Selfishness	Greedy, selfish, self-indulgent	Ag+/Cn−	−
	Stubbornness	Bullheaded, obstinate, stubborn	Ag+	NE+
	Thoughtlessness	Inconsiderate, tactless, thoughtless	Ag+/Sc−/Cn−	−
	Surliness	Caustic, curt, flippant, gruff, surly	Ag+/Sp+/Cn−	−
	Unfriendliness	Unfriendly, ungracious, unkind	Ag+/Sc−	−
	Prejudice	Bigoted, prejudiced	Ag+/Tr+	−
	Cunning	Crafty, cunning, devious, sly	Sp+/Ag+	−
	Deceit	Deceitful, dishonest, underhanded, unscrupulous	Ag+/Sc−	−
	Volatility	Explosive, tempestuous, volatile	Ag+/Sr+	NE+
	Stinginess	Miserly, stingy	Cn+/Sc−	−
III+				
	Efficiency	Concise, exacting, efficient, fastidious, self-disciplined	Ac+/Cn+	−
	Organization	Orderly, organized, systematic	Cn+	CO+
	Dependability	Dependable, reliable, responsible	Cn+	CO+
	Precision	Meticulous, perfectionistic, precise	Cn+/Ac+	−

(Continued)

APPENDIX B
(Continued)

	Goldberg Cluster	Terms Included in Each Cluster	Presumed Tellegen Factor Primary	Second-Order
	Decisiveness	Decisive, deliberate, firm, purposeful	Sp+/Cn+/Ac+	—
	Persistence	Industrious, persistent, tenacious, thorough	Ac+/Cn+	—
	Dignity	Dignified, formal, mannerly	Tr+/Cn+	CO+
	Caution	Careful, cautious	Cn+	CO+
	Punctuality	Prompt, punctual	Cn+	CO+
	Predictability	Consistent, predictable, steady	Cn+	CO+
	Thrift	Economical, thrifty	Cn+	CO+
	Logic	Analytical, logical	Cn+	CO+
	Conventionality	Conventional, traditional	Tr+	CO+
III−				
	Disorganization	Disorganized, haphazard, inefficient, scatterbrained, sloppy, unsystematic	Cn−/Sr+	—
	Negligence	Careless, negligent, undependable, unconscientious, unreliable	Cn−	CO−
	Inconsistency	Erratic, inconsistent, unpredictable	Cn−	CO−
	Recklessness	Foolhardy, rash, reckless	Cn−/Ha−	CO−
	Forgetfulness	Forgetful, absent-minded	Cn−/Sr+/Ab+	—
	Indecisiveness	Indecisive, wishy-washy	Sp−/Sr+	—
	Frivolity	Extravagant, frivolous, impractical	Cn−/Ab+	—
	Aimlessness	Aimless, unambitious	Ac−/Cn−	—
	Sloth	Lazy, slothful	Ac−	PE−[A−]
IV+				
	Placidity	Passionless, unexcitable, unemotional	Sr−/Wb−/Ab−	NE−/PE−
IV−				
	Emotionality	Emotional, excitable	Sr+/Wb+/Ab+	NE+/PE+
	Fear	Anxious, fearful, nervous	Sr+	NE+
	Instability	Temperamental, touchy, unstable	Sr+/Ag+	NE+
	Envy	Envious, jealous	Sr+/Al+	NE+
	Gullibility	Gullible, naive, suggestible	Sr+/Ab+/Sp−	—
	Intrusiveness	Intrusive, meddlesome, nosy	Sp+/Ag+	—
V+				
	Intellectuality	Contemplative, intellectual, introspective, meditative, philosophical	Cn+/Ab+	—
	Depth	Complex, deep	Cn+/Ab+	—
	Creativity	Artistic, creative, imaginative, innovative, inventive	Ab+/Ac+	—
	Intelligence	Bright, intelligent, smart	—	—
	Foresight	Foresighted, insightful, perceptive	Cn+/Ab+/Sp+	—
	Nonconformity	Nonconforming, rebellious, unconventional	Tr−/Ag+	—
	Sophistication	Cosmopolitan, cultured, refined, sophisticated, worldly	Tr−/Sp+/Ab+	—
	Curiosity	Curious, inquisitive	Ab+/Ha−	—
	Independence	Autonomous, independent, individualistic	Sc−/Ac+	—

(Continued)

APPENDIX B
(Continued)

Goldberg Cluster	Terms Included in Each Cluster	Presumed Tellegen Factor	
		Primary	Second-Order
V−			
Shallowness	Shallow, unintellectual, unreflective	Cn−/Ab−	−
Unimaginativeness	Uncreative, unimaginative	Ab−	−
Imperceptiveness	Imperceptive, unobservant	Ab−/Sp−	−
Stupidity	Dull, ignorant, unintelligent	−	−

Note. Locations of the clusters within the Tellegen system were provided by its author, Prof. Auke Tellegen. The primary factors are: Wb = Well-being; Sp = Social Potency; Sc = Social Closeness; Ac = Achievement; Sr = Stress Reaction; Al = Alienation; Ag = Aggression; Cn = Control; Ha = Harmavoidance; Tr = Traditionalism; and Ab = Absorption. The second-order factors are: PE = Positive Emotionality; NE = Negative Emotionality; and CO = Constraint. PE[A] = Agentic Positive Emotionality, and PE[C] = Communal Positive Emotionality.

APPENDIX C
The Big Five Factors Derived from the 100 Unipolar Markers ($N = 503$):
Varimax-Rotated Factor Loadings in Self Descriptions (z-Score Responses)

	I	II	III	IV	V
I+					
Talkative	.68*	.16	−.17	−.13	−.06
Extraverted	.65*	.09	−.08	.04	.01
Verbal	.58*	−.01	−.12	−.02	.04
Bold	.55*	−.11	.01	.21	.04
Assertive	.54*	−.12	.12	.10	.11
Unrestrained	.50*	.13	−.10	.03	.03
Energetic	.46*	.21	.17	.12	.02
Daring	.45*	−.03	.01	.12	.07
Active	.43*	.18	.20	.08	−.01
Vigorous	.40*	.08	.10	.11	.02
I−					
Shy	−.75*	.13	.06	−.04	−.01
Quiet	−.72*	.01	.17	.10	.08
Introverted	−.71*	−.04	.05	−.05	.01
Untalkative	−.69*	−.12	.14	.16	.02
Bashful	−.68*	.18	.06	−.06	−.03
Withdrawn	−.67*	−.13	−.04	−.03	.01
Reserved	−.66*	.04	.21	.11	.00
Timid	−.65*	.23	.00	−.11	−.15
Inhibited	−.55*	−.02	.04	−.14	−.11
Unadventurous	−.36*	.00	.00	−.02	−.21

(Continued)

APPENDIX C
(Continued)

	I	II	III	IV	V
II+					
Sympathetic	−.09	**.67***	−.02	−.10	.02
Kind	.00	**.64***	.12	−.04	.01
Warm	.16	**.60***	.08	−.07	.01
Helpful	.06	**.54***	.22	.13	.09
Considerate	−.11	**.54***	.17	.09	.04
Cooperative	−.10	**.53***	.23	.14	−.04
Trustful	.03	**.51***	.16	.23	−.08
Pleasant	.11	**.50***	.04	.21	−.06
Agreeable	−.16	**.45***	.02	.11	.00
Generous	.10	**.43***	.01	.16	.02
II−					
Cold	−.20	**−.61***	.03	.02	.00
Unsympathetic	−.02	**−.59***	−.01	.15	−.12
Unkind	−.06	**−.52***	−.08	.11	−.14
Harsh	.11	**−.49***	.02	−.12	−.06
Rude	.15	**−.48***	−.17	.00	−.02
Uncharitable	−.09	**−.42***	.00	−.02	−.13
Distrustful	−.17	**−.39***	−.18	−.14	.11
Uncooperative	.03	**−.38***	−.19	−.04	−.04
Selfish	−.12	**−.37***	−.12	−.27	.12
Demanding	.23	**−.35***	.11	**−.32**	.02
III+					
Organized	−.05	−.03	**.77***	−.02	−.04
Neat	−.09	.11	**.67***	−.11	−.04
Systematic	−.09	−.02	**.63***	.11	.01
Efficient	.04	.04	**.62***	.04	.02
Thorough	−.02	−.04	**.58***	.23	.07
Practical	−.03	.14	**.54***	.13	−.05
Prompt	−.05	.11	**.50***	−.05	−.06
Careful	−.22	.18	**.47***	−.02	.01
Steady	−.01	.15	**.44***	**.34**	−.08
Conscientious	−.12	.21	**.30***	.06	.09
III−					
Disorganized	.00	.05	**−.76***	.04	.02
Careless	.08	−.07	**−.61***	−.03	−.06
Unsystematic	−.02	.07	**−.60***	.01	−.06
Inefficient	−.17	−.06	**−.60***	.04	−.05
Sloppy	.01	−.05	**−.57***	.13	.04
Haphazard	.07	−.07	**−.53***	−.07	−.18
Inconsistent	−.03	−.10	**−.50***	−.24	−.07
Impractical	−.04	−.09	**−.49***	−.06	−.04
Negligent	−.06	−.14	**−.49***	−.06	−.09
Undependable	.02	−.20	**−.45***	.06	.04

(Continued)

APPENDIX C
(Continued)

	I	II	III	IV	V
IV +					
Unenvious	.03	.07	.01	**.60***	.04
Relaxed	.15	.21	.07	**.50***	−.10
Unemotional	−.19	**−.40**	.09	**.47***	−.10
Unexcitable	−.28	−.27	.00	**.45***	−.10
Undemanding	−.24	.26	−.10	**.43***	−.16
Imperturbable	−.09	.10	.05	**.39***	−.13
IV −					
Moody	−.12	−.15	−.07	**−.59***	.09
Temperamental	−.02	−.24	−.04	**−.55***	−.02
Jealous	−.08	−.06	−.05	**−.55***	−.12
Touchy	−.15	−.04	.03	**−.53***	−.06
Envious	−.16	−.02	−.05	**−.52***	−.11
Irritable	−.02	**−.32**	−.01	**−.51***	−.04
Fretful	−.21	.05	−.06	**−.49***	−.08
Emotional	.05	**.41**	−.09	**−.48***	.06
Self-pitying	**−.38**	−.07	−.08	**−.47***	−.04
Nervous	−.25	.05	−.03	**−.45***	−.04
Anxious	−.01	.01	.05	**−.44***	−.07
High-strung	.17	−.07	−.04	**−.42***	.02
Insecure	**−.38**	.03	−.23	**−.41***	−.02
Fearful	−.28	.12	−.05	**−.36***	−.12
V +					
Creative	.03	.04	.00	.17	**63***
Imaginative	.10	.03	−.02	.09	**.55***
Intellectual	−.03	−.02	.13	.17	**.54***
Philosophical	−.08	.03	−.03	.06	**.53***
Artistic	−.04	.02	.05	.11	**.50***
Complex	−.11	−.05	−.09	−.11	**.50***
Deep	−.12	.20	−.07	.02	**.44***
Innovative	.11	.00	.10	.21	**.44***
Bright	.08	.10	.03	.15	**.41***
Introspective	−.28	.03	−.07	−.01	**.35***
V −					
Uncreative	−.12	.04	.00	−.02	**−.60***
Unimaginative	−.17	−.03	−.03	.05	**−.58***
Unintellectual	−.03	.05	−.11	.05	**−.52***
Unintelligent	.00	−.02	−.07	−.01	**−.50***
Simple	−.14	.16	.07	.11	**−.41***
Unreflective	.08	−.07	.04	.14	**−.40***
Shallow	−.09	−.17	−.03	.02	**−.39***
Imperceptive	−.11	.02	−.06	.14	**−.38***
Unsophisticated	−.15	.00	−.21	.24	**−.34***
Uninquisitive	−.19	−.07	.00	.13	**−.33***

Note. Values equal to or larger than |.30| are listed in boldface.
*Highest factor loading of each variable.

REFERENCES

Allport, G. W., & Odbert, H. S. (1936). Trait-names: A psycho-lexical study. *Psychological Monographs, 47* (1, Whole No. 211).

Altemeyer, B. (1981). *Right-wing authoritarianism.* Winnipeg, Canada: University of Manitoba Press.

Block, J. (1961). *The Q-sort method in personality assessment and psychiatric research.* Springfield, IL: Thomas.

Borgatta, E. F., & Corsini, R. J. (1990). *Quick Word Test.* Seattle, WA: Edgar F. Borgatta, University of Washington.

Briggs, S. R. (1992). Assessing the five-factor model of personality description. *Journal of Personality, 60,* 253–293.

Cattell, R. B. (1943). The description of personality: Basic traits resolved into clusters. *Journal of Abnormal and Social Psychology, 38,* 476–506.

Cattell, R. B. (1947). Confirmation and clarification of primary personality factors. *Psychometrika, 12,* 197–220.

Costa, P. T., Jr., & McCrae, R. R. (1985). *The NEO Personality Inventory manual.* Odessa, FL: Psychological Assessment Resources.

Costa, P. T., Jr., & McCrae, R. R. (1988). Personality in adulthood: A 6-year longitudinal study of self-reports and spouse ratings on the NEO Personality Inventory. *Journal of Personality and Social Psychology, 54,* 853–863.

Digman, J. M. (1990). Personality structure: Emergence of the five-factor model. In M. R. Rosenzweig & L. W. Porter (Eds.), *Annual review of psychology* (Vol. 41, pp. 417–440). Palo Alto, CA: Annual Reviews.

Digman, J. M., & Inouye, J. (1986). Further specification of the five robust factors of personality. *Journal of Personality and Social Psychology, 50,* 116–123.

Eysenck, H. J. (1991). Dimensions of personality: Sixteen, 5, or 3?—Criteria for a taxonomic paradigm. *Personality and Individual Differences, 12,* 773–790.

Goldberg, L. R. (1981). Language and individual differences: The search for universals in personality lexicons. In L. Wheeler (Ed.), *Review of personality and social psychology* (Vol. 2, pp. 141–165). Beverly Hills, CA: Sage.

Goldberg, L. R. (1982). From Ace to Zombie: Some explorations in the language of personality. In C. D. Spielberger & J. N. Butcher (Eds.), *Advances in personality assessment* (Vol. 1, pp. 203–234). Hillsdale, NJ: Lawrence Erlbaum Associates.

Goldberg, L. R. (1990). An alternative "Description of personality": The Big-Five factor structure. *Journal of Personality and Social Psychology, 59,* 1216–1229.

Goldberg, L. R. (1992). The development of markers for the Big-Five factor structure. *Psychological Assessment, 4,* 26–42.

Hofstee, W. K. B., de Raad, B., & Goldberg, L. R. (1992). Integration of the Big Five and circumplex approaches to trait structure. *Journal of Personality and Social Psychology, 63,* 146–163.

John, O. P. (1990). The "Big Five" factor taxonomy: Dimensions of personality in the natural language and in questionnaires. In L. A. Pervin (Ed.), *Handbook of personality theory and research* (pp. 66–100). New York: Guilford.

McCrae, R. R., & Costa, P. T., Jr. (1985a). Comparison of EPI and psychoticism scales with measures of the five-factor model of personality. *Personality and Individual Differences, 6,* 587–597.

McCrae, R. R., & Costa, P. T., Jr. (1985b). Updating Norman's "adequate taxonomy": Intelligence and personality dimensions in natural language and in questionnaires. *Journal of Personality and Social Psychology, 49,* 710–721.

McCrae, R. R., & Costa, P. T., Jr. (1987). Validation of the five-factor model of personality across instruments and observers. *Journal of Personality and Social Psychology, 52,* 81–90.

McCrae, R. R., & John, O. P. (1992). An introduction to the five-factor model and its applications. *Journal of Personality, 60,* 175–215.

Norman, W. T. (1967). *2800 personality trait descriptors: Normative operating characteristics for a university population.* Department of Psychology, University of Michigan, Ann Arbor.

Peabody, D., & Goldberg, L. R. (1989). Some determinants of factor structures from personality-trait descriptors. *Journal of Personality and Social Psychology, 57,* 552–567.

Rosenberg, M. (1965). *Society and the adolescent self-image.* Princeton, NJ: Princeton University Press.

Saucier, G. (1992). Benchmarks: Integrating affective and interpersonal circles with the Big-Five personality factors. *Journal of Personality and Social Psychology, 62,* 1025–1035.

Trapnell, P. D., & Wiggins, J. S. (1990). Extension of the Interpersonal Adjective Scales to include the Big Five dimensions of personality. *Journal of Personality and Social Psychology, 59,* 781–790.

Tupes, E. C., & Christal, R. E. (1961). *Recurrent personality factors based on trait ratings* (Tech. Rep. No. ASD-TR-61-97). Lackland Air Force Base, TX: U.S. Air Force.

Wiggins, J. S., & Pincus, A. L. (1992). Personality: Structure and assessment. In M. R. Rosenzweig & L. W. Porter (Eds.), *Annual review of psychology* (Vol. 43, pp. 473–504). Palo Alto, CA: Annual Reviews.

Wiggins, J. S., & Trapnell, P. D. (in press). Personality structure: The return of the Big Five. In R. Hogan, J. A. Johnson, & S. R. Briggs (Eds.), *Handbook of personality psychology.* Orlando, FL: Academic Press.

Wilson, G. D. (Ed.). (1973). *The psychology of conservatism.* London: Academic Press.

CHAPTER

2

THE BIG FIVE OR GIANT THREE: CRITERIA FOR A PARADIGM

H. J. Eysenck
University of London

Science advances by the discovery of paradigms (Kuhn, 1962, 1974), which direct experimentation, serve to produce agreement on major theories, and guide the training of students. It is well known that such paradigms are almost unknown in the social sciences (Barnes, 1982), and in particular in the study of personality where the existence and use of thousands of quite different questionnaires and concepts attests to its absence, as does the existence of dozens of theories having very little in common (Hall & Lindzey, 1985). There is not even agreement on the meaning of the term *personality*. Where agreement on such fundamental points is missing, it becomes important to try and discover what *criteria* might be used to discover which theoretical scheme comes closest to forming a paradigm in this field. I have tried to do just that in a recent publication (H. J. Eysenck, 1991a). I have also argued for the possibility of such a paradigm (H. J. Eysenck, 1983a).

Many approaches are ruled out immediately because they contravene elementary psychometric rules. Thus the Minnesota Multiphasic Personality Inventory (MMPI), the California Psychological Inventory (CPI), or the Myers–Briggs Temperament Inventory are not based on a factor analysis of their items. And where such analyses have been done, they do not verify the alleged traits or types suggested by their authors (H. J. Eysenck & M. W. Eysenck, 1985). This is also true of the Cattell 16 Personality Faction (PF) system; although based on factor analytic foundations, it has been found impossible for many independent investigations to replicate Cattell's original findings. Usually there are 7 to 10 factors that emerge from such analyses, none resembling the Cattell factors; at the second-order level, 3 factors are found resembling Extraversion, Neuroticism, and Psychoticism, the three factors postulated by H. J. Eysenck's (1952) P-E-N theory (Matthews, 1989; McKenzie, 1988). Factor analysis is a necessary but not a sufficient method for arriving at the basic dimensions of personality.

H. J. Eysenck (1991a) suggested that only two major systems survive this psychometric holocaust, namely the P-E-N system and the Big Five (John, 1990), which also contain E and N as two of their five major factors or dimensions. This agreement suggests that we may be approaching enough accord to bring us somewhat nearer to a paradigm in this field. Yet there are some important differences, and a consideration of the differences may lead us to a more detailed look at criteria for a paradigm. Our major differences, in particular, may be useful in suggesting the importance of such criteria.

Given that almost everyone is agreed that E and N are undoubtedly two major dimensions of personality, we are faced with the question raised by Zuckerman, Kuhlman, and Camac (1988): What lies beyond E and N? My own suggestion has been that psychoticism is the third major factor dimension (H. J. Eysenck & S. B. G. Eysenck, 1976); Costa and McCrae (1992) suggested "Four ways five factors are basic" without specifying what "basic" means. H. J. Eysenck (1992b) responded by pointing out "four ways five factors are *not* basic," in an attempt to define more closely the meaning of "basic." It may be best to consider this problem in the light of the position taken by Costa and McCrae, namely that there are two basic factors: Agreeableness (A) and Conscientiousness (C). These show some covariance with P, which is a mere artifact, combining variance from A and C. This view is shown in Fig. 2.1b.

According to my view, A and C are some of the many primaries that go to define higher order Factor P; this view is shown in Fig. 2.1a. There is no doubt about the existence of considerable overlap between A and C on the one hand, and P on the other. McCrae and Costa (1987) reported correlations of $-.45$ and $-.31$, respectively, and Goldberg and Rosolack (in press) reported a disattenuated correlation of $-.85$ between P and Agreeableness and Conscientiousness combined. There is thus agreement on the facts, but disagreement on their interpretation. How can this disagreement be resolved? Note that we are here in the field of taxonomy, which historically has given rise to exceptionally fierce battles, the fierceness of which is probably a consequence of the simple fact that they are destined to be inconclusive as long as we remain in the field of taxonomy (Sokal & Sneath, 1963). What is needed is the inclusion of causal theories to explain the origins of our taxonomy; only by enlarging our viewpoint in this manner are we likely to arrive at some consensus that must precede the growth of a paradigm.

In biology, such a causal factor was the *theory of evolution*; this explained and verified the lines of growth of the different branches of the evolutionary tree. It also made intelligible the relations based on morphological similarity that led to so many differences of opinion. Of course there were gaps in the historical evidence, but now the use of DNA similarities and the extension of taxonomy

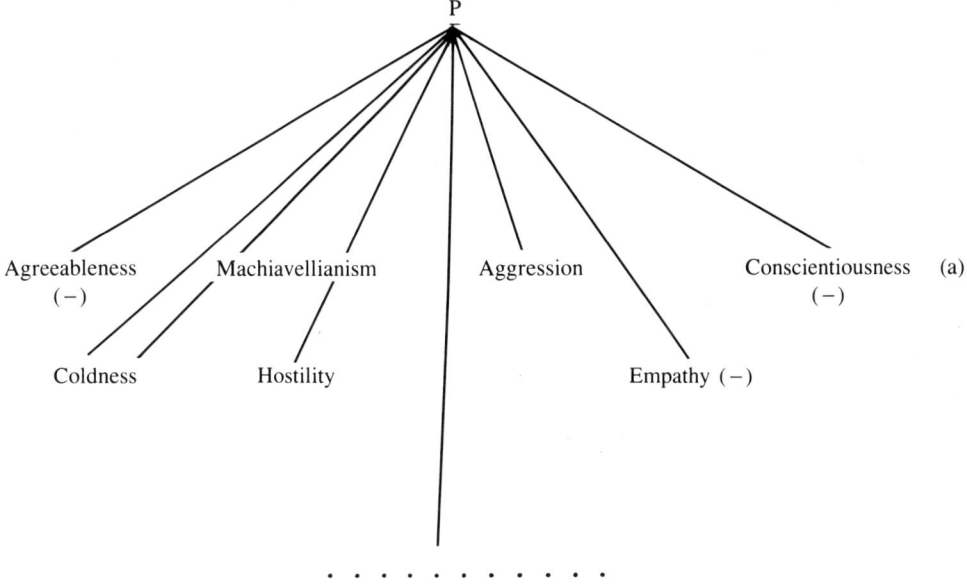

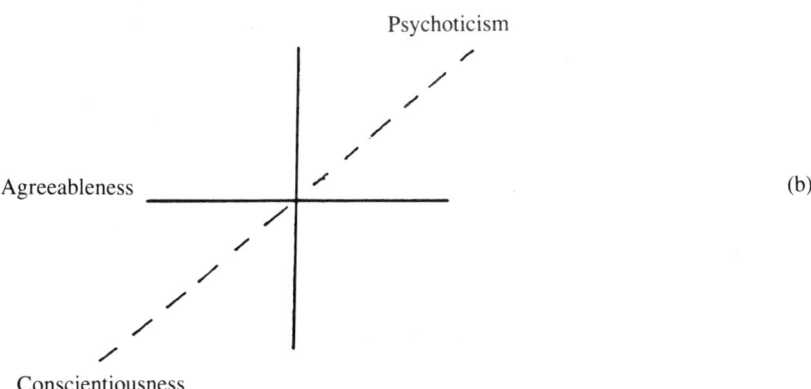

FIG. 2.1. Alternative psychometric conception of the P vs. A + C correlation. Fig. 2.1a shows the hypothetical position of Agreeableness and Conscientiousness as subfactors of P; Fig. 2.1b shows P as an artifact, combining variance from A and C.

to include causal theories have provided a reasonable paradigm (Sokal & Sneath, 1963).

In a similar manner, the taxonomy of stars (white dwarf, giants, red dwarfs, super giants, etc.) was systematized in the famous Hertzsprung–Russell diagram, which gives a good picture of stellar evolution (Hoyle, 1975; Vaucouleurs, 1956). Morphological similarities only become meaningful by means of theoretical advances explaining their origins, and taking the argument beyond simple taxonomy. It is suggested that what is true in biology and physics is equally true of psychology; if we wish to find agreed answers to taxonomic problems, we must transcend taxonomy.

This brings us back to Fig. 2.1, which may be used as a typical problem in the field of taxonomy. Arguments on both sides have been forthcoming in profusion, but as long as they remain within the narrow confines of psychometric taxonomy, they clearly are not sufficient to command universal agreement. Indeed, I would suggest that no such agreement is conceivable as long as we remain within these confines. No argument has been suggested that would help us decide which of the two alternatives in Fig. 2.1 is the correct one; indeed, there is no meaning to the adjective "correct," because psychometrically both are equally descriptive of the true state of affairs. Staying in the taxonomic field must mean that our decisions on how to distribute observed variance must be subjective—there are no rules we can appeal to prove that our way is best.

The favorite argument of Big Five advocates—namely that there is a natural language of trait description, given by lexical approaches—is clearly unacceptable; it states an axiom, but fails to give evidence in its favor. If we are prepared to make such a major assumption, we might proceed from there, but if we ask for proof, as scientists should, we are offered dry bread and water instead of nutritious fare. Cattell, Eber, and Tatsuoka (1970) started with a similar axiom, but landed in territories far removed from the Big Five—why? Why does his work culminate with three factors resembling P-E-N, rather than those advocated by Costa and McCrae? Even accepting their axiom apparently does not create agreement.

There are other objections to the lexical approach. DeRaad (1992) asked the pertinent question: "Why adjectives?" He used other lexical categories (nouns and verbs descriptive of personality), and found some resemblance to the Big Five structure with nouns, but a completely different two-dimensional structure with verbs. There is nothing in the axiom to favor adjectives over verbs, so the very different structures that emerge seem fatal to an easy acceptance of the lexical axiom. Much more research seems needed in order to classify these and other points of difference raised by DeRaad (1992).

What can be said in favor of P having A and C as primary factors, defining the superfactor in combination with many others? Note that the two theories portrayed in Fig. 2.1 have quite different origins. The A and C factors emerged from observed correlations between adjectives, applied to various samples; they are the product of factor analysis in its hypothesis-producing aspects, and have advanced but little from this unpropitious ancestry. Psychoticism, on the other hand, started as a theoretical concept based on a number of testable assumptions. According to the first of these assumptions, all functional psychoses have some fundamental psychological property in common (Crow, 1986). In the second, this property is not categorical or qualitative, opposing psychotic to normal, but is dimensional or continuous, going from one extreme (psychosis) to its opposite (Claridge, 1985). Figure 2.2 illustrates this conception. Both these assumptions have found strong support in the literature (H. J. Eysenck, 1992a, 1992b), and may thus be used to support the notion of *psychoticism*. P, in consequence, has a proper parentage in very numerous, large-scale empirical studies, which give it credence.

Having noted the different ways these two sets of factors were derived, we must also note the different ways they have been labeled. Apparently the parents of the A and C concepts simply looked at the items having high loadings, and proceeded to christen the factors rather arbitrarily. The arbitrary nature of such christening has always been an argument against factor analysis; it can be obviated by subjecting the naming process to a proper scientific examination following an experimental paradigm. This process is described in some detail in order to demonstrate the difference between the purely taxonomic approach, and the more inclusive experimental–theoretical approach advocated here.

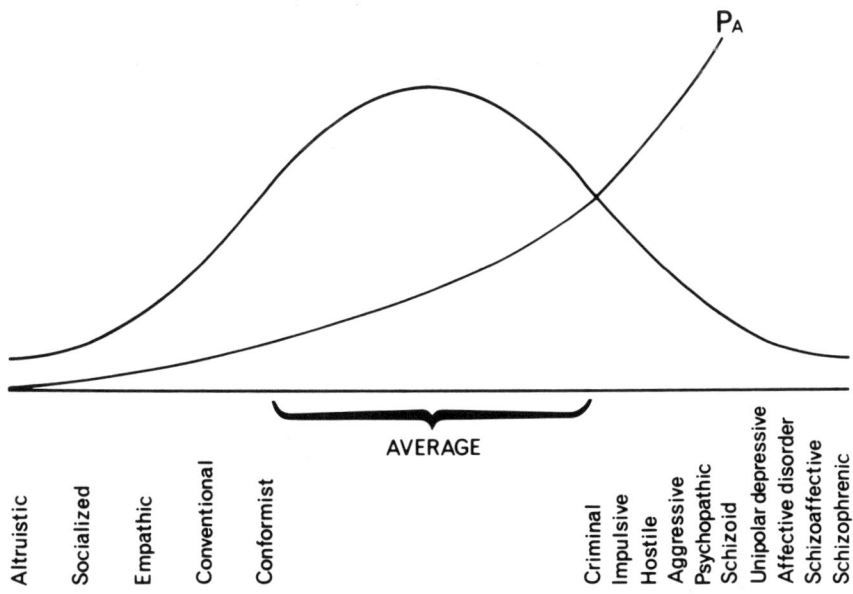

FIG. 2.2. Psychoticism (abscissa) as a continuous variable (P); P_A shows probability of developing psychosis as a function of P.

The argument relating to testable derivations from the model is as follows: Let us postulate that Trait T is colinear with the abscissa in Fig. 2.2, X; if $X = P$, then T should correlate with P in a normal population. It should also correlate with P in a schizophrenic-psychotic population. Finally, it should differentiate between normal and psychotic subjects. This is part of the method of criterion analysis (H. J. Eysenck, 1950, 1952a). Let us take a few tests that have been shown to differentiate between normals and psychotics (usually schizophrenics) to illustrate the method. The intention is to demonstrate a method that enables us to determine whether a personality inventory scale (P) assumed to measure psychoticism does in fact do so.

As an example, consider HLA B27, a subsystem of the human leukocyte antigen system, which is found more frequently in schizophrenics than in normal, nonpsychotic subjects (Gattaz, Ewald, & Beckman, 1980; McGuffin, 1979). Gattaz (1981) showed that in a comparison of schizophrenic patients with and without HLA B27, those with the antigen had significantly higher P scores ($p < .02$, $n = 11:29$). In another study (Gattaz, Seitz, & Beckman, 1985), 17 B27 positive and 16 B27 negative nonpsychotic subjects showed a difference on P scores in the expected direction ($p < .01$). This example shows the expected effects of an association between P and T in both a normal and a psychotic group, and may serve to illustrate the method.

Another study concentrated on the prevalence of hallucinations. Slade (1976) contrasted three groups—normals, and psychotics both with and without auditory hallucinations; on the P-test normals had the lowest scores (2.80), hallucinatory psychotics the highest (7.25), with nonhallucinatory psychotics in between (4.80). In a later study, Launay and Slade (1981) correlated scores on a 12-item questionnaire testing hallucinatory predispositions with the P scale. The correlations were .21 for 100 male prisoners and .46 for 100 female prisoners, making a combined $r = .35$. Thus here again there is an association between T (hallucinations) and P in both psychotic and nonpsychotic groups.

Eye-tracking is another variable that has been related to P and the general psychoticism continuum. Lipton, Levy, Holzman, and Levin (1983) showed that not only schizophrenics, but often also their relatives, show faulty lack of smoothness in the pursuit or tracking eye movements required when, say, following a swinging pendulum. Similarly, twin discordant schizophrenics may nevertheless be concordant for this test. Iacono, Peloquin, Lumry, Valentine, and Tuason (1982) found this symptom in patients with unipolar and bipolar affective disorder in remission. Bosch (1984) and Iacono and Lykken (1979) reported positive correlations with psychoticism questionnaires in schizophrenic and normal subjects, as did Yasamy (1987). There are some contradictions in the data, and a large-scale replication would seem suggested (see also Siever et al., 1982; Simons & Katkin, 1989).

Hemisphere differences provide another example. Jutai (1988) specifically examined the lateralized cerebral dysfunction in schizophrenic and affective disorders postulated by Flor-Henry and Gruzelier (1983), and based on a model suggested by Venables (1980). Jutai concluded that the results of his study supported Venables' notion that in the development of schizophrenic disorders, there may be an initial disturbance of right-hemisphere mechanisms of attentional control. Psychosis-prone young adults diagnosed on the Chapman tests tended to use visual search strategies similar to those of right-brain damaged patients. He added the usual disclaimer that at present it is not certain they do so for similar reasons.

A different technique for investigating hemisphere differences is the dichotic shadowing technique (Rawlings & Borge, 1987). The theory that schizophrenics are characterized by left-hemisphere overactivation (Flor-Henry & Gruzelier, 1983) has been tested by Rawlings and Claridge (1984) and shows that subjects scoring high on a measure of schizotypal personality responded more quickly to verbal material presented tachistopically to their left visual field than to their right, whereas subjects with low scores showed the usual superiority for material presented to the right visual field. Broks (1984) found a similar difference. Rawlings and Borge (1987) reported two experiments using the dichotic shadowing technique. Both gave positive results, showing differential responding in the two ears, with high P scorers failing to show the right ear superiority shown by the low P scorers; the second experiment gave similar results for the male subjects but gave little evidence for the females. Overall, the studies give support for the theory, but leave many questions unanswered. It is worth mentioning that Hare and McPherson (1984) found that a group of criminal psychopaths showed a significantly smaller right-ear advantage on a dichotic listening task than did groups of criminals who were not clearly psychopathic; this adds to the evidence that psychopaths belong to the schizophrenic *Erbkreis* (H. J. Eysenck, 1987a).

Related to these studies of attention deficit in schizophrenics is an experiment carried out by Hinton and Craske (1976), who argued that "attentional effort" is positively correlated with the magnitude of action potentials in those muscles that are not involved in the tasks being undertaken (Eason & White, 1961), and that "degree of effort" in attentional tasks would lead schizophrenics to show higher action potentials in a simple attention task (Goldstein, 1965; Malmo, Shagass, & A. A. Smith, 1951). They predicted and found positive correlations between their EMG index and P score for both males ($r = .56$) and females ($r = .44$), concluding that P score related directly to increase in generalized muscle action potentials on attending to simple perceptual discrimination tasks.

Attentional processes may also be involved in an interesting experiment reported by Babcock, G. A. Smith, and Rawlings (1988). The topic selected was the effect of a masking stimulus (backward masking) on exposure of a target stimulus, with a specified interstimulus interval intervening. Saccuzzo and Schubert (1981) used the presence of a masking deficit within various subgroups of schizophrenic and schizotypals to verify the existence of spectrum disorder.

Babcock et al. successfully extended this research to include high P scorers, who showed significantly more deficit than low P scorers.

Low platelet monoamine oxydase (MAO) has been found in psychotic patients, and also in their relatives and inpatients who have recovered, suggesting that low MAO activity may be a marker for "vulnerability" (Buchsbaum, Coursey, & Murphy, 1976; Schalling, Edman, & Aesberg, 1987). In a recent study of 61 healthy high school volunteers, Klinteberg, Schalling, Edman, Oreland, and Aesberg (1987) found correlations of $-.30$ in females and $-.27$ in males between MAO and psychoticism. It may also be noted that low MAO activity was found related to extraversion, impulsiveness, and sensation-seeking, as well as monotony avoidance, and that Lidberg, Modin, Oreland, Tucker, and Gillner (1985) found it related to psychopathy, again suggesting a relationship between psychopathy and schizophrenia. (See also Checkley, 1980, for a review of MAO in relation to depressive illness.)

These results may be related to serotonin levels, which seem to have similar behavioral correlates as MAO, and hence may be predicted to correlate inversely with P (Zuckerman, 1991). Schalling et al. (1987) found that cerebrospinal fluid (CSF) 5-HIAA levels were inversely related to P scores; similarly, CSF levels of 5-HIAA were found to be positively related to a measure of inhibition of aggression, suggesting that in humans, P is related inversely to the functioning of the serotonergic system, as is much psychopathology.

In this connection it may be useful finally to list two psychological systems that have received much theoretical attention and may have a causal influence on schizophrenia, as well as being related to P. The first of these is *negative priming* (Beech & Claridge, 1987), a concept widely used to explain the schizophrenic's failure to use inhibitory material early in the information-processing system, thus allowing material in the preconscious to gain conscious representation (Frith, 1979). The general nature of the effect is as follows: First, a distractor is used in a priming display; when next used as a target stimulus, response latency to the latter is increased compared with trials where no such relation is present (Tipper, 1985; Tipper & Cranston, 1985). This concept may be used as a measure of individual differences (Tipper & Baylis, 1987), and if it is true that schizophrenia is associated with a weakening of the inhibitory mechanism, then we would predict a negative correlation between measures of negative priming and interference, and a positive correlation between psychoticism or schizotypy and interference. In other words, negative priming is a precondition of effective inhibition of interfering stimuli, and inefficient negative priming, as in schizophrenics and high P scorers, would lead to interference and hence poor performance.

Beech and Claridge (1987) demonstrated a significant relationship between the effect and schizotypy, using the Claridge and Broks (1984) scale; subjects scoring high on the schizotypy scale demonstrated *reduced* negative priming, as predicted. Beech, Baylis, Smithson, and Claridge (1989) demonstrated similar effects in a replication study, and Beech, Powell, McWilliam, and Claridge (1989) extended the paradigm to schizophrenics with positive results. Here again, then, the proportionality criterion is satisfied.

The next measure is based on the Venables (1963, 1964) and Claridge (1972) theory that psychotic patients differ from normals not so much in their absolute levels on the range they cover on given psychophysical measures, but rather in the way in which different measures co-vary. Thus in psychosis, whether natural or LSD induced, there occurs a peculiar inversion of the co-variation between autonomic and perceptual function. The most widely used measures were the two-flash threshold and the electrodermal response. Claridge and Chappa (1973) extended this model to normal subjects and showed that high P scorers do indeed behave, when compared with low P scorers, as schizophrenics do when compared with normals. They concluded: "The results provide evidence for psychoticism as a normal personality dimension having, as its biological basis, a particular kind of nervous typological organization seen, in its extreme form, in the psychotic disorders" (p. 175). Later studies have extended this peculiar inversion of perceptual and autonomic functioning to relatives of psychotic patients, that is, to members of the psychotic *Erkbreis* (Claridge, Robinson, & Birchall, 1985). A more detailed discussion of the whole theory and its relevance to the concept of psychoticism is given in Claridge (1985).

The final concept to be discussed here is that of *latent inhibition*, a close relation of negative priming (Weiner, 1990). Passive pre-exposure of a stimulus reduces its ability to enter into new associations when that opportunity is offered in the same context as the initial pre-exposure (Macintosh, 1975; Pearce & Hall, 1980). This phenomenon, originally studied in animals, has now also been widely investigated in human subjects, both adults and children (Lubow, 1989). Lack of latent inhibition would promote attentional deficits, such as those that occur in schizophrenics, and it has been shown that schizophrenics not under medication, or at an early stage of medication, do indeed show less latent inhibition than controls (Baruch, Hemsley, & Gray, 1988). It was found that medication, as expected, reversed this trend.

When the same procedure was tried on normal subjects, using the Claridge schizotypy scale and the Eysenck psychoticism measure as psychosis-prone scales, these were negatively correlated with latent inhibition, supporting the hypothesis. Lubow, Ingberg-Sachs, Zalstein, and Gewirtz (in press) replicated the Baruch, Hemsley, and Gray (1988) study, showing that latent inhibition was weaker in high-P than in low-P subjects. Here also predictions of proportionality are successfully verified (Lubow, 1989).

Here, then, we have an attempt to prove along the lines of hypothetico-deductive demonstration that our factor-analytic P is in fact colinear with a dimension of personality properly called psychoticism, because P behaves, in a large number of experiments exploring many different aspects of psychosis (cognitive, physiological, hormonal, behavioral, etc.), exactly as a measure of psychoticism should behave (H. J. Eysenck, 1992a). This way of experimenting takes us away from the purely subjective "naming" process of customary factor analysis, and imbues the process with a great deal of objectivity. It is not suggested that our proof is absolute and cannot be criticized; obviously it is imperfect, and may be wrong. It does suggest that our theory is testable; it can be shown to be wrong in a meaningful way. The appelations "agreeableness" and "conscientiousness" are not subject to any such disproof, and hence are not really scientific concepts at all in the Popperian sense.

I would extend this argument further. We start with a theoretical concept defining an important dimension of personality along which to measure individual differences. We go backward to study its biological roots (genetic determinants, physiological and hormonal causes, neurological sources), and forward to study its social consequences. Thus the biological causes of P, E, and N have been studied very widely (Zuckerman, 1991), as have many of their social consequences in criminology (H. J. Eysenck & Gudjonsson, 1989), education (H. J. Eysenck, 1978), psychopathology (H. J. Eysenck, 1973), sexual behavior (H. J. Eysenck, 1976), smoking and smoking-related diseases (H. J. Eysenck, 1985, 1991b), and many more (Wilson, 1981). I would not deny the *possibility* that A and C may in due course attract sufficient research to develop a similar nomological network that alone would serve to give them the status of major dimensions of personality. To name A and C as major dimensions of personality is to draw promissory notes on a nonexistent bank account; it assumes that the experimental and theoretical work that should be done to establish such dimensions has in fact been done, when clearly it had not. In psychology, concepts and theories often produce a bandwagon effect that attracts a great deal of support, only to fade away after awhile when the promised advances do not materialize. The Big Five have produced such a bandwagon effect; there seems little justification for it if we take an objective look at the achievements of its advocates to date.

The statement that such factors as Agreeableness lack a nomological network to support them and vouchsafe their validity may appear to be contradicted by claims such as those of Graziano (in press) concerning "the development of agreeableness as a dimension of personality." But essentially such arguments simply indicate that identification of such a factor can be traced through development; they are not concerned with the essential query underlying this chapter, namely whether agreeableness is a primary or higher order factor. This argument must rest on the question of whether Costa and McCrae were right in arguing that P is an artifactual shot-gun marriage between A and C, or whether there is good evidence of P being a meaningful dimension of personality, showing good support of its appropriate conceptualization. It is for this reason that I have given at some length a list of studies demonstrating that the principle of criterion analysis justifies such an assumption.

The major difference between myself and the Costa–McCrae–Goldberg group is part of a much wider conflict, namely Cronbach's (1957) famous division of scientific psychology into two disciplines: the *experimental* and the *correlational*.

As he pointed out, the former approach disregards individual differences, which only appear in the error terms, and the latter disregard theory and causal arguments. Only by joining the two together will we ever achieve the semblance at least of a genuine science (H. J. Eysenck, 1984, 1985). The Big Five adherents clearly favor the correlational side, basing all their arguments on psychometric issues that, although important, cannot in principle decide the issue.

One example may serve to illustrate the argument. I have suggested that the concept of psychoticism can solve the paradox that genius and psychopathology are closely related, but that psychosis is no more frequent among geniuses than ordinary people (H. J. Eysenck, 1983a, 1983b, 1993). Using the concept of latent inhibition, absent among psychotics and high P scorers (Lubow, 1989), I argued that it might serve to explain cognitive peculiarities of creative people, high P scorers, and psychotics. From these suggestions and many of the facts linking psychoticism and psychosis, I constructed a chain of events leading from DNA to genius. Is it seriously suggested that an assertion that genius and creativity are based on disagreeableness and lack of conscientiousness (which psychometrically might indeed appear to be so in the correlations) would lend itself to the construction of such a nomological network? There is more in science than mere correlations, and decisions about theories demand a consideration of all the available facts. It makes sense to link psychoticism and schizophrenia through latent inhibition (Lubow, 1989); it makes no sense to link latent inhibition to agreeableness and conscientiousness. Psychometrics, correlations, and factor analysis are good servants, but bad masters; let us never forget this simple precept!

REFERENCES

Babcock, J. C., Smith, G. A., & Rawlings, D. (1988). Temporal processing and psychosis-proneness. *Personality and Individual Differences, 9*, 709–719.
Barnes, B. (1982). *T. S. Kuhn and social science*. London: Macmillan.
Baruch, I., Hemsley, D. R., & Gray, J. (1988). Latent inhibition and "psychotic-proneness" in normal subjects. *Personality and Individual Differences, 9*, 777–789.
Beech, A., Baylis, G. C., Smithson, P., & Claridge, G. (1989). Individual differences in schizotypy as reflected in measures of cognitive inhibition. *British Journal of Clinical Psychology, 28*, 117–129.
Beech, A., & Claridge, G. (1987). Individual differences in negative priming. *British Journal of Psychology, 78*, 349–356.
Beech, A., Powell, T., McWilliam, J., & Claridge, G. (1989). Evidence of reduced "cognitive inhibition" in schizophrenia. *British Journal of Clinical Psychology, 28*, 109–116.
Bosch, R. van den. (1984). Eye-tracking impairment: Attentional and psychometric correlates in psychiatric patients. *Journal of Psychiatric Research, 18*, 277–286.
Broks, P. (1984). Schizotypy and hemisphere function: II. Performance asymmetry on a verbal divided visual-field task. *Personality and Individual Differences, 5*, 649–656.
Buchsbaum, M. S., Coursey, R. D., & Murphy, D. L. (1976). The biochemical high-risk paradigm: Behavioral and familial correlates of low platelet monoamine oxidase activity. *Science, 194*, 339–341.

Cattell, R. B., Eber, H. W., & Tatsuoka, M. Y. (1970). *Handbook for the 16 PF*. Champaign, IL: Institute for Personality and Ability Testing.
Checkley, S. A. (1980). Neuroendocrine tests of monoamine function in man: A review of basic theory and its application to the study of depressive illness. *Psychological Medicine, 10,* 35–53.
Claridge, G. S. (1972). The schizophrenias as nervous types. *British Journal of Psychiatry, 121,* 1–17.
Claridge, G. S. (1985). *Origins of Mental Illness.* Oxford: Basil Blackwell.
Claridge, G. S., & Broks, P. (1984). Schizotype and hemisphere function: I. Theoretical considerations and the measurement of schizotypy. *Personality and Individual Differences, 5,* 633–648.
Claridge, G. S., & Chappa, H. J. (1973). Psychoticism: A study of its biological basis in normal subjects. *British Journal of Social and Clinical Psychology, 12,* 175–187.
Claridge, G. S., Robinson, D. L., & Birchall, P. M. A. (1985). Psychophysiological evidence of "psychoticism" in schizophrenics' relatives. *Personality & Individual Differences, 6,* 1–10.
Costa, P. T., & McCrae, R. R. (1992). Four ways five factors are basic. *Personality and Individual Differences, 13,* 653–665.
Cronbach, L. J. (1957). The two disciplines of scientific psychology. *American Psychologist, 12,* 671–684.
Crow, T. J. (1986). The continuum of psychosis and its implications for the structure of the gene. *British Journal of Psychiatry, 149,* 419–429.
DeRaad, B. (1992). The replicability of the Big Five personality dimensions in three word-classes of the Dutch language. *European Journal of Personality, 6,* 15–29.
Eason, R. G., & White, C. T. (1961). Muscular tension, effort and tracking difficulty: Studies of parameters which affect tension level and performance efficiency. *Perceptual and Motor Skills, 12,* 331–372.
Eysenck, H. J. (1950). Criterion analysis: An application of the hypothetico-deductive method to factor analysis. *Psychological Review,* 57, 38–53.
Eysenck, H. J. (1952a). Schizophrenia-cyclothymia as a dimension of personality. II. *Experimental Journal of Personality, 20,* 345–384.
Eysenck, H. J. (1952b). *The scientific study of personality.* London: Routledge & Kegan Paul.
Eysenck, H. J. (Ed.). (1973). *Handbook of abnormal psychology (2nd ed.).* London: Pitman.
Eysenck, H. J. (1976). *Sex and personality.* London: Open Books.
Eysenck, H. J. (1978). The development of personality and its relation to learning. In S. Murray-Smith (Ed.), *Melbourne studies in education* (pp. 134–181). Melbourne, Australia: Melbourne University Press.
Eysenck, H. J. (1980). *The causes and effects of smoking.* London: Laurence Temple Smith.
Eysenck, H. J. (1983a). Is there a paradigm in personality research? *Journal of Research in Personality, 17,* 369–397.
Eysenck, H. J. (1983b). The roots of creativity: Cognitive ability or personality trait? *Roeper Review, 5,* 10–12.
Eysenck, H. J. (1984). The place of individual differences in a scientific psychology. In J. R. Royce & L. P. Mos (Eds.), *Annals of theoretical psychology* (Vol. 1, pp. 233–314). New York: Plenum.
Eysenck, H. J. (1985). The place of theory in a world of facts. In K. B. Madsen & L. P. Mos (Eds.), *Annals of theoretical psychology* (Vol. 3, pp. 17–114). New York: Plenum.
Eysenck, H. J. (1987). The definition of personality disorders and the criteria appropriate for their description. *Journal of Personality Disorders, 1,* 211–219.
Eysenck, H. J. (1991a). Dimensions of personality: Sixteen, 5, or 3?—Criteria for a taxonomic paradigm. *Personality and Individual Differences, 12,* 773–790.
Eysenck, H. J. (1991b). *Smoking, personality and stress: Psychosocial factors in the prevention of cancer and coronary heart disease.* New York: Plenum.
Eysenck, H. J. (1992a). The definition and measurement of psychoticism. *Personality and Individual Differences, 13,* 757–785.

Eysenck, H. J. (1992b). Four ways five factors are *not* basic. *Personality and Individual Differences, 13*, 667–673.
Eysenck, H. J. (1993). Creativity and personality: Suggestions for a theory. *Psychological Inquiry, 4*, 147–178.
Eysenck, H. J., & Eysenck, M. W. (1985). *Personality and individual differences: A natural science approach.* New York: Plenum.
Eysenck, H. J., & Eysenck, S. B. G. (1976). *Psychoticism as a dimension of personality.* London: Hodder & Stoughton.
Eysenck, H. J., & Gudjonsson, G. H. (1989). *The causes and cures of criminality.* New York: Plenum.
Flor-Henry, P., & Gruzelier, J. (Eds.). (1983). *Laterality and psychopathology.* New York: Elsevier.
Frith, C. D. (1979). Consciousness, information processing and schizophrenia. *British Journal of Psychiatry, 134*, 225–235.
Gattaz, W., Ewald, R., & Beckman, H. (1980). The HLA system and schizophrenia. *Archiv fuer Psychiatrie und NervenKrankheiten, 228*, 205–211.
Gattaz, W. F., Seitz, M., & Beckman, H. (1985). A possible association between HLA B-27 and vulnerability to schizophrenia. *Personality and Individual Differences, 8*, 283–285.
Goldberg, L., & Rosolack, T. (in press). The Big-Five factor structure as an integrative framework: An empirical comparison with Eysenck's P-E-N model. In C. F. Halverson, G. A. Kohnstamm, & R. P. Martin (Eds.), *Development of the structure of temperament and personality from infancy to adulthood.* Hillsdale, NJ: Lawrence Erlbaum Associates.
Goldstein, I. B. (1965). The relationship of muscle tension and autonomic activity in psychiatric disorders. *Psychosomatic Medicine, 27*, 39–52.
Graziano, W. G. (in press). The development of agreeableness as a dimension of personality. In C. F. Halverson, D. Kohnstamm, & R. Martin (Eds.), *Development of the structure of temperament and personality from infancy to adulthood.* Hillsdale, NJ: Lawrence Erlbaum Associates.
Hall, C. S., & Lindzey, G. (1985). *Introduction to theories of personality.* New York: Wiley.
Hare, R. D., & McPherson, L. M. (1984). Psychopathy and perceptual asymmetry during verbal dichotic listening. *Journal of Abnormal Psychology, 93*, 141–149.
Hinton, J., & Craske, B. (1976). A relationship between Eysenck's P scale and change in muscle action potentials with attention to perceptual tasks. *British Journal of Psychology, 67*, 461–466.
Hoyle, F. (1975). *Astronomy and cosmology.* San Francisco: Freeman.
Iacono, W. G., & Lykken, D. T. (1979). Eye-tracking and psychopathology, new procedures applied to a sample of normal monozygotic twins. *Archives of General Psychiatry, 36*, 1361–1369.
Iacono, W. G., Peloquin, L. J., Lumry, A., Valentine, B. H., & Tuason, V. B. (1982). Eye-tracking in patients with unipolar and bipolar affective disorder in remission. *Journal of Abnormal Psychology, 91*, 35–44.
Jutai, J. W. (1988). Spatial attention in hypothetically psychosis-prone college students. *Psychiatry Research, 27*, 207–215.
John, O. P. (1990). The "Big Five" factor taxonomy: Dimensions of personality in the natural language and in questionnaires. In L. Pervin (Ed.), *Handbook of personality theory and research* (pp. 66–100). New York: Guilford.
Klinteberg, B., Schalling, D., Edman, G., Oreland, L., & Aesberg, M. (1987). Personality correlates of platelet monoamine oxidase (MAO) activity in female and male subjects. *Neuropsychobiology, 18*, 89–96.
Kuhn, T. S. (1962). *The structure of scientific revolutions.* Chicago: University of Chicago Press.
Kuhn, T. S. (1974). Second thoughts in paradigms. In F. Suppe (Ed.), *The structure of scientific theories* (pp. 459–482). Illinois: University of Illinois Press.
Launay, G., & Slade, P. (1981). The measurement of hallucinatory predisposition in male and female prisoners. *Personality and Individual Differences, 2*, 221–234.
Lidberg, L., Modin, I., Oreland, L., Tucker, J. R., & Gillner, A. (1985). Platelet monoamine oxidase activities and psychopathy. *Psychiatry Research, 16*, 339–343.

Lipton, R. B., Levy, D. L., Holzman, P. S., & Levin, S. (1983). Eye-movement dysfunction in psychiatric patients: A review. *Schizophrenia Bulletin, 9*, 13–32.
Lubow, R. E. (1984). *Latent inhibition and conditioned and attention theory.* Cambridge, England: Cambridge University Press.
Lubow, R. E. (1989). *Latent inhibition and conditioned attention theory.* New York: Cambridge University Press.
Lubow, R. E., Ingberg-Sacks, V., Zalstein, N., & Gewirtz, J. (in press). Latent inhibition in low and high "psychotic-prone" normal subjects. *Personality and Individual Differences.*
McCrae, R. R., & Costa, P. T. (1987). Validation of the five-factor model of personality across instruments and observers. *Journal of Personality & Social Psychology, 52*, 81–90.
McGuffin, P. (1979). Is schizophrenia an HLA-associated disease? *Psychological Medicine, 9*, 721–728.
McKenzie, J. (1988). Three superfactors in the 16 PF and their relation to Eysenck's P, E and N. *Personality and Individual Differences, 9*, 843–850.
Macintosh, N. J. (1975). A theory of attention: Variations of the associability of stimuli with reinforcement. *Psychological Review, 82*, 276–298.
Malmo, R., Shagass, C., & Smith, A. A. (1951). Responsiveness in chronic schizophrenia. *Journal of Personality, 19*, 359–375.
Matthews, G. (1989). The factor structure of the 16 PF: Twelve primary and three secondary factors. *Personality and Individual Differences, 10*, 931–940.
Pearce, J. M., & Hall, G. (1980). A model of Pavlovian learning: Variations in the affectiveness of conditional but not of unconditional stimuli. *Psychological Review, 87*, 532–552.
Rawlings, D., & Borge, A. (1987). Personality and hemisphere function: Two experiments using the dichotic shadowing technique. *Personality and Individual Differences, 8*, 483–488.
Rawlings, D., & Claridge, G. (1984). Schizotypal and hemisphere function: III. Performance asymmetrics on task of letter recognition and local-global processing. *Personality and Individual Differences, 5*, 657–663.
Saccuzzo, D. P., & Schubert, D. L. (1981). Backward marking as a measure of slow processing in schizophrenic spectrum disorders. *Journal of Abnormal Psychology, 90*, 305–312.
Schalling, D., Edman, G., & Aesberg, M. (1987). Impulsive cognitive style and inability to tolerate boredom: Psychobiological studies of temperamental vulnerability. In M. Zuckerman (Ed.), *Biological bases of sensation seeking, impulsivity, and anxiety* (pp. 123–146). Hillsdale, NJ: Lawrence Erlbaum Associates.
Siever, L. J., Haier, R. J., Coursey, R. D., Sortek, A. J., Murphy, D. L., Holzman, P. E., & Buchsbaum, M. S. (1982). Smooth pursuit-tracking impairment: Relation to other "markers" of schizophrenic and psychological correlates. *Archives of General Psychiatry, 39*, 1001–1005.
Simons, R. F., & Katkin, W. (1989). Smooth pursuit eye movements in subjects reporting physical anhedonia and perceptual aberrations. *Psychiatry Research, 14*, 275–289.
Slade, P. D. (1976). An investigation of psychological factors involved in the predisposition to auditory hallucinations. *Psychological Medicine, 6*, 123–132.
Sokal, R., & Sneath, P. (1963). *Principles of numerical taxonomy.* London: Freeman.
Tipper, S. P. (1985). The negative priming effect: Inhibitory priming by ignored objects. *Quarterly Journal of Experimental Psychology, 37a*, 571–590.
Tipper, S. P., & Baylis, G. C. (1987). Individual differences in selective attention and priming. *Personality and Individual Differences, 8*, 667–675.
Tipper, S. P., & Cranston, G. C. (1985). Selective attention and priming: Inhibitory and facilitatory affects of ignored primes. *Quarterly Journal of Experimental Psychology, 37a*, 591–611.
Vaucouleurs, G. de (1956). *Discovery of the universe.* London: Faber & Faber.
Venables, P. (1963). The relationship between level of skin potential and fusion of paired light flashes in schizophrenics and normal subjects. *Journal of Psychiatric Research, 1*, 279–287.
Venables, P. (1964). Input dysfunction in schizophrenia. In B. A. Maber (Ed.), *Progress in experimental personality research* (pp. 182–195). New York: Academic Press.

Venables, P. (1980). Primary dysfunction and cortical laterilization in schizophrenia. In M. Kruckow, D. Lebusann, & J. Angst (Eds.), *Functional states of the brain: Their determinants* (pp. 214–231). Amsterdam: Elsevier.

Weiner, I. (1990). Neural substrates of latent inhibition: The switching model. *Psychological Bulletin, 108,* 442–461.

Wilson, G. D. (1981). Personality and social behavior. In H. J. Eysenck (Ed.), *A model for personality* (pp. 210–245). New York: Springer-Verlag.

Yasamy, M. T. (1987). Schizoaffective disorder: A dimensional approach. *Acta Psychiatrica Scandinavia, 76,* 609–618.

Zuckerman, M. (1991). *Psychobiology of personality.* Cambridge, England: Cambridge University Press.

Zuckerman, M., Kuhlman, D. M., & Camac, C. (1988). What lies beyond E and N? Factor analyses of scales believed to measure basic dimensions of personality. *Journal of Personality and Social Psychology, 54,* 96–107.

CHAPTER

3

AN ALTERNATIVE FIVE-FACTOR MODEL FOR PERSONALITY

Marvin Zuckerman
University of Delaware

The skepticism of some social-personality psychologists (e.g., Mischel, 1981) about the existence of broad personality traits has been reinforced by the inability of psychologists to agree on either the number or nature of the "basic traits" of personality. H. J. Eysenck (1947, 1967) represents one extreme of trait generality with a parsimonious, theoretically evolved system involving only three basic traits: Extraversion (E), Neuroticism (N), and Psychoticism (P). At the other extreme are Guilford and Zimmerman (1956) and Cattell (1957), with from 14 to 20 inductively developed primary factors.

H. J. Eysenck and S. B. G. Eysenck (1969) undertook a large factorial study of the primary factors in the same subjects using the items from the original tests. They found that the factors described in the Guilford and Cattell tests could not be replicated from factor analyses of the items in their tests. Many subsequent investigators also found that Cattell's factors were not recoverable from the items of his test. Factor analyses of the original scales in all three tests and the second-order factors derived from the factor analyses of items resulted in two primary factors corresponding to E and N. A closer examination of their results, however, shows that what they called the N factor included many subfactors like Impulsivity and Superego Strength, along with the classical N factors like Guilt, Depression, Tension, and Inferiority. The former set would be regarded by Eysenck today as components of P (H. J. Eysenck & M. W. Eysenck, 1985). Factors beyond the first two were not replicable from male to female samples. At that time the theory of Psychoticism had not been well developed and there was no P scale in Eysenck's test.

In the meantime, a new model was evolving from factor analyses of ratings using trait terms sampled from the English language. The history of the development of the Big Five is described in many of the other articles in this volume so there is no need to reiterate it in this chapter. Goldberg (1990) called the factors: Surgency (I), Agreeableness (II), Conscientiousness (III), Emotional Stability (IV), Intellect (V). The specific terms for the factors vary somewhat from one investigator to another (Hogan, 1982), but researchers are in fair agreement on the substance of the first four factors. The fifth factor has been variously called Intelligence, Intellectance, Inquiring Intellect, Culture, and Openness to Experience. More recently Goldberg (1992) suggested the term "Imagination," but admitted that "the disagreement about the specific nature of factor V is somewhat of a scientific embarrassment."

The original Big Five factors were developed from lexical analyses on the assumption that the basic trait concepts of personality are embodied in single words or simple phrases from any language or culture (Norman, 1963). Recently, Goldberg (1990) demonstrated the generality of the five-factor model using 100 refined clusters of words based on 339 trait adjectives. Factors I and II were relatively large in size, Factor III was intermediate, and Factors IV and V were relatively small, reflecting the paucity of words representing them. For Factor IV (Emotional Stability), for instance, there were only two words representing the positive pole and seven words for the negative pole of the dimension. Emotional Stability is identified with Neuroticism or Anxiety in other classifications.

Does this lack of factorial strength for Emotional Stability reflect its importance as a trait? In analyses of questionnaire scales Neuroticism (Emotionality) always emerges as one of the two strongest factors. Surgency and Agreeableness may be the most heavily represented in the language because they refer to important and salient cues in personal interactions whereas Emotionality is often concealed and subjective. It is easier to see when someone is disagreeable but not always obvious when someone is mildly anxious. Whatever the reason, it is questionable whether a lexical sampling approach can adequately represent traits in proportion to their behavioral importance. Traits such as Impulsivity and Sensation Seeking, which have proven to be important in terms of their biological bases (Zuckerman, 1979a, 1983, 1991), are only represented as single scales within the larger factors of the Big Five, but they might be at least as important as the primary traits like Conscientiousness and Intellect. When we developed state scales for the Sensation-Seeking scale (SSS; Zuckerman, 1979a) we found few single adjectives to represent the specific construct. Costa and McCrae (1992a) reported a similar difficulty in finding words to represent the fifth factor, which they called Openness to Experience.

Whether we regard traits as organized in a hierarchy (e.g., H. J. Eysenck, 1967) or a circumplex (Wiggins, 1979), a decision must be made as to which traits are superordinate or subordinate in the hierarchy or where to place the primary dimensions in a circumplex. Factor analysis alone cannot answer this question because the strength or appearance of factors will depend on the sampling of scales or ratings. H. J. Eysenck (1992a) argued that the Big Five traits of Conscientiousness and Agreeableness are subtraits of his broad P factor, and Goldberg and Rosolack (chapter 1 of this volume) countered with the idea that P is a combination of low Conscientiousness and Agreeableness. However, it is clear that the P dimension represents more than Conscientiousness and Agreeableness.

Both H. J. Eysenck (1992a) and Zuckerman (1992) agreed that the determination of "which factors are basic" must go beyond psychometric analyses to the nomological networks tying them to other variables deduced from theories. In the case of H. J. Eysenck's (1967) and Zuckerman's (1991) models these are psychobiological theories. As yet, no comparable theories have been constructed for the Big Five.

The use of single trait words to represent components of traits has an intrinsic limitation in not being able to specify precisely what kinds of behaviors, attitudes, or feelings are described by the trait. Given the importance of person–situation interactions (Magnusson & Endler, 1977), personality questionnaires are superior to single word ratings because they can be more specific in the prototypical situation responses defining a trait.

QUESTIONNAIRE MEASURES OF THE BIG FIVE (OR SIX)

Hogan (1982) developed a questionnaire based on a six-factor model, splitting the Extraversion factor into Surgency and Sociability. In addition to these two he included factors of Likability (Agreeableness?), Conformity (Conscientiousness?), Adjustment (Neuroticism or Emotional Stability?), and Intellectance (Culture or Intellect?). Conformity included a number of sensation-seeking types of items that loaded negatively on the factor.

Costa, McCrae, and Arenburg (1980) started with a three-factor model and devised a questionnaire (NEO; Costa & McCrae, 1985) that included Eysenck's N and E factors and added a third factor called Openness to Experience. Later they enlarged their model to one resembling the Big Five by adding scales for Agreeableness and Conscientiousness. A comparison of their five-factor scales with Eysenck's scales showed near equivalence of E and N in the two questionnaires (McCrae & Costa, 1985). Eysenck's P scale correlated negatively with Agreeableness and Conscientiousness.

AN ALTERNATIVE FIVE-FACTOR MODEL

Three- and five-factor models are not incompatible within a hierarchal model of personality. Since the landmark H. J. Eysenck and S.B.G. Eysenck (1969) study, few others have attempted to analyze traits at more than one level and to trace the relationships between the levels. The next studies to be described explicitly addressed the problem of how broader factors emerge from narrower ones.

First Study (Zuckerman, Kuhlman, and Camac, 1988)

In contrast to the origin of the original five-factor model in lexical analyses of the language, an alternative five-factor model has emerged from factor analyses of personality or temperament questionnaire scales with established empirical validity and evidence of biological correlates (Zuckerman et al., 1988; Zuckerman, Kuhlman, Thornquist, & Kiers, 1991). These studies were begun to provide a structural framework for *Psychobiology of Personality* (Zuckerman, 1991). Eysenck's three scales, E, N, and P, were included because of their theoretical relevance and evidence of a biological basis, but also included were other scales used in assessing other dimensions of Temperament such as Activity, Impulsivity, Anxiety, Hostility, Aggression, Socialization, and Sensation Seeking (Zuckerman et al., 1988). The original five-factor model was considered as a framework for this book on psychobiology, but there was practically no research on the biological bases of traits like Conscientiousness and Agreeableness. We also decided not to include markers for Intellect or Culture because, like Eysenck, we preferred to regard personality traits related to intelligence or educational background apart from the realm of personality.

The first study included seven hypothesized factors represented by 46 scales from eight different questionnaires. Several Social Desirability scales were also included. Each proposed factor had from three to nine potential scale markers. Both oblique and orthogonal rotations were used with nearly identical results from both. The results using oblique rotations were presented in order to show the correlations among factors. Although a scree test suggested only four or five factors, we decided to compare the results from seven-, five-, and three-factor solutions in order to fit the results into a hierarchal structure with the superordinate factors represented by the three-factor solution.

At the three-factor level the factors were clearly identified as Eysenck's Big Three because his E and N scales had the highest loadings on two of the factors and the P scale had the second highest loading on the third factor. The E factor consisted of scales measuring Sociability and Activity; the N factor contained scales assessing Neuroticism, Anxiety, Anger, Hostility, general Emotionality, Dependency, Conformity, and inhibition of Aggression or Assertiveness, and a lack of Emotional Control and Work Efficiency. The P factor consisted of Autonomy (Independence), and nearly all of the Sensation-Seeking and Impulsivity scales. At the opposite pole the P dimension was defined by Socialization, Planning, Responsibility, Restraint, and Social Desirability. The factor was labeled in terms of the three main kinds of scales defining it: *Impulsive Unsocialized Sensation Seeking* (ImpUSS). The three factors were nearly identical in men and women.

The five-factor solution divided the Extraversion factor into its Sociability and Activity components, and split the P-ImpUSS factor into Impulsive Sensation-Seeking and Aggressive Sensation-Seeking factors. The seven-factor solution divided the N-Emotionality factor into Anger and Anxiety factors and the P-ImpUSS factor into Autonomy versus Conformity and a P-Impulsivity one.

Second Study (Zuckerman et al., 1991)

In order to further replicate and clarify the model, we undertook another study with a large sample of subjects ($n = 525$ compared to 271 in the first study) and a reduced number of variables (33 scales compared to 46 in the first study). Scales were included that were good markers for the narrower factors in the first study. We used orthogonal rotations in this one in order to define the factors more clearly. In both studies the results using orthogonal and oblique rotations were nearly identical. Factor rotations were done for three, four, five, six, and seven factors in order to track the factors within a hierarchal scheme.

The factors recovered from the scales at each level from six to three factors are shown in Fig. 3.1, with some of the stronger scale markers for the six- and three-factor solutions indicated. The seven-factor solution produced a factor consisting of only one scale and therefore was ignored. Factor scores were computed for subjects for each solution and these scores were correlated across solutions. The Sociability factor was identified at the six-factor level and remained unchanged through five, four, and three-factor solutions. Sociability is a superordinate trait at any level of analysis. The only change from the first study is that Eysenck's E scale was no longer the best marker for the factor and, in contrast to the other Sociability scales, had a substantial secondary loading on the P factor.

A separate Activity factor was identified at the six- and five-factor levels. The scales comprising the factor split up at the four-factor level with the strongest drift to the negative pole of the N-Anxiety factor. At the three-factor level, two of the three scales defining the factor loaded primarily on the Sociability dimension, whereas the third scale (energy level) loaded primarily on N-Emotionality with only a secondary loading on Sociability.

N-Anxiety and Aggression-Hostility formed two separate factors at the six-, five-, and four-factor levels, but they merged into a broad N-Emotionality factor in the three-factor solution. Eysenck's N scale was the strongest marker for the dimension, as in the first study. Aggression-Hostility was defined by scales for Aggression, Hostility, and Anger at the positive pole, and scales for Social Desirability, Responsibility, and Inhibitory Control at the opposite pole.

The P-Unsocialized Sensation Seeking (P-USS) at the six-factor level consisted of the P and autonomy scales and all of the Sensation-Seeking scales, and socialization at the opposite pole. Impulsivity scales constituted a separate Impulsivity (Imp) factor at this level. The P-USS and Imp factors merged at the five-factor level to form the P-ImpUSS factor that persisted relatively unchanged to the

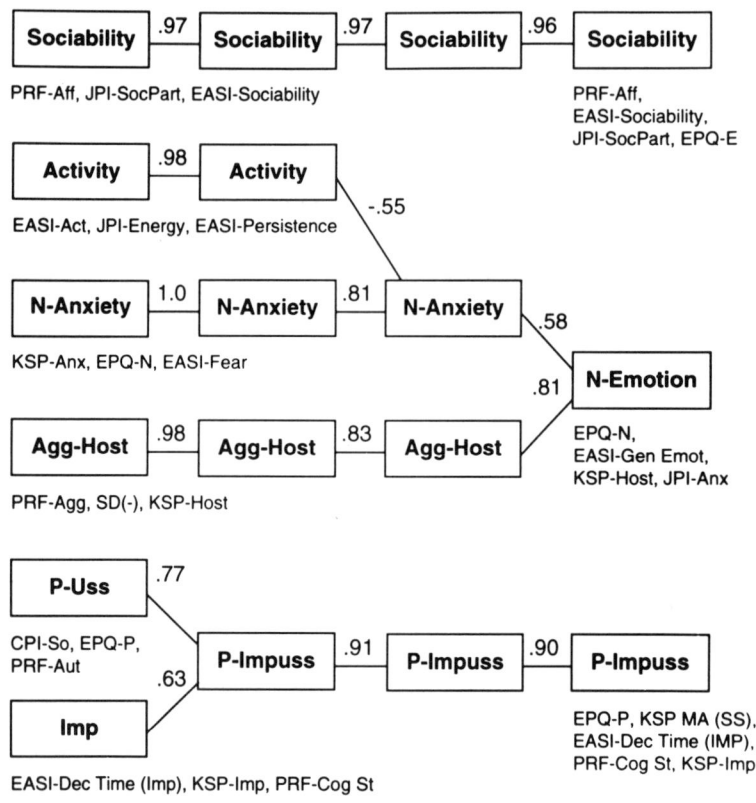

FIG. 3.1. Factors from factor analyses with three-, four-, five-, and six-factor levels (rotations). The numbers over the lines connecting factors at different levels are the correlations of factor scores of subjects at the different levels. Abbreviations for this and subsequent figures are: For factors: Emotion = Emotionality, Agg-Host = Aggression-Hostility, USS = Unsocialized Sensation Seeking, Imp = Impulsivity, ImpUSS = Impulsive Unsocialized Sensation Seeking, N = Neuroticism, P = Psychoticism (or Psychopathy) dimension. For questionnaires: PRF = Personality Research Form, JPI = Jackson Personality Inventory, EASI = Emotionality Activity Sociability Impulsivity (Buss–Plomin temperament inventory), EPQ = Eysenck Personality Questionnaire, KSP = Karolinska scales of Personality, CPI = California Personality Inventory, SSS = Sensation Seeking Scale. For scales: Aff = affiliation, SocPart = social participation, E = extraversion, Act = activity, Anx = anxiety, N = neuroticism, Agg = aggression, SD = social desirability, host = hostility, Gen Emot = general emotionality, So = socialization, P = psychoticism, Aut = autonomy, Dec Time (Imp) = decision time (impulsivity), Imp = impulsivity, Cog St = cognitive structure, MA (SS) = monotony avoidance (sensation seeking).

Note. From M. Zuckerman (1993) "Personality From Top (Traits) to Bottom (Genetics) With Stops at Each Level Between." In J. Hettema and I. J. Deary (Eds.) *Foundations of Personality,* p. 77. Dordrecht, The Netherlands: Kluwer Academic Publishers. Reprinted by permission of Kluwer Academic Publishers.

three-factor level. Eysenck's P scale provided the strongest marker for the broad factor.

Both five- and three-factor solutions were equally robust comparing male and female subjects, with high congruence coefficients (average .95 to .96) for corresponding factors and low coefficients for divergent factors averaging at about zero. The four-factor solution was not quite as good with an average coefficient of .86 and an average of divergent coefficients of .13.

Development of Scales to Assess the Alternative Five Factors

We decided to use the five-factor model to construct a questionnaire because it was as reliable as the three-factor one, but included potentially useful distinctions between Anxiety and Aggression-Hostility components of Emotionality, and between Sociability and Activity components of Extraversion in the three-factor model. The items of all of the scales used in the Zuckerman et al. (1991) study (except those from the EPQ) were correlated with the five-factor scores, calculated for each subject in the study. Twenty items were selected to represent each factor on the basis of high correlations with the factor scores for that factor and low correlations with the other factors. Some items were rewritten. The second form of the Zuckerman–Kuhlman Personality Questionnaire (ZKPQ II) was given to 589 subjects and item responses were factor analyzed. Scree tests clearly indicated a five-factor solution, as expected. Eighty-nine of the original 100 items loaded significantly on the factors to which they had been previously assigned on the basis of the results with the ZKPQ I. The sociability scale was revised with new items written in order to overcome a skewness in the distribution of scores and 10 new items were written for an ad hoc Social Desirability scale. The new 99-item ZKPQ III was given to new groups to assess reliabilities of the scales, sex differences, and correlations with Eysenck Personality Questionnaire (EPQ) scales.

Internal reliabilities of the five scales were good, ranging from .72 to .86. Relatively consistent sex differences were found for three scales: Men were significantly higher on Impulsive Sensation Seeking and Aggression-Hostility, and women scored higher on Neuroticism-Anxiety. These are consistent with the sex differences found previously on the component scales (Zuckerman et al., 1988, 1991).

A COMPARISON OF THREE MODELS: FACTOR ANALYSES OF SCALES FROM THE ZKPQ, EPQ, AND NEO

The study by Angleitner and Ostendorf (chapter 4 of this volume) provided a preliminary comparison of the new and old five-factor models. They included NEO scales along with some of the markers used by Zuckerman et al. (1988, 1991) like the Sensation-Seeking scales (SSS V; Zuckerman, 1979a) and the

Buss and Plomin (1984) EASI scales of temperament. Costa and McCrae (1992a) reanalyzed the data in the Zuckerman et al. (1991) study, realigning the factor axes along dimensions defined by putative markers for the Big Five. Both studies found some indication that scales defining the P-ImpUSS factor loaded on the Openness to Experience as well as the Conscientiousness factor. These studies were done before we developed questionnaire scales to directly measure the alternative five factors. The new questionnaire enabled us to do a direct test of the equivalence and divergence of the Eysenck three-factor, the Costa and McCrae five-factor, and the Zuckerman and Kuhlman five-factor models.

A class in personality psychology was tested with the S. B. G. Eysenck, H. J. Eysenck, and Barrett (1985) revised EPQ-R, the Zuckerman–Kuhlman Personality Questionnaire form III (ZKPQ), and the Costa and McCrae (1992b) revised NEO Personality Inventory (NEO-PI-R). The tests were given during class meetings on three consecutive weeks. Data on the 13 major scales in the three questionnaires (3 from the EPQ, 5 from the ZKPQ, and 5 from the NEO) from 157 students who took all three of the tests were factor analyzed.

Figure 3.2 shows the scree plot of the eigenvalues. Only four of the factors had eigenvalues greater than one. However, factor analyses were done for three, four, five, and six factors. Table 3.1 shows the results for the three-factor analysis with varimax rotations. Factor 1 is clearly Neuroticism with very high and nearly

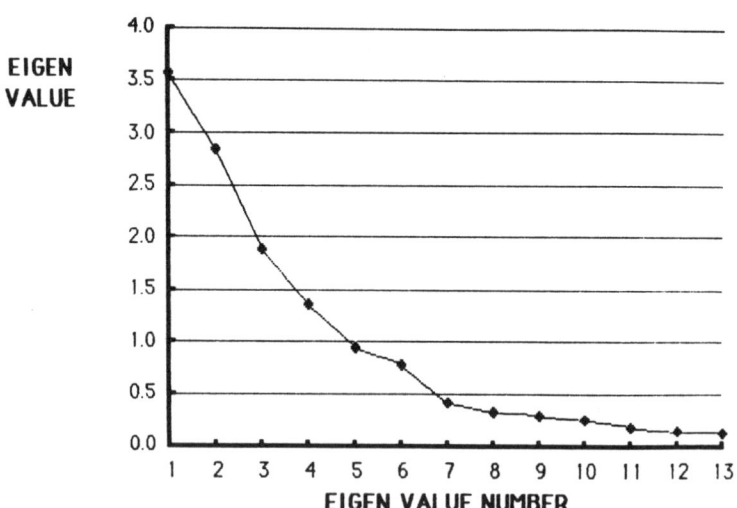

FIG. 3.2. Scree plot for the factor analysis of the five NEO, the three EPQ, and the five ZKPQ scales.

Note. From "A Comparison of Three Structural Models for Personality: The Big Three, the Big Five, and the Alternative Five" by M. Zuckerman, D. M. Kuhlman, J. Joireman, P. Teta, & M. Kraft, 1993, *Journal of Personality and Social Psychology, 65,* p. 762. Copyright 1993 by American Psychological Association. Reprinted by permission.

3. AN ALTERNATIVE FIVE-FACTOR MODEL

TABLE 3.1
Three-Factor Analysis* of EPQ, ZKPQ, and NEO Scales

	Factor Loadings		
	Factor 1	Factor 2	Factor 3
ZKPQ N-Anxiety	.93	−.09	−.03
EPQ Neuroticism	.92	−.13	.03
NEO Neuroticism	.90	−.13	.17
NEO Extraversion	−.16	.89	−.08
EPQ Extraversion	−.35	.76	.23
ZKPQ Sociability	−.19	.75	.17
ZKPQ Activity	.00	.60	−.11
NEO Openness	.11	.35	−.21
EPQ Psychoticism	−.11	−.12	.80
NEO Agreeable	−.07	.06	−.72
NEO Conscientious	−.03	.14	−.68
ZKPQ Impulsive Sensation Seeking	.03	.47	.65
ZKPQ Aggression-Hostility	.33	.27	.64

Note: EPQ = Eysenck Personality Questionnaire, ZKPQ = Zuckerman–Kuhlman Personality Questionnaire, NEO = Costa & McCrae NEO–PI–R. *Principal components, varimax rotation, three factors account for 63.5% of variance.

Note. From "A comparison of three structural models for personality: The big three, the big five, and the alternative five" by M. Zuckerman, D. M. Kuhlman, J. Joireman, P. Teta, and M. Kraft, 1993, *Journal of Personality and Social Psychology, 65*, p. 762; Copyright, 1993 by American Psychological Association. Reprinted by permission.

equivalent loadings from the N scales in all three tests. Factor 2 is Extraversion with high loadings from the NEO and EPQ Extraversion scales and the ZKPQ Sociability scale. The ZKPQ Activity scale also correlates with this factor and the NEO Openness scale has a minor loading on the factor. Factor 3 is identified by the highest positive loading from the EPQ P scale, high positive loadings from the ZKPQ Impulsive Sensation-Seeking and Aggression-Hostility scales, and high negative loadings from the NEO Agreeableness and Conscientiousness scales. Whatever one calls these factors, they seem to be a good fit to Eysenck's three-factor model.

Table 3.2 shows the results for the four-factor analysis. Factor 1 is Extraversion and Factor 2 is Neuroticism with variables loading as in the three-factor analysis. The third factor in the three-factor solution now splits into Factor 3 containing the NEO Conscientiousness, the EPQ P, and the ZKPQ Impulsive Sensation-Seeking scales; and Factor 4 identified by the ZKPQ Aggression-Hostility scale at one pole and the NEO Agreeableness and NEO Openness at the other.

Although the eigenvalues did not justify going further than four factors, a five-factor analysis was done. The first four factors were similar to those in the four-factor analysis and the fifth factor consisted of the ZKPQ Activity scale alone. In a six-factor analysis the NEO Openness scale alone defined the sixth factor. The absence of clear defining factors for activity and openness is clearly

TABLE 3.2
Four-Factor Analysis* of EPQ, ZKPQ, and NEO Scales

	Factor Loadings			
	Factor 1	Factor 2	Factor 3	Factor 4
NEO Extraversion	.88	−.13	−.05	.17
EPQ Extraversion	.79	−.32	.17	−.08
ZKPQ Sociability	.77	−.16	.10	−.07
ZKPQ Activity	.60	.01	−.18	.02
ZKPQ N-Anxiety	−.13	.93	−.01	.08
EPQ Neuroticism	−.16	.91	−.04	−.08
NEO Neuroticism	−.15	.90	.10	−.12
NEO Conscientiousness	.15	−.07	−.86	−.02
Eysenck Psychoticism	−.09	−.08	.80	−.28
ZKPQ Impulsive Sensation Seeking	.48	.08	.74	−.03
NEO Agreeableness	−.04	−.07	−.31	.81
ZKPQ Aggression-Hostility	.35	.34	.24	−.72
NEO Openness	.27	.14	.19	.67

Note: EPQ = Eysenck Personality Questionnaire, ZKPQ = Zuckerman–Kuhlman Personality Questionnaire, NEO = Costa & McCrae NEO–PI, N = Neuroticism, Host = Hostility.

*Principal Components, varimax rotation, four factors accounted for 74% of variance.

Note. From "A Comparison of Three Structural Models for Personality: The Big Three, the Big Five, and the Alternative Five" by M. Zuckerman, D. M. Kuhlman, J. Joireman, P. Teta, and M. Kraft, 1993, *Journal of Personality and Social Psychology, 65*, p. 762, Copyright 1993 by American Psychological Association. Reprinted by permission.

due to the lack of markers for these factors in more than one of the three tests. The NEO-PI-R scale contains six subscales or "facets" for each of the five major factors. A final factor analysis was done with the eight major scales from the EPQ and ZKPQ and the 30 facet scales from the NEO. Five factors accounted for 62% of the variance. These results are shown in Table 3.3.

The first factor consisted of the ZKPQ and EPQ N scores and four of the six N facet scales from the NEO. The second factor included all six of the NEO Conscientiousness facet scales, the ZKPQ Impulsive Sensation-Seeking scale, the EPQ P scale, and the Impulsiveness facet scale from the NEO. The third factor was defined by the ZKPQ Sociability and Activity scales, the EPQ E scale, and all six NEO Extraversion facet scales. The fourth factor contained the Aggression-Hostility scale of the ZKPQ, all six of the NEO Agreeableness facet scales, and the NEO N2 Anger-Hostility scale (which had a nearly equal loading on Factor 1). The sixth factor contained the six NEO Openness facet scales with no markers from the EPQ or the ZKPQ scales.

The results show a high degree of convergence of three of the factors in all three models: Extraversion or Sociability, Neuroticism or Anxiety, and Psychoticism or Impulsive Sensation Seeking, or Conscientiousness. Agreeableness and Aggression-Hostility appear to define two ends of the same factor in the two five-factor models. In Eysenck's three-factor model, Hostility and Anger would

TABLE 3.3
Five-Factor Analysis of EPQ, ZKPQ, and NEO Facet Scales*

	Factor 1	Factor 2	Factor 3	Factor 4	Factor 5
ZKPQ N-Anxiety	.89	−.02	−.07	.05	.06
EPQ Neuroticism	.86	.03	−.12	−.15	.04
N3-Depression	.84	−.18	−.20	−.07	.04
N1-Anxiety	.82	.18	−.06	.00	.11
N6-Vulnerability	.77	−.17	−.11	−.05	−.09
N4-Self-Conscious	.77	−.01	−.21	.12	−.03
C4-Achievement	−.02	.84	.20	−.13	.10
C5-Self-Discipline	−.18	.83	.02	.05	−.04
C6-Deliberation	.08	.76	−.25	.23	−.02
C3-Dutifulness	.00	.74	.14	.10	.09
C1-Competence	−.36	.73	.16	−.01	.09
C2-Order	.07	.66	−.01	.00	−.04
ZKPQ ImpUSS	−.06	−.59	.41	−.24	.12
EPQ Psychoticism	−.13	−.58	−.14	−.43	.07
N5-Impulsivity	.30	−.44	.29	−.27	.36
ZKPQ-Sociability	.16	−.11	.81	−.03	−.14
E2-Gregariousness	−.09	−.05	.80	.12	−.07
E1-Warmth	−.05	.14	.76	.36	.19
EPQ Extraversion	−.37	−.09	.73	−.21	.04
E4-Activity	−.07	.32	.65	−.18	.18
E5-Excitement Seeking	.01	−.32	.64	−.17	.27
E6-Positive Emotions	−.24	.13	.59	.25	.36
E3-Assertiveness	−.29	.20	.58	−.41	.10
ZKPQ-Activity	−.10	.29	.41	−.07	.09
A4-Compliance	−.08	−.02	−.18	.81	.13
ZKPQ Aggression-Hostility	.25	−.08	.25	−.74	−.13
A2-Straightforward.	.10	.26	−.11	.67	.02
A1-Trust	−.39	.16	.23	.61	.04
A3-Altruism	.08	.29	.35	.61	.35
N2-Anger-Hostility	.57	−.01	−.04	−.60	−.06
A5-Modesty	.34	−.10	−.17	.57	−.07
A6-Tendermindedness	.01	.07	.32	.50	.21
O2-Aesthetics	.08	.08	.06	.14	.80
O5-Ideas	−.29	.15	−.09	.01	.69
O3-Feelings	.31	.23	.21	.07	.68
O1-Fantasy	.14	−.33	.00	−.01	.62
O6-Values	.02	−.04	.13	.28	.50
O4-Actions	−.28	−.21	.25	.04	.43

*Numbered scales are from NEO–PI–R and designated by their placement among the five major trait scores: N = Neuroticism, C = Conscientiousness, E = Extraversion, A = Agreeableness, O = Openness to Experience.

Note. From "A Comparison of Three Structural Models for Personality: The Big Three, the Big Five, and the Alternative Five" by M. Zuckerman, D. M. Kuhlman, J. Joireman, P. Teta, and M. Kraft, 1993, Journal of Personality and Social Psychology, 65, p. 764, Copyright 1993 by American Psychological Association. Reprinted by permission.

be subsumed under Emotionality and Aggression under Psychoticism. In the three-factor analysis both Conscientiousness and Agreeableness as well as Aggression-Hostility fall mostly in the P dimension. Openness can be identified as a factor if enough markers are included, but it has little in common with the factors in the Eysenck or Zuckerman–Kuhlman models. The analyses of Angleitner and Ostendorf (chap. 4 this volume) and Costa and McCrae (1992a) showed some convergence of Sensation-Seeking and Impulsivity scales with Openness, but the Sensation-Seeking scale convergence was highly weighted by one of the four subscales, Experience Seeking. Although the new ImpSS scale correlated about equally with all of the SSS subscales in the current study, only the Experience Seeking subscale of the SSS correlated with the NEO Openness scale.

DISCUSSION

Extraversion (or Sociability) and Neuroticism (or Negative Emotionality) dimensions are common to all three- and five-factor models. The main disagreements concern the question of "what lies beyond E and N" (Zuckerman et al., 1988). However, there are still some disagreements about the components of E and N in Eysenck's three-factor model and the five-factor models of Costa and McCrae and Zuckerman and Kuhlman. Sociability is a component of E in all models. Sensation Seeking and Venturesomeness in Eysenck's model (H. J. Eysenck & M. W. Eysenck, 1985) and Excitement Seeking in Costa and McCrae's (1992b) model are regarded as components of Extraversion. In our model, sensation seeking in all its aspects belongs in the P dimension of personality and, along with impulsivity and antisocial tendencies, constitutes one of the main components of this dimension. The antisocial personality may represent the extreme manifestation of what may be regarded as a normal dimension of personality (Zuckerman, 1989, 1991). My conception of the P dimension is somewhat different from that of H. J. Eysenck (1992b). Whereas the dimension includes antisocial and impulsive traits, according to Eysenck it also includes a diathesis for schizophrenia and affective psychoses. In fact, schizophrenic psychoses are said to be the extreme manifestation of the dimension. This point is in dispute (Zuckerman, 1989).

Eysenck also placed aggression as central to the P dimension. In our five-factor analyses aggression, hostility, and trait anger form a separate dimension from the one characterized as impulsive unsocialized sensation seeking and more strongly associated with P. If we go to the three-factor level, Aggression-Hostility falls in the high N–high P quadrant whereas Anxiety is located in the high N–low P quadrant (Zuckerman et al., 1991). One might think that aggression and hostility represent the opposite of Agreeableness, but Costa and McCrae place their Angry-Hostility facet in the Neuroticism factor.

All of these models use a hierarchal system, but they differ in terms of which traits are regarded as superordinate and which are subordinate, and where subordinate traits are classified among the "supertraits." Is Sensation Seeking a subordinate trait under Extraversion and is Impulsivity a subtrait of Psychoticism, as maintained by Eysenck, or do Sensation Seeking and Impulsivity form a major trait dimension and comprise the core of what Eysenck called the P dimension? Are Conscientiousness and Agreeableness facets of the supertrait of Psychoticism or does Psychoticism represent a blend of the major dimensions of Conscientiousness and Agreeableness? Factor analyses of personality tests or ratings alone will not answer these questions because the results are ultimately dependent on the sampling of tests that go into the analyses.

Psychology is not the only science that argues about taxonomy. Biology also has its taxonomic territorial fights: "Taxonomy is the science of classification. For some people it has an undeservedly dull reputation, a subconscious association with dusty museums and the smell of preserving fluid, almost as though it were being confused with taxidermy. In fact it is anything but dull. It is, for reasons that I do not fully understand, one of the most acrimoniously controversial fields in all of biology" (Dawkins, 1986, p. 255).

Dawkins went on to describe the role of taxonomy in developing the theory of evolution. If psychologists were only interested in using personality traits to predict behavior, the debate about how many traits there are and how they should be classified would be a sterile exercise. Narrow traits, specifically designed in terms of the behaviors to be predicted, are usually (but not always) more accurate in prediction even if they have little theoretical interest (Zuckerman, 1979b). But if we want to understand traits themselves, in terms of their psychobiological or social determinants, it is important to find the ones that are universal and generalizable across many kinds of situations.

The Psychobiological Utility of the Alternate Five-Factor Model

Whereas it is easy to manipulate subjects' states in experiments, it is quite difficult to change their traits within a laboratory, and even if we could, it would be quite unethical unless it were done for therapy. Of necessity, we must take a naturalistic approach to the study of traits and their behavioral expressions. There is nothing unscientific in nonexperimental science; if there were, then astronomy is no science. I think social psychologists resist the idea of generalized traits mainly because they cannot manipulate them as easily as they can affect behavior or attitudes.

Psychobiological research with humans is similarly limited to correlational studies. Even if we assume that the amygdala is an important center of emotionality, we cannot go around removing subjects' amygdalas to prove our point. Psychobiological science needs animal models because brain experimentation is possible with other species (Zuckerman, 1984, 1991). Finding appropriate models of behavior in other species is difficult if constructs are conceptualized in uniquely human terms. Animals may be described as sociable, but not extraverted; as emotional, but not neurotic; as aggressive, but not agreeable; as impulsive, but not conscientious; as exploratory or sensation seeking, but certainly not cultured, intellectual, or open to experience.

One could argue that this is just semantics. Whatever you call a trait there is an enormous difference between general behavioral expressions in humans and other species. But trait descriptions and taxonomies should provide the possibility of distinguishing behavioral systems that are distinct in other species. It is important, for instance, to distinguish between fear and anger, or avoidance and aggression. When both are subsumed under a general trait of neuroticism, something important is lost in comparative possibilities. General Activity or Energy Level is considered a major trait in both animals (Royce, 1977) and young children (Buss & Plomin, 1984; Thomas & Chess, 1977), and is regarded as a basic aspect of temperament in neo-Pavlovian models of temperament for children or adults (Russalov, 1989; Strelau, 1983), but it tends to get lost or subsumed under Extraversion in the Big Three and the standard Big Five.

There is considerable evidence that Impulsivity and Sensation Seeking are linked to biological traits in humans (Barratt & Patton, 1983; Schalling, Edman, & Asberg, 1983; Zuckerman, 1979a, 1983, 1990, 1991; Zuckerman, Buchsbaum, & Murphy, 1980). Many of the biological, behavioral, and psychopathological correlates are similar for both traits, justifying the postulation of a combined trait like Impulsive Sensation Seeking. Evidence of common biological correlates of traits goes beyond the proof from factor analytic studies. Factor analysis alone cannot answer the question of which traits are basic or derived (H. J. Eysenck, 1992a; Zuckerman, 1992).

The discussion thus far has stressed the differences between the structural models of personality rather than their convergence. All 3 models are based on replicable factors. Three and 5 is a lot closer than 3 and 16, especially because 2 of the 3 and 5 are the same. The data presented here also suggest that Psychoticism, Impulsive Sensation-Seeking, and Conscientiousness factors have a high degree of similarity even though they sound different. Similarly, Agreeableness and Aggression-Hostility in the five-factor models are more similar than they are different. The next phase of research should be the search for common antecedents, and biological and behavioral correlates of factors in all models. This stage will take much more time and effort and the collaboration of scientists from different disciplines.

There is one important advantage of Eysenck's three-factor model and the alternative five-factor model. They have developed theories that have instigated a vast amount of research explicating the factors (H. J. Eysenck & M. W. Eysenck, 1985; Zuckerman, 1991). Hofstee (1991) regards the definition of individual differences as an end in itself: "The specific assignment of personality psychology is to explain behavior in terms of individual differences" (p. 177). Theorizing or investigating the source of these differences is interesting but not essential according to Hofstee. The problem with this view is that the definition of the individual differences depends on the level of analysis and what observations are accepted as significant ones. Recall the ancient Greeks' classification of the elements as earth, air, fire, and water. In the lexical approach to personality taxonomy, descriptive terms that go together are subsumed under a common classification, and the more terms involved in the cluster, the stronger the primacy of that factor. But things that go together are not necessarily members of the same species. Porpoises swim with fish but they are not fish. Fleas are often found in close association with dogs but they are not mammals. Hostility and anxiety are closely associated traits, but they are not the same, and the difference only appears if aggression is introduced as a trait and one goes to five factors.

Theory without classification is inaccurately simplistic. Classification without theory is sterile and formalistic. The standard five-factor model is a triumph of inductive taxonomy, but like a great pentagon standing in the middle of a conceptual desert we can only wonder and ask: What does it mean?

REFERENCES

Barratt, E. S., & Patton, J. H. (1983). Impulsivity: Cognitive, behavioral and psychophysiological correlates. In M. Zuckerman (Ed.), *Biological bases of sensation seeking, impulsivity, and anxiety* (pp. 77–116). Hillsdale, NJ: Lawrence Erlbaum Associates.

Buss, A. H., & Plomin, R. (1984). *Temperament: Early developing personality traits.* Hillsdale, NJ: Lawrence Erlbaum Associates.

Cattell, R. B. (1957). *Personality and motivation: Structure and measurement.* New York: Harcourt Brace.

Costa, P. T., Jr., & McCrae, R. R. (1985). *The NEO Personality Inventory manual.* Odessa, FL: Psychological Assessment Resources.

Costa, P. T., Jr., & McCrae, R. R. (1992a). Four ways five factors are basic. *Personality and Individual Differences, 13,* 653–656.

Costa, P. T., Jr., & McCrae, R. R. (1992b). *NEO–PI–R: Revised Personality Inventory manual.* Odessa, FL: Psychological Assessment Resources.

Costa, P. T., Jr., McCrae, R. R., & Arenberg, D. (1980). Enduring dispositions in adult males. *Journal of Personality and Social Psychology, 38,* 793–800.

Dawkins, R. (1986). *The blind watchmaker.* New York: Norton.

Eysenck, H. J. (1947). *Dimensions of personality.* New York: Praeger.

Eysenck, H. J. (1967). *The biological basis of personality.* Springfield, IL: Thomas.

Eysenck, H. J. (1992a). Four ways five factors are *not* basic. *Personality and Individual Differences, 13,* 667–673.

Eysenck, H. J. (1992b). The definition and measurement of psychoticism. *Personality and Individual Differences, 13,* 757–785.

Eysenck, H. J., & Eysenck, M. W. (1985). *Personality and individual differences: A natural science approach.* New York: Plenum.

Eysenck, H. J., & Eysenck, S. B. G. (1969). *Personality structure and measurement.* San Diego, CA: Knapp.

Eysenck, S. B. G., Eysenck, H. J., & Barrett, P. (1985). A revised version of the psychoticism scale. *Personality and Individual Differences, 6,* 21–29.

Goldberg, L. R. (1990). An alternative "description of personality": The Big-Five factor structure. *Journal of Personality and Social Psychology, 59,* 1216–1229.

Goldberg, L. R. (1992, June 16-19). *The structure of phenotypic personality traits (or the magical number five, plus or minus zero).* Keynote address to the sixth European Conference on Personality, Groningen, The Netherlands.

Guilford, J. P., & Zimmerman, W. S. (1956). Fourteen dimensional temperament factors. *Psychological Monographs, 70*(10), 1-26.

Hofstee, W. K. B. (1991). The concepts of personality and temperament. In J. Strelau & A. Angleitner (Eds.), *Explorations in temperament: International perspectives on theory and measurement* (pp. 177-188). New York: Plenum.

Hogan, R. (1982). A socioanalytic theory of personality. In M. M. Page (Ed.), *Personality: Current theory and research. Nebraska Symposium on Motivation* (pp. 55-89). Lincoln, NE: University of Nebraska Press.

Magnusson, D., & Endler, N. S. (1977). *Personality at the crossroads: Current issues in interactional psychology.* Hillsdale, NJ: Lawrence Erlbaum Associates.

Mischel, W. (1981). *Introduction to personality* (3rd ed.). New York: Holt, Rinehart & Winston.

Norman, W. T. (1963). Toward an adequate taxonomy of personality attributes: Replicated factor structure. *Journal of Abnormal and Social Psychology, 66,* 574-583.

Royce, J. R. (1977). On the construct validity of open-field measures. *Psychological Bulletin, 84,* 1098-1106.

Rusalov, V. M. (1989). Object-related and communicative aspects of human temperament: A new questionnaire of the structure of temperament. *Personality and Individual Differences, 10,* 817-827.

Schalling, D., Edman, G., & Asberg, M. (1983). Impulsive cognitive style and inability to tolerate boredom. In M. Zuckerman (Ed.), *Biological bases of sensation seeking, impulsivity, and anxiety* (pp. 125-147). Hillsdale, NJ: Lawrence Erlbaum Associates.

Strelau, J. (1983). *Temperament, personality, activity.* London: Academic Press.

Thomas, A., & Chess, S. (1977). *Temperament and development.* New York: Brunner/Mazel.

Wiggins, J. S. (1979). A psychological taxonomy of trait-descriptive terms: The interpersonal domain. *Journal of Personality and Social Psychology, 37,* 395-412.

Zuckerman, M. (1979a). *Sensation seeking: Beyond the optimal level of arousal.* Hillsdale, NJ: Lawrence Erlbaum Associates.

Zuckerman, M. (1979b). Traits, states, situations, and uncertainty. *Journal of Behavioral Assessment, 1,* 43-54.

Zuckerman, M. (1983). A biological theory of sensation seeking. In M. Zuckerman (Ed.), *Biological bases of sensation seeking, impulsivity, and anxiety* (pp. 37-76). Hillsdale, NJ: Lawrence Erlbaum Associates.

Zuckerman, M. (1984). Sensation seeking: A comparative approach to a human trait. *Behavioral and Brain Sciences, 7,* 413-471.

Zuckerman, M. (1989). Personality in the third dimension: A psychobiological approach. *Personality and Individual Differences, 10,* 391-418.

Zuckerman, M. (1990). The psychophysiology of sensation seeking. *Journal of Personality, 58,* 313-345.

Zuckerman, M. (1991). *Psychobiology of personality.* New York: Cambridge University Press.

Zuckerman, M. (1992). What is a basic factor and which factors are basic? Turtles all the way down. *Personality and Individual Differences, 13,* 675-681.

Zuckerman, M., Buchsbaum, M. S., & Murphy, D. L. (1980). Sensation seeking and its biological correlates. *Psychological Bulletin, 88,* 187-214.

Zuckerman, M., Kuhlman, D. M., & Camac, C. (1988). What lies beyond E and N? Factor analyses of scales believed to measure basic dimensions of personality. *Journal of Personality and Social Psychology, 54,* 96-107.

Zuckerman, M., Kuhlman, D. M., Thornquist, M., & Kiers, H. (1991). Five (or three) robust questionnaire scale factors of personality without culture. *Personality and Individual Differences, 12,* 929-941.

CHAPTER

4

TEMPERAMENT AND THE BIG FIVE FACTORS OF PERSONALITY

Alois Angleitner
Fritz Ostendorf
Universität Bielefeld

In the history of personality psychology, the terms *temperament* and *personality* have sometimes been used as synonyms. Strelau (1987) argued for a distinction between the concepts of temperament and personality. According to his view, temperament refers to early developing, stable individual differences that relate to more stylistic behavioral tendencies based on the constitutional or biologically determined makeup of individuals. In contrast, personality is seen as the broader concept, containing characteristics that are primarily determined by social factors like values, attitudes, and interests.

Among personality psychologists there is a growing consensus that the domain of individual differences as measured by rating scales or questionnaire items is almost completely accounted for by five broad factors (Digman & Takemoto-Chock, 1981; John, 1989; McCrae, 1989; McCrae & Costa, 1985a, 1987; Ostendorf, 1990). This five-factor model of personality has proved to be robust across different groups of subjects, item pools, various instruments, and methods of factor analysis, as well as across different languages and cultures.

Past research has concentrated primarily on discussing the *conceptual* relations between temperament and personality. Although various measurement tools have been developed in both research paradigms, there are only a few studies that related the concepts of temperament and personality empirically. This state of affairs also applies to the comparison between temperament and the five-factor model of personality. Until now, different researchers have stated their expectations about more or less specific relationships between temperament factors and the Big Five personality factors, but these speculations have only been based on rational considerations.

For example, John (1989, p. 263), referring to the temperamental factors of Buss and Plomin (1975), assumed a correspondence between these temperament and personality factors: Activity corresponds to Extraversion (I), Sociability to Agreeableness (II), Impulsivity to low Conscientiousness (III), and Emotionality to Neuroticism (IV).

These assumptions are quite plausible, and other experts like Digman (1990), Goldberg (1980), and Hogan (1983) made similar assumptions. We may note, however, that John (1990) revised his assumptions. According to his revised view, the factors "Activity and Emotionality can easily be matched to Factors I and IV. . . . Impulsivity may be related to Extraversion (expressive spontaneity), low Conscientiousness (distractability) or low Emotional Stability (inability to delay of gratification)" (p. 85).

But all these hypothesized relations have never been subjected to a thorough empirical examination. The goal of the present study was to remedy some of these omissions by empirically testing the correspondence between the temperament and personality spheres.

There is one other important reason to examine the relations among the Big Five and various temperament traits. Some of the proponents of the five-factor model have claimed that the Big Five factors account for almost all the individual differences as measured by self- or peer-reports (Digman & Inouye, 1986). The validity of this assumption has been partially confirmed by studies in which the five-factor model was compared to representative samples of trait-descriptive terms or large numbers of questionnaire scales. It may be the case that the five factors represent universal dimensions of personality language that describe the structure of all temperament and personality data, as long as the data are based on questionnaire items, adjective rating scales, or interviews. If this assumption holds, the domain of temperament should be completely accounted for by the Big Five factors as well and the concept of temperament will be subsumed under the broader concept of personality.

THE STRUCTURE OF TEMPERAMENT: EMPIRICAL STUDIES

Ruch, Angleitner, and Strelau (1991) investigated the structure of temperament in a factor analytic study of various temperamental inventories. This study employed the following questionnaires: the Strelau Temperament Inventory, revised version (STI-R; Strelau, Angleitner, Bantelmann, & Ruch, 1990); the EASI–III Temperament Survey (Buss, 1988; Buss & Plomin, 1975); the Dimensions of Temperament Survey (DOTS–R; Windle & Lerner, 1986); the STQ developed by Rusalov (1989).[1]

---

[1] Unrevised German Form for the last three.

A factor analysis of the scales of all these temperament inventories yielded the following five varimax-rotated factors:

I. *Emotional Stability*, marked by positive loadings of the STI scales Strength of Excitation (SE) and Mobility (MO), as well as the DOTS–R scale Flexibility. The negative pole of the factor was marked by the STQ Emotionality scales and the EASI Emotionality scale.

II. *Rhythmicity*, marked by positive loadings of the DOTS–R Rhythmicity scales and by negative loadings of the DOTS–R Activity Level Sleep scale.

III. *Activity and Tempo*, positively loaded by the STQ scales Tempo and the object-related Ergonicity and Plasticity scales, by EASI-Activity, DOTS–R Distractibility, and DOTS–R Persistence.

IV. *Sociability*, with positive loadings from the following scales: EASI Sociability, DOTS–R Mood, and DOTS–R Approach-Withdrawal, and STQ Social Ergonicity.

V. *Impulsivity Versus Impulse-Control*, with positive loadings from the scales: EASI Impulsivity, DOTS–R Activity Level General, STQ Social Plasticity and with negative loadings from the STI Strength of Inhibition scale (SI).

The results of this factor analysis underline the following points: (a) The scales of the EASI–III Temperament Survey were orthogonal, (b) the STI scales were related to Emotionality and Impulsivity, and (c) some DOTS–R scales measured some specific variance not covered by other temperament inventories, especially the Rhythmicity scales.

EYSENCK AND TEMPERAMENT

Most previous studies of temperament and personality have used Eysenck's personality model as a standard for their empirical comparisons. For example, there may be several reasons for choosing this model. First, Eysenck's three-factor model contains at least two robust factors (Extraversion and Neuroticism) that have been confirmed in numerous studies. Further, Eysenck interpreted these factors as temperament dimensions. Some of the primary marker variables of these factors (e.g., Emotionality, Impulsivity, Sociability) have been conceptualized as separate temperament dimensions in some temperament theories. Moreover, Eysenck assumed that the interindividual differences described by these factors are largely inherited, and such biological determination is usually seen as one of the critical features of temperament traits.

Windle (1989) compared the relationships between two temperament inventories (DOTS–R, EASI–II) and Eysenck's Personality Inventory (EPI). Corulla (1988) presented correlational and factor analytic evidence for a broad general

Sensation-Seeking factor, independent from the three factors Psychoticism, Extraversion, and Neuroticism of Eysenck's P-E-N model.

Questionnaires Based on Different Personality Theories and Temperament

Birenbaum and Montag (1986) tried to locate the Sensation-Seeking (SSS) construct in the Cattellian personality domain. They found that Sensation Seeking can be located in the broad second-order factor of Independence. If the subscales of the SSS were analyzed, these scales showed also strong loadings in the superfactors Super Ego (Disinhibition) and Pathemia (Experience Seeking). The authors speculated that the SSS may be found between the quadrants of Psychoticism and Extraversion. The second-order factor Independence consisted of two primaries (Q1 and N). In the view of the authors, these two primaries represent cognitive social attitudes rather than temperamental characteristics.

Based on factor analyses of selected self-report scales mostly belonging to the temperamental domain, an alternative five-factor model was suggested by Zuckerman, Kuhlman, and Camac (1988); Zuckerman, Kuhlman, Thornquist, and Kiers (1991); and Zuckerman (1991). The temperament inventories used in this study were the following: the Sensation-Seeking Scale Form V (Zuckerman, S. B. G. Eysenck, & H. J. Eysenck, 1978), the EASI–III (Buss & Plomin, 1975), the Karolinska Scales of Personality (KSP) (Magnusson, 1986), and the Strelau Temperament Inventory (Strelau, 1983).[2]

In addition, selected scales were taken from these personality inventories: the Personality Research Form (PRF; Jackson, 1984), the Jackson Personality Inventory (JPI; Jackson, 1976), the California Personality Inventory (CPI; Gough, 1964), and the Eysenck Personality Questionnaire (EPQ; H. J. Eysenck & S. B. G. Eysenck, 1975).

In their studies, Zuckerman et al. replicated clearly the factors of Sociability (or Extraversion) and Emotionality (or Neuroticism). Within a five-factor solution, a third factor was labeled Impulsive-Unsocialized Sensation Seeking (ImpSS). This factor had replicable loadings from the temperament scales SSS Experience Seeking, KSP Monotony Avoidance, as well as from the personality scales CPI-Socialization, PRF Cognitive Structure, and EPQ Psychoticism. The loading pattern suggested some correspondence of this factor to both Factor III (Conscientiousness) and Factor V (Openness to Experience) of the five-factor model of personality (McCrae & Costa, 1987). A fourth factor had strong replicable loadings from the PRF Aggression scale and the JPI Responsibility scale. This factor was called Aggression-Hostility and may have some similarity with a reversed version of the Agreeableness dimension. According to Eysenck's

---

[2] The Strelau Temperament Inventory was scored in a nonauthorized fashion according to a factor analysis by Carlier (1985).

model, however, Aggression should be located in the Psychoticism domain. A factor similar to the Conscientiousness dimension was not detected. A distinct factor called Activity was replicated in these studies. The reference made to the five-factor model, however, was not convincing because no measure specifically designed to assess the five-factor model was employed.

Temperament and the Big Five Factors of Personality: Empirical Studies

McCrae and Costa (1985b) conducted a joint factor analysis of Buss and Plomin's (1975) temperament scales with various self-control scales (measuring Conscientiousness), the scales of the Experience Inventory (a precursor of the NEO Openness scales), and a Positive Emotion scale. In this study the EASI Activity (Tempo, Vigor) and Sociability scales related to Extraversion, and the Emotionality scales related most strongly to the factor Neuroticism. Contrary to Buss and Plomin's assumption, the EASI Impulsivity scales did not form a homogeneous cluster. Persistence and Decision Time were related to Conscientiousness, EASI Impulse Inhibition to both Conscientiousness and Neuroticism, and EASI Sensation Seeking to Extraversion. In summary, this study revealed that temperament defined by the EASI was covered by three of the Big Five personality factors. John (1990) proposed one possible interpretation of this finding, suggesting that the nontemperamental factors Agreeableness and Openness "summarize less heritable, and later-appearing, individual differences" (p. 86).

McCrae and Costa (in press) presented data on different personality and temperament scales and their relations to Openness to Experience as measured with the NEO Personality Inventory. As temperament scales they used the SSS Form V. They reported significant correlations between the SSS and the NEO-PI Openness scale ranging from .20 (Boredom Susceptibility) to .55 (Experience Seeking), and between the SSS Experience Seeking scale and Openness facets of Actions and Values of .43 and .46.

For the first time, Ruch, Angleitner, and Strelau (1991) reported correlations between the revised STI scales and the NEO Personality Inventory (NEO–PI; Costa & McCrae, 1985; German adaptation by Borkenau & Ostendorf, 1991). With the exception of Openness to Experience, all other scales of the NEO-PI were correlated with the Pavlovian CNS properties implicated by the STI scales. The scales Strength of Excitation and Mobility showed positive relations to Extraversion and Conscientiousness and a negative relation to Neuroticism. Strength of Inhibition correlated positively with Agreeableness and negatively with Neuroticism, whereas Mobility correlated positively with Agreeableness. These relations paralleled relations between the STI and the Eysenckian superfactors. Ruch et al. (1991) concluded that the scales Strength of Excitation and Mobility are related to Neuroticism, Extraversion, and Conscientiousness and that Strength of Inhibition is associated with Agreeableness and Neuroticism.

In the current study we investigated the replicability of these earlier findings and the assumption that the domain of temperament and personality traits can be represented in one common framework, namely the Big Five factor structure. For the purpose of the study we collected a new sample of subjects, independent from that analyzed in the study of Ruch et al. (1991).

METHOD

Subjects

The sample consisted of 323 adults (111 men, 208 women, and 4 participants who did not report gender). Participants ranged in age from 17 to 67, with a mean age of 24.6 years and a standard deviation of 6.0 years. They were requested to answer all questionnaires at home and to return them to the experimenter within 1 week.

Instruments

The participants in our present study completed the following personality and temperament inventories: the revised short version of the Strelau Temperament Inventory (STI-RS);[3] the EASI–III Temperament Survey (Buss & Plomin, 1975);[4] the Sensation-Seeking scale (SSSR–LE), developed and revised by Zuckerman (Zuckerman, 1979; Zuckerman et al., 1978);[5] and the Dimensions of Temperament Survey (DOTS) developed by Windle and Lerner (1986).[6] In addition, the following instruments were used as marker variables for measuring the Big Five factors: the short-form of the NEO Personality Inventory (NEO Five-Factor Inventory, NEOFFI), developed by Costa and McCrae (1989);[7] a German version of an Adjective Rating Inventory, published by McCrae and Costa (1985a, 1987),[8] containing 80 bipolar rating scales designed to measure the Big Five factors in self or peer descriptions.

The participants answered all the items on all questionnaires with a set of 5-point Likert scales. The exception was for the items of the SSSR, which were

---

[3] The STI–RS was developed by Strelau, Angleitner, Bantelmann, and Ruch (1990) and contains a total of 84 questionnaire items. Research concerning the original STI is documented in Strelau, Angleitner, and Ruch (1990). The STI-R has been renamed as Pavlovian Temperament Survey (PTS).

[4] The German EASI–III was adapted by Angleitner, Harrow, Hoffmann, Köhler, Schäfer, and Thiel and contains 60 items. The Sociability II scale refers to the items reported in Buss (1988).

[5] The 56 items of the SSSR–LE were translated to German by Unterweger (1980).

[6] Translated and revised by Angleitner, Köhler, Hoffman, Schäfer, Thiel ,and Harrow (54 items).

[7] The NEOFFI was adapted by Borkenau and Ostendorf (1991) and contains 60 items, that is, 12 items to measure each of the five factors.

[8] Translated by Ostendorf (1990).

4. TEMPERAMENT AND THE BIG FIVE   75

presented in a forced-choice format. The adjective ratings were presented on 6-point Likert scales ranging from −3 (not at all applicable) to +3 (fully applicable).

RESULTS

Reliability of Scales and Factors

Table 4.1 shows the Cronbach-Alpha reliability coefficients.

The Alpha coefficients of the NEO rating factors were estimated with a formula published by Serlin and Kaiser (1976). The reliabilities of the 34 questionnaire scales and the 5 rating-factors ranged from .41 to .89 with a median of .74. The lowest reliability coefficients were found for the three EASI Impulsivity scales of Inhibition Control (.46), Decision Time (.41), and Sensation Seeking (.42), and for the EASI Activity subscale Tempo (.42). The highest reliabilities were obtained for the NEO rating factor Conscientiousness (.89), the Mood scale of the DOTS Inventory (.87), and the Mobility scale of the STI (.87).

The Factor Structure of the NEO Rating Scales

For all questionnaire inventories, the scale values were calculated on the basis of the corresponding item keys, that is, by calculating the unweighted sum-scores. In the case of the NEO Rating Inventory, however, such a procedure seemed to be inadequate as the original NEO Rating scales have been shown to have a factor structure that in some ways differs considerably from the scale key originally proposed by McCrae and Costa (1985a). For example, they classed the item "emotionally stable vs. unstable" with the Conscientiousness factor. This is obviously a clear misclassification of the item, both for rational and empirical reasons. Like McCrae and Costa (1985a, 1987), we used factor scores in the present study.

A principal component analysis of the 80 NEO Rating scales yielded a plot of eigenvalues that showed a clear break between the fifth and the sixth factors. The first seven eigenvalues were as follows: 13.09, 7.16, 5.79, 4.50, 3.14, 1.98, and 1.82.

The varimax-rotated components or factors in the present study (for the sake of simplicity, we label components "factors") were compared empirically with the respective factor structure of the original American NEO scales reported by McCrae and Costa (1987) for a sample of 738 peer ratings. To test the robustness of the five-factor structure over different languages, coefficients of congruence (Harman, 1970, p. 270) were calculated between each corresponding factor of the American and German sample. The congruence coefficients between the five factors of the present study (self ratings) and the corresponding factors of the

TABLE 4.1
Coefficient Alpha Reliabilities of Various Temperament
and Personality Questionnaire Scales

	Alpha	
	I	II
STI-RS		
Strength of Excitation	.86	(.88)[a]
Strength of Inhibition	.80	(.85)[a]
Mobility	.87	(.91)[a]
SSSR-LE		
Thrill & Adventure Seeking	.75	(.84)[b]
Disinhibition	.67	(.74)[b]
Experience Seeking	.71	(.80)[b]
Boredom Susceptibility	.59	(.60)[b]
EASI-III		
Emotionality		
General	.69	(.48)[b]
Fear	.74	(.71)[b]
Anger	.70	(.52)[b]
Distress	.73	(.72)[b]
Activity		
Tempo	.42	(.44)[b]
Vigor	.64	(.64)[b]
Sociability I	.66	(.69)[b]
Sociability II	.58	(.55)[b]
Impulsivity		
Inhibition Control	.46	(.41)[b]
Decision Time	.41	(.44)[b]
Sensation Seeking	.42	(.45)[b]
Persistence	.60	(.73)[b]
DOTS-R		
Activity-Level General	.72	(.69)[b]
Activity-Level Sleep	.77	(.78)[b]
Approach/Withdrawal	.76	(.75)[b]
Flexibility/Rigidity	.71	(.59)[b]
Mood	.87	(.85)[b]
Rhythmicity-Sleep	.79	(.79)[b]
Rhythmicity-Eating	.86	(.86)[b]
Rhythmicity-Daily Habits	.64	(.71)[b]
Distractibility	.79	(.80)[b]
Persistence	.77	(.68)[b]
NEOFFI		
Neuroticism	.85	(.85)[c]
Extraversion	.78	(.79)[c]
Openness to Experience	.71	(.75)[c]
Agreeableness	.73	(.72)[c]
Conscientiousness	.85	(.86)[c]
NEO-Rating Factors		
Neuroticism	.84	(.86)[d]
Extraversion	.85	(.89)[d]
Openness to Experience	.83	(.85)[d]
Agreeableness	.85	(.88)[d]
Conscientiousness	.89	(.91)[d]

Note: Column I: Alpha Reliabilities of scales in the present study ($N = 323$).
Column II: Alpha Coefficients of the scales in previous studies.
[a]$N = 76$. [b]$N = 85$. [c]$N = 578$. [d]$N = 401$.

American study (McCrae & Costa, 1987, peer ratings) were as follows: .88 (N), .88 (E), .89 (O), .91 (A), and .91 (C).

Factor Analysis of Temperament and Personality Scales

To test the correspondence of the temperament and personality trait-sphere we applied a principal component analysis to the intercorrelation matrix of the 34 temperament and personality questionnaire scales and the factor scores calculated on the basis of the NEO adjective ratings. An inspection of the plot of eigenvalues showed that six rather than five factors should be extracted from the intercorrelation matrix of the variables. The eigenvalues of the first eight unrotated components were 6.95, 6.45, 3.07, 3.02, 2.24, 1.65, 1.19, and 1.14. Two further tests were used to determine the number of components to be extracted. First, in a Parallel Analysis (Horn, 1965) a mean plot of eigenvalues was calculated on the basis of 50 intercorrelation matrices that were previously computed from data sets of randomly distributed variables. This plot of averaged random eigenvalues was compared with the scree of eigenvalues in our sample data. Second, the Minimum Average Partial method (Velicer, 1976) was applied to our data set. Both methods, which have been shown to be superior (Zwick & Velicer, 1986) to other methods (e.g., the Kaiser rule of thumb) yielded six significant principal components. Therefore, we extracted six factors and rotated them using the varimax criterion. Table 4.2 shows the results of the principal component analysis.

The six factors explained 59.9% of the total variance. On the basis of the factor patterns shown in Table 4.2, the first five components were clearly interpretable as the hypothesized Big Five factors. The analysis also yielded a very specific sixth factor defined by the three Rhythmicity scales of the DOTS Inventory. Only two additional scales (DOTS: Activity-Level Sleep, Flexibil-

TABLE 4.2
Six-Factor Structure Derived from Questionnaire Scales of Major Temperament Theories, the Scales of the NEO Five-Factor Inventory, Plus the NEO Adjective Rating Factors

Scales	Factors						
	N	E	O	A	C	RHY	h^2
STI-RS							
Excitation	−46	23	51	−30	20	10	67
Inhibition	−52	−11	03	44	01	16	50
Mobility	−40	50	44	15	19	−19	69
SSS-LE							
Thrill & Adventure Seeking	−23	12	51	05	−05	−06	35
Disinhibition	03	13	42	−41	−32	00	47
Experience Seeking	07	05	73	−10	−15	−15	60
Boredom Susceptibility	04	−16	64	−10	−24	03	50

(Continued)

TABLE 4.2
(Continued)

Scales	Factors						
	N	E	O	A	C	RHY	h^2
EASI-III							
Emotionality							
General	80	16	02	−08	−10	−06	68
Fear	73	−14	−24	10	−20	−02	66
Anger	44	13	03	−64	−04	−03	62
Distress	76	−18	05	−28	−17	−01	72
Activity							
Tempo	24	18	15	−30	45	04	40
Vigor	−18	36	28	−18	59	08	63
Sociability I	−10	81	12	02	−07	−01	69
Sociability II	16	68	02	06	−30	07	59
Impulsivity							
Non Inhibition Control	60	16	14	−25	−25	−09	54
Short Decision Time	−14	37	47	−01	−22	−10	44
Sensation Seeking	14	27	61	−23	−17	−08	55
Non Persistence	10	08	03	−03	−71	−11	54
DOTS-R							
Activity-Level General	38	15	25	−41	−12	−04	42
Activity-Level Sleep	11	−08	03	−12	−14	−34	17
Approach/Withdrawal	−23	57	48	02	11	−17	65
Flexibility/Rigidity	−28	28	39	18	08	−40	50
Mood	−11	68	02	10	10	−10	50
Rhythmicity-Sleep	01	−17	−16	−01	18	75	66
Rhythmicity-Eating	−17	−05	−14	08	10	75	64
Rhythmicity-Daily Habits	−07	01	−08	−01	12	83	72
Distractibility	−33	−12	08	12	51	28	48
Persistence	−25	−08	−01	07	72	20	64
NEOFFI							
Neuroticism	77	−22	−13	01	−24	−04	72
Extraversion	−01	87	14	−05	15	04	81
Openness to Experience	21	−07	57	30	30	−19	59
Agreeableness	−01	30	−06	79	06	02	72
Conscientiousness	−21	05	−29	10	75	13	72
NEO-Rating Factors							
Neuroticism	87	−14	−01	04	09	−14	80
Extraversion	09	85	−03	−06	−03	−04	74
Openness to Experience	−03	04	71	03	28	−14	60
Agreeableness	01	10	−03	85	−08	09	74
Conscientiousness	−11	−02	−34	06	77	06	73
% of explained variance	22.0	19.7	18.0	12.6	16.9	10.9 /	59.9%

Note: N of subjects = 323. Varimax-rotated principal components. Eigenvalues (unrotated PC): 6.95, 6.45, 3.07, 3.02, 2.24, 1.65, 1.19, 1.14. Factors: N = Neuroticism, E = Extraversion, O = Openness to Experience, A = Agreeableness, C = Conscientiousness, RHY = Rhythmicity. Scales: STI-RS = Revised short form of the Strelau Temperament Inventory (Strelau, Angleitner, Bantelmann, & Ruch, 1990); SSS = Sensation-Seeking scales (Zuckerman, 1979); EASI = EASI Temperament Survey (Buss & Plomin, 1984); DOTS-R = Revised Dimensions of Temperament Survey (Windle & Lerner, 1986); NEOFFI = NEO Five-Factor Inventory (Costa & McCrae, 1989; Borkenau & Ostendorf, 1991); NEO–R = NEO Adjective Rating Scales (McCrae & Costa, 1987; Ostendorf, 1990).

ity/Rigidity) had secondary loadings on this factor greater than .30. This sixth factor could unambiguously be interpreted as a Rhythmicity factor.

Each of the first five factors correlated highest with one of the two NEO scales measuring the dimensions N, E, O, A, and C. The NEO scales exhibit a loading pattern of high convergent and discriminant validity or simple structure, that is, in almost every case the NEO scales had their highest loading on only one factor with negligible loadings on the remaining four factors. The Openness and Agreeableness scales of the NEOFFI, however, did show secondary loadings on Extraversion, Conscientiousness, and Agreeableness.

On the basis of explained variance, the Neuroticism factor could be considered the most important (22.0%), followed by Extraversion (19.7%), Openness (18.0%), Conscientiousness (16.9%), and Agreeableness (12.6%). Rhythmicity (10.9%) was the least important factor.

An examination of the factor pattern for the first five factors also revealed the following:

1. *Neuroticism.* In addition to the respective NEO scales, the following temperament scales appeared to be primary markers of Neuroticism: EASI Emotionality scales General Emotionality, Fear and Distress as well as the EASI Non-Inhibition Control subscale of the Impulsivity dimension.

2. *Extraversion.* Extraversion correlated highest with the appropriate NEO scales, and with the following temperament scales as well: the Sociability subscales of the EASI, the DOTS scales Mood and Approach/Withdrawal, and the Mobility scale of the STI.

3. *Openness to Experience.* Openness showed many high loadings. This result was unexpected, because it is usually assumed this factor is a personality rather than a temperament factor (Ruch et al., 1991). Besides its correlations with the respective NEO scales, this factor correlated highly with the Sensation-Seeking scales by Zuckerman (1979), with the scales Sensation Seeking and Decision Time of the EASI Inventory, and with the STI scale Strength of Excitation and with the DOTS scales Approach/Withdrawal and Flexibility/Rigidity.

4. *Agreeableness.* Next to the Rhythmicity factor, Agreeableness explained the lowest proportion of variance in the analysis. The Agreeableness factor correlated strongest with the respective NEO scales, followed by the correlations with the EASI scale Emotionality-Anger, the STI scale Strength of Inhibition, the SSS scale Disinhibition, and the DOTS scale Activity Level/General.

5. *Conscientiousness.* Primary marker scales of the Conscientiousness factor were the respective NEO scales, the Persistence scales of the EASI, and the DOTS inventories. In addition, the factor was correlated significantly with the Vigor and Tempo scales of the EASI and the Distractibility scale of the DOTS questionnaire.

Compared to the results of Ruch et al. (1991), the present analysis yielded some discrepant correlations among the STI scales and the Big Five factors. Like prior results, we also found negative correlations between all STI scales and Neuroticism. In addition, we replicated the positive correlations between STI-Strength of Inhibition and Agreeableness and STI-Mobility and Extraversion. Departures from the previous findings of Ruch et al. (1991) included high correlations between Openness to Experience and STI-Strength of Excitation and Mobility.

The Rhythmicity factor appeared to be a quite specific factor. The factor was loaded almost exclusively by the Rhythmicity scales of the DOTS Inventory. Have we found an additional robust factor that has been overlooked by personality researchers until now? Must the five-factor model be expanded?

Five or Six Temperament Factors of Personality

It may be necessary to enlarge the five-factor model by another factor. Because the five-factor model of personality was initially found in lexical studies, the absence of a sixth Rhythmicity factor may indicate that ordinary people are insensitive to individual differences in rhythmicity in their daily transactions. Consequently, commonly used words for Rhythmicity have failed to enter into the lexicon.

Nevertheless, several considerations raise doubts about the robustness of an enlarged six-factor model. Our main concern is that Rhythmicity, in contrast to other dimensions, was measured several times. That is, the construct was operationalized by three scales or facets of Rhythmicity, each measuring three very concrete and specific domains of behavior (Sleep, Eating, and Daily Habits). The relatively narrow Rhythmicity construct was perhaps overweighted in the common factor analysis of all scales compared to, say, the constructs of Mood or Persistence of the DOTS Inventory. Therefore, it may not be surprising that three narrow and highly correlated scales formed a specific factor. It would be reasonable to assume that one could find a comparable specific factor "Decision Time" for example in an analysis in which the construct Decision Time of the EASI Inventory was operationalized by multiple scales.

The results from factor-analyzing scales unfortunately depend heavily on the broadness or inclusiveness of the analyzed scales, for example, on the level of abstraction of the operationalization of the different domains of behaviors that are structured and combined into scales. In contrast, an item-factor analysis avoids this problem because the analysis is *not* based on item pools already prestructured into scales. This is not to say that one cannot bias an item factor analysis by including many items of similar, specific content. If however, the ratio of the number of items of many specific scales to the number of items of a few global scales is lower (e.g., the 16 items of the specific Rhythmicity scales/the 24 items of the global STI-SE scale = .67), than the ratio of the number of specific to global scales (three Rhythmicity scales/one STI-SE scale = 3.0), a more adequate representation of the range of content within the items can most probably be achieved through an item-factor analysis.

To demonstrate the reality of an independent Rhythmicity factor, it must be shown that this factor can also be recovered from a factor analysis of the entire pool of all questionnaire items.

Factor Analysis of the Total Item Pool

For this reason, we performed a principal component analysis of the total pool of 394 questionnaire items. Colleagues have pointed out to us the small subject-to-variable ratio that our analyses—especially our item-factor analysis—were founded. On the other hand, several studies have shown that the usual rules of thumb concerning the subject-to-variable ratio (e.g., 5:1, Gorsuch, 1983; 3 to 6:1; Cattell, 1978; 10:1, Nunnally, 1978) have little effect on the robustness of factors (Arrindell & van der Ende, 1985; Barrett & Kline, 1981). It is not the variable-to-observation ratio that is important for stability but rather the absolute number of observations, which, in turn, has an effect on the interval of confidence of the correlation coefficients. Of course, it is advisable to reduce the confidence interval for the correlation coefficients by use of the largest possible sample.

Five- and six-factor solutions (varimax rotated) were examined. Factor scores from both item-factor solutions were correlated with factor scores derived from the factor analysis of the questionnaire scales. Table 4.3 shows the correlations among these factor scores.

There was a high correspondence among the item and scale factors N, E, O, A, and C across the analyses with five factors with some exceptions for the factor Openness. The high correspondence of the first five factors remained quite stable if the five item factors are correlated with the six scale factors. In this comparison of item and scale factors, the sixth scale factor (Rhythmicity) correlated negatively with the item factor Openness (−.50). The correlation of the six item factors with the respective scale factors, seemed to confirm a Rhythmicity factor, but a closer examination of the lower left quadrant of Table 4.3 showed that the sixth factor of the item-factor analysis can best be considered a specific facet of a more general Openness factor. The item factor was substantially correlated with the scale factor Openness (−.63), and this correlation was nearly as high as the correlation between the third factors (.65). The results shown in Table 4.3, therefore seem to imply only five broad and robust factors across both kinds of factor analysis.

Table 4.4 presents the pattern matrix of a component analysis of the scales with five factors. A comparison of this matrix with the factor structure of the six-factor solution presented in Table 4.2 revealed the main discrepancy was due to the Rhythmicity factor included in the six-factor model but excluded in the five-factor model. As could be expected, the Rhythmicity scales showed significant negative loadings on the Openness factor of the five-factor solution. The loading pattern of all other scales remains quite stable.

TABLE 4.3
Correlations Among Item-Factor Scores and Scale-Factor Scores Derived
From Five- and Six-Factor Solutions

Item Factors	Scale Factors										
	Five Factors					Six Factors					
	N	E	O	A	C	N	E	O	A	C	RHY
N	91	−09	−02	31	−08	89	−08	−24	23	−06	−19
E	04	97	01	12	−02	04	97	00	12	−03	−00
O	−03	−03	92	−12	−25	−05	−00	79	13	−18	−50
A	−35	−10	07	89	−01	−33	−10	−19	89	01	−08
C	05	01	23	00	92	05	01	14	02	93	−04
N	90	−04	09	06	−06	96	−04	02	12	−06	−02
E	05	97	−03	09	−04	03	97	−04	06	−04	−01
O	−25	13	65	−43	−07	−09	08	90	−06	−06	−01
A	−26	−03	14	83	−01	−17	−04	−02	94	00	04
C	06	02	22	03	91	06	03	12	03	93	−06
RHY	−13	03	−63	−19	30	−04	02	−19	−12	19	77

Note: N = 323 subjects. Factors: N = Neuroticism, E = Extraversion, O = Openness to Experience, A = Agreeableness, C = Conscientiousness, RHY = Rhythmicity.

Whether the evidence for additional robust factors beyond the Big Five can be substantiated will be a task for future research. To furnish proof of a robust and broad sixth factor it may be necessary to detect additional domains of behavior that are closely related to Rhythmicity but are almost uncorrelated with the first five temperament or personality factors. From a developmental perspective, one may argue that Rhythmicity may have its special importance for young children. Unfortunately, we do not have samples of subjects of children differing in age to make a comparison. In our sample we do have, however, an age range from 17 to 67 years. Therefore, we computed the correlations between age and the factor scores of the factor analytic studies reported in Tables 4.2 and 4.5. Rhythmicity showed a significant positive correlation with age in both analyses ($r = .20$ and $.21, p < .01$). The other factors were not correlated with age. This implies that the other factors, at least in adult populations, are highly robust and do not change with age (see Costa & McCrae, chap. 7 in this volume). The correlation with the Rhythmicity factor suggests that with increasing age Rhythmicity increases.

The Structure of Temperament Revisited

In our study we used clear and reliable marker variables for the Big Five personality factors. Of course, these markers have influenced the analyses in such a way that the Big Five had a good chance to be the major factors. What would happen to the factor structure if the Big Five markers are eliminated? We

TABLE 4.4
Five-Factor Structure Derived from Questionnaire Scales of Major
Temperament Theories, the Scales of the NEO Five-Factor Inventory,
Plus the NEO Adjective Rating Factors

	\multicolumn{6}{c}{Factors}
Scales	N	E	O	A	C	h^2
STI-RS						
Excitation	−52	25	25	−47	21	66
Inhibition	−58	−10	−01	36	02	48
Mobility	−43	51	46	02	16	69
SSS-LE						
Thrill & Adventure Seeking	−31	14	39	−24	−11	33
Disinhibition	−01	15	20	−55	−31	46
Experience Seeking	−04	08	61	−37	−17	55
Boredom Susceptibility	−09	−13	42	−38	−23	40
EASI-III						
Emotionality						
General	78	16	06	−10	−10	65
Fear	73	−15	−13	16	−20	64
Anger	48	12	−07	−58	−02	59
Distress	74	−18	01	−31	−16	70
Activity						
Tempo	23	18	08	−32	46	40
Vigor	−20	36	16	−25	60	63
Sociability I	−11	82	08	−02	−07	69
Sociability II	13	69	−05	02	−28	58
Impulsivity						
Non Inhibition Control	59	17	12	−29	−26	53
Short Decision Time	−20	39	38	−18	−24	43
Sensation Seeking	05	29	45	−45	−17	52
Non Persistence	10	08	02	−05	−72	54
DOTS-R						
Activity-Level General	37	16	13	−47	−12	42
Activity-Level Sleep	18	−09	21	−06	−18	12
Approach/Withdrawal	−28	58	46	−13	08	65
Flexibility/Rigidity	−28	29	57	10	02	49
Mood	−08	67	09	13	08	49
Rhythmicity-Sleep	−10	−15	−57	−11	28	45
Rhythmicity-Eating	−29	−03	−56	−03	20	44
Rhythmicity-Daily Habits	−20	03	−57	−15	23	45
Distractibility	−39	−11	−05	04	53	46
Persistence	−27	−08	−07	06	74	64
NEOFFI						
Neuroticism	76	−23	−05	02	−24	70
Extraversion	−03	88	07	−09	16	81
Openness to Experience	10	−05	64	07	27	50
Agreeableness	−07	30	10	72	05	63
Conscientiousness	−17	03	−22	22	76	70

(Continued)

TABLE 4.4
(Continued)

Scales	Factors					h^2
	N	E	O	A	C	
NEO-Rating Factors						
Neuroticism	86	−14	14	04	07	78
Extraversion	12	85	−02	−02	−02	73
Openness to Experience	−13	06	65	−22	26	56
Agreeableness	−09	11	08	73	−08	56
Conscientiousness	−04	−04	−21	22	77	69
% of explained variance	25.0	21.6	18.4	16.0	19.0 /	55.7%

Note: N of subjects = 323. Varimax-rotated principal components. Eigenvalues (unrotated PC): 7.32, 5.92, 3.28, 3.15, 2.21, 1.82, 1.37, 1.23. Factors: N = Neuroticism, E = Extraversion, O = Openness to Experience, A = Agreeableness, C = Conscientiousness. Scales: STI-RS = Revised short form of the Strelau Temperament Inventory (Strelau, Angleitner, Bantelmann, & Ruch, 1990); SSS = Sensation-Seeking scales (Zuckerman, 1979); EASI = EASI Temperament Survey (Buss & Plomin, 1984); DOTS-R = Revised Dimensions of Temperament Survey (Windle & Lerner, 1986); NEOFFI = NEO Five Factor Inventory (Costa & McCrae, 1989; Borkenau & Ostendorf, 1991); NEO-R = NEO Adjective Rating scales (McCrae & Costa, 1987; Ostendorf, 1990).

investigated the factor structure of the 29 temperament scales only to answer this question. We used principal component analysis as well as all methods used to determine the number of significant factors in the earlier analyses (MAP, Velicer, 1976; Parallel Analysis, Horn, 1965; Scree-Test, Cattell, 1966). The first seven eigenvalues were as follows: 5.25, 5.19, 2.37, 1.89, 1.65, 1.09, 1.00. Table 4.5 shows the varimax-rotated factor structure.

The five factors explained 56.3% of the total variance. The first factor seemed to be a blend of the factors Neuroticism and Agreeableness. High loading scales were the EASI Emotionality subscales (marker scales of Neuroticism) as well as EASI Inhibition Control, a measure of Impulsivity versus Impulse Control in interpersonal situations. Further, the STI-SI showed a strong negative loading and the DOTS Activity Level-General a positive loading.

Factor III showed a clear correspondence to the Openness factor of the common analysis of temperament and personality scales. Scales with high loadings on that factor were, for example, the SSS, the EASI Sensation-Seeking scales and the STI-SE scale.

Similar high correspondences were found for the second and the fourth factors, which we labeled Extraversion and Conscientiousness. Examples of high loading scales were EASI Sociability and DOTS Mood for Extraversion; the Persistence scales of the DOTS and EASI as well as the EASI activity scales for the Conscientiousness factor.

The fifth factor was comprised of the three Rhythmicity scales.

TABLE 4.5
Five-Factor Structure Derived from Temperament Questionnaire Scales

Scales	N/A−	E	O	C	RHY	h^2
STI-RS						
Excitation	−22	26	57	47	07	67
Inhibition	−69	−00	−00	−03	12	50
Mobility	−34	62	30	28	−20	71
SSS-LE						
Thrill & Adventure Seeking	−15	16	55	08	−12	37
Disinhibition	26	08	66	−16	01	53
Experience Seeking	10	10	71	−02	−23	57
Boredom Susceptibility	06	−16	72	−11	−05	57
EASI-III						
Emotionality						
General	74	05	−09	−16	−09	59
Fear	57	−24	−31	−29	−08	57
Anger	71	04	12	04	04	52
Distress	76	−29	04	−15	−06	69
Activity						
Tempo	38	07	06	60	−01	51
Vigor	−03	34	16	71	08	65
Sociability I	04	80	11	01	02	65
Sociability II	25	66	03	−25	09	56
Impulsivity						
Non Inhibition Control	69	08	14	−22	−10	56
Short Decision Time	−03	48	45	−13	−10	45
Sensation Seeking	30	30	60	05	−15	56
Non Persistence	14	10	20	−70	−09	57
DOTS-R						
Activity-Level General	58	01	31	10	−12	46
Activity-Level Sleep	14	−11	09	−10	−35	18
Approach/Withdrawal	−12	68	35	21	−17	67
Flexibility/Rigidity	−28	43	25	10	−40	50
Mood	−02	73	−09	06	−03	54
Rhythmicity-Sleep	−03	−21	−14	15	75	65
Rhythmicity-Eating	−19	−06	−08	06	77	65
Rhythmicity-Daily Habits	−05	−02	−04	07	86	75
Distractibility	−41	−11	00	51	24	49
Persistence	−30	−08	−15	70	19	65
% of explained variance	14.6	11.9	11.4	9.7	8.7 /	56.3%

Note: N of subjects = 323. Varimax-rotated principal components. Eigenvalues (unrotated PC): 5.25, 5.19, 2.37, 1.89, 1.65. Factors: N = Neuroticism, E = Extraversion, O = Openness to Experience, A = Agreeableness, C = Conscientiousness. Scales: STI–RS = Revised short form of the Strelau Temperament Inventory (Strelau, Angleitner, Bantelmann, & Ruch, 1990); SSS = Sensation-Seeking scales (Zuckerman, 1979); EASI = EASI Temperament Survey (Buss & Plomin, 1984); DOTS–R = Revised Dimensions of Temperament Survey (Windle & Lerner, 1986).

To supply empirical proof to our factor interpretations, we correlated the temperament factors (Table 4.5) with the six factors shown in Table 4.2. Substantial factor–score correlations were found between N/A and Neuroticism (.85), N/A and Agreeableness (−.47), as well as between the factors Openness (.85), Extraversion (.94), Conscientiousness (.88), and Rhythmicity (.97).

DISCUSSION

Our results confirm the structural validity of the five-factor model of personality. First, we showed that most of the temperament scales used fit reasonably well within the structure of these five factors. Second, this FFM model represents a comprehensive framework that can be used for a systematic classification and interpretation of single temperament or personality measures.

In agreement with previous studies (Corulla, 1988; Ruch et al., 1991; Zuckerman et al., 1988, 1991) we can assert that the three-factor P-E-N model proposed by Eysenck neglects some major factors necessary for an adequate description of the structure of personality and temperament traits. In addition to Extraversion and Neuroticism, at least three supplementary factors are needed for this purpose (see also Goldberg & Rosolak, chap. 1 in this vol.).

Are temperament and personality trait spheres completely congruent or is there only a partial overlap between both spheres? Can possibly one of the trait spheres be conceived of as a segment of the other? The findings of our study cannot provide final, unequivocal answers to these questions. It would be necessary to demonstrate that both domains are perfectly represented. Nevertheless, our results show that there is more congruence between both domains than many authors have previously believed.

One unexpected finding pertains to the Openness factor. Most authors previously assumed that this factor is not related to the temperament domain. Nevertheless, close relationships between Openness and temperament might have been predicted simply by looking more closely at the labels and contents of some of the temperament scales. For example, persons with high scores on Openness to Experience are described by Costa and McCrae (1985, 1989) as being actively and continuously searching for new experiences. Predictably, the Sensation-Seeking scales—in particular the Experience Seeking scale by Zuckerman (1979)—exhibit the highest loadings on this factor, followed by the Openness scale of the NEO. The loading patterns of variables was compatible with an interpretation of the fifth factor as General Openness to Experience as well as Experience Seeking. This factor may, however, represent a more specific facet of the broader Openness construct of Costa and McCrae: Openness to Actions. An inspection of temperament items that load on this factor supports this interpretation. It would appear that the Openness factor in our study pointed to some sample specificity in the sense that high factor scores described a kind of behavior that can be characterized as a surgent way of being open-minded to new experiences.[9] This state of affairs may elucidate the pronounced similarity of Openness to Experience with the Sensation-Seeking scales in our study (cf. Zuckerman et al., 1988, 1991).

Agreeableness was the weakest factor in our study. This finding stands in contrast to results from studies in which a broad spectrum of personality measures is analysed; in these studies, Agreeableness is usually one of the strongest factors. In the present study, only the temperament scale Anger of the EASI Inventory shows a substantial loading on the Agreeableness factor. When the temperament scales were factor analyzed separately, no single independent Agreeableness factor emerged. In fact, most of the temperament marker variables for Agreeableness emerge from such an analysis as markers for a factor that can be seen as a combination of Neuroticism (N) and Non-Agreeableness (A−). It would seem then that an analysis disregarding personality scales corresponds more to the findings of McCrae and Costa (1985b), whose analysis of the EASI scales within the domain of N, E, O, and C also failed to detect an Agreeableness factor.

Furthermore, our results demonstrated that the EASI domain scales do not form homogeneous subsets. As in the study by McCrae and Costa (1985b), we also found significant loadings of the Emotionality subscales on the Neuroticism factor corresponding to the hypothesis of Buss and Plomin (1975). Contrary to Buss and Plomin's assumption that the Inhibition-Control scale should be a marker of an independent Impulsivity factor, however, we found that the Inhibition-Control scale loads highest on the Neuroticism factor. McCrae and Costa (1985b) reported the same pattern together with a finding of similar correspondence, that the Impulsivity-Persistence scale is a central marker variable of the Conscientiousness factor. In addition to several concurrent results, our findings suggest some differences to those of McCrae and Costa (1985b). Whereas EASI Emotionality-Anger was a primary marker for Agreeableness in our study, it was a primary marker for Neuroticism in McCrae and Costa's study (1985b). The EASI Sensation-Seeking scale primarily marked the Openness factor in our study; in McCrae and Costa's study (1985b) the Sensation-Seeking scale marked primarily Extraversion. It may be that Openness in the present study was, however, predominantly Openness to Actions. A related reason may be that McCrae and Costa (1985b) analyzed a selection of scales that covered only the domains of four of the Big Five factors. Another possible explanation may be found in the low reliability of the EASI Impulsivity subscales.

Our empirical results contradict John's (1989, 1990) hypotheses about the relations among the EASI scales and the Big Five. For example, John's (1989) suggestions concerning the correspondence of the EASI dimensions Activity and Impulsivity to one of the Big Five factors respectively could not be clearly substantiated. Furthermore, Sociability clearly belongs on Extraversion and not at all on the Agreeableness factor.

---

[9]See De Raad, Hendriks, and Hofstee (chap. 5 in this vol.) for a structural model combining Factors I and V that may also describe this factor.

We might add that most of the other temperament scales also had highly complex loading patterns. Quite frequently, we found nearly comparable loadings of a single temperament scale on two or three of the Big Five factors. The salience of the loadings refer to a substantial interlacing of temperament and personality constructs.

Factoring the temperament scales alone yielded a broad factor that was a blend of Neuroticism and low Agreeableness. This finding supports the contention that Emotionality is strongly related to temperament in adults as well as children. The emotionality concepts introduced by Thomas and Chess (1977) for distinguishing easy from difficult children may also have some value for adults. As it stands, our study helps to solve the disagreements about the kind and number of dimensions needed beyond Extraversion and Neuroticism for structuring individual differences in the temperament domain. However, marker variables for Eysenck's P-E-N model were not included in our study. Joint factor analyses on the basis of item and scale scores including the relevant Eysenck scales are the next step to solve the debate about the appropriate number of factors in the temperament and personality domain.

ACKNOWLEDGMENTS

We would like to thank Jeff McCrae, Willem K. B. Hofstee, Jan Strelau, and Michael Windle for their various comments and suggestions on this chapter. The research was supported in part by the Deutsche Forschungsgemeinschaft (grant An 106-10/1, OZ 27230), and by the University of Bielefeld (grant 2794/2).

REFERENCES

Arrindell, W. A., & Van der Ende, J. (1985). An empirical test of the utility of the observation-to-variables ratio in factor and component analysis. *Applied Psychological Measurement, 9*, 165–178.

Barrett, P. T., & Kline, P. (1981). The observation to variable ratio in factor analysis. *Personality Study and Group Behaviour, 1*, 23–33.

Borkenau, P., & Ostendorf, F. (1991). Ein Fragebogen zur Erfassung fünf robuster Persönlichkeitsfaktoren [An inventory to measure five robust factors of personality]. *Diagnostica, 37*, 29–41.

Birenbaum, M., & Montag, I. (1986). On the location of the sensation seeking construct in the personality domain. *Multivariate Behavioral Research, 21*, 357–373.

Buss, A. H. (1988). *Personality: Evolutionary heritage and human distinctiveness.* Hillsdale, NJ: Lawrence Erlbaum Associates.

Buss, A. H., & Plomin, R. (1975). *A temperament theory of personality development.* New York: Wiley-Interscience.

Carlier, M. (1985). Factor analysis of Strelau's questionnaire and an attempt to validate some of the factors. In J. Strelau, F. H. Farley, & A. Gale (Eds.), *The biological bases of personality and behavior: Theories, measurement techniques, and development* (Vol. 1, pp. 145–160). Washington, DC: Hemisphere.

4. TEMPERAMENT AND THE BIG FIVE

Cattell, R. B. (1966). The Scree-Test for the number of factors. *Multivariate Behavioral Research, 1*, 140–161.
Cattell, R. B. (1978). *The scientific use of factor analysis*. New York: Plenum.
Corulla, W. J. (1988). A further psychometric investigation of the Sensation Seeking Scale Form-V and its relationship to the EPQ-R and the I.7 Impulsiveness Questionnaire. *Personality and Individual Differences, 9*, 277–288.
Costa, P. T., Jr., & McCrae, R. R. (1985). *The NEO Personality Inventory*. Manual. Form S and Form R. Odessa: Psychological Assessment Resources.
Costa, P. T., Jr., & McCrae, R. R. (1989). *NEO PI/FFI manual supplement*. Odessa, Fl: Psychological Assessment Resources.
Digman, J. M. (1990). Personality structure: Emergence of the five-factor model. *Annual Review of Psychology, 41*, 417–440.
Digman, J. M., & Inouye, J. (1986). Further specification of the five robust factors of personality. *Journal of Personality and Social Psychology, 50*, 116–123.
Digman, J. M., & Takemoto-Chock, N. K. (1981). Factors in the natural language of personality: Re-analysis and comparison of six major studies. *Multivariate Behavioral Research, 16*, 149–170.
Eysenck, H. J., & Eysenck, S. B. G. (1975). *Manual of the Eysenck Personality Questionnaire*. London: Hodder & Stoughton.
Goldberg, L. R. (1980, May). Some ruminations about the structure of individual differences: Developing a common lexicon for the major characteristics of human personality. *Meeting of the Western Psychological Association, Honolulu, Hawaii*.
Gorsuch, R. L. (1983). *Factor analysis*. Philadelphia: W. B. Saunders.
Gough, H. G. (1964). *California psychological inventory manual*. Palo Alto, CA: Consulting Psychologists Press.
Harman, H. H. (1970). *Modern factor analysis* (2nd ed.). Chicago: University of Chicago Press.
Hogan, R. T. (1983). A socioanalytic theory of personality. In M. Page (Ed.), *1982 Nebraska symposium on motivation* (pp. 55–89). Lincoln, NE: University of Nebraska Press.
Horn, J. L. (1965). A rationale and test for the number of factors in factor analysis. *Psychometrika, 30*, 179–185.
Jackson, D. N. (1976). *JPI—Jackson Personality Inventory—Manual*. Goshen, NY: Research Psychologists Press.
Jackson, D. N. (1984). *Personality Research Form Manual*. Port Huron, MI: Research Psychologists Press.
John, O. P. (1989). Towards a taxonomy of personality descriptors. In D. M. Buss & N. Cantor (Eds.), *Personality psychology: Recent trends and emerging directions* (pp. 261–271). New York: Springer.
John, O. P. (1990). The "Big Five" factor taxonomy: Dimensions of personality in the natural language and in questionnaires. In L. A. Pervin (Ed.), *Handbook of personality: Theory and research* (pp. 66–100). New York: Guilford.
Magnusson, D. (1986). *Individual development and adjustment* (Tech. Rep. No. 64). Stockholm: University of Stockholm, Department of Psychology.
McCrae, R. R. (1989). Why I advocate the five-factor model: Joint factor analyses of the NEO-PI with other instruments. In D. M. Buss & N. Cantor (Eds.), *Personality psychology: Recent trends and emerging directions* (pp. 237–245). New York: Springer.
McCrae, R. R., & Costa, P. T., Jr. (1985a). Updating Norman's adequate taxonomy: Intelligence and personality dimensions in natural language and in questionnaires. *Journal of Personality and Social Psychology, 49*, 710–721.
McCrae, R. R., & Costa, P. T., Jr. (1985b). Openness to experience. In R. Hogan & W. II. Jones (Eds.), *Perspectives in personality* (Vol. 1, pp. 145–172). Greenwich, CT: JAI Press.
McCrae, R. R., & Costa, P. T., Jr. (1987). Validation of the five-factor model of personality across instruments and observers. *Journal of Personality and Social Psychology, 52*, 81–90.

McCrae, R. R., & Costa, P. T., Jr. (in press). Conceptions and correlates of Openness to Experience. In R. Hogan, J. A. Johnson, & S. R. Briggs (Eds.), *Handbook of personality psychology*. Orlando, FL: Academic Press.

Nunnally, J. C. (1978). *Psychometric theory* (2nd ed.). New York: McGraw-Hill.

Ostendorf, F. (1990). *Sprache und Persönlichkeitsstruktur: Zur Validität des Fünf-Faktoren-Modells der Persönlichkeit* [Language and personality structure: On the structural validity of the five-factor model of personality]. Roderer: Regensburg.

Ruch, W., Angleitner, A., & Strelau, J. (1991). The Strelau Temperament Inventory—Revised (STI-R): Validity studies. *European Journal of Personality, 5,* 287–308.

Rusalov, V. M. (1989). Object-related and communicative aspects of human temperament: A new questionnaire of the structure of temperament. *Personality and Individual Differences, 10,* 817–827.

Serlin, R. C., & Kaiser, H. F. (1976). A computer program for item selection based on maximum internal consistency. *Educational and Psychological Measurement, 36,* 757–759.

Strelau, J. (1983). *Temperament personality activity*. New York: Academic Press.

Strelau, J. (1987). The concept of temperament in personality research. *European Journal of Personality, 1,* 107–117.

Strelau, J., Angleitner, A., & Ruch, W. (1990). Strelau Temperament Inventory (STI): General review and studies based on German samples. In C. D. Spielberger & J. N. Butcher (Eds.), *Advances in personality assessment* (Vol. 8, pp. 187–241). Hillsdale, NJ: Lawrence Erlbaum Associates.

Strelau, J., Angleitner, A., Bantelmann, J., & Ruch, W. (1990). The Strelau Temperament Inventory—Revised (STI-R): Theoretical considerations and scale development. *European Journal of Personality, 4,* 209–235.

Thomas, A., & Chess, S. (1977). *Temperament and development*. New York: Brunner/Mazel.

Unterweger, E. (1980). *Rigidität und Reizsuche* [Rigidity and sensation seeking]. Unpublished doctoral dissertation, University of Graz, Austria.

Velicer, W. F. (1976). Determining the number of components from the matrix of partial correlations. *Psychometrika, 41,* 321–327.

Windle, M. (1989). Temperament and Personality: An exploratory interinventory study of the DOTS-R, EASI-II, and EPI. *Journal of Personality Assessment, 53,* 487–501.

Windle, M., & Lerner, R. M. (1986). Reassessing the dimensions of temperament individuality across the life span: The Revised Dimensions of Temperament Survey (DOTS-R). *Journal of Adolescent Research, 1,* 213–230.

Zuckerman, M. (1979). *Sensation seeking: Beyond the optimal level of arousal*. Hillsdale, NJ: Lawrence Erlbaum Associates.

Zuckerman, M. (1991). *Psychobiology of personality*. New York: Cambridge University Press.

Zuckerman, M., Eysenck, S. B. G., & Eysenck, H. J. (1978). Sensation seeking in England and America: Cross-cultural, age and sex comparisons. *Journal of Consulting and Clinical Psychology, 46,* 139–149.

Zuckerman, M., Kuhlman, D. M., & Camac, C. (1988). What lies beyond E and N? Factor analysis of scales believed to measure basic dimensions of personality. *Journal of Personality and Social Psychology, 54,* 96–107.

Zuckerman, M., Kuhlman, D. M., Thornquist, H., & Kiers, H. (1991). Five (or three) robust questionnaire scale factors of personality without culture. *Personality and Individual Differences, 12,* 929–941.

Zwick, W. R., & Velicer, W. F. (1986). Comparison of five rules for determining the number of components to retain. *Psychological Bulletin, 99,* 432–442.

CHAPTER

5

THE BIG FIVE: A TIP OF THE ICEBERG OF INDIVIDUAL DIFFERENCES

Boele De Raad
A. A. Jolijn Hendriks
Willem K. B. Hofstee
University of Groningen

One of the major programs of the trait approach to personality during the last few decades has been the study of taxonomies of personality traits. This persistent and longtime endeavor toward a comprehensive mapping of individual differences began in the seminal work of Allport and Odbert (1936). Cattell (1943), a pioneer in the field, formulated the rationale behind this approach: "All aspects of human personality which are or have been of importance, interest, or utility have already become recorded in the substance of language" (p. 483). Another pioneer in the field of individual differences, Eysenck (1947) pursued a similar goal, namely to strive after a system to "cover all the diverse features of personality" (p. 20).

Although like-minded toward full coverage of the field, these two pioneers were radically opposed to each other over the number of dimensions needed to describe all personality traits. For full and satisfactory coverage, Cattell (1945) considered 12 as the minimum number of factors, but in terms of modern standards it has become clear that Cattell extracted too many factors from his data (cf. Digman & Takemoto-Chock, 1981; Eysenck, 1991; Howarth, 1976; Matthews, 1989). In contrast, Eysenck (1967, 1990, 1991, chap. 2 in this vol.) recurrently claimed no more than three factors necessary for a full accounting of important personality characteristics. The basic factors postulated by Eysenck (1952)—Psychoticism, Extraversion, and Neuroticism (P-E-N)—form the highest level of aggregation of a hierarchical model of personality (Eysenck, 1947). Although this P-E-N model seems to provide an attractive framework for the accommodation of the diverse features of personality, the aspect of hierarchy is overemphasized (Hofstee, 1990).

Empirical studies show at best partial hierarchy for the domain of traits (Hampson, John, & Goldberg, 1986).

The third movement claiming full capturing of all relevant individual differences, the lexical approach to personality (John, Angleitner, & Ostendorf, 1988), also found its origin in the work of Allport and Odbert (1936). The history of the movement is well documented in, inter alia, John et al. (1988). At present, consensus rapidly grows over its most important feat, the creation of the Big Five dimensional structure as the leading system for the assessment of important individual differences (Briggs, 1992; Goldberg, 1990, chap. 1 in this vol.; McAdams, 1992; McCrae & John, 1992).

The first thing that strikes one in a comparison between the P-E-N model and the Big Five system is the identification of Extraversion and Emotional Stability (Neuroticism) in both systems and the complete absence of the dimension *Intellect* in the P-E-N system. The reason for the omission of this dimension seems to be the position held by both Eysenck and Zuckerman, who consider "traits related to intelligence or educational background to be apart from the realm of personality" (Zuckerman, chap. 3 in this vol.). Contrary to this position is the one expressed by Brand and Egan (1989), who advocated adding and distinguishing "fluid" and "crystallized" intelligence to the taxonomy, thus arriving at six dimensions. Psychoticism, Eysenck's third dimension, appears to be a blend of the Factors II and III of the Big Five, Disagreeableness and Unconscientiousness (Goldberg & Rosolack, chap. 1 this volume; McCrae & Costa, 1985). This latter finding is representative of the main type of dispute now occurring among the most influential researchers in the field of personality, that is, the dispute about the factor interpretations and the equivalence (or nonequivalence) across studies (e.g., Costa & McCrae, 1992; Eysenck, chap. 2 in this vol.; Zuckerman, chap. 3 in this vol.).

In the present chapter we do not question the Big Five taxonomy. Rather, we emphasize the pervasiveness of the five-dimensional trait structure as it has emerged from the lexical approach. The Big Five system is rooted in thorough, large-scale, independent empirical studies in three Germanic languages: English (Goldberg, 1982, 1990), Dutch (Brokken, 1978; De Raad, 1992), and German (Ostendorf, 1990). We accept the system as the most generalizable model, emerging as it has through different data-gathering formats and different samples (Digman & Inouye, 1986; Goldberg, 1982; McCrae & Costa, 1985).

We have two goals in the present chapter. The first is to articulate further the dimensionality of the Dutch trait domain (De Raad, 1992). The second is to refine the Dutch trait structure into a conveniently arranged and detailed mapping of individual differences, one that provides clear niches for the various nuances of the trait language and for the different interpretations of the main factors of personality language (cf. Goldberg, 1990; Hofstee, De Raad, & Goldberg, 1992; John, 1989). In this respect, we discuss the comprehensiveness and the economy of trait representation and the model to be used in structuring the trait domain. The advantages and disadvantages of the two most popular models of the trait domain, the simple structure model and the circumplex model, are discussed, and we present a new framework that integrates these two models. This new framework enables us to clarify much of the dispute about the identification of factors from different studies, as indicated earlier. Hofstee et al. (1992) gave a full description of the framework, and Johnson and Ostendorf (1993) presented an extended documentation of its explanatory power.

TRAIT REPRESENTATION

Characteristic of the lexical approach is the conservative attitude toward the information contained in the comprehensive sets of salient personality descriptors: The reduction on the basis of self or peer ratings of the large numbers of distinct terms takes place in such a way that a maximum amount of information is captured by a minimum number of underlying dimensions. The most frequently used structural model serving this goal is the simple structure model, in which factors obtain their meaning from their primary loadings. The main problem with this approach is that the usual trait-descriptive data tend to deviate significantly from the simple structure model: The majority of trait variables can best be described by two factors. As a consequence of the simple structure treatment, a large amount of trait-descriptive information is disregarded.

The second model, the circumplex model, explicitly takes secondary factor loadings into account. The circumplex representation is a two-dimensional array in which traits are distributed around a circle with each concept merging into its neighboring ones. The circumplex is best exemplified in structuring the interpersonal trait domain (Wiggins, 1979, 1980), in which trait concepts are circularly ordered in a plane of which the dimensions Dominance and Nurturance form the coordinates. The two Big Five factors, corresponding to these dimensions, Extraversion/Surgency and Agreeableness, also may serve to produce a matching circumplex by taking those pairs of factor loadings as coordinate values, the sum of squares of which exceed a certain threshold. Traditionally, the circumplex model is used for a two-dimensional representation, whereas for the trait domain five factors have been established.

In this chapter, we integrate the five-factor model and the circumplex model in a common framework. McCrae and Costa (1989) argued that the circumplex model and the five-factor model play complementary roles. Trapnell and Wiggins (1990) provided empirical support for a fruitful combination of the two models. In both of these studies juxtaposition of the two models was emphasized over synthesis. The logical step would be to integrate the five-factor model and the circumplex model into a five-dimensional circumplex. Such a model, however, is hard to conceptualize and is uneconomical. It presupposes that each trait concept is five-dimensionally represented on the basis of its five loadings as coordinate values. As indicated, most trait variables substantially correlate with only *two* factors, even after varimax rotation (Hofstee & De Raad, 1991; Hofstee et al., 1992).

Traditionally, circumplex planes are partitioned into eight segments (octants) of 45° each (Wiggins & Broughton, 1991). Such a partitioning is necessary for discriminatory purposes, and it enhances interpretation of the results. In principle, the number of segments can be extended, the restriction being the extent to which the segment variables can be reliably distinguished (cf. Wiggins, 1979). A simple structure design would yield a partitioning into quadrants, which is clearly too broad a segmentation. The octants conception, which was dictated by Foa's facet design (U. G. Foa & E. B. Foa, 1974), accommodates blends of dimensions, but it does not distinguish among different sorts of blends: Items that load primarily on one dimension and secondarily on the other are put in the same category as items that load primarily on the other dimension. The model to be presented here takes into account the fact that most trait variables load on two factors, and it represents different sorts of blends between the two factors.

THE ABRIDGED BIG FIVE CIRCUMPLEX MODEL

The Abridged Big-Five Circumplex model (AB5C) (Hofstee & De Raad, 1991; Hofstee et al., 1992) comprises the 10 two-dimensional circumplexes that are produced by taking all possible pairs of the Big Five factors as coordinates. The trait variables are represented on the basis of their two highest loadings.

The circumplex planes of the AB5C model are partitioned into duodecants of 30°. Each circumplex provides segments for the four factor poles, and in addition, the blends of each pole with the two poles of the other factor. For example, the circumplex plane based on the Factors I and II includes trait concepts defined by the positive pole of Factor I (the I+ segment), the blend of the positive pole of I with the positive pole of II (the segment I+II+), and the segments II+I+, II+, II+I−, I−II+, I−, I−II−, II−I−, II−, II−I+, and I+II− (see Fig. 5.1).

The procedure for assigning trait concepts to segments relies upon the varimax-rotated matrix of loadings on the Big Five factors. In each circumplex plane, four additional quasi-factors (henceforth also called factors for convenience) are inserted at angles of 30° and 60° with the two respective Big Five factors serving as circumplex coordinates (see Fig. 5.2). Next, the loadings of the trait concepts on all the 40 inserted factors are calculated. The calculation is exemplified in Fig. 5.2 for the trait concept *cheerful* (opgewekt), which has loadings of .61 and .23 on the first two Big Five factors (see Table 5.1). The loading of *cheerful* on the inserted Factor I+II+ is obtained by computing the length of the projection of the trait concept: $(.61 * \cos 30°) + (.23 * \sin 30°) = .64$. The full procedure consists of postmultiplying the matrix of varimax-rotated factor loadings by a 5×45 matrix comprising the appropriate sines and cosines. This yields a matrix of loadings on the five original factors and the 40 inserted

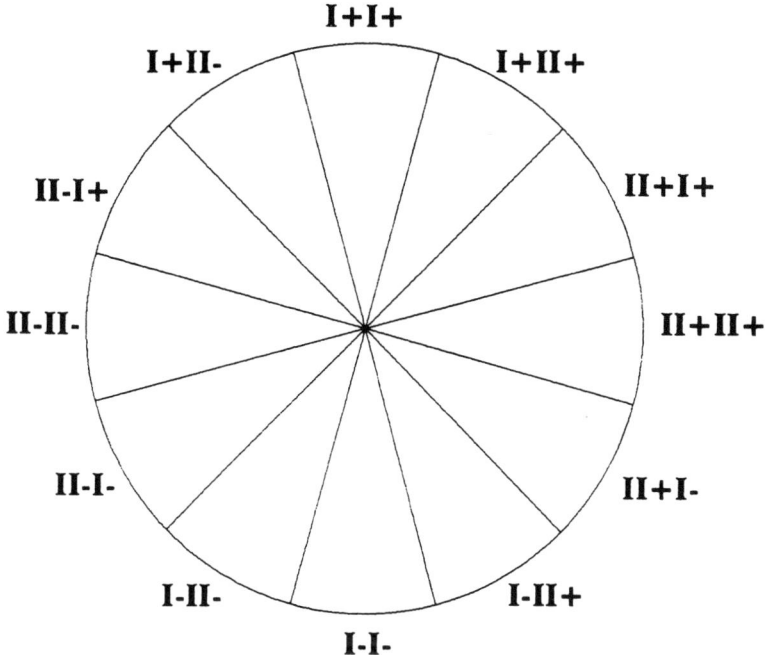

FIG. 5.1. The AB5C partitioning.

factors. The trait concepts are assigned to the segments belonging to the factor poles on which they have their highest loading. Trait concepts that load below .25 were omitted.

METHOD

In The Netherlands, Hofstee and Brokken were among the first to follow the lexical approach, providing the first factor structure in the Dutch language (Brokken, 1978; Hofstee, Brokken, & Land, 1981). Recently, a first test of the Big Five factor structure in the Dutch language domain was undertaken (De Raad, 1992; Hofstee & De Raad, 1991). The present results consist of an amplification and refinement of these studies.

For the Big Five representation of the Dutch trait structure, we started with a sample of 600 subjects that had provided self and peer ratings on a subset of 551 trait-descriptive adjectives out of a more comprehensive list of 1,203 (Brokken, 1978), that was considered more central to personality. The selection criteria are described in detail elsewhere (De Raad, 1992; De Raad, Mulder, Kloosterman, & Hofstee, 1988) and amount to a confinement to those terms that were considered as of more central importance to personality description. Next,

$a_1 = 0.61$

$a_2 = 0.23$

$a_3 = a_1 \cos 30° + a_2 \sin 30° = 0.64$

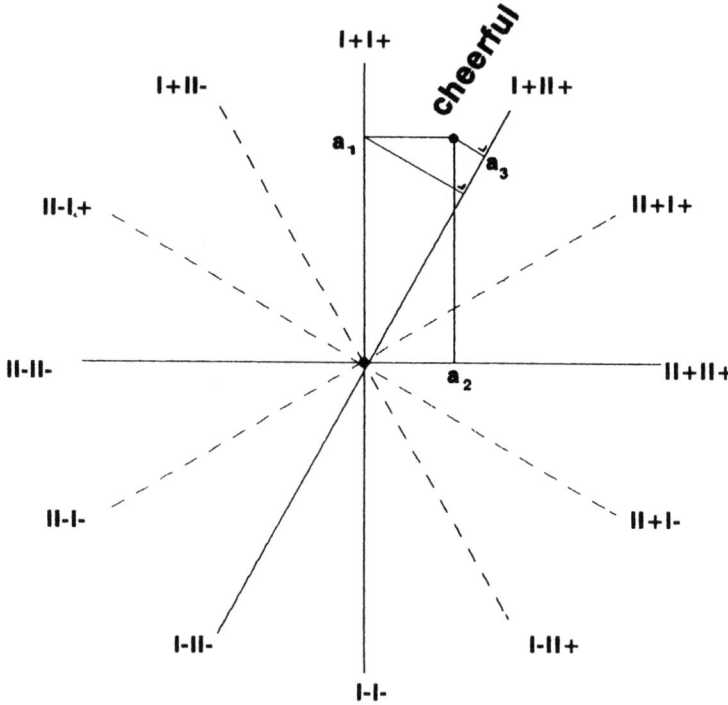

FIG. 5.2. Projection on inserted factor.

in order to refine and amplify this structure, the AB5C procedure was applied to the resulting five-factor matrix, yielding 45 factors. In addition, self and peer ratings of 400 subjects on the remaining 652 (1,203 − 551) were correlated with the 45 factors.

THE DUTCH TRAIT STRUCTURE

Subjects and Materials

For this set of 551 trait descriptors, we used the self and peer ratings by 400 subjects from Brokken (1978) and the self ratings by 200 subjects from De Raad et al. (1988). The ratings of the 600 subjects were standardized by subject to remove systematic differences with respect to means and standard deviations.

TABLE 5.1
Five-Factor Solution: Varimax Rotation

	Factors				
	I	II	III	IV	V
cheerful (opgewekt)	.61	.23	−.01	.17	−.02
exuberant (uitbundig)	.59	.02	−.07	−.14	.13
merry (vrolijk)	.57	.17	.03	.15	.03
spontaneous (spontaan)	.56	.10	−.01	−.04	1.05
jovial (joviaal)	.55	.22	−.04	.05	−.01
somber (somber)	−.55	−.02	.03	−.25	.02
aloof (terughoudend)	−.56	.01	.04	−.04	−.16
silent (zwijgzaam)	−.60	.21	.06	.05	−.20
introverted (introvert)	−.61	.15	−.07	.03	−.07
uncommunicative (gesloten)	−.65	.15	−.07	.08	−.12
mild (mild)	.06	.53	.00	−.05	−.15
tolerant (verdraagzaam)	.08	.53	−.04	.13	−.04
good-natured (goedaardig)	.14	.51	.05	.10	−.02
peaceful (vreedzaam)	.06	.50	.09	.07	−.11
peace-loving (vredelievend)	.00	.50	.00	−.08	−.03
dictatorial (dictatoriaal)	.04	−.45	−.04	.23	.04
autocratic (autoritair)	.03	−.46	−.01	.22	.15
imperious (heerszuchtig)	.08	−.50	−.04	.17	.07
domineering (baasachtig)	.14	−.54	.08	.11	.09
bossy (bazig)	.12	−.55	.11	.08	.07
careful (zorgvuldig)	.02	.09	.63	.12	−.07
prompt (stipt)	.04	.00	.60	.08	−.08
meticulous (nauwgezet)	−.08	.02	.60	.06	−.03
industrious (vlijtig)	.15	.09	.60	.04	−.05
precise (secuur)	.02	−.01	.60	.10	−.10
foolish (onnozel)	−.05	.26	−.44	−.15	.01
thoughtless (onbedachtzaam)	.07	.02	−.45	−.26	.04
lax (laks)	−.20	.05	−.47	−.15	−.05
nonchalant (nonchalant)	.11	.12	−.51	−.02	.05
indolent (gemakzuchtig)	−.10	.07	−.51	.00	−.13
steady (evenwichtig)	.06	.23	.19	.63	−.02
stable (stabiel)	.14	.20	.12	.63	−.07
assured (zelfverzekerd)	.26	−.11	.01	.62	.16
decisive (besluitvaardig)	.19	.03	.21	.50	.28
determined (vastberaden)	.11	−.01	.28	.49	.27
vulnerable (kwetsbaar)	−.15	.16	.05	−.55	.11
insecure (onzeker)	−.37	.13	−.08	−.58	−.12
unstable (instabiel)	−.21	−.03	−.21	−.58	.02
unbalanced (onevenwichtig)	−.25	.00	−.21	−.58	−.01
panicky (paniekerig)	−.07	−.06	.10	−.59	−.04
critical (kritisch)	−.09	.09	.11	.20	.50
mutinous (opstandig)	−.05	−.32	−.19	−.14	.46
fierce (fel)	.23	−.34	.08	−.05	.44
rebellious (rebels)	.02	−.24	−.38	.04	.41
dynamic (dynamisch)	.31	.00	.09	.24	.38
slavish (slaafs)	−.06	.11	−.03	−.17	−.43
shallow (oppervlakkig)	.05	−.01	−.17	−.01	−.44
virtuous (braaf)	−.02	.13	.31	−.03	−.46
meek (gedwee)	−.08	.22	.06	−.22	−.50
docile (volgzaam)	.06	.20	.06	−.25	−.52

The ipsatized data matrix of the 600 ratings on 551 adjectives was subjected to principal components analysis and varimax rotation of five factors. Other solutions were less satisfactory: The first four factors of the five-factor solution were almost identical to the four-factor solution. The fifth factor simply added new meaning. A six-factor solution was less clearcut in that it did not provide for new meaning, but rather showed blends of the factors from the five-factor solution.

Results and Discussion

The eigenvalues for the first five factors, respectively expressed in percentages, were: 6.85, 5.93, 3.88, 2.51, and 2.33. The relatively low total amount of variance thus explained (21.50%) was due to the ipsatization. Table 5.1 summarizes the first five varimax-rotated adjective factors, represented by their typical adjectives. Given the 10 highest positive and negative loading adjectives, there is no doubt about the interpretation of the five factors. Factor I expresses Extraversion with terms running from *cheerful* and *exuberant* to *introverted* and *uncommunicative*. Factor II represents *Agreeableness* with trait terms like *mild* and *tolerant* on the positive side and on the negative side terms like *domineering* and *bossy*. Next is *Conscientiousness* with terms like *careful* and *prompt*, on the positive pole, and *nonchalant* and *indolent*, on the other. The fourth factor is called *Emotional Stability* with positive terms like *steady* and *stable* and with negative terms like *unbalanced* and *panicky*. The fifth factor is the *Intellect* factor, with positive loadings on terms such as *critical* and *mutinous*, and with negative loadings on terms such as *meek* and *docile*.

The present results are a convincing independent confirmation of the existence of five major dimensions that cover the trait domain, the Big Five: Extraversion or Surgency (I), Agreeableness (II), Conscientiousness (III), Emotional Stability (IV), and Intellect or Openness to Experience (V). With respect to the interpretation of the factors, there is no real doubt about their general nomenclature. As regards the naming of the fifth factor the usual reserve is in order.

The usual guide for the interpretation of factors, the Thurstonian concept of simple structure, is not, however, very helpful in coping with variables that have more than one substantial loading, particularly those with mainly primary and secondary loadings. Even among the 50 adjectives listed in Table 5.1 that closely approximates simple structure, half of the adjectives have secondary loadings above .20, meaning that their location is similar to the example shown in Fig. 5.2. To fulfill the requirements of simple structure, variables with substantial secondary loadings are often termed deviant, less important, ambiguous, or fuzzy in meaning in terms of the underlying simple framework of factors. Such a practice of interpretation of factors is wasteful of good data and not too accurate either.

AMPLIFICATION AND REFINEMENT OF THE DUTCH TRAIT STRUCTURE

The application of the AB5C principle optimizes the use of the factor matrix. The simple structure evaluation of the factor matrix is largely replaced by the analytic procedure of inserting factors according to the described algorithm. After the first assessment of the AB5C structure on the basis of the ratings from the 600 subjects that yielded a fine-grained portrait of trait-relationships, a further articulation of the refined structure was pursued based on a sample of ratings from a subset of 400 of the 600 subjects on the additional set of 652 personality-descriptive adjectives.

Procedure

First, the AB5C procedure was applied to the five-factor solution. Each of the 551 personality descriptive-adjectives with a loading of at least .25 on one of the 45 factors was assigned to one of the 90 different segments of the 10 circumplexes. Next, the ratings of the 400 subjects on the 652 adjectives were correlated with the five factors, and the resulting 652 by 5 matrix of correlations was likewise subjected to the AB5C algorithm. The resulting two sets of 551 and 652 adjectives with projections on the 45 factors were examined together in a joint representation.

Results and Discussion

Of the total number of 1,203 adjectives, 321 (26%) loaded less than .25 on *all* five varimax factors (see Table 5.2). Of these, 173 had projections of at least .25 on one of the inserted factors. Thus, only 148 terms (12%) of the 1,203 were excluded from the AB5C representation. Only two adjectives loaded at least .25 on four of the varimax factors, and 32 adjectives loaded above .25 on three. The rest (71%) loaded at least .25 on one or two varimax factors. These results confirm the significance of the multiple two-dimensional representation according to the AB5C.

Instead of using the 10 two-dimensional circumplexes that resulted from the insertion method for a complete AB5C presentation, a matrix form of presentation was chosen, containing the same information more economically. The matrix is a 10 × 10 design, of which both the columns and the rows represent the 10 poles of the 5 factors. The cells of the matrix correspond to the 90 segments (opposite poles of the same factor do not produce existing blends) of the circumplexes. The 10 diagonal cells represent the segments to which factor-pure adjectives were assigned; the off-diagonal cells represent the blends of the 10 factor poles. Table 5.3 contains the numbers of adjectives assigned to the various segments of the matching circumplexes. Only those adjectives were counted that had a projection of at least .25 on the corresponding factor pole. The factors differed in the number of adjectives they contained, from 279 for Factor II (column II+ and II−) to 161 for Factor V, and they differed in the distribution of adjectives over the cells.

The observed differences in numbers of adjectives per factor can be understood in part from the order in which factors explained variance. For the Dutch Big Five, this order was II, I, IV, III, and V, which deviates from the order in English and in German. The negative poles contained more adjectives (570) than the positive poles (485). The combination of Factor I and II was comprised of most adjectives, and the combination IV and V was comprised of the smallest number. Moreover, the combination of I and II strongly deviated from the rest of the combinations in terms of spread of adjectives over the segments: There was a firm emphasis on the blends of the positive (I+I+ and II+II+ with 35 and 56 terms respectively) and negative poles (with 21 and 29 terms) of I and II. The most even spreads over the segments were found for the combination of II and IV, with an average of 11 ($SD = 4.9$) terms in the corresponding cells. The diagonal factor-pure cells had a tendency to be characterized by fewer adjectives, compared to the general average of 11.7 per cell with the diagonal average of 7.6 per cell.

Table 5.4 gives the trait adjectives placed in the cells on the basis of their two highest loadings on the original five factors. The matrix should be read vertically, meaning the adjectives have a primary loading on the column factors and a

TABLE 5.3
AB5C Representation: Numbers of Trait Terms

	I+	II+	III+	IV+	V+	I−	II−	III−	IV−	V−	Totals
I+		4	56	5	14	14		6	10	6	4	119
II+	35	8	16	7	11	3		3	11	6	100
III+	3	20	13	13	2	6	8		6	12	83
IV+	16	10	16	5	16	3	24	5		3	98
V+	22	9	4	23	0	7	23	11	4		103
I−		0	3	7	4	10	29	18	25	24	120
II−	6		6	12	15	21	10	23	10	8	111
III−	9	0		8	12	8	21	13	18	12	101
IV−	8	7	1		2	31	16	17	8	11	101
V−	1	15	21	6		29	17	6	19	5	119
Totals	104	125	85	95	76	118	154	106	107	85	1055

TABLE 5.4
AB5C Scheme: The Five Varimax Factors and Their Blends

	I+	II+	III+	IV+	V+
I+	59 exuberant 56 spontaneous 54 open 40 *funny*	55 *nice* 53 sympathetic 52 *big-hearted* 52 *supple* 52 good-natured 51 amiable	53 *laborious* 40 attentive 37 able 29 religious 27 *courteous*	66 assured 65 *certain* 42 *manful* 41 *mettlesome* 39 brave 39 adroit	49 dynamic 43 *militant* 43 frank 42 combative 40 *wild* 38 pugnacious
II+	64 cheerful 62 *joyous* 61 *sunny* 61 gay 60 high-spirited 59 *pleasant*	53 tolerant 50 peaceful 50 peace-loving 47 forgiving 42 good 41 unselfish	58 *precautious* 49 *cleanly* 48 caring 47 *well-mannered* 46 *respectable* 46 virtuous	66 steady 64 stable 57 calm 49 even-tempered 49 realistic 45 controlled	39 *constructive* 37 *freedom-loving* 37 advanced 35 *subtle* 33 *liberal-minded* 31 creative
III+	50 *brisk* 50 *busy* 31 charming	56 modest 47 sincere 46 faithful 44 *polite* 44 *sensitive* 41 honest	63 careful 60 prompt 60 meticulous 60 industrious 60 precise 59 punctilious	61 *resolved* 56 determined 53 perseverant 50 strong-willed 48 down-to-earth 42 well-advised	34 perceptive 26 straight
IV+	57 optimistic 54 buoyant 53 *vigorous* 44 lively 43 *comical* 43 happy	52 patient 51 composed 51 quiet 48 *fair* 44 *reasonable* 35 unprejudiced	59 accurate 59 *exact* 58 *systematic* 56 *close* 55 *efficient* 52 *purposeful*	51 *perfectly sober* 48 sober 48 imperturbable 48 unshakable 41 cold	53 critical 49 *strong-minded* 48 sharp 43 hardy 43 versatile 43 *radical*
V+	58 *communicative* 57 vivacious 52 *talkative* 51 enthusiastic 51 *eloquent* 50 *mobile*	43 broad-minded 42 just 42 humane 40 *interested* 34 unaffected 34 incorruptible	50 *observant* 35 principled 29 inquisitive 27 skillful	58 decisive 54 vigorous 54 resolute 50 independent 49 self-reliant 49 *strong*	
I−			46 serious 42 grave 35 finical	50 rational 49 stoical 47 *rationalistic* 34 icy 34 cool-headed 32 intellectualistic	42 profound 40 ironical 33 philosophical
II−	52 *garrulous* 51 *noisy* 45 chatty 32 *verbose* 29 *spirited* 25 sturdy		45 perfectionistic 42 stern 40 ambitious 36 *overzealous* 33 fastidious 30 snappish	50 rock-hard 49 obdurate 48 tough 48 *flinty* 42 unrelenting 38 *unruly*	56 *mutinous* 56 fierce 52 *intemperate* 46 explosive 42 obstinate 42 self-willed

(Continued)

TABLE 5.4
(Continued)

	I+	II+	III+	IV+	V+
III–	52 loud 51 uninhibited 45 clownish 43 light-hearted 42 impertinent 37 reckless			43 *masculine* 38 *carefree* 32 *thick-skinned* 31 *laconic* 31 *slippery* 28 felonious	54 rebellious 47 *free-and-easy* 43 *nonconformistic* 41 *revolutionary* 39 *disobedient* 37 *progressive*
IV–	49 *gossipy* 49 *gabby* 47 *loquacious* 47 *flirtatious* 41 *giggly* 38 *loose-lipped*	48 *feeling* 44 gentle 43 good-tempered 33 *highly-strung* 31 *pacifistic* 30 *philantropic*	29 *niggling*		39 *evasive*
V–	41 *presumptuous*	57 *willing* 57 *ready to laugh* 54 mild 53 *permissive* 52 mild-mannered 52 *indulgent*	64 *neat* 60 disciplined 58 *well-ordered* 58 tidy 57 orderly 53 *law-abiding*	59 *perfectly calm* 49 *equable* 41 *emotionless* 33 insensitive 31 fatherly 27 patriarchal	

	I–	II–	III–	IV–	V–
I+		52 *heated* 46 dominant 41 meddlesome 35 *defiant* 32 obtrusive	49 rash 48 lawless 46 frivolous 43 lazy 41 *loose* 35 *daring*	43 impulsive 34 *affectionate* 31 *sweet* 29 *coquettish* 26 *amorous*	40 kind-hearted 33 *suave* 31 zealous 26 *chauvinistic*
II+	62 silent 38 austere		51 foolish 42 careless 30 *forgetful*	56 vulnerable 46 sensitive 42 tender-hearted 42 *delicate* 41 attached 37 romantic	54 meek 48 compliant 46 good to a fault 40 *willing* 33 *ordinary* 29 servile
III+	48 reserved 43 earnest 36 thoughtful 34 *peaceable* 32 stiff 29 retiring	45 *thrusting* 41 *fault-finding* 37 fanatical 35 aspiring 32 *preachy*		54 *tearful* 52 *nervy* 44 *overanxious* 41 worrisome 40 *feminine* 38 concerned	55 virtuous 50 obedient 45 conventional 45 conservative 44 bourgeois 39 *overpolite*
IV+	42 detached 33 *analytic*	52 imperious 51 autocratic 51 *hard-handed* 50 dictatorial 45 hard 41 arrogant	34 criminal 34 *worriless* 28 destructive 27 violent		38 old-fashioned 29 stuck-up 29 *secretive*

(Continued)

TABLE 5.4
(Continued)

	I−	II−	III−	IV−	V−
V+	51 *complex*	49 *cross-grained*	53 *undisciplined*	37 uncontrolled	
	42 sceptical	48 demanding	50 reckless	37 restless	
	40 *maladjusted*	45 temperamental	40 *incautious*	26 sensual	
	39 individualistic	45 angry	39 *unashamed*		
	39 complicated	44 aggressive	37 *unrestrained*		
	35 *contemplative*	44 quick-tempered	36 *boyish*		
I−	65 uncommunicative	42 *grumbling*	51 lax	68 insecure	45 bashful
	61 introverted	39 egocentric	47 *weak-willed*	63 unbalanced	43 *unresisting*
	59 *difficult*	39 selfish	42 *indifferent*	61 *wavering*	42 submissive
	55 *unyielding*	38 intolerant	41 idle	60 nervous	41 sedate
	52 surly	37 *snappish*	41 antisocial	57 tensed	40 *one-sided*
	49 *impersonal*	36 unmannerly	38 *workshy*	54 indecisive	40 *moderate*
II−	53 *peevish*	55 bossy	35 shameless	46 touchy	32 hypocritical
	47 *resentful*	54 domineering	34 devious	44 irritable	31 short-sighted
	47 negativistic	39 *self-important*	34 *undecent*	38 *hurried*	27 stingy
	46 curt	39 interfering	34 perverted	38 *whining*	27 *obtuse*
	45 gruff	38 *quarrelsome*	33 immodest	36 *fretful*	27 condescending
	43 distrustful	38 rigid	33 coarse	36 *theatrical*	26 sneaky
III−	47 apathetic	41 conceited	55 *disorganized*	60 unstable	46 shallow
	46 *inactive*	39 bragging	52 *slovenly*	60 erratic	42 soggy
	42 dull	39 bluffing	51 indolent	58 inconstant	41 characterless
	39 vague	39 boastful	51 nonchalant	51 fickle	38 underhand
	38 *strange*	38 egoistic	49 *disorderly*	50 *confused*	34 cringing
	36 *nihilistic*	37 swanking	42 *boisterous*	48 *irrational*	33 twofaced
IV−	67 *depressive*	51 short-tempered	53 *chaotic*	59 panicky	57 docile
	66 dejected	46 hot-headed	52 *inaccurate*	55 emotional	46 slavish
	64 heavy-handed	44 *sulky*	52 thoughtless	52 oversensitive	45 subservient
	63 meloncholy	44 *snarly*	49 unthinking	51 hypersensitive	44 soft-boiled
	61 gloomy	43 *carping*	49 *muddle-headed*	50 jumpy	39 humble
	60 sombre	42 impatient	46 scatterbrained	44 sentimental	38 inane
V−	65 mute	45 greedy	37 unreliable	52 *frightened*	48 *uncritical*
	56 aloof	41 faithful	35 deceitful	51 dependent	48 *taciturn*
	52 boring	35 avaricious	33 *unprincipled*	50 *afraid*	42 *quotidian*
	52 unsociable	34 prejudiced	31 cowardly	48 fearful	39 mealy-mouthed
	50 shy	34 *gaudy*	28 perverse	46 credulous	31 *simple*
	49 passive	33 grasping	26 dishonest	43 naive	

secondary loading on the row factors. Each trait adjective is provided with the projection on the segment factor pole that corresponds to the cell. Only adjectives with projections of at least .25 are listed in the cells with a maximum of six terms per cell. Adjectives originating from the 652 sample are given in italics.

Some interesting observations can be made in a comparison of Tables 5.1 and 5.4. Even some of the highest loading adjectives of the five-factor solution do not appear on the diagonal but have moved to off-diagonal cells. Good examples are adjectives loading high on Factor IV, namely, *well-balanced, stable*, and *self-assured*, which terms are usually considered as typical of the dimension of Emotional Stability. This not only means that much of what has been called Emotional Stability is actually a mixture of Emotional Stability with other Big Five factors, it also means the characterization of the diagonal cells may need some reformulation.

Of special interest is Factor V, Intellect. The cell V+V+ remained empty, meaning that the positive pole of Factor V is defined in terms of blends with other factors. All of the terms contributing to the positive pole of Factor V also contribute to another factor. This observation may explain much of the dispute on the meaning of the fifth factor (e.g., McCrae, 1990; Saucier, 1992): It only appears under disguises.

A highly interesting observation that can be made from the structure of Table 5.4 is that all of the five pairs of factor columns, the fifth factor included, contain many adjectives implicating temperament constructs, witness such terms as *spontaneous* and *enthusiastic* (I), *composed* and *good-tempered* (II), *careful* and *meticulous* (III), *controlled* and *perseverant* (IV), and *militant* and *obstinate* (V).

Of the 50 highest loadings in Table 5.1 that contribute to the meanings of the five factors, less than half are found in the diagonal cells of Table 5.4. This confirms the idea that a simple structure approach to personality structure is too simple to arrive at a fair, economical, and comprehensive representation of the meanings of the personality domain. Not only do more than half of the highest loadings on the varimax factors find a more adequate accommodation in off-diagonal cells, the latter cells in turn give a much more subtle and comprehensive picture of the factors.

For example, all the adjectives in the off-diagonal cells of the first column of Table 5.4 are related to the factor-pure terms of cell I+I+, *exuberant, spontaneous, open*, and *funny*. The nine corresponding row cells each represent the different variations of the same theme. *Cheerful, joyous* and *sunny* together represent a facet of Factor I, namely Factor I with a Factor II leitmotif. *Brisk, busy*, and *charming* form another facet of Factor I, in this case with the leitmotif of Factor III. The conclusion is that next to the meaning of each diagonal cell or factor pole, a complete spectrum of facets of that core meaning is obtained by adding the meanings of the other nine diagonal cells respectively. The matrix as a whole thus represents the entire spectrum of personality descriptive *etymons* and their *derived meanings* in the form of a facet structure (U. G. Foa & E. B. Foa, 1974).

CONCLUSION

The most influential determinant of a factor structure is the selection of variables used for obtaining ratings (Peabody & Goldberg, 1989). It is therefore of utmost importance that great care is taken in composing an instrument that undoubtedly captures the most important individual differences in an unbiased way. Of the different approaches to trait structure, it is the lexical approach that pre-eminently reflects the essence of this guiding principle. The repeatedly confirmed Big Five factor framework can be considered as the best working hypothesis for further studies in personality structure. From the data in the present study we can say that the Big Five personality dimensions are only the tip of the iceberg of the language of individual differences. The five dimensions do form the constituting framework within which nearly all verbal descriptions of personality are likely to find accommodation. In their studies on the validation of the five factor model of personality, McCrae and Costa (1987) called for the systematic description of the substance of traits and proposed that the investigation of the five-factor model would be the most promising candidate to subsume the main themes and their variations in the description of the structure of personality. The current study provides both an affirmation of that assertion and an excellent starting point to do just that.

Our findings indicate that one should stop thinking merely in terms of the Thurstonian concept of simple structure categories that lend support to the idea of distinct faculties of personality. The method followed here optimizes the use of the factor matrix. The present approach adopts the simple-structure-guided varimax rotation for the production of the five-factor framework. For the purpose of interpreting the rich assortment of meanings in the factor matrix, however, simple structure is too imprecise. Instead, simple structure is replaced by an analytic procedure of inserting factor vectors according to a specified algorithm.

The newly refined facet structure of personality descriptors accommodates most of the nuances and differences of opinion with respect to the meaning of the personality language space. The structure also enables one to subsume other sorts of trait descriptors as well (De Raad, 1992; De Raad et al., 1988; De Raad & Hofstee, 1993; De Raad & Hoskens, 1990), thereby clarifying and articulating the meaning of poorly sampled areas of personality.

The trait approach to personality has long been known for its disputes, inter alia, on the concepts and substance of the discipline (e.g., state versus trait, personality or temperament, abilities and intelligence, bandwidth-fidelity). These examples cover many of the significant issues, attesting to the relevance of the approach, on the one hand, and the comprehensiveness of the approach, on the other. The general lexical approach lays claim to comprehensive coverage of the content domain of personality. The well-established Big Five framework and the numerous studies in that field (cf. John, 1990) do provide the required descriptive standard. The present results not only confirm again the framework, but also form an intriguing demonstration of its inclusive potential.

Many of the recurring disputes (cf. Costa & McCrae, 1992; Eysenck, 1992; Zuckerman, 1992) about the nature of factors and their proper interpretations are clarified by the present AB5C system. With respect to interpretations, the present system not only provides a solution to many of the disputes about the naming and the substance of the five factors (Johnson & Ostendorf, 1992), but also cautions that it may be wiser to abstain from interpretation at all, because of the promiscuity of the concepts comprising the factors. Instead, reference by numbers may be better. As to the nature of the Big Five factors, some are interpreted as mainly interpersonal in character (Wiggins, 1979), whereas at other times the temperamental character of some (cf. Eysenck, 1990) or all is stressed (Angleitner & Ostendorf, 1991). Our present findings suggest a temperamental flavor to all the five factors.

With respect to the relevance of the Big Five factors, some of the factors, usually Surgency and Agreeableness, are proposed as the major interpersonal axes that result "from the advantage humans gain from discerning others' hierarchical positions and proclivities to form reciprocal alliances" (Buss, 1991, p. 472). Digman (1989) discussed the role of Factor III, Conscientiousness, in determining variations in educational achievement. Peabody and Goldberg (1989) stressed the importance of the Big Five factors by relating them to the realms of Power, Love, Work, Affect, and Intellect.

The "small explosion of interest" (McCrae, 1991) in the Big Five model during the past decade reflects the increasing understanding among investigators of the utility of the model in various applied fields, especially in clinical and organizational settings. Costa (1991) argued that the five-factor model is a valuable common language for clinicians, and Barrick and Mount (1991) and Tett, Jackson, and Rothstein (1991) demonstrated the utility of the five dimensions in personnel psychology. These latter studies assume the validity of the five dimensions as the resource units of communication. For this purpose, we need sets of markers as adequate representations of the five factors. Goldberg (1990, 1992) developed different sets of markers based on the recent state of affairs of the English-language personality taxonomy. The AB5C model may enhance the process of filtering out appropriate factor-pure markers and of sampling nonpure terms in a rigorous way.

Most crucial in this respect is the cross-cultural validity of the Big Five. Simply translating items (i.e., Big Five markers) from one language to another, is not only extremely precarious as far as finding satisfactory translations (Hofstee, 1990), it also creates a suboptimal coverage of intended meanings in the different languages. The possibility of transposing the results from one language and culture to the other and of having comparable results between cultures has only recently started to take form. A significant step was taken by Hofstee, De Raad, Kiers, Goldberg, and Ostendorf (in preparation), who developed a cross-national AB5C solution, a joint Big Five structure on the basis of the English, Dutch, and German data sets. Although the cross-cultural enterprise is still in its infancy, it is hoped that the Hofstee et al. study stimulates further research on finding a common basis for the international communication on personality structure.

REFERENCES

Allport, G. W., & Odbert, H. S. (1936). Trait-names: A psycho-lexical study. *Psychological Monographs, 47* (Serial No. 211).

Angleitner, A., & Ostendorf, F. (1991, June 17–20). *Temperament and the Big Five factors of personality*. Paper presented at the Invited Workshop on the Development of the Structure of Temperament and Personality from Infancy to Adulthood, Wassenaar, The Netherlands.

Barrick, M. R., & Mount, M. K. (1991). The Big Five personality dimensions and job performance: A meta-analysis. *Personnel Psychology, 44*, 1–26.

Brand, C. R., & Egan, V. (1989). The "Big Five" dimensions of personality? Evidence from ipsative, adjectival self-attributions. *Personality and Individual Differences, 10*, 1165–1171.

Briggs, S. R. (1992). Assessing the five-factor model of personality description. *Journal of Personality, 60*, 253–293.

Brokken, F. B. (1978). *The language of personality*. Unpublished doctoral dissertation, University of Groningen, The Netherlands.

Buss, D. M. (1991). Evolutionary personality psychology. *Annual Review of Psychology, 42*, 459–491.

Cattell, R. B. (1943). The description of personality: Basic traits resolved into clusters. *Journal of Abnormal and Social Psychology, 38*, 476–506.

Cattell, R. B. (1945). The description of personality: Principles and findings in a factor analysis. *American Journal of Psychology, 58*, 69–90.

Costa, P. T., Jr. (1991). Clinical use of the five-factor model: An introduction. *Journal of Personality Assessment, 57*, 393–398.

Costa, P. T., Jr., & McCrae, R. R. (1992). Four ways five factors are basic. *Personality and Individual Differences, 13*, 653–665.

De Raad, B. (1992). The replicability of the Big Five personality dimensions in three word-classes of the Dutch language. *European Journal of Personality, 6*, 15–29.

De Raad, B., & Hofstee, W. K. B. (1993). A circumplex approach to the five factor model: A facet structure of trait adjectives supplemented by trait verbs. *Personality and Individual Differences, 15*, 493–505.

De Raad, B., & Hoskens, M. (1990). Personality-descriptive nouns. *European Journal of Personality, 4*, 131–146.

De Raad, B., Mulder, E., Kloosterman, K., & Hofstee, W. K. B. (1988). Personality-descriptive verbs. *European Journal of Personality, 2*, 81–96.

Digman, J. M. (1989). Five robust trait dimensions: Development, stability, and utility. *Journal of Personality, 57*, 195–214.

Digman, J. M., & Inouye, J. (1986). Further specification of the five robust factors of personality. *Journal of Personality and Social Psychology, 50*, 116–123.

Digman, J. M., & Takemoto-Chock, N. K. (1981). Factors in the natural language of personality: Re-analysis, comparison and interpretation of six major studies. *Multivariate Behavioral Research, 16*, 149–170.

Eysenck, H. J. (1947). *Dimensions of personality*. London: Routledge & Kegan Paul.

Eysenck, H. J. (1952). *The scientific study of personality*. London: Routledge & Kegan Paul.

Eysenck, H. J. (1967). *The biological basis of personality*. Springfield, IL: Thomas.

Eysenck, H. J. (1990). Biological dimensions of personality. In L. A. Pervin (Ed.), *Handbook of personality: Theory and research* (pp. 244–276). New York: Guilford.

Eysenck, H. J. (1991). Dimensions of personality: Sixteen, 5 or 3?—criteria for a taxonomic paradigm. *Personality and Individual Differences, 12*, 773–790.

Eysenck, H. J. (1992). Four ways five factors are *not* basic. *Personality and Individual Differences, 13*, 667–673.

Foa, U. G., & Foa, E. B. (1974). *Societal structures of the mind*. Springfield, IL: Thomas.

Goldberg, L. R. (1982). From Ace to Zombie: Some explorations in the language of personality. In C. D. Spielberger & J. N. Butcher (Eds.), *Advances in personality assessment* (Vol. 1, pp. 203–234). Hillsdale, NJ: Lawrence Erlbaum Associates.

Goldberg, L. R. (1990). An alternative "Description of personality": The Big-Five factor structure. *Journal of Personality and Social Psychology, 59*, 1216–1229.

Goldberg, L. R. (1992). The development of markers for the Big-Five factor structure. *Psychological Assessment, 4,* 26–42.

Hampson, S. E., John, O. P., & Goldberg, L. R. (1986). Category breadth and hierarchical structure in personality: Studies of asymmetries in judgments of trait implications. *Journal of Personality and Social Psychology, 51,* 37–54.

Hofstee, W. K. B. (1990). The use of everyday personality language for scientific purposes. *European Journal of Personality, 4,* 77–88.

Hofstee, W. K. B., Brokken, F. B., & Land, H. (1981). Constructie van een standaard-persoonlijkheidseigenschappenlijst (SPEL) [Construction of a standard list of personality descriptive adjectives]. *Nederlands Tijdschrift voor de Psychologie, 34,* 443–452.

Hofstee, W. K. B., & De Raad, B. (1991). Persoonlijkheidsstructuur: De AB5C-taxonomie van Nederlandse eigenschapstermen [Personality structure: The AB5C-taxonomy of Dutch trait terms]. *Nederlands Tijdschrift voor de Psychologie, 46,* 262–274.

Hofstee, W. K. B., De Raad, B., & Goldberg, L. R. (1992). Integration of the Big Five and Circumplex approaches to trait structure. *Journal of Personality and Social Psychology, 63,* 146–163.

Hofstee, W. K. B., De Raad, B., Kiers, H. A. L., Goldberg, L. R., & Ostendorf, F. (in preparation). A cross-national Big Five structure of personality traits.

Howarth, E. (1976). Were Cattell's "personality sphere" factors correctly identified in the first instance? *British Journal of Psychology, 67,* 213–230.

John, O. P. (1989). Towards a taxonomy of personality descriptors. In D. M. Buss & N. Cantor (Eds.), *Personality psychology: Recent trends and emerging directions* (pp. 261–271). New York: Springer-Verlag.

John, O. P. (1990). The Big Five factor taxonomy: Dimensions of personality in the natural language and in questionnaires. In L. A. Pervin (Ed.), *Handbook of personality: Theory and research* (pp. 66–100). New York: Guilford.

John, O. P., Angleitner, A., & Ostendorf, F. (1988). The lexical approach to personality. *European Journal of Personality, 2,* 171–205.

Johnson, J. A., & Ostendorf, F. (1993). *Clarification of the five factor model with the abridged Big Five-dimensional Circumplex.* Unpublished manuscript.

Matthews, G. (1989). The factor structure of the 16 PF: Twelve primary and three secondary factors. *Personality and Individual Differences, 10,* 931–940.

McAdams, D. P. (1992). The five-factor model *in* personality: A critical appraisal. *Journal of Personality, 60,* 329–361.

McCrae, R. R. (1990). Traits and trait names: How well is Openness represented in natural languages? *European Journal of Personality, 4,* 119–129.

McCrae, R. R. (1991). The five-factor model and its assessment in clinical settings. *Journal of Personality Assessment, 57,* 399–414.

McCrae, R. R., & Costa, P. T., Jr. (1985). Upgrading Norman's "Adequate Taxonomy": Intelligence and personality dimensions in natural language. *Journal of Personality and Social Psychology, 49,* 710–721.

McCrae, R. R., & Costa, P. T., Jr. (1987). Validation of the five-factor model of personality across instruments and observers. *Journal of Personality and Social Psychology, 52,* 81–90.

McCrae, R. R., & Costa, P. T., Jr. (1989). The structure of interpersonal traits: Wiggins's Circumplex and the five-factor model. *Journal of Personality and Social Psychology, 56,* 586–595.

McCrae, R. R., & John, O. P. (1992). An introduction to the five-factor model and its applications. *Journal of Personality, 60,* 175–215.

Ostendorf, F. (1990). *Sprache und Persönlichkeitsstruktur: zur Validität des Fünf-Faktoren-Modells der Persönlichkeit* [Language and personality structure: Towards the validity of the five-factor model of personality]. Regensburg, FRG: S. Roderer Verlag.

Peabody, D., & Goldberg, L. R. (1989). Some determinants of factor structures from personality-trait descriptors. *Journal of Personality and Social Psychology, 57,* 552–567.

Saucier, G. (1992). Openness versus intellect: much ado about nothing? *European Journal of Personality, 6*, 381–386.

Tett, R. P., Jackson, D. N., & Rothstein, M. (1991). Personality measures as predictors of job performance: A meta-analytic review. *Personnel Psychology, 44*, 703–742.

Trapnell, P. D., & Wiggins, J. S. (1990). Extension of the interpersonal adjective scales to include the Big Five dimensions of personality. *Journal of Personality and Social Psychology, 59*, 781–790.

Wiggins, J. S. (1979). A psychological taxonomy of trait-descriptive terms: The interpersonal domain. *Journal of Personality and Social Psychology, 37*, 395–412.

Wiggins, J. S. (1980). Circumplex models of interpersonal behavior. In L. Wheeler (Ed.), *Review of personality and social psychology* (Vol. 1, pp. 265–294). Beverly Hills, CA: Sage.

Wiggins, J. S., & Broughton, R. (1991). A geometric taxonomy of personality scales. *European Journal of Personality, 5*, 343–365.

Zuckerman, M. (1992). What is a basic factor and which factors are basic? Turtles all the way down. *Personality and Individual Differences, 13*, 675–681.

CHAPTER

6

STRUCTURAL MODELS FOR MULTIMODE DESIGNS IN PERSONALITY AND TEMPERAMENT RESEARCH

A. T. Panter
University of North Carolina, Chapel Hill

J. S. Tanaka
University of Illinois, Champaign-Urbana

Rick H. Hoyle
Unversity of Kentucky

Previous chapters in this volume have focused on conceptual models that will serve to integrate research in personality and temperament. Those models constitute emerging paradigms that will help to organize future directions for research. We view our chapter as complementary to the other work in this volume in that our interests lie in forwarding methodological and statistical models that allow for strong tests of competing conceptual models in personality and developmental personality research. In particular, we hope to demonstrate how such models should be considered, both conceptually and analytically, in the presence of method variance (such as when data are obtained across multiple measures, occasions, and/or informants).

A common theme of "structure" underlies much of contemporary work in personality. Hypothesized and unobserved structures are thought to be responsible for much of the observed regularities in behavior over time and contexts. For example, when researchers refer to the Big Five structure in personality, they are defining abstract concepts meant to summarize multiple related behaviors and trait descriptions. Taken literally, these structural assumptions have implications for relations among observed measures, and an important research goal is to identify and test the referents for these structures.

One plausible referent might be the features shared by members of a set that allow for the organizational hierarchy implied by a model such as the Big Five. For example, the trait descriptors "active" and "assertive" must share common features to be considered markers of a more abstract dimension labeled Extraversion. A research program interested in identifying such common features might focus on these linkages across the data modes where they occur. Examination of features aggregated across data modes would then lead to what we might describe as internal structural analyses. Such models and analysis strategies focus on the internal coherence of data, without regard to the data mode.

In contrast to determining the universality of a hypothesized structure, one might instead investigate the extent to which a consistent structure based on common features can be obtained across data mode (e.g., instrument, time, informant). This second approach focuses on the replicability and invariance of structures across data modes, not on the more general question of whether structure can be detected. Models under this second approach provide an external perspective, in that coherent structures are obtained only when common and shared agreement exists about the underlying structure across data modes. Reliance on covariation or common information as a criterion for structure is consistent with factor analytic tradition. However, this emphasis on convergence (in our case, across-mode) does not necessarily relate to accuracy, a criterion that may also be of interest (for a discussion, see e.g., Kenny, 1991).[1]

There is robust evidence for the Big Five structure for personality data from the perspective of an internal referent (e.g., Digman, 1990; John, 1990; McCrae & John, 1992). Joint factor analyses (McCrae, 1989) across instruments and across data source have provided impressive evidence for the five-factor model. There remains little question regarding the structural robustness of the Big Five model from an internal perspective.

However, less conclusive evidence exists regarding the Big Five factors from an external perspective. As researchers interested in the robustness of this structure, we are interested in whether the same robust five-factor structure can be obtained from the shared covariation across personality measures (e.g., Battery A vs. Battery B), time (e.g., fourth graders vs. sixth graders), and data source (e.g., self-report vs. peer-report). In other words, does the five-factor structure emerge despite the covariation that exists due to the multiple methods (e.g., across batteries, time points, informants) employed as part of the data collection?

This chapter focuses on representative designs, models, and analytic strategies for analyzing the information available in the shared covariation across instruments, time, and/or informants. The proposed approach allows explicit evaluation of structural models for agreement that will likely characterize future personality research (e.g., Funder, 1991). In some respects, we are presenting a multivariate perspective on the convergent and discriminant validity problem presented in Campbell and Fiske (1959) and are recognizing the multiplism that is explicitly part of the design. Consistent with our beliefs that data can be informative both for hypothesis development as well as for hypothesis testing, we discuss both explora-

---

[1]We thank Bill Graziano for reminding us of this point.

tory and confirmatory approaches to testing shared covariation components and common structure models in the context of multimode designs in personality and temperament.

We begin by contrasting the "total" covariation (internal referent) models typically employed to evaluate structural models in personality and temperament with our "shared" covariation (external referent) models and by showing an array of representative designs in personality research that we believe will be useful. We next demonstrate both exploratory and confirmatory statistical models for evaluating structural hypotheses in personality data. Whereas our two empirical examples concentrate on the shared covariation across batteries in a Big Five context, this external referent emphasis also extends to analogous structural questions concerning convergence across developmental stages in personality and across informants. We conclude with a discussion about the utility of these models for contributing to the understanding of personality and temperament structures from an external referent perspective.

FACTOR ANALYSIS: A METAPHOR FOR STRUCTURE

The approach developed in this chapter can be contrasted with what has been the typical strategy for ascertaining structure in personality and temperament data. Factor analytic paradigms have dominated structural searches to the extent that personality texts refer heavily to factor analytically derived models (e.g., Royce & Powell, 1983). Indeed, empirical evidence for the Big Five personality structure emerges largely through a series of factor analyses of trait ratings derived from both the lexical and questionnaire traditions (cf. McCrae & John, 1992).

The use of factor analysis models as a metaphor for the detection of structure in personality data has directed the way in which analyses in this literature are conceived. For example, in a study designed to examine personality structure, one might obtain a set of ratings on adjectival markers of the Big Five obtained from self-report. To rule out the possibility of self-report biases, an additional informant might be used to rate the target individual (e.g., the report of a best friend on a target individual). The factor analysis metaphor would suggest that we would form the complete correlation matrix of adjectival ratings from both self- and peer-report and factor analyze the entire matrix.

It is our belief that the use of a factor analytic model in such a context ignores important features of the study design. When data are obtained by both self- and peer-report, a critical design feature is the availability of multiple informants. Such crossed designs are relatively common in personality research and are likely to become increasingly common given the dissatisfaction with monomethod, monoagent reporting. One might examine whether a core personality structure can be detected in the covariation that self-reports and peer-reports share in common. However, as is shown here, analyses typically focus on evaluating structural hypotheses based on the joint data, without consideration of the source information provided in the design. The methods we propose present exploratory and confirmatory factor analytic models that incorporate design features and provide more focused evaluations of structural hypotheses.

The next section discusses some representative designs in personality research for which the methodological and statistical ideas presented later in the chapter may prove useful.

Representative Crossed Designs in Personality Research

In the literature on crossed experimental designs, one can think of data (typically scores on individuals) as being observed under specific conditions obtained from combining different levels of a particular mode of observation.[2] For example, if men and women are observed in treatment and control experimental conditions, a 2×2 design results with the two levels of Mode 1 (men, women) combined with the two levels of Mode 2 (treatment, control) to obtain four different conditions under which data are observed.

Though it may be less apparent in the correlations of self- and peer-ratings on trait adjectives, these data can also be thought of as emanating from this type of study design. Specifically, one is observing data (in this case, correlations) that come from a crossing of self-report data with peer-report data. This design leads to three different types of correlations that can be identified in the full data correlation matrix: (1) Intercorrelations among trait adjectives coming from self-report data (heterotrait, monomethod with convergent validities on the diagonal); (2) Intercorrelations among trait adjectives coming from peer-report data (heterotrait, monomethod with validities on the diagonal); and (3) Cross-correlations among the same trait adjectives obtained from self-report and peer-report. In Campbell and Fiske (1959) terms, the first two types of intercorrelations can be thought of as heterotrait, monomethod relations with convergent validities on the diagonal. The third type, reflecting the cross-correlations, maps the agreement between self-report and peer-report and describes heterotrait, heteromethod relations with reliabilities on the diagonal.

Within the context of the study design, it would seem natural to ask about structure underlying the agreement component of the correlation matrix. For our Big Five example, we might ask about the extent to which the Big Five factor structure describes the agreement of self-report and peer-report. However, standard factor analytic approaches ignore this particular subcomponent and instead factor analyze the complete correlation matrix. The resulting structures that are obtained from an analysis of the complete data matrix contains covariation

---

[2]We will use the term *crossed designs* to have the same meaning that it has in the experimental design literature (e.g., Winer, 1971), with the slight modification that we use "factor" to denote an unobserved, latent variable as in factor analysis. The corresponding use of "factor" in the experimental design literature to refer to predictor variables will be replaced in this chapter by the term *mode*.

attributable to the within-source components of the model (due to the self-report ratings, due to the peer-report ratings), in addition to the more interesting (from a convergent validity perspective) between-source aspects of the model. The original study design that focused on agreement between peer- and self-report has been lost to the statistical method used to analyze the data. Here, the conceptual model guiding the original study design is not consistent with the statistical model being employed to analyze the data given the design. To the extent that the within-source component is large, the use of such a strategy may greatly distort the nature of the solution obtained for data.

Multiple design modes are endemic to much of contemporary personality research. It is our feeling that, to date, many of these designs have been either underanalyzed (e.g., simply presenting the bivariate associations between self-report and peer-report data—convergent validities) or analyzed employing models that are not particularly well-suited to studying questions of across-mode agreement (e.g., factor analyses conducted on complete data matrices). We first consider some representative designs in which such problems occur and then present ways to analyze such designs.

Multiple Measure Designs. A very common multimode design in personality occurs when one obtains data crossing modes that are defined by instruments or batteries. In our empirical examples, we demonstrate this design by employing alternative measures, each constructed to tap the Big Five.

A goal of multiple measure designs is to insure that the resulting structures are attributable to constructs of interest rather than to instrumentation. Interest is focused on the common variability shared across measures of the same construct. This across-measure covariation is thought to come from the dependence of each measurement on the underlying construct. From this perspective it is clear that analyses in multiple measure designs should focus on the across-measure overlap, rather than the shared within-measure covariation. Note that the analysis assumes a symmetry across batteries, by allowing the between-measure convergence to be unaffected by differential contributions of within-measure variability.

Multiple measure designs are well-known to personality psychologists in terms of the Campbell and Fiske (1959) multitrait, multimethod approach to determining convergent and discriminant validity (e.g., Kenny & Kashy, 1992; Rudinger & Dommel, 1986; Schwarzer, 1986). Although the differentiation between variance sources due to instrumentation has typically been better articulated and modeled than in the corresponding multiple informant designs, it still remains the case that many analyses either follow the eyeball detection heuristic suggested by Campbell and Fiske or employ restrictive statistical models that have been less than well supported in empirical data (e.g., Kenny & Kashy, 1992). We demonstrate an intermediate and exploratory approach that still allows investigators to evaluate structural hypotheses.

Designs for Personality Processes. Beyond the psychometric referents provided by the multiple measure designs, the models we introduce in this chapter have some interesting implications for theoretical models of developmental personality process and personality process models more generally. When time and/or context is introduced as a design mode, the following question arises: To what extent does underlying structure remain stable or invariant across developmental levels and/or experimental contexts?

The stability of personality structure over the life span continues to be a key issue in contemporary personality research. For example, a special *Journal of Personality* issue on this topic (West & Graziano, 1989) presents an excellent series of articles looking at age-related change for a variety of individual differences, including those postulated by the Big Five model (Digman, 1989). Sections of this book attest to the importance of this issue in understanding the extent to which the Big Five structure describes how individuals view themselves and others across developmental levels. The exploratory and confirmatory approaches presented in this chapter allow a researcher to isolate the within-stage variability and focus on the between-stage variability and the structure that underlies it. By dealing with the communalities without the within-stage idiosyncracies, researchers have a test for structural change and/or growth over time.

Similarly, personality process can also be examined without invoking the longitudinal component. In an experimental investigation of implicit personality theories, Romer and Revelle (1984) presented a design where raters were asked to employ different coding schemes and to map these coding schemes into memory-based judgments of target individuals. In this study, Romer and Revelle considered the bias introduced by frequency counts in assessing behavioral observations (for a more a recent critique of the same logic, see Block, 1989).

We believe the models presented here can be fruitfully extended to consider important theoretical ideas that have emerged in personality theory such as implicit personality theory as evaluated in the Romer and Revelle study or the "fundamental attribution error" (Jones & Nisbett, 1971). At the core of each of these theoretical models are issues related to construct consistency. The actor–observer difference in the fundamental attribution error hypothesizes a null relation between the congruence of trait attributions made by an actor and an observer. The statistical models that we present are well-suited for evaluating such consistency as it exists at the construct level rather than at the level of the specific measures.

Multiple Informant Designs. An alternative conceptualization of the multimode situation is the experimental design where one obtains data from multiple informants on a target individual. Indeed, Funder (1991) suggested that this particular experimental design is critical for personality research to develop, and a special issue of *Journal of Personality* conveys the critical thinking in this area (Funder & West, 1993). A standard design is to obtain both self- and other-informant data (e.g., peer, teacher, parent, spouse) on a set of personality attributes.

An experimental design that generates a correlation matrix that contains both self and peer ratings can be thought of crossing two observer modes or sources: A self-report mode and a peer-report mode. From this design metaphor, it can easily be argued that interest in this design is not the within-observer covariation (or the "main effects" of observer mode), but the data that come from crossing self-report and peer-report modes (or the "interaction" of the two observer modes).

The idea of triangulating constructs of interest using multiple informants has been used in a number of different research contexts. In work on child socialization, Patterson and his colleagues (e.g., Bank, Dishion, Skinner, & Patterson, 1990) referred to the problem of "monoagent" data contamination that leads to "gloppy" data. The fundamental goal is to obtain multiple operationalizations of study constructs such that the focus can be on the overlapping common variation and not on the idiosyncrasies attributable to the reporter source. From this perspective, the within-source idiosyncrasies are viewed as "noise" or nuisance variance that interferes with the detection of the "signal" of the construct.

Multiple informant designs have been used to provide information about trait construct consensus and agreement. In the personality literature, for example, it is typical to obtain self- and peer-ratings on adjectival markers of the Big Five factors. However, typical analysis strategies have not addressed the problem of the within-source idiosyncrasies that motivated the multiple informant design. We have seen numerous examples of such designs that do not use data in an efficient manner for tests of structural hypotheses. These examples include either the selective reporting of bivariate correlations that demonstrate convergent validity (e.g., presenting only correlations between self- and peer-report) or the failure to address the problem of within-informant or method variance by the use of a simultaneous factor analysis of the full, self–peer correlation matrix.[3] We discuss this factor analytic issue in more detail later.

TESTING STRUCTURES

The next sections present two factor analytically based approaches that may be employed to evaluate hypotheses of the structural invariance of personality. Both approaches are sensitive to the cases where assessments are obtained across modes, where modes can refer to different batteries of instruments, points in time, and/or raters. The first method reviewed, interbattery factor analysis (Browne, 1979, 1980; Tucker, 1958), is appropriate for exploring structural hypotheses in multimode designs.

The second method, structural equation modeling with multiple modes, typically considers confirmatory tests of hypotheses. Although there are a number

---

[3]Though we have employed an experimental design metaphor to illustrate some conceptual ideas, we cannot formally speak of interactions operating on the correlational data unless we evaluate models of considerably greater complexity (cf. Browne, 1984).

of different ways in which modes might be crossed, our discussion in this chapter focuses on trait and method modes as has been discussed in the literature on the analysis of multitrait, multimethod data (e.g., Kenny & Kashy, 1992; Marsh, 1989; Marsh & Hocevar, 1983; Widaman, 1985). Structural equation modeling with latent variables has become increasingly popular and accessible over the past decade (e.g., Tanaka, Panter, Winborne, & Huba, 1990) and is well-suited for specific, confirmatory hypotheses based on a priori ideas about underlying structures. For each of these analytic strategies, we provide examples using some familiar multiple method, Big Five designs.

Exploring Structures Across Modes: An Overview

A critical issue for investigations of Big Five factor structure has been determining the extent to which this particular structure holds—or is invariant—across various measurement situations. For instance, interest may be in structural similarity across instruments, each designed to tap the Big Five factors (e.g., Briggs, 1992). Or, across content domains of instruments, one might have exploratory hypotheses about how the Big Five "fit" in the space of the other instruments, such as the space occupied by psychopathology instruments (cf. Widiger & Trull, 1992) or other models of personality (e.g., Hofstee, DeRaad, & Goldberg, 1992). Parallel issues can be raised for data collected across developmental level; for example, does a particular Big Five dimension and its referents remain stable over developmental stage (e.g., Agreeableness; see Graziano & Eisenberg, in press). Across for multiple informant designs, one might ask: To what extent is there evidence for convergence in peer-reports versus self-reports of the Big Five (e.g., Borkenau & Ostendorf, 1990; McCrae & Costa, 1987)?

The question of structural invariance across domains is not new in the factor analytic tradition. L. L. Thurstone (1947), who devoted an entire chapter to the issue in his classic factor analysis book, described the problem as follows (also cited in Tucker, 1958): "It is a fundamental criterion of a valid method of isolating primary abilities for a test must remain invariant when it is moved from one test battery to another test battery" (p. 361). Viewing primary abilities as primary factors in personality, one can conclude that a key to demonstrating structural invariance is providing clear evidence that the structure (as in Thurstone's words) "transcends" the chosen methods of data collection. Although impressive evidence exists for the Big Five factors within and across measurement modes, there is considerably less evidence on the extent to which the "five robust factors" of personality emerge when only looking at the common association across assessment modes.

Demonstrating across-domain generalizability of the Big Five using exploratory factor analysis requires modeling data in a manner that makes the most of the multimode research design. Surprisingly, despite the central role of exploratory methods in the history and development of this view of personality (e.g., in shaping

6. STRUCTURAL MODELS FOR MULTIMODE DESIGNS

and providing clearer understanding of structure, in attempting to show across-domain generalizability of this structure, in providing clues about the appropriate level of abstraction for personality), the issue of "what to do about method variance" in Big Five research has not been fully pursued. Typically, variance partitioning among measures into components due to traits or constructs (common to both methods) and to method, independent of trait, has not been standard fare for personality researchers in applications of exploratory factor analysis.

A (very) typical example of the aggregation problem and the neglect of method variance-related problems can be seen in the simple case where exploratory factor analysis is employed to compare two batteries assessing the Big Five (five scale scores from each battery). When the entire 10×10 correlation or covariance matrix of scale scores is factor analyzed (using what has been called "joint factor analysis"), the resulting solution is based on the variability contained in three distinct types of bivariate relations. Figure 6.1 illustrates this "supermatrix" and enumerates these types of relations.

The full factor analysis on the 10×10 matrix (R_{AB}) consists of: (1) within-scale (mono- and heterotrait, monomethod) correlations for the first Big Five battery (R_{11}); (2) within-scale (mono- and heterotrait, monomethod) correlations for the second Big Five battery (R_{22}); and (3) a block of between-scale (mono- and heterotrait, heteromethod) relations across the two batteries (R_{21}). The first two types of correlations on the block-diagonal of this supermatrix contain method or battery-specific variance and are thus both likely to reflect higher intercorrelations (relative to the R_{21} correlations) for this reason.

The third type of correlations, contained in a block rather than a triangular matrix, expresses convergent and divergent information, without the shared effects of method—that is, across the two batteries, the extent to which theoretically similar

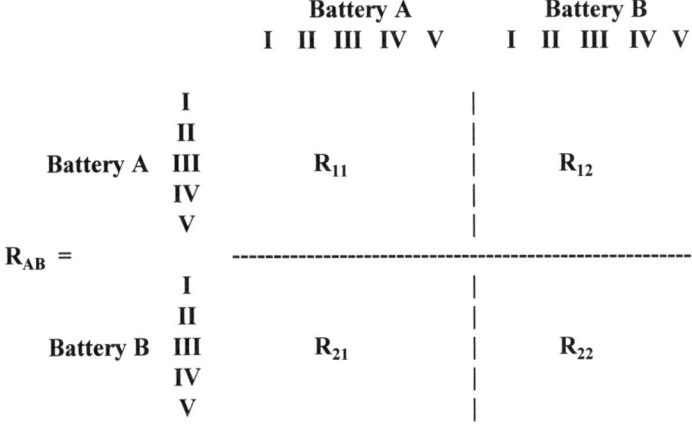

FIG. 6.1. Supermatrix of two personality batteries (A and B), each with five scores.

scales agree and theoretically dissimilar scales disagree. The diagonal elements of the R_{21} block express the traditional convergent validities (cf. Campbell & Fiske, 1959) between corresponding scales in each battery (e.g., Extraversion from Battery A with Extraversion with Battery B). The off-diagonal elements in this block express the relation or predictability between each scale from one battery with each scale from the second battery and vice versa. Note that we are dealing with a block because the triangular matrix above the convergent diagonal need not be the same as below the diagonal (e.g., the relation between Battery A Extraversion and Battery B Agreeableness may not be the same as the relation between Battery B Extraversion and Battery A Agreeableness). Thus, the R_{21} matrix is not symmetric about its diagonal and, in a more general case with different numbers of tests comprising each battery, need not even be square.

In performing a joint factor analysis with scale scores from two batteries, one might be tempted to claim support for structural invariance when corresponding subscales load on specific dimensions—that is, when Extraversion from Battery A and Extraversion from Battery B load on one dimension and not others, and so on. However, such an analysis and its resulting factor solution does not directly speak to whether the same Big Five structure underlies the two batteries. The reason is that this type of strategy simultaneously evaluates information within methods and across methods, confounds trait relations and structure, and does not consider variability differences that are built into the study design. Such a distortion can manifest itself in a number of ways in a factor solution. Loadings of scales on factors can be larger (or smaller!) than they might otherwise be. Scales may load on more factors than might be expected as well, leading to a less "clean" solution. Thus, although the external referent approach provides a strong link between theory, design, and analysis, it may lead to an interpretationally more complex picture of underlying structure. Though the amount of variability to be analyzed will be greater when method factors are ignored (in the internal referent situation), the distribution of this variability in the solution cannot be determined without an empirical comparison.

Interbattery Factor Analysis

An exploratory factor analytic method that can address explicitly the invariance of personality structure across methods is interbattery factor analysis (Browne, 1979, 1980; Tucker, 1958). Conceptually, the interbattery approach differs substantially from the type of exploratory factor analytic strategies that are generally employed to address this question in this literature. In the interbattery case, only the variability across the methods (the R_{21} block from Fig. 6.1) is considered, making the operating question: Does the common variance between modes (e.g., battery, time, data source) yield the Big Five factor structure? Thus, the method is appropriate in situations where information on traits are collected across method(s), where across-method variance can be analyzed.

Historical Background. Tucker (1958) outlined the problem and solution for the interbattery problem using as an example data collected by L. L. Thurstone and T. G. Thurstone (1941) comprised of nine word fluency and verbal tasks distributed across two batteries. Much of the original article concentrates on solutions to some factor analytic problems that, in our age of "point and click" canned factor analysis programs, are perhaps of less consequence now than they were in the 1950s. Tucker's work showed that one could decompose a correlation matrix in a way that could isolate across-domain variability and within-domain variability and use factor analysis to describe the dimensions underlying each source of variance.

Whereas across-battery variability is most directly relevant for the question of factor invariance of the Big Five, the residual within-battery variability, can also be factor analyzed separately to entertain hypotheses about the nature of the residual variance to determine if systematic structure can be obtained. If clear method factors are obtained in an analysis of the residual variance, it would suggest the extent to which these systematic components may influence structures obtained from a joint factor analysis of the same data.

In an important series of papers, Browne (1979, 1980) reanalyzed the Thurstone and Thurstone data and showed that Tucker's interbattery factor analysis model could be related to a broader (and more familiar) class of models and could be generalized to the more-than-two battery case. In particular, Browne demonstrated that maximum likelihood interbattery factor loadings were simply a rescaling of the loadings that would be obtained from a canonical correlation (CC) analysis.

While the interbattery factor analysis model and the CC model are related, they are, by no means, identical. In CC analysis, the analysis is strictly based on the across-set (or domain) structure of observed variables. Here, a set refers to scores obtained on a battery, at a time point, or from an informant. The goal in CC is to find a linear combination of variables within one set that is maximally associated with a corresponding linear composite from the second set. In the CC model, one refers to the canonical variable pair (the linear combinations from both sets). A sequence of such CCs can be obtained with each subsequent pair orthogonal to earlier pairs.

In the interbattery factor analytic model, one hypothesizes underlying latent variables or factors that represent the common structure only in the across-set covariation. In contrast to the CC model, which maximizes the association between paired linear combinations of observed variables, the interbattery model considers maximized associations between observed variables and underlying (and unobserved) factors.

A major contribution of Browne (1979) was to demonstrate that although CC and interbattery procedures were based on different models, maximum likelihood estimates for the interbattery solution could be obtained as a rescaling of CC solution. The particular rescaling suggested by Browne "corrects" for the fact that the observed scales are measured with error. Specifically, one can obtain interbattery factor loadings by first conducting a CC analysis between the two sets of scale scores. Next, each column of the canonical loading matrix obtained in that analysis should be multiplied by the square root of the CC associated with that column. It might also be noted in passing that, given the close numerical relation between CC and this specific implementation of a more general factor analytic model, the kinds of interpretational concerns that are thought to be endemic to CC (e.g., the "bouncing beta" problem; cf. Thorndike & Weiss, 1973) would be equally applicable to the factor analysis problem, although such instabilities in a factor analytic context have not been widely recognized to date.

In the implementation of an interbattery solution proposed in this chapter, we suggest an additional follow-up step that we do not believe has been suggested in the literature on interbattery analysis, but is closely related to general models for the residual analysis (e.g., Mosteller & Tukey, 1977). After the interbattery loadings are obtained, one can also remove the interbattery information from the original correlation matrix of scale scores and factor analyze the residual or battery-specific variability. In our specific interbattery context, the interpretability of factors from such a residual analysis would provide information about the extent to which a factor solution obtained from an analysis including within-method information (i.e., a joint factor analysis) might be influenced by a remaining systematic component.

Over the 40 years since the interbattery factor solution surfaced in the psychometric literature, the number of applications of this method in the more general psychological literature has been relatively small. Issues that are addressed with the interbattery method are illustrative and highly related to the type of questions that are asked in Big Five investigations. For example, researchers have identified factors that are shared between batteries of ability and personality measures (Hakstian & Cattell, 1978), learning tasks and intelligence measures (Hundal & Horn, 1977), sensation-seeking measures and reported drug use (Huba, Newcomb, & Bentler, 1981), measures of information-processing strategies and daydreaming styles (Tanaka, Panter, & Winborne, 1987), and most recently, two widely used clinical batteries, the Millon Clinical Multiaxial Inventory and the Symptom Checklist-90 (Strauman & Wetzler, 1992). The interbattery method has also been employed in the context of multiple-informant designs such as across parent and child reports of parental behavior (Kojima, 1975) and the child's competence (Tanaka & Westerman, 1988). Whereas all of the cited applications have included only two sources of method variance (across two batteries, across two sources), the interbattery model has been generalized to the more-than-two domain case (Browne, 1980), and the general model is implemented in a computer program by Cudeck (1982). This also appears to be related to work by Escofier and Pages (1989).

Testing Factor Invariance: An Interbattery Example

To demonstrate differences between the joint factor analytic method and the interbattery method, we use a dataset comprised of two assessment instruments, the NEO Personality Inventory (NEO-PI; Costa & McCrae, 1985) and the Goldberg bipolar adjectives (Goldberg, 1992).[4] Given the robustness of the Big Five, we would expect that the between-battery variability would tap the same Big Five factor structure.

The two batteries, the NEO-PI and the Goldberg bipolar adjectives, each consist of five scales: Extraversion, Agreeableness, Conscientiousness, Neuroticism (for NEO-PI)/Emotional Stability (for Goldberg adjectives), and Openness to Experience (for NEO-PI)/Intellect (for Goldberg adjectives). In theory, it is reasonable to question (as it has been done elsewhere; see McCrae & Costa, 1985) whether the two self-report instruments, derived from distinct traditions in personality and of different formats (behavioral statements versus bipolar adjective dimensions), would show the expected dimensionality and pattern of loadings.

We analyzed the data in two ways to examine to what extent a common factor structure exists across these two Big Five batteries. First, a joint factor analytic approach was taken, which considers the entire 10×10 correlation matrix of NEO-PI and Goldberg scale scores. Second, the interbattery factor analytic approach, which makes use of only across-battery information, is demonstrated and followed by an analysis of the residual variance after the interbattery information is removed (e.g., the variability attributable to each method).

Respondents and Measures. Respondents for this example were 248 undergraduates from a large, public university in the southern United States who received partial course credit for their participation and completed the measures as part of a larger study on personality and nonverbal cue use in a social decoding task.

The NEO-PI is comprised of 181 statements or phrases to which respondents are to indicate on a five-point Likert-type scale the extent to which they disagree or agree. Neuroticism ("I often feel tense and jittery"; $\alpha = .91$), Extraversion ("I enjoy talking to people"; $\alpha = .90$), and Openness ("I often enjoy playing with theories or abstract ideas"; $\alpha = .88$) each have 48 items, whereas Agreeableness ("I believe that most people are basically well-intentioned"; $\alpha = .76$) and Conscientiousness ("I keep my belongings neat and clean"; $\alpha = .88$) have just 18 items each.

The Goldberg adjectives have 10 items per scale, with a total of 50 items. Each item is anchored by a trait term and its opposite and is rated on a nine-point Likert-type scale ranging from "very" (one pole) to "very" (the other pole). Examples of trait terms (positive pole) for each scale are extraverted, energetic, active (Extraversion; $\alpha = .90$), warm, cooperative, flexible (Agreeableness; $\alpha = .85$), organized, responsible, practical (Conscientiousness; $\alpha = .83$), calm, relaxed, secure (Emotional Stability; $\alpha = .86$), and intelligent, analytical, creative (Intellect; $\alpha = .73$).

---

[4]Descriptive information (means, standard deviations, and correlations) for these data, as well as the data discussed in the next empirical example are available from the first author.

Results

Joint Factor Analysis. When the correlations among the ten scales (from the two Big Five measures) are analyzed in a joint factor analysis, all traditional factor analysis "signs," both descriptive and statistical (e.g., scree plot, eigenvalue-one rule, significance tests, extraction convergence), show that a four-factor solution is most appropriate for these data. These factors, in the unrotated solution, account for a very large proportion (78.7%) of the common variance.[5]

Table 6.1 presents the factor loadings for a varimax-rotated four-factor solution for this analysis. Note that one of the four factors (Factor 1) is a combined Extraversion-Openness factor. The failure to identify cleanly the Openness factor is a finding that has been replicated in a number of other analyses (e.g., McCrae, 1990). When factors are forced to be uncorrelated as is the case in most applications of joint factor analysis to Big Five data, the solution shows high loadings for scales on corresponding factors; however, Agreeableness (Goldberg adjectives) loads on two additional factors.

The situation changes somewhat when an oblique solution is employed that allows factors to be intercorrelated. In that case, although corresponding scales load on corresponding dimensions, there are three double loadings, one triple loading, and one quadruple loading (using a criterion of at least $|.30|$). Moreover, in three cases, the factor intercorrelations were moderate. In all cases except for Agreeableness (where the quadruple loading occurs for the Goldberg adjectives), the Goldberg scales show higher loadings on their factors than the NEO-PI scales.

Interbattery Factor Analysis: Across-Domain Structure. The interbattery solution given in Table 6.2 was obtained by first conducting a CC analysis between the two batteries and rescaling the canonical loadings following Browne (1979). Results from the CC analysis provide clear evidence that each of the five possible dimensions between the two sets of variables should be retained. Step-down F tests for the number of interbattery factors reveal that all of the possible five between-set dimensions are statistically significant, and CCs for the five dimensions are high ranging from .52 to .84.

The varimax-rotated interbattery solution in Table 6.2, when compared to the joint factor analysis solution in Table 6.1, shows a pattern that is more consistent with Big Five theory and the idea of simple structure in factor analysis. Unlike the joint factor analysis solution, the magnitude of the interbattery loadings on each factor is comparable for both batteries, suggesting that neither instrument dominates in determining the structure underlying the scales across the batteries. This shift in loadings across batteries seen in this example will not necessarily emerge in all joint factor analysis–interbattery comparisons. However, with the

---

[5]Eigenvalues for the first five factors were 3.89, 1.73, 1.23, 1.02 and .81. A five-factor solution would not converge within a reasonable number of iterations.

TABLE 6.1
Joint Factor Analysis of NEO–PI and Goldberg Instruments:
Factor Loadings From Varimax Rotation

Scale	F1	F2	F3	F4
Extraversion (Goldberg)	**.88**	.29	.10	.05
Extraversion (NEO–PI)	**.83**	.14	.14	.09
Intellect (Goldberg)	**.46**	.15	.19	.01
Openness to Experience (NEO–PI)	**.35**	−.10	−.19	.21
Emotional Stability (Goldberg)	.21	**.96**	.16	.13
Neuroticism (NEO-PI)	−.15	**−.77**	−.12	−.15
Conscientiousness (Goldberg)	.08	.18	**.97**	.12
Conscientiousness (NEO–PI)	.11	.09	**.74**	.03
Agreeableness (NEO–PI)	.10	.18	.06	**.98**
Agreeableness (Goldberg)	**.36**	**.35**	.26	**.50**

Note: For clarity, factor loadings greater than |.30| are in bold. The unrotated four-factor solution accounts for 78.7% of the total variance in the correlations among scales.

TABLE 6.2
Interbattery Factor Analysis for the NEO–PI and the Goldberg Instruments:
Factor Loadings for Varimax Rotation

Scale	F1	F2	F3	F4	F5
Neuroticism (NEO–PI)	**−.86**	−.14	−.13	−.17	−.05
Emotional Stability (Goldberg)	**.84**	.22	.14	.23	.01
Extraversion (NEO–PI)	.12	**.84**	.10	.17	.20
Extraversion (Goldberg)	.25	**.83**	.09	.12	.20
Conscientiousness (NEO–PI)	.09	.09	**.85**	.04	.01
Conscientiousness (Goldberg)	.15	.08	**.84**	.18	−.02
Agreeableness (NEO–PI)	.15	.07	.06	**.76**	.04
Agreeableness (Goldberg)	.23	.25	.17	**.70**	.18
Openness to Experience (NEO–PI)	−.08	.13	−.18	.14	**.71**
Intellect (Goldberg)	.15	.22	.18	.03	**.69**

Note: For clarity, factor loadings greater than |.30| are bolded. The unrotated four-factor solution accounts for 71.8% of the total variance in the correlations among scales.

interbattery solution one can be sure the loadings are not affected by variability due to method idiosyncrasies.

While one can be lulled by the as-hypothesized structure for the interbattery varimax solution, this clarity is in part due to the orthogonal rotation scheme. When the factors are permitted to correlate in an oblique rotation, the picture is, if anything, equally as complex as the obliquely rotated joint factor analysis solution—in terms of double, triple, and quadruple loadings across factors. In both solutions, the factors are not defined just by the two salient loadings from corresponding scales across the two batteries. In addition, as is the case for the joint factor analysis solution, half the factor intercorrelations that describe this five-factor solution are at least |.30| in magnitude.

Interbattery Factor Analysis: Within-Domain Structure. In this section, we demonstrate what happens when the across-battery information is removed from the original 10 × 10 correlation matrix and is analyzed using exploratory factor analysis. Because the shared between-instrument variability has been removed, only the battery-specific information should remain.

These two instruments are distinct in terms of the stimuli to be rated (phrases versus natural language adjectives), and there is no expectation that the method variance associated with each should be related. Indeed, when the residual, battery-specific information is factored, two large and independent factors emerge, each corresponding precisely to its respective battery. The factor loadings from the varimax solution for this analysis are provided in Table 6.3, but even the obliquely rotated solution shows the same pattern and the same near-zero correlation between factors. The only scales that do not show loadings of at least |.30| on their expected factor are for the NEO-PI Neuroticism and Conscientiousness scales. Interestingly, these two scales break off to form their own separate method factor when a three-factor solution is retained for these data. Thus, when across-battery variability is removed from the original data, two separate dimensions emerge, one describing covariance due to responding to the NEO-PI scales and the other describing covariance due to responding to the Goldberg adjectives. The ability to detect this systematic covariation in the residual marks the extent to which method variance may alter factor structures obtained from a joint factor analysis.

Benefits of the Interbattery Approach

When the research interest is in describing the factor structure that underlies two (or more) instruments, it is important that within-instrument variability is not

TABLE 6.3
Interbattery Factor Analysis of the Residual (Method) Variance From the NEO–PI and Goldberg Instruments: Factor Loadings for Varimax Rotation

Scale	F1	F2
Agreeableness (Goldberg)	**.60**	<.01
Extraversion (Goldberg)	**.54**	<.01
Emotional Stability (Goldberg)	**.53**	<.01
Intellect (Goldberg)	**.50**	<.01
Conscientiousness (Goldberg)	**.45**	<.01
Extraversion (NEO–PI)	<.01	**.53**
Openness to Experience (NEO–PI)	<.01	**.49**
Agreeableness (NEO–PI)	<.01	**.45**
Neuroticism (NEO–PI)	<.01	−.20
Conscientiousness (NEO–PI)	<.01	.12

Note: For clarity, factor loadings greater than |.30| are bolded. Three eigenvalues were greater than 1.0, but two factors were extracted for interpretation purposes. When obliquely rotated, these two factors correlate < .01 with each other. The unrotated solution accounts for 36.5% of the total variance in the residuals.

indiscriminantly incorporated into solution. A correlation matrix describing two batteries can be decomposed into variability due to the constructs being measured and the other due to the methods by which the assessments are collected. The latter source of variation is typically thought to be not substantively interesting. The interbattery factor method described earlier treats between-battery variability separately from battery-specific variability. Even though obtained factor solutions may be interpretationally complex (e.g., the oblique interbattery five-factor solution), an interbattery approach more accurately depicts the research design and describes the dimensionality of the across-method information.

Confirming Structures Across Modes: An Overview

In cases where confirmatory hypotheses are being advanced based on multiple method data, the interbattery factor analysis approach described previously is not appropriate. An alternative approach to separating trait from method variance in interbattery studies of personality structure is Structural Equation Modeling (SEM) with latent variables. SEM can be thought of as a multivariate generalization of multiple regression analysis that allows tests of linear relations between observed and unobserved variables (i.e., factors). Unlike other more exploratory approaches, SEM is used most effectively as a confirmatory technique—one in which an a priori set of relations is proposed and is then compared against the relations observed in data from a sample. To the extent that a proposed set of relations do not conform to the observed relations, with proper precautions (MacCallum, Roznowski, & Necowitz, 1992) a model may be adjusted to more closely approximate the observed data.

A particular SEM application that has received considerable attention among researchers interested in the structure of multivariate data is confirmatory factor analysis (CFA). CFA considers the relations between a set of observed variables and the latent variables, or factors, believed to account for the shared covariation among the observed variables. CFA can be thought of as a special case of traditional factor analytic models in which the number of factors and the variables that load on particular factors are specified in advance. By imposing an a priori simple structure criterion (single nonzero loading, off-factor loadings constrained to zero) in a CFA model, mathematical problems associated with solutions from traditional factor analyses are overcome. Moreover, an omnibus test of model fit and tests of loadings and correlations among factors may be calculated.

Our interest in this chapter is the application of CFA to interbattery data in which multiple facets of personality have been assessed using multiple modes such as test batteries, points in time, and informants. The resulting multitrait-multimethod (MTMM; Campbell & Fiske, 1959) matrix can be analyzed as a CFA model in which each observed measure loads on one trait factor and one "method" factor (Kenny & Kashy, 1992). That model has the virtue that trait and method variance components are estimated separately so that the relations between observed measures and their corresponding trait factor, relations between trait factors, and relations between trait factors and variables outside the CFA model are less likely to be attributable to spurious relations due to shared method variance. In sum, then, using CFA it is possible to operationalize personality factors using multiple measures, developmental levels, or informants, control for covariation among measures from the same source, then model the structural relations between personality factors and other variables of interest.

Empirical Example

Data. We analyzed responses by 351 college students' to the NEO-PI (Costa & McCrae, 1985), the Interpersonal Adjective Scales-Big Five version (IAS-B5; Trapnell & Wiggins, 1988), and the revised Personality Diagnostic Questionnaire (PDQ-R; Hyler & Rieder, 1987), a self-report measure of *DSM-III-R* (American Psychiatric Association, 1987) Axis II disorders.[6] From the PDQ-R we extracted scores for antisocial, dependent, and schizoid personality disorders to demonstrate the inclusion of exogenous variables in interbattery analyses of personality structure.

Model Specification. CFA of interbattery personality data begins with the formal specification of a structural model. At the most general level, the model must account for the fact that each personality score is a function of at least two influences: (1) the respondents' standing on one of the five personality factors; and (2) the method by which their standing was assessed. Fig. 6.2 depicts a path diagram of a model that accounts for the role of trait and method variance in the structure of interbattery personality data. Near the middle of the figure are five circles representing the Big Five personality factors. Note that each factor influences two measured variables, represented by boxes: the NEO-PI and the IAS-B5 assessments of the factor. Beneath each box is a small circle, labeled "e," which represents the influence of error on the measured variables. Error may encompass a variety of influences, ranging from uniqueness to method. Note that the errors associated with the NEO-PI measures are connected by arrows, as are the errors associated with the IAS-B5. Those arrows represent the fact that some portion of the error associated with measures from a single battery is shared method variance.[7] Because, in this case, the NEO-PI and the IAS-B5 represent different "methods" of assessment, there is no reason to suspect shared method variance across batteries. Moving back to the Big Five personality factors, note

---

[6]We thank James Stokes and Kristopher West for making these data available to us.

[7]We could have modeled two methods factors (Marsh & Hocevar, 1983) rather than a series of correlations among within-battery errors; however, Kenny and Kashy (1992) questioned the integrity of estimates obtained in such a model.

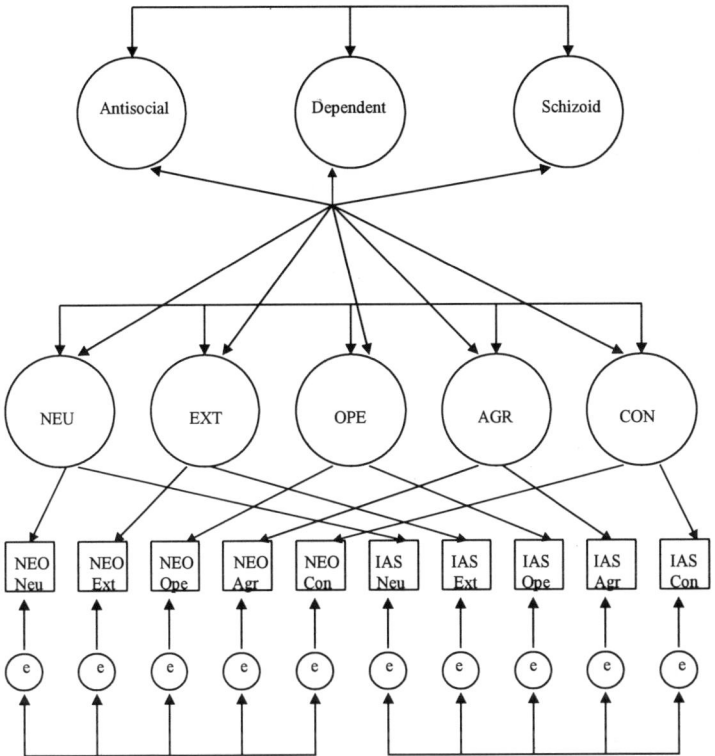

FIG. 6.2. Hypothesized model of personality interbattery relations.

that the larger circles are connected by arrows, representing the fact that they are likely correlated (as revealed in our previous analysis). Finally, note the three circles at the top of the figure. Those circles represent the three personality disorders we selected as exogenous variables. The arrows that connect them reflect our expectation that the factors are intercorrelated, and the arrows that run between the personality disorders and the Big Five factors represent correlations between them. Thus, in a single analysis, it is possible to test a model in which simple structure is imposed, method variance is accounted for, and relations between personality factors and exogenous variables are examined.

Estimation. Our next step is to estimate the hypothesized model parameters in the model. Of most interest are the factor loadings, correlations among errors, correlations among Big Five factors, and correlations between the Big Five factors and the personality disorders. We obtained estimates using the maximum likelihood method in EQS (Bentler, 1989). As noted by Kenny and Kashy (1992) and others, analyses of CFA models that include only two indicators of factors are likely to present estimation problems (Anderson & Gerbing, 1984). Indeed, our first pass at estimating the model revealed three Heywood cases: negative estimates of error variances. The data were then screened for outliers (e.g., Bollen, 1989), and the model was reestimated excluding outlying cases; that strategy failed to correct the estimation problems. We imposed constraints on the model that would increase the likelihood of plausible error variance estimates. Errors associated with each pair of indicators of a factor were constrained to be equal. That strategy eliminated Heywood cases, but resulted in out-of-range estimates of the correlations between errors. We next reasoned that, because the NEO-PI and IAS-B5 assess personality on such different metrics, weighted equality constraints were more appropriate. Indeed, when equality constraints were imposed, plausible estimates and standard errors resulted.

The degree to which a model fits a set of observed data is evaluated by an approximation of the χ^2 statistic and one of several descriptive indexes of fit. A nonsignificant value of χ^2 signifies that the relations in a proposed model are consistent with the relations in the observed data. For various reasons associated with the questionable performance of the χ^2 statistic, adjunct fit indexes such as Bentler's (1990) comparative fit index (CFI) are consulted to evaluate further model fit (cf. Tanaka, 1993) for a review of the CFI and other fit indices). Values of CFI greater than .90 (range: 0 to 1.0) typically signify an acceptable fit of a model to a set of data. Estimation of the model displayed in Fig. 6.2 revealed that the model is reasonably consistent with the observed data, $\chi^2(25, N = 351) = 109.12, p < .001$, CFI = .95.

Individual parameter estimates are displayed in Table 6.4. Looking to the left side in the top panel of Table 6.4, the loadings of the NEO-PI and IAS-B5 scores on the five factors are large and statistically significant. There is some tendency for the IAS-B5 to dominate the Openness and Agreeableness factors and the NEO-PI to dominate the Neuroticism factor; however, the overall pattern of loadings is clearly consistent with expectations. On the right side in the top panel are the estimates of the correlations among errors. Of note is the fact that the correlations among errors associated with the NEO-PI are uniformly high, whereas only 3 of the 10 correlations among errors associated with the IAS-B5 were significant. In the middle panel of Table 6.4 are the estimates of the correlations among the Big Five factors. Note that 9 of the 10 correlations are significant and that the Extraversion factor is moderately correlated with each of the remaining four factors. Finally, displayed in the bottom panel of Table 6.4 are the correlations between the Big Five factors and the personality disorders. Though the relations between dependent and schizoid and the Big Five are relatively uniform, the pattern of correlations between antisocial personality and the Big Five are not. Consistent with results of the analysis by Wiggins and Pincus (1989), our analyses show that antisocial personality scores are unrelated to Neuroticism, Extraversion, and Openness, but moderately negatively correlated with Agreeableness and Conscientiousness.

TABLE 6.4
Completely Standardized Maximum Likelihood Solution

	Factor Loadings					Error Correlations								
	1	2	3	4	5	1	2	3	4	5	6	7	8	9
NEO-PI														
1. neu	.98***	0	0	0	0									
2. ext	0	.76***	0	0	0	.23								
3. ope	0	0	.57***	0	0	.84***	.58***							
4. agr	0	0	0	.48***	0	-.55***	.66***	.42***						
5. con	0	0	0	0	.78***	-.70**	.42***	.29***	.42***					
IAS-B5														
6. neu	.61***	0	0	0	0	0	0	0	0	0				
7. dom	0	.80***	0	0	0	0	0	0	0	0	-.04			
8. ope	0	0	.95***	0	0	0	0	0	0	0	0	.23		
9. nur	0	0	0	.93***	0	0	0	0	0	0	.16	-.77***	.50**	
10. con	0	0	0	0	.87***	0	0	0	0	0	.24**	-.06	-.39	.09
													-.10	

Correlations among personality factors

	1	2	3	4	5
1. neu					
2. ext	-.42***				
3. ope	-.11	.35***			
4. agr	-.14*	.31***	.35***		
5. con	-.15*	.25***	.14*	.34***	

Correlations between personality factors and personality disorders

	1	2	3	4	5
ant	.09	-.06	-.04	-.41***	-.26***
dep	.43***	-.30***	-.24***	-.15**	-.20***
sch	.19**	-.42***	-.13*	-.33***	-.16**

Note: neu = Neuroticism; ext = Extraversion; ope = Openness to Experience; agr = Agreeableness; con = Conscientiousness; dom = Dominance; nur = Nurturance; ant = Antisocial; dep = Dependent; sch = Schizoid. Values of 0 were fixed a priori. $N = 351$.
*$p < .05$. **$p < .01$. ***$p < .001$.

Model Comparisons. Although our model is consistent with the observed data, there may be additional, perhaps more parsimonious, models that account for the data equally well (Breckler, 1990). By imposing various constraints on the model shown in Fig. 6.2, we produced plausible alternative models that are nested in the full model and, therefore, can be statistically compared using chi-square difference test ($\Delta\chi^2$). We first compared the full model to one in which the correlations among factors are constrained to zero, a model consistent with varimax rotation of exploratory factor solutions. Those constraints resulted in a significant decline in overall fit, $\Delta\chi^2(10, N = 351) = 117.09, p < .001$. Moreover, the CFI value for that model was only .88. We next compared the full model to one in which the correlations among within-battery errors were constrained to zero. Those constraints also resulted in a significant decline in overall fit, $\Delta\chi^2(20, N = 351) = 362.59, p < .001$; the value of CFI for that model was .74. Finally, we examined the fit of a model in which the correlations among the Big Five factors were constrained to zero, and the correlations among within-battery errors were constrained to zero. This model is of particular interest because it can be thought of as representing the status quo in analyses of interbattery personality data: the assumption of orthogonal factors and the neglect of method variance. The model failed to account for the relations in the observed data, $\chi^2(55, N = 351) = 642.39, p < .001$, CFI = .64 and provided a much poorer account of the data than the model that included correlated personality factors and correlated within-battery errors, $\Delta\chi^2(30, N = 351) = 533.27, p < .001$.

Finally, we conducted an informal comparison between the structure supported by the CFA and the structure indicated by a joint factor analysis, as might be typically conducted with such data. Factors were extracted using both principal-components and principal-factors methods and rotated to both varimax (orthogonal) and promax (oblique) criteria. Before describing the EFA five-factor solution, we should note that the principal-components analysis produced four eigenvalues greater than 1.0, and the principal-factors analysis produced three eigenvalues greater than 1.0. Thus, an uninformed examination of the solutions would not likely lead one to rotate five factors. Nevertheless, as is customary, we rotated five factors. The solution was similar regardless of extraction or rotation method: Although one pair of indicators loaded prominently on each factor, there were between two and four double loadings ($> |.30|$) and several off-loadings between $|.20|$ and $|.30|$. Thus, whereas the CFA produced a clear picture of the complexities of the structure in the interbattery data, the joint factor analysis produced some doubts about the five-factor structure.

The Role of Exogenous Variables. Ours is not the first interbattery analysis to include exogenous variables. For instance, Wiggins and Pincus (1989) assessed the Big Five personality factors and several personality disorders each with two batteries, then submitted the entire complement of scores to a principal-components analysis. The resultant solution consisted of components defined by both

6. STRUCTURAL MODELS FOR MULTIMODE DESIGNS 133

personality factors and personality disorders and was interpreted as representing the contribution of the personality disorders to the structure of personality. The approach we have demonstrated is an alternative to the analysis by Wiggins and Pincus and, we believe, provides a useful method for relating the Big Five factors of personality and personality disorder. Of course, a more complete model would include multiple measures of the exogenous variables so that the structure of personality disorder controlling for method variance could be evaluated in the context of the model.

SUMMARY AND CONCLUSIONS

In this chapter, we have presented two general strategies for evaluating multimode designs in personality. We first considered structural models for correlational data with an emphasis on crossed designs (e.g., across batteries, time, and source). Next, an exploratory analysis strategy for evaluating Big Five structure across assessment methods was demonstrated. Finally, similar structural issues were considered employing confirmatory structural models.

We feel that a strength of the external referent, multimode emphasis suggested at the outset of this chapter is to encourage investigators of personality and developmental personality to think critically about the designs typically employed in their research. Designs employed in personality and temperament research are often multimode (and when they are not, they should be; cf. Funder, 1991), in that they generally include data obtained from more than one assessment method (e.g., multiple measures of an underlying construct), from more than one period of time (e.g., temperament assessments made in infancy and in early childhood), and/or from more than one source (e.g., self- and other-ratings on personality attributes). We have argued that one can think of these data as arising from designs with crossed modes where modes refers to informants, measures, and time in the three examples provided.

An exploratory approach to multimode data, which isolates structural components due to construct invariance, controlling for other modes, was presented using Tucker's (1958) interbattery factor analysis model. Here, we take the view that a more accurate, but not necessarily more clearly interpretable, description of structural hypotheses with multimode data will be obtained when variability irrelevant to the initial question is excluded. To the extent that method variance represents an interesting aspect of a research question, this external referent position that we adopt will be less appropriate.

The exploratory example, which compared Big Five factor structure across two batteries (statement- versus adjective-based self-reports), showed how this method can be operationalized and the nature of the factor solution when only construct-related variance is analyzed. The analysis allowed a more direct and appropriate link between research question and analysis strategy, but did not uncover a more "clean" view of the underlying Big Five structure, compared to the joint factor analysis approach. We also demonstrated how the predicted factor solution emerges when just method variance is considered.

We then provided an empirical example from a confirmatory perspective of how multimode designs in personality and temperament can be addressed. This dataset related two Big Five batteries, as well as the exogenous personality disorder variables. Our intention was not simply to suggest that these methods might be used in personality and temperament research—such a recommendation would be "old news" at this date. Structural equation modeling-based approaches can be employed in a complementary way to the exploratory methods earlier outlined. A strength of both approaches is their concentration on modeling variability due to mode-specific sources.

In both of our interbattery factor analytic and the confirmatory factor analytic examples we found that a five-factor solution was reasonable, but that: (1) within-battery variability is considerable; and (2) the five factors are by no means orthogonal, as is implied by the continual use of the varimax rotation in exploratory analyses. When both interbattery datasets were analyzed without regard to the presence of within-battery variance (i.e., using a joint factor analysis), a four-factor, not a five-factor, solution was retained. This latter result suggests that basic issues such as the dimensionality of the personality space described by the batteries may be at issue when design features are not taken into consideration.

Although our focus has been exclusively in the domain of personality structure, we feel these ideas are equally relevant for the study of temperament. For example, Lerner (1986) discussed dimensional models of temperament, and Windle (1989) employed confirmatory factor analytic methods to provide critical evaluation of Lerner's model. Similar strategies can and have been adopted in tests of other temperament models (cf. Goldsmith, Rieser-Danner, & Briggs, 1991).

A more important contribution that we hope might be made concerns strategic analyses of personality and temperament data. As noted by Funder (1991), it is likely that future work in personality is likely to incorporate multiple modes of observation. Whereas Funder focuses on the actor–observer design mode, other modes are equally plausible within study designs. For example, longitudinal research and design has long been of interest to personality and temperament research (e.g., Block, 1971), with corresponding interest in statistical methods for analyzing such data (e.g., Collins & Horn, 1991; Harris, 1963; Von Eye, 1990). Methods for analyzing longitudinal data can be easily incorporated into the models we have discussed. In fact, all of these models can be considered as special cases of the multimode data methods discussed in the 1950s by Tucker and presented in more recent statistical literature by Coppi and Bolasco (1989).

Much effort is typically expended in collecting high-quality data from across multiple observational modes, whether they involve multiple measures, multiple time points, and/or multiple informants. However, strategies for analyzing the data that emanate from these designs do not always optimize the available information. We hope the ideas discussed in this chapter help to provide an introductory framework for understanding the structural models and hypotheses that are central to contemporary work in personality and temperament research.

ACKNOWLEDGMENTS

We wish to thank Chuck Halverson for inviting us to prepare this chapter and for his valuable editorial suggestions. Thanks also to Bill Graziano for clarifying our thinking throughout this chapter and Tom Widiger for useful comments on an earlier draft. Some of the ideas in this chapter were presented by A. T. Panter at the 1992 Nags Head Conference on Personality and Social Behavior, Highland Beach, Florida. J. S. Tanaka gratefully acknowledged the support provided to him through the University Scholars program at the University of Illinois. R. H. Hoyle was supported by a fellowship from the University of Kentucky Fund for Excellence during the preparation of the chapter.

REFERENCES

American Psychiatric Association. (1987). *Diagnostic and statistical manual of mental disorders* (3rd rev. ed.). Washington, DC: American Psychiatric Association.

Anderson, J., & Gerbing, D. W. (1984). The effects of sampling error on convergence, improper solutions, and goodness-of-fit indices for maximum likelihood factor analysis. *Psychometrika, 49*, 155–173.

Bank, L., Dishion, T., Skinner, M., & Patterson, G. R. (1990). Method variance in structural equation modeling: Living with "glop." In G. R. Patterson (Ed.), *Depression and aggression in family interaction* (pp. 247–279). Hillsdale, NJ: Lawrence Erlbaum Associates.

Bentler, P. M. (1989). *EQS structural equations program manual.* Los Angeles: BMDP Statistical Software.

Bentler, P. M. (1990). Comparative fit indexes in structural models. *Psychological Bulletin, 107*, 238–246.

Block, J. (1971). *Lives through time.* Berkeley, CA: Bancroft.

Block, J. (1989). Critique of the act frequency approach to personality. *Journal of Personality and Social Psychology, 56*, 234–245.

Borkenau, P., & Ostendorf, F. (1990). Comparing exploratory and confirmatory factor analysis: A study on the five-factor model of personality. *Personality and Individual Differences, 11*, 515–524.

Bollen, K. A. (1989). *Structural equations with latent variables.* New York: Wiley.

Breckler, S. J. (1990). Applications of covariance structure modeling in psychology: Cause for concern? *Psychological Bulletin, 107*, 260–273.

Briggs, S. R. (1992). Assessing the five-factor model of personality description. *Journal of Personality, 60*, 252–293.

Browne, M. W. (1979). The maximum-likelihood solution in interbattery factor analysis. *British Journal of Mathematical and Statistical Psychology, 32*, 75–86.

Browne, M. W. (1980). Factor analysis of multiple batteries by maximum likelihood. *British Journal of Mathematical and Statistical Psychology, 33*, 184–199.

Campbell, D. T., & Fiske, D. W. (1959). Convergent and discriminant validation by the multitrait-multimethod matrix. *Psychological Bulletin, 56*, 81–105.
Collins, L. M., & Horn, J. L. (Eds.). (1991). *Best methods for the analysis of change.* Washington, DC: American Psychological Association.
Coppi, R., & Bolasco, S. (Eds.). (1989). *Multiway data analysis.* Amsterdam: North-Holland.
Costa, P. T., & McCrae, R. R. (1985). *The NEO Personality Inventory manual.* Odessa, FL: Psychological Assessment Resources.
Cudeck, R. (1982). Methods for estimating between-battery factors. *Multivariate Behavioral Research, 17*, 47–68.
Digman, J. M. (1989). Five robust trait dimensions: Development, stability, and utility. *Journal of Personality, 57*, 195–214.
Digman, J. M. (1990). Personality structure: Emergence of the five-factor model. *Annual Review of Psychology, 41*, 417–440.
Escofier, B., & Pages, J. (1989). Multiple factor analysis: Results of a three-year utilization. In R. Coppi & S. Bolasco (Eds.), *Multiway data analysis* (pp. 277–285). Amsterdam: North Holland.
Funder, D. C. (1991). Global traits: A neo-Allportian approach to personality. *Psychological Science, 2*, 31–39.
Funder, D. C., & West, S. G. (Eds.). (1993). Viewpoints on personality: Consensus, self-other agreement, and accuracy in personality judgment. *Journal of Personality, 61.*
Goldberg, L. R. (1992). The development of markers of the Big-Five factor structure. *Psychological Assessment, 4*, 26–42.
Goldsmith, H. H., Rieser-Danner, L. A., & Briggs, S. (1991). Evaluating convergent and discriminant validity of temperament questionnaires for preschoolers, toddlers, and infants. *Developmental Psychology, 27*, 566–579.
Graziano, W. G., & Eisenberg, N. H. (in press). Agreeableness: A dimension of personality. In S. Briggs, R. Hogan, & W. Jones (Eds.), *Handbook of personality psychology.* San Diego: Academic Press.
Hakstian, A. R., & Cattell, R. B. (1978). An examination of inter-domain relationships among some ability and personality traits. *Educational and Psychological Measurement, 38*, 275–290.
Harris, C. W. (Ed.). (1963). *Problems in measuring change.* Madison: University of Wisconsin.
Hofstee, W. K. B., DeRaad, B., & Goldberg, L. R. (1992). Integration of the Big Five and circumplex approaches to trait structure. *Journal of Personality and Social Psychology, 63*, 146–163.
Huba, G. J., Newcomb, M. D., & Bentler, P. M. (1981). Comparison of canonical correlation and interbattery factor analysis on sensation seeking and drug use domains. *Applied Psychological Measurement, 5*, 291–306.
Hundal, P. S., & Horn, J. L. (1977). On the relationships between short-term learning and fluid and crystallized intelligence. *Applied Psychological Measurement, 1*, 11–21.
Hyler, S. E., & Rieder, R. O. (1987). *PDQ-R: Personality Diagnostic Questionnaire-Revised.* New York: New York State Psychiatric Institute.
John, O. P. (1990). The "Big Five" factor taxonomy: Dimensions of personality in the natural language and in questionnaires. In L. A. Pervin (Ed.), *Handbook of personality: Theory and research* (pp. 66–100). New York: Guilford.
Jones, E. E., & Nisbett, R. E. (1971). *The actor and the observer: Divergent perceptions of the causes of behavior.* Morristown, NJ: General Learning.
Kenny, D. A. (1991). A general model of consensus and accuracy in interpersonal perception. *Psychological Review, 98*, 155–163.
Kenny, D. A., & Kashy, D. A. (1992). Analysis of the multitrait-multimethod matrix by confirmatory factor analysis. *Psychological Bulletin, 112*, 165–172.
Kojima, H. (1975). Inter-battery factor analysis of parents' and childrens' reports of parental behavior. *Japanese Psychological Research, 17*, 33–48.
Lerner, R. M. (1986). *Concepts and theories of human development* (2nd ed.) New York: Random House.

MacCallum, R. C., Roznowski, M., & Necowitz, L. B. (1992). Model modifications in covariance structure analysis: The problem of capitalization on chance. *Psychological Bulletin, 111*, 490–504.

Marsh, H. W. (1989). Confirmatory factor analyses of multitrait-multimethod data: Many problems and a few solutions. *Applied Psychological Measurement, 13*, 335–361.

Marsh, H. W., & Hocevar, D. (1983). Confirmatory factor analysis of multitrait-multimethod matrices. *Journal of Educational Measurement, 20*, 231–248.

McCrae, R. R. (1989). Why I advocate the five-factor model: Joint factor analyses of the NEO-PI with other instruments. In D. M. Buss & N. Cantor (Eds.), *Personality psychology* (pp. 236–245). New York: Springer-Verlag.

McCrae, R. R. (1990). Traits and trait names: How well is Openness represented in natural languages? *European Journal of Personality, 4*, 119–129.

McCrae, R. R., & Costa, P. T. (1985). Updating Norman's "adequate taxonomy": Intelligence and personality dimensions in natural language and in questionnaires. *Journal of Personality and Social Psychology, 49*, 710–721.

McCrae, R. R., & Costa, P. T. (1987). Validation of the five-factor model of personality across instruments and observers. *Journal of Personality and Social Psychology, 52*, 81–90.

McCrae, R. R., & John, O. P. (1992). An introduction to the five-factor model and its applications. *Journal of Personality, 60*, 175–215.

Mosteller, F., & Tukey, J. W. (1977). *Data analysis and regression.* Reading, MA: Addison-Wesley.

Romer, D., & Revelle, W. (1984). Personality traits: Fact or fiction? A critique of the Shweder and D'Andrade systematic distortion hypothesis. *Journal of Personality and Social Psychology, 47*, 1028–1042.

Royce, J. R., & Powell, A. (1983). *Theory of personality and individual differences: Factors, systems, and processes.* Englewood Cliffs, NJ: Prentice-Hall.

Rudinger, G., & Dommel, N. (1986). An example of convergent and discriminant validity of personality questionnaires. In A. Angleitner & J. S. Wiggins (Eds.), *Personality assessment by questionnaires: Current issues in theory and measurement* (pp. 214–234). Berlin: Springer Verlag.

Schwarzer, R. (1986). Evaluation of convergent and discriminant validity by use of structural equations. A. Angleitner & J. S. Wiggins (Eds.), *Personality assessment by questionnaires: Current issues in theory and measurement* (pp. 191–213). Berlin: Springer-Verlag.

Strauman, T. J., & Wetzler, S. (1992). The factor structure of the SCL-90 and MCMI scale scores. *Multivariate Behavioral Research, 27*, 1–20.

Tanaka, J. S. (1993). Multifaceted conceptions of fit in structural equation models. In K. A. Bollen & J. S. Long (Eds.), *Testing structural equation models* (pp. 10–39). Newbury Park, CA: Sage.

Tanaka, J. S., Panter, A. T., & Winborne, W. C. (1987). Associations between daydreaming style and information processing predispositions. *Imagination, Cognition, and Personality, 6*, 161–168.

Tanaka, J. S., Panter, A. T., Winborne, W. C., & Huba, G. J. (1990). Theory testing in personality and social psychology with latent variable models. *Review of Personality and Social Psychology, 11*, 217–242.

Tanaka, J. S., & Westerman, M. A. (1988). Common dimensions in the assessment of competence in school-aged girls. *Journal of Educational Psychology, 4*, 579–584.

Thorndike, R. M., & Weiss, D. J. (1973). A study of the stability of canonical correlations and canonical components. *Educational and Psychological Measurement, 33*, 123–134.

Thurstone, L. L. (1947). *Multiple factor analysis.* Chicago: University of Chicago.

Thurstone, L. L., & Thurstone, T. G. (1941). Factorial studies of intelligence. *Psychometric Monographs*, No. 2.

Trapnell, P., & Wiggins, J. S. (1988). *Extension of the Interpersonal Adjective Scales to include the Big Five dimensions of personality (IASR-B5).* Unpublished manuscript, University of British Columbia, Vancouver, Canada.

Tucker, L. R. (1958). An inter-battery method of factor analysis. *Psychometrika, 23*, 111–136.

Von Eye, A. (Ed.). (1990). *Statistical methods in longitudinal research.* New York: Academic Press.

West, S. G., & Graziano, W. G. (Eds.). (1989). Long-term stability and change in personality. *Journal of Personality, 57*.

Widiger, T. A., & Trull, T. J. (1992). Personality and psychopathology: An application of the five factor model. *Journal of Personality, 60*, 363–393.

Widaman, K. F. (1985). Hierarchically nested covariance structure models for multitrait-multimethod data. *Applied Psychological Measurement, 9*, 1–26.

Wiggins, J., & Pincus, A. (1989). Conceptions of personality disorders and dimensions of personality. *Psychological Assessment: A Journal of Consulting and Clinical Psychology, 1*, 305–316.

Windle, M. (1989). A factorial replications study of the adult Revised Dimensions of Temperament Survey. *Journal of Personality Assessment, 53*, 685–692.

Winer, B. J. (1971). *Statistical principles in experimental design* (2nd ed.). New York: McGraw-Hill.

CHAPTER

7

STABILITY AND CHANGE IN PERSONALITY FROM ADOLESCENCE THROUGH ADULTHOOD

Paul T. Costa, Jr.
Robert R. McCrae
Gerontology Research Center
National Institute on Aging, NIH

The study of development normally presupposes an understanding of the fully developed individual. In normative studies, adult structure dictates the variables that developmentalists must attend to: A theory of language acquisition, for example, must be able to account for the mastery of grammatical rules that competent adult speakers show. In studies of individual differences, adult status is the ultimate criterion that developmental variables must predict: Adult vocabulary scores might be the outcome in a study of educational enrichment.

But until recently, psychologists concerned with the development of personality were in the unfortunate position of not knowing exactly what they were supposed to explain. There was little consensus on the structure of adult personality and almost no information on when, if ever, personality should be considered fully developed. Many of the chapters in this book provide arguments for the superiority of the five-factor model of personality as a guide to the structure of personality traits in adults; they imply that theories of personality development must explain the emergence of Neuroticism (N), Extraversion (E), Openness (O), Agreeableness (A), and Conscientiousness (C). Our purpose here is to present evidence on stability and change in these five factors, and to suggest that personality development is not complete until the end of the decade of the 20s.

THE STRUCTURAL INVARIANCE OF PERSONALITY

Before considering change or stability in individuals' standing on a set of trait dimensions, it is first necessary to establish the cross-time invariance of the dimensions themselves. This is a particularly complex issue in the early years of development. It is probably meaningless to ask if there is a general increase or decrease in Conscientiousness between 1 and 6 months of age, because adult traits such as dutifulness, organization, and achievement striving are not relevant to the behavior of infants. Basic dimensions of infant temperament may be precursors of the five adult personality factors, but in this case, we might better speak of continuity than of high or low stability.

Several studies (e.g., Digman & Inouye, 1986; Graziano & Ward, 1992) have recovered the five-factor structure in adults' ratings of school children. Although the results have generally (and plausibly) been interpreted as evidence that children's personality shows the same structure as adults', the fact that the data are ratings by adults makes other interpretations possible. After all, as Passini and Norman (1966) demonstrated, the five factors can be recovered in ratings of complete strangers through the operation of implicit personality theories. The same might be true of ratings of children. Validation of child personality factors through behavioral observation or studies of cross-observer agreement would be useful.

Personality structure in adults is usually measured by self-report inventories. The reliability and validity of self-report scales is questionable in children under age 10 (H. J. Eysenck & S. B. G. Eysenck, 1975), perhaps because the self-concept is poorly defined at that age. By adolescence, however, self-report is a useful technique, and studies on the structure of personality in junior high and high school students could probably be conducted with the same instruments that have been used for adults.

By college age, the similarity of adolescent and adult personality structure is clear. Table 7.1 reports a factor analysis of data from the college-age normative sample for the Revised NEO Personality Inventory (NEO–PI–R; Costa & McCrae, 1992b). Five factors had eigenvalues greater than 1.0; after varimax rotation, all NEO–PI–R facet scales loaded on the intended factor, and 28 had their highest loading there. Coefficients of congruence between this factor structure and that found in the analysis of the adult normative sample (Costa & McCrae, 1992b) range from .94 to .98. The small deviations from the adult structure could be largely corrected by a 15° rotation of the E and A factors. Variations in the placement of these two axes of the interpersonal circumplex (McCrae & Costa, 1989) are common and probably unrelated to the age of the sample.

This finding is hardly surprising. Goldberg's (1990, 1992) studies of trait adjectives have repeatedly recovered the five factors in self-reports from college students. Costa, McCrae, and Dye (1991) showed that the same factor structure for the NEO–PI–R was found in adults age 21 to 29 and adults 30 to 64, and

TABLE 7.1
Factor Analysis of Revised NEO Personality Inventory (NEO–PI–R)
Facet Scales in the College-Age Normative Sample

NEO–PI–R Scale	Varimax-Rotated Principal Component				
	N	E	O	A	C
Neuroticism (N) Facets:					
N1: Anxiety	.80				
N2: Angry Hostility	.61			−.51	
N3: Depression	.79				
N4: Self-Consciousness	.69				
N5: Impulsiveness	.60				
N6: Vulnerability	.76				
Extraversion (E) Facets:					
E1: Warmth		.83			
E2: Gregariousness		.75			
E3: Assertiveness		.46		−.53	
E4: Activity		.49			.45
E5: Excitement Seeking		.60			
E6: Positive Emotions		.72			
Openness (O) Facets:					
O1: Fantasy			.55		
O2: Aesthetics			.75		
O3: Feelings	.49		.53		
O4: Actions			.68		
O5: Ideas			.72		
O6: Values			.53		
Agreeableness (A) Facets					
A1: Trust		.47		.47	
A2: Straightforwardness				.71	
A3: Altruism		.58		.52	
A4: Compliance				.75	
A5: Modesty				.62	
A6: Tender-Mindedness				.51	
Conscientiousness (C) Facets:					
C1: Competence					.75
C2: Order					.64
C3: Dutifulness					.71
C4: Achievement Striving					.83
C5: Self-Discipline					.81
C6: Deliberation					.70

Note. N = 148 male, 241 female college students age 17 to 20. All loadings ≥ .40 in absolute magnitude are reported.

Costa and McCrae (1992a) recovered the NEO–PI–R's factor structure in a third group age 19 to 96. The structure of personality appears to be invariant, at least from adolescence through adulthood.

PERSONALITY CHANGES IN THE DECADE OF THE 20s

Questions of structure and stability are largely independent. It is possible that individuals could change their standing on basic dimensions of personality repeatedly without affecting the factor structure of trait measures at any given time. Stressful life events, for example, might make one higher in characteristic levels of anxiety, anger, and depression, whereas psychotherapy might lower one's standing on all these traits. But the covariation of anxiety with anger and depression would remain, and it is this covariation that defines Neuroticism, one of the five basic factors.

If status on the five personality factors changed often and unpredictably, like mood, it would hardly make sense to study its "development" at all. In fact, however, we know that—barring such catastrophes as Alzheimer's disease (Siegler et al., 1991)—people do not change dramatically in their standing on basic dimensions after they reach adulthood. Like intelligence and height, personality traits appear to have a point of full maturity. This fact was clear sometime ago (Costa & McCrae, 1980), and has been consistently supported by subsequent longitudinal studies (McCrae & Costa, 1990). The major issue has been determining precisely when personality reaches maturity.

During the 1960s and 1970s, the concept of adult development was popular, and belief in continuing personality growth was fueled not only by the theories of Jung (1933) and Erikson (1950), but also by the empirical findings of Vaillant (1977), who showed increasing maturity of defenses in three periods of life, and Whitbourne and Waterman (1979), who demonstrated changes in psychosocial maturity in a college sample recontacted 10 years later. These findings were at odds with our own research, which had shown predominant stability in men over age 25 (Costa & McCrae, 1978). It was not clear at that time whether the differences were due to the age of the subjects or the nature of the variables measured.

After the publication of the NEO–PI (Costa & McCrae, 1985), the instrument began to be used in college samples; several investigators reported that their groups differed noticeably from the published adult norms. Data from four different college samples showed consistent trends across colleges and gender: Young people were higher on N, E, and O scales, and lower on A and C scales (Costa & McCrae, 1989). The most marked difference was on the Excitement Seeking facet of E, which was almost two standard deviations higher in students than in older adults. A subsequent analysis of data from a college-age military recruit sample suggested that most of these differences were not restricted to college students: Individuals in late adolescence appear to be more intensely emotional (high N and E) and less socialized (low A and C) than older adults (Costa & McCrae, in press), regardless of educational status.

In preparing a revision of the NEO-PI that provides new facet scales for A and C, we obtained data from a large employment sample (Costa, McCrae, & Dye, 1991) and from two new college samples. The college students ranged in age from 17 to 20; the employment sample subjects were subdivided into a group age 21 to 29 and a group age 30 to 64. Figures 7.1 and 7.2 show the mean values of the three groups plotted on adult male and female norms; in these large samples, most differences are significant.

The results are remarkably consistent. The same pattern is seen for men and for women, and replicates findings from our earlier sample (Costa & McCrae, 1989). Adolescents are higher in N and E and lower in A and C than older adults. Men and women in their 20s are in most cases intermediate between adolescents and mature adults, suggesting a smooth developmental progression.

These are cross-sectional comparisons, and it is possible that they reflect recent generational changes. Several longitudinal studies have covered roughly the same age period, and provide a check on our findings. Mortimer, Finch, and Kumka (1982) studied the self-concept of 368 men as college freshmen and again at 10

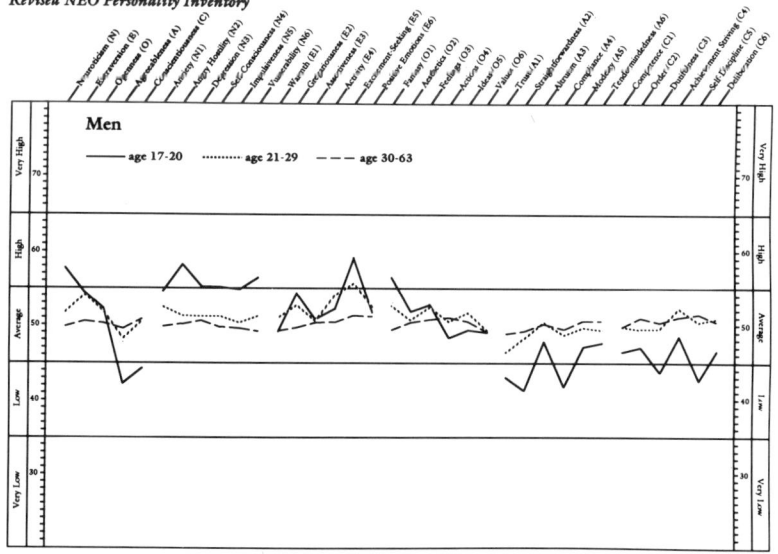

FIG. 7.1. Mean NEO-PI-R scale scores for 148 men age 17 to 20, 271 men age 21 to 29, and 272 men age 30 to 63. Reproduced by special permission of the publisher, Psychological Assessment Resources, Inc., 16204 North Florida Avenue, Lutz, Florida 33549, from the NEO Personality Inventory-Revised, by Paul Costa and Robert McCrae, Copyright © 1978, 1985, 1989, 1992 by PAR, Inc. Further reproduction is prohibited without permission of PAR, Inc.

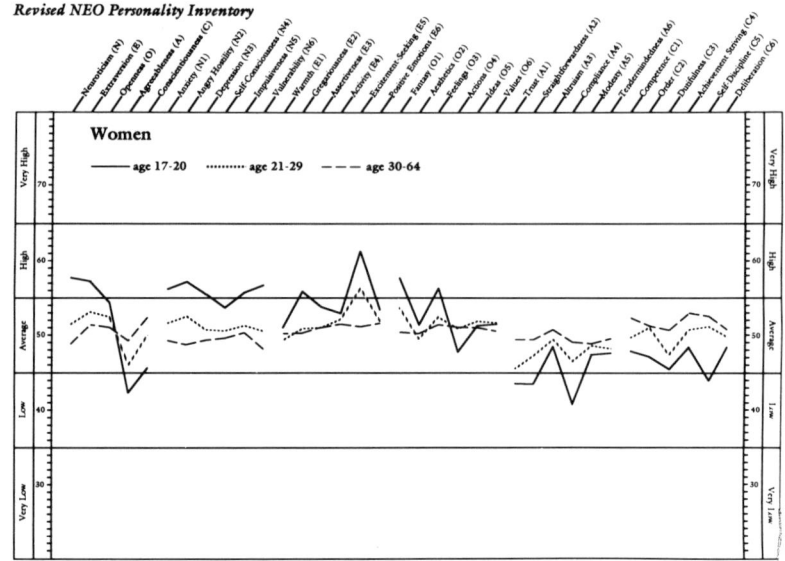

FIG. 7.2. Mean NEO-PI-R scale scores for 241 women age 17 to 20, 445 women age 21 to 29, and 551 women age 30 to 64. Reproduced by special permission of the publisher, Psychological Assessment Resources, Inc., 16204 North Florida Avenue, Lutz, Florida 33549, from the NEO Personality Inventory-Revised, by Paul Costa and Robert McCrae, Copyright © 1978, 1985, 1989, 1992 by PAR, Inc. Further reproduction is prohibited without permission of PAR, Inc.

years after graduation. Haan, Millsap, and Hartka (1986) reported California Q-Set (CQS) data on 118 men and women over a long period, including an interval from high school to the mid-30s. Jessor (1983) conducted a follow-up of 596 junior high and college students when in their mid-20s. Helson and Moane examined California Psychological Inventory (CPI; Gough, 1987) scores for 81 college seniors at a women's college followed at age 27 and 43.

Although these various investigators used different instruments and somewhat different segments of the lifespan, many similarities to the present cross-sectional findings can be found. Figures 7.1 and 7.2 show lower N scores for older adults, suggesting better psychological adjustment; these age differences are paralleled in longitudinal age changes: Mortimer et al. reported an increase in well-being, Jessor found that alienation decreased, and Helson and Moane found that CPI Self-control (a scale negatively related to NEO–PI-R Angry Hostility and Impulsiveness; see McCrae, Costa, & Piedmont, 1993) increased. Our data show lowered E, Mortimer found declines in Sociability. The higher levels of A seen in our samples resemble the increased warmth that Haan et al. reported and may be related to the decline in social criticism noted by Jessor. Finally, our age differences in C are also seen in an increased value on achievement (Jessor,

1983), increased competence (Mortimer et al., 1982), and increased dependability (Haan et al., 1986). Jessor (1983) summarized these trends by noting that "the course of personality development across the developmental and historical interval examined is theoretically away from involvement in problem behavior and toward commitment to conventional behavior" (p. 329). Vaillant (1977) and Whitbourne and Waterman (1979) might say there is increasing maturity.

THE STABILITY OF INDIVIDUAL DIFFERENCES

The discussion so far has focused on normative age trends that affect adolescents as a group, such as the general decline in excitement seeking that occurs with age. But stability and change can also be examined in terms of the rank ordering of individuals: Do those who are highest in excitement seeking in college remain highest, relative to their peers, at age 40? Or, having sown their wild oats early, are they the most settled and staid? These questions require longitudinal samples measured on at least two occasions.

A simple generalization seems to be that the older the individual, the higher the retest stability for a given interval. Jessor (1983) reported 7-year retest correlations for 13 personality variables in a high school sample and a college sample; the median correlations were .25 and .23 for male and female high school students, and .35 and .34 for college students. Haan et al. (1986) found median retest correlations on rated CQS dimensions of .40 for the interval from 17 to mid-30s; the same dimensions in the same sample showed a median retest correlation of .52 in a subsequent 10-year follow-up, and .55 in a further 14-year follow-up. Finn (1986) examined 30-year stability coefficients for Minnesota Multiphasic Personality Inventory (MMPI) factor scales and found a median coefficient of .35 for the group who were initially college students. By contrast, the median 30-year coefficient was .56 for a group initially assessed in their 40s. Helson and Moane (1987) reported retest correlations on CPI scales of .50 or above "for 15 of 20 scales between ages 21 and 27 and on 16 scales between ages 27 and 43, even though the latter correlations span a period about three times as long" (p. 179). In a subsequent 9-year follow-up of this sample, Helson and Wink (1992) noted that all the CPI scales except Communality showed stability coefficients above .56, with a median of .73.

Siegler et al. (1990) used path analysis to estimate the stability of personality from college to mid-40s. Cross-lagged correlations between college MMPI scales and NEO–PI factors measured 24 years later were compared to contemporaneous MMPI/NEO–PI correlations in a second sample. The cross-lagged correlations were about half as large as the contemporaneous correlations, suggesting that about half the variance in individual differences was stable from college on. Conversely, almost half the variance was not stable: College students have not yet reached the final configuration of their adult personality.

THE STABILITY OF PERSONALITY IN LATER ADULTHOOD

The generalization that individuals become increasingly stable with age has a limit: By about age 30, maximal stability is shown. Costa, McCrae, and Arenberg (1980) examined the 12-year retest stability of 10 Guilford–Zimmerman Temperament Survey (GZTS; J. S. Guilford, Zimmerman, & J. P. Guilford, 1976) scales in young (20–44), middle-aged (45–59), and older (60–76) men. The median stability coefficients for the three groups were .72, .75, and .73. Similarly, Costa and McCrae (1988) compared 6-year stability coefficients on NEO–PI scales for men and women age 25 to 56 versus 57 to 84. The median values were .74 and .74 for the younger groups, .75 and .69 for the older. In each of these studies, the number of subjects under age 30 was too small for a separate analysis; smaller correlations would probably have been seen in the younger groups if individuals in their 20s had been better represented.

Recently we reported a 7-year longitudinal study of peer ratings on the NEO–PI (Costa & McCrae, 1992c). Our subjects ranged in age from 31 to 81 when the first ratings were obtained. Unlike most longitudinal studies of rated personality (e.g., Field & Millsap, 1991; Haan et al., 1986), in which different raters assess personality at different times, our design used the same raters on both occasions. In addition, we relied on long-term acquaintances rather than on expert raters as our source of data. For the group as a whole, rated personality showed about the same level of stability as is typically seen in self-reports of adults: Stability coefficients for the five NEO–PI domain scores ranged from .63 to .84.

Is there differential stability for younger and older individuals? For subjects initially age 31 to 57, correlations for N, E, O, A, and C were .80, .81, .77, .65, and .78, respectively, $N = 77$, $p < .001$. For subjects initially age 58 to 81, the corresponding figures are .66, .78, .82, .76, and .72, $N = 80$, $p < .001$. There are no significant differences between the five pairs of correlations.

Figure 7.3 illustrates the same point in a different way. Here are the peer-rated domain profiles of the youngest and oldest men and women in the sample. It is clear from inspection that there are few remarkable changes for any of the subjects; the differences from one occasion to the other might well be attributed to chance. In fact, when retest correlations are corrected for retest unreliability, they often approach unity (Costa & McCrae, 1988, 1992c; Costa, McCrae, & Arenberg, 1980). That personality among 60-year-olds is no more stable than personality among 30-year-olds is attributable to a ceiling effect: By age 30, personality is essentially fixed.

Nothing in life is really permanent, however. Although the rate of change in personality apparently does not change after age 30, small changes do accumulate over the life span. Using 20-year retest data on the GZTS, we projected that the stability of true scores would average about .60 over the 50-year period from 30 to 80 (Costa & McCrae, 1992c). About three-fifths of the variance in individual differences in adult personality is apparently stable.

7. STABILITY AND CHANGE

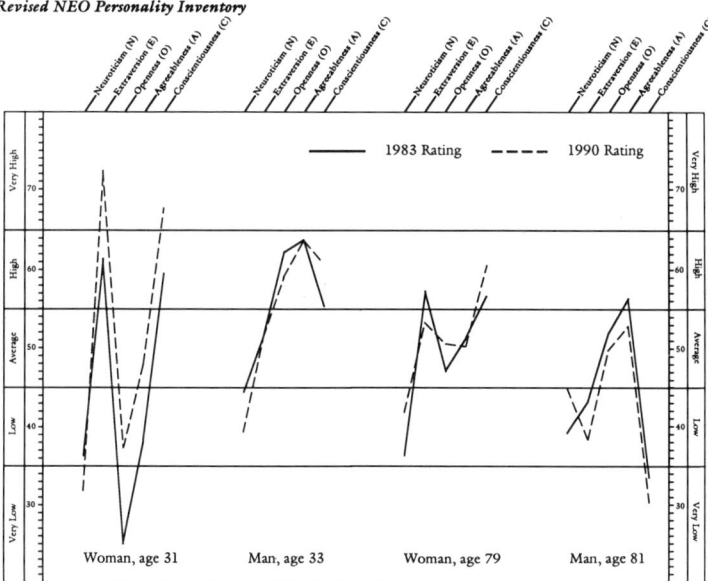

FIG. 7.3. Peer-rated domain profiles for four individuals rated in 1983 and 1990. Reproduced by special permission of the publisher, Psychological Assessment Resources, Inc., 16204 North Florida Avenue, Lutz, Florida 33549, from the NEO Personality Inventory-Revised, by Paul Costa and Robert McCrae, Copyright © 1978, 1985, 1989, 1992 by PAR, Inc. Further reproduction is prohibited without permission of PAR, Inc.

MEAN LEVEL CHANGES IN OLDER ADULTS

Once again, the issue of stability of mean levels must be considered separately. Helson and Wink looked for changes in personality between age 43 and 52 in a sample of 101 women, using the CPI and the Adjective Checklist (Gough & Heilbrun, 1983). Only 5 of the 23 CPI scales showed significant changes, and four of these changes were smaller than one-third standard deviation. A one-half standard deviation decline was found on the CPI Femininity scale. Analyses of the ACL scales showed small decreases in needs for Succorance and Abasement, and small increases in the Favorableness, Dominance, Self-Confidence, and Ideal Self scales, suggesting improved self-esteem and confidence. However, there were no changes in 31 other ACL scales (including Femininity).

Further, the Helson and Wink study is strictly longitudinal, and the results might be attributed to time-of-measurement effects. Perhaps women learned to describe themselves in more positive, less stereotypically feminine terms in the decade of the 1980s. If so, Helson and Wink's 52-year-olds would not differ from 43-year-olds measured at the same time—a cross-sectional analysis. A combination of cross-sectional and longitudinal methods is a better basis for inferring developmental changes (Costa & McCrae, 1982).

In our 6-year longitudinal study of self-reports and spouse ratings on the NEO–PI (Costa & McCrae, 1988), we found that only 3 of 23 scales—Activity, Positive Emotions, and Openness to Actions—changed with age in both cross-sectional and longitudinal analyses. The decline in activity level has been noted by other researchers (Douglas & Arenberg, 1978; Field & Millsap, 1991), and is probably attributable to health problems in the elderly. The declines in Positive Emotions and Openness to Actions were small, with age accounting for less than 10% of the variance in either variable across the age span from 19 to 93.

We do not wish to suggest that the mean levels of all personality variables are fixed after age 30: Small changes may occur in some, such as those noted by Helson and Wink (1992), and these may be theoretically meaningful to the adult developmentalist. But from the perspective of the child psychologist seeking a fixed endpoint, development appears to be essentially finished by age 30. Kagan and Moss (1962), in their classic *Birth to Maturity*, assessed subjects as adults in their mid-20s. Today's longitudinal researchers would be well-advised to wait just a few more years.

ACKNOWLEDGMENTS

Thanks are due to Brian Little, David Watson, and Lee Anna Clark for providing college student data.

REFERENCES

Costa, P. T., Jr., & McCrae, R. R. (1978). Objective personality assessment. In M. Storandt, I. C. Siegler, & M. F. Elias (Eds.), *The clinical psychology of aging* (pp. 119–143). New York: Plenum.

Costa, P. T., Jr., & McCrae, R. R. (1980). Still stable after all these years: Personality as a key to some issues in adulthood and old age. In P. B. Baltes & O. G. Brim, Jr. (Eds.), *Life span development and behavior* (Vol. 3, pp. 65–102). New York: Academic Press.

Costa, P. T., Jr., & McCrae, R. R. (1982). An approach to the attribution of age, period, and cohort effects. *Psychological Bulletin, 92*, 238–250.

Costa, P. T., Jr., & McCrae, R. R. (1985). *The NEO Personality Inventory manual*. Odessa, FL: Psychological Assessment Resources.

Costa, P. T., Jr., & McCrae, R. R. (1988). Personality in adulthood: A 6-year longitudinal study of self-reports and spouse ratings on the NEO Personality Inventory. *Journal of Personality and Social Psychology, 54*, 853–863.

Costa, P. T., Jr., & McCrae, R. R. (1989). *The NEO-PI/NEO-FFI manual supplement*. Odessa, FL: Psychological Assessment Resources.

Costa, P. T., Jr., & McCrae, R. R. (1992a). Four ways five factors are basic. *Personality and Individual Differences, 13*, 653–665.

Costa, P. T., Jr., & McCrae, R. R. (1992b). *Revised NEO Personality Inventory (NEO-PI-R) and NEO Five-Factor Inventory (NEO–FFI) professional manual*. Odessa, FL: Psychological Assessment Resources, Inc.

Costa, P. T., Jr., & McCrae, R. R. (1992c). Trait psychology comes of age. In T. B. Sonderegger (Ed.), *Nebraska symposium on motivation: Psychology and aging* (pp. 169–204). Lincoln, NE: University of Nebraska Press.

Costa, P. T., Jr., & McCrae, R. R. (in press). Longitudinal stability of adult personality. In R. Hogan, J. A. Johnson, & S. R. Briggs (Eds.), *Handbook of personality psychology*. New York: Academic Press.

Costa, P. T., Jr., McCrae, R. R., & Arenberg, D. (1980). Enduring dispositions in adult males. *Journal of Personality and Social Psychology, 38*, 793–800.

Costa, P. T., Jr., McCrae, R. R., & Dye, D. A. (1991). Facet scales for Agreeableness and Conscientiousness: A revision of the NEO Personality Inventory. *Personality and Individual Differences, 12*, 887–898.

Digman, J. M., & Inouye, J. (1986). Further specification of the five robust factors of personality. *Journal of Personality and Social Psychology, 50*, 116–123.

Douglas, K., & Arenberg, D. (1978). Age changes, cohort differences, and cultural change on the Guilford-Zimmerman Temperament Survey. *Journal of Gerontology, 33*, 737–747.

Erikson, E. H. (1950). *Childhood and society.* New York: Norton.

Eysenck, H. J., & Eysenck, S. B. G. (1975). *Manual of the Eysenck Personality Questionnaire.* San Diego: EdITS Publishers.

Field, D., & Millsap, R. E. (1991). Personality in advanced old age: Continuity or change? *Journals of Gerontology: Psychological Sciences, 46*, P299–P308.

Finn, S. E. (1986). Stability of personality self-ratings over 30 years: Evidence for an age/cohort interaction. *Journal of Personality and Social Psychology, 50*, 813–818.

Goldberg, L. R. (1990). An alternative "description of personality": The Big-Five factor structure. *Journal of Personality and Social Psychology, 59*, 1216–1229.

Goldberg, L. R. (1992). The development of markers for the Big-Five factor structure. *Psychological Assessment, 4*, 26–42.

Gough, H. G. (1987). *California Psychological Inventory administrator's guide.* Palo Alto, CA: Consulting Psychologists Press.

Gough, H. G., & Heilbrun, A. B., Jr. (1983). *Adjective Check List manual.* Palo Alto, CA: Consulting Psychologists Press.

Graziano, W. G., & Ward, D. (1992). Probing the Big Five in adolescence: Personality and adjustment during a developmental transition. *Journal of Personality, 60*, 425–439.

Guilford, J. S., Zimmerman, W. S., & Guilford, J. P. (1976). *The Guilford-Zimmerman Temperament Survey Handbook: Twenty-five years of research and application.* San Diego, CA: EdITS Publishers.

Haan, N., Millsap, R., & Hartka, E. (1986). As time goes by: Change and stability in personality over fifty years. *Psychology and Aging, 1*, 220–232.

Helson, R., & Moane, G. (1987). Personality change in women from college to midlife. *Journal of Personality and Social Psychology, 53*, 176–186.

Helson, R., & Wink, P. (1992). Personality change in women from the early 40s to the early 50s. *Psychology and Aging, 7*, 46–55.

Jessor, R. (1983). The stability of change: Psychosocial development from adolescence to young adulthood. In D. Magnusson & V. L. Allen (Eds.), *Human development: An interactional perspective* (pp. 321–341). New York: Academic Press.

Jung, C. G. (1933). *Modern man in search of a soul* (W. S. Dell & C. F. Baynes, Trans.). New York: Harcourt Brace Jovanovich.

Kagan, J., & Moss, H. A. (1962). *From birth to maturity.* New York: Wiley.

McCrae, R. R., & Costa, P. T., Jr. (1989). The structure of interpersonal traits: Wiggins's circumplex and the five-factor model. *Journal of Personality and Social Psychology, 56*, 586–595.

McCrae, R. R., & Costa, P. T., Jr. (1990). *Personality in adulthood.* New York: Guilford.

McCrae, R. R., Costa, P. T., Jr., & Piedmont, R. L. (1993). Folk concepts, natural language, and psychological constructs: The California Psychological Inventory and the five-factor model. *Journal of Personality, 61*, 1–26.

Mortimer, J. T., Finch, M. D., & Kumka, D. (1982). Persistence and change in development: The multidimensional self-concept. In P. B. Baltes & O. G. Brim, Jr. (Eds.), *Life-span development and behavior* (Vol. 4, pp. 264–315). New York: Academic Press.

Passini, F. T., & Norman, W. T. (1966). A universal conception of personality structure? *Journal of Personality and Social Psychology, 4*, 44–49.

Siegler, I. C., Welsh, K. A., Dawson, D. V., Fillenbaum, G. G., Earl, N. L., Kaplan, E. B., & Clark, C. M. (1991). Ratings of personality change in patients being evaluated for memory disorders. *Alzheimer Disease and Associated Disorders, 5*, 240–250.

Siegler, I. C., Zonderman, A. B., Barefoot, J. C., Williams, R. B., Jr., Costa, P. T., Jr., & McCrae, R. R. (1990). Predicting personality in adulthood from college MMPI scores: Implications for follow-up studies in psychosomatic medicine. *Psychosomatic Medicine, 52*, 644–652.

Vaillant, G. E. (1977). *Adaptation to life*. Boston: Little, Brown.

Whitbourne, S. K., & Waterman, A. S. (1979). Psychosocial development during the adult years: Age and cohort comparisons. *Developmental Psychology, 15*, 373–378.

PART

II

EMERGING CONCEPTIONS OF THE CHILDHOOD PRECURSORS OF PERSONALITY STRUCTURE

The study of temperament in childhood has long been dominated by the nine-dimensional structure proposed by Thomas, Chess, and Birch (1968; Thomas & Chess, 1977). Interviews and questionnaires assessing the strength of each of these dimensions were developed by these psychiatrists and by the pediatrician Carey and his co-workers (e.g., 1970). Initially, factor analytic techniques were only used on the correlations among the nine subscale scores, not on the 72 or more individual items. Analysis of the interrelations among the nine subscale scores produced the now famous clusters *difficult, easy,* and *slow-to-warm-up*. When psychologists, however, began to use these same instruments, they questioned the robustness of the nine-dimensional structure. Several large-scale studies in the United States, Europe, Australia, and China have shown that when factor analysis was applied to the intercorrelations among all items, only five to seven factors could be meaningfully extracted. This section opens with the first integrative review of such studies by Martin and his co-workers. The conclusions of this review are clear: Only five factors are consistently replicable over studies, and two smaller ones appear occasionally.[1]

---

[1]Because this section does not address questions of clinical relevance we do not discuss here the relative merit for clinical practice of either the original nine dimensions, including the clusters easy, difficult, and so forth, or the empirically proven five factors that result from the meta-analysis presented here. Obviously, much work remains to be done on the clinical aspects of a developmentally derived Big Five scheme and existing schemes. See the chapters by Havill et al. and Victor this volume.

The five factors derived from the limited set of items selected by Thomas and Chess may not necessarily resemble the Big Five of adulthood. First, items were not systematically derived from a comprehensive set of temperamental characteristics as can be found in dictionaries, or as can be derived from interviews held with parents or teachers (see section V). Second, children are different from adults. The dimensions that have become the deep structure underlying the perceived personality characteristics of adults need not be manifest when adults describe individual differences among children. Nevertheless, some of the precursors of the Big Five seem to be recognizable in the results of the integrative review presented in the first chapter of this section.

One of the prominent and replicable factors in infancy and childhood is motor activity, a factor that seems to lose its prominence and/or separate identity in late adolescence and adulthood. The second chapter of this section is devoted to an analysis of individual differences as well as the developmental trajectory of activity level. Eaton discerns a common core in the diversity of definitions of activity level: the customary energy expenditure through movement. During the first 2 years of life, activity level appears to grow in importance as a dimension of difference. The dimension meets all the criteria for being acknowledged as a truly temperamental one, and for this reason was selected by Buss and Plomin as one of their three dimensions: emotionality, activity, and sociability (EAS; Buss & Plomin, 1975; 1984). At the beginning of this century Heymans (1910; Heymans & Wiersma, 1916) also made it one of his three dimensions: activity, emotionality, and primary versus secondary function. Early in the new wave of interest in temperamental differences, Fries (1954; Fries & Woolf, 1953) and Escalona (1968; for a summary, see Rothbart, 1989) identified activity level as a major dimension of individual differences. In the Thomas–Chess paradigm, activity level is the first of their nine dimensions.

Eaton shows how in childhood motor activity level begins to lose its favorable connotation because high levels of activity become associated with undercontrol, inattentiveness, and aggression. In the Digman and Inouye (1986) study, the adjectives *energetic* and *lethargic* loaded high on an Extraversion factor (.73 and −.50) just as the Energy Level cluster does in Goldberg's work with adults (.60). But, as in childhood, activity level also becomes associated with other Big Five factors, most notably with conscientiousness, and seems to diminish in importance as a primary, independent personality dimension. Eaton sketches a developmental trajectory of activity level across the life span. Adults are much less motorically active than children because their energy has shifted from motor schemes to symbolic schemes, reducing the saliency of the trait. The energy is no longer clearly expressed in motor activity, but rather in several less-visible activities of a more symbolic nature. Some of the variance in motor activity may be transformed into variance in talking, but longitudinal studies tracing this metamorphosis are still missing. Eaton's chapter in this volume is the first written from a truly developmental perspective. In combination with the previous chapter by Martin et al., it leads to the possibility that motor activity level probably belongs to a "Little Five" in infancy and childhood diminishing as a prime dimension in the course of adolescence, yet remaining as an important "multiplier" of several of the Big Five personality factors in adulthood.

In the third chapter of this section, Ahadi and Rothbart discuss possible developmental precursors of later personality factors and the systems likely to be involved in their functioning. Rothbart was among the first to explore the relations between major temperamental differences in infancy and the Big Five in adulthood (Rothbart, 1989). Ahadi and Rothbart consider precursors, including positive affect and the approach tendency underlying Extraversion, negative affect behaviors underlying Emotional Instability, and the attentional self-regulatory systems underlying Conscientiousness. Together with the chapter by Graziano in Section IV on the development of Agreeableness, this completes the quartet of the first four of the Big Five.

Ahadi, Rothbart, and Ye (1993) gave Rothbart's Children's Behavioral Questionnaire (CBQ) to mothers of 6- and 7-year-old children in the United States ($N = 156$) and China ($N = 468$). In a three-factor solution on the Chinese data set, a first factor was obtained that consisted of a mixture of approach, smiling and laughter, high intensity pleasure, activity and impulsivity, and a negative loading on shyness. Kohnstamm, Van der Kamp, Zhang, and Martin (in press) gave a Chinese version of the Thomas and Chess questionnaire to Chinese mothers of 3- to 7-year-old children ($N = 966$). In a five-factor solution, the approach-withdrawal items clearly formed a separate (fourth) factor. this approach-withdrawal factor is similar to the approach factor based on the Thomas and Chess items described by Martin et al. (chap. 8 in this vol.). Thus, the Rothbart et al. factor of approach, activity, and positive mood may be due to either the nature or number of items for each of these extraversion facets in the CBQ, or to the fact that only three factors were extracted when more could have been. Consensus on both instruments given to Chinese mothers (for all of whom this was probably the first experience with rating scales!) came from what Ahadi and Rothbart labeled as individual differences in Effortful Control. In their three-factor solution, Effortful Control consisted of scales for inhibitory control, attention, low pleasure, and perceptual sensitivity. This composition matches the structure of the largest factor found by Kohnstamm et al., using a different instrument and a different Chinese sample. This construct of Effortful Control seems closely related to Task Persistence, and matches this factor as discussed by Martin et al. (chap. 8 in this vol.). In the words of Ahadi and Rothbart: "Operationally, Effortful Control is reflected in individual differences in the ability to voluntarily sustain focus on a task, to voluntarily shift attention from one task to another, to voluntarily initiate action, and to voluntarily inhibit action." This phrasing reminds us of the label *Will*, originally preferred by Digman for the Big Five factor of Conscientiousness.

Ahadi and Rothbart (chap. 10 in this vol.) quote a longitudinal study (Shoda, Mischel, & Peake, 1990) in which preschool children's delay of gratification behavior was correlated with their self-regulatory capacities in adolescence as judged by their parents. Though in this study the highest correlations accounted for no more than 25% of the variance, a coherent pattern of statistically significant correlations emerged. Ratings on questions, such as "When trying to concentrate, how distractible is your son or daughter?", were predicted by observed preschool self-imposed delay time. Of course, many more such longitudinal studies need to be done before we will know the continuity and/or precursors of adult Conscientiousness. Also, it may prove useful to explore existing longitudinal databases. These may be able to shed light on the question of whether individual differences in adulthood, organized according to the five-factor model, can indeed be predicted from temperamental differences in childhood. As stated by Ahadi and Rothbart: "The Big Five taxonomy has provided us with a target framework for attempting to identify how infant and child temperamental dimensions may interact with each other and the environment to create variation in (adult) personality." From the outset, these authors reject an approach in which temperamental dimensions in infancy and childhood are conceived as variations of *separate* systems, each developing in its own way into similar separate dimensions of adult personality.

In an interesting and important theoretical analysis. Ahadi and Rothbart propose that Effortful Control moderates other systems such as the expression of approach-related tendencies, the expressions of anger and other negative emotions, and the expressions of love and hate (Agreeableness). Their neurobiological orientation leads them to expect dependencies among the Big Five factors (more so between their precursors). They remind us that the orthogonality of the factors is statistical and not necessarily reflective of underlying processes. In this, their orientation seems to be more akin to the one promoted by the circumplex adherents (see, e.g., De Raad, Hendriks, & Hofstee, chap. 5 in this vol.) rather than to the more conventional and, in a logical sense, more "neat" hierarchical orientation of most Big Five theorists. As Ahadi and Rothbart state: "In our attempt to describe the psychological processes that may underlay the Big Five, we hope to have conveyed a sense of the dynamics of personality development and functioning that can be lost in static taxonomic models."

In the last chapter of this section, Wachs opens with a sobering reminder of the relatively low stability coefficients usually found in longitudinal temperament research. If stability and continuity over a period of a few years in childhood is so modest, what can be expected of empirical relations between childhood temperament and adult personality? The process is complicated by changing biological systems during growth, and by differential reactions to changing environments within which the individual develops. To illustrate the latter: For the great majority of temperament traits, available evidence does not suggest a great deal of consistency between individual child temperamental characteristics and subsequent caregiver behaviors. Only when temperamental characteristics elicit or match "stabilizing" environmental characteristics can continuity from childhood temperament to adult personality be expected.

Wachs uses Inhibition as an example one of the best studied temperamental differences. He sketches what environmental qualities might stimulate an inhibited child into becoming a shy adult, and what qualities may, on the contrary, promote development toward extraversion. Wachs ends his chapter with a strong plea to develop specific hypotheses about how contextual factors will strengthen or attenuate linkages among specific domains in early temperament and subsequent personality.

REFERENCES

Ahadi, S. A., Rothbart, M. K., & Ye, R. M. (1993). Child temperament in the U.S. and China: Similarities and differences. *European Journal of Personality, 7,* 359–378.

Buss, A. H., & Plomin, R. (1975). *A temperament theory of personality development.* New York: Wiley.

Buss, A. H., & Plomin, R. (1984). *Temperament: Early developing personality traits.* Hillsdale, NJ: Lawrence Erlbaum Associates.

Carey, W. B. (1970). A simplified-method for measuring infant temperament. *Journal of Pediatrics, 77,* 188–194.

Digman, J. M., & Inouye, J. (1986). Further specification of the Five robust factors of personality. *Journal of Personality and Social Psychology, 50,* 116–123.

Escalona, S. K. (1968). *The roots of individuality: Normal patterns of development in infancy.* Chicago: Aldine.

Fries, M. E. (1954). Some hypotheses on the role of congenital activity types in personality development. *International Journal of Psychoanalysis, 35,* 206–207.

Fries, M. E., & Woolf, P. (1953). Some hypotheses on the role of congenital activity type in personality development. In R. Eissleratal (Ed.), *The psychoanalytic study of the child* (Vol. 8, pp. 48–62). New York: International Universities Press.

Heymans, G. (1910). *Die Psychologie der Frauen* [The psychology of women]. Heidelberg: Carl Winter's Universitatsbuch: Handlung.

Heymans, G., & Wiersma, E. (1916). Verschiedenheiten der Altersent wicklung De'l Mannlichen und weiblichen Mitschulern [Differences in development between male and female high school pupils]. *Zeitschrift Fur Angewandte Psychologie, 11,* 441–464.

Kohnstamm, G. A., Van der Kamp, L., Zhang, Y., & Martin, R. P. (in press). The structure of temperament based on parental ratings of preschool children in Finland, Australia and China.

Rothbart, M. K. (1989). Temperament in childhood: A framework. In G. A. Kohnstamm, J. Bates, & M. K. Rothbart (Eds.), *Temperament in childhood* (pp. 59–73). Chichester, England: Wiley.

Shoda, Y., Mischel, W., & Peake, P. K. (1990). Predicting adolescent cognitive and self-regulatory competencies from preschool delay of gratification: Identifying diagnostic conditions. *Developmental Psychology, 26,* 978–986.

Thomas, A., & Chess, S. (1977). *Temperament and development.* New York: Brunner/Mazel.

Thomas, A., Chess, S., & Birch, H. (1968). *Temperament and behavior: Disorders in children.* New York: New York University Press.

CHAPTER

8

REVIEW OF FACTOR ANALYTIC STUDIES OF TEMPERAMENT MEASURES BASED ON THE THOMAS–CHESS STRUCTURAL MODEL: IMPLICATIONS FOR THE BIG FIVE

Roy P. Martin
Joseph Wisenbaker
University of Georgia

Matti Huttunen
University of Helsinki

In a new area of research in personality, the fundamental tasks are to build a measure of the construct of interest, then to provide a body of research that demonstrates the validity of the construct. Adult personality researchers, faced with a large number of constructs developed through this process, have begun to address questions about the relationship among these constructs. In the process, questions about the fundamental structure of personality have been debated. Interest in the Big Five adult personality model described in this volume and elsewhere (e.g., Digman, 1990; John, 1990) is the most current manifestation of the search for this structure.

Temperament researchers also have made progress in both instrument construction and construct validation. Hundreds of validation studies of perhaps 15 to 20 constructs have appeared in the literature, and several integrative summaries are available (e.g., Buss & Plomin, 1975, 1984; Ciba Foundation Symposium No. 89, 1982; Garrison & Earls, 1987; Kohnstamm, Bates, & Rothbart, 1989). Concern about the structure has only recently begun to appear in the literature. The recency of this concern seems attributable to two factors. First, temperament research has only recently matured to the point that basic questions about the importance of the phenomena have been put to rest. The existence of a body of positive findings provides researchers with the impetus to continue to refine their concepts. Second, issues of structure are conceptually more complicated in childhood due to the rapid developmental changes. Third, much temperament research is based on measurement instruments derived from the nine-dimensional structural model of Thomas and Chess (Thomas & Chess, 1977; Thomas, Chess, Birch, Hertzig, & Korn, 1963). This list of measurement tools includes the Behavioral Style Questionnaire (McDevitt & Carey, 1978), Infant Temperament Questionnaire (Carey & McDevitt, 1978), Middle-Childhood Temperament Questionnaire (Hegvik, McDevitt, & Carey, 1980); Teacher and Parent Temperament Questionnaires (Thomas & Chess, 1977), Temperament Assessment Battery for Children (Martin, 1988), Toddler Temperament Scale (Fullard, McDevitt, & Carey, 1984). Questions of structure were slow to arise, because a structural model was built into the measurement tools.

Structural questions began to arise in the temperament literature as second- and third-generation instrument builders turned to factor analytic instrument development methods. Many of these instrument builders began with one of the original instruments, and factor analyzed the items in an attempt to verify the nine-dimensional structure (e.g., Presley & Martin, in press), or augmented the items in minor ways to more fully assess the structure (e.g., Lerner, Palermo, Sprio, & Nessleroade, 1982). As this kind of research has accumulated, it has become clear that only some of the Thomas and Chess dimensions have held up under factor analysis. The senior author reviewed some of the strongest of this type (Martin, 1990; Presley & Martin, in press). However, additional large sample factor analytic studies have recently become available that were not available when the previous reviews were prepared. Furthermore, the stronger recent studies reported item content in a more detailed manner, so that it is now possible to study the specific content of factors and make cross-study comparison in a more precise manner than was previously possible.

One of the purposes of this chapter is to briefly present this review of the strongest available factor analytic studies of instruments based on the Thomas and Chess item pool. Strong studies are reviewed at each age level of childhood based on samples from Australia, Scandinavia, and the United States. These data provide an opportunity to speculate, more completely than has been done before, on developmental aspects of temperament based on patterns of factor structure from across ages ranging from infancy to adolescence. Finally, hypotheses are offered suggesting relationships between a proposed structural model of temperament in childhood and the Big Five adult model of personality.

REVIEW OF FACTOR ANALYTIC STUDIES

Table 8.1 presents the results of 12 large sample factor analyses of the original Thomas, Chess, and Korn Parent and Teacher Questionnaires, or instruments based largely on these questionnaires. A sizable number of factor analytic studies were eliminated from the review, because they were not based on item pools derived from the Thomas and Chess measures, they were based on scale scores

TABLE 8.1
Selected Factor Analytic Studies of Parental and Teacher Temperament Ratings

Reference	Subjects N	Subjects Age	Instrument	Factor Names
Parents' Ratings of Infants				
Bohlin et al. (1981)	381 410	3–6 months 6–10 months Sweden	Baby Behavior Questionnaire	Intensity/Activity Manageability Regularity Approach/Withdrawal Sensory Sensitivity Attentiveness Sensitivity to New Foods
Hagekull et al. (1980)	357	11–15 months Sweden	Toddler Behavior Questionnaire	(Same as above except Adaptability also found)
Martin et al. (1991)	1372	6–8 months Finland	Finnish version of Carey Infant Temp. Quest.	Negative Emotionality Rhythmicity Threshold (sensitivity to wet or soiled diapers) Agreeableness/Adaptability
Sanson et al. (1987)	2,443	2–4 months Australia	Revised Infant Temp. Quest.	Approach/Withdrawal Rhythmicity Cooperation/Manageability Activity/Reactivity Irritability
Parent Ratings of Preschoolers				
Martin et al. (1991)	439	5 years Finland	Thomas, Chess, & Korn Parent Temp. Questionnaire	Negative Emotionality Social Inhibition Task Persistence (boys only) Threshold (boys only) Agreeableness/Adaptability Rhythmicity (girls only) Activity Level (girls only)
Presley & Martin (in press)	1,808	3–7 years U.S.	Temperament Assessment Battery for Children	Social Inhibition Negative Emotionality Agreeableness/Adaptability Activity Level Task Persistence
Parent Ratings of School Age Children				
Lambert & Windmiller (1977)	327	Grade 2,4,6 U.S.	interview based on Thomas & Chess model	Attention Span Threshold Activity Distractibility Rhythmicity/Adaptability Approach/Withdrawal
McClowry, Hegvik, & Teglasi (in press)	957	7–11 years U.S.	Middle Childhood Temperament Quest.	Task Persistence Negative Reactivity Approach Activity Responsiveness

(Continued)

TABLE 8.1
(Continued)

Reference	Subjects		Instrument	Factor Names
	N	Age		
Self-Ratings by Children, Adolescents, and Adults				
Lerner et al. (1982)	161 508 717	preschool grade 4 & 6 college students U.S.	item pool based on Thomas & Chess model	Activity Attention Span/ Distractibility Adaptability Approach/Withdrawal Rhythmicity Reactivity

Windle (1992)	975	Grade 10,11
		U.S.
			Dimensions of Temperament Survey—Revised	Activity
				  General and Sleep
				Approach/Withdrawal
				Flexibility/Rigidity
				Mood
				Rhythmicity
				  Sleep, Eating, and
				  Daily Habit
				Distractibility
				Persistence

Teacher Ratings of Elementary School Students				
Baker & Velicer (1982)	118 155	5–7 years 5–6 years U.S.	Thomas & Chess Teacher Temp. Questionnaire	Compliance with Task Demands Interpersonal Affect Extraversion Environmental Sensitivity
Martin et al. (1991)	1007	11–12 years Finland	Keogh Teacher Temperament Survey	Task Persistence Inhibition Reactivity
Presley & Martin (in press)	514	3–7 years U.S.	Temperament Assessment Battery for Children	Task Persistence Inhibition

as opposed to item scores, or the sample size was judged to be too small to allow for stable results. When large-scale item-level analyses were available on several versions of an instrument, data obtained from early versions of the instrument were not considered. Further, only studies in which items and loadings for each factor were available (either in the published research or from the authors) were considered.

Based on factor labels, the first impression obtained from glancing at Table 8.1 is that there is considerable uniformity across ages and subject nationality for parental and self ratings. Second, whereas researchers uniformly obtained fewer factors from teachers' ratings than parental ratings, there appears to be considerable consistency in factors extracted from teacher studies. The third impression obtained from the data presented in Table 8.1 is that there is very little evidence for the Thomas and Chess nine-factor structure, although some of the original nine dimensions appear to be strongly represented.

It appears that there is evidence for seven factors, although the support for some factors is not as strong as for others. Tables 8.2 and 8.3 attempt to capture the consistencies appearing in Table 8.1 by categorizing all factors listed in Table 8.1 into these seven categories. Table 8.2 contains the five most commonly assessed factors in the temperament literature, and Table 8.3 contains two factors that have appeared with some regularity, but about which there is considerable theoretical controversy.

Each of these seven factors and issues related to them are discussed. The names of these seven factors, of course, are somewhat arbitrary, but were selected based on the authors' understanding of common nomenclature among temperament researchers and consideration of item content.

Activity Level

Although almost all temperament theorists include a construct of motor vigor in their list of temperament constructs, the results of factor analytic studies demonstrates that the measurement of this factor is complicated by considerations of the age of child and the person doing the ratings. The results are, however, strongly supportive of an activity level factor that can be isolated from the preschool period through adolescence, when the measurement is through parental or self ratings.

Table 8.4 presents the three items that loaded most strongly on a factor labeled Activity Level, or factors containing items clearly indicative of activity level. The items tap problems in control of gross motor activity, frequency of vigorous gross motor activity, and speed of gross motor activity. Researchers working with the Dimensions of Temperament Survey and its revisions (e.g., Windel, 1992) have found robust measures of motor vigor as manifest in both waking and sleeping states.

Motor activity level is not easily assessed in infancy, independent of emotional responses. Tables 8.1 and 8.2 reveal that no homogeneous activity level factor was found in any study, but in several studies, an item indicative of activity level formed part of a factor that was heavily loaded with items taping the strength of emotional expression. Such a finding is consistent with the observation that emotional arousal in infancy is often expressed through movement of arms, legs, and torso. Further, motor movements may be interpreted by parents as signs of discomfort among young infants. These data do not address the issue of whether motoric activity can be rated separately from emotional activity by parents given some specialized training, but it does indicate that this distinction is problematic in the item sets used.

TABLE 8.2
Comparisons of Five Major Factors Across Studies

Study	Activity Level	Negative Emotionality	Task Persistence	Adaptability/ Agreeableness	Inhibition
Parental Ratings of Infants					
Bohlin et al. (1981)	Activity/ Intensity	Manageability	Attentiveness	Manageability	Approach-Withdrawal
Hagekull et al. (1980)	Activity/ Intensity	Manageability	Attentiveness	Adaptability	Approach-Withdrawal
Martin et al. (1991)	—[1]	Negative Emotionality	—	Agreeableness	
Sanson et al. (1987)	Activity/ Reactivity	Irritability	Persistence	Cooperation/ Manageability Placidity	Approach
Parental Ratings of Preschoolers					
Martin et al. (1991)	Activity Level[2]	Negative Emotionality	Task Persistence[3]	Adaptability/ Agreeableness	Social Inhibition
Presley & Martin (in press)	Activity Level	Negative Emotionality	Task Persistence	Adaptability/ Agreeableness	Social Inhibition
Parental Ratings of School-Age Children					
Lambert & Windmiller (1977)	Activity Level	Threshold	Attention Span	Adaptability	Approach/ Withdrawal
McClowry et al. (in press)	Activity	Negative Reactivity	Persistence	—	Approach
Self-Ratings of Adolescents					
Windle (1992)	Activity Level-General Activity Level-Sleep	Mood	Persistence Distractibility	Flexibility/ Rigidity	Approach/ Withdrawal
Teachers' Ratings of Elementary School Students					
Baker & Velicer (1982)	—	Interpersonal Affect	Compliance	—	Extraversion
Martin et al. (1991)	—	Reactivity	Task Persistence	—	Inhibition
Presley & Martin (in press)	—	Reactivity	Task Persistence	—	Inhibition

[1]No factor similar to the construct was found in this research.
[2]Factor obtained for girls only.
[3]Factor obtained for boys only.

TABLE 8.3
Comparison of Two Controversial Factors Across Studies

Study	Rhythmicity	Threshold
Parental Ratings of Infants		
Bohlin et al. (1981)	Regularity	Sensory Sensitivity
		Sensitivity to New Foods
Hagekull et al. (1980)	Regularity	Sensory Sensitivity
Martin et al. (1991)	Biological Rhythmicity	Threshold (wet diapers)
Sanson et al. (1987)	Rhythmicity	Food Fussiness
		Threshold (wet diapers)
Parental Ratings of Preschoolers		
Martin et al. (1991)	Rhythmicity[1]	Threshold[2]
Presley & Martin (in press)	—[3]	—
Parental Ratings of School-Age Children		
Lambert & Windmiller (1977)	Rhythmicity/Adaptability	Threshold
McClowry et al. (in press)	—	Responsiveness
Self-Ratings of Adolescents		
Windle (1992)	Rhythmicity – Sleep	—
	Rhythmicity – Eating	
	Rhythmicity – Daily Habits	
Teacher's Ratings of Elementary School Students		
Baker & Velicer (1982)	—	Environmental Sensitivity
Martin et al. (1991)	—	Reactivity
Presley & Martin (in press)	—	—

[1]This factor was present only for girls.
[2]This factor was present only for boys.
[3]No factor similar to the construct was found in this research.

The response of teachers to temperament measurement instruments of activity level is a good demonstration of the effect of situation on behavior, observer, and item covariance. None of the studies reviewed found an independent Activity Level factor. In each case, activity level items covary with items tapping distractibility and task persistence to such an extent that a single factor often labeled Task Persistence is produced. This occurs, we believe, because the classroom is not a place in which a full range of motor activity is permitted; most teachers spend a good deal of time controlling and minimizing gross motor activity. The elementary school classroom was designed to maximize concentrated mental activity in the context of a crowded space. Thus, gross motor

TABLE 8.4
Items Loading Highest on Factors Conceptually Related to Activity Level

Study	Factor Name	Highest Loading Item	Loading
Parental Ratings of Infants			
Bohlin et al. (1982)	Intensity/ Activity	(No activity items in top three loading items.)	
Hagekull et al. (1980)	Intensity/ Activity	Intensity of reactions during bath.[1]	.51
		Mood during play.	.45
		Activity during bath.	.45
Martin et al. (1991)	No Similar Factor		
Sanson et al. (1987)	Activity/ Reactivity	The baby greets a new toy with a loud voice and much expression of feeling.	.52
		The baby actively reaches for or touches (Hair, spoon, glasses, toy, etc.) close to him/her.	.52
		Baby keeps trying to get a desired toy, which is out of reach, for 2 minutes or more.	.52
Parental Ratings of Preschoolers			
Martin et al. (1991)	Activity Level[2]	On the playground the child runs, climbs, swings, and is moving all the time.	.57
		When there is bad weather and the child has to stay inside he/she runs around and doesn't like to play quietly.	.45
		When parents promise to do something, the child reminds all the time.	.43
Presley & Martin (in press)	Activity Level	When sitting, my child swings his/her legs, fidgets, or has hands in constant motion.	.60
		My child can sit quietly through a family meal.	−.51
		My child sits still to have a story read or told.	−.49
Parental Ratings of School-Age Children			
Lambert & Windmiller (1977)	Activity Level	How would you rate the activity level of your child as an infant?	.59
		Would you say your child is generally quick or slow moving?	.51
		When child was a baby and wanted something, how insistent was he?	.35
	Distractibility	How well does your child do on things that require sitting still—can he sit still for a whole meal?	.54
		Does child get side-tracked when he sets out to do something?	.52
		Does child complain very much or is he usually pretty happy with things?	.30
McClowry et al. (in press)	Activity	Runs when entering home.[3]	.68
		Runs to where he/she wants to go.	.65
		Bursts loudly into a room.	.59

(Continued)

TABLE 8.4
(Continued)

Study	Factor Name	Highest Loading Item	Loading
Self-Ratings of Adolescents			
Windel (1992)	Activity Level-General	I can't stay still for long.	.71
		Even when I am supposed to be still, I get very fidgety after a few minutes.	.67
		I often stay still for long periods of time.	−.64
	Activity Level-Sleep	I move a lot in bed.	.86
		I move a great deal in my sleep.	.84
		I don't move around much at all in my sleep.	−.75
Teachers' Ratings of Elementary School Students			
Baker & Velicer (1982)	(No similar factor)		
Martin et al. (1991)	(No similar factor)		
Presley & Martin (in press)	(No similar factor)		

[1]The items presented are the highest loading items related to activity level. The highest rated items in the factor appear under Negative Emotionality.
[2]This factor appeared only for girls in this sample.
[3]Only the key phrase from the item was reproduced, not the entire item.

activity is seen by the teacher as an indication of off-task behavior, and as disruptive of the on-task behavior of other students.

We do not believe that the absence of an independent activity level factor in infants and in teachers ratings indicates that activity level is not a dimension of temperament. There is a great deal of evidence to the contrary (see Eaton, chap. 9 this volume). However, the factor structure evidence does point out some difficulties in isolating this factor through rating technology in all contexts. (Tables listing the core items for each of the seven factors from each study in this review are available from the senior author.)

Negative Emotionality

There is ample evidence that a factor that taps variation in the tendency to express negative emotional reactions can be obtained from infancy through adolescence, whether assessed via parental, self, or teacher ratings. This factor is composed of items focused on the negative quality of the emotional reaction, the intensity of negative emotional reactions, and the persistence of the negative reaction. Further, the items sample factors that foster these reactions such as frustration, novelty, or stress.

Task Persistence

In 11 of the 12 studies reviewed, a factor tapping attentiveness or task persistence was isolated. The factor becomes clearer in content in ratings of children ranging in age from the preschool period through adolescence, than it is in infancy. It is the dominant factor in ratings provided by teachers.

The consistency with which this factor is obtained belies the complexity of the behavioral phenomena being rated. In infancy, the core items are related to the ability to notice variation in the environment, based on reaction to this variation. Attention is obviously involved in this process. Some items tap continuity of attention. At the preschool level, items assessing ability to control motoric activity, and to continue a frustrating learning experience begin to appear. In later childhood and adolescence, the emphasis is on attention span. The most central behavior assessed by these items at all ages is continuity of activities related to learning or productive activity. Attentional processes can be inferred from these behaviors.

Adaptability

A set of factors has been isolated in many studies that seems to depict an adaptable and an easy-to-manage child. A tentative label of Adaptability has been given to this set of factors, although the authors are less convinced of the uniformity of this cluster of factors than any other cluster considered here.

Items designed to assess the original Adaptability scale of Thomas, Chess, and Korn (Thomas & Chess, 1977) are clearly represented in factors isolated by a number of researchers. These items deal with the speed of adjustment to environmental change, or the lack of a negative reaction to environmental change. Another theme that seems to run through these items is one of placidity; that is, in infancy there is evidence of quiet, and emotionally mild responses to a variety of environmental events.

An argument could be put forth that these factors share a common theme distinguished by the manner in which the child adjusts to change or disturbance. At one end of the continuum is an easily managed child, who appears placid and easygoing because self-regulatory processes are in place that allow the child to keep arousal at manageable levels. At the other end is a difficult child, who creates management problems for caretakers because self-management processes are not in place.

According to another interpretation, some of these factors are more parsimoniously interpreted as another component of negative emotionality; that is, the factors consist of positively worded items tapping the absence of negative emotionality (e.g., My child's emotional expressions are mild.), whereas the factors more clearly in the Negative Emotionality cluster were worded in the negative direction (e.g., Child generally objects with fussing or cries to any new procedure.). If this hypothesis were correct, there should be a moderate to high negative correlation between the factors based on positively and negatively worded items from the same study. Data relevant to this question are available from four studies. Hagekull, Lindhagen, and Bohlin (1980) found that none of their obliquely extracted factors correlated above .22, so it can be assumed that Activity/Intensity, related here to the Negative Emotionality Factor, and Adaptability were negligibly related. Presley and Martin (in press), factor analyzing a large sample of preschool parental ratings, utilized an oblique rotation procedure that allows extracted factors to correlate. They obtained a −.54 correlation between the Adaptability and Negative Emotionality Factors. Lambert and Windmiller (1977) found a factor they labeled Threshold, but this is more related to the Negative Emotionality cluster. It contains items related to negative reactions to noise, high frequency of nightmares, and poor adaptability to change. In this study, which utilized a very small sample of items, poor adaptability and negative emotional reactions were found in the same factor, and thus were clearly correlated. Finally, Windle (1992), using confirmatory factor analyses procedures on a large adolescent sample, obtained a mood quality factor that is part of what we have called the Negative Emotionality cluster, and a Flexibility-Rigidity factor that we have placed in the Adaptability cluster. These two factors are correlated .42, when mood was scored in the positive direction. A second-order factor labeled Adaptability/Positive Affect is composed of these two factors plus the Approach/Withdrawal factor.

These findings indicate that the Negative Emotionality factors and the Adaptability factors are moderately negatively related. The evidence is not conclusive, but leads us to interpret the Adaptability factor as assessing a continua ranging from children who adjust quickly to altered circumstances, to those who have difficulty making this adjustment. We hypothesize that the psychological process underlying this ability to adjust may relate to individual differences in the extent to which novelty results in emotional reactions, and the extent to which the child successfully engages in self-control techniques. This interpretation has elements in common with those in Graziano's (chap. 17 in this vol.) discussion of the origins of the Agreeableness construct found in adulthood.

Inhibition

The original Thomas, Chess, and Korn scales on which many later measurement instruments were based had a scale labeled "Approach/Withdrawal," which described the initial response made by the child to novel environmental circumstances. This scale has proven to be one of the most robust in factor analytic studies. The items that have been found to load heavily on this factor across a wide age range include those that deal with the positive versus negative initial reaction to strangers, persistence of anxious or fearful reactions to strangers, and tendency to seek out novel situations.

We believe the primary psychological process underlying this factor is the tendency of the neurological system to respond to novelty in such a way as to produce strong fear or anxiety reactions. This factor does not seem to tap the sociability dimension assessed by others (e.g., Buss & Plomin, 1984), although it may be a developmental antecedent to the tendency to seek or need social contact versus the tendency to seek social isolation.

Biological Rhythmicity and Threshold

The five-factor clusters described so far are found in one form or another in most temperament theories of childhood. The two factors of Rhythmicity and Threshold have had somewhat less enthusiastic acceptance among temperament theorists based on theoretical and psychometric criteria. For example, some theorists believe that Biological Rhythmicity is an important characteristic of infancy, but that its importance is reduced by the preschool years because the diurnal timing of feeding, elimination, and sleep are thought to respond to socialization pressures after infancy (Buss & Plomin, 1984). The Threshold variable was designed to assess individual differences in sensitivity of visual, auditory, tactical, and olfactory (taste and smell) processes. However, some researchers have argued that there is little reason to believe that if the child is particularly sensitive in one modality, they also are as sensitive in another. Some psychometricians attempting to construct threshold scales have found poor internal consistency of this scale apparently for this reason (e.g., Martin, 1988).

Despite these concerns, the factor analytic evidence is supportive for both factors. For example, Biological Rhythmicity in the form of time to fall asleep, time to awake, and feeding times, can be found in most studies of infants and preschoolers, and is an important factor in the measurement efforts of the group working on the Dimensions of Temperament Survey–Revised (DOTS–R) (e.g., Windle, 1992). This factor is not seen in teacher ratings as would be expected, because they do not have the opportunity to observe these behaviors. The psychological processes are not clear, although we speculate that in infancy in particular they may relate to the maturity, intactness, and integration of neurological systems. This speculation is based, in part, on the finding that arrhythmic infant girls were found in a large longitudinal study to have more behavior and attentional problems as school-age children than girls who were rhythmic as infants (Martin, 1991).

The Threshold factor has also been given significant support in factor analytic studies. In infancy, it is often seen in items related to sensitivity to new foods or to reactions to wet or soiled diapers. In later periods of development, items relating to sensitivity to temperament and light predominate. The senior author also has come into contact with several clinical cases of children who are exceptionally sensitive to the feel of clothing, although this type of item has not been found in many factor analytic studies.

We have speculated whether this variable is related to heightened sensory sensitivity or to a slow process of habituation. There is little evidence to help differentiate between these hypotheses. In any event, those low on this variable may experience the world as more irritating than others, and this may combine with other processes to create heightened expression of negative emotionality or slower adaptation. In fact, some studies have found threshold items mixed with other items indicative of negative emotionality (e.g., Baker & Velicer, 1982; Keogh, Pullis, & Cadwell, 1982; Lambert & Windmiller, 1977; Martin et al. 1991).

RELATIONSHIP OF SEVEN-FACTOR MODEL OF TEMPERAMENT TO THE BIG FIVE

The discussion to this point has set the stage for a seven-factor model of temperament in childhood and adolescence. No assumption is made that this seven-factor model encompasses all infant, preschool, childhood, or adolescent temperament factors that have currently been isolated or will be isolated. We argue, however, that it represents the major portion of those factors that have been assessed to date, even through means other than the item pool derived from Thomas, Chess, and Korn (e.g., Rothbart, 1989). Given a seven-factor model of temperament in childhood, we have a set of characteristics that have been empirically verified as a starting point for the discussion of development of adult personality. The Big Five model of personality provides a target to predict. Unfortunately, there have not been empirical tests in long-term longitudinal studies of the relationship between Big Five factors and any of the seven factors of this temperament model. There has been a little research, including that reported in this volume, that can, at least tangentially, be used to develop hypotheses about relations among these characteristics. The remainder of this chapter presents our hypotheses about these relations.

Activity Level

From a logical point of view, it would appear that activity level assessed in childhood and adolescents should developmentally precede Factor 1 (Extraversion) of the Big Five (see Hagekull, chap. 12 in this vol., for a similar conclusion). Activity level is a major aspect of Factor 1 of the Neuroticism, Extraversion, Openness-to-Experience Personality Inventory (NEO-PI) (Costa & McCrae, 1985), and is one of the 100 synonym clusters defining Factor I of Goldberg (see Goldberg & Rosolack, chap. 1 in this vol.).

Such a logical analysis glosses over many potential complexities. In infancy, some manifestations of activity level are associated with arousal that is related to intense negative emotional expression (e.g., crying). Thus, high activity level in infancy may be a poor predictor of extraversion or activity level in adults. It may be predictive of negative emotionality. It is our opinion, however, that during the preschool years, activity level becomes firmly associated with gross-motor vigor, and it will prove to be a strong predictor of Factor 1 in adulthood. Eaton's work (see chap. 9 in this vol.) also points out that after puberty, activity level sometimes becomes related to talkativeness in social contexts, which seems particularly strongly related to the social aspects of Factor 1.

Negative Emotionality

Negative emotionality measured in childhood is characterized by intense fussing, anger, low threshold of frustration, loudness, and general irritability. There are two likely adult manifestations for this kind of behavior found in childhood; one is some facets of Factor II (Agreeableness) and the other is some facets of Factor IV (Neuroticism). Adults scoring low on some facets of Factor II are described as irritable, manipulative, uncooperative. Likewise, adults scoring low on some facets of Factor IV are described as hot-tempered, angry, easily frustrated, and unable to deal with stress.

Task Persistence

Task persistence as a childhood characteristic is primarily descriptive of attentive behavior that is focused on learning or mental skill performance. This characteristic, seen in rudimentary form in infancy, is clearly more easily observed by parents and teachers beginning in the preschool years. This temperamental factor logically seems related to Factor III (Conscientiousness) in adulthood. Costa and McCrae (1985) utilized words like hard-working, self-disciplined, and persevering to describe the positive end of this factor. Goldberg's synonym clusters describing this factor include persistence on the positive pole and aimless on the negative. However, there have been no strong studies aimed at investigating whether Task Persistence in childhood is related to Conscientiousness in adulthood, although that is our hypothesis.

Adaptability

As discussed previously, we interpret this factor to be related to the tendency for the child to experience fear and anxiety in novel situations, and also to be related to self-soothing abilities. Thus, we hypothesize that this factor assessed in childhood will be found to be related to Neuroticism in adulthood. Further, we argue that the tendency to be adaptable in childhood is related to the Agreeableness factor in adulthood, in that highly agreeable adults are characterized by high flexibility, and enhanced self-control of negative affect.

Inhibition

Social inhibition is one of the clearest factors obtained from childhood temperament questionnaires, and seems unequivocally related to the Extraversion factor found in adulthood. Social inhibition is a defining aspect of this factor (see Costa &

McCrae, 1985). However, social inhibition is based in a fearlike response to novelty; it is not simply a preference for solitary activity. Therefore, it seems likely that it would also be an antecedent to Neuroticism in adulthood.

Biological Rhythmicity and Threshold

It is very difficult to form hypotheses about the relationship between the characteristics of biological rhythmicity and threshold and adult Big Five factors because there is so little surface similarity among these concepts. Perhaps the most likely hypothesis is that low threshold may relate to Neuroticism in that heightened sensory sensitivity might be a precursor to the experience of more frequent aversive stimulation, and thus lead to fearful, anxious, and avoidant behavior.

SUMMARY

Based on a review of some of the strongest factor analytic research available, a seven-factor model of childhood and adolescent temperament is suggested. Hypotheses are then offered regarding the developmental connections between these temperamental characteristics and adult Big Five personality factors. Theoretical considerations lead to the hypothesis that the adult Extraversion factor will be predicted by the child temperament factors of Activity Level and Inhibition, and that Agreeableness in adulthood is predicted by Adaptability in childhood. Neuroticism is hypothesized to have multiple childhood antecedents, including the temperament factors of Negative Emotionality, Activity level (in infants), Adaptability, and Inhibition. Conscientiousness in adulthood is probably developmentally preceded by behaviors conceptualized under the rubric of Task Persistence in childhood. Finally, the Big Five factors of Openness to Experience is not thought of as highly related to temperamental factors of childhood, but will probably be best predicted from measures of childhood intellectual ability.

REFERENCES

Baker, E. H., & Velicer, W. F. (1982). The structure and reliability of the Teacher Temperament Questionnaire. *Journal of Abnormal Child Psychology, 10*, 531–546.

Bohlin, G., Hagekull, B., & Lindhagen, K. (1981). Dimensions of infant behavior. *Infant Behavior and Development, 4*, 83–96.

Buss, A. H., & Plomin, R. (1975). *A temperament theory of personality.* New York: Wiley.

Buss, A. H., & Plomin, R. (1984). *Temperament: Early developing personality traits.* Hillsdale, NJ: Lawrence Erlbaum Associates.

Carey, W. B., & McDevitt, S. C. (1978). Revision of the infant temperament questionnaire. *Pediatrics, 61*, 735–739.

Ciba Foundation Symposium No. 89 (1982). *Temperament in infants and young children.* London: Pitman.

Costa, P. T., Jr., & McCrae, R. R. (1985). *The NEO Personality Inventory manual*. Odessa, FL: Psychological Assessment Resources.

Digman, J. M. (1990). Personality structure: Emergence of the five-factor model. *Annual Review of Psychology, 41*, 417–440.

Fullard, W., McDevitt, S. C., & Carey, W. B. (1984). *Toddler temperament scale*. Temple University, Philadelphia, PA.

Garrison, W. T., & Earls, F. J. (1987). *Temperament and child psychopathology*. Newbury Park, CA: Sage.

Hagekull, B., Lindhagen, K., & Bohlin, G. (1980). Behavioral dimensions in 1-year-olds and dimensional stability in infancy. *International Journal of Behavioral Development, 3*, 351–364.

Hegvik, R. L., McDevitt, S. C., & Carey, W. B. (1980). *Middle Childhood Temperament Questionnaire*. Unpublished instrument.

John, O. P. (1990). The "big five" factor taxonomy: Dimensions of personality in the natural language and in questionnaires. In L. A. Pervin (Ed.), *Handbook of personality: Theory and research* (pp. 67–100). New York: Guilford.

Keogh, B. K., Pullis, M. E., & Cadwell, J. (1982). A short form of the teacher temperament questionnaire. *Journal of Educational Measurement, 19*, 323–329.

Kohnstamm, G. A., Bates, J. E., & Rothbart, M. K. (1989). *Temperament in childhood*. Chichester, England: Wiley.

Lambert, N. M., & Windmiller, M. (1977). An exploratory study of temperament traits in a population of children at risk. *Journal of Special Education, 11*, 37–46.

Lerner, R. M., Palermo, M., Sprio, A., & Nessleroade, J. (1982). Assessing the dimensions of temperamental individuality across the life-span: The Dimensions of Temperament Survey (DOTS). *Child Development, 53*, 149–160.

Martin, R. P. (1988). *The Temperament Assessment Battery for Children*. Brandon, VT: Clinical Psychology Publishing Company.

Martin, R. P. (1990). *The macrostructure of childhood temperament*. Paper presented at the Eighth Occasional Temperament Conference, Scottsdale, AZ.

Martin, R. P. (1991, August). *The education of ladybugs and killerbees: Early personality and schooling*. Presidential address to the membership of Division 16 of APA, at the annual meeting of APA, San Francisco, CA.

Martin, R. P., Huttunen, M. O., Wisenbaker, J., Salonen, R., Tanskanen, A., & Lorys, A. (1991, June). *The structure of temperament ratings in infancy, preschool, and early adolescence: A large scale longitudinal study*. Paper presented at an international meeting entitled "The developing structure of temperament and personality in childhood," Wassenaar, The Netherlands.

McDevitt, S. C., & Carey, W. B. (1978). The measurement of temperament in 3- to 7-year-old children. *Journal of Child Psychology and Psychiatry, 19*, 245–253.

McClowry, S. G., Hegvik, R. L., & Teglasi, H. (in press). An examination of the construct validity of the Middle Childhood Temperament Questionnaire. *Merrill-Palmer Quarterly*.

Presley, R., & Martin, R. P. (in press). Toward a structure of preschool temperament: Factor structure of the Temperament Assessment Battery for Children. *Journal of Personality*.

Rothbart, M. K. (1989). Temperament and development. In G. A. Kohnstamm, J. E. Bates, & M. K. Rothbart (Eds.), *Temperament in childhood* (pp. 187–248). Chichester, England: Wiley.

Sanson, A., Prior, M., Garino, E., Oberklaid, F., & Sewell, J. (1987). The structure of infant temperament: Factor analysis of the Revised Infant Temperament Questionnaire. *Infant Behavior and Development, 10*, 97–104.

Thomas, A., & Chess, S. (1977). *Temperament and development*. New York: Brunner/Mazel.

Thomas, A., Chess, S., Birch, H. G., Hertzig, M., & Korn, S. (1963). *Behavioral individuality in early childhood*. New York: New York University Press.

Windle, M. (1992). Revised dimensions of temperament survey (DOTS-R): Simultaneous group confirmatory factor analysis for adolescent gender groups. *Psychological Assessment, 4*, 1–14.

CHAPTER

9

TEMPERAMENT, DEVELOPMENT, AND THE FIVE-FACTOR MODEL: LESSONS FROM ACTIVITY LEVEL

Warren O. Eaton
University of Manitoba

The search for between-individual differences that, by definition, show stability over time and situations characterizes the study of personality and temperament. Indeed, without such stability, knowledge of a person's characteristics in one situation or at one age would be of little use in predicting their characteristics in another situation or at a later age. Stability in this context is the stability of the individual's rank within the group, and though everyone could change in concert on the characteristic in question, stability of the ranking within the group could remain stable. Age-related change, though generally ignored by the personologist, is of central concern to most developmentalists. In short, personologists and developmentalists tend to study opposite sides of the same coin. Such a division of labor can be scientifically productive, but an understanding of the changing structure of temperament and personality from infancy to adulthood will benefit from a knowledge of developmental changes. This lesson can be seen in a core dimension of individual difference in infancy, activity level (AL).

Adults watching children at play are struck by how motorically active the youngsters are. Less noticeable, but still apparent, are individual differences in the characteristic levels of motor activity from child to child. Some will seem to be in almost constant motion whereas others will be more calm and deliberate. Thus, there are two types of difference, one of the developmental difference between children and adults, the other of individual differences among children. The latter difference has received the most attention from temperament and personality researchers; indeed, activity level (AL) is one of the focal noncognitive dimensions of individual differences in infancy and childhood (Buss & Plomin, 1975; Goldsmith et al., 1987; Thomas & Chess, 1977), but its status as a dimension of adult difference is far less clear. How AL fits within the dimensional framework of temperament and personality at various ages is summarized first. Then a developmental perspective is described and applied.

Activity level has been defined in many ways, and though definitional distinctions may be important, a comprehensive, general definition of AL provides both understanding and heuristic value. The common element to the diversity of definitions of AL is customary energy expenditure through movement. Attention here is directed at individual differences and developmental changes in customary energy expenditure for the purposes of movement (energy expended for growth and system maintenance is excluded from consideration). Just as one's overall financial expenditures may vary among individuals and change across the life span, customary energy output expressed in behavioral motility also displays meaningful individual differences and follows a developmental trajectory.

ACTIVITY LEVEL IN INFANCY

As a component of individual difference, activity level emerges to prominence very early in life, perhaps even before birth. Indeed, aggregated fetal movement counts appear to meet the criteria for a dimension of temperament (Eaton & Saudino, 1992), namely that such a dimension of individual difference emerges early in life, reflects broad behavioral tendencies, has a constitutional foundation, and demonstrates continuity of expression across time (Goldsmith et al., 1987). Early in postnatal life, neonates can be characterized by individual differences in activity, but differences in the first postnatal days and weeks appear to be uncorrelated with later infancy differences (Birns, Barten, & Bridger, 1969). Distress in newborns accompanies a high level of activity (see Rothbart, 1989), and even later at 6 months, instrumented measures of 48-hour in-home activity level are positively correlated with diary records of infant crying and fussing (McKeen, 1988). However, once the neonatal period is passed, motor activity also comes to be associated with a pattern of positive affect and vocalizing in social contexts (Rothbart, 1989), and parent ratings of aspects of positive emotionality such as infant smiling and laughing are positively associated with AL (Crockenberg & Acredolo, 1983; Eaton & Dureski, 1986).

During the first 2 years of life, activity level appears to grow in importance as a dimension of difference. Matheny (1980) analyzed the behavior rating scales that comprise Infant Behavior Record component of the Bayley Scales of Infant Development for a sample of several hundred infants assessed from 3 to 24 months. An Activity factor emerged at each of six 3-month intervals; AL ranked third in accounting for total variance at 3 months with 8% of the variance, and it grew in prominence with age until it ranked first and accounted for 22% of the variance at 24 months.

It is important to note that infant activity often correlates positively with measures of developmental maturity. For example, a 48-hr mechanical measure of AL (actometer) correlated +.24 on the Bayley Psychomotor Development Index and +.26 with chronological age (Saudino & Eaton, 1991). Such findings are corroborated by Matheny (1989), who reported positive correlations between tester-rated activity and Bayley Mental test scores at 12 and 18 months. Such relations suggest there are maturational aspects to this individual difference dimension in infancy.

ACTIVITY LEVEL IN CHILDHOOD

In the later preschool and early school years, AL begins to take on a more pejorative flavor because high levels of AL are generally associated with undercontrol, inattentiveness, and aggression. Buss, J. H. Block, and J. Block (1980) measured activity in a sample of children with actometers at 3 and 4 years. The children were assessed with the California Child Q-Set by different sets of teachers at ages 3, 4, and 7 years. The actometer data showed significant longitudinal stability (+.40s). Moreover, highly active children were less inhibited, more aggressive, more assertive, more competitive, more restless, and less cautious than their less active agemates at all three ages. The negative flavor of high activity level is not limited to teacher judgments, but can be found in the peer evaluations. Eaton and Pressé (1985) found that observed activity correlated −.43 with a composite peer popularity score in a group of 3- to 5-year-olds. Highly active children are often not much liked by their peers.

It will be recalled that activity level was positively associated with measures of motor maturity in infancy, and though evidence of a linkage between AL and maturity remains in the preschool years, it seems to reverse itself from a positive to a negative association. for example, Butcher and Eaton (1989) collected actometer and behavioral observations of activity choices from children during free play in a nursery school and then assessed the children on standardized tests of motor proficiency. High actometer scores and preferences for highly active play were positively associated with running speed and agility but negatively associated with balance, visual motor control, and upper limb speed and dexterity. Aspects of motor proficiency that require controlled movements, that rely heavily on perceptual abilities and feedback from proprioceptive, vestibular, and visual systems were associated with lower levels of activity. These results suggest that high AL is associated with immaturity because the ability to control and inhibit movement improves with age and reflects greater physical maturity.

In this same vein, the well-replicated association between activity level and distractibility points to high AL as a marker for immaturity. For example, Martin

(1989) reported correlations between the adult-rated activity and distractibility that range from .5 to .7 across five different samples of schoolchildren. Given that attention and task persistence facilitate performance on mental test scores, the commonly observed negative association between mental ability performance and AL during the school years (Martin, 1989) is not surprising. It is noteworthy that a modest negative AL–IQ relation can also be found between verbal and performance IQ scores and activity level at 5 years, before the more structured demands of the classroom are typically encountered (Matheny, 1989).

Childhood activity is also linked to social behavior. Tsoi and Nicholson (1982) had teachers rate 240 children on 70 adjectives. Two adjectives that clearly reference motor activity, *action-loving* and *vigorous*, loaded positively and most strongly on an Extraversion factor. Two other adjectives that reference both activity and attention, *hyperactive* and *restless*, also loaded positively on Extraversion (.49 and .44, respectively). However, *hyperactive*'s strongest loading was on Psychoticism, .58, and *restless* loaded most strongly on Good Pupil, –.55. These associations of AL with both extraversion and being a bad pupil illustrate the paradoxical nature of the activity factor in childhood samples.

Digman and Inouye (1986) also linked activity to extraversion. They factor analyzed teacher ratings of sixth grade children on 43 unipolar adjectives, two of which are clear activity items, *energetic* and *lethargic*. Both loaded on an extraversion factor, .73 and –.50 respectively. *Restless*, which is somewhat more ambiguous with reference to pure energy expenditure, loaded positively on Extraversion, .32, but in a more negative twist, loaded negatively on Conscientiousness, –.38, and positively on Neuroticism, .34. Once again positive and negative aspects of AL emerge.

In sum, during the late preschool years and in middle childhood, AL presents a somewhat mixed picture. High activity level is linked to extraversion, distractibility, undercontrol, and poorer academic performance.

ACTIVITY LEVEL IN ADULTHOOD

As detailed in other chapters, adult personality can be well described with five major factors. How, then, does activity level fit within this framework? Goldberg (1990), in arguing for the generality of a five-factor structure, examined synonym clusters drawn from trait terms. The *energy level* cluster, which included the terms *active*, *energetic*, and *vigorous*, loaded most strongly on Extraversion (.60), followed by Agreeableness (.18), Conscientiousness (.16), Emotional Stability (.15), and Intellect (–.09).

Similar patterns have been found by other investigators. Conley (1985) utilized data from Kelly's Personality Rating Scale and found that the most AL-relevant category, *energetic*, loaded most strongly on an Extraversion dimension, followed by Impulse Control (Conscientiousness). McCrae and Costa (1987) used 40-item bipolar adjective scales, two of which are closely related to activity level, *unenergetic–energetic* and *passive–active* with peer ratings and self-reports. The *passive–active* adjective pairing loaded .42 on Extraversion, .37 on Conscientiousness, .28 on Openness, −.23 on Agreeableness, and −.26 on Neuroticism. The *unenergetic–energetic* pairing loaded .34, .46, .27, −.06, and −.14 on these same dimensions respectively. Such results indicate that higher adult activity is associated with enjoyment of social contact, dependability, an achievement orientation, broad interests, and positive emotional affect.

Under some circumstances, Activity can emerge as a factor in its own right. For example, Zuckerman, Kuhlman, and Camac (1988) factor analyzed 46 personality scales from eight major tests, and applied seven-, five- and three-factor solutions to the data. When only three factors were extracted, Activity was subsumed under a general Extraversion factor but emerged in its own right with the five- and seven-factor solutions. Other investigators (Comrey, 1973; Howarth, 1976) have also found Activity to emerge as a seventh factor (see Mershon & Gorsuch, 1988).

As one moves from early childhood to adulthood, activity retreats from the first to the second row of personality dimensions. The consistent theme that emerges from the studies of the Big Five in adulthood is that AL is a second-tier trait, one primarily related to Extraversion and secondarily to several other traits, most notably Conscientiousness. Furthermore, by adulthood the valence for high activity has shifted from the negative pole in childhood to the positive pole, and favorable attributes like sociability, dependability, and openness appear to characterize the active adult.

The preceding review of activity level and the structure of individual differences from infancy to adulthood raises several major questions. Why the transition from a primary dimension of childhood temperament to a secondary dimension of adult personality? Why the shift from the positive AL correlates of infancy to the negative ones of childhood and back to more positive correlates in adulthood? Tentative answers to such questions emerge from a consideration of the developmental course of the person's mean level of activity.

THE DEVELOPMENTAL TRAJECTORY OF ACTIVITY LEVEL

Despite activity level's status as one of the most studied of individual difference variables in childhood, the literature has largely neglected the question of age change in mean level of activity. To remedy that neglect, a review that combines the results of many studies in a kind of developmental meta-analysis are described with the intent of identifying the trajectory of activity level across the life span. This analysis was inspired, oddly enough, by a set of rules for displaying data badly (Wainer, 1984). One of his rules for bad data display is to organize information along an irrelevant dimension. At the time I read his work, I had my age-AL notes sorted by author name, and could only see a jumble of inconsistent findings. Reorganization of the notes along a relevant dimension led to greater clarity and the following analysis.

AL studies are characterized by diversity, and I sought to identify a scale-independent age pattern by combining study outcomes on a common index. In most studies only the general direction of the relation could be determined, and faced with a choice between a precise index from a small number of studies or a crude index from a large set of studies, I chose the latter and classified studies only as to the direction of the age-AL relation. Included for review were those measures that, in one form or another, operationalized energy expenditure through movement; these encompassed measures of frequency, duration, amplitude, and type of movement, and included rater judgments. The set of studies were then ranked by the age of the study samples to determine if some regularity in study outcome was evident. Such a methodology offers a heuristic exploration of broad developmental change.

Method

Studies included for analysis were selected from a much larger set of empirical, English-language research reports on normal participants. Work on hyperactivity is not included, but the control groups used in some studies of hyperactives were often suitable and were included. An initial computer search of the *Psychological Abstracts* database for descriptors like *activity level*, *motility*, and so forth, was undertaken. From this start, more traditional bibliographic search procedures were followed. Each of several hundred studies was read to identify every possible publication with a measure of activity and an age comparison; forty-one such publications were found, one reporting two experiments, which left 42 age-AL comparisons for integration.

Observable behavior that, however crudely, reflects energy expenditure through movement was viewed as an instance of AL. Typically, such behavior involves gross postural changes such as those involved in walking or running; and acceptable measures of AL could entail the measurement of type, frequency, duration, or amplitude of movement, and could include specific limb movements or whole body actions. Variables such as attentiveness and impulsiveness often covary with AL, but in so far as possible, such correlated variables were excluded. If a rating scale included items other than motor activity items, the study was coded only if a majority of the constituent items were primarily concerned with motor activity.

To summarize the chronological age distribution of a study, the minimum and maximum ages as well as the average age of the participants were recorded. Mean CA was used if reported or calculable, otherwise the midpoint of the minimum–maximum interval was employed. Where school grades rather than ages were reported, it was assumed that Grade 1 began at 72 months and that observations were collected at midyear.

AL measures were partitioned into three categories: instrument measures, which include actometers, pedometers, stabilimeters, and all automatic recording devices; observation measures, which include counts within *a priori*, low-inference categories and generally utilize some form of time-based sampling; and rating measures, which include both subjective judgments about others and self-reports on questionnaires and inventories. If more than one type of measure was used in a study, a fourth category, combination, was coded.

The age-AL relationships were coded as *positive*, *negative*, or *unclear*. Significance level, though noted, was ignored for purposes of coding, and all nonzero correlations were reported as positive or negative. When AL information was presented in the form of means from three or more groups, the overall mean of the younger half of the groups was compared to the overall mean for the older half. Again, direction was almost always apparent because significance level, though noted, was ignored. When outcomes from several AL variables within a study were scorable, direction was coded only if all outcomes were directionally consistent. If outcomes for multiple AL variables within a given study were inconsistent, the unclear category was used. Where AL was assessed under various stimulus conditions, the outcome for the least restrictive circumstance was recorded.

A second reader coded 26 studies for design, measurement type, and outcome. The percentage of interjudge agreement for these three variables was 92%, 85%, and 92%, respectively. The more stringent, chance-corrected reliability coefficient, kappa, was also calculated, the resulting coefficients being .85, .78, and .87, respectively.

Results

The studies are arrayed by age and presented in Table 9.1. The first column reveals a pattern in the outcomes, with several breaks suggested, the first at 24 months, and the second at 60 months. Using these breaks, the array of studies was partitioned into three age groups as shown. The first 24 months after birth are characterized, with three exceptions, by positive outcomes. The preschool years, however, show a mixed pattern of results with no clear preponderance of positive or negative relationships. After age 5 years, the study outcomes are, with one exception, consistently negative.

Conclusion

The reviewed studies have few things in common apart from the fact that they all included some kind of measure of motor activity level for normal humans of varying ages. The studies were conducted by different investigators at different times with different methodologies for different purposes. The outcome measure for this review was an extremely crude trichotomy, yet with the exception of the preschool period, those studies with overlapping and adjacent age ranges generally report the same outcome. The pattern of results implies the presence of a curvilinear trajectory in the mean level of customary motor activity level of humans, a path characterized by increasing activity from the early days of postnatal life to sometime between 2 and 5 years and by decreasing motor activity levels thereafter (see Fig. 9.1).

Corroboration for a curvilinear pattern in activity can be found in other research. Curvilinear age patterns in activity have been reported in longitudinal studies of short-lived animal species (Campbell & Mabry, 1972; Owens, 1975;

TABLE 9.1
Activity Trend Over Within-Study Age Range

AL Trend[a]	Citation	CA (months)	n	Meas[b]	Desgn[c]
		Less than 2 years			
≈	Korner et al. (1981)	<1	72	Inst	Lg
↑*	Campbell (1968)	<1	43	Inst	Lg
↑*	Kessen et al. (1961)	<1	11	Obs	Lg
↑	Gatewood & Weiss (1930)	<1	78	Obs	Lg
≈	Irwin (1930)	<1	4	Comb	Lg
↑*	Richards (1936)	<1	17	Inst	Cs
↑*	Sander & Julia (1966)	<1	6	Inst	Lg
↑*	Campbell et al. (1971)	1	59	Inst	Lg
↓	Ohyabu (1976)	3	2	Inst	Lg
↑	Turnure (1971)	6	33	Obs	Cs
↑	Partington et al. (1971)	12	57	Comb	Cs
↑	Clarke-Stewart (1973)	14	36	Obs	Lg
↑*	Kagan (1971)	17	134	Obs	Lg
		2 to 5 years			
↑*	Routh et al. (1978)	30	100	Obs	Cs
↓*	Lytton (1980)	32	90	Obs	Cs
↑	Manwell & Mengert (1934)	32	35	Obs	Cs
↓*	Milar et al. (1981)	33	48	Comb	Cs
↓*	Cohen et al. (1977)	36	754	Rate	Cs
↑*	Rheingold & Eckerman (1970)	36	48	Obs	Cs
↓*	Fales (1937)	40	32	Obs	Cs
↓	Garvey (1939)	42	22	Inst	Lg
↑	Goodenough (1930)	43	33	Obs	Cs
↑*	Koch & Streit (1932)	46	50	Comb	Cs
≈	Routh et al. (1978)	48	96	Obs	Cs
↓*	Eaton (1983)	50	27	Comb	Cs
≈	Toner et al. (1977)	51	55	Obs	Cs
↑*	Langlois & Downs (1979)	54	64	Obs	Cs
↑	Paulsen & Johnson (1980)	55	55	Rate	Cs
↓	Hatfield et al. (1967)	57	40	Rate	Cs

(Continued)

TABLE 9.1
(Continued)

AL Trend[a]	Citation	CA (months)	n	Meas[b]	Desgn[c]
		Over 5 years			
↓*	Routh et al. (1974)	78	140	Comb	Cs
↓	Victor et al. (1973)	84	8	Inst	Cs
↓*	Spring et al. (1977)	90	1337	Rate	Cs
↓	MacFarlane et al. (1962)	96	77	Rate	Cs
↓	LaPouse & Monk (1964)	114	482	Rate	Cs
↓*	Grinsted (1939)	114	123	Obs	Cs
↑*	Walker (1967)	120	368	Rate	Lg
↓*	Kendall & Brophy (1981)	121	49	Inst	Cs
↓*	Achenbach & Edelbrock (1981)	126	1300	Rate	Cs
↓	McGhee (1900)	150	8718	Rate	Cs
↓*	Rapoport et al. (1980)	251	45	Inst	Cs
↓*	Wessel & Van Huss (1969)	534	47	Obs	Cs
↓*	Douglas & Arenberg (1978)	690	842	Rate	Mx

Note: Citations ordered by mean chronological age of sample.
[a]Relation code: ↑ = positive, ↓ = negative, and ≈ = unclear.
[b]Type of activity level measurement: *Inst* = instrumentation, *Rate* = rating, *Obs* = observation, and *Comb* = combination.
[c]Design: *Cs* = cross-sectional, *Lg* = longitudinal, *Mx* = mixed.
*Age-AL relation reported as significant at $p < .05$.

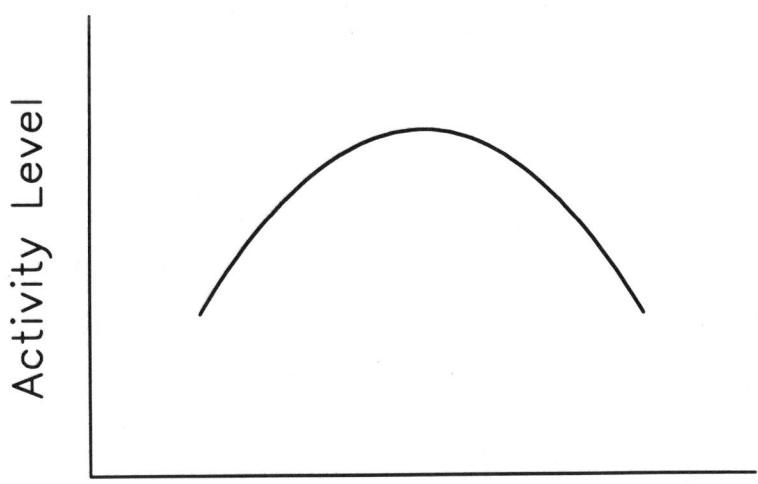

FIG. 9.1. Hypothesized developmental trajectory of activity level across the life span.

Reed, 1947). There is also at least one human study that covers the necessary age range and has a measure of activity level that points to a curvilinear developmental trajectory. Macfarlane, Allen, and Honzik (1954) longitudinally studied behavioral problems in children between 2 and 14 years. One such problem was overactivity, and Macfarlane et al. found a curvilinear pattern like the one implied in the meta-analysis; overactivity peaks as a behavior problem for both boys and girls between 3 and 5 years (Macfarlane et al., 1954).

Methodological objections can, of course, be raised to this developmental meta-analysis. Despite its limitations, such as the combination of heterogeneous measures, the preceding analysis does what a good exploratory analysis should do: It suggests hypotheses, questions, and explanations. Moreover, some implications of the activity trajectory can inform understanding of the development of temperament and personality.

IMPLICATIONS FOR TEMPERAMENT AND PERSONALITY

One question that emerged from the earlier review of activity and its correlates at various ages was: Why does AL change from a primary to secondary dimension of individual difference? The developmental perspective suggests a reason: Adults are much less motorically active than children. To the observer, motor activity is simply less important for meaningful description of adults. Most developmentalists acknowledge a shift from predominantly motor schemes in infancy to predominantly symbolic schemes during childhood and adolescence. This shift to symbolic schemes is apparently accompanied by a decline in motor activity. A more colloquial way of putting it is that the individual, in the course of development, shifts from mostly moving to mostly talking, and the residue of AL variance in adults is seen in the context of social and verbal interactions rather than in motor behavior.

Perhaps it is fortunate that Activity is subsumed in the more symbolic, energy-efficient social exchanges of adult life. Energy efficiency is increasingly important for the aging organism as speed of response slows and as basal metabolism drops. Individual differences in motor exuberance give way to individual differences in level of social engagement, and this analysis suggests that the motorically active child becomes the extroverted adult.

How can a developmental analysis be informative about the shifting valence of high activity from positive to negative to positive? As infants follow the developmental trajectory up, higher AL is positively associated with greater maturity. However, after the AL peak has been passed, the more mature child will be less active by virtue of being farther along and down the developmental trajectory. From this maturity perspective, Matheny's (1989) finding that activity level has a positive relation with mental test scores in infancy, but a negative one in childhood becomes understandable. Children differ in their maturational timing, some being more advanced than others. Thus, some of what may appear to be individual difference variance in activity is probably linked to maturational timing differences. For example, because mental abilities are standardized by chronological age groups, the less mature child will be more likely to lag more mature agemates in cognitive performance—and on the activity trajectory. If this is so, the infant who is lagging maturationally is less active and performs more poorly on age-normed tests, and a positive correlation between activity and cognitive performance results. The child who is lagging maturationally is more active and performs more poorly on the tests, and a negative correlation results.

The preceding analysis does not explain the valence shift across the transition from childhood to adulthood, when, as noted earlier, high activity has generally positive connotations. Several points are relevant. First, by the time adulthood is reached, maturational timing differences between individuals are probably of much less importance than they are during childhood, at least as far as activity level is concerned. Thus, the maturationally delayed child eventually closes the gap on more mature agemates, and maturity-linked differences are likely attenuated. Furthermore, once adulthood is reached, delays in development (staying young) are perceived very positively. Because activity declines across adulthood, higher activity is associated with being younger, which is viewed quite favorably.

CONCLUSIONS

Temperament and personality research, with its attention to individual differences, has tended to be independent of the body of developmental research that emphasizes age-related changes common to all. A developmental perspective, I have tried to argue, can bring some insight to issues of individual difference.

Perhaps activity level is an anomaly among personality traits in having, as I have tried to demonstrate, important developmental characteristics. However, activity may have indirect influences on other behaviors. Jacobs and Dunlap (1976) suggested that activity is a multiplier of other characteristics and noted that someone who is highly active will bring that level of behaving to bear on other traits. For example, the highly active, friendly individual will probably engage in more social interchanges than the quiescent and equally friendly peer. Thus, if a trait is tied to the frequency of certain behaviors (e.g., socializing with others), activity level may well play a mediating role with other, less age-sensitive personality traits.

In conclusion, I offer the general observation that developmental variance may play an important role in understanding individual differences among children and adults. The search for temporal stabilities in traits is worthy of the attention it has received, but perhaps a significant part of individual variability lies with individual variation in the traversing of developmental pathways. That is the lesson of activity level for the developing structure of temperament and personality.

ACKNOWLEDGMENTS

Preparation of this chapter was supported by research grants from the Social Sciences and Humanities Research Council of Canada and by University of Manitoba/SSHRC Funds.

REFERENCES

Achenbach, T. M., & Edelbrock, C. S. (1981). Behavioral problems and competencies reported by parents of normal and disturbed children aged four through sixteen. *Monographs of the Society for Research in Child Development, 46* (Serial No. 188).

Birns, B., Barten, S., & Bridger, W. (1969). Individual differences in temperamental characteristics of infants. *Transactions of the New York Academy of Sciences, 31,* 1071–1082.

Buss, A. H., & Plomin, R. (1975). *A temperament theory of personality development.* New York: Wiley.

Buss, D. M., Block, J. H., & Block, J. (1980). Preschool activity level: Personality correlates and developmental implications. *Child Development, 51,* 401–408.

Butcher, J. E., & Eaton, W. O. (1989). Gross and fine motor proficiency in preschoolers: Relationships with free play behavior and activity level. *Journal of Human Movement Studies, 16,* 27–36.

Campbell, D. (1968). Motor activity in a group of newborn babies. *Biology of the Neonate, 13,* 257–270.

Campbell, D., Kuyek, J., Lang, E., & Partington, M. W. (1971). Motor activity in early life: II. Daily motor activity output in the neonatal period. *Biology of the Neonate, 18,* 108–120.

Campbell, B. A., & Mabry, P. D. (1972). Ontogeny of behavioral arousal: A comparative study. *Journal of Comparative and Physiological Psychology, 81,* 371–379.

Clarke-Stewart, K. A. (1973). Interactions between mothers and their young children: Characteristics and consequences. *Monographs of the Society for Research in Child Development, 38* (Serial No. 153).

Cohen, D. J., Dibble, E., & Grawe, J. M. (1977). Fathers' and mothers' perceptions of children's personality. *Archives of General Psychiatry, 34,* 480–487.

Comrey, A. L. (1973). *A first course in factor analysis.* New York: Academic Press.

Conley, J. J. (1985). Longitudinal stability of personality traits: A multitrait-multimethod-multioccasion analysis. *Journal of Personality and Social Psychology, 49,* 1266–1282.

Crockenberg, S., & Acredolo, C. (1983). Infant temperament ratings: A function of infants, or mothers, or both? *Infant Behavior and Development, 6,* 61–72.

Digman, J. M., & Inouye, J. (1986). Further specification of the five robust factors of personality. *Journal of Personality and Social Psychology, 50,* 116–123.

Douglas, K., & Arenberg, D. (1978). Age changes, cohort differences, and cultural change on the Guilford–Zimmerman Temperament Survey. *Journal of Gerontology, 33,* 737–747.

Eaton, W. O. (1983). Measuring activity level with actometers: Reliability, validity, and arm length. *Child Development, 54,* 720–726.

Eaton, W. O., & Dureski, C. (1986). Parent and actometer measures of motor activity level in the young infant. *Infant Behavior and Development, 9,* 383–393.

Eaton, W. O., & Pressé, M. C. (1985). *Impact, behavioral quality, and popularity in preschool children.* Unpublished manuscript, Department of Psychology, University of Manitoba, Winnipeg, Canada.

Eaton, W. O., & Saudino, K. J. (1992). Prenatal activity level as a temperament dimensions? Individual differences and developmental functions of fetal movement. *Infant Behavior and Development, 15,* 57–70.

Fales, E. (1937). A comparison of the vigorousness of play activities of preschool boys and girls. *Child Development, 8*, 144–158.

Garvey, C. R. (1939). *The activity of young children during sleep: An objective study* (Institute of Child Welfare, Monograph No. 18). Minneapolis: University of Minnesota Press.

Gatewood, M. C., & Weiss, A. P. (1930). Race and sex differences in newborn infants. *Journal of Genetic Psychology, 38*, 31–49.

Goldberg, L. R. (1990). An alternative "description of personality": The Big-Five factor structure. *Journal of Personality and Social Psychology, 59*, 1216–1229.

Goldsmith, H. H., Buss, A. H., Plomin, R., Rothbart, M. K., Thomas, A., Chess, S., Hinde, R. A., & McCall, R. B. (1987). Roundtable: What is temperament? Four approaches. *Child Development, 58*, 505–529.

Goodenough, F. L. (1930). Inter-relationships in the behavior of young children. *Child Development, 1*, 29–47.

Grinsted, A. D. (1939). *Studies in gross bodily movement.* Unpublished doctoral dissertation, Louisiana State University.

Hatfield, J. S., Ferguson, L. R., & Alpert, R. (1967). Mother–child interaction and the socialization process. *Child Development, 38*, 365–414.

Howarth, E. (1976). Were Cattell's "personality sphere" factors correctly identified in the first instance? *British Journal of Psychology, 2*, 213–230.

Irwin, O. C. (1930). The amount and nature of activities of newborn infants under constant external stimulating conditions during the first 10 days of life. *Genetic Psychology Monographs, 8*, 1–92.

Jacobs, A., & Dunlap, D. N. (1976). The clinical interpretation of the GZTS Scales. In J. S. Guilford, W. S. Zimmerman, & J. P. Guilford (Eds.), *The Guilford–Zimmerman Temperament Survey handbook* (pp. 287–299). San Diego: EdITS Publishers.

Kagan, J. (1971). *Change and continuity in infancy.* New York: Wiley.

Kendall, P. C., & Brophy, C. (1981). Activity and attentional correlates of teacher ratings of hyperactivity. *Journal of Pediatric Psychology, 6*, 451–458.

Kessen, W., Williams, E. J., & Williams, J. P. (1961). Selection and test of response measures in the study of the human newborn. *Child Development, 32*, 7–24.

Koch, H. L., & Streit, H. (1932). A study in rating technique with special reference to activity in preschool children. *Journal of Genetic Psychology, 41*, 330–357.

Korner, A. F., Hutchinson, C. A., Koperski, J. A., Kraemer, H. C., & Schneider, P. A. (1981). Stability of individual differences of neonatal motor and crying patterns. *Child Development, 52*, 83–90.

Langlois, J. H., & Downs, A. C. (1979). Peer relations as a function of physical attractiveness: The eye of the beholder or behavioral reality? *Child Development, 50*, 409–418.

LaPouse, R., & Monk, M. A. (1964). Behavior deviations in a representative sample of children: Variation by sex, age, race, social class, and family size. *American Journal of Orthopsychiatry, 34*, 436–446.

Lytton, H. (1980). *Parent–child interaction.* New York: Plenum.

MacFarlane, J. W., Allen, L., & Honzik, M. P. (1954). *A developmental study of the behavior problems of normal children between 21 months and 14 years.* Berkeley: University of California Press.

Manwell, E. M., & Mengert, I. G. (1934). A study of the development of 2- and 3-year-old children with respect to play activities. *University of Iowa Studies in Child Welfare, 9*, 67–111.

Martin, R. P. (1989). Activity level, distractibility, and persistence: Critical characteristics in early schooling. In G. A. Kohnstamm, J. E. Bates, & M. K. Rothbart (Eds.), *Temperament in childhood* (pp. 451–461). New York: Wiley.

Matheny, A. P., Jr. (1980). Bayley's Infant Behavior Record: Behavioral components and twin analyses. *Child Development, 51*, 1157–1167.

Matheny, A. P., Jr. (1989). Temperament and cognition: Relations between temperament and mental test scores. In G. A. Kohnstamm, J. E. Bates, & M. K. Rothbart (Eds.), *Temperament in childhood* (pp. 263–282). New York: Wiley.

McCrae, R. R., & Costa, P. T., Jr. (1987). Validation of the five-factor model of personality across instruments and observers. *Journal of Personality and Social Psychology, 52*, 81–90.

McGhee, Z. (1900). A study in the play life of some South Carolina children. *Journal of Genetic Psychology, 7*, 459–478.

McKeen, N. A. (1988). *Infant motor activity: Temperament and wake–sleep behaviour.* Unpublished master's thesis, University of Manitoba, Winnipeg, Canada.

Mershon, B., & Gorsuch, R. L. (1988). Number of factors in the personality sphere: Does increase in factors increase predictability of real-life criteria? *Journal of Personality and Social Psychology, 55*, 675–680.

Milar, C. R., Schroeder, S. R., Mushak, P., & Boone, L. (1981). Failure to find hyperactivity in preschool children with moderately elevated lead burden. *Journal of Pediatric Psychology, 6*, 85–95.

Ohyabu, Y. (1976). The relation between motor activity and behaviors of infants. *Journal of Child Development, 12*, 24–31.

Owens, N. W. (1975). Social play behaviour in free-living baboons, papio anubis. *Animal Behavior, 23*, 387–408.

Partington, M. W., Lang, E., & Campbell, D. (1971). Motor activity in early life: I. Fries' congenital activity types. *Biology of the Neonate, 18*, 94–107.

Paulsen, K., & Johnson, M. (1980). Impulsivity: A multidimensional concept with developmental aspects. *Journal of Abnormal Child Psychology, 8*, 269–277.

Rapoport, J. L., Buchsbaum, M. S., Weingartner, H., Zahn, T. P., Ludlow, C., & Mikkelsen, E. J. (1980). Dextroamphetamine: Its cognitive and behavioral effects in normal and hyperactive boys and normal men. *Archives of General Psychiatry, 37*, 933–943.

Reed, J. D. (1947). Spontaneous activity in animals. *Psychological Bulletin, 44*, 393–412.

Rheingold, H. L., & Eckerman, C. O. (1970). The infant separates himself from his mother. *Science, 168*, 78–83.

Richards, T. W. (1936). The relation between bodily and gastric activity of newborn infants: I. Correlation and influence of time since feeding. *Human Biology, 8*, 368–380.

Rothbart, M. K. (1989). Temperament and development. In G. A. Kohnstamm, J. E. Bates, & M. K. Rothbart (Eds.), *Temperament in childhood* (pp. 187–247). New York: Wiley.

Routh, D. K., Schroeder, C. S., & O'Tauma, L. A. (1974). Development of activity level in children. *Developmental Psychology, 10*, 163–168.

Routh, D. K., Walton, M. D., & Padan-Belkin, E. (1978). Development of activity level in children revisited: Effects of mother presence. *Developmental Psychology, 14*, 571–581.

Sander, L. W., & Julia, H. L. (1966). Continuous interactional monitoring in the neonate. *Psychosomatic Medicine, 28*, 822–835.

Saudino, K. J., & Eaton, W. O. (1991). Infant temperament and genetics: An objective twin study of motor activity level. *Child Development, 62*, 1167–1174.

Spring, C., Blunden, D., Greenberg, L. M., & Yellin, A. M. (1977). Validity and norms of a hyperactivity rating scale. *Journal of Special Education, 11*, 313–321.

Thomas, A., & Chess, S. (1977). *Temperament and development.* New York: Brunner/Mazel.

Toner, I. J., Holstein, R. B., & Hetherington, E. M. (1977). Reflection-impulsivity and self-control in preschool children. *Child Development, 48*, 239–245.

Tsoi, M. M., & Nicholson, J. N. (1982). A factor analytic study of teachers' ratings of the personality of school children. *Personality and Individual Differences, 3*, 53–63.

Turnure, C. (1971). Response to voice of mother and stranger by babies in the first year. *Developmental Psychology, 4*, 182–190.

Victor, J. B., Halverson, C. F. Jr., Inoff, G., & Buczkowski, H. J. (1973). Objective behavior measures of first- and second-grade boys' free play and teachers' ratings on a behavior problem checklist. *Psychology in the Schools, 10,* 439–443.

Wainer, H. (1984). How to display data badly. *American Statistician, 38,* 137–147.

Walker, R. N. (1967). Some temperament traits in children as viewed by their peers, their teachers, and themselves. *Monographs of the Society for Research in Child Development, 36*(6, Serial No. 114).

Wessel, J. A., & Van Huss, W. D. (1969). The influence of physical activity and age on exercise adaptation of women, 20–69 years. *Journal of Sports Medicine and Physical Fitness, 9,* 173–179.

Zuckerman, M., Kuhlman, D. M., & Camac, C. (1988). What lies beyond E and N? Factor analyses of scales believed to measure basic dimensions of personality. *Journal of Personality and Social Psychology, 54,* 96–107.

CHAPTER
10

TEMPERAMENT, DEVELOPMENT, AND THE BIG FIVE

Stephan A. Ahadi
Mary K. Rothbart
University of Oregon

A rich tradition has developed in the study of personality attempting to identify a taxonomy of individual differences. As has been noted (Briggs, 1992; Cattell, 1965; Goldberg, 1981; Norman, 1967), identification of a structure of personality and the development of a taxonomy of trait descriptors and behavior patterns is important to the field for at least two reasons. First, knowledge of structure establishes the very domain of inquiry for personality psychology. Second, the development of a taxonomy provides a common language allowing acceleration of progress in the field. The current zeitgeist of the Big Five attests that much progress has been made toward the development of a comprehensive taxonomy of personality trait descriptors and behavior patterns.

To the extent that a domain of inquiry has been defined by this activity, however, it becomes necessary for the field to turn its attention to additional levels of analysis. These levels include the investigation of psychological processes underlying dimensions of personality and, when possible, identification of neural systems supporting these processes. By adopting this approach we may further illuminate our understanding of individual differences and their tendencies to cluster together. Temperament researchers have traditionally attempted to adopt this framework (for a historical review, see Rothbart, 1989a). Goals of temperament researchers have traditionally been to identify the psychological processes by which individual differences arise, the neuropsychological systems underlying these psychological processes, the developmental course of these processes, and the interaction of these processes and the environment. When the goals of temperament research are defined in this manner, a rather broad and diverse set of approaches is included within the temperament area, including the biologically based models of H. J. Eysenck (1967; H. J. Eysenck & M. W. Eysenck, 1985), the animal models of Gray (1982, 1987), the behavior genetic models of Buss and Plomin (1975, 1984), and the developmental models of Campos and his associates (Campos, Barrett, Lamb, Goldsmith, & Stenberg, 1983) and Rothbart and Derryberry (Derryberry & Rothbart, 1984; Rothbart, 1991; Rothbart & Derryberry, 1981).

In this chapter, we take a developmental view of temperamental processes that may prove to be related to the Big Five. We take the Big Five to include the factors of Extraversion, Agreeableness, Conscientiousness, Neuroticism, and Openness to Experience. We have previously attempted to relate temperament in childhood to the Big Five (Rothbart, 1989c), and have noted that the simpler factor structure emerging from item-level analyses of parent-report infant temperament questionnaires appears especially suitable for considering longitudinal similarities and differences in structure (Rothbart & Mauro, 1990).

Even if temperament is viewed as the matrix from which later child and adult personality develops, however, a direct mapping of temperament dimensions on the Big Five traits may not be straightforward. First, assessment of personality, especially in adults, often involves assessment of a cognitive self-concept. This self-concept may include beliefs about how the individual would ideally like to be or should be (Higgins, 1987) in addition to beliefs about how the individual is, and the three may not be readily separable. More importantly, interaction between cognition and self-regulation in the adult personality allows for coping strategies that may serve to inhibit or facilitate underlying temperamental tendencies (Carver & Scheier, 1981; Lazarus, 1991; Thomas & Chess, 1977).

In addition, there remains some confusion as to how the Big Five are defined. This problem may be exemplified in the currently overworked construct of "impulsivity," included in both the Extraversion and Conscientiousness dimensions of the Big Five. Costa and McCrae (1985) included a form of impulsivity as a facet of Neuroticism, so that impulsivity is implicated in at least three of the Big Five dimensions. One source of such problems is the absence of a process-oriented approach to personality. Whereas tools like factor analysis have proven fruitful for broadly identifying the dimensions of personality, and indeed that has been the goal of this research, more fine-grained categorizations of traits will need to be made on the basis of common underlying processes rather than behavioral similarity.

Regardless of difficulties involved in directly mapping childhood temperament dimensions onto the Big Five, we might expect overlap of basic temperamental processes on at least a subset of the Big Five dimensions of personality. We approach this issue by considering possible developmental precursors of later personality factors and the systems likely to be involved in their functioning. In addition, we consider a dimension of temperamental variability in infants that does not appear to be well accounted for in adult models.

The precursors we consider include the positive affect and approach underlying what is variously labeled Extraversion, Surgency, or Positive Emotionality, the negative affect and related behaviors underlying what is variously labeled Neuroticism, Anxiety, or Negative Emotionality, and the attentional self-regulatory systems underlying what may be described as Constraint or Effortful Control. Temperament systems will be described with reference to the affective, arousal, and self-regulatory components thought to underlie them (Derryberry & Rothbart, 1988). Because Effortful Control is thought to have superordinate regulative functions over other temperament systems, we then turn to a discussion of how Effortful Control may modulate the expression of temperamental tendencies in the course of personality development.

APPROACH SYSTEMS

The first set of temperament systems addressed are those thought to underlie the broad personality dimension of Extraversion, Surgency, or Positive Emotionality. As these labels imply, this dimension reflects an underlying positive emotion, approach, or reward orientation. The temperamental system is reflected conceptually by what Gray (1981) labeled the Behavioral Activation System. In general, approach orientation subsumes a sensitivity to signals of reward in the environment and an active engagement of the environment by the individual. Approach is manifested behaviorally through sociability (to the extent that other people provide one of the richest sources of both reward and engagement), through a form of impulsivity reflecting immediate responsiveness to signals of reward in the environment, through sensation seeking (engaging in activities that increase levels of cortical arousal whether through sky-diving or daydreaming in a boring class), and activity level (for a review, see H. J. Eysenck & M. W. Eysenck, 1985; Zuckerman, 1991). The dimension may also be partly related to intensity of affective response, especially positive affect.

Some have argued that this dimension is synonymous with the dimension of positive affect underlying emotional experience (Tellegen, 1985; Watson & Tellegen, 1985). However, we feel that defining this dimension simply in terms of Positive Emotionality is too restrictive and fails to take into consideration other nonaffective components. Derryberry and Rothbart (1988) argued that temperament must be understood with respect to not only its affective components, but also with respect to arousal and self-regulatory aspects of individual differences. Our approach indeed views temperament in terms of the functioning of affective-motivational systems. While Positive Emotionality clearly captures the affective component underlying this dimension, it ignores other properties of this temperament system. H. J. Eysenck's (1967) Extraversion label, with its accompanying cortical arousal hypothesis, addresses the arousal component, while Gray's (1987) Behavioral Activation System nicely captures the self-regulative nature of the temperament system with its sensitivity to signals of reward in the environment. Clearly, the complexity and richness of the affective-motivational system is lost when we narrow our focus to only one aspect of the temperament process.

We have found recent evidence for an approach factor in parents' reports of temperament for 6- to 7-year-old children (Ahadi, Rothbart, & Ye, 1993). In a cross-cultural study of temperament, we administered the Children's Behavior Questionnaire (CBQ) to mothers of 6- and 7-year-olds in the United States and China. We employed a principal axis factor analysis, with commonalities estimated through iteration, to identify the latent structure of the CBQ scales. We employed an oblique rotation to identify possible differences in structural relations among the latent factors. (Definitions of the CBQ scales referred to in this chapter are included in Table 10.1.) In both cases a clear three-factor structure emerged. For the larger Chinese sample ($N = 468$), the first factor was defined primarily by Approach, High Intensity Pleasure, Smiling and Laughter, Activity Level, Impulsivity, and a negative loading for Shyness (Table 10.2). In the U.S. sample ($N = 156$), the first factor was defined similarly with two major exceptions. Approach and Smiling and Laughter loaded only moderately on the first factor. Approach in the U.S. sample loaded moderately on all three factors and Smiling and Laughter loaded highly on the third factor.

We have also used laboratory measures of infant temperament to predict parent ratings of temperament on the Children's Behavior Questionnaire at age seven for a small sample of 26 subjects for whom follow-up data was obtained (Rothbart, Derryberry, & Hershey, 1993). Smiling and laughter was assessed in infancy in the laboratory through children's positive reactivity to novel objects and auditory stimuli, and to interaction with an experimenter. A composite measure was formed reflecting the latency, intensity, and duration of emotional reaction. This positive affect measure predicted significantly 7-year-old Approach, Impulsivity, and Activity Level as reported by the mother.

As noted previously, in our cross-cultural study of child temperament, the Smiling and Laughter scale of the CBQ did not load on the first approach-related factor in the U.S. sample. Consistent with that finding, smiling and laughing in infancy did not predict 7-year scores on the Smiling and Laughter scale of the CBQ. Further, infant latency to approach objects in the laboratory predicted 7-year Approach and Impulsivity as well as (negatively) Inhibitory Control and Attentional Focusing. It is interesting to note that what would appear to be a relatively pure measure of approach in infancy is implicated in facets of two of the major temperament systems (i.e., approach and effortful control). Infant Activity Level, assessed via locomotion across a grid at 13 months predicted 7-year Activity Level, Approach, Anger/Frustration, Impulsivity, and (negatively) Sadness.

TABLE 10.1
CBQ Scale

	Description	Example
Activity Level	Level of gross motor activity including rate and extent of locomotion.	Seems always in a big hurry to get from one place to another.
Anger/Frustration	Amount of negative affect related to interruption of ongoing tasks or goal blocking.	Has temper tantrums when s/he doesn't get what s/he wants.
Approach	Amount of excitement and positive anticipation for expected pleasurable activities.	Gets so worked up before an exciting event that s/he has trouble sitting still.
Attentional Focusing	Tendency to maintain attentional focus on task-related channels.	When picking up toys or other jobs, usually keeps at the task until it's done.
Discomfort	Amount of negative affect related to sensory qualities of stimulation, including intensity, rate, or complexity of light, movement, sound, and texture.	Is not very bothered by pain.
Fear	Amount of negative affect, including unease, worry, or nervousness related to anticipated pain or distress and/or potentially threatening situations.	Is not afraid of large dogs and/or other animals.
High Intensity Pleasure	Amount of pleasure or enjoyment related to situations involving high stimulus intensity, rate, complexity, novelty, and incongruity.	Likes going down high slides or other adventurous activities.
Impulsivity	Speed of response initiation	Usually rushes into an activity without thinking about it.
Inhibitory Control	The capacity to plan and to suppress inappropriate approach responses under instructions or in novel or uncertain situations.	Can lower his/her voice when asked to do so.
Low Intensity Pleasure	Amount of pleasure or enjoyment related to situations involving low stimulus intensity, rate, complexity, novelty, and incongruity.	Rarely enjoys just being talked to.
Perceptual Sensitivity	Amount of detection of slight, low intensity stimuli from the external environment.	Notices the smoothness or roughness of objects s/he touches.
Sadness	Amount of negative affect and lowered mood and energy related to exposure to suffering, disappointment, and object loss.	Cries sadly when a favorite toy gets lost or broken.
Shyness	Slow or inhibited approach in situations involving novelty or uncertainty.	Often prefers to watch rather than join other children playing.
Smiling and Laughter	Amount of positive affect in response to changes in stimulus intensity, rate, complexity, and incongruity.	Laughs a lot at jokes and silly happenings.
Soothability and Falling Reactivity	Rate of recovery from peak distress, excitement, or general arousal.	Has a hard time settling down for a nap.

TABLE 10.2
Factor Pattern of CBQ Scales in the PRC Sample

Scale	Factors		
	1	2	3
Approach	.69	.26	.25
High Pleasure	.68		
Smiling	.65		
Activity	.64		−.35
Impulsivity	.63		−.25
Shyness	−.46	.39	
Discomfort		.71	
Fear		.64	
Anger	.30	.59	
Sadness		.58	
Soothability		−.40	
Inhibitory Control			.73
Attention			.64
Low Pleasure			.61
Perceptual Sensitivity	.33		.49

Note: $N = 468$. Only loadings greater than or equal to .25 are presented.

It should also be noted that the approach system likely involves an inhibitory function in addition to its obvious approach functions. H. J. Eysenck (1967) adopted the Pavlovian concept of transmarginal inhibition to account for the decreased responsiveness of introverts to high intensity signals from the environment. Although the operation of this system has by no means been firmly established, it does suggest that we should be careful in our interpretation of the negative loading, for example, of the CBQ Shyness scale on the Approach factor. Although Shyness may reflect absence of approach or reward tendencies, it may also reflect inhibition in response to novel and to high intensity stimuli (Rothbart, 1988, 1989b, 1991).

ANXIETY SYSTEMS

The second temperament system has been variously labeled Neuroticism, Negative Emotionality, or Anxiety. Gray (1981, 1987) identified a Behavioral Inhibition System (BIS) that is sensitive to cues of punishment, frustrative nonreward, and novel stimuli. Activation of the BIS generates fear, inhibits ongoing behavior, increases readiness for action, and increases attention to environmental stimuli (Gray, 1987). H. J. Eysenck (1967) postulated that the basic personality dimension of Neuroticism reflects the underlying reactivity of the limbic system. In general, however, this set of systems can be conceptualized as general threat sensitivity with accompanying negative affect.

The correspondence between this system and the major dimension of negative emotionality underlying the structure of mood has led some to suggest these dimensions are synonymous and that we should label this temperament Negative Affectivity (Tellegen, 1985; Watson & Clark, 1984). Again, focusing on the affective component of this system ignores the self-regulative aspects underlying this temperament system. Effects of BIS activation in Gray's model nicely illustrate the multiplicity of functions associated with this system. Although the affective component, generation of anxiety or negative affect, is clearly important, also important are somatic and autonomic arousal components involving increasing readiness for action, and two self-regulative components, inhibition of ongoing behavior and heightened attention to environmental stimuli. Again, it is important to take a broad consideration of the complexities of this temperament system.

In our cross-cultural study of temperament, the second factor extracted in the Chinese sample of 6- and 7-year-olds was defined by positive loadings for Discomfort, Fear, Anger/Frustration, Sadness, Shyness, and a negative loading for Soothability (Table 10.2). This pattern of relationships was also found for the U.S. sample. Interestingly, in both samples, Approach loaded moderately on this second factor. This may be due to the presence of Anger/Frustration on this dimension, which from infancy onward is an approach-related reaction. Consistent with this, in both samples Anger/Frustration loaded moderately and positively on the first factor.

In the small sample follow-up of children assessed at infancy and at age 7, fear was assessed during infancy in the laboratory through children's negative affective reactions to stimuli that were both novel and intense, composited across the parameters of latency, intensity, and duration. The fear measure in infancy predicted 7-year Fear and Sadness as well as (negatively) Activity Level, Impulsivity, and Approach. Infant behavioral inhibition to novel and intense toys, a response related to fearfulness in infancy, predicted 7-year Attentional Focusing and (negatively) Approach, Anger/Frustration, Risk Enjoyment, and Impulsivity. That infant behavioral inhibition in the laboratory did not predict later fear may illustrate the ambiguity involved in the use of a single overt behavioral marker to identify latent temperament dimensions. Behavioral inhibition in this setting could also have reflected decreased responding to the environment in introverted infants in response to high intensity stimulation or even the cautious, attentional self-regulation in infants high on precursors of Effortful Control.

SELF-REGULATIVE SYSTEMS

Rothbart and Posner (1985) proposed temperamental individual differences in Effortful Control that reflect individual differences in attentional self-regulation. Very generally, self-regulation refers to processes such as attention, approach, withdrawal, attack, behavioral inhibition, and self-soothing that can serve to modulate (facilitate or inhibit) reactivity (Rothbart, 1991; Rothbart & Derryberry, 1981). Self-regulation in this general sense is an integral component of all temperament systems. Effortful Control as a temperamental dimension in itself, however, refers to superordinate self-regulatory systems that can assert control over the reactive and self-regulatory processes of other temperament systems, so that an analogy to "effort" or "will" is appropriate. As noted earlier, Effortful Control as a general dimension in temperament is thought to reflect individual differences in related, but anatomically distinct attentional systems, perhaps most importantly, the anterior attention system (Posner & Petersen, 1990; Posner & Rothbart, 1992). Operationally, Effortful Control is reflected in individual differences in the ability to voluntarily sustain focus on a task, to voluntarily shift attention from one task to another, to voluntarily initiate action, and to voluntarily inhibit action. Although the maturation of this system undergoes rapid growth during the last half of the infant's first year, this system appears to continue to mature throughout at least the preschool period (Rothbart, 1989a, 1989b).

Interestingly, attentional self-regulating systems, unlike the approach and avoidance systems, do not appear to have an affective component. (There are, however, affective aspects of interest and boredom involved in the maintenance of attention to rewarding stimuli.) Moreover, because the self-regulatory nature of this temperament system is, under at least some conditions, superordinate to the other temperament systems, individual differences in Effortful Control can have important consequences for the developing personality.

Evidence has been found for longitudinal stability of Effortful Control. Shoda, Mischel, and Peake (1990) did a 10-year follow-up study of adolescents who had participated as preschoolers (mean age 4;4) in various delay of gratification experiments. They found that children who were able to self-impose delay of gratification when rewards were exposed during the waiting period were rated 10 years later by their parents on the California Child Q-Sort as being more planful, attentive, able to concentrate, to delay gratification, and to maintain composure under stress. Parents rated these children on the Adolescent Coping Questionnaire as being able to exhibit self-control in frustrating situations, unlikely to yield to temptation, and relatively undistractible when trying to concentrate. They also found that these children scored higher on both the verbal and quantitative measures of the Scholastic Aptitude Test.

In our cross-cultural study of temperament, the third latent dimension underlying the CBQ scales in the Chinese sample was defined primarily by Inhibitory Control, Attentional Focusing, Low Intensity Pleasures, and Perceptual Sensitivity. A somewhat similar pattern was found for the U.S. sample, except that Attentional Focusing did not load on this factor, whereas Smiling and Laughter loaded strongly. One explanation for the dissociation of Smiling and Laughter from the first approach factor to the third factor is that the U.S. sample is simply much smaller so that the extracted solution is less reliable. However, the loading of Smiling and Laughter on the third factor was strong enough to suggest that in the U.S. sample, Smiling and Laughter may be associated with the third factor. In a culture like the United States, where socialization pressures are toward being outgoing, sociable, and even gregarious, Smiling and Laughter might be a better index of self-regulation of behavior than of positive affect.

In considering relationships among factors in our study, this third factor was correlated negatively with the approach factor in the Chinese sample and was uncorrelated with the anxiety factor, whereas in the U.S. sample, the structural relation was reversed. The self-regulation factor in the United States was negatively correlated with the anxiety factor and uncorrelated with the approach factor. Such differences in structural relations among the factors may be reflective of prevailing cultural values. If cultural values, such as those in the United States, tend to discourage avoidant, fearful, and negative behaviors, one might expect individuals' self-regulative capacities to work to suppress such behavioral responding. Conversely, if Chinese cultural values tend to discourage approach, impulsive, and high activity level behaviors (Ho, 1986), then one might expect individual's self-regulative capacities to work to suppress those behavioral tendencies.

EFFORTFUL CONTROL AND PERSONALITY DEVELOPMENT

As noted previously, Effortful Control as a temperament system is thought to be superordinate to the approach and negative affect systems. As a superordinate system, it should have observable consequences for individual differences in the expression of underlying temperamental tendencies specifically, and personality development more generally (Rothbart, 1991). This section discusses the possible role of attentional self-regulation in the modulation of temperamental tendencies as well as in the development of later personality characteristics. We begin by considering possible moderating effects of attentional self-regulation on the approach and anxiety temperament systems. We then discuss the possible role of attentional self-regulation in the development of Conscientiousness and Agreeableness.

Effortful Control and Approach

Developmentally, approach tendencies require self-regulation. The child's capacity to inhibit crossing the street in compliance with parental rules invokes a process whereby attention to the "reward" contingency of playing with one's friends across the street becomes reoriented to possible consequences of violating parental rules. The capacity to self-regulate approach tendencies become increasingly more important as strength of the approach system increases.

Cultural norms or values concerning approach tendencies may influence the relationship between attentional self-regulation and approach. As noted previously, although the latent factors of self-regulation and approach were uncorrelated in the U.S. sample of 6- and 7-year-olds, these latent factors were negatively correlated in the Chinese sample. Reviews of Chinese socialization patterns point rather clearly to devaluation of approach tendencies in the Chinese culture where "active and exploratory demands tend to be thwarted even during the period of infancy and early childhood" (Ho, 1986, p. 4).

Effortful Control and Anxiety

Attentional self-regulation also appears to have important moderating influences on negative affect systems. While the anxiety systems appear to operate in such a way as to orient attention to the environment (Gray, 1987) or even more specifically to threatening signals in the environment (Christianson, E. F. Loftus, Hoffman, & G. R. Loftus, 1991; Kramer, Buckhout, & Eugenio, 1990), a superordinate attentional system is necessary to reorient attention away from the threatening signal to evaluate the nature of the threat and to identify and implement appropriate coping strategies.

In a study by Christianson et al. (1991, Experiment 3), subjects were presented a series of slides "depicting everyday scenes that a person might see on his or her way to or from work" (p. 697). A critical eighth slide depicted either a woman riding a bike (control condition), a woman lying on the ground beside her bike bleeding from a head injury (emotion condition), or a woman carrying a bicycle on her shoulder (novel condition). Subjects were exposed to each slide for 2.7 sec and subjects' eye movements were recorded to identify the frequency and duration of subjects' eye fixations on the central detail (i.e., the woman). The mean duration of eye fixations on the central detail for subjects in the emotion condition was significantly less than the mean duration of eye fixation in the other two conditions. Interestingly, however, the mean number of eye fixations on the central detail was significantly greater for subjects in the emotional condition. Whereas subjects in the emotional condition spent less time attending to the central detail per fixation, they reoriented attention to the central detail more frequently. More than one process may be involved in this situation. Threat stimuli may draw attention but also repel it due to their association with punishment. An anxiety system may also serve to orient attention while attentional self-regulation may serve to override this "automatic" response. Relative strength of attentional self-regulation versus anxiety may serve to determine ability to cope with negative affectivity attentionally (Derryberry & Rothbart, 1988).

In a number of studies using adult and adolescent measures of self-reported temperament, we have found that persons who report the ability to easily shift and focus their attention also report lower distress susceptibility (e.g., Derryberry & Rothbart, 1988). We have also seen attentional disengagement working to oppose distress in infants, as adults soothe their infants through distraction or as the infants move their own attentional focus from one location to another (Rothbart, Ziaie, & O'Boyle, 1992). In adults, there is laboratory evidence of individual differences in flexibility of attention (Keele & Hawkins, 1982) and further laboratory evidence that individuals who report high negative affect have difficulty moving their attention away from a negative location (MacLeod & Matthews, 1988). These latter findings suggest that an inability to regulate attentional control may be implicated in anxiety disorders.

The ability to shift and focus attention seems not to be limited to "objective" environmental signals. Larsen (1992) had subjects complete a symptom checklist three times a day (at noon for symptoms experienced during the morning, at dinnertime for symptoms experienced during the afternoon, and before going to bed for symptoms experienced during the evening) for 2 months. Following the 2 months of online ratings, subjects were asked to rate retrospectively how often they had experienced each of the symptoms during the past 2 months. Although Neuroticism, as measured by the Eysenck Personality Questionnaire-Revised (S. B. G. Eysenck, H. J. Eysenck, & Barrett, 1985), was correlated with symptoms reported online, retrospective ratings of symptoms were exaggerated relative to online reports. Moreover, this exaggeration was also systematically related to Neuroticism, suggesting that the relationship between Neuroticism and memory for symptoms is not simply determined by individual differences at the time of encoding. Similarly, Ahadi, Fujita, and Diener (1992) found that whereas Neuroticism accounted for substantial unique variation in global and daily ratings of subjective well-being, it did not account for significant unique variation in ratings of well-being from moment to moment. Attentional self-regulation may have an important role in determining the kinds of "work" individuals perform on their memories, consistent with the "neurotic" characterization that appears to go beyond simply "negative emotionality."

Because attentional self-regulation appears to have important moderating effects on the anxiety systems, we might ask whether anxiety can be overregulated. Recent research on repressive style is informative on this question. This research utilizes the Marlowe–Crowne scale as a measure of defensiveness, in addition to the Taylor Manifest Anxiety Scale to identify repressive style (for a review, see Weinberger, 1990). The Marlowe–Crowne scale assesses "behaviors which are culturally sanctioned and approved but which are improbable of occurrence" such as "I never hesitate to go out of my way to help someone in trouble" (Crowne & Marlowe, 1960, p. 350). Repressors are identified as individuals who report very low susceptibility to negative affect in both trait and state measures, but score high on the Marlowe–Crowne social desirability scale.

In fact, these identified repressors tend to score even lower on measures of negative affectivity than Negative Affectivity (NA) low scorers who do not score high on the measure of social desirability. They also tend to see themselves as "maintaining firm control over their negative affects and egoistic impulses. There is also considerable evidence ... that repressors report very little discrepancy between ratings of their actual and ideal selves" (Weinberger, 1990, p. 349). Interestingly, repressors report low susceptibility to negative affectivity, but are physiologically reactive (spontaneous skin resistance, heart rate), similar to subjectively distressed individuals under stressful circumstances. On at least one measure, the repressors were more reactive (forehead electromyograph, EMG; Weinberger, Schwartz, & Davidson, 1979). Thus, it would seem that at least some people who are temperamentally susceptible to negative affectivity may be able to keep others, and possibly themselves, unaware of it.

This repressive mechanism can have implications for personality measurement, especially if one is concerned about psychological processes underlying personality. While repressors may give self-reports, and even be rated by others, as being behaviorally and emotionally nonanxious, the processes by which these descriptively similar outcomes occur may be quite different for true low anxious individuals than for repressors.

Effortful Control and Conscientiousness

Traits making up the broad personality dimension variously labeled Conscientiousness, Constraint, or Superego Strength appear to be strongly self-regulative in function and may be developmentally related to Effortful Control. Tellegen and Waller (in press) reported a factor analysis of the scales in their Multidimensional Personality Questionnaire (MPQ), Cattell's 16PF, and Jackson's Personality Research Form (PRF). Loading on their factor of Constraint were the MPQ scales of Control, Harm Avoidance, and Traditionalism, the 16PF scales of G (conscientiousness) and Q3 (controlled), and the PRF scales of Need for Cognitive Structure, Harm avoidance, Need for Order, and, loading negatively, Impulsivity. These constructs appear to have a strong self-regulatory nature that, as some of the trait labels suggest, may be crucial for effective socialization of the individual.

The adolescent personality correlates of childhood self-imposed delay of gratification in the Shoda et al. (1990) study bear a striking resemblance to the constellation of traits making up the Conscientiousness dimension. In the Shoda et al. study, children who were able to spontaneously delay gratification when rewards were exposed, were rated 10 years later as being persistent, planful, attentive and able to concentrate, and using and responding to reason, among others. These characteristics are virtually synonymous with traits such as persistent, organized, self-disciplined, and logical, which define the positive pole of Conscientiousness (Goldberg, 1990). It may also be the case that one's ability to control attention facilitates internalization of societal values. Conversely, inability to control attention may lead to the more disorganized, inconsistent, and nonconformist characterization of individuals low on Conscientiousness.

Effortful Control and Agreeableness

Although the Anger/Frustration scale of the CBQ loaded on the second, "negative affect" factor for both the U.S. and Chinese samples of 6- and 7-year-old children, it is interesting to note that Anger/Frustration and Fear appear to be separable in infancy (Rothbart & Mauro, 1990) and they also appear to be separable in adulthood, with anger appearing to reside in the negative pole of Agreeableness. By the second half of the first year of life there are differential tendencies that, in the case of fear, appear to be related to later internalizing characteristics such as fearfulness, shyness, and sadness, and in the case of anger, to later externalizing characteristics, including proneness to anger, aggression, and general lack of control. We have evidence from the longitudinal work of Bates and his colleagues (Bates, Freeland, & Lounsbury, 1979; Bates, Maslin, & Franke, 1985) that we can predict from these two kinds of parent-reported infant negative affect to the two major kinds of reported behavior problems from 3 to 6 years. Fearful children (those relatively unadaptable to new people and places) have a tendency to show later internalizing behavior problems. Children with early frequent and intense expressions of irritable distress later have a tendency toward both internalizing and externalizing behavior problems.

In our small sample follow-up, infant anger/frustration was assessed in the laboratory through composited negative affect to objects placed out of reach, behind a plexiglas barrier, or removed from infants. The infant measures (at 10 but not 13 months) predicted 7-year Anger/Frustration, Activity Level, Impulsivity, and Risk Enjoyment as well as (negatively) Soothability, Attentional Focussing, and Sadness. These correlates seem to suggest that while anger and frustration are structurally related to high negative affect, they may also be related to high Approach and low Effortful Control, which may account for the externalizing nature of the anger/frustration response.

In considering the possible developmental role of Effortful control on Conscientiousness and Agreeableness, it is interesting to note that Eysenck's Psychoticism factor includes components of both Conscientiousness and Agreeableness. When Eysenck's dimensions are mapped onto the Big Five domain, Psychoticism is consistently represented as a blend of Conscientiousness and Agreeableness (e.g., Digman, 1990; John, 1989). If it is the case that Effortful Control is implicated in the development of both Conscientiousness and Agreeableness, this might account for why Eysenck is able to account with one dimension what Big Five researchers insist are two conceptually unique dimensions.

Zuckerman, Kuhlman, and Camac (1988) factor analyzed 46 scale scores from eight personality tests. They reported three-, five-, and seven-factor solutions, although here we are interested in the most differentiated of these, the seven-factor solution. Specifically, we are interested in three primary factors that, in a second-order factor analysis, clustered to form a superfactor that might be labeled Psychoticism. One of these factors was defined positively by Autonomy, Experience Seeking, and Risk Taking, and negatively by Conformity, Succorance, Socialization, and Inhibition of Aggression. A second of these three primary factors was defined by Impulsivity, Monotony Avoidance, quick Decision Time, Psychoticism, lack of Persistence, and negatively by need for Cognitive Structure. The third factor was defined by Aggression, Disinhibition, Boredom Susceptibility, and negatively by Responsibility, Social Desirability, and a Lie scale (probably also reflecting social desirability).

Thus, even in the most differentiated structure model presented, characteristics associated with Conscientiousness and Agreeableness did not, in at least two of these primary factors, differentiate, but rather consistently remained as opposite poles of the "mini-factors." We have no desire to enter into the debate as to the correct structural model of personality description, but it would be interesting to determine whether Conscientiousness and Agreeableness may share developmentally at least one common matrix, that of Effortful Control. At the same time, the descriptive contents of Conscientiousness and Agreeableness are different enough to indicate that they do not share other important developmental inputs. It is interesting to note that Robins, John, and Caspi (chap. 14 in this vol.) found both Conscientiousness and Agreeableness to be strongly negatively correlated with adolescent antisocial personality. It should be noted, however, that they also found Conscientiousness and Agreeableness to account for unique variation in adolescent self-reported delinquency.

CONCLUSIONS AND SUGGESTIONS FOR FUTURE RESEARCH

We hope this chapter has reflected both the importance of developing a taxonomy of trait descriptors and behavior patterns as well as the importance of identifying the processes underlying these traits and behavior patterns. The Big Five taxonomy has provided us with a target framework for attempting to identify how infant and child temperamental dimensions may interact with each other and the environment to create variation in personality.

We have attempted an initial mapping with respect to four of the Big Five dimensions. Approach-related dimensions of infant and child temperament appear to map fairly directly onto the Big Five dimension of Extraversion/Surgency. However, the temperamental dimension of Effortful Control may also play a role in modulating the expression of approach-related tendencies. Similarly, anxiety-related dimensions of infant and child temperament appear to map fairly directly on the Big Five dimension of Neuroticism/Negative Emotionality. However, the modulating influence of Effortful Control may lead to lower negative affect, and possibly at the extreme, to repressive tendencies for those high on Effortful Control. We have suggested that Effortful Control may be implicated in the regulation of anger/frustration tendencies that may emerge as Agreeableness, and that Effortful Control may also serve to facilitate internalization and identification of social norms and values in the developing personality, to emerge as Conscientiousness. We have not attempted to map infant and child temperament onto Openness to Experience/Intellectance. To date, few have even looked for temperamental variation along this dimension in children (for a notable exception, see Digman & Inouye, 1986; Digman & Takemoto-Chock, 1981) or infants.

We do want to reinforce, however, that having a taxonomic framework of trait descriptors and behavior patterns is not sufficient for a model of personality. Efforts to describe the psychological processes and developmental influences on these dimensions are essential (Rothbart & Ahadi, 1994). In our attempt to describe the psychological processes that may underly the Big Five, we hope to have conveyed a sense of the dynamics of personality development and functioning that can be lost in static taxonomic models. Especially with respect to the temperamental dimension of Effortful Control, we have suggested that superordinate regulatory systems may have powerful influences on the modulation of other temperamental tendencies and on the effectiveness of social learning.

In considering a process-based approach, we have also had cause to consider some assumptions that guide researchers in their studies of individual differences. When Allport and Odbert (1936) compiled their list of trait adjectives, they were guided by the very reasonable, and eventually fruitful, assumption that important individual differences will be encoded through time in language. From this assumption the conclusion comes easily that the more words existing to describe a characteristic behavior pattern, the more important that behavior pattern. Consequently, Big Five taxonomies have generally found the most "important" dimension to be Surgency/Extraversion, followed by Agreeableness, Conscientiousness, Negative Emotionality/Neuroticism, and Openness to Experience.

The problem with this assumption is that importance in this model is strongly confounded with observability. It seems more than plausible to us that many of the most important psychological processes result in covert behavior and thought that are more difficult to label. Because anxiety serves to inhibit behavior, it could be said that anxiety is related to absence of behavior, and absence of behavior may not lend itself to rich description. Furthermore, except in the case of severe psychopathology, most of the rumination and worry characteristic of anxiety is also covert (we admit our personal fears and worries only to those closest to us), further detracting from the observability and rich description of variation along this dimension. Consequently, we question the value of imparting a sense of "importance" to a personality dimension based on its representation in the language. In fact, a brief scan of the research literature would suggest that trait Factor IV (Neuroticism) is probably one of the two or three most important trait dimensions.

In addition, as noted previously, the constellation of traits that make up the Big Five dimensions reflect the outcomes of temperamental and environmental interactions. Viewing the Big Five as conceptually independent dimensions of variation in personality denies the possibility that these trait dimensions may evolve from common sources of temperamental variation. For example, we have discussed temperamental variation in Effortful Control as a superordinate regulatory system that may be represented diffusely across the Big Five dimensions of personality. Only by adopting a process approach can we determine whether the Big Five develop from relatively independent temperamental and environmental factors or whether they share some common underlying matrix. Defining the Big Five as conceptually independent via varimax rotations does not make them independent in reality. It may be possible that by identifying processes underlying the Big Five, the empirical relationships among the Big Five will become meaningful.

Finally, although we are only just beginning to get a grasp of the kinds of psychological processes that may underly the major dimensions of personality, it seems important to also consider additional levels of analysis in the development of personality. A neural systems level of analysis, for example, might add a good deal more to our understanding of the interactions between emotion and attention in personality development (Rothbart, Derryberry & Posner, 1994). We are currently studying the development of attentional control in infancy as it relates to both neural development and the development of individual differences in temperamental emotionality (Johnson, Posner, & Rothbart, 1991; Posner, Rothbart, & Harmon, in press; Rothbart, Posner, & Boylan, 1990).

In cognitive neuroscience terms, emotion can be seen as a data-processing (cognitive) system that provides information about what environmental and internal events mean to us. This information is relayed to consciousness both directly (amygdala to cortex) and indirectly via feedback from somatic reactivity programmed via the hypothalamus. Different distributed brain systems have been found for attentional than for emotional analysis although the systems are linked (LeDoux, 1989; Posner & Rothbart, 1992). We thus may or may not be aware of the output of the emotional analysis, depending on what we code as emotion and/or what we attend to. The emotional analysis appears to be closely related to motivational outcomes: This is dangerous, I'm going to stay away from it; this is bad, it should be destroyed; this is good, it should be appreciated and preserved; this is interesting, it should be explored; I don't know what this is, but (depending to a degree on individual differences in temperament) I'm either going to go right after it or I want nothing to do with it.

By studying the interaction of emotion and attention from multiple levels of analysis we may gain greater insight into the stability and instability of temperament in development. For example, our research has already demonstrated that some forms of attentional self-regulation (the posterior attention system; Posner & Peterson, 1990) appear to develop rapidly from 3 to 6 months of age (Johnson et al., 1991; Rothbart et al., 1990). However, a complete maturation of structures comprising the executive attention system may not occur until adolescence (Chugani, Phelps, & Mazziotta, 1987; Huttenlocher, 1990). Consequently, not only are there individual differences in adult levels of attentional processes that may be seen to underly Effortful Control (Rothbart & Posner, 1985), but we would also expect maturational differences in levels of Effortful Control as well as differences in maturation rate.

By beginning to observe temperament from a cognitive neuroscience perspective, we realize that personality development is not simply a dynamic environment acting on a static temperament system, but rather that both environmental and neurophysiological substrates of temperament are dynamic. From this perspective, extremely high levels of behavioral stability, especially in the developing child, are not to be expected, and our ultimate understanding of the development of personality will be complex.

REFERENCES

Ahadi, S. A., Fujita, F., & Diener, E. (1992). *The Big Five and their relationship to global, daily, and momentary well-being.* Unpublished manuscript.

Ahadi, S. A., Rothbart, M. K., & Ye, R. M. (1993). Child temperament in the U.S. and China: Similarities and differences. *European Journal of Personality, 7,* 359–378.

Allport, G. W., & Odbert, H. S. (1936). Trait-names: A psycho-lexical study. *Psychological Monographs, 47* (1, Whole No. 211).

Bates, J. E., Freeland, C.A.B., & Lounsbury, M. L. (1979). Measurement of infant difficultness. *Child Development, 50,* 794–803.

Bates, J. E., Maslin, C. A., & Franke, K. A. (1985). Attachment security, mother–child interaction, and temperament as predictors of behavior-problem ratings at age 3 years. In I. Bretherton & E. Waters (Eds.), Growing points in attachment theory and research. *Society for Research in Child Development Monographs, 50* (Serial No. 209), 167–193.

Briggs, S. R. (1992). Assessing the five-factor model of personality description. *Journal of Personality, 60,* 253–293.

Buss, A. H., & Plomin, R. (1975). *A temperament theory of personality development.* New York: Wiley.

Buss, A. H., & Plomin, R. (1984). *Temperament: Early developing personality traits.* Hillsdale, NJ: Lawrence Erlbaum Associates.

Campos, J. J., Barrett, K. C., Lamb, M. E., Goldsmith, H. H., & Stenberg, C. (1983). Socioemotional development. In P. H. Mussen (Series Ed.) & M. M. Haith & J. J. Campos (Vol. Eds.), *Handbook of child psychology: Vol. 2. Infancy and developmental biology* (pp. 783–916). New York: Wiley.

Carver, C. S., & Scheier, M. F. (1981). *Attention and self-regulation: A control-theory approach to human behavior.* New York: Springer-Verlag.

Cattell, R. B. (1965). *The scientific analysis of personality.* Baltimore: Penguin.

Christianson, S. A., Loftus, E. F., Hoffman, H., & Loftus, G. R. (1991). Eye fixations and memory for emotional events. *Journal of Experimental Psychology: Learning, Memory, and Cognition, 17,* 693–701.

Chugani, H. T., Phelps, M. E., & Mazziotta, J. C. (1987). Positron emission tomography study of human brain functional development. *Annals of Neurology, 22,* 487–497.

Costa, P. T., Jr., & McCrae, R. R. (1985). *The NEO Personality Inventory manual.* Odessa, FL: Psychological Assessment Resources.

Crowne, D. P., & Marlow, D. A. (1960). A new scale of social desirability independent of psychopathology. *Journal of Consulting Psychology, 24,* 349–354.

Derryberry, D., & Rothbart, M. K. (1984). Emotion, attention, and temperament. In C. Izard, J. Kagan, & R. Zajonc (Eds.), *Emotion, cognition and behavior* (pp. 132–166). Cambridge, England: Cambridge University Press.

Derryberry, D., & Rothbart, M. K. (1988). Arousal, affective and attentional components of adult temperament. *Journal of Personality and Social Psychology, 55,* 953–966.

Digman, J. M. (1990). Personality structure: Emergence of the five-factor model. *Annual Review of Psychology, 41,* 417–440.

Digman, J. M., & Inouye, J. (1986). Further specification of the five robust factors of personality. *Journal of Personality and Social Psychology, 50,* 116–123.

Digman, J. M., & Takemoto-Chock, N. K. (1981). Factors in the natural language of personality: Re-analysis, comparison, and interpretation of six major studies. *Multivariate Behavioral Research, 16,* 149–170.

Eysenck, H. J. (1967). *The biological basis of personality*. Springfield, IL: Thomas.
Eysenck, H. J., & Eysenck, M. W. (1985). *Personality and individual differences: A natural science approach*. New York: Plenum.
Eysenck, S. B. G., Eysenck, H. J., & Barrett, P. (1985). A revised version of the psychoticism scale. *Personality and Individual Differences, 6*, 21–29.
Goldberg, L. R. (1981). Language and individual differences: The search for universals in personality lexicons. In L. Wheeler (Ed.), *Review of personality and social psychology* (Vol. 2, pp. 141–165). Beverly Hills, CA: Sage.
Goldberg, L. R. (1990). An alternative "Description of Personality": The Big-Five factor structure. *Journal of Personality and Social Psychology, 59*, 1216–1229.
Gray, J. A. (1981). A critique of Eysenck's theory of personality. In H. J. Eysenck (Ed.), *A model for personality* (pp. 246–276). Berlin: Springer-Verlag.
Gray, J. A. (1982). *The neuropsychology of anxiety: An enquiry into the functions of the septo-hippocampal system*. New York: Oxford University Press.
Gray, J. A. (1987). *The psychology of fear and stress*. New York: Cambridge University Press.
Higgins, E. T. (1987). Self-discrepancy: A theory relating self and affect. *Psychological Review, 94*, 319–340.
Ho, D.Y.F. (1986). Chinese patterns of socialization: A critical review. In M. H. Bond (Ed.), *The psychology of the Chinese people* (pp. 1–37). New York: Oxford University Press.
Huttenlocher, P. R. (1990). Morphometric study of human cerebral cortex development. *Neuropsychologia, 28*, 517–527.
John, O. P. (1989). Towards a taxonomy of personality descriptors. In D. M. Buss & N. Cantor (Eds.), *Personality psychology: Recent trends and emerging directions* (pp. 261–271). New York: Springer-Verlag.
Johnson, M. H., Posner, M. I., & Rothbart, M. K. (1991). Components of visual orienting in early infancy: Contingency learning, anticipatory looking and disengaging. *Journal of Cognitive Neuroscience, 3*, 335–344.
Keele, S. W., & Hawkins, H. L. (1982). Explorations of individual differences relevant to high level skill. *Journal of Motor Behavior, 14*, 3–23.
Kramer, T. H., Buckhout, R., & Eugenio, P. (1990). Weapon focus, arousal, and eyewitness memory: Attention must be paid. *Law and Human Behavior, 14*, 167–184.
Larsen, R. J. (1992). Neuroticism and selective encoding and recall of symptoms: Evidence from a combined concurrent-retrospective study. *Journal of Personality and Social Psychology, 62*, 480–488.
Lazarus, R. S. (1991). *Emotion and adaptation*. New York: Oxford University Press.
LeDoux, J. E. (1989). Cognitive-emotional interactions in the brain. *Cognition and Emotion, 3*, 267–289.
MacLeod, C., & Mathews, A. (1988). Anxiety and the allocation of attention to threat. *Quarterly Journal of Experimental Psychology, 40A*, 653–670.
Norman, W. T. (1967). *2800 personality trait descriptors: Normative operating characteristics for a university population*. Department of Psychology, University of Michigan, Ann Arbor.
Posner, M. I., & Peterson, S. E. (1990). The attention system of the human brain. *Annual Review of Neuroscience, 13*, 25–42.
Posner, M. I., & Rothbart, M. K. (1992). Attention mechanisms and conscious experience. In M. Rugg & A. D. Milner (Eds.), *Consciousness and cognition* (pp. 91–112). London: Academic Press.
Posner, M. I., Rothbart, M. K., & Harmon, C. (in press). Cognitive science contributions to culture and emotion. In S. Kitayama & H. Markus (Eds.), *Culture and emotion*. Washington, DC: American Psychological Association.
Rothbart, M. K. (1988). Temperament and the development of inhibited approach. *Child Development, 59*, 1241–1250.

Rothbart, M. K. (1989a). Biological processes of temperament. In G. Kohnstamm, J. Bates, & M. K. Rothbart (Eds.), *Temperament in childhood* (pp. 77–110). Chichester, England: Wiley.

Rothbart, M. K. (1989b). Temperament and development. In G. A. Kohnstamm, J. E. Bates, & M. K. Rothbart (Eds.), *Temperament in childhood* (pp. 187–247). Chichester, England: Wiley.

Rothbart, M. K. (1991). Temperament: A developmental framework. In A. Angleitner & J. Strelau (Eds.), *Explorations in temperament: International perspectives on theory and measurement* (pp. 61–74). New York: Plenum.

Rothbart, M. K., & Ahadi, S. A. (1994). Temperament and the development of personality. *Journal of Abnormal Psychology, 103*, 55–66.

Rothbart, M. K., & Derryberry, D. (1981). Development of individual differences in temperament. In M. E. Lamb & A. L. Brown (Eds.), *Advances in developmental psychology* (Vol. 1, pp. 37–86). Hillsdale, NJ: Lawrence Erlbaum Associates.

Rothbart, M. K., Derryberry, D., & Hershey, K. (1993). *Stability of temperament in childhood: Laboratory infant assessment to parent report at seven years.* Unpublished manuscript.

Rothbart, M. K., Derryberry, D., & Posner, M. I. (1994). A psychobiological approach to the development of temperament. In J. E. Bates & T. D. Wachs (Eds.), *Temperament: Individual differences at the interface of biology and behavior* (pp. 83–116). Washington, DC: American Psychological Association.

Rothbart, M. K., & Mauro, J. A. (1990). Questionnaire measures of infant temperament. In J. W. Fagen & J. Colombo (Eds.), *Individual differences in infancy: Reliability, stability and prediction* (pp. 411–429). Hillsdale, NJ: Lawrence Erlbaum Associates.

Rothbart, M. K., & Posner, M. (1985). Temperament and the development of self-regulation. In Hartlage, L. C. & Telzrow, C. F. (Eds.), *The neuropsychology of individual differences: A developmental perspective* (pp. 93–123). New York: Plenum.

Rothbart, M. K., Posner, M. I., & Boylan, A. (1990). Regulatory mechanisms in infant development. In J. Enns (Ed.), *The development of attention: Research and theory* (pp. 139–160). Amsterdam: Elsevier.

Rothbart, M. K., Ziaie, H., & O'Boyle, C. G. (1992). Self-regulation and emotion in infancy. In N. Eisenberg & R. A. Fabes (Eds.), Emotion and its regulation in early development, *New Directions in Child Development, 55*, 7–24.

Shoda, Y., Mischel, W., & Peake, P. K. (1990). Predicting adolescent cognitive and self-regulatory competencies from preschool delay of gratification: Identifying diagnostic conditions. *Developmental Psychology, 26*, 978–986.

Tellegen, A. (1985). Structures of mood and personality and their relevance to assessing anxiety, with an emphasis on self-report. In A. H. Tuma & J. D. Maser (Eds.), *Anxiety and the anxiety disorders* (pp. 681–706). Hillsdale, NJ: Lawrence Erlbaum Associates.

Tellegen, A., & Waller, N. G. (in press). Exploring personality through test construction: Development of the Multidimensional Personality Questionnaire. In S. R. Briggs & J. M. Cheek (Eds.), *Personality measures: Development and evaluation* (Vol. 1). Greenwich, CT: JAI Press.

Thomas, A., & Chess, S. (1977). *Temperament and development.* New York: Brunner/Mazel.

Watson, D., & Clark, L. A. (1984). Negative affectivity: The disposition to experience aversive emotional states. *Psychological Bulletin, 96*, 465–490.

Watson, & Tellegen, A. (1985). Toward a consensual structure of mood. *Psychological Bulletin, 98*, 219–235.

Weinberger, D. A. (1990). The construct validity of the repressive coping style. In J. L. Singer (Ed.), *Repression and dissociation* (pp. 337–386). Chicago: University of Chicago Press.

Weinberger, D. A., Schwartz, G. E., & Davidson, R. J. (1979). Low-anxious, high-anxious, and repressive coping styles: Psychometric patterns and behavioral and physiological responses to stress. *Journal of Abnormal Psychology, 88*, 369–380.

Zuckerman, M. (1991). *Psychobiology of personality.* New York: Cambridge University Press.

Zuckerman, M., Kuhlman, D. M., & Camac, C. (1988). What lies beyond E and N? Factor analyses of scales believed to measure basic dimensions of personality. *Journal of Personality and Social Psychology, 54*, 96–107.

CHAPTER

11

FIT, CONTEXT, AND THE TRANSITION BETWEEN TEMPERAMENT AND PERSONALITY

Theodore D. Wachs
Purdue University

Both historically (Strelau, 1987), and in modern theory (Buss, 1991), temperament has been viewed as that biologically based domain of personality that appears early in life and is stable across time. If temperament traits are the earliest manifestation of later personality characteristics we should expect to find specific linkages between early temperament and later personality (Buss & Plomin, 1984). The hypothesized linkage between temperament and personality is thought to be direct and biologically driven; specifically, it is assumed that common genetic structures drive physiology, neurology, and hormones, which in turn govern the expression of both personality and temperament (Eysenck, 1991; Netter, 1991; also see introduction to this section).

The hypothesized linkage between personality and temperament receives support from both behavioral genetic research and personality theory. In terms of genetics, although heritability figures vary across traits and ages, available evidence does suggest at least moderate heritability for a number of commonly accepted temperament traits in infancy and early childhood (Buss & Plomin, 1984; Goldsmith, 1983, 1989; Saudino & Eaton, 1991). Strelau (1987) has argued that personality is more environmentally driven than temperament, but available evidence also points to a moderate degree of genetic influence on a wide variety of personality traits (Loehlin, Willerman, & Horn, 1988; Plomin & Rende, 1991). Given that both temperament and personality appear to be, in part, heritable, it does not require a large leap of faith to assume a common genetic linkage between specific temperament and personality dimensions. Indeed, Matheny (1989) has presented evidence indicating genetic regulation of transitions in patterns of inhibitory behavior between 12 and 30 months.

The hypothesized linkage between temperament and personality also has been strengthened by recent theoretical advances in the classification of personality itself. Specifically, there has been an increasing convergence on the idea that the overall domain of personality can be encompassed by five major factors, the so-called Big Five (Digman, chap. 16 in this vol.; 1990).

Delineation of five replicable dimensions of adult personality allows for the possibility of mapping specific early temperament characteristics onto specific adult personality traits, rather than relating "temperament" to "personality" in a vague and global fashion (Digman, 1989). For example, Rothbart (1989) hypothesized that there will be linkages between the temperament dimension of Positive Emotionality and the personality dimension of Extraversion, between the temperament dimension of Negative Emotionality and the personality dimension of Neuroticism, and between the temperament dimension of Inhibition and the personality dimension of Conscientiousness. Similarly, Hagekull (chap. 12 in this vol.) hypothesized links between the temperament dimension of Manageability (persistence, negative mood) and personality Factor III (Conscientiousness), between the temperament dimensions of Shyness and Activity and personality Factor IV (Negative Emotionality) and between the temperament domain of Sociability and personality Factor II (Friendliness).

It is clear that both temperament and personality are partially influenced by genetic-biological factors. It is also clear that, on a conceptual level, we can find potential linkages between specific domains of temperament and specific dimensions of personality. Does this mean there is continuity between early temperament and later personality? Unfortunately there is little evidence available on this question (Prior, Crook, Stripp, Power, & Joseph, 1986). For the most part, available evidence is centered around the stability of temperament per se, rather than on the transition from temperament to personality. Further, most stability studies involve a relatively constrained time period, often less than 12 months. At least in regard to the stability of temperament, in infancy and childhood the majority of short-term stability coefficients are modest at best ($r = +.2 - +.3$), and begin to decline when stability intervals greater than 6 months are utilized, or when different instruments or different raters are used at different ages (Slabach, Morrow, & Wachs, 1991). The same modest relations are found when temperament and personality domains are assessed concurrently (Prior et al., 1986). When continuity of temperament or personality is assessed across age periods (e.g., from infancy to preschool, from childhood to adulthood), for the most part modest correlations are again the rule (Caspi, Elder, & Bem, 1988; Hagekull, 1991). Although stability coefficients can be raised into the $r = .5$ range, for the most part these occur only when aggregated measures are utilized with a temperamentally extreme group of children (Kagan, Reznick, & Snidman, 1988). These modest stability correlations suggest that a strong direct mapping from early temperament to later personality is not a likely possibility. It is, however, still possible to argue that whatever the degree of transition from specific early temperament traits to specific later personality domains, this transition is primarily driven by common biological-genetic processes (Eysenck, 1991).

Whereas there may well be some biological linkages between early temperament and later personality, I argue that the linkage process is more likely to be indirect, mediated both by changing biological systems and the nature of the environmental context within which the individual develops. Put another way, it may be a mistake to look for relations between temperament and personality without considering those factors that promote individual variability in both temperament and personality.

BIOLOGICAL PROCESSES

From a genetic-biological viewpoint, the idea of a common genetic-biological substrate governing the transition from temperament to personality is problematic in two ways. First, advances in molecular genetics suggest that the concept of gene systems beginning to operate at conception, and continuing on unchanged throughout the life span, may be incorrect. A more appropriate model may be one where different gene systems become operative at different time periods across the life span (Goldsmith, 1988; Plomin, 1986). If gene systems are actively changing across the life span, this makes the assertion of a common genetic-biological substrate underlying both early temperament and later personality quite problematical.

Moreover, the concept of gene-guided behavioral programs appears to be based on an outmoded deterministic model of gene action. In place of deterministic gene-driven behavioral models we find an increasing emphasis on probabilistic models that encompass multiple bidirectional influences among genes, biological processes, environment, and behavior (Horowitz, 1987; Oyama, 1989; Plomin, 1990; Wachs, 1992; Wachs & Plomin, 1991).

An excellent example of a probabilistic systems model, with clear implications for understanding the nature of the transition from temperament to personality, is seen in Gottlieb's (1991) concept of *experiential canalization*. Experiential canalization refers to a situation where maintenance of genetic influences across time is a function both of genes, and of the impact of the organism's own behavior on subsequent transactions with the environment. What are the implications of the experiential canalization model for the study of the transition from temperament to personality? One obvious implication is that the transition process will be facilitated or inhibited by the degree to which individuals having specific biologically based temperament traits are able to elicit responses from the environment that serve to maintain these traits across time. For example, Caspi, Elder, and Bem (1988) hypothesized that temperamentally shy children are less likely to experience rules and roles governing standard social interaction patterns. Over time, because these children have not experienced these rules and roles, they are less likely to respond appropriately to social overtures, thus furthering their sense of isolation and shyness. Their social problems may also result in the development of a sense of social inadequacy, leading to even greater isolation and shyness in social situations. In adulthood these individuals would be more likely to marry individuals with similar traits, leading to further stabilization (Caspi & Herbner, 1990). Thus, the original biological substrate underlying the temperament trait of shyness becomes strengthened by the children's subsequent transactions with their environment, leading to a continuity of shyness and an increased probability of later introversion.

It must be emphasized that a probabilistic experiential canalization model, as described earlier, stands in sharp contrast to deterministic gene-driven models (e.g., Scarr, 1992). The difference lies in the fact that the elicitation process is not an automatic one. For the great majority of temperament traits, available evidence does not suggest a great deal of consistency between individual child temperament characteristics and subsequent caregiver behaviors (Crockenberg, 1986; Slabach et al., 1991). Whether individual children's temperament traits are accepted (which should lead to continuity), or rejected (which should lead to discontinuity), is a function of *multiple factors*. These include but are not limited to:

1. Caregiver (Hubert & Wachs, 1985) or culturally based (Super & Harkness, 1986) preferences for specific types of temperamental behavioral patterns; children whose individual characteristics do not fit caregiver or cultural preferences would more likely be pressured to change these characteristics.
2. The degree of family stress; caregivers experiencing higher stress levels may be either less sensitive (Crockenberg & McCluskey, 1986) or less able to consistently respond to their children's individual characteristics (Bell & Chapman, 1986).
3. Parental belief systems; parents who believe they can have little influence on their child's development will exert very little effort to change developmental patterns (Fry, 1988).
4. How extreme are the child's temperament characteristics; whereas extreme temperament characteristics may be less changeable (Buss & Plomin, 1984), children with extreme characteristics may experience greater amounts of "lower" and "upper level" parental controls, which are designed to move children toward less extreme behavioral patterns (Bell & Chapman, 1986).

Although there appear to be no existing studies illustrating how the transition from temperament to personality is influenced by multiple factors governing the degree of fit between child temperament characteristics and their subsequent context, several examples suggest *analogues* for this process. Research by Kagan, Reznick, and Snidman (1988) suggests that infants who are biologically predisposed to be inhibited are more likely to display inhibited behavioral styles later in life, if they have encountered repeated environmental stressors. Although not directly studying developmental transitions, Lerner and colleagues showed how it becomes increasingly difficult to document simple linear connections between temperament and adjustment for older children. Rather, we find that adolescents whose temperament qualities fit (match) the qualities demanded by peers or adults are more likely to develop adequate adjustments than are adolescents whose temperament qualities do not fit these demands (J. Lerner, Nitz, Talwar, & R. Lerner, 1989).

Looked at in terms of the transition from temperament to personality, children whose temperament characteristics elicit or match "stabilizing" environmental characteristics are more likely to be those for whom we can demonstrate a consistent transition from temperament to personality; those whose temperament does not elicit or match environmental stabilizing characteristics will be less likely to demonstrate consistent transitions from temperament to personality. The degree to which children with a specific temperament characteristic are able to elicit stabilizing reactions from their environments appears to be a function of multiple factors, including not only the child's temperament, but also the individual and ecological factors already noted. Implications of this probabilistic system for generating future research on the transition between temperament and personality are discussed later.

TEMPERAMENT AND ENVIRONMENT

The hypothesis that the transition between temperament and personality is primarily due to a common underlying biological substrate is based, in part, on research showing a genetic-biological influence on both temperament and personality. Particularly for temperament, however, even theories with strong biological assumptions clearly accept the possibility that environmental variability can promote individual variability in temperament across time (e.g., Buss & Plomin, 1984; Rothbart & Derryberry, 1981). The possibility that variability in temperament is related to variability in environment adds another layer of complexity beyond the biological, in terms of understanding the transition from temperament to personality.

What evidence is there that variability in temperament or personality can be influenced by the environment? As noted previously, Kagan, Reznick, and Snidman (1989) argued that behavioral changes shown by extremely inhibited children may be a function of unspecified environmental stress factors. Similarly, behavioral genetic studies have reported that shared environmental variance can influence twin concordance on various measures of temperament (Goldsmith,

1988) and personality (Rose, Koskenvuo, Kaprio, Sarna & Langinvainio, 1988). These studies, although suggesting a role for environment in promoting variability in temperament and personality, tell us little about which specific environmental variables are relevant.

In terms of specific environmental variables, several studies have reported relations between caregiver *involvement* and measures of children's emotionality (Crockenberg & Acredolo, 1983) and persistence (Bathhurst, Gottfried, Guerin, & Hobson, 1988). Other research indicates that family *conflict* tends to increase the probability of difficult temperament (Matheny, Wilson, & Thobin, 1987), whereas *direct maternal teaching* appears to reduce difficult temperament, at least for boys (Maccoby, Snow, & Jacklin, 1984).

The aforementioned studies, although illustrating the relevance of specific environmental variables for variability in temperament, assess only the microenvironment of the child. Current conceptual formulations stress the need for a more differentiated view of the environment, encompassing both the child's immediate microenvironment and the ongoing context within which the microenvironment is nested (Wachs, 1992). Looking at the broader environmental context, several studies have implicated changes in *maternal employment* as relevant for influencing variability in children's temperament (Lerner et al., 1989; Thompson & Lamb, 1982). Along the same lines, Caspi et al. (1988) documented different developmental transitions from childhood to adulthood for shy males and females. Caspi et al. suggested that these sex differences are a function of *differential cultural supports* and *cultural prohibitions* for the different sexes. That is, cultural support for certain patterns of behavior in males versus females leads to different transition patterns across time.

Although the previous results could be used to argue that the transition from temperament to personality will be influenced by environmentally related changes in temperament, from a deterministic viewpoint it could be argued that environment–temperament relations are themselves biologically driven. That is, it could be argued either that genetic factors may structure the nature of the environment within which the child functions (Scarr, 1992), or that it is not so much the environment influencing the child's temperament as it is the child's biologically driven temperament that influences the subsequent environment. Whereas these arguments are logical, available evidence still suggests a role for the environment in promoting individual differences in temperament. In terms of the first possibility—namely, common genes driving both environment and temperament—behavior genetic studies have documented a number of environment–temperament relations (such as low maternal sociability and high infant shyness) occurring even in adoptive families where there is no common genetic substrate between caregiver and child (Daniels & Plomin, 1985; Plomin, DeFries, & Fulker, 1988).

In terms of the second argument that temperament drives environment, the probabilistic nature of this relation has been documented in the previous section. In terms of additional evidence, Power, Gershenhorn, and Stafford (1990) reported that maternal inflexibility predicts subsequent infant fussiness, even after controlling for initial levels of infant fussiness. Wachs (1988) argued that certain dimensions of the physical environment such as crowding (e.g., rooms-to-people ratio, number of sibs), which occur prior to the birth of a specific child, are less likely to be influenced by that child's temperament characteristics. Wachs' (1988) finding that crowding in the home predisposes to lower approach, less adaptability, and greater negative moods in young infants, even after partialling out the influence of maternal temperament, also supports an independent role for environmental influences on variability in temperament.

The evidence documenting relations between environment and temperament further contradicts the hypothesis that the transition from temperament to personality is main effect in nature, being primarily the result of a shared biological substrate. The overall pattern of results summarized in this chapter suggests the need for changes, both in our conceptual scheme and in the way in which we study the transition from temperament to personality. Potential changes are discussed in the final section.

THE TRANSITION FROM TEMPERAMENT TO PERSONALITY: FUTURE DIRECTIONS

Bates (1989) demonstrated that temperament is best viewed as a multilevel phenomenon, encompassing both biological and behavioral components. An analysis of the transition from temperament to personality must encompass these multiple levels as well. Three dimensions seem particularly salient in terms of understanding the process of transition. First, there is the degree of stability in the biological substrates underlying both temperament and personality. Among the questions that are necessary for an understanding at this level are the degree of overlap of the functional genotype influencing both temperament and personality, and whether the same genetically driven biological mechanisms influence the expression of both temperament and personality traits. Questions in this domain, although undoubtedly critical, perhaps may be more in the realm of molecular genetics and developmental neurobiology than in the realm of the behavioral sciences.

At a behavioral level, input from two other domains appears to be critical. First, to the extent that variability in temperament is influenced by the nature of the child's environment, it is critical to assess whether subsequent experiences strengthen or weaken particular temperament attributes. Second, to the extent that children's temperament characteristics have the potential to influence the nature of the subsequent environment, it is equally essential to assess the degree of "fit" or match between the child's temperament and the child's subsequent environment; as suggested earlier, temperament–environment fits may be likely to sustain the transition process, whereas temperament–environment mismatches may be more likely to weaken this process.

The aforementioned means that we will never understand the nature of the transition between temperament and personality simply by looking at correlations between early temperament and later personality. Rather, in order to predict accurately whether transitions between specific temperament and personality dimensions will or will not occur, it is critical to assess the nature of the intervening context during the time the transition is taking place.

Although this call for more contextually based transition research could be seen as an excuse for fishing expeditions, this need not be the case. The specific dimensions characterizing early temperament have been delineated in some detail (Bates, 1989); research on the Big Five personality structure has yielded an impressive list of characteristics encompassing these specific domains (Digman, 1990; chap. 16 in this vol.). With both a beginning and an endpoint, it is possible to derive specific hypotheses about which types of contextual factors should strengthen or attenuate linkages between specific domains of early temperament and subsequent personality. Rothbart (1989) did precisely this with the area of negative emotionality. Specifically, Rothbart hypothesized that children who show low levels of negative emotionality in infancy may show high levels of emotionality in adulthood, if they encounter high levels of criticism or frustration during childhood. In contrast, children who are highly susceptible to distress may show low levels of distress in adulthood, if they are able to carve out environmental niches that allow them to avoid unpleasantness.

A similar set of predictions for other potential temperament-personality transitions can also be derived, particularly within the framework of a multilevel environmental system.[1] Taking the dimension of Temperamental Inhibition (Shyness) as a starting point we can trace two potential transition processes, depending on the nature of the subsequent environment and the fit between child temperament and environmental characteristics. One transition leads from inhibition to behavioral manifestations of Extraversion (Factor I) and Emotional Stability (Factor IV); the other leads from early inhibition to the other poles of these bipolar factors, namely Introversion and Neuroticism. These separate paths are illustrated in Table 11.1.

Table 11.1 illustrates an identical initial starting point with two distinctly different outcomes, depending on both context and fit. Inhibited children who encounter sensitive caregivers, varied physical contexts, and mesosystem structures and peer groups that fit the child's temperament should show a distinctly different transition pattern than inhibited children who encounter insensitive

---

[1]Although precise predictions can be made about which environmental factors should influence transitions between specific temperament and personality dimensions, we should not necessarily assume that all temperament and personality domains can be linked in this fashion. Certain primary temperament dimensions, such as Activity Level, although stable in their own right, may bear only a tangential relation to Big Five personality factors (see Eaton, chap. 9 in this vol.). Similarly, certain Big Five dimensions, such as Intellect-Openness, may have few behavioral referents in early development when temperament first emerges.

TABLE 11.1
Proposed Transition Paths Between Early Temperament and Later Personality

Initial Temperamental Trait	Inhibition	
	Potential Environments:	
Social microenvironment	Caregivers (parents) who are sensitive and let the children set their own pace	Caregivers who use inappropriate "low level control" (Bell & Chapman, 1986), and attempt to force the children into new situations
Physical microenvironment	Presence of "stimulus shelters" or "defensible spaces" (Wachs, 1987), which the children can retreat to when there is too much stimulation	The children continually encounter noisy, chaotic environments that allow no escape from stimulation
Nonfamily: Peer Groups	Peer groups have other inhibited children with common interests, so the children feel accepted	Peer groups consist of athletic extraverts so the children feel rejected
Mesosystem: School environment	School is "undermanned" (Schoggen, 1989) so children are more likely to be tolerated and feel they can make a contribution	School is "overmanned" so children less likely to be tolerated and feel undervalued
Personality Outcomes	Individuals closer to extraversion and emotional stability poles	Individuals closer to introversion and neuroticism poles

caregivers, restricted physical contexts, and mesosystem structures and peer groups that do not fit the child's temperament characteristics.

Besides context and fit, two other factors also need to be considered. First, Buss and Plomin (1984) hypothesized that children in the middle ranges of temperament are more likely to be influenced by their environment, whereas those at the extremes of temperament are more likely to influence their environment. If this hypothesis is correct, to the extent that the child's temperament characteristics are not extreme, I would predict a greater likelihood of the transition process being more influenced by subsequent context than by fit. To the extent that the child's temperamental characteristics are extreme, I would predict that the transition process will be more influenced by fit than by context.

Second, given the nature of the environmental system, there is likely to be at least some degree of covariance among the different levels of the environment shown in Table 11.1. For example, available evidence consistently indicates that caregivers in noisy-chaotic homes are less likely to be sensitive to children's needs than are caregivers in quiet, non-chaotic homes (Wachs, 1992). To the extent that there is positive covariance across the different levels of the environment, we are more likely to see contextual influences governing the transition from temperament to personality.

The critical point is that without studying the child and the child's context simultaneously, research on the transition between temperament and personality is likely to reveal only low level relations. Research studying the child and the context simultaneously not only will be more powerful, but also will tell us more about the nature of the processes governing the transition between temperament and personality.

REFERENCES

Bates, J. (1989). Concepts and measures of temperament. In G. Kohnstamm, J. Bates, & M. Rothbart (Eds.), *Temperament in childhood* (pp. 3–26). New York: Wiley.

Bathurst, K., Gottfried, A., Guerin, D., & Hobson, L. (1988, April). *Home environment and infant temperament*. Paper presented at the Sixth International Conference on Infant Studies, Washington, DC.

Bell, R., & Chapman, M. (1986). Child effects in studies using brief longitudinal approaches to socialization. *Developmental Psychology, 22*, 599–603.

Buss, A. (1991). The EAS theory of temperament. In J. Strelau & A. Angleitner (Eds.), *Exploration in temperaments* (pp. 43–60). London: Plenum.

Buss, A., & Plomin, R. (1984). *Temperament: Early developing personality traits.* Hillsdale, NJ: Lawrence Erlbaum Associates.

Caspi, A., Elder, G., & Bem, D. (1988). Moving away from the world: Life course patterns of shy children. *Developmental Psychology, 24*, 824–831.

Caspi, A., & Herbner, E. (1990). Continuity and change: Assortative marriage and the consistency of personality in adulthood. *Journal of Personality and Social Psychology, 58*, 250–258.

Crockenberg, S. (1986). Are temperamental differences in babies associated with predictable differences in caregiving. In J. Lerner & R. Lerner (Eds.), *Temperament and psychosocial interactions in children* (pp. 53–73). San Francisco: Josey-Bass.

Crockenberg, S., & Acredolo, C. (1983). Infant temperament ratings: A function of infants, or mothers, or both. *Infant Behavior and Development, 6*, 61–72.

Crockenberg, S., & McClusky, K. (1986). Change in maternal behavior during the baby's first year of life. *Child Development, 57*, 746–753.

Daniels, D., & Plomin, R. (1985). Origins of individual differences in infant shyness. *Developmental Psychology, 21*, 118–121.

Digman, J. (1989). Five robust factors dimensions. *Journal of Personality, 57*, 195–214.

Digman, J. (1990). Personality structure: Emergence of the five factor model. *Annual Review of Psychology, 41*, 417–440.

Eysenck, H. J. (1991). Dimensions of personality: The biosocial approach to personality. In J. Strelau & A. Angleitner (Eds.), *Explorations in temperament* (pp. 87–104). London: Plenum.

Fry, D. (1988). Intercommunity differences in aggression among Zapotec children. *Child Development, 59*, 1008–1019.

Goldsmith, H. (1983). Genetic influences on personality from infancy to adulthood. *Child Development, 54*, 331–355.

Goldsmith, H. (1988). Human developmental behavior genetics. *Annals of Child Development, 5*, 187–227.

Goldsmith, H. (1989). Behavior genetic approaches to temperament. In G. Kohnstamm, J. Bates, & M. Rothbart (Eds.), *Temperament in childhood* (pp. 111–132). New York: Wiley.

Gottlieb, G. (1991). Experiential canalization of behavioral development. *Developmental Psychology, 27*, 4–13.

Hagekull, B. (1991, June). *Infant temperament and the Big Five dimension of personality.* Paper presented at the Conference on the Development of the Structure of Temperament and Personality from Infancy to Adulthood, Wassenaar, The Netherlands.

Horowitz, F. (1987). *Exploring developmental theories.* Hillsdale, NJ: Lawrence Erlbaum Associates.

Hubert, N., & Wachs, T. D. (1985). Parental perceptions of the behavioral components of infant easiness–difficultness. *Child Development, 56*, 1525–1537.

Kagan, J., Reznick, S., & Snidman, N. (1988). Biological basis of childhood shyness. *Science, 240*, 167–171.

Kagan, J., Reznick, S., & Snidman, N. (1989). Issues in the study of temperament. In G. Kohnstamm, J. Bates, & M. Rothbart (Eds.), *Temperament in childhood* (pp. 133–144). New York: Wiley.

Lerner, J., Nitz, K., Talwar, R., & Lerner, R. (1989). On the functional significance of temperamental individuality. In G. Kohnstamm, J. Bates, & M. Rothbart (Eds.), *Temperament in childhood* (pp. 509–522). New York: Wiley.

Loehlin, J., Willerman, L., & Horn, J. (1988). Human behavior genetics. *Annual Review of Psychology, 39*, 101–133.

Maccoby, E., Snow, M., & Jacklin, C. (1984). Childrens dispositions and mother–child interaction at 12 and 18 months. *Developmental Psychology, 20*, 459–472.

Matheny, A. (1989). Childrens behavioral inhibition over ages and across situations. *Journal of Personality, 57*, 215–235.

Matheny, A., Wilson, R., & Thobin, A. (1987). Home and mother: Relations with infant temperament. *Developmental Psychology, 23*, 323–331.

Netter, P. (1991). Biochemical variables in the study of temperament. In J. Strelau & A. Angleitner (Eds.), *Explorations in temperaments* (pp. 147–162). New York: Plenum.

Oyama, S. (1989). Ontogeny and the central dogma. In M. Gunnar & E. Thelen (Eds.), *Systems and development: Minnesota Symposium* (Vol. 22, pp. 1–34). Hillsdale, NJ: Lawrence Erlbaum Associates.

Plomin, R. (1986). *Development, genetics and psychology.* Hillsdale, NJ: Lawrence Erlbaum Associates.

Plomin, R. (1990). The role of inheritance in behavior. *Science, 248*, 183–188.

Plomin, R., DeFries, J., & Fulker, D. (1988). *Nature and nurture: Infancy and early childhood.* New York: Cambridge University Press.

Plomin, R., & Rende, R. (1991). Human behavioral genetics. *Annual Review of Psychology, 42*, 161–190.

Power, T., Gershenhorn, S., & Stafford, D. (1990). Maternal perceptions of infant difficultness: The influence of maternal attitudes and attributions. *Infant Behavior and Development, 13*, 421–437.

Prior, M., Crook, G., Stripp, A., Power, M., & Joseph, M. (1986). The relationship between temperament and personality. *Personality and Individual Differences, 7*, 875–881.

Rose, B., Koskenvuo, M., Kaprio, J., Sarna, S., & Langinvainio, H. (1988). Shared genes, shared experiences and similarity of personality. *Journal of Personality and Social Psychology, 54*, 161–171.

Rothbart, M. (1989). Temperament and development. In G. Kohnstamm, J. Bates, & M. Rothbart (Eds.), *Temperament in childhood* (pp. 187–248). New York: Wiley.

Rothbart, M., & Derryberry, D. (1981). Development of individual differences in temperament. In M. Lamb & A. Brown (Eds.), *Advances in developmental psychology* (Vol. 1, pp. 37–86). Hillsdale, NJ: Lawrence Erlbaum Associates.

Saudino, K., & Eaton, W. (1991). Infant temperament and genetics. *Child Development, 62*, 1167–1174.

Scarr, S. (1992). Developmental theories for the 1990's. *Child Development, 63*, 1–19.

Schoggen, P. (1989). *Behavior settings.* Stanford, CA: Stanford University Press.

Slabach, E., Morrow, J., & Wachs, T. D. (1991). Questionnaire measurement of infant and child temperament: Current status and future directions. In J. Strelau & A. Angleitner (Eds.), *Explorations in temperament* (pp. 205–234). New York: Plenum.

Strelau, J. (1987). The concept of temperament in personality research. *European Journal of Personality, 1*, 107–117.

Super, C., & Harkness, S. (1986). Temperament, development and culture. In R. Plomin & J. Dunn (Eds.), *The study of temperament* (pp. 131–150). Hillsdale, NJ: Lawrence Erlbaum Associates.

Thompson, R., & Lamb, M. (1982). Stranger sociability and its relationship to temperament and social experience in the second year. *Infant Behavior and Development, 5*, 277–287.

Wachs, T. D. (1987). Developmental perspectives on designing for development. In C. Weinstein & T. Davids (Ed.), *Spaces for children* (pp. 291–308). New York: Plenum.

Wachs, T. D. (1988). Relevance of physical environmental influences for toddler temperament. *Infant Behavior and Development, 11*, 431–445.

Wachs, T. D. (1992). *The nature of nurture*. Newbury Park, CA: Sage.

Wachs, T. D., & Plomin, R. (1991). *Conceptualization and measurement of organism environment interaction*. Washington, DC: American Psychological Association.

PART

DERIVING THE FIVE-FACTOR MODEL FROM PARENTAL RATINGS OF CHILDREN AND ADOLESCENTS

In this section, four empirical studies are presented, all based mostly on parental ratings of temperament and personality in infancy, childhood, or adolescence. In the first two chapters investigators used ratings from questionnaires, whereas in the last two chapters they used Q-sort methodology to assess parental views of their children's temperament and personality.

In the preceding section, readers may have noticed how the words temperament and personality were used in mutually exclusive ways. Though no one will deny that we can still speak appropriately of an adult's *temperament*, most authors now seem to reserve the word for more or less stable individual differences in infancy and childhood. This is more than just a matter of efficiency and convention. Hagekull, in the opening of her chapter, nicely shows the usefulness of conceptualizing temperament as early appearing personality traits. She presents data from her Swedish longitudinal study over the first 4 years of life, focusing on how early appearing infant temperament could be related to the later emerging five-factor model. The correlation coefficients in Table 12.1 provide an example of what Wachs (chap. 11) meant in writing that "when continuity of temperament is assessed across age periods, for the most part modest correlations are the rule." Maternal ratings in infancy, using a Thomas-and-Chess-based questionnaire (see chap. 8), correlated modestly with parental ratings at preschool age, using the Emotionality, Activity, Sociability, Impulsivity (EASI) scale by Buss and Plomin (1984). The highest correlations found were between activity scales at both times ($r = .40$) and between infant *manageability* and preschool *impulsivity* ($r = .42$). Even infancy shyness (Approach-Withdrawal) did not correlate above .25 with later shyness. What might we expect if we were to extrapolate to adult Extraversion? We currently lack longitudinal data for all ages between the preschool period and adulthood, but we might speculate that the correlations would be low. Would this be due to the weakness of our instruments, the fact that the parental questionnaires were given to mostly inexperienced users of rating scales, or the instability of temperamental characteristics in those first years of life? Would we improve measurement with multiple methods and sources? We simply lack the data to choose among these alternative explanations.

Hagekull derives optimism from her data, suggesting that such continuities between temperamental differences in early childhood and Big Five dimensions in adulthood await testing in longitudinal studies. We must, however, be mindful of the cautions given by Wachs: Very little may be obtained from simply correlating rating scales over longer time spans. Unless we take environmental factors and differential interactions between specific temperaments and specific contextual characteristics into account, our predictions to adult personality from infancy and childhood may indeed be limited.

Goldsmith et al. represent the behavior-genetic approach to personality in this volume, though we must also refer the reader to Graziano (chap. 17) for an extensive treatment of the question of the differential heritability of Agreeableness. Goldsmith et al. present data from several studies. In the first study, the genetic resemblance between adult twins was studied using Goldberg's bipolar adjective scales for the Big Five. Comparing resemblances for identical and nonidentical twins, heritability estimates were calculated. Those adult twins with children between 3 and 8 years old were asked to rate their children on Rothbart's Children's Behavioral Questionnaire (CBQ), the same instrument described in her earlier chapter. Correlations between parental self-ratings on the Goldberg scales and parental ratings of their children on the CBQ were in the .2 to .3 range, with one exception: a correlation of .46 between parental Emotional Stability and child Soothability.

The authors rightfully discuss the intrinsic weakness of data derived solely from parents. After discussing several processes that may account for similarities between parental personality and offspring temperament—note again this distinction—the authors present data from two other questionnaire studies where parents were sole informants. Goldsmith et al. describe three replicable associations emerging from their data: (a) Parental positive affect was associated with reported positive affect in the child; and parental negative affect was associated with negative affect in the child (b) in infants and toddlers only, parental negative affect correlated with higher offspring activity level; (c) in toddlers and young children, parental overcontrol, constraint, and conscientiousness correlated with inhibition in offspring.

The authors believe these replicated effects "justify a search for mediating variables. For example, do more anxious, suspicious, or aggressive parents engage in behaviors that heighten infant motoric behavior?" The strategy embodied by this quote resembles the differential approach ("contextual") recommended by Wachs.

The California Child Q-Set (CCQ; J. H. Block & J. Block, 1980) is discussed in the next two chapters. Both research groups set out to see if the Big Five could be replicated from CCQ data sets obtained for adolescents and children, just as McCrae, Costa, and Busch (1986) had done for the adult version of this instrument, the California Adult Q-Set (CAQ). Robins, John, and Caspi have chosen an unconventional question and answer format, introducing a hypothetical skeptic to question their findings and interpretations. Their first step was to distribute intuitively the CCQ items over the Big Five. Because 44 items in the CCQ correspond with similar items in the CAQ, they could compare their groupings with the empirically demonstrated factors by McCrae et al. (1986). The result was one of close correspondence.

They then go on to provide impressive construct validity evidence for the adolescent CCQ items, showing how developmental constructs like Ego Resiliency, Control, and Antisocial Behavior can be located in Big Five dimensions. Further buttressing the validity of the Big Five are the reported real-world predictions possible from knowing an adolescent's position on the Big Five dimensions—variables like delinquency, school performance, and IQ have significant and important relations to Big Five dimensions (see also Graziano, chap. 17, and Victor, chap. 18, for more criterion validity data).

The authors also report the outcome of a factor analysis on the full 100-item CCQ, obtained for a large sample of young adolescent boys. A five-factor solution replicated only three of the Big Five factors (Extraversion, Agreeableness, and Conscientiousness), but in a seven-factor principal component analysis the Big Five were more or less clearly reproduced, supplemented by two extra factors labeled Activity and Irritability. The authors argue that in early adolescent boys, Activity and Irritability are not simply facets of Extraversion and Emotional Stability, but may be relatively independent dimensions of personality, stable from an earlier period in life. Concerning activity, the present CCQ result should be interpreted in the context of the discussion of developmental changes in Activity by Eaton in the preceding section.

Finally, these authors discuss the fact that only half of the 100 CCQ items could be clearly located in any one of the Big Five. The other half either fell outside the Big Five domain, or were related to two or more factors. The authors refer to the circumplex approach to the Big Five by investigators like Wiggins (1979) and Hofstee (see De Raad, Hendriks, & Hofstee, chap. 5) to account for these results.

There is more than a bit of irony that J. Block, a devoted skeptic regarding the validity of the five-factor model, has his CCQ further analyzed in a Big Five trial in the Netherlands. We have placed this Dutch report in the present section, though it is based on both parental and teacher ratings, and could have just as easily been placed in the next section. It is in this section, however, because it compares so nicely with the preceding chapter on the CCQ.

Van Lieshout and Haselager present results for teacher ratings and parental ratings separately, by different age groups and by gender. The data are summarized from six different studies in which a total of 1,836 CCQ descriptions were obtained for 720 children and adolescents. The sample was split into three age levels: 3–6, 7–10, and 11–16 years. A factor analysis using the total sample was interpreted as revealing seven factors: the Big Five, plus Motor Activity and Dependency. It is tempting to compare the items in the first five factors of the Dutch CCQ descriptions (Table 15.2) with the intuitive ordering of these same items in Table 14.1. Agreeableness and Emotional Stability compare across the two studies fairly well, though many high loading items in the Dutch study did not appear at the same magnitude for Robins et al. For Extraversion and Conscientiousness, about half of the items selected by Robins et al. did not show up among the high loading items on these factors in the overall Dutch analysis.

Least agreement is found for Openness: Both factors, the intuitive American one, and the empirical Dutch one, have only two items in common. The appearance of some typical Openness items (*high intellectual capacity* and *is curious and explores*) in the Dutch Conscientiousness factor reminds us of results obtained by Mervielde in Belgium (Mervielde & DeFruyt, in press) indicating that school-age children rating peers do not yet differentiate between Conscientiousness and Openness dimensions. The separate Motor Activity factor is a replication of the factor reported by Robins et al. in the previous chapter, and again supports the contention that activity is a major child factor (see Eaton, chap. 9, and Martin et al., chap. 8).

We note here that, in the parental Q-sorts done on young adolescents, no Motor Activity factor was present. However, it was clearly present in their sorts of children below 11 years. It is also of interest that no Activity factor was detected for girls when they were analyzed separately. Motor Activity is apparently an independent factor for young boys only (at least in the Netherlands).

When separate analyses were done for subgroups, the two larger factors, Agreeableness and Emotional Stability, replicated best over specific groups. The smaller factors, Extraversion and Conscientiousness, showed somewhat more variability. The factor Irritability that was found in the American CCQ study, was found in the Dutch study but only for girls. The authors warn us, however, that the differences in factor solutions between specific subsamples may be due to varying sample sizes for various analyses. Overall, both the CCQ studies reported in this section indicate that a version of the Big Five dimensional structure seems to be operating latently in the minds of the adults who are asked to sort the cards of the CCQ for their children and pupils.

REFERENCES

Block, J. H., & Block, J. (1980). The role of ego-control and ego resiliency in the organization of behavior. In W. A. Collins (Ed.), *Minnesota symposium on child psychology* (Vol. 13, pp. 39–101). Hillsdale, NJ: Lawrence Erlbaum Associates.

Buss, A. H., & Plomin, R. (1984). *Temperament: Early developing personality traits*. Hillsdale, NJ: Lawrence Erlbaum Associates.

McCrae, R. R., Costa, P. T., & Busch, C. M. (1986). Evaluating comprehensiveness in personality systems: The California Q-set and the five factor model. *Journal of Personality, 54*, 430–446.

Mervielde, I., & DeFruyt, F. (in press). The "Big Five" personality factors as a model for structure and development of peer nominations. *Child Development*.

Wiggins, J. S. (1979). A psychological taxonomy of trait descriptive terms: The interpersonal domain. *Journal of Personality and Social Psychology, 37*, 395–412.

CHAPTER

12

INFANT TEMPERAMENT AND EARLY CHILDHOOD FUNCTIONING: POSSIBLE RELATIONS TO THE FIVE-FACTOR MODEL

Berit Hagekull
Uppsala University

A lucid description of the conceptual relation between early temperament and the construct of personality has been given by Buss (1989), "Temperaments are the subclass of personality traits that are inherited. . . . Temperaments also differ from other personality traits in their initial appearance during the first year of life. The combination of inheritance and early appearance suggests that they are basic building blocks for personality" (p. 49). From the perspective of temperament theory, Bates (1986) had a similar formulation of the relationship between temperament and personality. "Some users of temperament are primarily interested in discovering basic constitutional substrates to a child's personality. . . . Others . . . are interested in basic description of the individuality of very young children. For them, temperament concepts stand in for the personality concepts used with older children and adults" (p. 2f.). Thus, there is a clear conceptual connection between temperament and personality in which personality is seen as the broader concept encompassing temperament in more mature individuals. Temperament refers to early appearing personality traits that may or may not have a biological origin. A meeting between the two areas is facilitated by methodological similarities such as the use of questionnaire approaches and factor analysis.

The two areas of research have existed without much contact. Working within the personality area, Digman (1989; 1990) compared the Big Five personality traits, generally extracted from factor analyses of adult samples, with the genetically based temperament dimensions of Buss and Plomin (1975; 1984). Digman (1989) also conducted studies with teacher ratings of the personality of school-age children and found that five to seven factors typically emerge; the dimensions closely resemble the Big Five dimensions found in studies of adults. From the perspective of child temperament research, few attempts (see, however, Buss & Plomin, 1975, 1984; Martin, 1990) have been made to theoretically link infant temperament dimensions to personality, let alone to empirically link early temperament dimensions in longitudinal contexts to later personality traits.

The purpose of this chapter is to present data from a longitudinal study of socioemotional development during the first 4 years in order to arrive at propositions about the relationships between infant temperament dimensions, early childhood functioning, and the Big Five personality dimensions. The previous work of Digman (1989, 1990) constitutes the theoretical link between the early childhood data and the Big Five dimensions.

APPROACHES TO INFANT TEMPERAMENT

According to McDevitt (1982), three main conceptualizations can be distinguished within the child temperament area: the behavioral style concept (e.g., Thomas & Chess, 1977) describing temperament as the *how* of behavior, the social perception approach (e.g., Bates, 1980) stressing parental perception and personality as important contributors to infant temperament descriptions, and the constitutional approach in which the genetic-biological basis for dimensions of temperament has been emphasized (e.g., Buss & Plomin, 1984; Rothbart, 1989). Despite theoretical and methodological differences in these approaches, they all study the behavioral repertoire of the young child, they all employ parental questionnaire ratings, and in most cases factor analysis has been used at some point in the development of dimensions and measures. Measures from all three approaches have been used in the study to be reported here.

THE UPPSALA LONGITUDINAL STUDY

The main aim of the longitudinal study conducted at Uppsala University is the delineation of factors influencing early socioemotional development. One of the theoretical perspectives stresses the importance of early individual behavioral differences (e.g., Hagekull & Bohlin, 1990). A sample of 123 mainly middle-class, Swedish families with a child born during 1985 has so far been followed from the time the infants were 6 weeks old until they were 4 years old (attrition about 17%).

Temperament data have been collected with three different types of questionnaires. During infancy, the Baby and Toddler Behavior Questionnaires (BBQ for age 4 months and TBQ for ages 10, 15, and 20 months; Hagekull & Bohlin, 1981) were used. These parental rating scales are based on factor analytic studies, in which the behavioral style conceptualization of temperament (Carey, 1970;

Thomas, Chess, Birch, Hertzig, & Korn, 1963) was used in selecting the original item pool. Six dimensions are measured: Intensity/Activity, Regularity, Approach-Withdrawal, Sensory Sensitivity, Attentiveness, and Manageability.

From 20 months and onward (28, 36, 43, and 48 months) the Emotionality, Activity, Sociability, Impulsivity (EASI) questionnaires from the constitutional approach (Buss & Plomin, 1975, 1984) comprising the Emotionality, Activity, Sociability, and Impulsivity scales, were utilized. In the present context, the 20-month data are excluded to avoid age overlap in measures. Finally, at the 43-month data collection we employed the Fussy/Difficult scale from the social perception approach. This dimension emerged as the most important factor in factor analytic treatment of the Child Characteristics Questionnaire (Lee & Bates, 1985). The construct of Difficultness has a prominent place in both the behavioral style and the social perception approach to temperament, being a predictor of later behavior problems (Bates, Maslin, & Frankel, 1985; Thomas, Chess, & Birch, 1968).

Ratings of temperament were obtained from mothers and, in 85% of the cases, from 10 months onward also from the fathers of the children. In the majority of the analyses reported here, maternal and paternal TBQ ratings from the three ages (10, 15, and 20 months) were averaged to give a single score for each of the six infancy dimensions. The EASI ratings were collapsed across parents and ages; the 28- and 36-month data yielded one score for each dimension, which is referred to as the early childhood scores, and the 43- and 48-month data were similarly averaged to give scores for 4-year-olds.

As one of the outcome measures for the 48-month-old children, a questionnaire was developed to study externalizing and internalizing problem behaviors as well as positive aspects of child functioning. Items from the Preschool Behavior Questionnaire (PBQ; Behar & Stringfield, 1974) were merged with items measuring the concepts of social competence and ego strength/effectance (see Waters, Wippman, & Sroufe, 1979, for original items, and Hagekull & Bohlin, in press, for a description of the dimensionality of the instrument). In supplementing the temperament measure with the Ego Strength/Effectance and Problem measures in the present context (Social Competence was excluded due to dimensional overlap with Anxiousness/Fearfulness behaviors), we obtained a broader picture of the child's personality at age 4 years, which might add to the discussion about early childhood personality and the Big Five personality traits. Averaged maternal and paternal ratings were used also for measures of Ego Strength/Effectance and Problem Behaviors.

DESCRIPTION OF THE DIMENSIONS

In order to facilitate a discussion of relationships between the temperament and the personality constructs, the relevant dimensions are briefly described.

BBQ/TBQ Dimensions

In the behavioral-style approach, a description of the young infant's total behavioral repertoire as seen in specified situations is the basis for measurement (cf. Thomas et al., 1963). In factor analytic studies of the BBQ and the TBQ, we adhered to the general definition of temperament as a collection of broad descriptive traits (Bohlin, Hagekull, & Lindhagen, 1981). Only factors composed by items covering behaviors in several situations were retained and seen as temperamental dimensions:

1. Intensity/Activity: intensity and vigor in both negative and positive reactions and amount of activity shown.
2. Regularity: rhythmicity in biologically influenced behaviors such as sleeping, eating, and elimination.
3. Approach-Withdrawal: positive or negative behaviors in new, mostly social, situations.
4. Sensory Sensitivity: intensity of both positive and negative reactions to strong environmental stimulation such as strong light, noise, and so forth.
5. Attentiveness: reactivity to minor changes in the environment possibly reflecting attention-getting processes.
6. Manageability: persistence, mood, and adaptability behaviors, possibly reflecting irritability or negative emotionality level in the young infant.

More extensive conceptual analyses of the dimensions can be found in Hagekull (1985, 1989).

EASI Dimensions

The EASI instrument is tailored to cover a broader age range than questionnaires within the behavioral-style tradition usually do, and the behavioral descriptions are therefore more generally worded. Three of the dimensions—Emotionality, Activity, and Sociability—are considered to have a genetic origin; the case for a genetic base of the fourth dimension, Impulsivity, is less clear (Buss & Plomin, 1984). Impulsivity has nevertheless been retained in our study because of its assumed relevance for the functioning of the child and for the Big Five comparison. Buss and Plomin state that Impulsivity becomes an individual difference dimension of importance around the child's fourth year. In the 43- and 48-month data collections, the Sociability scale was split into two measures, a Sociability scale and a Shyness scale, as motivated by the distinction between the two constructs made by Buss and Plomin (1984). The following dimensions were measured:

1. Emotionality: general distress behaviors indicating negative emotionality pertaining to the components of fear and anger.
2. Activity: tempo and vigor in the child's movements.
3. Sociability: the tendency to affiliate with others. In the earlier version of the EASI (Buss & Plomin, 1975) used in our early childhood measure, Sociability was operationalized with an emphasis on responsivity to others in new social situations. This resulted in conceptual overlap with Shyness. In the later EASI version (Buss & Plomin, 1984) used in our 4-year measure, the Sociability scale is a pure measure of the tendency to prefer the presence of others to being alone. Shyness, which is assumed to develop from the Sociability and Emotionality traits, is operationalized in the 4-year ratings as behaviors with casual acquaintances or strangers.
4. Impulsivity: four components are proposed as underlying this construct: inhibitory control, decision time, persistence, and sensation seeking. In the EASI, the questionnaire items concern mainly behaviors reflecting persistence in various activities.

The Fussy/Difficult Dimension

To operationalize the Fussiness/Difficultness dimension, mainly negative emotionality behaviors are used together with one general item asking for how difficult an average parent would find the child (Lee & Bates, 1985).

The Ego Strength/Effectance and Problem Behavior Dimensions

Early childhood functioning was further studied in the following dimensions:

1. Ego Strength/Effectance: reflects parts of the J. H. Block and J. Block (1980) concepts of ego control and ego resiliency (Waters et al., 1979). The items, void of interactional content, concern curiosity and involvement, interest in learning new skills, confidence, and self-directedness.
2. Externalizing Problems: the PBQ dimensions of Hostility/Aggressiveness and Hyperactivity/Distractibility (Behar & Stringfield, 1974) have, based on factor analytic work (Hagekull & Bohlin, in press) been combined into one scale.
3. Internalizing Problems: the PBQ dimension of Anxiousness/Fearfulness.

The Big Five Dimensions

Recent reports (e.g., Digman, 1990; John, 1989; Wiggins & Trapnell, in press) about personality structure emphasize the consensus concerning the number of high-level personality dimensions, but point to some disagreement concerning interpretation and content of the five dimensions usually found in the literature. Following Digman's (1990) review, the Big Five dimensions are in the present context labeled and conceptualized as follows:

1. Extraversion/Introversion (or Surgency): Emphasis is given to the H. J. Eysenck (1947) conception of the term. Factor labels such as Social Adaptability and Assertiveness have also been used in the reviewed research. The EASI dimension of Activity is included. In a previous paper Digman (1989) placed EASI Sociability in this dimension.

2. Friendliness/Hostility (or Agreeableness): Other factor labels for this dimension include Likability, Love, and Level of Socialization. The EASI Sociability dimension is included here in the later paper by Digman (1990).

3. Conscientiousness (or Will): Task interest, Work, Superego Strength, Thinking Introversion, and the Buss and Plomin Impulsivity dimension are among the factors found here.

4. Neuroticism/Emotional Stability: Together with Factor 1, this is the factor whose content is most generally agreed on in the research literature. It reflects the presence and effects of negative affect and is comparable to H. J. Eysenck's (1947) Neuroticism dimension. The EASI dimension of Emotionality clearly belongs to this grouping of factors.

5. Intellect (or Openness): Culture, Intelligence, and Inquiring Intellect are other factors in this grouping. No EASI dimension is related to Intellect according to Digman (1990).

HYPOTHESIZED RELATIONSHIPS BETWEEN INFANT AND CHILDHOOD TEMPERAMENT

From a stability perspective, infant temperament can be hypothesized to be related to childhood temperament. The following relations are proposed: infant Intensity/Activity predicts childhood Activity; Approach-Withdrawal in infancy predicts Sociability/Shyness in early childhood and Shyness in the 4-year period; infant Attentiveness predicts later Impulsivity; early Manageability predicts Impulsivity, Emotionality, and Shyness in childhood. We furthermore hypothesize a predictive relationship from early Intensity/Activity to Sociability and possibly also to Shyness. This hypothesis is based on the idea put forth by Buss and Plomin (1975) that the temperament traits of Activity and Sociability may be related because "other things being equal, active persons do more of everything, including interacting socially" (p. 121).

No predictions are made from Sensory Sensitivity and Regularity. Buss and Plomin (1984) described the Regularity dimension as an early appearing but later disappearing trait and have not included Rhythmicity behaviors in their instrument. Neither is a Reactivity/Sensitivity measure included in the EASI.

In the present context, Fussiness/Difficultness will be treated as a supplementary aspect of childhood temperament, which via the EASI scales will be linked to the Big Five dimensions.

PREDICTIONS FROM INFANT TEMPERAMENT TO CHILDHOOD TEMPERAMENT

The correlations between TBQ and EASI dimensions are shown in Table 12.1. Concentrating on significant coefficients found in predictions to both the early childhood period and the 4-year period, a clear pattern emerges: Childhood Emotionality is predicted by infant Manageability and Attentiveness scales, Activity is predicted by early Intensity/Activity tendencies, and Impulsivity seems to have its roots in infant Manageability. The Sociability/Shyness predictions are more complicated. The Sociability dimension in the early childhood period has the same roots as Shyness, measured in the 4-year period; that is, withdrawing behaviors and low degrees of Intensity/Activity are predictive of both constructs. This confirms the previous assumption that what is measured in the Buss and Plomin (1975) Sociability scale is in fact Shyness. The revised Sociability measure, emphasizing the tendency to need social contacts, is positively related to early Intensity/Activity.

TABLE 12.1
Significant Product-Moment Correlations Between Infant Temperament Dimensions (TBQ) and Childhood Temperament Dimensions (EASI)

TBQ (10–15 months)	EASI (28–36 months; n = 110)			
	Emotionality	Activity	Sociability/Shyness	Impulsivity
Intensity/Activity	–	.33***	–.21*	–
Regularity	–	–	–	–
Approach-Withdrawal	–.25**	–	–.40***	–
Sensory Sensitivity	–	–	–	–
Attentiveness	.24*	–	–	–
Manageability	–.33***	–	–	–.52***

TBQ (10–20 months)	EASI (43–48 months; n = 105)				
	Emotionality	Activity	Sociability	Shyness	Impulsivity
Intensity/Activity	–	.40***	.32***	–.21*	.20*
Regularity	–	–	–	–	–
Approach-Withdrawal	–	–	–	–.25*	–
Sensory Sensitivity	.23*	–	–	–	–
Attentiveness	.28**	–	–	–	–
Manageability	–.33***	–	–	–	–.42***

*$p < .05$. **$p < .01$. ***$p < .001$, two-tailed tests.

Going back even further in infancy to the 4-month period, we find that early Manageability (based on one maternal BBQ rating) significantly predicts, in both periods of childhood, Emotionality ($r = -.24$ and $r = -.20$; $df = 106-110$; $p < .05$) and Impulsivity ($r = -.19$ and $r = -.23$; $df = 106-110$; $p < .05$). Shyness in 4-year-olds is significantly related to low Intensity/Activity during the first 4 months of life ($r = -.22$; $df = 106$; $p < .05$). None of the other predictive relationships found from the later infancy period were evident as early as from 4 months.

Relating the presented results to the hypotheses, we find that the majority of our hypotheses were supported by the data: The more intense and active the infant, the higher the probability that the 2- and 4-year-old will be an active child. An infant showing negative reactions when facing new social situations has an increased tendency to be shy in childhood. Impulsivity and Emotionality in childhood have roots in early Manageability, that is, in irritability and persistence behavior during infancy. It is of interest to note that these roots could be detected already during the first months of life, as shown in the BBQ ratings of Manageability. The Intensity/Activity and Sociability/Shyness correlations provide, together with the predictive relationship from Approach-Withdrawal to Shyness, a nice illustration of the similarities and differences in the origin of these two social dimensions. Active and intense infants might later show tendencies to be dependent on social contacts for good functioning, whereas the not-so-energetic infants are likely to become shy children, especially if they are also socially withdrawn. This interpretation is consistent with that of Buss and Plomin (1984).

No relation between the early Manageability tendencies and Shyness was found. In so far as Manageability incorporates the fear aspect of Negative Emotionality, the notion that Shyness is based on fear was not corroborated in our study. Neither was there a significant relation between Attentiveness and Impulsivity. A nonhypothesized association was, however, found between early Attentiveness and Emotionality, meaning that an infant noticing small environmental changes tends to show Negative Emotionality later on. A possible explanation for this outcome might be that early attention-getting processes could be expressed as negative behaviors that are later seen in a more general negative behavior tendency.

RELATIONSHIPS BETWEEN EASI DIMENSIONS AND FUSSINESS/DIFFICULTNESS

The relationships between Fussiness/Difficultness and the EASI dimensions are clear. Predictions from early childhood EASI measures to fussy/difficult temperament and predictions from the Fussiness/Difficultness scale at 43 months to EASI scales at 48 months show the same pattern: Emotionality is substantially correlated with Fussiness/Difficultness ($r = .66$ and $r = .57$; $df = 93-96$; $p < .001$). Somewhat lower correlations are obtained with Impulsivity ($r = .32$; $df = 96$; $p < .01$, and $r = .43$; $df = 93$; $p < .001$).

RELATIONSHIPS BETWEEN CHILDHOOD TEMPERAMENT AND EGO STRENGTH/EFFECTANCE AND PROBLEM BEHAVIORS

Product-moment correlations between EASI dimensions from the two age periods during childhood and the Ego Strength/Effectance and Behavioral Problem dimensions measured at age 4 years are reported in Table 12.2. Replicated temperament associations with Ego Strength/Effectance are found for Impulsivity and Shyness. This indicates that the shy and impulsive child is likely to be low in curiosity and interest in learning new things and in confidence and self-directedness.

Table 12.2 also indicates that high degrees of outgoing conduct disordered behaviors are related to high Impulsivity, Activity, and Emotionality in both age periods. Shyness, Negative Emotionality, and Passivity have been characteristics of anxious and fearful children during a large part of their early childhood.

PROPOSED RELATIONSHIPS BETWEEN INFANT TEMPERAMENT, CHILDHOOD FUNCTIONING, AND THE BIG FIVE DIMENSIONS

In Figs. 12.1 through 12.4 the predictive relationships between infant and childhood temperament as well as the relationships between childhood temperament and Ego Strength/Effectance and Problem Behaviors have been summarized

TABLE 12.2
Significant Product-Moment Correlations Between Childhood Temperament Dimensions (EASI) and Childhood Ego Strength/Effectance and Externalizing and Internalizing Problem Behavior Dimensions

	48 months		
	Ego Strength/ Effectance	Externalizing Problems	Internalizing Problems
EASI 28–36 months			
Emotionality	−.21*	.35***	.30**
Activity	−	.32***	−.27**
Sociability/Shyness	−.21*	−	.26**
Impulsivity	−.40***	.51***	−
EASI 43–48 months			
Emotionality	−	.37***	.38***
Activity	−	.41***	−.21*
Shyness	−.36***	−	.52***
Sociability	−	−	−
Impulsivity	−.35***	.57***	−

*$p < .05$. **$p < .01$. ***$p < .001$, two-tailed tests; $n = 105$–110.

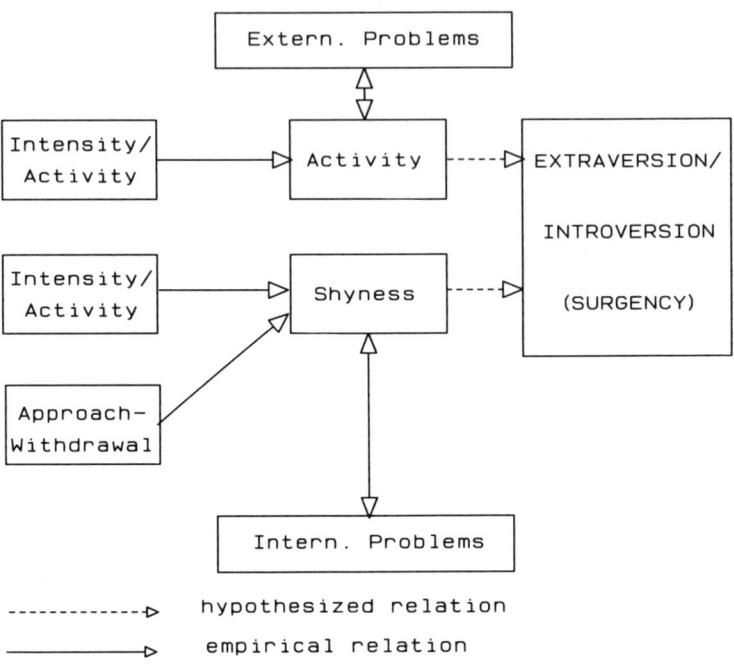

FIG. 12.1. Proposed relationships between infant and childhood temperament and behavior dimensions and the Big Five personality dimension of Extraversion/Introversion (Surgency).

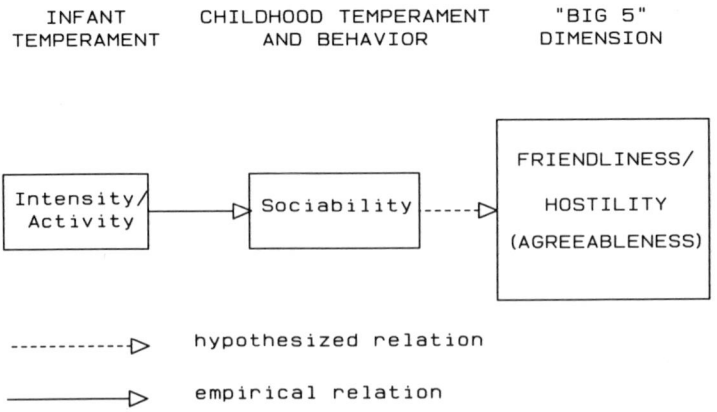

FIG. 12.2. Proposed relationships between infant and childhood temperament and behavior dimensions and the Big Five personality dimension of Friendliness/Hostility (Agreeableness).

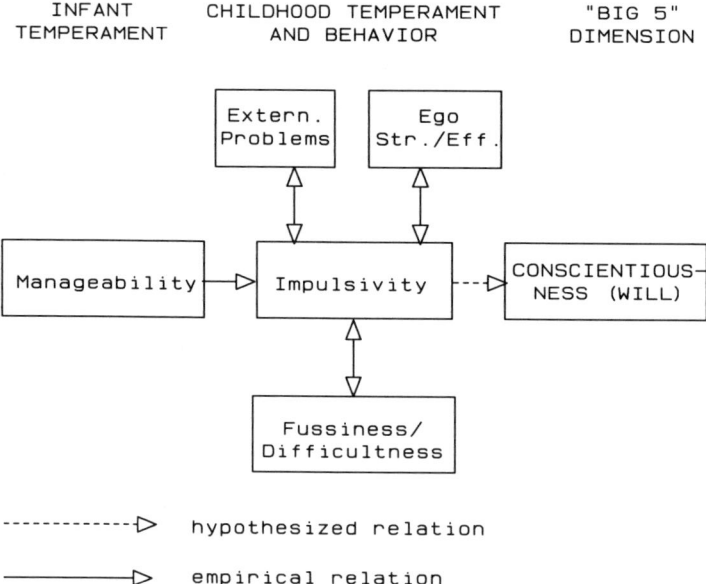

FIG. 12.3. Proposed relationships between infant and childhood temperament and behavior dimensions and the Big Five personality dimension of Conscientiousness (Will).

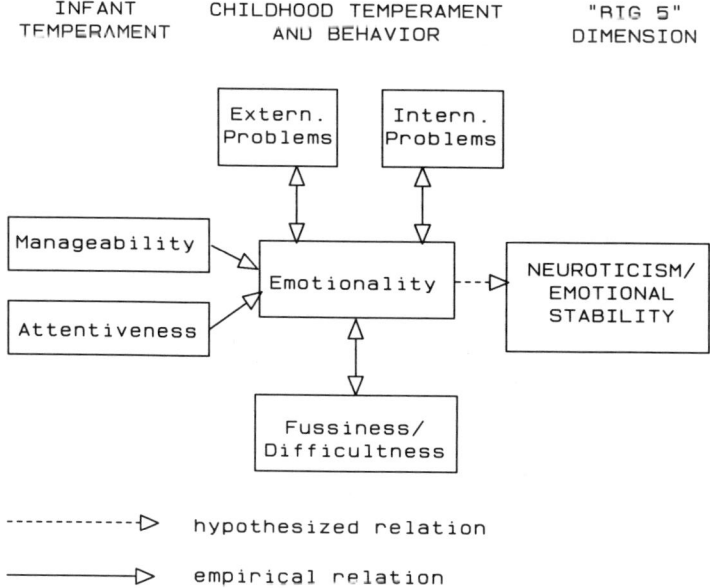

FIG. 12.4. Proposed relationships between infant and childhood temperament and behavior dimensions and the Big Five personality dimension of Neuroticism/Emotional Stability.

and hypothetically related to the Big Five dimensions of personality. The EASI dimensions have been connected to the Big Five personality structure as in Digman (1989; 1990), which excludes Intellect (Openness) from this discussion.

What we see as roots of the first two of the Big Five factors (Figs. 12.1 and 12.2) reflects the conceptual problems with the EASI Sociability dimension. It should be noted again that Buss and Plomin (1984) stated that Shyness could be seen as a derivative emerging from the more generic temperament traits of Emotionality and Sociability. In Buss and Plomin (1975) this thinking was not clearly spelled out. This concept and measurement ambiguity might have contributed to Digman's ambivalence when relating Sociability to the Big Five. In the present discussion, we assume the Shyness trait together with Activity conceptually belongs under the heading of Extraversion/Introversion and Surgency, and that Sociability (the tendency to prefer company to being alone) is related to Friendliness/Hostility.

Given the distinction between Shyness and Sociability, we find that both Introversion and Friendliness could have roots in early Intensity/Activity tendencies. The Extraversion/Introversion personality trait also seems to have a background in early approaching or withdrawing behaviors in new social situations. Furthermore, this trait might be related to both types of behavior problems in childhood, via Activity and Shyness characteristics.

The results further suggest that the dimensions of Conscientiousness and Emotional Stability (Figs. 12.3 and 12.4) both could be expected to have roots in Manageability (persistence and mood behaviors, tapping a negative emotionality disposition) during infancy, as inferred from the relationships between early Manageability and later Impulsivity and Emotionality. It is also in these areas (Neuroticism and lack of Conscientiousness) that precursors such as the fussy/difficult temperament of early childhood and the Externalizing Problem Behaviors described at age 4 years are found. Distinguishing Neuroticism from Conscientiousness is early Attentiveness, which might be a predictor of emotional instability, and also the differential relations between the EASI dimensions and other childhood behaviors. Neuroticism could be related to both Externalizing and Internalizing Problem Behaviors. Conscientiousness may have precursors in early signs of Ego Strength/Effectance, and low degrees of Externalizing Problem Behaviors.

CONCLUDING COMMENTS

The presented relationships are based on aggregated maternal and paternal data from several ages, meaning that the results represent a fairly broad picture of parents' views of their infants and young children. Variance attributable to other factors than child behavior is likely to have influenced this picture (cf. Bates & Bayles, 1984), but there is also ample evidence in favor of the validity of parental data as descriptions of actual infant behaviors (e.g., Hagekull, Bohlin, & Lindhagen, 1984; Matheny, Wilson, & Nuss, 1984; Wolk, Zeanah, Garcia Coll, & Carr, 1992). Given this state of affairs, and accepting the Digman (1989; 1990) conceptualization of the relationships between the EASI dimensions and the Big Five dimensions of personality, the present discussion is suggestive for a research program to study the roots of the Big Five in infancy and early childhood. The proposed continuities should be tested in a longitudinal approach, spanning from infancy to childhood and adolescence, and eventually into adulthood.

ACKNOWLEDGMENTS

This research was financed by the Swedish Council for Research in the Humanities and Social Sciences and by the Bank of Sweden Tercentenary Foundation.

REFERENCES

Bates, J. E. (1980). The concept of difficult temperament. *Merrill-Palmer Quarterly, 26*, 299–319.

Bates, J. E. (1986). The measurement of temperament. In R. Plomin & J. Dunn (Eds.), *The study of temperament: Changes, continuities and challenges* (pp. 1–11). Hillsdale, NJ: Lawrence Erlbaum Associates.

Bates, J. E., & Bayles, K. (1984). Objective and subjective components in mothers' perceptions of their children from age 6 months to 3 years. *Merrill-Palmer Quarterly, 30*, 111–130.

Bates, J. E., Maslin, C. A., & Frankel, K. A. (1985). Attachment security, mother–child interaction, and temperament as predictors of behavior-problem ratings at age 3 years. In I. Bretherton & E. Waters (Eds.), Growing points of attachment theory and research. *Monographs of the Society for Research in Child Development, 50*(1–2, Serial No. 209).

Behar, L., & Stringfield, S. (1974). A behavior rating scale for the preschool child. *Developmental Psychology, 10*, 601–610.

Block, J. H., & Block, J. (1980). The role of ego control and ego resiliency in the organization of behavior. In A. Collins (Ed.), *Minnesota symposium on child psychology* (Vol. 11, pp. 39–101). Hillsdale, NJ: Lawrence Erlbaum Associates.

Bohlin, G., Hagekull, B., & Lindhagen, K. (1981). Dimensions of infant behavior. *Infant Behavior and Development, 4*, 83–96.

Buss, A. H. (1989). Temperaments as personality traits. In G. A. Kohnstamm, J. E. Bates, & M. K. Rothbart (Eds.), *Temperament in childhood* (pp. 49–58). New York: Wiley.

Buss, A. H., & Plomin, R. (1975). *A temperament theory of personality development.* New York: Wiley.

Buss, A. H., & Plomin, R. (1984). *Temperament: Early developing personality traits.* Hillsdale, NJ: Lawrence Erlbaum Associates.

Carey, W. B. (1970). A simplified method for measuring infant temperament. *Journal of Pediatrics, 77*, 188–194.

Digman, J. M. (1989). Five robust trait dimensions: Development, stability, and utility. *Journal of Personality, 57*, 195–214.

Digman, J. M. (1990). Personality structure: Emergence of the five-factor model. *Annual Review of Psychology, 41*, 417–440.

Eysenck, H. J. (1947). *Dimensions of personality.* New York: Praeger.

Hagekull, B. (1985). The Baby and Toddler Behavior Questionnaires: Empirical studies and conceptual considerations. *Scandinavian Journal of Psychology, 26*, 110–122.

Hagekull, B. (1989). Longitudinal stability of temperament within a behavioral style framework. In G. A. Kohnstamm, J. E. Bates, & M. K. Rothbart (Eds.), *Temperament in childhood* (pp. 281–297). New York: Wiley.

Hagekull, B., & Bohlin, G. (1981). Individual stability in dimensions of infant behavior. *Infant Behavior and Development, 4*, 97–108.

Hagekull, B., & Bohlin, G. (1990). Early infant temperament and maternal expectations related to maternal adaptation. *International Journal of Behavioral Development, 13*, 199–214.

Hagekull, B., & Bohlin, G. (in press). Behavioral problems and competences in 4-year-olds: Dimensions and relationships. *International Journal of Behavioral Development.*

Hagekull, B., Bohlin, G., & Lindhagen, K. (1984). Validity of parental reports. *Infant Behavior and Development, 7*, 77–92.

John, O. P. (1990). Towards a taxonomy of personality descriptors. In D. M. Buss & N. Cantor (Eds.), *Personality psychology* (pp. 261–271). New York: Springer-Verlag.

Lee, C. L., & Bates, J. E. (1985). Mother–child interaction at age 2 years and perceived difficult temperament. *Child Development, 65*, 1314–1325.

Matheny, A. P., Wilson, R. S., & Nuss, S. M. (1984). Toddler temperament: Stability across settings and over ages. *Child Development, 55*, 1200–1211.

Martin, P. (1990, October). *Toward a macro-structure of childhood temperament.* Paper presented at the Eighth Occasional Temperament Conference, Scottsdale, AZ.

McDevitt, S. D. (1982, November). *On questionnaire reports.* Paper presented at the Fourth Occasional Temperament Conference, Salem, MA.

Rothbart, M. K. (1989). Temperament in childhood: A framework. In G. A. Kohnstamm, J. E. Bates, & M. K. Rothbart (Eds.), *Temperament in childhood* (pp. 59–73). New York: Wiley.

Thomas, A., & Chess, S. (1977). *Temperament and development.* New York: Brunner/Mazel.

Thomas, A., Chess, S., & Birch, H. G. (1968). *Temperament and behavioral disorders in children.* New York: New York University Press.

Thomas, A., Chess, S., Birch, H. G., Hertzig, M. E., & Korn, S. (1963). *Behavioral individuality in early childhood.* New York: New York University Press.

Waters, E., Wippman, J., & Sroufe, L. A. (1979). Attachment, positive affect, and competence in the peer group: Two studies in construct validation. *Child Development, 50*, 821–829.

Wiggins, J. S., & Trapnell, P. D. (in press). Personality structure: The return of the Big Five. In S. R. Briggs, R. Hogan, & W. H. Jones (Eds.), *Handbook of personality psychology.* Orlando, FL: Academic Press.

Wolk, S., Zeanah, C. H., Garcia Coll, C. T., & Carr, S. (1992). Factors affecting parents' perceptions of temperament in early infancy. *American Journal of Orthopsychiatry, 62*, 71–82.

CHAPTER

13

GENETICS OF PERSONALITY: A TWIN STUDY OF THE FIVE-FACTOR MODEL AND PARENT–OFFSPRING ANALYSES

H. H. Goldsmith
University of Wisconsin–Madison

Sandra H. Losoya
University of Oregon

Donna L. Bradshaw
Harvard University

J. J. Campos
University of California, Berkeley

Despite the ontogenetic emphases of pioneers such as Allport (1937), until recently personality theorists and researchers regularly went about their work without concern for its developmental implications. Similarly, behavioral genetics of personality was also typically studied in isolation from the field of personality development. These tides have slowly turned. The pages of mainstream personality journals now reveal attention to developmental issues, and developmental journals incorporate individual differences approaches to personality development. Also, behavioral geneticists have extended their investigations to young family members and consequently confronted issues about genetic influences on personality continuity and discontinuity. To help lay a better foundation for this interdisciplinary research, we offer family data on the relation of parental personality to childhood temperament. Because few genetic analyses have focused on the five-factor model directly, we first provide twin data on parents for the five-factor model.

TEMPERAMENT AND PERSONALITY

Temperament refers to early appearing dimensions of individual variability that are variously defined, but have as their core individual differences in emotional reactivity and activity (Goldsmith, in press; Goldsmith & Campos, 1982, 1986).

Included by many investigators are such traits as fearfulness, persistence, sociability, soothability, and positive affectivity (Bates, 1987; Bornstein, Gaughran, & Homel, 1986; Buss & Plomin, 1984; Chess & Thomas, 1984; Goldsmith et al., 1987; Rothbart & Derryberry, 1981). Temperamental dimensions are generally expected to have biological origins and to be relatively stable, although stability is expected primarily within, but not necessarily across, periods of major developmental reorganization (Goldsmith & Campos, 1982). Thus, temperament is primarily an individual construct, but one that is not impervious to social influence (Stevenson-Hinde, 1986).

We believe temperament constitutes the "emotional core" of later personality characteristics. Thus, we should ultimately be able to specify a course of development whereby early proneness to anger predisposes toward later aggressiveness (Goldsmith & Davis, 1991), early behavioral inhibition predisposes toward later guilt proneness (Kochanska, 1991), and so forth for the various temperamental constructs. These transformations will be probabilistic tendencies rather than deterministic blueprints.

Given the chapters on the structure of personality in this volume, it seems unnecessary to discuss adult personality in detail. Suffice it to note that the availability of new and more sophisticated adult personality measures invites new examinations of familial resemblance. Indeed, Loehlin (1992) organized the behavior–genetic literature on personality according to the five-factor model although only one study (Bergeman et al., in press, cited in Loehlin, 1992) that he reviewed used an instrument specifically designed to tap the five-factor model.

A TWIN STUDY OF THE BIG FIVE FACTORS OF ADULT PERSONALITY

Sample

The sample for the behavior–genetic analyses comprised 236 individuals, divided into 63 identical and 55 fraternal pairs. Females comprised 74.6% of the sample. Disproportionate numbers of females and identical pairs are often recruited in mail surveys requiring voluntary cooperation (Lykken, McGue, & Tellegen, 1987; Lykken, Tellegen, & DeRubeis, 1978). Twin zygosity diagnosis was based on each twin's report of physical traits (e.g., eye color, height, hair color, and texture) and appearance similarity on an adult version of Goldsmith's (1991) extensive Zygosity Questionnaire for Young Twins. Because the sample was highly restricted, we recruited via newspaper advertising. Thus, the sample cannot be considered random or representative.

Assessment of Personality

Parent personality was assessed with Goldberg's (1992) inventory. This instrument contains 50 transparent scales anchored by bipolar adjectives, 10 for each of the five domains that subsume most English personality-trait terms. In our study, reliability estimates for the scores formed by unweighted summing of items varied between .82 and .89, which compares to Goldberg's (1992) range of .84 to .89. Goldberg also reported that scores correlated highly (median $r = .67$) with the five domain scores of the NEO–Personality Inventory (PI), an alternative measure of the five domains (Costa & McCrae, 1985). Twins were instructed not to confer while completing the questionnaires. Because they lived apart, collaboration between the twins was unlikely.

Twin Similarity

Table 13.1 shows intraclass correlations that reflect cotwin similarity. We computed the intraclass correlations from a double entry data file and estimated the additive genetic (heritability) and shared environmental effects from a separate regression analysis on the same double entry data file (DeFries & Fulker, 1985). The regression formula predicts one twin's score from the cotwin's score, the pair's zygosity coded as .5 for fraternal pairs and 1.0 for identical pairs, and the interaction of zygosity by cotwin score. The partial regression coefficient for the cotwin's score estimates the shared environmental effect, the partial regression coefficient for zygosity reflects any mean difference between identicals and fraternals, and the partial regression coefficient for the interaction term estimates the heritability. In separate analyses, we found that entering sex into the regression equation had very minimal effects on the other parameter estimates. Assumptions of the method include a linear polygenic model, minimal assortative mating, and equal shared environmental influences for identical and fraternal twins. The results for the Extraversion, Pleasantness/Agreeableness, and Emotional Stability factors are very similar to those in the literature on adult personality (see reviews cited earlier). That

TABLE 13.1
Twin Similarity and Genetic and Environmental Variance Estimates for Markers of the Five-Factor Model as Assessed by a 50-item Bipolar Rating Scale (Sample 1)[a]

Scales	Identical R[b]	Fraternal R[b]	Heritability	Shared Environment
I. Extraversion	.43 (.10)	.18 (.13)	.50	.00*
II. Pleasantness or Agreeableness	.56 (.09)	.07 (.14)	.46	.03
III. Conscientiousness or Dependability	.59 (.08)	.40 (.11)	.39	.20
IV. Emotional Stability	.44 (.10)	.15 (.13)	.57	.00*
V. Intellect or Sophistication	.34 (.11)	.33 (.12)	.02	.32

[a]Ns = 63 identical and 55 fraternal pairs.

[b]Value of 1 standard error of the correlation is given in parentheses.

*Parameter takes negative values in model that includes shared environmental effect and is thus set to zero.

is, genetic effects account for about one half the variance and all or almost all the environmental variance is unshared by cotwins. Factor III, Conscientiousness or Dependability, shows a moderate genetic variance as well as a shared environmental component estimated at .20. Is this shared environmental component real? Perhaps not, because the .20 effect is not statistically significant with our sample size, and the Bergeman et al. (in press, cited in Loehlin, 1992) results using the NEO–PI questionnaire did not implicate shared environmental variance in a study of (mostly) older Swedish twins. However, the facets of conscientiousness (organized, reliable, practical, thrifty, etc.) have seldom been investigated from a genetic perspective, and further attention to the possibility of shared environmental variance for this factor is perhaps justified. The most interesting finding is the *lack* of greater identical than fraternal similarity for Factor V, Intellect or Sophistication. Little data have been organized to address the biometric architecture of Factor V, partly because it has an alternate conceptualization as Culture/Openness (Costa & McCrae, 1985) rather than Intellect/Sophistication (Goldberg, 1990). The correlation of Goldberg's measure of Intellect with Costa and McCrae's (1985) NEO–PI domain scale of Openness is only .46 (Goldberg, 1992). An analysis of individual items on Goldberg's Intellect marker scale revealed that the item "unintelligent vs. intelligent" does show greater identical than fraternal similarity, but that the other facets of the Intellect marker scale (perceptive, analytic, and inquisitive, as well as cultured, refined, and sophisticated) are no more similar in identical than fraternal pairs.

With these twin analyses as background, we address the issue of parent–offspring resemblance for personality/temperament.

RELATION OF FIVE-FACTOR MARKER SCALES TO CHILDHOOD TEMPERAMENT

The adult twins in the sample discussed were parents, who also reported on their children's temperament. These twins were recruited via newspaper advertisements in Oregon and Washington. Their average age was 34.5 years (range: 22.5 to 46.5; $SD = 4.81$). To maximize sample size for the parent–offspring analyses, we used different criteria for inclusion of subjects. We had data from 236 adult twin individuals with children, regardless of whether or not the cotwin participated in the study. This sample, referred to hereafter as Sample 1, was 53.8% female. Sample 1 had three cross-sectional cohorts, with the three divided according to the age of their children. For the first analysis, we used the 132 parents with children who were in the age range (3–8 yrs) covered by Rothbart's Children's Behavior Questionnaire (CBQ) (see Ahadi & Rothbart, chap. 10 in this vol.). We began our investigation with these older children rather than infants and toddlers because the behaviors captured by the childhood scales are more similar to those in adult questionnaires. The CBQ is a caregiver-report measure that assesses the following dimensions: Activity Level, Anger, Approach/Anticipation, Attentional Shifting and Focusing, Discomfort, Fear, Pleasure to High and Low Stimulus Intensities, Impulsivity, Inhibitory Control, Falling Reactivity/Soothability, Sadness, Shyness, and Smiling and Laughter. The format of the CBQ is illustrated by items such as: "My child easily gets irritated when s/he has trouble with some task (e.g., building, drawing, dressing)." Responses range from extremely untrue (1), to neither true nor untrue (4), to extremely true (7), in addition to a "not applicable" option.

Table 13.2 shows the significant ($p < .05$) correlations of parental self-report of personality on the Goldberg (1992) instrument used in the previous twin similarity analysis with parentally reported childhood temperament as assessed by the CBQ.

The 19 significant correlations in Table 13.2 were extracted from a 5 (Five-Factor Model) by 16 (CBQ scales) matrix, and thus a few might be expected to differ from zero only by chance. Thus, we limit interpretation to systematic patterns in the data. Heritabilities in the range of .40 to .50 predict parent–offspring correlations in the range of .20 to .25, if genetic transmission is the only underlying source of similarity.

Fortunately, correlations in this range are significant with our sample size. The 16 scales of the CBQ are somewhat unwieldy to interpret, but the strength of the CBQ lies in its differentiated view of the child's temperament. Thus, Table 13.2 shows results of individual scales rather than factors derived from the CBQ. However, knowledge of the CBQ factor structure aids interpretation, and the reader may wish to consult chapter 10 in this volume. We also refer to our own factor analyses, which are not presented here.

The most salient finding concerns the tendency of parents high on Factor IV. Emotional Stability to report their children as expressing less negative affect and being more soothable. Various factor solutions for the CBQ indicate that Anger, Fear, Sadness, and Soothability (and sometimes other scales) load a broad negative affect factor. Parents with low scores on Emotional Stability endorse self-descriptors such as angry, nervous, irritable, discontented, insecure, and emotional, so the parent–offspring association involves like content predicting like content. A second finding that might reflect similar content in both parental and offspring scales is the association of parental extraversion with positive hedonic CBQ scales (Smiling and Laughter, and Low Pleasure). A third finding from Table 13.2 is more complex. We have noted that CBQ Inhibitory Control, Attentional Focusing, Perceptual Sensitivity, and sometimes Low Pleasure (a tendency to derive pleasure from low intensity stimulation) are correlated. Subsets of this cluster of CBQ scales in children are associated with parental Agreeableness, Conscientiousness, and Intellect. These findings for Agreeableness, Conscientiousness, and Intellect perhaps reflect one underlying association with CBQ Inhibitory Control and its related scales because the three adult factor markers are substantially intercorrelated (mean $r = .37$) in our data. That is, a broad tendency to view the self in terms that are

TABLE 13.2
Correlations of Parental Five-Factor Markers with 16 CBQ Scales (Sample 1)

Marker Scales	CBQ Correlates	Observed Correlation
FI. Extraversion	Low Intensity Pleasure	.20
	Smiling & Laughter	.18
FII. Pleasantness or Agreeableness	Soothability	.34
	Inhibitory Control	.29
	Anger	−.22
	Attentional Focusing	.21
	Low Intensity Pleasure	.18
FIII. Conscientiousness or Dependability	Inhibitory Control	.27
	Low Intensity Pleasure	.26
FIV. Emotional Stability	Soothability	.46
	Anger	−.30
	Fear	−.27
	Sadness	−.23
FV. Intellect or Sophistication	Inhibitory Control	.31
	Anger	−.25
	Attentional Focusing	.23
	Perceptual Sensitivity	.21
	Smiling & Laughter	.18
	Sadness	−.18

[a]N = 132 parent–offspring pairs; each of the correlations presented in the table is significant at p = .04 (2-tailed).

socially valued is associated with a tendency to view the child as controlled, task oriented, and sensitive. The explanations for this association could obviously take different forms, especially given that the parent is the source of all information.

We now turn to consideration of these explanations before presenting additional data from parents with younger children.

WHY MIGHT PARENTAL PERSONALITY RELATE TO TEMPERAMENT?

At least four processes could account for associations between parental personality and offspring temperament. Although each of the processes may be important, they are likely to be reflected in only subtle empirical relations.

Parental Personality Characteristics as Biasing Factors

The least interesting of these processes is that certain parental traits may bias the assessment of offspring behavior. This explanation looms most prominently when the parents contribute to the assessment process, as they do in all our analyses. When parents complete a temperament questionnaire about their child, they are potentially susceptible to the same response sets that apply to self-report of mature personality, most notably, social desirability. Certain other parental characteristics might also bias perception and/or report of infant temperament. For example, aggressive fathers might be reluctant to report their offspring as fearful. The other three processes represent more developmentally interesting lines of influence.

Genetic Transmission of Personality Characteristics

A substantial literature indicates that most adult and adolescent personality traits are moderately heritable (for reviews, see Eaves, Eysenck, & Martin, 1989; Goldsmith, 1983; Loehlin, 1992; McCartney, Harris, & Bernieri, 1990; Plomin, 1986). Most of this evidence comes from twin studies, but model-fitting approaches that include data from nontwin siblings, parents, and their mature offspring, and, in some cases, adoptees, also implicate moderate genetic effects.

The genetic relation between adult personality traits and their anlagen that presumably exist early in life is a more complex matter. Infant temperamental traits are often considered to be the affective cores of adult personality traits. The postulation of a genetic relation between infant and adult forms presupposes some form of continuity from infant behavioral patterns to adult personality traits. The adult traits undoubtedly entail more complex cognitive, social, and self-related components.

Parental Personality as Part of the Developmental Context for Children's Personality Development

In addition to genetic transmission, parents' personality characteristics might be socially transmitted to their children, either directly through the processes of modeling and identification emphasized in social learning and psychoanalytic theory (Bandura, 1971; Sears, Maccoby, & Levin, 1957), or more broadly by mediating parenting behavior (Belsky, 1984; Heinicke, 1984). Parental maturity, ego strength, and other indicators of healthy personality integration predict maternal responsiveness and other parenting behaviors (Brunnquell, Crichton, & Egeland, 1981; Feldman & Nash, 1986; Heinicke, Diskin, Ramsey-Klee, & Given, 1983).

Parental personality is also part of the developmental context for temperament, as emphasized by the goodness-of-fit conceptualization (J. V. Lerner & R. M. Lerner, 1983; Thomas & Chess, 1977). According to this conceptualization, similar initial temperamental characteristics will lead to different outcomes depending on the fit between the child's characteristics and environmental factors, including parental personality as well as parents' and teachers' attitudes and expectations and ecological variables.

Effect of Children on Parental Personality

Although it is more common and probably more realistic to think of parental effects on children and, especially, infants, the direction of influence may also be reversed. Our study does not address this possibility, but some temperament literature suggests that child-to-parent effects may occur (e.g., Sirignano & Lachman, 1985).

ANALYSES OF PARENT–OFFSPRING SIMILARITY FOR INFANTS AND TODDLERS IN MULTIPLE SAMPLES

Samples: Overview

The data come from the study of adult twin personality described previously plus two studies of infant development that included assessment of parents (Bradshaw, Goldsmith, & Campos, 1987; Goldsmith & Campos, 1986).

Methods in the Bradshaw (Sample 2) Study

Sample 2 comprised a subset of 48 mothers and their 12-month-olds participating in a laboratory study of the relations among infant temperament, attachment, and emotional communication processes (Bradshaw et al., 1987). All of the mothers were married, Caucasian, and almost exclusively middle class (100% high school and 72% college graduates; 91% with annual family incomes > $16,000). The infants were all born full-term and had experienced no perinatal illnesses or birth complications. Twenty-one (44%) were firstborns, and half were boys.

Maternal personality was assessed with Tellegen's (1982) 300-item Multidimensional Personality Questionnaire (MPQ). The MPQ is notable for its careful derivation and coverage of normal range personality dimensions. The eleven internally consistent content scales are the result of successive cycles of trait conceptualization, item writing, data collection, item factor analysis, and item selection. Tellegen (1982) reported extensive standardization data, reasonable levels of internal consistency and test–retest reliability, and convergent validity correlations of the MPQ scales with other established instruments. The MPQ incorporates perhaps the most sophisticated validity scales of any self-report inventory. One of these validity scales assesses tendency to respond in a socially desirable fashion and is central to our analyses.

The MPQ also has a well-replicated higher order factor structure. The three MPQ factor scales play a large role in our study. Tellegen (1985) interpreted these factors—Positive Emotionality, Negative Emotionality, and Constraint—in temperamental terms. The two emotionality factors are particularly congruent with our theoretical view of temperament as individual differences in emotional expression (Goldsmith & Campos, 1982, 1986). Since its introduction, evidence for the external validity of the MPQ scales and their higher order structure has steadily accumulated (e.g., Gjerde, J. Block, & J. H. Block, 1988; Hall, 1977; Tellegen, 1982, 1985; Tellegen & Waller, in press; Watson, Clark, & Carey, 1988).

We chose Rothbart's (1981) Infant Behavior Questionnaire (IBQ) as the most appropriate parental report measure of temperament because it emphasizes individual differences in emotionality and shows good psychometric qualities. The IBQ includes scales that assess fear, anger, pleasure, persistence, soothability, and activity level; it asks the caregiver to report the frequency of certain situationally specified behaviors during the past week, or, in some cases, 2 weeks. Thus, a scale score reflects averaged responses across situations that were rationally expected to elicit related emotional expressions or motoric acts. The following IBQ Fear item exemplifies the form used: "How often during the last week did the baby cry or show distress at a loud sound (blender, vacuum cleaner, etc)?" Rothbart constructed the IBQ using a standard technique that combines rational selection of candidate items with subsequent item analytic procedures designed to maximize internal consistency and discriminant validity. By age 9 months, internal consistency and stability correlations are satisfactory (Rothbart, 1981), and IBQ scales correlate moderately with behaviors recorded during home observations (Rothbart, 1986).

Mothers were given the IBQ and the MPQ to complete at home after a 1-hour laboratory session focused on social referencing behavior. They returned the completed questionnaires at a second testing session approximately 10 days later ($M = 9.6$ days). Forty mothers completed the IBQ and 35 completed the MPQ.

Methods in the Goldsmith and Campos (Sample 3) Study

From a larger sample that included infant twins (Goldsmith & Campos, 1990), we used a group of singleton subjects who were initially studied for comparison with the twins, hereafter called Sample 3. They were identified and recruited in the same manner as the subjects in Sample 2. For most analyses, about 35 singletons were available; precise information is given in each table. As in Sample 2, this study utilized the IBQ and the MPQ. When the infants reached age $8\frac{1}{2}$ months, mothers completed the IBQ; when she returned it, we sent the father an IBQ form. Then, both parents completed the MPQ at home. A 2-week interval typically separated parental rating of infant temperament from self-rating of adult personality.

When the children in Sample 3 reached age 21 to 22 months, we again assessed temperament with a parental report questionnaire. This questionnaire comprised only three scales: Pleasure, Activity Level, and Fearfulness. The questionnaire was constructed especially for this study, using an independent sample. The methods of construction were modeled directly after those of the IBQ, which has three conceptually comparable scales. Item content was modified extensively to ensure that it was age appropriate. Later these three scales were further revised and combined with two others to form the Toddler Behavior Assessment Questionnaire (TBAQ) (Goldsmith, 1988; Goldsmith, Elliott, & Jaco, 1986;

Goldsmith & Rothbart, 1991). We refer to the version of the toddler questionnaire used in Sample 3 as the Preliminary-TBAQ (P-TBAQ).

Additional Methods in Sample 1

The sample for this study has already been described. As reported previously, parental personality was assessed with Goldberg's markers of the five-factor model. For parents with infants under 17 months of age, we used the IBQ to assess temperament, as in Samples 2 and 3. The companion instrument chosen to measure temperament in children ages 17 months to 3 years was Goldsmith's (1988) TBAQ. The TBAQ scales include Anger, Proneness, Pleasure, Social Fear, Interest-Persistence, and Activity Level. Reported estimates of internal consistency were .82, .80, .83, .79, and .78, respectively. A sample item (from the Social Fear scale) is: "When your child was being approached by an unfamiliar adult while shopping or out walking, how often did your child show distress or cry?"

Associations of Parental Personality and IBQ Scales

Our main basis for inference is constructive replication. Based on considerations in the personality literature (e.g., Funder, 1987) and on the nature of our variables, we selected correlational effect sizes that are likely to be meaningful and focused on those that replicated. We began by calculating the 11 by 6 matrix of MPQ content scales by IBQ scales in both Samples 2 and 3. We augmented this with the 3 by 6 matrix for the MPQ factor scales and the IBQ. We observed several modest-to-moderate correlations between MPQ content scales and IBQ scales, practically all of which were reflected in the pattern of correlations between MPQ factor scales and the IBQ scales. For example, in Sample 2, the individual MPQ content scale Achievement correlated .51 with the IBQ Smiling and Laughter scale, and the MPQ factor scale Positive Emotionality (which loads Achievement) correlated .56 with IBQ Smiling and Laughter. Thus, we can simply present the results for MPQ factor scales without distorting the overall pattern of findings.

Section I of Table 13.3 displays the mothers' data for Samples 2 and 3 in the first two rows under each of the three MPQ factor scale headings. The third row under each heading shows correlations of Sample 3 fathers' MPQs with their spouses' reports of infant temperament; in parentheses are correlations with fathers' own reports.[1] The five associations that we judged to be possibly

---

[1] In agreement with other reports in the early temperament literature (Bates, 1987), mothers' and fathers' reports of infant temperament were often only moderately correlated in the entire Goldsmith and Campos (1986) sample. In Sample 3, the correlation between mothers' and fathers' perceptions as reported on the IBQ were as follows: Activity Level ($r = .22$); Smiling and Laughter ($r = .35$); Fear ($r = .15$); Distress to Limitations ($r = .25$); Soothability ($r = .12$); and Duration of Orienting ($r = .12$). Reasons for this lack of correspondence have been discussed elsewhere (e.g., Rothbart & Goldsmith, 1985). This result led us to keep maternal and paternal report of infant temperament separate in these analyses.

noteworthy and reasonably replicable are printed in a boldfaced font. The first replicated finding was that parents who rated themselves higher on Positive Emotionality reported their infants as smiling and laughing more frequently in a number of everyday situations. Although Tellegen distinguished communal and agentic components of the Positive Emotionality factor (as represented by the Social Closeness and Achievement scales, respectively), we found no trend for the communal component to account for the association with IBQ Smiling and Laughter (cf. Mangelsdorf, Gunnar, Kestenbaum, Lang, & Andreas, 1990).

The second and third replicated findings were that parents higher on Negative Emotionality reported their infants motorically active and distressed by limitations (more prone to anger). The fourth and fifth replicated findings were that parents higher on Constraint reported their infants as more soothable and affectively positive.

Two other findings from Section I of Table 13.3 deserve mention. In Sample 2, the maternal Constraint factor predicted several of the IBQ scales. The pattern of prediction corresponds to the one-factor structure underlying the largely independent IBQ scales (Rothbart, 1986); that is, the 12-month-old offspring of more constrained mothers scored toward the positive pole of a broad IBQ hedonic tone factor. Main components of the Constraint factor are tendencies to avoid dangerous situations, to be controlled rather than spontaneous, and to endorse traditional attitudes. We also note that parental MPQ Positive Emotionality predicted Soothability and Duration of Orienting with correlations of .20 or above in the fathers' data ($rs = .46$ and .41) and in one of the maternal samples.

Turning now to Section II of Table 13.3, we provide the data from the Sample 1 parents with infants. Parents were, of course, assessed by markers of the five-factor model. These data present a challenging opportunity for replication. First, Goldberg's markers of the five-factor model and the MPQ factors do not match neatly, so the results pertain more to generalization than to replication. Second, only 35 parents with infants were available from Sample 1 so the possibility of falsely concluding that findings do not generalize is substantial.

Rather than relying entirely on rational matching of content in the MPQ versus the markers of the five-factor model, we are informed by recent findings of Tellegen and Waller (in press) concerning the relation of markers of the five-factor model with the MPQ. Their results show that MPQ Positive Emotionality overlaps substantially with Extraversion, that MPQ Negative Emotionality is associated chiefly with (low) Emotional Stability but also with some aspects of (low) Agreeableness. MPQ Constraint matches best with Conscientiousness, but the degree of association is rather weak because it is only the control (nonimpulsiveness) aspect of Conscientiousness that relates to Constraint. Complicating matters somewhat is the finding is that the nonimpulsiveness aspect of Conscientiousness was also associated with MPQ Positive Emotionality.

Considering these correspondences of the MPQ and five-factor model in conjunction with Sections I and II of Table 13.3, we find two cases of clear gener-

TABLE 13.3
Prediction of Infant Temperament from Parental Personality[a,b]

	IBQ Scales					
	Activity Level	Smiling & Laughter	Fear	Distress to Limitations	Soothability	Duration of Orienting
	I. Correlations of Parental MPQ Factor Scales with Maternal IBQ Scales[c]					
Positive Emotionality						
Sample 2: Mothers	-.02	**.56**	.07	-.11	.01	.20
Sample 3: Mothers	.15	**.29**	.14	.07	.22	-.02
Sample 3: Fathers	.14 (.13)	**.10 (.21)**	.31 (.04)	-.02 (-.10)	-.03 (.46)	-.04 (.41)
Sample 3: Mean Parent[d]	.16 (.19)	**.24 (.03)**	.33 (-.02)	.04 (-.04)	.14 (.50)	-.09 (.18)
Negative Emotionality						
Sample 2: Mothers	**.38**	.18	.05	**.02**	-.15	.12
Sample 3: Mothers	**.20**	-.24	.03	**.29**	-.16	-.07
Sample 3: Fathers	**.34 (.44)**	-.01 (.39)	.14 (.07)	**.31 (.11)**	.21 (.38)	.07 (.26)
Sample 3: Mean Parent	**.34 (.40)**	-.23 (.15)	.13 (.11)	**.39 (.29)**	.01 (.31)	-.01 (.14)

Constraint					
Sample 2: Mothers	-.36	**.21**	-.11	-.41	.51
Sample 3: Mothers	.17	**.21**	-.16	-.02	-.01
Sample 3: Fathers	.14 (.17)	**.18** (-.10)	.01 (.18)	.15 (-.00)	-.01 (.10)
Sample 3: Mean Parent	.16 (.12)	**.28** (-.08)	-.03 (.05)	.14 (.11)	-.06 (-.04)

II. Correlations of Parental Five-Factor Marker Scales with IBQ Scales[e]

I. Extraversion	-.20	**-.11**	-.11	.19	-.33
II. Agreeableness	.02	-.17	-.14	-.07	-.31
III. Conscientiousness	.27	**.04**	.08	-.21	-.01
IV. Emotional Stability	**-.24**	-.04	-.46	**-.23**	-.28
V. Intellect/Culture	-.28	-.02	-.63	-.26	-.07

[a]Correlations with paternal report of toddler temperament are provided in parentheses.
[b]Boldfaced values suggest a pattern of replicated findings.
[c]$N = 35$ for Sample 2; $N = 34$ for Sample 3 mothers; $N = 30$ for Sample 3 fathers (with maternal report of temperament); $N = 31$ for averaged parent values; $N = 30$ for Sample 3 fathers and averaged parent values with paternal report of temperament (values in parentheses).
[d]The mean parent scores are averages of maternal and paternal z scores for corresponding MPQ scales. Note that only the parent personality – not the infant temperament – scales are cross-parent composites.
[e]$N = 35$ (combined mothers and fathers) for Sample 1.

alization: Infants of parents high on Emotional Stability were rated as less active and less prone to anger (less distressed to limitations). Other boldfaced values in Section II might be considered cases of nongeneralization of findings. Other correlations are possibly worthy of note (e.g., the finding, $r = -.46$, that parents high on Emotional Stability reported their infants as less fearful), but the correlation of $-.63$ between parental Intellect/Culture and infant fear was substantially influenced by one extreme outlier.

What characterizes the best replicated associations that we have observed? As regards scale content, there are some obvious correspondences. Parental Positive Emotionality is associated with infant Smiling and Laughter, both of which tap hedonically positive response tendencies despite quite different, age-appropriate item content. Also, parental Negative Emotionality or low Emotional Stability is associated with infant high activity level and distress to limitations. Distress to limitations clearly involves negative hedonic tone, as do the parental scales. High activity is sometimes associated with high reactivity in infancy, and this combination predicts later inhibition (Kagan & Snidman, 1991). A strong interpretation of our results suggests neurotic tendencies in the parents of such children.

Attempts to Extend the Findings

A small subgroup of Sample 3, which had initially been tested as age 9 months, was followed up about 1 year later, at age 21 to 22 months. Toddler temperament was assessed via the P-TBAQ, and parental personality was not reassessed. The number of singletons was greatly diminished. Parental personality might change over the 1-year period, or the underlying temperament constructs measured by similarly named IBQ and P–TBAQ scales might differ subtly. Despite the corresponding scales, the TBAQ items were not derived from the IBQ items, with a few exceptions. The correlations between corresponding IBQ and P-TBAQ scales over time was modest. For the full longitudinal sample, which included twins that do not otherwise enter into this report ($N = 79$ for maternal report and $N = 70$ for paternal report), the correlations predicting the P-TBAQ from the IBQ were as follows: For Fear, $r = .36$ for mothers and .22 for fathers; for the pleasure-related scales, $r = .16$ for mothers and .19 for fathers; and for Activity Level, $r = .20$ for fathers and .02 for fathers. It is also possible that the relation of parental personality and offspring temperament might change from midinfancy to early toddlerhood. Finally, the P–TBAQ, with its three scales, limits the associations that we can attempt to replicate. Nevertheless, we performed analyses corresponding to those in Table 13.3. For the 13 mother–singleton pairs available, two of the three replicable associations from Table 13.2 produced high correlations (MPQ Positive Emotionality by P-TBAQ Pleasure, $r = .48$; MPQ Constraint by P-TBAQ Pleasure, $r = .57$). For the 12 father-singleton pairs, a .61 correlation between MPQ Constraint and P-TBAQ Fearfulness could be

TABLE 13.4
Correlations of Parental Five-Factor Marker Scales with
TBAQ Scales for Sample 1 Toddlers[a]

Parental Five-Factor Markers	TBAQ Scales					
	Activity	Pleasure	Social Fear	Interest	Anger	Social Desirability
I. Extraversion	.04	**.26**	−.12	.05	.05	.11
II. Agreeableness	**−.29**	.20	−.06	.27	**−.25**	.22
III. Conscientiousness	−.21	.10	−.08	.07	.02	.21
IV. Emotional Stability	−.04	.12	−.04	.01	−.03	.27
V. Intellect	−.07	.27	−.09	.05	−.05	.23

[a]$N = 69$ (combined mothers and fathers); correlational estimates > 1.191 are significant at $p = .05$ (1-tailed).

considered a replication. The tiny follow-up sample of singletons obviously renders these findings tenuous, and it is only their confirmation of earlier findings that justifies their report.[2]

In the portion of Sample 1 with toddler data, there are several correlations that buttress other findings already reported. For instance, positive affect in the parent and toddler are related (parental Extraversion and offspring TBAQ Pleasure). As in the infant data, parental negative emotionality (in the form of low Agreeableness but not low Emotional Stability) was associated with activity and anger. These correlations that seem consistent with the infant results are boldfaced in Table 13.4. Note also that results for the TBAQ Social Desirability scale are given in Table 13.4 (discussed later).

---

[2]The total follow-up of twins and singletons in Sample 3 was large enough to support inference, so we examined the relevant associations. Only the MPQ Constraint factor seemed to predict toddler temperament. The most striking feature was that fathers' Constraint scores significantly predicted their own report of their toddlers' higher Fearfulness ($r = .44$) and lower Activity ($r = −.39$). The mothers' data showed a moderate correlation of .21 between MPQ Constraint and P-TBAQ Fearfulness. The link between MPQ Constraint and P-TBAQ Fearfulness may be especially noteworthy because of the surface similarity of the behaviors involved. The primary reason for the discrepancy between the infant and toddler fear associations with MPQ Constraint is probably that the fear system is undergoing change in most infants at the age of 9 months. A large developmental literature documents the onset of wariness to strangers and other fear-related phenomena in the second half-year of life. By the time of the toddler assessment, the fear system is better organized and probably more reflective of stable individual differences. Another possible contributing explanation of the stronger associations of MPQ Constraint with fearfulness in the toddler data is that the P-TBAQ Fear scale contains more items dealing with social contexts than does the IBQ Fear scale. Because the parental personality data were collected 1 year before the toddler temperament data, situational variables, responses sets, parental mood states, or other unstable aspects of parental personality are unlikely to account for any associations.

Summary of Findings Thus Far

Across all our samples, instruments, and age groups, three replicable associations have emerged, although they are not apparent in every case where we have searched for them. Parental positive affect is associated with report of positive affect in the child; and parental negative affect is associated with report of negative affect in the child. In infants and toddlers only, parental negative affect predicts higher offspring activity level. Finally, in toddlers and young children, parental overcontrol, constraint, and conscientiousness predict inhibition in offspring.

WHAT ACCOUNTS FOR ASSOCIATIONS BETWEEN PARENTAL PERSONALITY AND INFANT OR TODDLER TEMPERAMENT?

Analyses of Parental Rating Bias

The immediate question that arises is whether our findings are due to parental reporting bias. But what form is reporting bias expected to take? A straightforward, but probably incorrect, idea is that parents might project their own personalities onto their infants (Lyon & Plomin, 1981). Indeed, the modest size of the significant parent–offspring correlations suggests that there is no strong tendency toward projection.

What is needed is an independent measure of parental rating bias, such as a validity scale. The only validity scale that exists for a temperament questionnaire is the TBAQ Social Desirability scale, and it has not yet been adequately validated (Goldsmith, 1988). Nevertheless, the content-balanced TBAQ Social Desirability scale is correlated with several five-factor markers (Table 13.4), raising the possibility that parents with certain personality characteristics are prone to describe their children in a socially desirable light. Or, perhaps, the TBAQ Social Desirability scale has some substantive interpretation that is not yet understood.

Another approach to the issue involves the MPQ validity scales, the most relevant of which seem to be the Unlikely Virtues scale, a lie scale with fairly obvious items, and the content-balanced Desirable Response Inconsistency (DRIN) scale, a more subtle social desirability measure, which the TBAQ Sociability Desirability scale was modeled after. In the infant data, we made the strong assumption that parents who tended to distort self-report of their own personalities would also be biased in reporting about their children's personalities. Then, we approached the issue in the traditional manner of personality researchers by identifying and deleting potentially invalid records. In Sample 2, raw scores two standard deviations above the mean on either of these validity scales or scores approaching that level on both scales led to disqualification of only three cases. We then recalculated all of the MPQ by IBQ correlations. The resulting correlations for this purified sample were minimally different from the values in the full sample; none of the larger correlations were notably reduced. To examine the issue in more detail, we used regression analyses to predict specific IBQ scales from MPQ factors and the DRIN scale in Sample 2. The results should be understood in reference to Table 13.3. Inclusion of DRIN did not reduce the predictive power of MPQ Positive Emotionality for IBQ Smiling and Laughter. Moving to the other stronger correlations in Table 13.3, we found that DRIN did diminish the predictive power of MPQ Negative Emotionality for IBQ Activity Level, but the degree of reduction was insignificant and less socially desirable responding was associated with report of higher infant activity. Partialling out the effect of DRIN from both predictor and criterion resulted in a partial correlation of .27 (compared to .38) for MPQ Negative Emotionality and IBQ Activity Level. Turning to the associations of the MPQ Constraint factors mentioned in footnote 2, we performed similar regression and partial correlation analyses. In correlational terms, DRIN led to a .11 to .12 reduction in the prediction of IBQ Activity Level and Soothability. Prediction of the other scales was undiminished. We conducted similar analyses with similar results in Sample 3. The tentative conclusion from these analyses with the MPQ validity scales is that social desirability, at least as detected in maternal self-ratings, has a very modest effect on prediction of activity level from parental personality, but it is clearly not a major bias in these analyses.

Effect of Averaging Mothers' and Fathers' MPQ Scales

In Sample 3, both mothers and fathers completed the MPQ. We uncovered one clue to the meaning of observed MPB by IBQ correlations by simply averaging the standardized maternal and paternal MPQ scores and repeating the correlational analyses shown in Table 13.3. Unless the same types of interpersonal interactions occur in both mother–infant and father–infant relationships, this averaging should dilute the effects due to specific interactions between parents and their offspring. In contrast, the averaging process should strengthen effects due to joint parental contribution. Joint parental contribution is exemplified by genetic contribution or, perhaps, by general emotional atmosphere of the home. Table 13.3 presented these correlations between "Mean Parent" and report of infant temperament. Comparing the "Mean Parent" correlations with individual parent values in Sample 3 leads to a consistent and remarkable discovery: Averaging the parental MPQs, which then reflect the personality of no particular individual, typically left the strength of parent personality–infant temperament correlations undiminished. In fact, about as often as not, the averaged values were higher than the individual values. The same phenomenon occurred in the toddler data from Sample 3. This finding demands some attempt at explanation.

Are Parent Personality–Infant Temperament Associations Genetically Mediated?

A genetic explanation is that averaging parental scores more accurately predicts the infant's genetic constitution. In examining the issue of genetic transmission, we face the issue of developmental continuity, and lack thereof, between infant temperament and adult personality. This issue has received extensive treatment (e.g., Plomin & DeFries, 1985). Here, our approach is empirical.

First, we reasoned that a genetic explanation for parent–infant resemblance is likely only for trait pairs that show heritability during both infancy and adulthood. Heritabilities for the markers of the five-factor model are given in Table 13.1. For the MPQ scales, Tellegen, Lykken, Bouchard, Wilcox, Segal, and Rich's (1988) model-fitting analyses using adult twins (some reared together and others reared apart) yielded moderate estimates of heritability ranging narrowly from 39% to 55%. Genetic variance estimates for the Positive Emotionality, Negative Emotionality, and Constraint factor scores were, respectively, .40, .55, and .58. For the IBQ, heritabilities have been estimated from three relatively small twin samples, including the Sample 3 twins (Goldsmith, 1986; Goldsmith & Campos, 1986; Goldsmith et al., 1986). We derived mean IBQ heritabilities by subtracting a weighted average of the fraternal twin intraclass correlations in the three samples from a corresponding identical mean correlation, and doubling the difference. Activity Level, Fear, and Distress to Limitations showed moderate heritabilities similar to those estimated for MPQ. However, the other three, more affectively positive IBQ scales were apparently less heritable, casting some doubt as to whether their associations with parental personality are substantially due to genetic mechanisms.

This reasoning can be represented quantitatively. Genetic theory places constraints on the expected degree of kin similarity. For instance, sibling, parent–offspring, and fraternal twin correlations should be similar and no less than one-half the identical twin correlation. The relevant genetic constraint is that the regression of offspring on midparent values (b_{PO}) is equal to the product of the square roots of the infant (h_i) and adult (h_a) heritabilities and the genetic correlation (r_g) from infancy to adulthood, or $b_{PO} = h_i\, h_a\, r_g$. The midparent value is simply the mean of fathers' and mothers' scores. The nature of genetic correlations is somewhat complex (Carey, 1988). Under certain fairly restrictive assumptions about the genetic architecture of the traits involved, the genetic correlation can be interpreted as "an index of the proportion of loci [genes] that two variables have in common" (Carey, 1988). More generally, in the context of our study, the strength of the genetic correlation reflects the degree of genetic variance common to the temperament trait measured in infancy and the personality trait measured in adulthood.

We can analyze the formula $b_{PO} = h_i\, h_a\, r_g$ to ascertain what range of values of b_{PO} are reasonable from a genetic perspective. Assume that both the offspring and adult heritabilities (h_i^2 and h_a^2) are .50; then $b_{PO} = .5\, r_g$. Because r_g cannot exceed 1.0, b_{PO} must be less than .50, and any values close to .50 would be suspect from the perspective of a solely genetic explanation due to the less-than-perfect reliability of the measures. We undertook these analyses for several of the parent–offspring associations observed. For analyses involving infant IBQ Smiling and Laughter, the derived values of r_g were too high to be accounted for by genetic transmission (a rarity in psychological research—a finding too strong to support the theoretical explanation being tested). In other cases, the results were consistent with—but did not compel—an hypothesis of genetic transmission. Values of r_g tended to vary around the .40 to .50 range, suggesting substantial genetic correlation between the unattenuated childhood and adult versions of the various trait pairings.

SUMMARY OF KEY FINDINGS

Our report analyzes parent–offspring resemblance for the IBQ, which is currently widely used to assess infant temperament (Goldsmith & Rothbart, 1991). It offers an explicit treatment of the effect of social desirability response tendencies on infant temperament report. We examined many possible associations between parent personality and infant temperament. The nature of our variables dictated that effect sizes would be modest because the relation between parental personality tendencies and infant or toddler behavioral patterns must be mediated by unmeasured variables. We uncovered moderate relations between parental personality and infant or toddler temperament, and several of these relations replicated across samples that differed in age of assessment, respondent (mother versus father), and the questionnaire used to assess temperament. Some of the findings replicate those of Mangelsdorf et al. (1990), who used the MPQ in a different design. An important caveat is that different parent–offspring associations sometimes held in the infant, toddler, and childhood data. The associations of IBQ Smiling and Laughter with MPQ Positive Emotionality and of P-TBAQ Fearfulness with MPQ Constraint measured 1 year earlier might reflect similar but developmentally transformed content. Less isomorphic were other relations, such as the replicated associations between IBQ Activity Level and the parental scales related to negative affect. The MPQ social desirability measure did not account for the relations we observed to a significant degree, but the TBAQ social desirability measure was associated with societally valued features of the adult five-factor markers. An important finding was that averaging the parental MPQs did not substantially diminish the strength of any of these associations. Additional analyses suggested that genetic factors could account for the modest parent–offspring resemblance we observed in most analyses but that the parent–offspring similarity on the pleasure dimension in infancy was too strong to be accounted for by genetic factors alone.

Despite these findings, our study has limitations. For example, more direct observational measures of parental personality would undoubtedly have enriched our report, but use of self-report inventories does allow closer connections with the personality literature. Also, validity scales on all the temperament questionnaires would have allowed shorter chains of inference.

RELATED RESEARCH IN THE TEMPERAMENT LITERATURE

Behavior–genetic studies often investigate parent–offspring similarity, but the offspring are usually adults, adolescents, or older children who can be assessed via methods similar to those used for parents. However, a few studies focus on infants or young children. For example, Plomin (1976) found significant parent–offspring correlations for several EASI (Emotionality Activity, Sociability, Impulsivity) temperament survey scales in 2- to 6-year-old twins, and Lyon and Plomin (1981) demonstrated that the similarity was generally not due to a direct "projection" of parental characteristics onto their children. This conclusion is consistent with our results. Neale and Stevenson (1989) undertook a more extensive analysis of rater bias using the EASI scales with twin and parent–offspring data. Like the simpler Lyon and Plomin (1981) correlational analyses, Neale and Stevenson's (1989) model-fitting analyses depended on mothers' and fathers' ratings of themselves, each other, and both twins. The latter study did reveal rater bias effects, but differences in the design, as compared with our study, and differences in the EASI versus the questionnaires we used preclude reconciliation of findings. In the two studies mentioned as well as others that used the EASI, fraternal twin correlations tended to be low or even negative. This is not the case for the IBQ (Goldsmith & Campos, 1986) or TBAQ (Goldsmith et al., 1986). Also, the EASI calls for rather global ratings of the child's tendencies whereas the IBQ and TBAQ items inquire about specific types of responses in defined situations. It seems plausible that the latter might be less susceptible to bias.

Using an infant adaptation of the Colorado Childhood Temperament Inventory (CCTI) and the EASI for mothers, Field, Vega-Lahr, Scafidi, and Goldstein (1987) found infant–mother similarity (r's in the .40s) for all four EASI scales with corresponding infant CCTI scales when the infants were 4 months of age. The infants were followed up at 8 and 18 months of age, but correlations of these later temperament assessments with parental personality were not included in Field et al.'s (1987) brief report. Other analyses indicated instability of emotionality and sociability ratings across infancy, which implies that parent–infant correlations will also change, as we found in some cases in the Sample 3 data.

The Colorado Adoption Project employed the CCTI for offspring and the EAS (a descendant of the EASI) for parents. Low, almost negligible mother–offspring similarity was found for most scales at ages 1, 2, 3, and 4 years (Plomin, DeFries, & Fulker, 1988). One of the few notable points of mother–infant resemblance emerged for the Sociability scale, a finding that probably reinforces our results that MPQ Positive Emotionality predicted IBQ Smiling and Laughter (Table 13.3) and that Factor I, Extraversion, predicted TBAQ Pleasure (Table 13.4).

Moderate correlations between self-report of maternal temperament and maternal-report of infant temperament obtained for several scales of the original Dimensions of Temperament Scale (DOTS) (Weber, Levitt, & Clark, 1986). They reported significant correlations in the .30s and .40s for Activity, Adaptability,

Reactivity, and Rhythmicity for 13-month-olds. Of these DOTS scales, only Adaptability and Activity have counterparts on the IBQ (Fearfulness and Activity Level). The MPQ has no counterpart for DOTS Activity, but we have previously argued that MPQ Constraint may reflect adult fearfulness. If so, Weber et al.'s results support the generalizability our P-TBAQ Fear by MBQ Constraint correlations reported in footnote 2.

Bates, Freeland, and Lounsbury (1979) analyzed parent–infant associations using the Personality Research Form (PRF) and their own Infant Characteristics Questionnaire (ICQ). They employed a similar strategy to ours in trying to assess parental personality with state-of-the-art adult instruments rather than adult versions of questionnaires developed chiefly for infants or children. Low maternal scores on PRF Extraversion and Achievement significantly predicted high infant scores on the Fussy-Difficult scale, another finding consistent with results reviewed previously. Bates and Bayles (1984) later expanded the scope of their analyses to investigate several correlates of maternal report, not only of temperament but also of other infant and toddler characteristics. Maternal data included selected scales or factors from both the PRF and MMPI. Three features of their findings are relevant to our report: "there was a consistent trace of [maternal] personality throughout the dimensions of maternal report" (p. 122); the magnitude of significant correlations between maternal personality variables and temperamentlike variables tended to fall just below .20; and maternal social desirability was the personality variable most frequently linked to temperamentlike child characteristics. The first two of these features again confirm that this domain is one in which small, but widespread, effect sizes predominate. At first blush, the social desirability findings seem to contradict our negative results. However, the MPQ DRIN (Desirability) scale is content-balanced, whereas the PRF desirability scale may represent "a positive trait, and not just a response bias," (p. 127), as noted by Bates and Bayles (1984). Thus, the predictive power of maternal hedonic tone, as captured by our MPQ findings, may influence the social desirability findings in Bates and Bayles' analyses.

In summary, when we survey a literature that was motivated by other goals, we find substantial support for the gist of our results: little evidence for strong rater bias but a modest degree of parent–infant similarity. In several cases, the literature supports the specific parent personality–infant temperament relations that we uncovered.

IMPLICATIONS FOR FUTURE INVESTIGATIONS

Our results weaken the common objection that parentally reported temperament is overwhelmingly biased due to parental characteristics. Rather, relations between parental characteristics and parent-reported infant temperament are modest. Furthermore, these modest relations seem not to be specific to the particular parent involved, based on our results using averaged parental scores. This finding does not deny the impact of specific environmental effects of parental personality characteristics on infant or toddler temperament, but it does imply that such effects simply are not general enough to affect group data. Thus, effects on infant temperament specific to parental personality characteristics may only hold in more homogeneous subgroups. Despite conducting extensive graphical analyses, we did not detect such subgroups. However, a focus on extreme groups of either parents or infants might prove fruitful, as exemplified by the research of Kagan, Reznick, and Gibbons (1989).

Our replicated effects, such as the prediction of high infant motoric activity by Negative Emotionality of fathers and mothers (Table 13.3), now justify a search for mediating variables. For example, do more anxious, suspicious, or aggressive parents engage in behaviors that heighten infant motoric behavior? If such mediating variables are discovered, they should be highly correlated with both the relevant parental and offspring scales. The recurring appearance of the MPQ Constraint variable in several of our findings and in Mangelsdorf et al.'s (1990) results suggests that this personality variable, and its relation to parenting, deserves fuller investigation. Assuming the relation between, for example, toddler fearfulness and adult constraint scales is real, developmental personality researchers face a substantial task in specifying how the affective core of fearfulness is modified to yield the more differentiated traits of control (vs. impulsivity), low risk-taking, and traditional social attitudes. Tracing the developmental transformations through childhood and adolescence is even more daunting than simply mapping the five-factor model onto early temperament. What is beginning to emerge is a series of empirical issues that require the joint perspectives of personality psychology, developmental psychology, and behavioral genetics for successful resolution.

ACKNOWLEDGMENTS

Our research was supported by the Spencer Foundation, NIMH (MH35270 to Campos and Goldsmith; MH23556 to Campos; and MH08239 to Goldsmith), and seed funds from the Developmental Psychobiology Research Group of the University of Colorado Health Sciences Center. Goldsmith was supported by a NICHD Research Career Development Award (HD00694) during preparation of the article. Losoya was supported by an NIMH predoctoral traineeship in emotion research (MH18935).

We are grateful for the excellent assistance of Charlotte Henderson, Patricia East, Nancy Benson, and Kate Duncan Rogers in assessing Samples 2 and 3.

REFERENCES

Allport, G. W. (1937). *Personality: A psychological interpretation*. New York: Holt.
Bandura, A. (1971). *Psychological modeling: Conflicting theories*. New York: Aldine-Atherton.

Bates, J. E. (1987). Temperament in infancy. In J. D. Osofsky (Ed.), *Handbook of infant development* (2nd ed., pp. 1101–1149). New York: Wiley.

Bates, J. E., & Bayles, K. (1984). Objective and subjective components in mothers' perceptions of their children from age 6 months to 3 years. *Merrill-Palmer Quarterly, 30*, 111–130.

Bates, J. E., Freeland, C. A., & Lounsbury, M. L. (1979). Measurement of infant difficultness. *Child Development, 50*, 794–803.

Belsky, J. (1984). The determinants of parenting: A process model. *Child Development, 55*, 83–96.

Bornstein, M. H., Gaughran, J. M., & Homel, P. (1986). Infant temperament: Theory, tradition, critique, and new assessments. In C. E. Izard & P. B. Read (Eds.), *Measuring emotions in infants and children* (Vol. 2, pp. 172–199). Cambridge, England: Cambridge University Press.

Bradshaw, D. L., Goldsmith, H. H., & Campos, J. J. (1987). Attachment, temperament, and social referencing: Interrelations among three domains of infant behavior. *Infant Behavior and Development, 10*, 223–231.

Brunnquell, D., Crichton, L., & Egeland, B. (1981). Maternal personality and attitude in disturbances of child rearing. *American Journal of Orthopsychiatry, 51*, 680–691.

Buss, A. H., & Plomin, R. (1984). *Temperament: Early appearing personality traits*. Hillsdale, NJ: Lawrence Erlbaum Associates.

Carey, G. (1988). Inference about genetic correlations. *Behavior Genetics, 18*, 329–338.

Chess, S., & Thomas, A. (1984). *Origins and evolution of behavior disorders: From infancy to adult life*. New York: Brunner/Mazel.

Costa, P. T., & McCrae, R. R. (1985). *The NEO Personality Inventory manual*. Odessa, FL: Psychological Assessment Resources.

DeFries, J. C., & Fulker, D. W. (1985). Multiple regression analysis of twin data. *Behavior Genetics, 15*, 467–473.

Eaves, L. J., Eysenck, H. J., & Martin, N. G. (1989). *Genes, culture, and personality*. London: Academic Press.

Feldman, S. S., & Nash, S. C. (1986). Antecedents of early parenting. In A. Fogel & G. F. Melson (Eds.), *Origins of nurturance: Developmental, biological, and cultural perspectives on caregiving* (pp. 209–232). Hillsdale, NJ: Lawrence Erlbaum Associates.

Field, T., Vega-Lahr, N., Scafidi, F., & Goldstein, S. (1987). Reliability, stability, and relationships between infant and parent temperament. *Infant Behavior and Development, 10*, 117–122.

Funder, D. C. (1987). Errors and mistakes: Evaluating the accuracy of social judgment. *Psychological Bulletin, 101*, 75–90.

Gjerde, P. F., Block, J., & Block, J. H. (1988). Depressive symptoms and personality during late adolescence: Gender differences in the externalization–internalization of symptom expression. *Journal of Abnormal Psychology, 97*, 475–486.

Goldberg, L. R. (1990). An alternative "Description of Personality": The Big-Five factor structure. *Journal of Personality and Social Psychology, 59*, 1215–1229.

Goldberg, L. R. (1992). The development of markers for the Big-Five factor structure. *Psychological Assessment, 4*, 26–42.

Goldsmith, H. H. (1983). Genetic influences on personality from infancy to adulthood. *Child Development, 54*, 331–355.

Goldsmith, H. H. (1986). Heritability of temperament: Cautions and some empirical evidence. In G. A. Kohnstamm (Ed.), *Temperament discussed: Temperament and development in infancy and childhood* (pp. 83–96). Lisse, The Netherlands: Swets & Zeitlinger.

Goldsmith, H. H. (1988). *Preliminary manual for the Toddler Behavior Assessment Questionnaire* (Oregon Center for the Study of Emotion Tech. Rep. No. 88-04). Department of Psychology, University of Oregon, Eugene.

Goldsmith, H. H. (1993). Temperament: Variability in developing emotion systems. In M. Lewis & J. M. Haviland (Eds.), *Handbook of emotions* (pp. 353–364). New York: Guilford.

Goldsmith, H. H., Buss, A. H., Plomin, R., Rothbart, M. K., Thomas, A., Chess, S., Hinde, R. A., & McCall, R. B. (1987). Roundtable: What is temperament? Four Approaches. *Child Development, 58*, 505–529.

Goldsmith, H. H., & Campos, J. J. (1982). Toward a theory of infant temperament. In R. N. Emde & R. J. Harmon (Eds.), *The development of attachment and affiliative systems* (pp. 161–193). New York: Plenum.

Goldsmith, H. H., & Campos, J. J. (1986). Fundamental issues in the study of early temperament: The Denver Twin Temperament Study. In M. E. Lamb, A. L. Brown, & B. Rogoff (Eds.), *Advances in developmental psychology* (Vol. 4, pp. 231–283). Hillsdale, NJ: Lawrence Erlbaum Associates.

Goldsmith, H. H., & Campos, J. J. (1990). The structure of infant temperamental dispositions to experience fear and pleasure: A psychometric perspective. *Child Development, 61*, 1944–1964.

Goldsmith, H. H., & Davis, A. L. (1991, April). *Predicting representation of social emotions at ages 4 and 5: A longitudinal study.* Seattle, WA: Society for Research in Child Development.

Goldsmith, H. H., Elliott, T. K., & Jaco, K. L. (1986). Construction and initial validation of a new temperament questionnaire. *Infant Behavior and Development, 9*, 144 (Abstract).

Goldsmith, H. H., & Rothbart, M. K. (1991). Contemporary instruments for assessing early temperament by questionnaire and in the laboratory. In J. Strelau & A. Angleitner (Eds.), *Explorations in temperament* (pp. 249–272). New York: Plenum.

Hall, C. A. (1977). *Differential relationships of pleasure and distress with depression and anxiety over a past, present, and future time framework.* Unpublished doctoral dissertation, University of Minnesota, Minneapolis.

Heinicke, C. (1984). Impact of prebirth parent personality and marital functioning on family development: A framework and suggestions for further study. *Developmental Psychology, 20*, 1044–1053.

Heinicke, C., Diskin, S. D., Ramsey-Klee, D. M., & Given, K. (1983). Pre-birth parent characteristics and family development in the first year of life. *Child Development, 54*, 194–208.

Kagan, J., Reznick, J. S., & Gibbons, J. (1989). Inhibited and uninhibited types of children. *Child Development, 60*, 838–845.

Kagan, J., & Snidman, N. (1991). Temperamental factors in human development. *American Psychologist, 46*, 856–862.

Kochanska, G. (1991). Socialization and temperament in the development of guilt and conscience. *Child Development, 62*, 1379–1392.

Lerner, J. V., & Lerner, R. M. (1983). Temperament and adaptation across life: Theoretical and empirical issues. In P. B. Baltes & O. G. Brim (Eds.), *Lifespan development and behavior* (Vol. 5, pp. 197–231). New York: Academic Press.

Loehlin, J. C. (1992). *Genes and environment in personality development.* Newbury Park, CA: Sage.

Lykken, D. T., McGue, M., & Tellegen, A. (1987). Recruitment bias in twin research: The rule of two-thirds reconsidered. *Behavior Genetics, 17*, 343–362.

Lykken, D. T., Tellegen, A., & DeRubeis, R. (1978). Volunteer bias in twin research: The rule of two-thirds. *Social Biology, 25*, 1–9.

Lyon, M., & Plomin, R. (1981). The measurement of temperament using parent ratings. *Journal of Child Psychology and Psychiatry, 22*, 47–54.

Mangelsdorf, S., Gunnar, M., Kestenbaum, R., Lang, S., & Andreas, D. (1990). Infant proneness-to-distress temperament, maternal personality and mother–infant attachment: Associations and goodness of fit. *Child Development, 61*, 820–831.

McCartney, K., Harris, M. J., & Bernieri, F. (1990). Growing up and growing apart: A developmental meta-analysis of twin studies. *Psychological Bulletin, 107*, 226–237.

Neale, M. C., & Stevenson, J. (1989). Rater bias in the EASI temperament scales: A twin study. *Journal of Personality and Social Psychology, 56*, 446–455.

Plomin, R. (1976). A twin and family study of personality in twins and young children. *Journal of Personality, 94*, 233–235.

Plomin, R. (1986). *Development, genetics, and psychology.* Hillsdale, NJ: Lawrence Erlbaum Associates.

Plomin, R., & DeFries, J. C. (1985). *Origins of individual differences in infancy: The Colorado Adoption Project.* New York: Academic Press.

Plomin, R., DeFries, J. C., & Fulker, D. W. (1988). *Nature and nurture during infancy and early childhood.* Cambridge, England: Cambridge University Press.

Rothbart, M. K. (1981). Measurement of temperament in infancy. *Child Development, 52,* 569–578.

Rothbart, M. K. (1986). Longitudinal observation of infant temperament. *Developmental Psychology, 22,* 356–366.

Rothbart, M. K., & Derryberry, D. (1981). Development of individual differences in temperament. In M. E. Lamb & A. L. Brown (Eds.), *Advances in developmental psychology* (Vol. 1, pp. 37–86). Hillsdale, NJ: Lawrence Erlbaum Associates.

Sears, R. R., Maccoby, E. E., & Levin, H. (1957). *Patterns of child rearing.* Evanston, IL: Row, Peterson.

Sirignano, S. W., & Lachman, M. E. (1985). Personality change during the transition to parenthood: The role of perceived infant temperament. *Developmental Psychology, 21,* 558–567.

Stevenson-Hinde, J. (1986). Towards a more open construct. In G. A. Kohnstamm (Ed.), *Temperament discussed: Temperament and development in infancy and childhood* (pp. 97–106). Lisse, The Netherlands: Swets & Zeitlinger.

Tellegen, A. (1982). *Brief manual for the Differential Personality Questionnaire.* Department of Psychology, University of Minnesota, Minneapolis.

Tellegen, A. (1985). Structures of mood and personality and their relevance to assessing anxiety, with an emphasis on self-report. In A. H. Tuma & J. D. Maser (Eds.), *Anxiety and the anxiety disorders* (pp. 681–706). Hillsdale, NJ: Lawrence Erlbaum Associates.

Tellegen, A., Lykken, D. T., Bouchard, T. J., Jr., Wilcox, K. J., Segal, E. L., & Rich, S. (1988). Personality similarity in twins reared apart and together. *Journal of Personality and Social Psychology, 54,* 1031–1039.

Tellegen, A., & Waller, N. G. (in press). Exploring personality through the process of test construction: Development of the Multidimensional Personality Questionnaire. In S. R. Briggs & J. R. Cheek (Eds.), *Personality measures: Development and evaluation* (Vol. 1). Greenwich, CT: JAI Press.

Thomas, A., & Chess, S. (1977). *Temperament and development.* New York: Brunner/Mazel.

Watson, D., Clark, L. A., & Carey, G. (1988). Positive and negative affectivity and their relation to anxiety and depressive disorders. *Journal of Abnormal Psychology, 97,* 346–353.

Weber, R. A., Levitt, M. J., & Clark, M. C. (1986). Individual variation in attachment security and strange situation behavior: The role of maternal and infant temperament. *Child Development, 57,* 56–66.

CHAPTER

14

MAJOR DIMENSIONS OF PERSONALITY IN EARLY ADOLESCENCE: THE BIG FIVE AND BEYOND

Richard W. Robins
Oliver P. John
University of California at Berkeley

Avshalom Caspi
University of Wisconsin at Madison

Personality psychologists have long sought to generate a taxonomy of personality traits that would provide an integrative framework for personality research. This search for the basic building blocks of personality has led many researchers down a contentious and often confusing path, plagued by methodological maelstroms such as determining the number of factors needed to account for personality ratings and complex theoretical issues such as defining what makes a personality dimension basic. Over the past decade the debates and confusion have waned as considerable progress has been made toward the development of a generally accepted trait taxonomy. The repeated identification of the "Big Five" factors in personality ratings has led to the beginning of a consensus that most personality traits fall within five broad content domains: Extraversion, Agreeableness, Conscientiousness, Neuroticism, and Openness to Experience (for recent reviews, see Digman, 1990; Goldberg, 1993a; John, 1990). According to the five-factor model (FFM) of personality, these broad factors are basic dimensions of personality that represent "the major variables that have been studied by psychologists as well as those traits that are used by laypersons to characterize themselves and their acquaintances" (Costa & McCrae, 1992a, p. 4). The available research suggests that the FFM provides a generalizable and comprehensive representation of personality trait structure in adulthood (McCrae & John, 1992).[1]

---

[1]In this chapter, "personality structure" refers to the patterns of covariation of traits across individuals, not to the organization of traits within the individual (cf. John & Robins, 1993).

A large body of research supports the replicability of the FFM in self-reports and ratings, in natural languages and theoretically based questionnaires, in college students and older adults, in men and women, and in English, Dutch, German, and Japanese samples (John, 1990). As the chapters in this volume show, attention has turned recently toward understanding the Big Five dimensions during childhood and adolescence (see also Digman, 1989; Graziano & Ward, 1992; John, Caspi, Robins, Moffitt, & Stouthamer-Loeber, 1994). During these developmentally critical periods, personality is formed and shaped through myriad complex processes involving the reciprocal influences of a person's innate predispositions, early family experiences, peer interactions, social roles, and cultural environment. Because these biological and social-contextual factors change over time, the structure of personality might change accordingly and the Big Five dimensions that characterize the adult personality may not appear in earlier ages. Thus, more research is needed on the emergence and development of the Big Five structure. For example, we do not know whether it originates in an earlier developmental period, perhaps through the expression of early emerging temperamental traits, or, alternatively, whether it emerges in adolescence, perhaps as a consequence of the internal maturational changes, shifting societal expectations, and conflicting role demands that influence the developing adolescent. The research program described in this chapter represents an attempt to trace back to early adolescence the developmental origins of the adult Big Five dimensions and to examine their replicability and behavioral expression at the beginning of the transition from childhood to adulthood.

The data used in this research come from the Pittsburgh Youth Study (PYS), an ongoing longitudinal study of several hundred Caucasian and African-American boys focusing on the antecedents and correlates of early forms of delinquency (for details about the PYS study, see Loeber, Stouthamer-Loeber, Van Kammen, & Farrington, 1989). When the subjects were between 12 and 13 years old, they were described by their mothers using the 100 items of the California Child Q-Set (CCQ; J. Block & J. H. Block, 1980), as adapted for use by laypersons (Caspi et al., 1992). The CCQ-set provides a comprehensive, standardized language for describing the behavioral, affective, and cognitive characteristics of adolescents and children. It is ideal for exploring the FFM in our adolescent sample because the instrument was developed independently of research on the Big Five and the development of the item pool was guided by psychodynamic theory whereas the Big Five dimensions were identified through empirical analyses of the natural language. Therefore, if we find evidence of the replicability of the Big Five factors in early adolescence it cannot be because the five dimensions were "built into" the CCQ-set.

This chapter reviews some of our recent findings (John et al., 1994) and presents additional analyses to explore the FFM in a large, heterogeneous sample of adolescents. Our aims are to extend previous FFM research by (a) developing measures of the Big Five for use with adolescents, (b) relating the Big Five dimensions to several constructs from the literature on personality development,

(c) improving our understanding of the relations between the Big Five dimensions and important real-world variables (e.g., juvenile delinquency), and (d) exploring unresolved issues concerning the possible existence of additional broad dimensions in adolescence.

In discussing these issues, we adopted a question and answer format: We first pose a question, then present empirical evidence to address the question, and then allow a hypothetical skeptic to question our findings and interpretations. The skeptic is dubious of the generalizability of the FFM to adolescence, and the usefulness of the FFM in research on personality development.

Question 1: Can the Big Five personality dimensions be measured in adolescence using the CCQ set?

To address this question, we first determined whether the CCQ—an instrument developed to assess the behavioral, cognitive, and affective characteristics of children and adolescents—contains items relevant to each of the Big Five dimensions as they have emerged in adulthood. In a previous study (John et al., 1994), we described the development of Big Five scales for the CCQ. Using the definitions of the dimensions established in adult samples, the CCQ items were categorized rationally into one of the Big Five domains. The vast majority (78%) of the 100 items could be categorized in this way; the largest number of items (22) was assigned to Agreeableness and the fewest number (10) to Openness. Thus, the CCQ set seems to contain items that represent each of the five factors. (CCQ items not related to any of the Big Five dimensions are examined later in this chapter.)

The initial rational scales were refined through item analyses. The items scored on the final Big Five scales are shown in Table 14.1, and their coefficient alpha reliabilities are shown in Table 14.2. Of the 48 items on the final scales, 46 had been categorized correctly in the initial classification.

Skeptic: The scales may be reliable, but do they have content validity? Besides the judgment of the sorter, how do you know your CCQ–Big Five scales measure the same content as that covered by the Big Five dimensions as they appear in adulthood?

Question 2: Do our CCQ Big Five scales actually resemble the Big Five dimensions in adulthood?

An inspection of the items in Table 14.1 suggests that the content of the scales closely resembles the definitions of the Big Five factors in the adult literature (e.g., McCrae & John, 1992, Table 1). Yet, such impressionistic claims of content validity are unlikely to satisfy our skeptic. How could one show that our CCQ scales indeed represent the Big Five as they are defined in the adult literature? An attractive feature of the CCQ is that about half of the items have equivalent

TABLE 14.1
Big Five Scales for the California Child Q-Set

Item Number	Item Text (Common-Language Version of the CCQ-set)
	Extraversion (9 items)
1.	He shows his thoughts and feelings in the way he looks and acts, but he does not talk much about what he thinks and about how he feels. (R)
8.	He likes to keep his thoughts and feelings to himself. (R)
28.	He is energetic and full of life.
35.	He holds things in. He has a hard time expressing himself; he is a little bit uptight. (R)
58.	He openly shows the way he feels, whether it's good or bad. He shows his emotions openly.
63.	He is fast-paced; he moves and reacts to things quickly.
84.	He is a talkative child; he talks a lot.
86.	He likes to be by himself; he enjoys doing things alone. (R)
98.	He is shy; he has a hard time getting to know people. (R)
	Agreeableness (13 items)
2.	He is considerate and thoughtful of other people.
3.	He is a warm person and responds with kindness to other people.
4.	He gets along well with other people.
6.	He is helpful and cooperates with other people.
9.	He makes good and close friendships with other people.
14.	He tries hard to please other people.
22.	He tries to get others to do what he wants by playing up to them. He acts charming in order to get his way. (R)
29.	He is protective of others. He protects people who are close to him.
30.	Most adults seem to like him.
32.	He gives, lends, and shares things.
80.	He teases and picks on other kids (including his own brothers and sisters). (R)
90.	He is stubborn. (R)
93.	He's bossy and likes to dominate other people. (R)
	Conscientiousness (9 items)
36.	He finds ways to make things happen and get things done.
41.	He is determined in what he does; he does not give up easily.
47.	He has high standards for himself. He needs to do very well in the things he does.
59.	He is neat and orderly in the way he dresses and acts.
66.	He pays attention well and can concentrate on things.
67.	He plans things ahead; he thinks before he does something. He "looks before he leaps."
76.	He can be trusted; he's reliable, and dependable.
89.	He's able to do many things well; he is skillful.
99.	He thinks about his actions and behaviors; he uses his head before doing or saying something.

(Continued)

TABLE 14.1
(Continued)

Item Number	Item Text (Common-Language Version of the CCQ-set)
	Neuroticism (10 items)
23.	He is nervous and fearful.
24.	He worries about things for a long time.
39.	He freezes up when things are stressful, or else he keeps doing the same thing over and over.
43.	He can bounce back or recover after a stressful or bad experience. (R)
46.	He tends to go to pieces under stress; he gets rattled when things are tough.
48.	He needs to have people tell him that he's doing well or ok. He is not very sure of himself.
50.	He tends to get sick when things go wrong or when there is a lot of stress. (For example, he gets headaches, stomach aches, throws up.)
60.	He gets nervous if he's not sure what's going to happen or when it's not clear what he's supposed to do.
77.	He feels unworthy; he has a low opinion of himself.
78.	His feelings get hurt easily if he is made fun of or criticized.
	Openness to Experience (7 items)
40.	He is curious and exploring; he likes to learn and experience new things.
68.	He is a very smart kid (even though his grades in school might not show this).
69.	He has a way with words; he can express himself well with words.
70.	He daydreams; he often gets lost in thought or a fantasy world.
74.	He usually gets wrapped up in what he's doing.
96.	He is creative in the way he looks at things; the way he thinks, works or plays is very creative.
97.	He likes to dream up fantasies; he has a good imagination.

Note. Adapted from John, Caspi, Robins, Moffitt, and Stouthamer-Loeber (1994). (R) = Item is reversed keyed.

adult versions on Block's California Adult Q-sort (CAQ; Block, 1961). Moreover, CAQ items defining the five factors have previously been identified by McCrae, Costa, and Busch (1986) in their factor analysis of self-report Q-sorts. We used this information to construct five Adult Equivalence Factor (AEF) scales from the 44 CCQ items that corresponded to the CAQ items defining the five factors in the McCrae et al. study. Congruence between our scales and these AEF scales would provide impressive evidence of content validity because the comparison involves four different facets of generalizability: age (adolescence to adulthood), instrument (CCQ to CAQ), data source (mothers' descriptions of their sons to self-reports), and demographic characteristics of the sample (from McCrae et al.'s sample of well-educated, Caucasian middle-aged men and women to our racially and economically diverse sample of adolescent boys).

To assess the congruence between McCrae et al.'s AEF scales and our independently derived Big Five scales, we correlated each of our Big Five scales with the corresponding AEF scale. These congruence correlations ranged from

TABLE 14.2
Reliability and Validity of the Big Five Scales for the CCQ

	Reliability	Content Validity	Construct Validity				Criterion Validity			
Big Five Scale	Coefficient Alpha	Congruence With AEF Factors[a]	Undercontrol	Ego Resiliency	Antisocial	Delinquency	School Performance[b]	IQ	SES	Race[c]
E: Extraversion (9)	.73	.86[E]	.51*	.38*	.04	.17*	-.07	.03	.06	-.01
A: Agreeableness (13)	.83	.90[A]	-.62*	.62*	-.87*	-.27*	.06	.02	.04	-.05
C: Conscientiousness (9)	.78	.85[C]	-.60*	.76*	-.71*	-.27*	.22*	.20*	.01	-.11
N: Neuroticism (10)	.71	.75[N]	-.05	-.68*	.22*	-.02	-.08	-.11	.04	-.13
O: Openness (7)	.53	.70[O]	-.14*	.44*	-.31*	-.16*	.20*	.39*	.04	.14*

Note: The numbers in this table are correlations, except for the alpha reliabilities. $N = 350$ for all variables except School Performance ($N = 188$). Reliabilities and correlations with IQ, SES, and Race were previously reported in Tables 2 and 4 of John et al. (1994).

[a] The Adult Equivalence Factors (AEF) are Big Five scales scored from the CCQ-set items; the scales are based on the equivalent adult items defining the five factors in McCrae, Costa, and Busch's (1986) factor analysis of self-report CAQ-sorts by adults participating in the Baltimore Longitudinal Study of Aging. Superscript letters indicate which AEF factor was correlated with the scale.
[b] Composite of teacher ratings of school performance in reading, writing, spelling, and math (alpha reliability = .95).
[c] Race was coded: African American = 1 ($n = 181$); Caucasian = 2 ($n = 160$); Other = missing ($n = 9$).
*$p < .01$.

.90 for Agreeableness to .70 for Openness (see Table 2); even the congruence correlation for Openness is substantial given that the AEF Openness scale has only three items. These findings demonstrate that the Big Five dimensions as they have emerged in research in adulthood can be measured in adolescence from the CCQ-set. More generally, the findings show that mothers perceive systematic patterns in their son's behavior that reflect the five personality factors.

Skeptic: The CCQ is a comprehensive assessment instrument and therefore contains items related to almost any personality dimension conceptualized by psychologists. It is not surprising, then, that dimensions resembling the Big Five can be measured with the CCQ. However, I am dubious about the value of these dimensions to developmental psychologists. Do they have meaningful relations with constructs used in research on personality development such as resilience, undercontrol, and antisocial personality? More generally, does the nomological network of relations surrounding the Big Five in adolescence support their construct validity?

Question 3: Do the Big Five dimensions relate to constructs used in research on personality development?

The theoretical constructs of Ego Control and Ego Resiliency are conceptualized as dynamic individual differences variables that have powerful organizing effects on behavior across time and contexts (J. H. Block & J. Block, 1980). Ego Control refers to the tendency to contain rather than express emotional and motivational impulses, and Ego Resiliency refers to the tendency to respond flexibly rather than rigidly to changing situational demands, especially frustrating and taxing encounters (J. H. Block & J. Block, 1980). Although the constructs have enjoyed considerable utility in developmental research (see Funder, Tomlinson-Keasey, Parke, & Widaman, 1993), their relations with the Big Five have not yet been examined empirically.

To measure Ego *Under*control and Ego Resiliency, we computed the similarity between each boy's CCQ personality profile and the CCQ personality profile of the prototypical undercontrolled adolescent and the prototypical resilient adolescent, both of which had been specified previously (J. H. Block & J. Block, 1980). The correlations of Ego Undercontrol and Ego Resiliency with each of the Big Five are shown in Table 14.2. Ego Undercontrol correlated positively with Extraversion and negatively with Conscientiousness and Agreeableness; adolescents manifest their undercontrol in expressive, energetic, and outgoing behaviors but also in inattentive, careless, and undependable behaviors. Ego Resiliency was related to all five dimensions: resilient adolescents were conscientious, emotionally stable, agreeable, and somewhat extraverted and open, suggesting that resiliency represents a combination of the well-adjusted poles of all Big Five dimensions.

Another construct of considerable interest to developmental psychologists is Antisocial Personality. The Antisocial Personality is characterized by unempathic, egocentric, impersonal, and manipulative behavior; the psychological profile of antisocial youth also includes attentional problems (e.g., restless, fidgety, lacking concentration) and insufficient impulse control (Olweus, Block, & Radke-Yarrow, 1986). Thus, in terms of the Big Five, measures of antisocial personality should be negatively related to both Agreeableness and Conscientiousness. As with Ego Control and Ego Resiliency, we measured Antisocial Personality by assessing the similarity between the personality profile of each subject and the CCQ personality profile of the prototypical antisocial youth. We found that antisocial adolescent boys were less Agreeable and less Conscientious (see Table 14.2).

These relations between the Big Five dimensions and the developmental personality constructs support the construct validity of our Big Five scales. They also illustrate the usefulness of the Big Five in identifying conceptual similarities and differences between empirically related constructs. Consider Ego Undercontrol and Antisocial Personality as an example (see Block & Gjerde, 1986, for a more extensive analysis). As Table 14.2 shows, both undercontrolled and antisocial boys were low in Conscientiousness, but they differed in their levels of Extraversion and Agreeableness: Undercontrolled boys were more extraverted than antisocial boys, and antisocial boys were less agreeable than undercontrolled boys. Thus, our findings further delineate the meaning and behavioral consequences of these developmental constructs.

Skeptic: How can you compare a factor like Conscientiousness, which reflects observed regularities in manifest behavior, to a construct like Ego Control, which reflects a dynamic mechanism underlying a wide range of behaviors?

We agree that the Big Five dimensions are conceptually different from constructs such as Ego Control and Ego Resiliency: Whereas the Blocks have postulated regulatory processes within the individual that influence how an individual behaves in different situational contexts, the Big Five taxonomy provides a framework for describing and categorizing individual differences in behavior that result from these different regulatory processes. Thus, dynamic mechanisms such as the two dimensions of ego functioning can help explain the observed regularities in behavior that are represented by the Big Five (John & Robins, 1993). For example, the relation between Conscientiousness and Ego Overcontrol may indicate that adolescent boys who engage in the types of behaviors that define the Conscientiousness factor do so, or are capable of doing so, because they control and contain their emotional and motivational impulses. In other words, conscientious behaviors—such as paying attention, planning ahead, and so on—often require ego-control.

Skeptic: The Big Five and the theoretical variables you examined were both scored from the same instrument (the CCQ) and the same data source (mothers' reports). The relations you report may simply reflect item overlap and shared method variance.

Obviously, the magnitude of these correlations may be inflated. However, what is important here is not the absolute size of the correlations but their differential

14. PERSONALITY IN EARLY ADOLESCENCE   **275**

pattern, as our example of the differences between Ego Undercontrol and Antisocial Personality showed. In fact, the relations we have reported are informative because they show how constructs from personality theory, transcribed into the common language of the CCQ, correspond to the dimensions of the Big Five transcribed into the same language. Thus, from the perspective of the FFM, our findings provide information about the nomological network surrounding the Big Five dimensions in adolescence. From the perspective of personality development theory, our findings provide information about the behavioral regularities generated by Ego Control, Ego Resiliency, and Antisocial Personality in adolescence. Nonetheless, relying on the same instrument and data source is limiting, and we agree that the nomological network surrounding the Big Five dimensions can be strengthened considerably by examining their relations with real-world outcomes.

Question 4: Do the Big Five dimensions predict important real-world variables in adolescence?

Many psychologists consider the prediction of real-world variables critical for assessing validity. In a recent critique of the FFM, Eysenck (1991) argued that "it would be difficult to take seriously the claims of a factor to be of fundamental importance if that factor could not be shown to interact powerfully with social activities widely regarded as important.... Little is known about the social relevance and importance of openness, agreeableness, and conscientiousness" (p. 785). Eysenck (chap. 2 in this vol.) questions the validity of Agreeableness, Conscientiousness, and Openness as basic dimensions beyond Extraversion and Neuroticism, noting that there is a large body of evidence on the real-world correlates of Extraversion and Neuroticism but relatively little evidence for the other three factors: "Almost everyone is agreed that E and N are undoubtably two major dimensions of personality." The real question is "What lies beyond E and N?"

To address the concerns of Eysenck and others, we examined a set of criterion variables that on conceptual grounds should be related to Agreeableness, Conscientiousness, and Openness, allowing us to examine the predictive validity of these factors. In particular, we examined the relations between the Big Five dimensions and five real-world variables (which themselves could be considered "Big" given their central importance in developmental psychology): self-reported juvenile delinquency, teacher ratings of school performance, objectively measured intelligence, socioeconomic status (SES), and race. Note that all five criteria were measured from a different data source than the Big Five and thus the correlations we report cannot be confounded by method variance.

The correlations between the five criterion variables and the Big Five are shown in Table 14.2. Adolescents who had engaged in more severe delinquent behaviors were lower on Agreeableness and Conscientiousness; moreover, these two dimensions predicted delinquency independently when all five scales were entered in a multiple regression. In terms of mean-level differences, the 170 boys who had committed more severe delinquent behaviors were nearly one-half (.45) of a standard deviation lower on Agreeableness and nearly one-half of a standard deviation (.47) lower on Conscientiousness than the 180 boys who had engaged in few or no delinquent behaviors. These findings provide important corroboration that the Big Five dimensions, in particular Agreeableness and Conscientiousness, can identify youth who are at risk for juvenile delinquency and criminal behavior. They also provide further support for the link between Antisocial Personality and Agreeableness and Conscientiousness.

Next we examined the extent to which the Big Five predict school performance, measured by a composite of teacher ratings in four academic areas (reading, writing, spelling, and math). We found that boys who were higher on Conscientiousness and Openness performed better in school (see Table 14.2), and that Conscientiousness and Openness were independent predictors of school performance in a multiple regression analysis; these relations also held for each of the four academic areas considered separately. These findings replicate and extend previous research showing a link between teacher ratings of Conscientiousness and teacher ratings of school performance (Digman, 1989; Graziano & Ward, 1992). In the present research, however, *teacher* ratings of school performance predicted *mothers'* ratings of personality, thus extending these earlier findings, which had used a single method to assess both personality and school performance.

With respect to the relations between IQ and the Big Five, Table 14.2 shows that IQ, measured with an abbreviated form of the Wechsler Intelligence Scale for Children–Revised (WISC–R), was positively related to both Openness and Conscientiousness. Thus, boys scoring high on tests of cognitive ability differ from their less intelligent peers by their standing on the Big Five personality dimensions.

The correlations between SES and the Big Five scales were essentially zero (see Table 14.2), and did not replicate the small but significant relation between SES and Openness found in adult samples (McCrae & Costa, 1985). Although Openness to Experience was not influenced by the social class of the child's parents, Openness may influence the child's subsequent attainment in adulthood because individuals who score high on this factor do well in school, and actively seek out educational opportunities and challenging work experiences. Here, then, is a possible case in which personality is not influenced by characteristics of one's family of origin but does influence characteristics of one's family of destination (Caspi, Herbener, & Ozer, 1992).

The correlations between race (scored as African American versus Caucasian) and the Big Five scales were all nonsignificant except for Openness: Caucasians scored slightly higher on Openness to Experience than African Americans. However, this correlation was entirely accounted for by race differences in IQ; controlling for IQ reduced the correlation between race and Openness from .14 to –.02.

In conclusion, the findings summarized in Table 14.2 show a meaningful pattern of relations between the Big Five and the five criteria. These relations demonstrate the convergent and discriminant validity of our CCQ–Big Five scales. For example, our findings show that although Agreeableness and Conscientiousness have similar relations with Antisocial Personality and delinquency, they also show discriminant relations with school performance and IQ. More generally, the results support the external validity of the Big Five dimensions and extend the nomological network surrounding the Big Five into adolescence. Moreover, the findings demonstrate that Agreeableness, Conscientiousness, and Openness are truly consequential at this developmental period, predicting theoretically, socially, and developmentally important variables such as resiliency, academic achievement, and delinquency. Thus, in response to Eysenck's question—"What lies beyond E and N?"—our answer is: three very important and distinct dimensions of personality.

Skeptic: The relations you have reported are impressive given that the Big Five dimensions and the criteria were assessed using different methods. However, I am not clear how these relations further our understanding of the criterion variables. For example, what do we learn about delinquency by knowing that it is negatively related to Agreeableness and Conscientiousness?

It is important to recognize that the Big Five dimensions are not explanatory variables and thus do not provide a causal account of behavior (cf. John & Robins, 1993, for a distinction between the Big Five taxonomy and the FFM). Nonetheless, the Big Five can contribute to our understanding of a variable and help generate causal accounts. In some sense, the Big Five taxonomy provides a large nomological network within which all constructs can be related to each other; that is, locating constructs within the five-dimensional space represented by the Big Five facilitates comparisons across dimensions and helps identify conceptual differences between constructs. Consider the relation of delinquency with Agreeableness and Conscientiousness. We have located delinquency in the quadrant defined by low Agreeableness and low Conscientiousness. This allows us to extrapolate that personality dimensions related to Agreeableness and Conscientiousness should predict delinquency. Conversely, we can assume that variables related to delinquency (e.g., other indicators of moral character and socialization) should be predictable from Agreeableness and Conscientiousness. Going one step further, we can ask what are the psychological dynamics of agreeable and conscientious behaviors in adolescence, and we can then attempt to generate causal process models that can explain the observed relations. We know that, to some extent, agreeable behaviors reflect an altruistic and prosocial orientation toward others and conscientious behaviors reflect adherence to norms and authority; thus, it is easy to paint a portrait of the juvenile delinquent as a youth who does not care about harming others and who disregards the norms and rules of society. At a deeper explanatory level, we can then postulate that what produces agreeable, conscientious, *and* delinquent behavior is the inability or failure to adequately control impulses (e.g., ego control), which we have already shown is strongly related to both low Agreeableness and low

Conscientiousness. Thus, we have generated some ideas for a process model linking an important real-world outcome to a dynamically conceptualized variable and two personality dimensions representing observed regularities in behavior.

Skeptic: Although you have provided evidence that the five dimensions can be reliably and validly measured in adolescence, is this not simply a Procrustean exercise in which you impose the Big Five structure onto the CCQ-set? Doesn't the argument that the FFM is a comprehensive model of personality structure require evidence that five factors can account for personality ratings of adolescents? Otherwise, how do you know that there are not more than five broad dimensions, as Cattell argued, or less than five dimensions, as Eysenck argued?

Question 5: Does the Big Five taxonomy represent adolescent personality structure as revealed in mothers' CCQs?

Digman and Inouye (1986) claimed that "if a large number of rating scales is used and the scope of the scales is very broad, the domain of personality descriptors is almost completely accounted for by five robust factors" (p. 116). To examine this claim in our sample of young adolescents, we factor analyzed the full 100-item CCQ-set (see John et al., 1994). According to three different criteria, seven factors were needed to account for the relations among the items. To permit an empirically based interpretation of the seven factors of the CCQ, we computed factor scores and correlated them with the five Adult Equivalence Factor (AEF) scales, representing McCrae et al.'s (1986) Big Five in adulthood. Note that the AEF scales have not been empirically refined in the present data set and thus are independent of the seven empirically discovered CCQ factors; therefore, they provide a lower-bound estimate of the congruence between the present CCQ factors and the Big Five found in studies of adults.

Five of the seven empirical factors resembled the AEF versions of the Big Five. Empirical Factor 3 found its adult equivalent in the Extraversion AEF scale (congruence $r = .89$), Factor 1 in the Agreeableness AEF scale ($r = .84$), Factor 2 in the Conscientiousness AEF scale ($r = .66$), Factor 4 in the Neuroticism AEF scale ($r = .56$), and Factor 7 in the Openness AEF scale ($r = .76$). The items loading on Factor 1 (Agreeableness), Factor 2 (Conscientiousness), and Factor 7 (Openness) differed little from our rationally constructed Big Five scales. However, Factors 3 and 4, which resembled Extraversion and Neuroticism, respectively, covered a narrower range of content than our Big Five scales. In particular, Factor 3 was defined primarily by elements of sociability and expressiveness, and did not include items related to energy and activity level, which typically load on the Extraversion factor in adult samples. Therefore, Factor 3 may be interpreted as Sociability, a narrower version of the adult Extraversion factor. Factor 4 was defined primarily by anxiety, nervous worry, guilt feelings, and low self-esteem, representing a more limited range of negative affects than typically found on the Neuroticism factor in adulthood. Therefore, we suggest the label Anxious Distress for Factor 4.

Factors 5 and 6 were not strongly related to any of the AEF Big Five scales; Factor 5 correlated most highly with the AEF Neuroticism scale ($r = .38$) and Factor 6 correlated most highly with the AEF Extraversion scale ($r = .18$). Factor 5 was defined by items that indicate negative affect expressed in immature and age-inappropriate behaviors (such as whining, crying, and tantrums), being overly sensitive to teasing, and irritable, suggesting the label Irritability. Factor 6 was defined by items such as energy and activity level, suggesting the label Activity.

In summary, there may be as many as seven common factors in personality ratings of boys in early adolescence.[2] Five of these factors corresponded to the Big Five personality dimensions, whereas the two additional factors—Irritability and Activity—may be independent of the Big Five dimensions, at least in early adolescence.

Skeptic: The basic claim of the FFM is that at the broadest level of description there are five dimensions of personality. The seven-factor solution suggests to me that additional dimensions are needed to account for the structure of CCQ personality descriptions. Is there something beyond the Big Five in early adolescence?

Question 6: Do the two additional factors represent independent dimensions of adolescent personality beyond the Big Five?

There are several possible interpretations of the two additional factors: They may be error factors arising from spurious intercorrelations among a small subset of items; instrument-specific factors produced by overrepresentation of the Irritability and Activity content domains in the CCQ-set; facets or components of the broad Big Five dimensions; and age-specific personality dimensions that are independent of the Big Five in the early adolescent years.

---

[2] To examine whether more than seven factors were meaningful, we also extracted and rotated eight varimax factors. The first seven factors were identical to those found in the seven-factor solution and the eighth varimax factor was defined by seemingly unrelated characteristics such as having lasting friendships, having nervous habits, and not judging other people. We also examined the five-factor solution of the CCQ-set. The first three factors clearly resembled Extraversion, Agreeableness, and Conscientiousness; their congruence correlations with the corresponding AEF Big Five scales ranged from .72 to .90. Moreover, these three factors were essentially the same factors as the first three in the seven-factor solution (congruence correlations ranged from .92 to .99). The remaining two factors did not correspond directly to either Neuroticism or Openness. The fourth factor corresponded to the Activity factor from the seven-factor solution (congruence correlation = .84). The fifth factor combined Openness (correlation of .60 with the AEF Openness scale) and Irritability (.55 with the Irritability factor). Thus, the five-factor solution produced three factors resembling one of the Big Five dimensions, a factor combining Openness and Irritability, and no clear Neuroticism factor.

Digman and Takemoto-Chock (1981) reanalyzed a number of factor analytic studies in adulthood and found that additional factors beyond the Big Five did not replicate from study to study. Thus, they concluded that additional factors are often "error factors" representing narrow item clusters arising from spuriously high intercorrelations among a few items rather than broad, general factors. To examine this possibility for our additional factors, we used an item-deletion technique that tests whether the factors disappear when some of their defining items are omitted from the factor analysis. Specifically, for each of the two additional factors, we deleted one, then two, and finally three of the most defining items; each time we refactored the remaining set of items. In all of these analyses, both Irritability and Activity continued to emerge as separate factors, suggesting that the two factors are not narrow clusters dependent on just a few items. It also seems unlikely that the two additional factors are error factors because their item content is conceptually coherent; characteristics on the Irritability factor such as acting immature, crying easily, and whining form a psychologically meaningful dimension, as do characteristics on the Activity factor such as active, energetic, and fast-paced.

On the other hand, the correlations of Irritability and Activity with the five criterion variables and with the other variables scored from the CCQ were generally small. The only correlations exceeding .20 were with Ego Resiliency; the Irritability factor correlated −.25 and the Activity factor correlated .22 with Ego Resiliency. Thus, the external validity of these two factors remains to be demonstrated.

It is also possible that Irritability and Activity are instrument-specific factors. Such factors can arise when a specific content domain is represented by several highly similar items; the specific variance shared by these items can cause them to split off from the broad factors and form separate factors that would not be found with other instruments. Indeed, the items on the two additional factors do refer to a more narrow range of characteristics than the items on the Big Five factors. Most of the Irritability items specifically refer to an agitated form of distress in response to minor stress or frustration, and the Activity items specifically refer to physical activity. Thus, there is some evidence that the two additional factors are instrument specific, and they need to be replicated in other assessment instruments.

A third possibility is that the two additional factors are facets of the Big Five dimensions. In studies of adults, Activity items typically load on Extraversion and Irritability items typically load on Neuroticism. For example, the Extraversion domain scale on Costa and McCrae's (1992b) NEO-PI-R inventory includes a facet scale for Activity and their Neuroticism domain scale includes a facet scale for Angry Hostility, which resembles our Irritability factor. Similarly, in factor analyses of trait adjectives, *active* loads on Extraversion and *irritable* loads on Neuroticism (e.g., Hofstee, DeRaad, & Goldberg, 1992). Thus, in *adulthood*,

Activity and Irritability are facets of the broader Extraversion and Neuroticism factors.

The subjects in our study, however, were at the cusp of adolescence and many were psychosocially and biologically still children. At this developmental period, are Activity and Irritability lower level facets of Extraversion and Neuroticism just as in adulthood? If this facet interpretation is correct, Activity and Irritability should be positively related to the adolescent versions of Extraversion (Sociability) and Neuroticism (Anxious Distress). To evaluate this possibility, we computed unit-weighted nonoverlapping scales from the items defining Factors 3 (Extraversion/Sociability) and 6 (Activity), and Factors 4 (Neuroticism/Anxious Distress) and 5 (Irritability) in the seven-factor solution. For facet scales, one would expect intercorrelations of at least .35. However, the Activity scale correlated only .16 with the Extraversion/Sociability scale and the Irritability scale correlated .25 with the Neuroticism/Anxious Distress scale. These results suggest that in early adolescence Activity and Irritability are not simply facets of Extraversion and Neuroticism.[3] Rather, they are relatively independent dimensions of pre-adult personality that exist at the same level of breadth as the other five dimensions during adolescence. Presumably, these dimensions will eventually merge with Sociability and Anxious Distress, respectively, to form the superordinate dimensions of Extraversion and Neuroticism in adulthood.

Skeptic: You argue that the two additional factors cannot be dismissed as error factors or as lower level facets. If so, can you offer a substantive interpretation? As a developmental psychologist, I would like to know where these dimensions come from and where they go to in adulthood.

It is possible that Activity and Irritability are age-specific dimensions that over the course of adolescence become integrated into the broader adult dimensions of Extraversion and Neuroticism. In terms of the developmental roots of Activity and Irritability, temperament researchers have identified and measured similar dimensions in childhood. With respect to Neuroticism and Irritability, Rothbart and Mauro (1990) distinguished between *fearful distress* and *irritable distress*, implying a bifurcation of the broader domain of negative affect that is quite similar to the separation of Neuroticism into Anxious Distress and Irritability we found in early adolescence. Thus, there may be two distinct aspects of negative affectivity

---

[3]Researchers interested in scoring Activity and Irritability from the CCQ may use scales constructed from the items loading above .40 on the varimax factors. The Activity scale consists of the following five items: (5) Other kids look up to him and seek him out. (26) He is physically active. He enjoys running, playing, and exercise. (28) He is energetic and full of life. (51) He is well-coordinated. (For example, he does well in sports.) (63) He is fast-paced. He moves and reacts to things quickly. The Irritability scale consists of the following 5 items: (12) He starts to act immature when he faces difficult problems or when he is under stress. (For example, he whines or has tantrums.) (33) He cries easily. (78) His feelings get hurt easily if he is made fun of or criticized. (94) He whines or pouts often. (95) He lets little problems get to him and he is easily upset; it doesn't take much to get him irritated or mad.

in pre-adulthood—one linked closely to fear and wary reactions to novelty and the other linked to irritability and frustration—which eventually grow together into the broad adult Neuroticism factor sometime during adolescence. Similarly, our interpretation that the adult Extraversion dimension is foreshadowed by separate Sociability and Activity factors in adolescence is consistent with Buss and Plomin's (1984) view that sociability and activity level are distinct, early emerging temperamental traits. These observations suggest the provocative hypothesis that, contrary to the Orthogenetic Principle (Werner, 1957), the personality system may become less differentiated and more integrated during the course of development.

More generally, the expression of personality traits may change over the course of development (Caspi & Bem, 1990). For example, the temperament dimension of Rhythmicity is significant in infancy but of little importance in later developmental periods. Developmental research on the Big Five has focused on adults and aging (McCrae & Costa, 1990) and has tended to emphasize "homotypic continuity"—continuity of similar behaviors or phenotypic attributes over time—to the possible neglect of "heterotypic continuity"—continuity of an inferred genotypic attribute presumed to underlie diverse phenotypic behaviors. This emphasis may be reasonable when developmental questions are framed about adulthood, but it is restrictive when developmental questions are framed about the earlier years of life when the behavioral manifestations of an underlying trait are more likely to change over time.

The distinction between homotypic and heterotypic continuity is relevant to our findings. For example, the emergence of the Irritability factor suggests the possibility that the expression of negative emotionality, which forms the core of adult Neuroticism, may also change over time. Such heterotypic continuity is implied by the items in Block's child and adult versions of the California Q-set; for example, children who whine and pout often (CCQ) may become adults who are self-pitying and feel victimized by life (CAQ). Despite phenotypic discontinuities in specific manifestations of negative affect, there may still be continuity in their "central orientation" (Bronson, 1966). Similarly, the emergence of the Activity factor defined by energy, tempo, and athletic prowess suggests that the behavioral expression of Extraversion may change with age. In adolescence, when physical activity and athletics play a central role in peer relations and carry social-status implications, Extraversion manifests itself in part through social contact, and in part through physical vigor. In adulthood, when social contexts become the arena in which most individuals vie for social status and acceptance, Extraversion may be expressed primarily through social activity, assertiveness, and gregariousness.

Skeptic: Although you have attempted to explain what may lie beyond the Big Five at the level of broad dimensions, much of the richness and nuance of personality lies in the individual characteristics captured by each CCQ item. According to the FFM, most specific personality traits fall into one of the Big Five domains. But, the CCQ Big Five scales described in this chapter include only 48 of the 100 CCQ items. What happened to the other 52 items?

Question 7: Is there personality content "beyond" or "between" the Big Five in adolescence?

Seven of the 52 "missing" CCQ items defined the Irritability and Activity factors, and thus are related to the two additional personality dimensions. How are we to account for the remaining 45 items? There are several possible interpretations of these items: They may be unrelated to the Big Five dimensions (e.g., masculinity), individual differences not considered part of personality (e.g., physical appearance), primarily error (i.e., items with low reliability), or related to more than one Big Five dimension.

Table 14.3 shows the results of several analyses we conducted to help interpret these 45 items within the context of the FFM. The items are organized by their relations with the Big Five scales. The first 12 items in Table 14.3 are designated "non-Big Five" items because their low multiple correlation with the Big Five suggests they are largely independent of (i.e., "beyond") the Big Five.[4] Several of these items contain personality content not well represented by the Big Five dimensions (e.g., masculinity). Others contain content typically considered outside the domain of personality (e.g., physical appearance). The remaining items refer to behaviors or attributes that reflect multiple, psychologically complex motives (e.g., "Tries to copy and act like the people he admires and looks up to") or that may imply different attributes for different individuals (e.g., "Looks different from other kids his own age").

There is also evidence that these 12 "non-Big Five" items contain almost exclusively specific (or error) variance. These items share very little common variance with any of the other items in the CCQ-set, as indicated by their low communalities even when we extracted as many as 16 factors (cf. Cattell, Eber, Tatsuoka, 1970); of the 45 items, they had the lowest communalities (mean communality of .22 compared to a mean communality of .43 for the remaining 33 items). Moreover, as shown in Table 3, the 12 items had no more significant correlations (5%) with the five real-world criteria than would be expected by chance, whereas 20% of the correlations between the remaining 33 items and the criterion variables were significant. Together, the findings suggest that each of the 12 "non-Big Five" items contain unique variance, some of which reflects content other than personality and some of which reflects unreliability in the judgments of the mothers.

The remaining 33 items presented in Table 3 were related to the five factors; all had multiple correlations larger than .30 with the Big Five scales, and 79% had

---

[4] It is an oversimplification to label an item as either a Big Five item or not a Big Five item—items vary in the degree to which they share variance with the Big Five dimensions (or similarly the common factors in the CCQ) and the degree to which they have specific variance. Indeed, most of the items listed in Table 3 have primarily specific variance. We chose .30 as a cut-off because ratings of a single item by a single judge have low reliability and we assumed that a multiple correlation above .30 indicates that a substantial portion of the item's reliable variance reflects Big Five content.

TABLE 14.3
Analyses of the 45 CCQ Items Not Scored on the Big Five Scales or Defining the Irritability or Activity Factors

	Communality in the CCQ-Set[a]	Representation in FFM		Correlations With Real-World Criteria				
Abbreviated CCQ Item		Multiple R With Big Five[b]	Related Big Five Scales[c]	Delinquency	School Performance[d]	IQ	SES	Race[e]
Non-Big Five Content (Multiple R below .31)								
16. Proud of the things he's done and made	.22	.30*	N− C+ O+	−.01	−.04	−.01	−.02	−.05
61. Judges other people	.23	.30*	A−	.03	.10	−.03	−.02	−.09
83. Independent; does not rely on others	.28	.28*	N− C+	.01	−.00	.01	−.02	.01
79. Suspicious; doesn't trust others	.29	.27*	A−	.08	.08	−.13	−.14*	−.08
52. Careful not to get physically hurt	.17	.27*	C+	−.13	−.02	−.04	−.13	−.15*
38. Thinks about things in an unusual way	.26	.24*		.06	.00	.02	−.01	.00
17. Acts very masculine	.20	.21*		.04	−.13	−.14*	.06	−.11
42. Is an interesting child	.18	.20		.04	−.01	.01	.02	−.06
49. Has nervous habits (tics, stutters, etc.)	.20	.20		.05	.01	−.04	−.07	.01
27. Looks different from other kids his own age	.10	.15		.07	.03	−.05	−.06	.00
87. Tries to copy and act like the people he admires	.17	.13		.09	−.07	.02	.03	.06
92. Is attractive, good looking	.20	.10		−.06	.03	.06	.09	.05
Agreeableness and Conscientiousness								
62. Is obedient and does what he is told	.59	.65*	A+ C+	−.24*	.09	.08	−.04	−.05
31. Able to see how others feel; empathic	.40	.50*	A+ C+	−.21*	.04	.13	.03	.03
15. Concerned about right and wrong; tries to be fair	.50	.62*	A+ C+ N−	−.22*	.12	.15*	.10	.03

#	Description									
71.	Often asks grown-ups for help and advice	.34	.48*	A+ C+ N−	−.10	.04	.01	.00	.00	−.07
20.	Tries to take advantage of other people	.42	.52*	A− C−	.19*	−.12	.05	−.01	−.01	.05
10.	Friendships don't last long	.46	.37*	A− C−	.13	−.04	−.04	−.04	.00	.08
55.	Worries about getting enough for self	.30	.37*	A− C−	.14*	.07	−.06	.01	.01	−.04
85.	Aggressive; picks fights or starts arguments	.59	.67*	A− C− O−	.25*	−.06	−.08	−.08	−.04	.05
13.	Pushes limits and tries to stretch the rules	.52	.65*	A− C− O−	.24*	−.20*	−.11	−.08	.04	.01
21.	Tries to be center of attention	.46	.51*	A− C− O−	.21*	−.15*	−.16*	−.11	−.03	−.07
56.	Jealous and envious	.50	.49*	A− C− O−	.20*	−.05	−.08	−.16*	−.02	.07
65.	Has a hard time waiting for things he wants	.43	.48*	A− C− O−	.15*	−.08	−.01	−.08	.04	.11
54.	Moods change often and quickly	.50	.52*	A− C− O− N+	.13	−.06	−.19*	−.01	−.03	.03
11.	Tries to blame other people for things he has done	.49	.60*	C− A−	.19*	−.12	−.07	−.19*	.00	−.05
57.	Exaggerates and blows things out of proportion	.45	.46*	C− A−	.21*	−.16*	−.12	−.07	.02	.07
34.	Restless and fidgety	.39	.44*	C− A−	.10	−.02	−.07	−.12	−.02	.06
91.	Emotions don't fit the situation	.50	.52*	C− A− N−	.20*	−.08	−.17*	−.08	−.12	−.03

Conscientiousness and Neuroticism

#	Description									
25.	Thinks things out; can be reasoned with	.41	.42*	C+ N− A+	−.09	.22*	.19*	.04	.04	−.02
88.	Self-confident and sure of himself	.45	.50*	N− C+	−.11	.13	.11	−.03	−.08	−.08
100.	Other kids pick on him; victimized	.39	.32*	C− N+	.16*	−.07	−.18*	−.24*	.05	.05
45.	Gives up easily when under stress	.40	.47*	C− N+ E−	.02	.00	−.13	−.01	−.02	−.02
53.	Indecisive; changes his mind a lot	.34	.33*	C− N+ O−	.00	−.11	−.15*	−.08	−.08	−.02

Neuroticism and Extraversion

#	Description									
72.	Often feels guilty; quick to blame self	.36	.40*	N+ E−	−.08	.05	−.01	−.08	.03	.05
82.	Assertive; goes after what he wants	.42	.47*	N− E+	.12	−.03	−.08	.12	.04	−.12
73.	Has a sense of humor; likes to laugh	.35	.40*	N− E+ O+	.00	.05	.09	−.24*	.02	.08
19.	Straightforward and open, not deceitful	.36	.49*	E+ N− C+ A+	−.02	.03	.08	−.01	.05	.00
81.	Able to talk about unpleasant things	.44	.43*	E+ N− A+ C+	.07	.00	.03	−.08	.05	−.07

(Continued)

TABLE 14.3
(Continued)

Abbreviated CCQ Item	Communality in the CCQ-Set[a]	Representation in FFM		Correlations With Real-World Criteria				
		Multiple R With Big Five[b]	Related Big Five Scales[c]	Delinquency	School Performance[d]	IQ	SES	Race[e]

Other Factorial Combinations Involving Agreeableness

64. Is calm and relaxed, easy-going	.52	.60*	A+ N− C+ O+	−.20*	.08	.08	.01	−.09
75. Is cheerful	.43	.47*	A+ N− E+	−.04	.04	−.01	.06	.00
7. Likes physical affection	.36	.41*	A+ E+	−.03	.01	.11	.17*	.16*
44. Submissive; gives in to others	.48	.33*	E− A+	−.05	.06	−.12	−.13	.01
37. Likes to compete	.36	.33*	A− E+	−.01	.10	.06	.04	−.01
18. Expresses negative feelings toward peers directly	.37	.38*	A− O−	.21*	−.10	−.03	.01	−.03

Note: $N = 350$ for all variables except School Performance ($N = 188$). The items are organized by their two largest correlations with the Big Five.
[a] Final communality in a 16-factor varimax-rotated solution of the 100-item CCQ-set using principal-factors analysis.
[b] Multiple correlation with all five predictors entered as a set into the regression equation.
[c] Big Five scales with zero-order correlations above $|.20|$ ($p < .001$), listed in descending order of magnitude. E = Extraversion, A = Agreeableness, C = Conscientiousness, N = Neuroticism, and O = Openness; "+" indicates a positive correlation and "−" indicates a negative correlation.
[d] Composite of teacher ratings of school performance in reading, writing, spelling, and math (alpha reliability = .95).
[e] Race was coded: African American = 1; Caucasian = 2; Other = missing.
*$p < .01$.

correlations above .40. Although these items clearly contain Big Five content, they are not uniquely related to any *one* factor. Instead, they represent combinations of two or more factors. How are we to account for these interstitial items that fall *between* the factors?

Hofstee et al. (1992) suggested that the Big Five may be better understood as broad personality categories that partially overlap and have fuzzy boundaries. The vast majority of the interstitial items can be represented using a circumplex approach (Wiggins, 1979), which represents an item in two-dimensional space rather than on one unidimensional factor. In their analysis of 540 personality-descriptive adjectives, Hofstee et al. found that most of the adjectives (84%) were related to the Big Five factors. However, only 48% of the total were uniquely related to a single factor; 33% were related to two factors and 3% to more than two factors. Similarly, we found that 48% of the 100 CCQ items were related to only one of our Big Five scales whereas 33% were related to two or more of the Big Five factors.

Following Hofstee et al. (1992), the items in Table 14.3 are grouped by their two largest correlations with the Big Five scales. Of the 10 possible pairwise combinations of the five dimensions, we found four large subsets of items representing combinations of (a) Agreeableness and Conscientiousness, (b) Conscientiousness and Neuroticism, (c) Neuroticism and Extraversion, and (d) various other combinations involving Agreeableness. The combination of Agreeableness and Conscientiousness contained by far the largest number of items (17). All these items fell either into the low Agreeableness, low Conscientiousness "antisocial" quadrant or the high Agreeableness, high Conscientiousness "prosocial" quadrant. As shown in Table 14.3, most of these items were significantly related to our delinquency criterion variable, supporting our previous findings linking both low Agreeableness and low Conscientiousness to delinquency and Antisocial Personality. These items further portray the antisocial adolescent as selfish, aggressive, exploitative, rebellious, and immoral. The items in this domain were also related to school performance and intelligence; items in the antisocial quadrant were generally negatively correlated with these two variables and, conversely, all of the items in the prosocial quadrant were positively correlated with them.

The second largest group of items involved the Conscientiousness and Neuroticism factors. All of these items fell into two opposing quadrants, which contrast conscientious, emotionally stable boys who are confident and have good judgment with unconscientious, neurotic boys who are vulnerable and indecisive. The third group consisted of five items combining Neuroticism and Extraversion. The emotionally stable extravert is charismatic and assertive, whereas the introverted neurotic is humorless, guilt-ridden, and reticent. The remaining items all involved Agreeableness, combined with either Extraversion, Neuroticism, or Openness. The classic interpersonal circumplex (e.g., Wiggins, 1979), combining Extraversion (Power) and Agreeableness (Love), was represented in the CCQ by items such as "Likes to compete" (A−, E+) and "Is cheerful" (A+, E+).

In summary, although some of the 45 items are unreliable or contain content not represented by the FFM, many can be described as combinations of two of the Big Five dimensions. The advantage of these two-dimensional representations is that they allow us to classify behaviors and traits that cannot be adequately accounted for by just one Big Five factor. In general, then, an item (or personality characteristic) can be represented within the FFM both by its vertical location "beneath" one of the Big Five factors and by its horizontal location "between" two factors in a circumplex representation (Goldberg, 1993b). Combining these two approaches to the FFM provides a more integrative taxonomic framework within which the vast majority of personality trait terms can be classified.

Skeptic: Your initial explorations into the origins of the Big Five have convinced me that the Big Five dimensions can be measured from the CCQ in early adolescence. In addition to constructing Big Five scales, you have also begun to examine the nomological network of the Big Five in early adolescence. Your data reveal conceptually coherent relations between your scales and other personality constructs as well as delinquent behavior, school performance, and intelligence. On the other hand, your findings also suggest that the search for the basic dimensions of personality is even more complex in adolescence than it is in adulthood. In your factor analysis, you found a variant of the Big Five and two additional factors—Irritability and Activity. You offer a speculative account of the origins and subsequent development of these two additional dimensions, and you suggest the provocative hypothesis that they may be atavistic remnants from an earlier ontogenic period, temperamental features of childhood that have yet to become integrated into the personality structure observed in studies of adults.

A thorough evaluation of this speculative account, and of the development of the Big Five more generally, requires a longitudinal study in which personality assessments of the same subjects are charted over time from early childhood through adolescence to adulthood. Such data would allow you to map longitudinally how the dimensional structure of personality changes over time and to ask how temperamental variations in infancy and early childhood manifest themselves during the transitional phase of adolescence and into adulthood. Thus, you could examine many of the questions you have raised: Does the personality system indeed become less differentiated over time? Does the child high on the temperament dimension of Irritable Distress become an adolescent high on our dimension of Irritability, and eventually become an adult high on the broad Neuroticism dimension? When exactly do Sociability and Activity merge into Extraversion? It is, of course, possible that early temperamental qualities and later personality characteristics reflect the same genotype, and longitudinal studies that assess age-to-age genetic continuity will be needed to examine this issue (Plomin, 1986).

Clearly, you have a great deal of work ahead of you. First of all, you need to establish the generalizability of the present findings to samples of females, to assessment instruments other than the CCQ, and to raters other than mothers. Second, your future research should be guided more explicitly by theories of personality development to explain why *personality structure changes through childhood and adolescence, and it should focus on the changes that occur during developmental transitions such as puberty. Finally, to embed the Big Five into the broader field of developmental psychology, you should examine the developmental antecedents of the Big Five and their relations to other aspects of development that have been linked to personality in adolescence such as depression (Block, Gjerde, & Block, 1991) and self-esteem (Block & Robins, 1993).*

ACKNOWLEDGMENTS

The writing of this chapter was supported by a National Science Foundation Graduate Fellowship to Richard W. Robins, NIMH Grant MH49255 to Oliver P. John, and a Spencer Fellowship from the National Academy of Education to Avshalom Caspi. We are indebted to Rolf Loeber and Magda Stouthamer-Loeber for allowing us to explore these issues in their Pittsburgh Youth Study. This research was supported by several agencies: the Antisocial and Violent Behavior Branch of the NIMH (Grant MH45548 to Terrie Moffitt); the University of Wisconsin Graduate School; and the Office of Juvenile Justice and Delinquency Prevention, Office of Justice Programs, U.S. Department of Justice (Grant No. 86-JN-CX-0009 to Rolf Loeber and Magda Stouthamer-Loeber). Points of view or opinions in this document are those of the authors and do not necessarily represent the official position or policies of the U.S. Department of Justice. We also acknowledge the support and resources provided by the Institute of Personality and Social Research, University of California at Berkeley. We would like to thank Jack Block, Kenneth Craik, Lewis R. Goldberg, Robert Hogan, Robert R. McCrae, Terrie Moffitt, and Kristina Whitney for their comments on an earlier version of this chapter.

REFERENCES

Block, J. (1961). *The Q-sort method in personality assessment and psychiatric research.* (Reprint Edition 1978). Palo Alto, CA: Consulting Psychologists Press.

Block, J., & Block, J. H. (1980). *The California Child Q-set.* Palo Alto, CA: Consulting Psychologists Press. (Original work published 1969)

Block, J., & Gjerde, P. F. (1986). Distinguishing between antisocial behavior and undercontrol. In D. Olweus, J. Block, & M. Radke-Yarrow (Eds.), *Development of antisocial and prosocial behavior: Research, theories, and issues* (pp. 177–206). New York: Academic Press.

Block, J., Gjerde, P. F., & Block, J. H. (1991). Personality antecedents of depressive tendencies in 18-year-olds: A prospective study. *Journal of Personality and Social Psychology, 60,* 726–738.

Block, J., & Robins, R. W. (1993). A longitudinal study of consistency and change in self-esteem from early adolescence to early adulthood. *Child Development, 64*, 909–923.

Block, J. H., & Block, J. (1980). The role of ego-control and ego-resiliency in the organization of behavior. In W. A. Collins (Ed.), *Minnesota Symposium on Child Psychology* (Vol. 13, pp. 39–101). Hillsdale, NJ: Lawrence Erlbaum Associates.

Bronson, W. C. (1966). Central orientations: A study of behavior organization from childhood to adolescence. *Child Development, 37*, 125–155.

Buss, A. H., & Plomin, R. (1984). *A temperament theory of personality development* (rev. ed.). New York: Wiley.

Caspi, A., & Bem, D. J. (1990). Personality continuity and change across the life course. In L. A. Pervin (Ed.), *Handbook of personality: Theory and research* (pp. 549–575). New York: Guilford Press.

Caspi, A., Block, J., Block, J. H., Klopp, B., Lynam, D., Moffitt, T. E., & Stouthamer-Loeber, M. (1992). A "common language" version of the California Child Q-Set for personality assessment. *Psychological Assessment, 4*, 512–523.

Caspi, A., Herbener, E. S., & Ozer, D. J. (1992). Shared experiences and the similarity of personalities: A longitudinal study of married couples. *Journal of Personality and Social Psychology, 62*, 281–291.

Cattell, R. B., Eber, H. W., & Tatsuoka, M. M. (1970). *Handbook for the Sixteen Personality Factor Questionnaire (16PF)*. Champaign, IL: Institute for Personality and Ability Testing.

Costa, P. T., & McCrae, R. R. (1992a). Four ways five factors are basic. *Personality and Individual Differences, 13*, 653–665.

Costa, P. T., & McCrae, R. R. (1992b). *Revised NEO Personality Inventory (NEO-PI-R) and NEO Five-Factor Inventory (NEO-FFI) Professional Manual*. Odessa, FL: Psychological Assessment Resources.

Digman, J. M. (1990). Personality structure: Emergence of the five-factor model. *Annual Review of Psychology, 41*, 417–440.

Digman, J. M. (1989). Five robust trait dimensions: Development, stability, and utility. *Journal of Personality, 57*, 195–214.

Digman, J. M., & Inouye, J. (1986). Further specification of the five robust factors of personality. *Journal of Personality and Social Psychology, 50*, 116–123.

Digman, J. M., & Takemoto-Chock, N. K. (1981). Factors in the natural language of personality: Re-analysis, comparison, and interpretation of six major studies. *Multivariate Behavioral Research, 16*, 149–170.

Eysenck, H. J. (1991). Dimensions of personality: 16, 5, or 3?—Criteria for a taxonomic paradigm. *Personality and Individual Differences, 12*, 773–790.

Funder, D. C., Tomlinson-Keasey, C., Parke, R., & Widaman, K. (1993). *Studying lives through time: Approaches to personality and development*. Washington, DC: American Psychological Association.

Goldberg, L. R. (1993a). The structure of phenotypic personality traits. *American Psychologist, 48*, 26–34.

Goldberg, L. R. (1993b). The structure of personality traits: Vertical and horizontal aspects. In D. C. Funder, R. Parke, C. Tomlinson-Keasey, & K. Widaman (Eds.), *Studying lives through time: Approaches to personality and development* (pp. 169–188). Washington, DC: American Psychological Association.

Graziano, W. G., & Ward, D. (1992). Probing the Big Five in adolescence: Personality and adjustment during a developmental transition. *Journal of Personality, 60*, 425–439.

Hofstee, W. K. B., DeRaad, B., & Goldberg, L. R. (1992). Integration of the Big Five and circumplex approaches to trait structure. *Journal of Personality and Social Psychology, 63*, 146–163.

John, O. P. (1990). The "Big Five" factor taxonomy: Dimensions of personality in the natural language and questionnaires. In L. A. Pervin (Ed.), *Handbook of personality: Theory and research* (pp. 66–100). New York: Guilford Press.

John, O. P., & Robins, R. W. (1993). Gordon Allport: Father and critic of the Five-Factor Model. In K. H. Craik, R. T. Hogan, & R. N. Wolfe (Eds.), *Fifty years of personality research* (pp. 215–236). New York: Plenum.

John, O. P., Caspi, A., Robins, R. W., Moffitt, T. E., & Stouthamer-Loeber, M. (1994). The "Little Five": Exploring the nomological network of the Five-Factor Model of personality in adolescent boys. *Child Development, 65,* 160–178.

Loeber, R., Stouthamer-Loeber, M., Van Kammen, W., & Farrington, D. (1989). Development of a new measure for self-reported antisocial behavior for young children: Prevalence and reliability. In M. W. Klein (Ed.), *Cross-national research in self-reported crime and delinquency.* Dordrecht, The Netherlands: Kluwer.

McCrae, R. R., & Costa, P. T. (1985). Updating Norman's adequate taxonomy: Intelligence and personality dimensions in natural language and in questionnaires. *Journal of Personality and Social Psychology, 49,* 710–721.

McCrae, R. R., & Costa, P. T. (1990). *Personality in adulthood.* New York: Guilford Press.

McCrae, R. R., & Costa, P. T. (in press). Conceptions and correlates of Openness to Experience. In R. Hogan, J. A. Johnson, & S. R. Briggs (Eds.), *Handbook of personality psychology.* New York: Academic Press.

McCrae, R. R., Costa, P. T., & Busch, C. M. (1986). Evaluating comprehensiveness in personality systems: The California Q-Set and the five-factor model. *Journal of Personality, 54,* 430–446.

McCrae, R. R., & John, O. P. (1992). An introduction to the Five-Factor Model and its applications. *Journal of Personality, 60,* 175–215.

Olweus, D., Block, J., & Radke-Yarrow, M. (1986). *Development of antisocial and prosocial behavior: Research, theories, and issues.* New York: Academic Press.

Plomin, R. (1986). *Development, genetics, and psychology.* Hillsdale, NJ: Lawrence Erlbaum Associates.

Rothbart, M. K., & Mauro, J. A. (1990). Questionnaire approaches to the study of infant temperament. In J. Columbo & J. Fagen (Eds.), *Individual differences in infancy: Reliability, stability and prediction* (pp. 411–429). Hillsdale, NJ: Lawrence Erlbaum Associates.

Werner, H. (1957). *Comparative psychology of mental development.* New York: International Universities Press.

Wiggins, J. S. (1979). A psychological taxonomy of trait-descriptive terms: The interpersonal domain. *Journal of Personality and Social Psychology, 37,* 395–412.

CHAPTER

15

THE BIG FIVE PERSONALITY FACTORS IN Q-SORT DESCRIPTIONS OF CHILDREN AND ADOLESCENTS

Cornelis F. M. van Lieshout
Gerbert J. T. Haselager
University of Nijmegen

Language analyses, for example, in English (cf. Norman, 1963; Peabody & Goldberg, 1989) or in Dutch (cf. Brokken, 1978) have enabled taxonomers to reveal in adult self- and peer-ratings five personality factors or dimensions. These Big Five factors have been numbered and labeled as (I) Extraversion (or Power, Surgency), (II) Agreeableness (or Love), (III) Conscientiousness (or Work, Dependability), (IV) Emotional Stability (vs. Neuroticism, or Affect), and (V) Intellect (or Openness, Culture). Studies have been executed in a diversity of languages (cf. Brokken, 1978; John, Goldberg, & Angleitner, 1984), with different sets of person descriptive adjectives, nouns, and verbs (De Raad, 1991), with different types of judges, and with different factor analytic procedures (Goldberg, 1990). In addition, investigators have searched for the Big Five in clinical person descriptions of children and adults (cf. Digman, 1989; Digman & Inouye, 1986; McCrae, Costa, & Busch, 1986).

The purpose of this study was to determine the utility of the five-factor personality taxonomy in personality descriptions of children and adolescents. For person descriptions we used a Dutch version of the California Child Q-set (CCQ; J. H. Block & J. Block, 1980). The domain of phenomena covered in the CCQ consists of a large set of statements worded by J. H. Block and J. Block in common language and aimed at the comprehensive description of the wide range of affective, cognitive, and social attributes that manifest themselves in the behavior and personality of children and adolescents from the ages of 3 to 18 years. Two thirds of the statements of the CCQ have been adapted from the adult form of the

293

California Q-set (CAQ; J. Block, 1961/1978). Most of the other items were specifically devised for person descriptions of children and adolescents.

Over the past decades investigators have used the 100 CCQ items in studies of a great variety of personality characteristics such as ego resiliency and ego control (cf. J. Block, 1971; J. H. Block & J. Block, 1980; van Lieshout et al., 1986), social competence and social desirability (Waters, Garber, Gornal, & Vaughn, 1983), peer competence (Haselager, 1988; van Lieshout, van Aken, & van Seyen, 1990), depressive symptoms (J. Block, Gjerde, & J. H. Block, 1991; Jansen & van Aken, 1991), delay of gratification (Bem & Funder, 1978; Mischel & Ebbesen, 1970), as well as in studies of separate behaviors and experiences such as anxiety, stress, depressive feelings, hypersensitivity, withdrawal, imbalance, cooperation, aggression, disruption, shyness, help seeking, leadership, and intellectual competence (Cillessen, 1991; van Aken, van Lieshout, Roosen, & Roeffen, 1991; van IJzendoorn & Cillessen, 1991). The CCQ also has been used in studies of consistency in personality development (Ozer & Gjerde, 1989), and agreement of self-descriptions with descriptions by others (van Aken & van Lieshout, 1991; van Lieshout et al., 1990) as well as in studies of the background of agreement and differences in person descriptions by different judges (Asendorpf & van Aken, 1991; Funder & Dobroth, 1987). All these studies indicated that the CCQ covers a broad domain of behaviors and person characteristics of children and adolescents.

Characteristics of the Q-sort procedure as well as procedures followed in our study guarantee a broad sampling of children's and adolescents' behavior and personality characteristics. The Q-sort procedure of the CCQ results in an ipsative forced distribution of the items over the nine points of a scale. This scale ranges from extremely uncharacteristic (Category 1) to extremely characteristic (Category 9) for the observed child. It should be noted that extremely uncharacteristic statements also are very salient for the description of a person. A rectangular, forced distribution is used, that is, the same number of items are assigned to each category with the exception of Category 5, where 12 items are placed. This forced distribution leads to comparison of each statement or attribute with other attributes of the child. In contrast to the person-centered ipsative approach, variable-centered rating procedures compare each individual on a statement with a reference group. The Q-sort procedure focuses on a personality description based on within- rather than between-person differences. The ipsative procedure also results in suppression of response tendencies and observer biases (J. Block, 1961/1978). Before using the CCQ, observers must have had the opportunity to observe the child on a day-to-day basis, in a variety of settings, for several months. Also, in this study Q-sort descriptions of judges from different settings were compared, that is, from parents and teachers as well as self and peer descriptions of adolescents.

We had good reasons to suspect that our efforts would result in a factor structure of the CCQ descriptions of children and adolescents which was similar to the five-factor model (FFM). Using teachers' behavior ratings of children,

Digman (1989; Digman & Inouye, 1986) has shown that the five-factor structure was appropriate for describing children's personality. In addition, McCrae, Costa, and Busch (1986) factored self-CAQ-sorts for men and women. The resulting five factors—Neuroticism, Extraversion, Openness, Agreeableness, and Conscientiousness—closely resembled those found in earlier studies of adjectives and showed convergent and discriminant validity against self-, peer-, and spouse-ratings on other measures of the FFM. McCrae et al. considered their findings as strong support for the claim of comprehensiveness of the FFM of personality descriptions.

Three sets of research questions were studied. First, how universal is the FFM? Using an existing set of CCQ descriptions in this study, the generality of the FFM has been tested for adult observer descriptions of children and adolescents ranging in age from 3 to 17 years. If the FFM can be recovered, the generality of the model will be strengthened in several ways. The model will not only be recovered in self- and other-evaluations of adult academics using adjectives, nouns or verbs for personality descriptions, it also will be found in clinical personality assessments of children by lay observers as teachers and parents. In children and adolescents additional factors may cover behavior patterns and personality characteristics that are less relevant for adults. Therefore, we will also examine the nature of any additional factors beyond the first five.

A second set of research questions concerned the generality of the factors over observers, that is, teachers and parents, over gender of child, and over age of the children. Although the FFM may be recovered in an overall analyses of CCQ descriptions by teachers and parents of a large number of children and adolescents, further tests are required to determine whether the five-factor structure will be found in separate sets of CCQ descriptions from teachers and parents of both boys and girls at different age levels. Some factors may be environment specific (e.g., Openness and Conscientiousness in school or Emotional Stability at home). Some behaviors may be more specific for boys (e.g., motor activity), and others for girls (e.g., verbal skills; cf. Maccoby & Jacklin, 1974), leading to gender-specific factors or facets of factors. In addition, some behaviors may be more relevant for younger children and others for adolescents. Therefore, separate factor analyses of CCQ descriptions from parents and from teachers, of boys and girls, and for children of three age levels were compared with an overall factor analysis.

The third set of research questions concerned a comparison of the factor structure of CCQ descriptions of the same group of early adolescents by four different types of observers: for example, parents, teachers, best friends, and self descriptions. In early adolescence children become able to render self and peer descriptions using the CCQ. This comparison might reveal how early adolescents start using the FFM in self and peer descriptions. For this purpose, four separate factor analyses of CCQ descriptions from parents, teachers, best friends, and self were compared with an overall analysis.

METHOD

Subjects

In six separate studies (Studies 1–6) 937 parents and 899 teachers gave 1,836 CCQ descriptions of 720 children and adolescents (462 boys; 258 girls), predominantly attending regular schools. Only one CCQ description from each judge was included in the study. The children were split in three age groups: of 636 children (403 boys; 233 girls) between 3.2 and 7.0 years ($M = 5.8$), of 626 children (430 boys; 196 girls) between 7.1 and 11.6 years ($M = 9.7$), and of 574 adolescents (316 boys; 258 girls) between 11.7 and 16.10 years ($M = 13.5$). Further details concerning the separate samples are listed in Table 15.1.

Analyses concerning the early adolescent sample were based on 794 CCQ descriptions of 156 adolescents (76 boys and 80 girls) from two studies by 186 fathers and mothers, 229 teachers, 242 best friends and 137 adolescents themselves (see lower panel of Table 15.1).

Materials

CCQ Descriptions

Subjects provided CCQ descriptions on a Dutch translation (van Lieshout et al., 1986) of the California Child Q-Set (J. H. Block & J. Block, 1980), referred to as the Nijmegen California Child Q-set (NCCQ). The CCQ consists of 100 statements describing a wide range of behavior and personality characteristics. Each statement is printed on a separate card. The 100 cards were sorted by an observer into nine categories ranging from "least" (Category 1) to "most characteristic" (Category 9). Multiple observers independently described each child with the NCCQ, using a rectangular 9-point forced distribution. Eleven statements were placed in each category except Category 5, in which 12 statements were placed.

For each subject, one to eight NCCQ descriptions were available. To estimate item reliability in Study 4 for each separate item, a Cronbach's alpha was obtained over eight NCCQ descriptions. The mean alpha, averaged over 100 items, was .62 (range .16 to .87).

RESULTS

Overall Principal Component Analysis

To determine the number of factors best fitted to the NCCQ descriptions by parents and teachers, several steps were followed. First, a principal component analysis on the 1,836 NCCQ descriptions resulted in 19 factors with eigenvalues greater than 1.00. The cumulative percentage of explained variance amounted to

TABLE 15.1
Number of Subjects, Age, and Type of NCCQ description, per Study and per Measurement Wave

Study	N^a	Wave	Age[b]	NCCQ description[c]
Overall Sample				
1. Siebenheller (1990)	210(101, 109)	A	11.7 (6.0–16.10)	F/M(315)
2. Van IJzendoorn et al. (1987)	68(34, 34)	A	5.8 (4.10–6.4)	F/M(133), T(74)
3. Van IJzendoorn et al. (1991)	70(35, 35)	A	3.6 (3.2–3.11)	F/M(139)
4. Arnhem Study (van Aken, 1991)	97(47, 50)	A	7.3 (6.10–7.5)	T(96)
		B	10.2 (9.8–10.8)	F/M(94), T(91)
		C	11.11 (11.5–12.6)	T(80)
5. Nijmegen Study (van Lieshout et al., 1986)	59(29, 30)	A	12.2 (12.0–12.5)	T(58)
		B	14.0 (13.10–14.3)	F/M(99), T(149)
6. Cillessen (1991)	216(216, 0)	A	6.7 (4.7–9.3)	T(167)
		B	7.7 (5.9–9.10)	T(130)
		C	11.2 (9.5–13.7)	M(157), T(54)
Total	720(462, 258)			F/M(937), T(899)
Early Adolescent Sample				
4. Arnhem-Study (van Aken, 1991)	97(47, 50)	C	11.11 (11.5–12.6)	F/M(87), T(80), P(174), S(87)
5. Nijmegen-Study (van Lieshout et al., 1986)	59(29, 30)	B	14.0 (13.10–14.3)	F/M(99), T(149), P(68), S(50)
Total	156(76, 80)			F/M(186), T(229), P(242), S(137)

[a]Between parentheses number of boys and girls, respectively.
[b]Age in years/months; Between parentheses age range.
[c]NCCQ description by F = Father; M = Mother; T = Teacher; P = Best Friend; S = Self. Between parentheses number of NCCQ descriptions.

55.9%. Next, a scree plot indicated that at least four components might be extracted. The ipsative character of Q-sort data, however, lowers the average intercorrelations among Q-sort items. As a consequence, components typically will have comparatively low eigenvalues. One must choose between leaving much variance unexplained or retaining many components that may be quite unstable unless sample size is very large (cf. Ozer, 1993). Because our sample was very large, we considered the four-component solution as the minimum number of factors and we subsequently explored a five-, six-, seven-, eight-, and nine-factor solution. Two quantitative indicators were used to evaluate the similarity between the factors derived in subsequent solutions, that is, the number of common high loading (equal or higher than |.35|) items on factors in subsequent solutions and Tucker's φ (cf. Harman, 1967) as a coeffient of factor congruence.

The seven-factor solution fit our data best for a number of reasons. Eight- and nine-factor solutions did not have more than one item on the last factor with a unique factor loading higher than .35. In the four-, five-, six-, and seven-factor solutions, in subsequent solutions subgroups of items were regrouped under different components. In the eight- and nine-factor solutions no further regrouping occurred. On the contrary, subgroups of items split from earlier components. The mean Tucker's φ among corresponding factors in subsequent solutions increased from .78 to .94 between the four- and five-factor solution and between the seven- and eight-factor solutions, and subsequently decreased to .92 between the eight- and nine-factor solutions. The cumulative percentage of explained variance of the seven-factor solution was 40.5%. The varimax-rotated, seven-factor solution is presented in Table 15.2. Item loadings higher than .35 on each factor are printed boldface. Fourteen items did not reach the .35 criterion. These 14 items were a heterogeneous subset of items. The factors are reported in the order of factor extraction in the overall sample and are numbered with Arabic numbers to distinguish the factors of this study from the FFM. The latter are numbered with Roman numbers according to convention in FFM studies.

Factor 1 (32 items), contained by far the largest number of items and closely resembled Love or Agreeableness (Factor II). This bipolar factor covered the broad area of prosocial versus antisocial relationships, especially peer relationships. The factor contrasted a warm, empathic consideration of other people's needs, emotions and interests and open, trustful interpersonal orientations with aggressive, irritated and antisocial exploitations of others. The large number of items loading on this factor reflects the number of items related to agreeable behavior on the CCQ but also reflects the large number of person descriptors referring to agreeableness in the common language (cf. Goldberg, 1990; Hofstee & DeRaad, 1991).

Factor 2 (16 items) contained items that predominantly referred to Affect or Emotional Stability (Factor IV). Self-reliance, assertiveness, being easy-going, independent, and resourceful were opposed to being fearful, anxious, emotionally disorganized under stress, and having low self-esteem.

TABLE 15.2
Nijmegen California Child Q-Set Items Defining the Seven Factors in the Overall Sample

Item Number and Description	1 Agreeableness	2 Emotional Stability	3 Conscientiousness	4 Openness	5 Extraversion	6 Motor Activity	7 Dependency
Factor 1: Agreeableness							
2 Is considerate of other children	**76**	-02	03	09	-02	-07	00
6 Is helpful and cooperative	**72**	03	01	04	07	06	04
3 Is warm and responsive	**72**	05	-03	18	13	01	03
76 Can be trusted, is dependable	**68**	05	23	-03	-09	-10	-09
15 Shows concern for moral issues	**68**	-01	01	-07	09	-06	-09
31 Recognizes feelings of others	**64**	-01	-02	05	26	-06	-01
11 Attempts to transfer blame to others	**-64**	06	-18	-14	07	-01	16
32 Tends to give, lend and share	**63**	04	-16	03	-12	-02	-06
19 Open and straightforward	**61**	10	05	04	13	00	-09
29 Protective of others	**61**	07	-09	01	18	05	-05
56 Jealous and envious of others	**-60**	-06	-05	-12	12	-03	18
4 Gets along well with other children	**59**	17	-01	-10	-03	12	14
20 Tries to take advantage of others	**-55**	17	-12	-10	-06	01	25
85 Aggressive (physically or verbally)	**-54**	04	-23	-24	17	21	-15
62 Obedient and compliant	**54**	-08	18	-10	-34	-21	19
90 Is stubborn	**-54**	03	-13	-13	10	01	-17
55 Afraid of being deprived	**-54**	-14	-09	-09	13	-03	23
95 Overreacts to minor frustrations	**-52**	-21	-21	-14	27	-06	-08
30 Arouses liking in adults	**52**	08	05	-02	-03	00	07
80 Teases other children	**-51**	16	-23	-02	10	17	-07
25 Uses and responds to reason	**50**	21	**40**	00	-16	-10	05
9 Genuine and close relationships	**50**	11	10	28	04	08	01
93 Behaves in a dominating manner	**-47**	26	02	-10	**30**	18	04
13 Generally stretches limits	**-47**	23	-25	13	16	22	01

(Continued)

TABLE 15.2
(Continued)

Item Number and Description	1 Agreeableness	2 Emotional Stability	3 Conscientiousness	4 Openness	5 Extraversion	6 Motor Activity	7 Dependency
10 Transient interpersonal relations	**-45**	-01	-19	-32	-12	-04	02
61 Tends to be judgmental of others	**-42**	17	-14	-29	23	11	14
78 Easily offended	**-41**	-24	-11	**-37**	15	-03	00
21 Tries to be the center of attention	**-41**	20	-04	-01	33	18	27
91 Inappropriate in emotive behavior	**-38**	-21	-18	-34	-22	-06	-07
81 Can admit to own negative feelings	**38**	33	09	-15	09	-02	-10
57 Tends to exaggerate mishaps	**-36**	-18	-14	-12	30	-25	10
54 Emotionally labile	**-35**	-31	-34	-22	10	02	-06
Factor 2: Emotional Stability							
88 Self-reliant, confident	06	**64**	32	15	11	02	-16
23 Fearful, anxious	-05	**-63**	-10	-12	-21	-17	00
46 Tends to go to pieces under stress	-04	**-61**	-18	-18	-07	-10	00
24 Tends to brood and ruminate or worry	13	**-59**	06	-23	-18	-11	00
60 Anxious in unpredictable situations	06	**-58**	-13	-08	-19	-13	11
82 Self-assertive	-09	**57**	05	-14	27	16	-03
64 Calm and relaxed, easy-going	27	**53**	17	12	-27	-30	-03
77 Appears to feel unworthy	-07	**-47**	-21	-35	-29	-05	00
35 Inhibited and constricted	-13	**-47**	-08	-33	**-45**	-11	-05
72 Has a readiness to feel guilty	16	**-46**	00	-22	-15	-01	-01
50 Bodily symptoms from stress	06	**-45**	-04	-11	-02	-09	02
53 Indecisive, vacillating	00	**-42**	-33	-22	**-36**	-14	19
43 Recoups after stressful experiences	15	**41**	-06	03	-03	03	07
83 Seeks to be independent	-04	**40**	28	-03	-02	09	-27
33 Cries easily	-17	**-40**	-09	09	25	-33	-02
39 Immobilized under stress	-16	**-39**	-20	-31	-26	-13	-05
Factor 3: Conscientiousness							
66 Attentive, able to concentrate	24	16	**70**	11	-09	-10	-05
47 Performance standards for self high	20	-04	**68**	-01	-04	11	-08
67 Planful, thinks ahead	26	18	**65**	06	-16	-19	-17

300

89 Competent, skillful	16	23	**63**	26	−05	04	−15
68 High intellectual capacity	−04	16	**56**	33	−01	−01	−14
99 Is reflective	31	09	**51**	−02	**−36**	−30	−07
40 Is curious and exploring	08	20	**45**	29	24	14	−19

Factor 4: Openness

92 Physically attractive, good-looking	12	08	08	**53**	−04	06	11
97 Active fantasy life	−02	04	−03	**52**	17	07	−35
42 Interesting and arresting child	18	14	13	**52**	15	15	−19
96 Creative	11	12	16	**48**	10	03	**−37**
79 Suspicious of others	**−47**	−07	−07	**−47**	−14	−04	07
73 Responds to humor	22	28	−13	**43**	04	14	−12
36 Resourceful in initiating activities	08	21	19	**43**	19	21	−33
5 Admired and sought by other children	25	21	07	**41**	05	26	04
75 Cheerful	**35**	31	−12	**37**	13	20	13

Factor 5: Extraversion

8 Keeps thoughts and feelings to self	00	−06	00	−17	**−65**	−06	−07
98 Shy and reserved	03	−29	03	−20	**−59**	−25	−04
58 Emotionally expressive	06	18	−14	07	**55**	−06	02
18 Expresses negative feelings openly	−11	**41**	−17	−11	**43**	07	−09
86 Likes to be by him/herself	−03	03	12	−03	**−43**	**−35**	−31
44 Tends to yield and give in	27	−26	−05	−04	**−43**	−14	18
69 Verbally fluent	06	34	27	25	**38**	−05	−12
45 Withdraws under stress	−02	−28	−21	−10	**−37**	−20	12
84 Is a talkative child	−20	14	−27	05	**37**	20	09

Factor 6: Motor Activity

26 Physically active	−04	15	−09	27	08	**67**	02
28 Vital, energetic, lively	04	21	−07	**37**	26	**61**	−01
52 Physically cautious	15	−10	10	−09	−18	**−59**	02
51 Agile and well coordinated	06	21	05	29	−04	**53**	03
63 Rapid personal tempo	−07	15	31	−03	07	**49**	−04
37 Competitive	−24	16	34	−11	11	**42**	22
34 Is restless and fidgety	−28	−35	−29	−27	09	**38**	−02
70 Daydreams, gets lost in reverie	00	−12	**−36**	−09	−29	**−37**	−08

(Continued)

TABLE 15.2
(Continued)

Item Number and Description	1 Agreeableness	2 Emotional Stability	3 Conscientiousness	4 Openness	5 Extraversion	6 Motor Activity	7 Dependency
Factor 7: Dependency							
14 Eager to please	-14	02	-08	-06	05	05	**55**
48 Others sought to affirm self worth	-11	-12	-02	-17	08	04	**41**
22 Manipulates others by ingratiation	**-37**	11	-25	05	08	-07	**40**
38 Unusual thought processes	-24	-07	-21	-15	-17	-13	**-37**
87 Tends to imitate those admired	-17	-04	-13	12	-02	07	**36**
Items not in solution[a]							
7 Seeks physical contact with others	06	-01	-23	34	25	-10	06
65 Unable to delay gratification	-34	04	-28	08	19	02	04
1 Prefers non-verbal communication	01	-04	-27	-03	-34	03	-13
94 Tends to be sulky or whiny	-33	-33	-13	01	17	-32	-02
41 Persistent, does not give up	00	26	33	-11	-04	12	-18
71 Looks to adults for help	11	-13	-13	-04	-01	-23	33
74 Becomes involved in what (s)he does	23	-06	33	08	17	05	-16
100 Easily victimized by other children	-28	-24	-21	-32	-03	-14	-10
12 Immature behavior under stress	-25	-29	-21	04	14	-22	-03
49 Shows specific mannerisms	-12	-22	-28	-02	-11	-08	-12
59 Neat and orderly in dress	25	10	26	-16	-18	-24	20
16 Proud of own accomplishments	-01	24	23	01	08	03	16
17 Behaves in a sex-typed manner	-01	18	-04	01	-07	23	22
27 Visibly deviant from peers	-04	-01	-10	-23	-12	-08	-16

Note: Factors are reported in the order of the factor extraction in the overall sample. Within factors, items are sorted according to descending absolute factor loadings. Loadings ≥ .35 are printed in boldface. Decimal points are omitted.
[a] Loadings < .35 on all seven factors.

Factor 3 (7 items) was called Conscientiousness. Highest loading items concerned conscientiousness in work situations. This factor combined a concentrated, planful, reliable, and competent high achievement orientation with high intellectual capacity, reflection, and curiosity. This factor consisted of only items with positive loadings. Typical negative items concerning disorganization, negligence, carelessness, impracticality, irresponsibility, laziness, or extravagancy (cf. Goldberg, 1992) were not represented. Two items with their highest loading on this factor—*High intellectual capacity*, and *Is curious and exploring*—according to their content might better fit in the Openness factor in the FFM.

Factor 4 (9 items) combined openness to new ideas and experiences with physical attractiveness. The predominantly positive loading items emphasized nonscholastic openness in terms of fantasy, imagination, creativity, humor, and resourcefulness, along with attractiveness and good humor. The only negative loading item, *Suspicious of others*, had a similar negative loading on the first factor Agreeableness. The social items (e.g., Items 92, 79, 5, and 75) are usually not considered markers of Openness (cf. Goldberg, 1992). The absence of negative loading items on Openness is in agreement with the low number of negative openness descriptors in common language (cf. Goldberg, 1990; Hofstee & De Raad, 1991).

Factor 5 (9 items) concerned Extraversion versus Introversion. Emotional and verbal expressiveness were contrasted with shyness, inhibition, self-isolation, withdrawal, and nonassertiveness. Some aspects of Extraversion such as sociability, energy, and motor (in)activity did not load on the factor, being instead part of a separate factor (Factor 6).

Factor 6 (8 items) specifically referred to Motor Activity. This factor contrasted a high level of agility, physical activity, motor coordination, restlessness, and rapid personal tempo with physical cautiousness and daydreaming.

Factor 7 (5 items) was called Dependency. Most items were specifically oriented toward dependency on others and a strong tendency to seek support and affirmation from others.

Generality of Factors Over Observers, Gender of Child, and Age Level

Several steps were followed to determine the similarity of the varimax-rotated factor solutions within the overall sample with varimax-rotated factor solutions of NCCQ descriptions within seven subsamples, for example, NCCQ descriptions from parents and from teachers, for boys and for girls, and for three separate age groups. First, seven separate forced seven-factor principal component analyses were computed for each specific subsample. Subsequently, Tucker's ϕ matrices were computed between the seven factors within the overall sample and the seven factors within each specific factor solution. Next, the factor of a specific subsample with the highest Tucker's ϕ congruence coefficient was similarly labeled as the corresponding factor in the overall sample. When all φ coefficients of a factor within the subsample remained below .60, such a factor was not labeled with one of the seven factor labels of the overall sample. In those instances a factor was labeled according to its item content (e.g., Irritability), or received a number code according to the factor number in the factor solution of the specific subsample. The findings of the factor comparisons are reported in Table 15.3.

The factor and item orders are the same as in Table 15.2. The seven-factor solution within the overall sample is reported in the far left Column 1, using a letter code for each factor with a plus or minus sign for a negative or positive loading of an item on a factor. A high loading (equal or higher than .35) on the second highest loading factor is also reported using a letter and plus–minus code. High loadings on a third or a fourth factor were rare and are not reported. In all seven comparisons of the overall sample with the seven specific subsamples (see Table 15.3, Columns 2–8) Agreeableness had the highest average congruence (.99), followed by Emotional Stability (.97), Conscientiousness (.94), and Extraversion (.90). Of the FFM factors, Openness had the lowest average congruence (.85), lower than Motor Activity (.88). Dependency was the least stable factor of all seven (.83).

Parents' and Teachers' NCCQ Descriptions (Columns 7 and 8)

Within the teachers' subsample the seven-factor solution of the overall sample emerged quite clearly. The percentage of explained variance of the seven-factor solution for teachers (47.6%) was considerably higher than for parents (32.9%; see bottom line Table 15.3). The Tucker's φ congruence coefficients across the seven corresponding factors ranged for teachers from .91 (for Openness) to .99 (for Agreeableness) and averaged .96, indicating high congruence of the factor solution of the teachers' subsample with the overall sample. A somewhat lower congruence with factors within the overall sample was found for six out of seven factors within the parental subsample. For these six factors φ coefficients ranged from .79 (for Openness) to .98 (for Emotional Stability) and averaged .90. The seventh factor in the parental sample was related to Dependency (Tucker's φ = −.69) as well as to Openness (Tucker's φ = .68) in the overall sample. Therefore, a second factor in the parental solution in Table 15.3 (Column 7) was related to Openness and was indicated as O_2. Summarizing, teachers seem to be more proficient in describing children's personality than parents. As professionals, teachers more often than parents, provide behavior and personality descriptions of children. In general, they are better trained than parents, having more experience in describing children's behavior and personality and have had exposure to many more and to a greater diversity of children than parents. Parents have a broader view on Openness. Included in this parental factor are a number of items referring to social and relational skills of children: for example, *Gets along well with other children*; *Arouses liking in adults*; *Genuine and close*

TABLE 15.3
Forced Seven-Factor Solutions in Several Samples

	Overall Sample (1)	Gender		Subsamples from Overall Sample				Rater			Early-Adolescent Sample[e]			
				Age Group							Rater			
		Boys (2)	Girls (3)	< 7.0[b] (4)	7.0–11.5 (5)	11.5 < (6)	Parent (7)	Teacher (8)	Parent (9)	Teacher (10)	Peer (11)	Self (12)
Item Number and Description[a]												
Factor 1: Agreeableness												
2 Is considerate of other children	A+[c]	A+	A+	A+	A+	A+	A+	A+	A+	A+	A+	A_1+A_2+
6 Is helpful and cooperative	A+	A+	A+	A+	A+	A+	A+	A+	A+	A+	A+	.
3 Is warm and responsive	A+	A+	A+	A+	A+	A+	A+	A+	A+	A+	.	A_2+
76 Can be trusted, is dependable	A+	A+	A+	A+	A+	A+	A+	A+	A+	A+	A+	A_1+
15 Shows concern for moral issues	A+	A+	A+	A+	A+	A+	A+	A+	A+	A+	A+	A_2+A_1+
31 Recognizes feelings of others	A+	A+	A+	A+	A+	A+	A+	A+	A+	A+	A+	5–
11 Attempts to transfer blame to others	A–	A–	A–	A–	A–	A–	A–	A–	A–5–	A–	A–	$A_1–A_2–$
32 Tends to give, lend, and share	A+	A+	A+	A+	A+	A+	A+	A+	A+	A+	A+	.
19 Open and straightforward	A+	A+	A+	A+	A+	A+	A+	A+	A+	A+	A+	A_1+
29 Protective of others	A+	A+	A+	A+	A+	A+	A+	A+	A+	A+	A+	E+
56 Jealous and envious of others	A–	A–	A–	A–	A–	A–	A–	A–	A–	A–	A–	.
4 Gets along well with other children	A+O+	A+	A+O+	A+O+	A+	A+M+	O_1+	A+	5+	A+	O+*A+	A_2+E+
20 Tries to take advantage of others	A–	A–	A–	A–	A–	A–	A–	A–	A–	A–	A–	.
85 Aggressive (physically or verbally)	A–	A–	A–	A–M+*	A–	A–	A–	A+E–	A–	A–	A–	$A_1–$
62 Obedient and compliant	A+	A+	A+E–	A+M–*	A+	A+	A+	A+E–	7+A+	A+E–	A+	A_1+
90 Is stubborn	A–	A–	A–	A–	A–	A–	A–	A–	A–	A–	A–	$A_1–$
55 Afraid of being deprived	A–	A–	A–	I+A–	A–	A–	A–	A–	A–	A–E+	A–	$A_1–$
95 Overreacts to minor frustrations	A+O+	A+	A+	O+A+	A+	A+	O_1+	A+	.	A+	A+	E+
30 Arouses liking in adults	A–	A–	A–	A–	A–	A–	.	A–	5–	A–	A–	$A_1–$
80 Teases other children	A+C+	A+	A+C+	A+I–	A+	A+C+	C+A+	A+	C+	A+	A+	A_1+
25 Uses and responds to reason	A+	A+	A+	O+A+	A+	A+	O_1+	A+	A+5+	A+	A+O+*	A_2+E+
9 Genuine and close relationships												

(Continued)

TABLE 15.3
(Continued)

	Overall Sample (1)	Subsamples from Overall Sample							Early-Adolescent Sample[e]			
		Gender		Age Group			Rater		Rater			
		Boys (2)	Girls (3)	< 7.0[b] (4)	7.0–11.5 (5)	11.5 < (6)	Parent (7)	Teacher (8)	Parent (9)	Teacher (10)	Peer (11)	Self (12)
Item Number and Description[a]												
93 Behaves in a dominating manner	A–	A–	A–E+	A–S+	A–	A–	.	A–E+	A–	A–	A–	A_1–
13 Generally stretches limits	A–	A–	A–	A–	A–	A–	A–	A–	.	A–	A–	A_1–
10 Transient interpersonal relations	A–	A–	A–	0–	A–	A–	.	A–	A–	A–	A–	A_2–E–
61 Tends to be judgmental of others	A–	A–	A–E+	A–	A–	A–	0_1–	A–E+	0–	A–	S+	.
78 Easily offended	A–O–	A–	A–	0–A–	A–	A–S–	0_1–	A–	.	A–D+	A–	A_2–
21 Tries to be the center of attention	A–	A–	E+A–	D+A–	A–	A–	.	A–E+	A–	A–D+	A–	.
91 Inappropriate in emotive behavior	A–	A–	A–	0–	A–	A–	E–	A–	E–	A–	2–	.
81 Can admit to own negative feelings	A+	A+	A+	S+	S+	A+	.	A+	A+	A+D–	.	5–
57 Tends to exaggerate mishaps	A–	A–	1+	1+	A–	A–	.	A–	.	A–E+	A–	A_2–
54 Emotionally labile	A–	A–	.	.	A–	A–	.	A–S–	.	A–C–	.	.
Factor 2: Emotional Stability												
88 Self-reliant, confident	S+	S+	S+	S+	S+	S+C+	S+	S+	S+C+	S+	S+	S+
23 Fearful, anxious	S–	S–	S–	S–	S–	S–	S–	S–E–	S–	0–E–	S–	S–M–
46 Tends to go to pieces under stress	S–	S–	S–	S–	S–	S–	S–	S–	S–	S–	.	S–
24 Tends to brood, ruminate, or worry	S–	S–	S–	S–	S–	S–	S–	S–	S–	S–0–	S–	S–
60 Anxious in unpredictable situations	S–	S–	S–	S–	S–	S+E+	S–	S+E+	S–	E+S+	S–	S–
82 Self-assertive	S+	S+	E+S+	S+	S+	S+	S+	S+	7–S+	S+A+	S+	S+
64 Calm and relaxed, easygoing	S+	S+	S+	M–*	S–	S–	S+	S+	S+	0–S–	A+	S–
77 Appears to feel unworthy	S–	S–	S–	S–O–	S–	S–	S–O_1–	S–	S–	E–O–	.	S–
35 Inhibited and constricted	S–E–	S–	E–S–	S–O–	E–S–	E–S–	S–E–	E–S–	E–	S–	6+	S–
72 Has a readiness to feel guilty	S–	S–	S–	S–	S–	S–	S–	S–	S–	S–	S–	S–
50 Bodily symptoms from stress	S–	S–	S–	S–	S–	S–	S–	S–	S–	S–	.	S–
53 Indecisive, vacillating	S–E–	S–	C–S–	S–C–	C–E–	E–C–	S–	S–C–	E–7+	0–S–	.	C–*
43 Recoups after stressful experiences	S+	S+	S+	.	S+	S+	.	S+	.	S+	S+	.

83 Seeks to be independent	S+	S+	.	S+	S+	S+	S+	S+	C+	S+	6−	C+*
33 Cries easily	S−	S−	I+	I+	S−	.	.	S−	S−	S−	S−	A₂−
39 Immobilized under stress	S−	S−	S−	S−C−	.	S−	S−	E−	.	E−	.	.
Factor 3: Conscientiousness												
66 Attentive, able to concentrate	C+	C+	C+	C+M−*	C+	C+	C+	C+A+	C+	C+A+	C+A+	C+*
47 Performance standards for self high	C+	C+	C+	C+	C+	C+	C+	C+A+	C+	C+A+	.	C+*
67 Planful, thinks ahead	C+	C+	C+	M−* C+	C+	C+	C+	C+A+	C+	C+A+	A+	C+*
89 Competent, skillful	C+	C+	C+	C+	C+	C+	C+	C+O+	C+	C+O+	.	.
68 High intellectual capacity	C+O+	C+O+	C+	C+	C+	C+	C+	C+S+	C+S+	O+	6−	C+*S+
99 Is reflective	C+E−	C+M−	E−C+	M−*	C+A+	C+	C+	E−C+	C+E−	E−A+	A+	C+*
40 Is curious and exploring	C+	C+O+	C+	C+S+	O+C+	.	C+	C+O+	C+E+	O+C+	.	.
Factor 4: Openness												
92 Physically attractive, good-looking	O+	O+	O+	O+	.	O+	.	7+S+	O+	O+*	O+*	E+
97 Active fantasy life	O+	O+	D−	.	O+	O+	O₂+	O+	O+	O+	2+	.
42 Interesting and arresting child	O+	O+	O+	O+	O+	O+	O₂+	S+O+	S+O+	O+	2+	.
96 Creative	O+D−	O+	D−	C+	O+	O+	O₂+	O+	O+	O+	2+	A₂+
79 Suspicious of others	O−A−	A−O−	A−O−	A−O−	A−	A−	O₁−	A−O−	A−	A−	A−	5−
73 Responds to humor	O+	O+	.	O+	O+	O+	.	O+	S+	O+A+	2+	M+
36 Resourceful in initiating activities	O+	O+	.	C+O+	C+O+	O+	O₂+	O+	O+E+	O+	2+	E+
5 Admired and sought by other children	O+	O+	O+	O+	O+	M+	O₁+	O+	5+	A+	O+*	A₂+
75 Cheerful	O+A+	A+S+	O+	O+	A+	A+	O₁+	A+	.	A+S+	.	.
Factor 5: Extraversion												
8 Keeps thoughts and feelings to self	E−	E−	E−	.	E−	E−	E−	E−	E−	E−	O−*	E−
98 Shy and reserved	E−	E−S−	E−	S−M−*	E−	E−	E−	E−	E−	E−M−*	.	M−E−
58 Emotionally expressive	E+	E+	E+	S+	E+	E+	E+	E+	A+	E+	.	5−
18 Expresses negative feelings openly	E+S+	S+E+	E+	S+	E+S+	E+	S+	E+	E+	E+	.	5−
86 Likes to be by him/herself	E−M−	M−E−	E−	D−M−*	E−M−	M−	.	E−M−	E−	E−M−A+	.	E−
44 Tends to yield and give in	E−	E−	E−	S−	E−A+	E−	.	E−A+	.	E−A−	.	.
69 Verbally fluent	E+	O+S+	S+E+	C+S+	E+	E+	S−	E+O+	E+	E+O+	O+*	E+
45 Withdraws under stress	E−	.	E−	S−	E−	E−	E+	E−M−*	E−	E−M−*	O−*	E−
84 Is a talkative child	E+	.	E+	M+*	E+	E+	.	E+A−	E+	E+A−	A−	A₁−

(Continued)

307

TABLE 15.3
(Continued)

	Overall Sample (1)	Subsamples from Overall Sample							Early-Adolescent Sample[e]			
		Gender		Age Group			Rater			Rater		
		Boys (2)	Girls (3)	< 7.0[b] (4)	7.0–11.5 (5)	11.5 < (6)	Parent (7)	Teacher (8)	Parent (9)	Teacher (10)	Peer (11)	Self (12)
Item Number and Description[a]												
Factor 6: Motor Activity												
26 Physically active	M+	M+	O+	M+*	M+	M+	M+O$_1$+	M+	5+	M+*	2+	M+
28 Vital, energetic, lively	M+O+	M+	O+E+	M+*O+	M+	M+O+*	M+O$_1$+	M+	E+5+	M+*E+	2+	M+
52 Physically cautious	M–	M–	O–E–	M–*	M–	M–	M–	M–	E–	M–*	.	.
51 Agile and well coordinated	M+	M+	O+	I–O+	M+	M+	M+O$_1$+	M+	5+	M+*	2+	M+
63 Rapid personal tempo	M+	M+C+	I–	.	C+M+	M+	M+	C+M+	.	C+	C+	.
37 Competitive	M+	C+	.	D+	C+M+	M+	M+	C+M+	.	C+	7–	A$_1$–
34 Is restless and fidgety	M+	M+	S–	M+*	A–M+	S–	C–	M+S–	S–	M+*A–	.	C–*
70 Daydreams, gets lost in reverie	M–C–	C–M–	C–	.	C–	M–C–	M–	C–	E–	C–	C–	.
Factor 7: Dependency												
14 Eager to please	D+	D+	D+	D+	D+	D+	O$_2$–	D+	.	D+	7–	.
48 Others sought to affirm self worth	D+	D+	D+	D+	D+	D+	.	D+	.	D+	7–	.
22 Manipulates others by ingratiation	D+A–	D+	A–D+	C–	D+	.	.	D+A–	C–	D+A–	2–	.
38 Unusual thought processes	D–	.	D–	D–	A–	.	.	.	E–	A–S–	A–	.
87 Tends to imitate those admired	D+	D+	.	.	D+	.	.	D+	.	D+	.	.
Items not in Overall Sample Factor Solution[d]												
7 Seeks physical contact with others	.	.	I+	.	.	.	.	.	.	E+	.	.
65 Unable to delay gratification	.	.	.	I+	.	A–	A–	A–	A–	A–	A–	A$_1$–
1 Prefers non-verbal communication	.	.	.	.	E–	.	E–	.	.	C–	.	.

Item												
94 Tends to be sulky or whiny	.	.	.	.	.	.	.	.	.	.	.	S–
41 Persistent, does not give up	.	.	I+A–	.	.	.	A–	.	.	.	.	.
71 Looks to adults for help	.	.	.	I+	S–	S–	.	S–	S–	S–A–	S–	.
74 Becomes involved in what (s)he does	.	.	D+	C–	C+	C+	.	C+	7–	C+	.	.
100 Easily victimized by other children	.	.	.	C+	D+	D+	.	.	7+	D+	.	.
12 Immature behavior under stress	A–	.	O–	O–	.	.	.	.	.	A+C+	.	A_2–
49 Shows specific mannerisms	.	.	.	I+	A–	M–	O_1–	A–	5–	A–	.	.
59 Neat and orderly in dress	.	.	.	.	S–	.	.	S–	C–	S–	S–2–	.
16 Proud of own accomplishments	.	M+	.	M+	.	.	.	.	.	.	C–	.
17 Behaves in a sex-typed manner	M+	.	.	.	.	.	C+	C+	.	A+M–*	A+	A_1+
27 Visibly deviant from peers	.	D+	.	.	.	.	.	.	.	S+	5+	.
	.	O–	.	.	.	.	.	.	.	.	.	.
Number of Q-descriptions	1836	1149	687	636	626	574	937	899	186	134	242	137
% of Variance Explained by Solution	40.5	41.4	39.7	41.0	43.0	39.7	32.9	47.6	35.9	56.9	31.6	29.3

[a] Factors are reported in the order of the factor extraction in the factor solution in the overall sample. Within factors, items are sorted according to descending absolute factor loadings.

[b] Age in years.

[c] Factor codes (letter codes) are assigned according to the factor solution in the overall sample:
- Meaning of letters: A, A_1, A_2: Agreeableness; S: Emotional Stability; C: Conscientiousness; O, O_1: Openness; O_2: Openness & Dependency; E: Extraversion; M: Motor Activity; D: Dependency; I: Irritability and Immaturity.
- Codes are printed for items with loadings $\geq |0.35|$. Maximally two highest loading factors are coded on an item. Dots denote loadings $< |0.35|$ on all seven factors.
- Letter codes are assigned to factors with a congruence (Tucker's ϕ) > $|0.60|$ with one or more factors in the overall solution.
 In self-descriptions letter codes are assigned to factors with highest congruence with factor within overall sample.
 The rank-number of the factor of the concerning solution is assigned when no relation was found with any factor within the overall sample.
- Codes printed in boldface correspond with the same factor within the overall sample.
- Meaning of other codes: + Denotes a positive factor loading, – denotes a negative loading.
*Afterwards inverted sign of code (Tucker's ϕ with corresponding factor in overall sample was negative)

[d] Loadings $< |0.35|$ on all seven factors in overall sample

[e] Total number of Q-descriptions in early-adolescent sample: 794.

relationships; *Transient interpersonal relations* (reversed); and *Easily offended* (reversed).

Gender of Child (Columns 2 and 3)

The seven-factors solution within the subsample of boys is most similar to the overall seven-factors solution. For boys, the Tucker's φ coefficients across the seven corresponding factors ranged from .93 (for Dependency) to .99 (for Agreeableness), and averaged .97. For girls, the Motor Activity factor was not differentiated from Openness. In addition, some Openness items for girls intersected with negative Dependency. For girls, the six factors corresponding with factors within the overall sample reached φ coefficients ranging from .82 (for Openness) to .99 (for Agreeableness), and averaged .93. The higher average congruence for boys may result from the much larger number of NCCQ descriptions of boys in the overall sample. In Study 6 only boys were involved. Also the content of some factors was fairly different for boys and girls. The most striking difference was the absence of a Motor Activity factor in girls. Openness also had a different content. Four out of eight Motor Activity items within the overall sample loaded in the factor solution for girls on Openness (i.e., *Physically active*; *Vital, energetic, lively*; *Physically cautious* (reversed); and *Agile and well coordinated*). In contrast, some other items did not load on Openness (e.g., *Active fantasy life*; *Creative*; and *Resourceful in initiating activities*). These latter items were negatively related to Dependency.

Thus, in boys items with high loadings on Openness emphasized high intellectual skills, verbal fluency, creativity, and fantasy as well as social attractiveness. In girls Openness items referred to a broader content, that is, motor activity and motor coordination, social cognitive and social relational capacities and skills, as well as social and physical attractiveness. Imagination, fantasy, and resourcefulness was the opposite of Dependency in girls, that is, a tendency to seek support and affirmation from others. In addition, the girl seventh factor referred to irritability and immature behavior (cf. Robins, John, & Caspi, chap. 14 in this vol.) with high loading items as *Tends to exaggerate mishaps*; *Cries easily*; *Rapid personal tempo* (reversed); *Seeks physical contact with others*; and *Tends to be sulky or whiny*.

Age Differences (Columns 4, 5, and 6)

The overall sample was divided into three age groups: kindergarten age from 3.0 to 7.0 years of age middle childhood from ages 7.1 to 11.6 years; and adolescence from 11.7 to 17.0 years. For the youngest age group (see Column 4), the average congruence with the overall sample was the lowest (.82) and ranged from .66 (for Extraversion) to .89 (for Agreeableness). In this age group the largest number of items (24 items) had a high loading (equal or higher than .35) on a second factor. Many items had ambiguous or undifferentiated meanings in terms of the overall seven factors. Further, the Extraversion factor was not clearly differentiated from the Emotional Stability factor. The following six out of nine items of the Extraversion factor in the overall sample had a high loading on Emotional Stability in this young age group: *Shy and reserved* (reversed); *Emotionally expressive*; *Expresses negative feelings openly*; *Tends to yield and give in* (reversed); *Verbally fluent*; and *Withdraws under stress* (reversed). At this age, the Motor Activity factor had a diverse content. There were a few specific motor activity items: *Physically active*; *Vital, energetic, lively*; *Physically cautious* (reversed); and *Is restless and fidgety*. The factor also contained items related with (low) Conscientiousness: *Attentive, able to concentrate* (reversed); *Planful, thinks ahead* (reversed); and *Is reflective* (reversed) as well as items concerning low impulse control: *Aggressive*; *Obedient and compliant* (reversed); *Calm and relaxed, easy-going* (reversed); *Shy and reserved* (reversed); *Likes to be by him/herself* (reversed); and *Is a talkative child*. Finally, a sixth factor, unrelated to any of the overall seven factors was obtained and concerned irritability and immaturity (cf. Robins et al., chap. 14 in this vol.).

The middle childhood subsample (see Column 5) was most congruent with the overall sample. The ϕ coefficients with the corresponding factors within the overall sample ranged from .81 (for Openness) to .99 (for Agreeableness), and averaged .93. On the Openness factor the more social items were no longer high loaders (equal or higher than .35): items such as *Physically attractive, good-looking*; *Suspicious of others* (reversed); *Admired, sought out by other children*; and *Cheerful*, while the item *Is curious and exploring* was added to this factor. Thus, the item content of the Openness factor at this age was more in agreement with the content of the adult Openness factor (cf. Goldberg, 1992).

In adolescence (see Column 6) the factor structure was somewhat less congruent with the overall sample than in middle childhood. ϕ coefficients ranged from .73 (for Openness) to .99 (for Agreeableness), and averaged .90. As in middle childhood the content of the Openness items was more in agreement with the content of the adult Openness factor.

Different Observers in Early Adolescence (Columns 9–12)

To determine the factor structure of NCCQ descriptions within each subsample of parents, teachers, best friends, as well as self descriptions, forced seven-factor varimax-rotated, principal component solutions were compared to the seven-factor solution for the overall sample. The factor analysis of teachers' NCCQ descriptions explained the highest percentage of variance (56.9%) and those for best friends and for self the lowest percentages (31.6% and 29.3%, respectively; see bottom line Table 15.3).

Within the parental NCCQ descriptions, five factors revealed substantial congruence across six factors within the overall sample. They were Agreeableness (ϕ = .93), Conscientiousness (ϕ = .92), Emotional Stability (ϕ = .89), Extraversion (ϕs with Extraversion and Motor Activity in the overall sample were .80 and

.67, respectively), and Openness ($\phi = .62$). As Column 9 shows, in addition to the majority of the Extraversion items, items of Factor 5 loaded high on Extraversion (e.g., the motor activity items *Vital, energetic, lively*; *Physically cautious*; and *Daydreams, gets lost in reverie* (reversed); but also *Admired and sought by other children*; and *Easily victimized by other children* (reversed). For parents, motor activity and sociability were also highly related to Extraversion.

For the subsample of teacher NCCQ descriptions of early adolescents two forced varimax-rotated, seven-factor principal component analyses were computed. The first analysis was based on 229 separate NCCQ descriptions, that is, 80 NCCQ descriptions of 80 12-year-olds in Study 4 and 149 NCCQ descriptions of 54 14-year-olds in Study 5. This seven-factor solution explained 51.7% of the variance, but the factors Extraversion, Conscientiousness, Openness, and Motor Activity were not well differentiated. The reason for the low differentiation among factors may be that in high school the three NCCQ descriptions were done by teachers each of whom taught a different subject matter, each for only a few hours per week. Therefore, they might not be acquainted well enough with the adolescent to give differentiated descriptions. In contrast, the 12-year-olds were all in elementary school and each had one or two teachers who knew them well.

The second forced seven-factor principal component analysis was computed on 134 NCCQ descriptions. For 80 children in sixth grade the NCCQ description was given by their teacher. For the 54 14-year-old children, per subject mean scores per item over two or three teachers were computed. These mean scores were used in the factor analysis. This second factor analysis is reported in Table 15.3, Column 10. This solution explained 56.9% of the variance. The coefficients of congruence of the seven factors with the corresponding factors within the overall sample ranged from .77 (for Openness) to .98 (for Agreeableness), and averaged .86. In this sample many items had high loadings on more than one factor. Most items, however, had their highest loading on the same factor as in the overall sample. Deviant items often had their highest loading on a factor that was more in agreement with the content of the factor that was typical for adults: for example, *Self-assertive* and *Inhibited and constricted* (reversed) on Extraversion; *High intellectual capacity* and *Is curious and exploring* on Openness; and *Suspicious of others* (reversed), *Admired and sought by other children*; and *Cheerful* on Agreeableness. In teachers' views, early adolescents' Openness concerned high intellectual capacities, curiosity, fantasy, creativity, imagination, resourcefulness, and verbal fluency, and, negatively, some aspects of Neuroticism (e.g., anxiety, low self-esteem, and indecisiveness). In addition to the Big Five factors, teachers also distinguished Motor Activity and Dependency in early adolescents. Motor Activity is mainly restricted to physical activity, motor coordination, and, negatively, to aspects of Introversion such as shyness, self isolation, and withdrawal.

In NCCQ descriptions by best friends, four factors have a substantial congruence with factors in the overall sample. They are Agreeableness ($\phi = .93$), Emotional Stability ($\phi = .85$), Conscientiousness ($\phi = .68$) and Openness ($\phi =$

−.63). Extraversion is missing in best friends' person descriptions. In addition, a factor (coded as Factor 2, Column 11) had its highest congruence ($\phi = .59$) with Motor Activity, but also with Openness ($\phi = .57$). This factor combined items related to Motor Activity with Openness. Apparently, best friends do not differentiate between Motor Activity and Openness. A sixth and seventh factor each had only three high loading items.

Factor analysis of the adolescents' NCCQ self descriptions explained the lowest percentage of variance—29.3%. ϕ coefficients also were low but the factors were meaningfully related to the factors within the overall sample. Three factors had a substantial congruence with factors in the overall sample. They are Agreeableness (coded as A_1, $\phi = .74$), Emotional Stability ($\phi = .75$), and Conscientiousness ($\phi = .71$). An additional factor (coded as A_2) also had a high congruence score with Agreeableness ($\phi = .58$) and contrasted genuine and dependable relationships versus victimization by other children and irritability and immaturity. Another factor (coded as E) had the highest ϕ (.47) with Extraversion in the overall sample and contrasted sociability, social and physical attractiveness, and verbal fluency versus social withdrawal. Of the two residual factors one (Column 12, Factor 7) was related to Motor Activity ($\phi = .51$), whereas the other had no congruence relation with factors within the overall sample.

To summarize, although, in comparison to the other specific factor solutions, factors in self descriptions have lower coefficients of congruence with factors within the overall sample, the item content of five out of seven factors could be related to four of the five Big Five factors: Agreeableness, Emotional Stability, Conscientiousness, and Extraversion. None of the factors was clearly related to Openness. An additional factor was related to Motor Activity.

DISCUSSION

The first five principal components in factor analyses of NCCQ descriptions by teachers and parents of Dutch children and adolescents were clearly identifiable as the Big Five personality factors. Agreeableness appeared to be the most robust personality dimension followed by Emotional Stability. Conscientiousness and Extraversion were somewhat less robust and more sample and observer dependent. Openness was the least consistent factor. Openness in the overall sample and in the subsamples of girls, of youngest children, and in descriptions of parents contained a much broader range of items, including motor activity and/or social and physical attractiveness items. In middle childhood and adolescence, in the subsample of boys and in descriptions by teachers, the item content of Openness was much more oriented toward high intellectual capacities, curiosity, imagination, fantasy and creativity, resourcefulness and a sense of humor, clearly similar to the characteristics describing adult Openness.

The differences in robustness may be partly due to the number of relevant items for each factor that is represented in the CCQ. Also in the general language more person descriptors may be available for personality dimensions such as Agreeableness and Emotional Stability, whereas relatively few person descriptors are available for Openness (cf. Hofstee & De Raad, 1991; Hofstee, De Raad, & Goldberg, 1992).

Not all five factors contained positive as well as negative items. For Agreeableness and Extraversion both positive and negative items were equally represented. These factors were clearly bipolar in the CCQ. Emotional Stability was mainly determined by negative items and might be better indicated as Emotional Instability or Neuroticism. Conscientiousness and Openness mainly contained positive items. The unipolarity of Openness was in accordance with general language. Low Openness in general language is qualified as *un*intelligent, *un*imaginative, *un*inquisitive, *un*creative, and so forth (cf. Goldberg, 1992). Negative Conscientiousness items referring to person characteristics as disorganized, negligent, careless, and lazy (cf. Goldberg, 1992) seemed to be lacking in the CCQ or did not form a negative pole of the Conscientiousness factor.

The Big Five factors of Agreeableness and Emotional Stability were robust across age levels from preschool into adolescence, across gender of child, and across observers; other Big Five factors were more age, gender, or observer specific. In some subsamples, however, even robust factors had fewer high loading marker items, for example, Agreeableness in the parental subsample and Emotional Stability in girls. Some other factors were undifferentiated in some subsamples. For example, in the youngest age group Extraversion was undifferentiated from Emotional Stability and the Openness factor had a greater diversity, encompassing social cognition and social skills, social and physical attractiveness, and motor coordination. These skills were also more characteristic of Openness in girls, whereas the more usual characteristics typified Openness for boys.

Compared to adult person descriptions of children and adolescents, adolescent peer and self descriptions fitting the FFM were less clearly evident. Some factors could not be traced back to the FFM and coefficients of congruence were generally lower. The factors of Agreeableness, Emotional Stability, and Conscientiousness, however, were clearly identifiable in self and peer descriptions. In peer descriptions the Openness factor could also be found, and in self descriptions traces of Extraversion were present, especially sociability and social and physical attractiveness versus social withdrawal.

In addition to the Big Five factors, NCCQ descriptions provided several other factors. The most conspicuous factor was Motor Activity. Two more factors were Irritability and Dependency. Some authors (e.g., Eaton, chap. 9 in this vol.; Robins et al., chap. 14 in this vol.) claim that motor activity in childhood is linked with energetic elements in Extraversion in later life. Indeed, the Motor Activity factor was clearly present in our data in a changing composition over age. Gender differences in Motor Activity were also very obvious, as well as differences in emphasis on motor activity in person descriptions of different types of observers. In our youngest age group three facets of motor behavior were represented in the Motor Activity factor: specific physical and motor activity versus physical cautiousness; facets of low conscientiousness, such as low levels of concentration and low planful and reflective behavior versus talkativeness, hyperactivity, and restlessness; as well as low impulse control—aggressive versus obedient, shy, and reserved behavior. These three facets seemed clearly related to later Extraversion, Conscientiousness, and Emotional Stability. In middle childhood and adolescence, Motor Activity was more specifically displayed in motor activity in groups, including motor coordination and restlessness versus daydreaming and a tendency to isolate. At all ages, however, motor activity was much more relevant for boys than for girls. Compared to boys, girls' motor activity items were related to the broader content of Openness, including more social skills as well as physical and social attractiveness. In the early adolescent subsample, in parent and teacher descriptions most motor activity items were positioned in Extraversion, indicating that these items eventually may be considered as part of this factor.

The Dependency and Irritability and Immaturity factors tended to be sample and/or observer specific. The Dependency factor gradually disappeared over age and consisted of only two high loading items in adolescence. In teachers' views even at early adolescence, Dependency remained, however, an essential component in their description of pupil personality. The Irritability and Immaturity factor had a similar content as the same factor in Robins et al. (chap. 14 in this vol.). In contrast to their findings, however, this factor in our data seemed less robust, being more age and gender specific, than Dependency. Irritability and Immaturity was most characteristic of our youngest age group and more characteristic of girls.

For four of the five factors, similarity was found between our factors and the Big Five categories in the American common language CCQ as determined by Robins et al. (chap. 14 in this vol.). Openness was the exception. Eleven of the 13 Agreeableness items selected by Robins et al. were represented in our Agreeableness factor. The other two items—*Eager to please* and *Manipulates others by ingratiation*—were part of our Dependency factor. The latter item had a secondary loading (.37) on Agreeableness. Eight out of 10 Emotional Stability items were in the same factor. The item *Is easily offended* loaded on our Agreeableness factor, and the item *Others sought to affirm self worth*, was part of our Dependency factor. Five of our seven Conscientiousness items were also considered as such by Robins et al. They place the two missing items loading on our Conscientiousness factor, *Is curious and exploring* and *High intellectual capacity*, with the Openness factor. In several of our subsamples these items actually loaded on the Openness factor. The other four items identified by Robins et al. as belonging to the Conscientiousness category loaded on a diversity of our factors. The item *Can be trusted, is dependable* had a high loading on Agreeableness. The item *Resourceful in initiating activities* loaded on Openness. Two more items, *Persistent, does not give up*, and *Neat and orderly in dress* remained below the critical loading of .35 in the overall sample, but had their highest loading on Conscientiousness (.33 and .26, respectively). Five of our nine Extraversion items were also marked on this factor by Robins et al. Of the other four Extraversion items of Robins et al., the item *Inhibited and constricted* had a secondary high loading on Extraversion (–.45); two items—*Vital, energetic, lively,* and *Rapid personal tempo*—loaded high on Motor Activity; the item *Prefers nonverbal communication* had its highest—but below-criterion—loading on Extraversion (–.34). Only two out of seven Openness items of Robins et al. were represented in our Openness factor. Our Openness factor was the least consistent of all our Big Five factors and contained social cognitive capacities and physical and social attractiveness items in addition to items considered regular for this factor in adult studies. Reasons for the discrepancies between our results and those of Robins et al. may be deviations in our translation of the American CCQ version as well as differences between the common language CCQ (Robins et al., chap. 14 in this vol.) and the original CCQ. In addition, differences in the age and sex composition of the samples as well as differences in observers and cultural fluctuations may cause different results.

Finally, a few warnings are necessary. Although we had a large overall sample of NCCQ descriptions, in some respects the sample was not very well balanced. Our sample contained nearly twice as many boys as girls and nearly the same ratio of NCCQ descriptions of boys and girls. Also the numbers of parents and teachers were not precisely balanced over age groups and gender of child. The differences in factor solutions between specific subsamples underscore the importance of a large balanced sample of CCQ descriptions. Therefore, some of our findings may be partly determined by the composition of our sample.

ACKNOWLEDGMENTS

We are grateful to Marcel van Aken, Toon Cillessen, Eric Siebenheller, Marinus H. van IJzendoorn and co-workers, for making available NCCQ descriptions of their subjects. Part of the data were collected in a study granted by the Foundation for Educational Research (SVO BS560) to the first author and to J. M. A. Riksen-Walraven and in a study granted by the Netherlands Organization for Scientific Research (NWO-Psychon project 560-263-013).

An earlier version of this chapter was presented at the Symposium "The Development of the Structure of Temperament and Personality from Infancy to Adulthood," NIAS, Wassenaar, The Netherlands, June 17–20, 1991.

REFERENCES

Asendorpf, J. B., & van Aken, M. A. G. (1991). Correlates of the temporal consistency of personality patterns in childhood. *Journal of Personality, 59*, 689–703.

Bem, D. J., & Funder, D. C. (1978). Predicting more of the people more of the time: Assessing the personality of situations. *Psychological Review, 95*, 485–501.

Block, J. (1961/1978). *The Q-sort method in personality assessment and psychiatric research.* Palo Alto, CA: Consulting Psychologists Press.

Block, J. (1971). *Lives through time.* Berkeley, CA: Brancroft Books.

Block, J. H., & Block, J. (1980). The role of ego-control and ego-resiliency in the organization of behavior. In W. A. Collins (Ed.), Development of cognition, affect, and social relations. *Minnesota Symposia on child psychology* (Vol. 13, pp. 39–101). Hillsdale, NJ: Lawrence Erlbaum Associates.

Block, J., Gjerde, P. F., & Block, J. H. (1991). Personality antecedents of depressive tendencies in 18-year-olds: A prospective study. *Journal of Personality and Social Psychology, 60,* 726–738.

Brokken, F. B. (1978). *The language of personality.* Unpublished doctoral dissertation, University of Groningen, The Netherlands.

Cillessen, A. H. N. (1991). *The self-perpetuating nature of children's peer relationships.* Unpublished doctoral dissertation, University of Nijmegen, The Netherlands.

De Raad, B. (1991, June 17–20). *Personality language in different word classes (adjectives, verbs, and nouns) and their structuring according to the principles of the AB5C algorithm.* Paper presented at the Symposium "The Development of the Structure of Temperament and Personality From Infancy to Adulthood," Wassenaar.

Digman, J. M. (1989). Five robust trait dimensions: Development, stability, and utility. *Journal of Personality, 57,* 195–214.

Digman, J. M., & Inouye, J. (1986). Further specification of the five robust factors of personality. *Journal of Personality and Social Psychology, 50,* 116–123.

Funder, D. C., & Dobroth, K. M. (1987). Differences between traits: Properties associated with interjudge agreement. *Journal of Personality and Social Psychology, 52,* 409–418.

Goldberg, L. R. (1990). An alternative "Description of Personality": The Big-Five factor structure. *Journal of Personality and Social Psychology, 59,* 1216–1229.

Goldberg, L. R. (1992). The development of markers for the Big-Five factor structure. *Psychological Assessment, 4,* 26–42.

Harman, H. H. (1967). *Modern factor analysis* (2nd ed.). Chicago: University of Chicago Press.

Haselager, G. (1988). *Het appèl van de peer. Een longitudinaal onderzoek* [A longitudinal study on peer relations]. Unpublished masters thesis, Katholieke Universiteit, Nijmegen.

Hofstee, W. K. B., & De Raad, B. (1991). Persoonlijkheidsstructuur: De AB5C-taxonomie van Nederlandse eigenschapstermen [Personality structure: The AB5C-taxonomy of Dutch trait adjectives]. *Nederlands Tijdschrift voor de Psychologie, 46,* 262–274.

Hofstee, W. K. B., De Raad, B., & Goldberg, L. R. (1992). Integration of the Big Five and circumplex approaches to trait structure. *Journal of Personality and Social Psychology, 63,* 146–163.

Jansen, I. I., & van Aken, M. A. G. (1991). Depressieve gedragskenmerken bij onpopulaire kinderen [Depressive symptoms in unpopular children]. *Tijdschrift voor Orthopedagogiek, 30,* 123–136.

John, O. P., Goldberg, L. R., & Angleitner, A. (1984). Better than the alphabet: Taxonomies of personality-descriptive terms in English, Dutch, and German. In H. C. J. Bonarius, G. L. M. van Heck, & N. G. Smid (Eds.), *Personality psychology in Europe: Theoretical and empirical developments* (Vol. 1, pp. 83–100). Lisse: Swets & Zeitlinger.

Maccoby, E. E., & Jacklin, C. N. (1974). *The psychology of sex differences.* Stanford, CA: Stanford University Press.

McCrae, R. R., Costa, P. T., & Busch, C. M. (1986). Evaluating comprehensiveness in personality systems: The California Q-set and the five-factor model. *Journal of Personality, 54,* 430–446.

Mischel, W., & Ebbesen, E. B. (1970). Attention in delay of gratification. *Journal of Personality and Social Psychology, 16,* 329–337.

Norman, W. T. (1963). Toward an adequate taxonomy of personality attributes: Replicated factor structure in peer nomination personality ratings. *Journal of Abnormal and Social Psychology, 66,* 574–583.

Ozer, D. J. (1993). The Q-sort method and the study of personality development. In D. C. Funder, R. D. Parke, C. Tomlinson-Keasy, & K. Widaman (Eds.), *Studying lives through time: Personality and development* (pp. 147–168). Washington, DC: American Psychological Association.

Ozer, D. J., & Gjerde, P. F. (1989). Patterns of personality consistency and change from childhood through adolescence. *Journal of Personality, 57*, 483–507.

Peabody, D., & Goldberg, L. R. (1989). Some determinants of factor structures from personality-trait descriptors. *Journal of Personality and Social Psychology, 57*, 552–567.

Siebenheller, E. (1990). *Problematische opvoedingssituaties: Percepties, emoties en disciplineringsreacties van ouders* [Problematic pedagogical situations: Perceptions, emotions and disciplinary strategies from parents]. Unpublished doctoral dissertation, University of Nijmegen, The Netherlands.

Van Aken, M. A. G. (1991). *Competence Development in a transactional perspective: A longitudinal study.* Unpublished doctoral dissertation, University of Nijmegen, The Netherlands.

Van Aken, M. A. G. & van Lieshout, C. F. M. (1991). Children's competence and the agreement and stability of self- and child-descriptions. *International Journal of Behavioral Development, 14*, 83–99.

Van Aken, M. A. G., van Lieshout, C. F. M., Roosen, M. A., & Roeffen, J. T. W. M. (1991). Relaties met leeftijdgenoten van (semi-)residentieel behandelde kinderen [Peer relations of (semi-)residentially treated children]. *Pedagogische Studiën, 68*, 68–77.

Van IJzendoorn, M. H., van der Veer, R., & van Vliet-Visser, S. (1987). Attachment 3 years later: Relationships between quality of mother–infant attachment and emotional/cognitive development in kindergarten. In L. W. C. Tavecchio & M. H. van IJzendoorn (Eds.), *Attachment in social networks* (pp. 185–225). Amsterdam: Elsevier Science (North-Holland).

Van IJzendoorn, M. H., Kranenburg, M., Zwart-Woudstra, H., van Busschbach, A., & Lambermon, M. W. E. (1991). Parental attachment and children's socio-emotional development: Some findings on the validity of the Adult Attachment Interview in Holland. *International Journal of Behavioral Development, 14*, 375–394.

Van IJzendoorn, M. H., & Cillessen, A. H. N. (1991). Relaties met leeftijdgenoten over verloop van tijd [Consistency over time of peer relations]. *Pedagogische Studiën, 68*, 56–67.

Van Lieshout, C. F. M., Riksen-Walraven, J. M. A., ten Brink, P. W. M., Siebenheller, F. A., Mey, J. Th. H., Koot, J. M., Janssen, A. W. H., & Cillessen, A. H. N. (1986). Zelfstandigheidsontwikkeling in het basisonderwijs [Development of autonomy in middle childhood]. Nijmegen: ITS.

Van Lieshout, C. F. M., van Aken, M. A. G., & van Seyen, E. T. J. (1990). Perspectives on peer relations from mothers, teachers, friends and self. *Human Development, 33*, 225–237.

Waters, E., Garber, J., Gornal, M., & Vaughn, B. E. (1983). Q-correlates of visual regard among preschool peers: Validation of a behavioral index of social competence. *Developmental Psychology, 19*, 550–560.

PART

IV

DERIVING THE FIVE-FACTOR MODEL FROM TEACHER RATINGS OF CHILDREN AND ADOLESCENTS

This section contains three diverse chapters addressing the issue of the applicability of Big Five constructs to childhood. The editors chose to group these articles into one section because, to varying degrees, the data on which the articles are based were obtained from teachers. Much of the other research on childhood temperament and personality, including the bulk of the data reported here, is obtained from parents or from self ratings.

It is necessary to consider the source of these data for at least three reasons. First, the relations among parent, teacher, and self ratings of children and adolescents are very low. Achenbach, McConaughy, and Howell (1987) reviewed 119 studies presenting cross-informant data for ratings of behavior problems and temperament in children and adolescents and determined that the mean correlation between parent and teacher was .27, between parent and self was .25, and between teacher and self was .20.

Second, some researchers find different factor structures for the ratings of parents versus teachers on scales designed to measure the same constructs. For example, Martin, Wisenbaker, and Huttunen (chap. 8 in this vol.) found that factor analyses of parent ratings of temperament on measures derived from the Thomas and Chess paradigm typically produced five to seven factors, whereas ratings by teachers of measures from the same paradigm typically produced three factors.

Finally, there is some evidence that parental and teacher ratings have differential validity. For example, parental ratings of the temperamental characteristics of emotional intensity, mood, or negative emotionality in a nonclinical population have been found by a number of researchers to predict emotional problems or behavior problems in children (e.g., Thomas & Chess, 1977). Parental temperament ratings of task persistence, activity level, or distractibility have, however, typically been found to be weak or nonsignificant predictors of academic achievement (e.g., Burk, 1980). A reverse pattern seems to emerge from teacher ratings. That is, there is ample evidence that teacher ratings of activity level, distractibility, and task persistence of unselected schoolchildren relate substantially to academic achievement, whereas teachers often have difficulty even rating the factors of emotional intensity and mood (no factor or a weak factor is typically obtained, e.g., Presley & Martin, in press).

It is critical in the present context that these two classes of raters see behavior in different environments, and these environments differ in their demand characteristics. In intimate relationships involved in home life, issues of negative emotionality (mood, emotional intensity) are of great saliency. People express these emotions more readily at home, and prolonged and intense emotional expression makes home life much more difficult. These behaviors then have great salience for life with children and adolescents. In the school, most children inhibit intense emotional expression so this behavior is less easily observed and rated by teachers. Further, the classroom is an environment in which the environmental press is for prolonged attention and maximal performance. Issues of activity level are highly salient because high gross motor activity is disruptive to the attention of the learner and to other learners in the environment. Issues of task persistence and distractibility are highly salient because focused attention is the critical behavior in this environment. Therefore, it seems likely that teachers would be acutely aware of these behaviors, and, in fact, the first factor from most teachers' temperament ratings is a factor combining activity level, distractibility, and task persistence.

In addition, teachers observe the behavior of the child in the context of a same age cohort; thus, they have a normative group in front of them everyday with which to compare the behavior of a target child. Parents have little information about age cohorts of children, most of which is provided by observing the behavior of their other children at that age (should they have other children), or the behavior of a few children of friends, neighbors, or relatives.

Because parents and teachers observe the behavior of children and adolescents in different environments with different task demands and different social characteristics, is it reasonable to assume that the structure of the Big Five will emerge from both sets of ratings, and will be equally useful in both contexts? The data summarized by Digman, Graziano, and Mervielde in this section provide substantial support for the notion that the Big Five can be extracted from teacher ratings, and that ratings in this structure are useful for providing a frame of reference for better understanding the development of children's personalities.

PART IV

Digman (chap. 16) was one of the first researchers to determine that the Big Five could be obtained from ratings of children and adolescents. He begins with a brief discussion of the history of the Big Five and his research program. In particular, Digman reviews research on second-order factor analyses of the Big Five in which two factors are found. He interprets factor "a" as being "not difficult" (i.e., stable, friendly, conscientious). He suggests that the factor measures successful versus unsuccessful socialization. The second factor has elements of extraversion and intellect, and is thought to reflect personal growth versus personal constriction.

He also attempts to demonstrate empirically how temperament (interpreted as affect) plays a role in the Big Five. He extracts 18 scales from his list of 35 personality scales thought to assess most clearly feeling and emotion. In a reanalysis of previous teacher ratings of young children, he obtains a four-factor solution. As would be predicted from the previous discussion on the salience of attention in the classroom, the first factor assesses inattentive, impulsive behavior. The second factor seems to be Sociability, and the third is Fear, which is much like the inhibition factor found so often in temperament research (see Martin et al., chap. 8 in this vol.). The final factor was labeled "unpleasant attitude" and relates to the ease with which anger is aroused. The factor has much in common with the Presley and Martin (in press) factor labeled Emotional Reactivity, obtained from teacher ratings of a temperament measure. The similarity of these factors to those obtained by temperament researchers lend some support to Digman's hypothesis, and that of many temperament researchers, that temperament is the precursor of childhood and adult personality. With maturity and experience, the four temperament factors broaden, and the fifth factor appears, resulting in the Big Five.

In contrast to the other chapters in this section, Graziano explores conceptually the development of Agreeableness, one of the Big Five factors. Graziano chose this dimension because it is pervasive in Big Five research, particularly with children (see Mervielde, chap. 20); it is conceptually related to many other child personality constructs of considerable interest (e.g., self-concept, interpersonal motivation); and little is known about its origins.

First, Graziano considers the heritability of Agreeableness. Although there is no behavior genetics research in which this characteristic was measured directly, there are data on related constructs (e.g., altruism, empathy) that shows heritabilities of about .50. He then explores research from neuropsychology on self-regulation of excitation, making the case that these processes may relate to the development of agreeableness. Next, he explores the research on socialization and attachment looking for antecedents to Agreeableness. He ends his presentation with a summary of data from his own research program that shows moderate relations among agreeableness ratings of teachers and school counselors, and self-reports of self-concept and adjustment. The relations reported are impressive given the very low correlations typically found between self ratings and teacher ratings of even the same characteristics. The strength of this chapter is in the breadth of literature explored in seeking the origins of Agreeableness. It provides a model for others who would seek to explore the range of variables that contribute to the development of each of the Big Five factors.

Victor's chapter 18 is guided by the notion that measures of Big Five personality variables will share considerable variance with contemporaneously obtained measures of behavior problems in children. According to his hypothesis, the Big Five provides the more general frame of reference for social/emotional characteristics of school-age children, and behavior problems constitute a subset of this larger domain. In order to study the variance overlap among these domains, teacher ratings of a sizable sample of fifth- and sixth-grade children were obtained using the Behavior Problem Checklist developed by Quay and Peterson (1987), and a measure of the Big Five for children developed by Digman. Different teachers made these ratings of each child. Achievement scores were also obtained. To determine the extent of shared variance among the measurements obtained, a scale-level factor analysis of all measurements was carried out. A five-factor solution was produced. Inspection of the results of this analysis supported Victor's hypothesis because each of the five factors was anchored by Big Five scales, and the five factors seemed conceptually very close to the five-factor solutions of Digman and adult-oriented Big Five researchers. He also presents data that demonstrates in a multiple regression analysis (Big Five scales served as predictors and Conduct Problems served as criteria) that Big Five scores accounted for nearly 40% of the variance of the Conduct Problems scores. Further, Big Five scores and behavior problem scores accounted for approximately 50% of the variance in achievement, with the Big Five dimension of Openness to Experience making the largest contribution. These results add considerable support to the notion that Big Five measures correlate substantially with measures of behavior problems, and that the Big Five may serve as a useful frame of reference for a unified understanding of social and emotional behavior in school-age children.

Taken as a whole, these chapters provide strong initial support for the notion that the Big Five is a useful frame of reference for ratings of personality by teachers. They also break new ground by establishing models for the further exploration of the place of the Big Five in childhood.

REFERENCES

Achenbach, T. M., McConaughy, S. H., & Howell, C. T. (1987). Child/adolescent behavioral and emotional problems: Implications of cross-informant correlations for situational specificity. *Psychological Bulletin, 101*, 213–232.

Burk, E. (1980). *Relationship of temperamental traits to achievement and adjustment in gifted children.* Unpublished doctoral dissertation, Fordham University.

Presley, R., & Martin, R. (in press). Toward a structure of preschool temperament: Factor structure of the Temperament Assessment Battery for Children. *Journal of Personality.*

Quay, H. C., & Peterson, D. R. (1987). *The Revised Behavior Problem Checklist.* Coral Gables, FL.

Thomas, A., & Chess, S. (1977). *Temperament and development.* New York: Brunner/Mazel.

CHAPTER

16

CHILD PERSONALITY AND TEMPERAMENT: DOES THE FIVE-FACTOR MODEL EMBRACE BOTH DOMAINS?

John M. Digman
Oregon Research Institute

CONCERNING PERSONALITY

In recent years, the five-factor model (the Big Five) has emerged as a persuasive paradigm for the organization of personality concepts into a meaningful and heuristic *structure*. Like many scientific paradigms that often require a generation of consideration before adoption, the model is not at all new, having been clearly demonstrated in a series of studies that began more than 40 years ago (Fiske, 1949; Norman, 1963; Norman & Goldberg, 1966; Tupes & Christal, 1961). Seemingly assigned to oblivion by the antitrait movement of the 1970s, it has enjoyed a renaissance during the past decade, as many researchers became persuaded of its validity (e.g., Borkenau, 1988; Borkenau & Ostendorf, 1990; Costa & McCrae, 1985, 1988; Digman, 1990; Digman & Inouye, 1986; Goldberg, 1981, 1983, 1990; John, Angleitner, & Ostendorf, 1988; McCrae & Costa, 1985, 1989; Ostendorf, 1990; Wiggins & Trapnell, 1991).

Whereas most of the authors cited have been cautious about claiming that this is the ultimate model for personality, they would doubtless second Goldberg's (1981) remarks: "It should be possible to argue the case that *any* model for structuring individual differences will have to encompass—at some level of abstraction—something like these 'big five' dimensions. . . . We have here something reasonably solid and method resilient" (p. 159).

Goldberg's remarks have proved to be right on the mark. As noted in my review (Digman, 1990), the five-factor model has proved to be a very robust model, across ages (Digman & Takemoto-Chock, 1981) and across languages (Bond, Nakazato,

& Shiraishi, 1975; Ostendorf, 1990). It has also proved to be an effective model for ordering the many measures that have originated in the questionnaire domain: Thus, the classical systems of Cattell, Guilford, and Eysenck, based on questionnaire data, have been shown to fit the five-factor model very nicely (Borkenau & Ostendorf, 1990; Digman, 1979, 1988; McCrae & Costa, 1985). An important point here is that the five factors of the rating domain are usually found at the *second-order level* of the questionnaire domain. Thus, the 30 specific scales of the NEO Personality Inventory (Costa & McCrae, 1985) coalesce at a higher level of abstraction and utilization into the now familiar Extraversion, Agreeableness, Conscientiousness, Neuroticism, and Openness to Experience.

CONCERNING TEMPERAMENT

Although psychometric studies of *personality* have appeared in the literature for many years, finally culminating in the five-factor model, a parallel research effort over the past 25 years has been concerned with what has traditionally been called *temperament*. The Wassenaar Conference (Kohnstamm & Halverson, 1991) brought together researchers from both fields, not only to present recent research findings, but also to examine the possibility of finding some common ground.

Since much of the research on which the five-factor model has been established has come from studies of the language of personality, it is interesting to consider the roots of the word *temperament*. According to the *Oxford English Dictionary*, the word stems from the Latin *temperare*, which meant to blend. It was the four humors of ancient physiology, and differences in the mixture or blending of them, that were believed to produce differences in behavior and mood. Today, as we learn more about the biochemistry of the central nervous system, this ancient system strikes us as right in principle, if not in particulars. Just now, the neurohormone serotonin, for example, seems to be a better candidate than black bile for a latter-day "humor."

A view of temperament closer to our interests as psychologists was offered by Allport (1937): "Temperament refers to the characteristic phenomena of an individual's emotional nature, including his susceptibility to emotional stimulation, his customary strength and speed of response, the quality of his prevailing mood, and all peculiarities of fluctuation and intensity of mood; these phenomena being regarded as dependent on constitutional makeup and therefore largely hereditary in origin" (p. 54).

Another view has been offered by Rothbart and Derryberry (1981): "We will define temperament as constitutional differences in reactivity and self-regulation, with 'constitutional' seen as the relatively enduring biological makeup of the organism, as influenced over time by heredity, maturation, and experience" (p. 37).

Or, as Goldsmith, Losoya, Bradshaw, and Campos (see chap. 13) conceptualize it: "Temperament refers to early appearing dimensions of individual variability.

. . . Included by many investigators are such traits as fearfulness, persistence, sociability, soothability, and positive affectivity."

Although these definitions differ somewhat, it seems clear that many researchers in this field have been persuaded that individual differences in temperament are to a considerable degree constitutionally determined. It also seems clear that much of the work has been focused on basic emotions and the parameters of their expression, as these are observed to differ from one individual to another in, as Kohnstamm (1989, p. 558) put it in his history of the concept of temperament, "the affective side of personality."

Perhaps a reasonable distillation of these several views might be that temperament refers to affective aspects of personality, that individual differences in the expression of these aspects are based at least to some significant degree on individual differences in genetically determined constitution, that these differences are observable very early in life, and that they may become the framework, as it were, for the development of those individual differences in children and adults commonly considered under "personality."

Studies of Individual Differences in Temperament

Many investigators—and most parents of more than one child—have noted striking differences among infants and young children in their characteristic emotions and in the intensity with which they are expressed (e.g., Thomas & Chess, 1977; Rothbart, 1989). Analyses of such individual differences by Buss and Plomin (1984) led them to their three-fold EAS system, in terms of Emotionality (which subsequently differentiates into fear and anger), Activity, and Sociability.

Earlier, H. J. Eysenck (1953), although writing a book on "personality," was distilling nonintellective individual differences in terms of Neuroticism and Extraversion. Somewhat later, a third dimension, Psychoticism, was added (H. J. Eysenck & M. W. Eysenck, 1985).

Even earlier, illustrating the point that "temperament" to many researchers has meant the nonintellective aspects of personality, there was the popular Guilford–Zimmerman Temperament Survey (Guilford & Zimmerman, 1949), which is usually regarded as a personality inventory.

More recently, Tellegen (1985) offered a model of individual differences in terms of Positive Emotionality, Negative Emotionality, and Impulsiveness. Subsequently, in one of the first reports from the Minnesota Twin Study (Tellegen, Lykken, Bouchard, Wilcox, Segal, & Rich, 1988) these dimensions have been shown to have a rather strong hereditary basis.

The View From the Five-Factor Model of Personality

Investigators who are strong supporters of the so-called Big Five personality dimensions may appear to be imperialistic at times, in their efforts to subordinate all concepts of individual differences to the model of their choice. Nonetheless, these efforts have been quite successful (Digman, 1990), and the model appears to have fulfilled the hope that factor analysis would bring order to the complexities of personality structure. Thus, "regardless of whether teachers rate children, officer candidates rate one another, college students rate one another, or clinical staff members rate graduate trainees, the results are pretty much the same" (Digman & Takemoto-Chock, 1981, pp. 164–165).

To return to the question posed by the title of this chapter: In what way (or ways) is temperament related to personality? There appear to be at least three ways in which these concepts and fields of investigation may be related. First, temperament is simply the nonintellective aspect of personality, a distinction made by Guilford (1975) among others. Second, temperament represents a subfield of personality, concerning those concepts that denote emotion and feeling. And third, personality not only subsumes that aspect of personality known as temperament, but represents the effects of the interaction of the temperament base with maturation and the social environment. I believe this is the view of Rothbart (1989), whose attempts to link temperament to personality strike me as having great heuristic value here.

FACTOR REDUX: TWO EARLY STUDIES OF CHILD PERSONALITY REVISITED

Before examining further the apparent parallels of temperament systems and the Big Five system of personality, I should like to turn briefly to two studies of child personality traits. These studies were carried out more than 30 years ago. As analyzed at that time, they did not support the Big Five view of personality. As analyzed today, with today's methods, they provide striking confirmation of the five-factor model, as it is seen in young children. These studies, together with Goldberg's (1990) persuasive analyses of various sets of data, are convincing that a model in terms of five broad factors meets the basic criteria of an adequate scientific theoretical system: It is general and it is robust. More complex systems, in terms of six factors and more, thus far have not been able to meet these criteria.

Most of the recent studies of temperament have been carried out on infants and very young children, whereas almost all studies of personality, such as those that have demonstrated the value of the Big Five, have involved adults. My studies of personality structure in children, as seen in teachers' ratings of young children, may furnish a link between these two fields of research effort.

When I began these studies, I was substantially influenced by Cattell (1957) and his complex system. I considered myself something of a novice in this field and believed the best way to acquire skills here was to undertake a replication of one of his studies (Cattell & Coan, 1957). This was a factor analysis of 38 teacher rating scales, based upon first- and second-grade children. My analysis employed his complex bipolar scales and, as did Cattell and Coan, I added sex as a variable to the list. Two of the 38 rating scales involved teachers' perceptions of parental behavior.

Believing at the time that underextraction was a more serious sin than overextraction, I removed 11 common factors, spent many weeks in graphic rotation to simple structure, and finally concluded that 8 of the 11 were personality factors that could be meaningfully interpreted (Digman, 1963). [Subsequently, Cattell (1963) analyzed my data and reported a 12-factor solution that appeared to support his studies of adult personality structure.]

A year later, I conducted another, similar study. To the original 36 personality scales I added 17 others that I had designed. Factor analysis of the data provided by teachers' ratings of 149 children suggested that Cattell might be right—by the "eigenvalue of one" rule, there seemed to be at least 10 common factors present in the data. However, these factors did not seem to be very much like the factors of the first study—and Cattell's factors, even those based on my data, seemed different still.

Many years later, a meta-analysis of several studies (Digman & Takemoto-Chock, 1981) revealed the root of the difficulty: Reliance on the classic "eigenvalue of one" rule often leads to overextraction, particularly where the sample N's are modest in size (e.g., less than 500). Later, a study of teachers' ratings of a group of sixth-grade children provided a beautiful confirmation of the essential wisdom of the five-factor model (Digman & Inouye, 1986).

All of which led me to reconsider my first two studies, done many years before I came to see the wisdom of the Big Five model. Would their reanalysis demonstrate the correctness of the Big Five Model? Not available to me when the original analyses were done but available to me now were two new procedures for estimating the number of common factors: one was the Everett-Nunnally method (Everett, 1983; Nunnally, 1978); the other, parallel analysis (Montanelli & Humphreys, 1976; Zwick & Velicer, 1986).

First, the two studies were made more comparable by deletion of the parental behavior and sex variables. In addition, one of the complex Cattell scales of the first study had caused so much confusion for the raters that it was substantially edited for the second study. My reanalyses, then, were based on the remaining 35 scales common to both studies. (See Table 16.1.)

According to the "eigenvalue of one" rule, both sets of data contained at least six common factors, possibly seven (the seventh eigenvalues being .97 and .98, respectively). Because this eigenvalue rule is so commonly employed, I would expect the typical user of a canned computer program to proceed to extract six (possibly seven) factors and then to announce the discovery of one of two "new" factors of child personality.

Finding the Robust Factors

However, the question regarding the number of factors is not how many factors may be extracted from a *particular* study but the number of factors replicable across studies. Everett's (1983) procedure, used to relate factors across two

TABLE 16.1
The 35 Rating Scales Common to the Two Studies

Expressive	Secretive, reserved vs. expressive, frank
Outgoing	Shy, bashful, seclusive, aloof, remains fairly isolated from other children vs. outgoing, mixes freely with other children
Gregarious	Prefers solitary pursuits vs. gregarious, prefers games involving many children
Adventurous	Retiring, cautious, vs. adventurous, bold, willing to run the risk of possible rejection or injury
Alert	Lethargic, apathetic, easily tired or fatigued vs. alert, wide-awake, energetic
Noisy	Quiet vs. noisy, distracting in class
Ownsex	Associates mostly with children of opposite sex vs. associates mostly with children of own sex
Aggressive	Nonaggressive, kind, considerate vs. aggressive, tends toward fighting, bullying, teasing, cruelty
Cooperative	Negativistic, stubborn, disobedient, argumentative vs. cooperative, compliant, obedient
Untrustworthy	Conscientious, trustworthy vs. untrustworthy, dishonest
Suspicious	Trustful of others, readily accepts solicitude of others as sincere vs. suspicious of others, ungrateful, rejects affection or solicitude
Overactive	Calm, relaxed vs. overactive, excitable, perhaps irritable
Self-Centered	Self-abasive, deferent, minimizes own importance, vs. self-centered, conceited, boastful, "show-off"
Assertive	Submissive, follows lead of other children vs. self assertive, tends to dominate other children
Nervous	Lacks nervous habits vs. prone to nervous habits (e.g., thumbsucking, nail-biting, pulling and twisting hair, etc.)
Responsible	Irresponsible, frivolous vs. responsible
Stable	Changeable in interests, attitudes, opinions vs. stable in interests, attitudes, opinions
Persevering	Quitting, fickle vs. persevering, determined
Tidy	Untidy, careless with respect to appearance of self or possessions vs. neat, tidy, orderly
Careless	Careful with property of others vs. careless, destructive of property of others
Attentive	Inattentive, absent-minded, prone to daydreaming, shows poor concentration vs. very attentive to class proceedings
Follows Instructions	Has difficulty following instructions vs. follows instructions easily and accurately
Fearful	Placid, free from distress vs. fearful, worrying, anxious
Jealous	Free of jealousy, feels accepted vs. prone to jealousy
Rigid	Adaptable, flexible vs. rigid, has difficulty adjusting to changes or new situations
Depressed	Cheerful vs. depressed
Dependent	Self-sufficient, independent vs. dependent on teacher
Popular	Unpopular, generally disliked by other children vs. popular, generally well liked by other children
Demanding	Prefers not to be noticed vs. demanding of teacher's attention
Confident	Lacking in self-confidence, easily discouraged or defeated vs. confident (perhaps overconfident) of own ability and ideas
Health	Poor general health, prone to absence by reason of illness or physical complaints vs. of generally good health
Imaginative	Practical-minded vs. imaginative
Aesthetically Sensitive	Lacking in artistic feeling vs. aesthetically sensitive, aesthetically fastidious
Learns Quickly	Learns slowly vs. learns quickly
Polished	Socially awkward and clumsy vs. polished in manner

independent studies, is similar to the traditional method of cross-validation in regression analysis. Two sets of factor scores are composed for the same set of data. For one set the factor scores are formed from the data of the second study in accord with the salient variables of the first study; the second set is based on the factor analysis of the second study. If the model is robust across the two studies, then these two sets of factor scores should correlate substantially.

When the Everett method was applied to five-, six-, and seven-factor solutions of the two studies, the results indicated quite clearly that six- and seven-factor solutions were not robust across the two studies. However, a five-factor solution was (see Table 16.2), with strikingly high comparability coefficients for all factors except for Factor IV. The results of this five-factor solution for the first study may be seen in Table 16.3.

These results are completely in accord with the recent work of Goldberg (1990), who analyzed several sets of data by various methods, demonstrating clearly the robustness of the five-factor model: Regardless of method of extraction or rotation, it was the five-factor solution that was stable across studies.

Two Higher Order Factors of the Big Five

Impressed by the work of Hampson (1988) and a recent study by John, Hampson, and Goldberg (1991) on the hierarchical nature of personality attributes, I then obtained the correlations of these two sets of factor scores—by the method of weighted summation of salient variables—for the five-factor solutions and factored these to produce the two-factor pattern that may be seen in Table 16.4. I might add that the results are just as they emerged from the computer, without any attempt to bring them into further congruence. For now, I have labeled these factors α and β.

Interpretation of Factor α is not difficult; children who are empathic and friendly, rather than aggressive (a Friendliness/Hostility factor), who have sufficient ego strength to cope with adversity (Emotional Stability/Neuroticism), and who show steadfastness and purpose (Conscientiousness), rather than heedlessness have been well socialized, suggesting Successful versus Unsuccessful Socialization as the interpretation.

Factor β, which extracts certain common aspects of Extraversion (venturesomeness, activity, courage) and Intellect (creativity, esthetic interests, flexibility,

TABLE 16.2
Comparability Coefficients for the Five-Factor Solutions
Across the Two Studies

I: Extraversion	.99+
II: Friendliness	.95
III: Conscientiousness	.99+
IV: Emotional Stability	.85
V: Intellect	.96

TABLE 16.3
The Five-Factor Solution Of Study I
(Decimals Omitted; Values < |.30| Omitted)

Scale*	Factor				
	I	II	III	IV	V
Expressive	78				40
Outgoing	78				40
Gregarious	72				
Adventurous	66			-30	
Alert	63				40
Noisy	56	-60	-36		
Own sex	-35				
Fights		-84			
Cooperative		77	32		
Untrustworthy		-69	-43		
Suspicious		-67			
Overactive	30	-61	-37		
Self-centered	48	-54			
Assertive	46	-51			37
Nervous habits		-44	-39	44	
Responsible		34	80		
Stable			69	-33	
Persevering			68		
Tidy			69		
Careless		-52	-67		
Attentive			62		44
Follows instructions			53	-34	39
Fearful				84	
Jealous		-37		69	
Rigid		-34		69	-34
Depressed	-49			61	
Dependent			-40	59	
Popular				-56	33
Demanding	45			54	
Confident	36			-52	
Good health				-46	
Imaginative					77
Aesthetically sensitive					72
Learns quickly			48		63
Polished	38		40		45

*Abbreviated version of bipolar scale

TABLE 16.4
Higher Order Factor Analysis of the Correlations of the Five Factors
(Decimals Omitted)

	Study 1		Study 2	
	α	β	α	β
Extraversion	−22	77	−09	66
Friendliness	81	−36	68	−32
Conscientiousness	82	13	72	29
Neuroticism	−66	−46	−76	−12
Intellect	28	55	24	68

attention to learning) reminds one of the virtues extolled by Rogers (1961) and Maslow (1962). Possibly, this higher order factor is none other than the lofty concept of Personal Growth versus Personal Constriction.

Factors α and β and Eysenck's Factors

Because Eysenck (see chap. 2) has suggested that Big Five Factors A (Agreeableness or Friendliness) and C (Conscientiousness) are lower order factors of his P (Psychoticism) factor, a natural question is whether the α and β factors of the present study are the two Eysenck factors P and E. Readers who are acquainted with the content of the P factor—embodying, according to H. J. Eysenck (1975, p. 197), such characteristics as "solitary, not caring for people," "cruel, inhumane," and "lacks feeling, insensitive"—may see much of the P factor in what I have called "socialization." On the other hand, the Neuroticism factor, clearly present in all studies at the Big Five level of abstraction, has made its contribution to the α (Socialization) factor at the more abstract level here. More likely, as I have suggested elsewhere (Digman, 1990), Eysenck's Giant Three are nonintellective personality dimensions at the Big Five level, with the P factor being most similar in content to the negative (Hostility) end of the Friendliness factor.

LINKING TEMPERAMENT TO PERSONALITY

Now, back to the place where temperament may fit into the picture here. A close look at some of the scales used in the two studies suggests the raters often were drawing inferences about emotion and feeling. For example, consider some of the rating scales of the studies that are set forth in detail in Table 16.1. One may note emotional content in many of these scales. Is a child who is perceived as "rejecting of solicitude" also a child who would be rated as "not very sociable"? How about the child who is rated as "fearful"? Would this not fall under the Buss and Plomin (1984) dimension of Emotionality? and "expressive" and "alert" suggest the Activity dimension of Thomas and Chess (1977), Rothbart (1989), and Buss and Plomin (1984). It seems clear that ratings of 7-year-old children involve attributes of both emotion and its behavioral expression. It is also apparent that many of the scales refer to behavior that seems quite independent of emotion. For example, "imaginative" is dependent on language and artistic expression, as in storytelling and painting. The scale "follows instructions easily and accurately" seems quite unrelated to any conception of temperament.

Many years ago, Young (1936) began his influential treatise on motivation with the statement: "All behavior is motivated" (p. 1). Later, in the same chapter, he stated that "motivational psychology may be defined as the study of all conditions which arouse and regulate the behavior of organisms" (p. 45). The study of temperament is clearly in this tradition.

The study of personality, on the other hand, has involved "that which distinguishes and characterized a person" (White, 1976, p. 12). In this sense, the study of personality is more inclusive, incorporating behavior, motives, emotions, attitudes, and values. And yet, as the behaviorists are likely to remind us, our observations of these phenomena are usually based on behavior. For example, the scales that help to define Factor II of the Big Five, as seen in Tables 16.1 and 16.2, suggest that this personality dimension involves partly *descriptions* of behavior and partly *inferences* about emotion and feeling.

A Four-Factor Solution of Temperament Scales of Study 1

Of the 35 scales of Study 1, 18 were chosen as "temperament" scales.[1] Scales suggesting an Intellect factor in the five-factor solution were deleted. Temperament theory and research (Buss & Plomin, 1984, 1986) would suggest either a three- or four-factor solution for these scales, assuming of course these are indeed scales that reflect temperament.

Table 16.5 contains the results of a factor analysis of these scales. Four factors were clearly indicated, as evidenced by a strikingly large drop in eigenvalues of the correlation matrix between the fourth (1.20) and the fifth (.68). The first, marked by the negative ends of the scales that had helped to identify the Conscientiousness factor in the five-factor solution, suggests the child who is inattentive, "flighty," quick to quit tasks, and to shift orientation abruptly—in other words, impulsive. The second factor could be labeled Extraversion or, in keeping with temperament theory, Sociability. Factor 3 is an emotional factor, which appears to have *fear* as its core. Factor 4 hints at something that could be called an "unpleasant attitude." Perhaps easily aroused anger is the emotional core here?

Taking seriously the suggestions of Rothbart (1989), Buss (1989), and others that temperament matures into personality, I have labeled the factors (a bit impulsively, perhaps) Impulsivity, Sociability, Fear, and Anger. (For the Impulsiv-

---

[1] I wish to express my thanks to Dr. Berit Hagekull and Dr. Mary Rothbart for helpful suggestions here.

TABLE 16.5
Four-Factor Solution of 18 "Temperament" Scales
(Decimals Omitted; Values < |.30| Omitted)

Rating Scale	Factor			
	Impulsivity	Sociability	Fear	Anger
Quitting, fickle[a]	79			
Inattentive[a]	75	−35		
Changeable[a]	73		32	
Outgoing		90		
Expressive		87		
Alert	−34	79		
Adventurous		76		33
Cheerful[a]		72	−45	
Gregarious		65		
Noisy	31	58		61
Fearful		−34	72	
Jealous			72	31
Demanding		40	65	
Aggressive				84
Negativistic, stubborn	34			73
Suspicious				67
Overactive	37		38	59
Nervous	35		47	39

[a]Negative end of bipolar scale

ity factor the negative ends of three scales that helped to define the Conscientiousness factor of the preceding analyses have been used here.)

These results, based on quite young children, are in very good agreement with the work of Angleitner and Ostendorf (see chap. 4 in this vol.), despite great differences in subject age (their work was based on adults), in language (German versus English), and medium (questionnaires versus ratings). In addition, the children of the study reported here were predominantly of third-generation Oriental ancestry, living in Hawaii. Given all of these differences, the general agreement is striking.

If some aspects of Impulsivity, Sociability, and Emotionality (both fear and anger) appear in the five-factor solutions of characteristics of young children, what is in the Big Five that is not in the temperament studies—other than the Intellect dimension? One important cluster of characteristics is denoted by the positive pole of the Friendliness–Hostility dimension. These characteristics are emotions not often seen in 3-year-olds, but are easily noted in some 7-year-olds and help to form one of the major dimensions of the Big Five: They involve sensitivity to others' feelings, concern for others, and sympathy. One is not surprised to find these qualities missing in a 3-year-old; a considerable degree of cognitive development seems to be necessary before a child can experience grief upon learning what happened to Anna Frank, for example.

An important emotion that seems to be missing is love and its more moderate form, affection. Elsewhere (Digman, 1990) I have called attention to the lukewarm quality of the interpretation of Factor II as "agreeableness." Why have researchers shied away, it seems, from seeing this important dimension as love or something like loving kindness? Although Wiggins (1980) has not hesitated to see this as a love–hate dimension in interpersonal relations, many of the rest of us have avoided this interpretation, preferring the cooler interpretation of "agreeableness" or "friendliness." Given the origins of personality theory (Erikson, 1950; Freud, 1924; Horney, 1973), this strikes me as rather strange.

Another dimension of importance for the five-factor model is Conscientiousness. Although impulsivity may be the precursor of this personality dimension, the positive pole involves the ability to organize one's world in terms of space and time. Again, some cognitive development is necessary before 3-year-olds can relate their activity today to some event in the future and act in such a way as to make that future event likely.

Finally, although one may see gross differences in intellect in a set of infants and very young children, it will be some time before they can be characterized as imaginative, artistic, or creative, which are qualities related to Factor V, Intellect. Although the domain of intellect has usually been viewed as the rational, nonemotional (and nontemperamental) side of personality, one may infer from behavior in children, as well as adults, the "feeling of efficacy" (White, 1976), the "joy in being a cause" (Groos, 1901), that accompanies successful intellectual endeavor or the exercise of skill. For example, when attending my daughter's gymnastic class, I watched a 7-year-old practicing a triple backward flip. When she finally managed to bring it off, she smiled broadly and announced aloud to herself, "I did it!" Although this is seldom discussed as an aspect of temperament, it would seem to be an aspect of positive emotionality, of the feeling that accompanies successful performance.

The principal differences, then, between temperament dimensions of individual differences in infants and very young children and the five-factor model (as seen in the two studies already discussed and as seen in studies of adults) seem related to the different ages of the subjects of the studies. Temperament may indeed be the basis of personality, but some aspects of cognitive skills and temperament may require maturation beyond the years of the subjects in the typical temperament study of infants and very young children.

SOME REFLECTIONS ON HORSES, GENETICS, AND PERSONALITY

Ask any horse breeder whether horses differ in temperament, and the answer will be provided quickly and with authority. A first distinction, very likely, will be between the two main divisions of *equus cabbalus*, the so-called cold blooded and the hot-blooded (Lasley, 1976). These are traditional concepts used to describe temperament differences in horses produced by centuries of breeding. The cold-blooded are typically described as "placid and docile," and the latter are said to have a "fiery temperament." If a psychologist were to ask whether such temperament differences could be ascribed to heredity, the horse breeder would smile patiently and tell the psychologist something about the patient breeding of the past 200 years that resulted in the "high-strung, nervous—but *fast*" thoroughbred.

Social scientists, particularly anthropologists and psychologists, have been slow to generalize the implications of centuries of animal breeding for our own species. Centuries of religious dogma slowed the acceptance of Darwinian principles in the 19th century, even among biologists. In the United States and in the former Soviet Union, fervent hopes for the perfectibility of humankind, whether under the banner of behaviorism or the flag of Marxism, resulted in a half century of ideologically based ignoring or casual explaining away such studies as those of Freeman, Holzinger, and Mitchell (1928), or the Iowa Adoption Studies (Skodak & Skeels, 1945). However, the general conclusion reached from the more recent independent studies (Bouchard & McGue, 1990; Loehlin, 1986; Rushton, Fulker, Neale, Nias, & H. J. Eysenck, 1986; Tellegen et al., 1988) that heredity may account for something between 40% and 60% of the variability in adult personality traits can no longer be swept away.

Granted that this view is more commonly accepted today—we may be witnessing a real paradigm shift here—how does one explain the linkage between the molecular level of DNA and the complex system that is adult personality? I believe the focus of this conference points to an answer. Early temperament differences are, as Allport (1937) suspected, determined by genetics to a very large degree. The link between genetics and temperament is via structure (constitution), and the link with adult personality is through the interaction of temperament and individual experience (i.e., nonshared environment; Buss & Rende, 1991).

SUMMARY

To return to the question posed by the title: Does the five-factor model embrace the temperament domain, as well as the personality domain? The studies of child personality, which had led to quite complex interpretations when first analyzed, were reanalyzed, using contemporary methods of factor analysis and methods of comparing factors across studies. The five-factor model was clearly supported, whereas more complex solutions were not. The factors are identical with the Big Five at the adult level (see Goldberg, chap. 1 in this vol.).

Scales suggestive of temperament were abstracted out of the set of one study, following deletion of scales suggestive of intellect. A clear four-factor solution resulted. The factors were interpreted as Sociability, Fear, Anger, and Impulsivity, conceptual dimensions that have been in the temperament literature for some time.

REFERENCES

Allport, G. W. (1937). *Personality: A psychosocial interpretation.* New York: Holt.
Bond, M. H., Nakazato, H. S., & Shiraishi, D. (1975). Universality and distinctiveness in dirmenions of Japanese person perception. *Journal of Cross Cultural Psychology, 6,* 346–355.
Borkenau, P. (1988). The multiple classification of acts and the big five factors of personality. *Journal of Research in Personality, 22,* 337–352.
Borkenau, P., & Ostendorf, F. (1990). Comparing exploratory and confirmatory factor analysis: A study on the five-factor model of personality. *Personality and Individual Differences, 11,* 515–524.
Bouchard, T. J., McGue, M. (1990). Genetic and rearing influences on personality: An analysis of adopted twins reared apart. *Journal of Personality, 58,* 263–292.
Buss, A. (1989). Temperaments as personality traits. In G. A. Kohnstamm, J. E. Bates, & M. K. Rothbart (Eds.), *Temperament in childhood* (pp. 49–58). Wiley: New York.
Buss, A. H., & Plomin, R. (1984). *Temperament: Early developing personality traits.* Hillsdale, NJ: Lawrence Erlbaum Associates.
Buss, A. H., & Plomin, R. (1986). The EAS approach to temperament. In R. Plomin & J. Dunn (Eds.), *The study of temperament: Changes, continuities, and challenges* (pp. 67–79). Hillsdale, NJ: Lawrence Erlbaum Associates.
Buss, A. H., & Rende, R. (1991). Human behavioral genetics. *Annual Review of Psychology, 42,* 161–190.
Cattell, R. B. (1957). *Personality and motivation structure and measurement.* Yonkers-on Hudson: World Book.
Cattell, R. B. (1963). Teachers' personality description of 6-year-olds: A check on structure. *British Journal of Educational Psychology, 33,* 219–235.
Cattell, R. B., & Coan, R. A. (1957). Child personality structure as revealed in teachers' ratings. *Journal of Clinical Psychology, 13,* 315–327.
Costa, P. T., Jr., & McCrae, R. R. (1985). *The NEO Personality Inventory.* Odessa, FL: Psychological Assessment Resources.
Costa, P. T., Jr., & McCrae, R. R. (1988). From catalog to classification: Murray's needs and the five-factor model. *Journal of Personality and Social Psychology, 55,* 258–265.
Digman, J. M. (1963). Principal dimensions of child personality as inferred from teachers' judgments. *Child Development, 34,* 43–60.
Digman, J. M. (1979, November). *The five major domains of personality variables: Analysis of questionnaire data in the light of the five robust factors emerging from studies of rated characteristics.* Paper presented at the Annual Meeting of the Society for Multivariate Experimental Psychology, Atlanta, GA.
Digman, J. M. (1988, August). *Classical theories of trait organization and the Big Five factors of personality.* Paper presented at the annual convention of the American Psychological Association, Atlanta, GA.
Digman, J. M. (1990). Personality structure: Emergence of the five-factor model. *Annual Review of Psychology, 41,* 417–440.
Digman, J. M., & Inouye, J. (1986). Further specification of the five robust factors of personality. *Journal of Personality and Social Psychology, 50,* 116–123.
Digman, J. M., & Takemoto-Chock, N. K. (1981). Factors in the natural language of personality: Re-analysis, comparison, and interpretation of six major studies. *Multivariate Behavioral Research, 16,* 149–170.
Erikson, E. (1950). *Childhood and society.* New York: Norton.
Everett, J. E. (1983). Factor comparability as a means of determining the number of factors and their rotation. *Multivariate Behavioral Research, 18,* 197–218.
Eysenck, H. J. (1953). *The structure of human personality.* New York: Wiley.
Eysenck, H. J. (1975). *The inequality of man.* San Diego: EdITS Publishing.

Eysenck, H. J., & Eysenck, M. W. (1985). *Personality and individual differences.* New York: Plenum.
Fiske, D. W. (1949). Consistency of the factorial structures of personality ratings from different sources. *Journal of Social and Abnormal Psychology, 44,* 329–344.
Freeman, F. N., Holzinger, K. J., & Mitchell, B. C. (1928). The influence of environment on the intelligence school achievement, and conduct of foster children. *27th Yearbook, National Society for Studies in Education,* Part 1, 103–217.
Freud, S. (1924). *A general introduction to psychoanalysis.* New York: Permabooks.
Goldberg, L. R. (1981). Language and individual differences: The search for universals in personality lexicons. In L. Wheeler (Ed.), *Review of personality and social psychology* (Vol. 2, pp. 141–165). Beverly Hills, CA: Sage.
Goldberg, L. R. (1983). *The magical number of five, plus or minus two: Some conjectures on the dimensionality of personality descriptors.* Paper presented at a research seminar, Gerontology Research Center, Baltimore.
Goldberg, L. R. (1990). An alternative "description of personality": The Big Five factor structure. *Journal of Personality and Social Psychology, 59,* 1216–1229.
Groos, K. (1901). *The play of man* (E. L. Baldwin, Trans.). New York: Appleton.
Guilford, J. P. (1975). Factors and factors of personality. *Psychological Bulletin, 82,* 802–814.
Guilford, J. P., & Zimmerman, W. S. (1949). *The Guilford-Zimmerman Temperament Survey.* Beverly Hills, CA: Sheridan Supply.
Hampson, S. E. (1988). *The construction of personality* (2nd ed.). London: Routledge.
Horney, K. (1973). *Feminine psychology.* New York: Norton.
John, O. P., Angleitner, A., & Ostendorf, F. (1988). The lexical approach to personality: A historical review of personality taxonomic research. *European Journal of Personality, 2,* 171–205.
John, O. P., Hampson, S. E., & Goldberg, L. R. (1991). The basic level in personality-trait hierarchies: Studies of trait use and accessibility in different contexts. *Journal of Personality and Social Psychology, 60,* 349–361.
Kohnstamm, G. A. (1989). Historical and international perspectives. In G. A. Kohnstamm, J. E. Bates, & M. K. Rothbart (Eds.), *Temperament in childhood* (pp. 567–566). New York: Wiley.
Kohnstamm, G. A., & Halverson, C. F. (1991, June). Conference on "The Development of the Structure of Temperament and Personality from Infancy to Adulthood," Wassenaar, The Netherlands.
Lasley, J. F. (1976). *Genetic principles in horse breeding.* Houston, TX: Cordovan Corporation.
Loehlin, J. C. (1986). Are California Psychological Inventory items differentially heritable? *Behavior Genetics, 16,* 599–603.
Maslow, A. H. (1962). *Toward a psychology of being.* New York: Van Nostrand.
McCrae, R. R., & Costa, P. T., Jr. (1985). Comparison of EPI and psychoticism scales with measures of the five-factor theory of personality. *Personaltiy and Individual Differences, 6,* 587–597.
McCrae, R. R., & Costa, P. T. (1989). Reinterpreting the Myers–Briggs Type Indicator from the perspective of the five-factor model of personality. *Journal of Personality, 57,* 17–40.
Montanelli, R. G., & Humphreys, L. G. (1976). Latent roots of correlations matrices with squared multiple correlations on the diagonal: A Monte-Carlo study. *Psychometrika, 41,* 341–348.
Norman, W. T. (1963). Toward an adequate taxonomy of personality attributes. *Journal of Abnormal and Social Psychology, 66,* 574–583.
Norman, W. T., & Goldberg, L. R. (1966). Raters, ratees, and randomness. *Journal of Personality and Social Psychology, 52,* 574–583.
Nunnally, J. C. (1978). *Psychometric theory* (2nd ed.). New York: McGraw-Hill.
Ostendorf, F. (1990). *Sprache und Persönlichkeitsstruktur, zur Validität des Funf-Faktoren-Modells der Persönlichkeit.* Unpublished doctoral dissertation, University of Bielefeld, Germany.
Rogers, C. R. (1961). *On becoming a person.* Boston: Houghton-Miflin.
Rothbart, M. K. (1989). Temperament in childhood: A framework. In G. A. Kohnstamm, J. E. Bates, & M. K. Rothbart (Eds.), *Temperament in childhood* (pp. 59–73). New York: Wiley.

Rothbart, M. K., & Derryberry, D. (1981). Development of individual differences in temperament. In M. E. Lamb & A. L. Brown (Eds.), *Advances in developmental psychology* (Vol. 1, p. 37). Hillsdale, NJ: Lawrence Erlbaum Associates.

Rushton, J. P., Fulker, D. W., Neale, M. C., Nias, D.K.B., & Eysenck, H. J. (1986). Altruism and aggression: The heritability of individual differences. *Journal of Personality and Social Psychology, 50,* 1192–1198.

Skodak, M., & Skeels, H. M. (1945). A follow-up study of children of adoptive homes. *Journal of Genetic Psychology, 66,* 21–58.

Tellegen, A. (1985). Structures of mood and personality and their relevance to assessing anxiety with an emphasis on self report. In A. Tuma & J. Maser (Eds.), *Anxiety and the anxiety disorders* (pp. 681–706). Hillsdale, NJ: Lawrence Erlbaum Associates.

Tellegen, A., Lykken, D. T., Bouchard, T. J., Wilcox, K. J., Segal, E. L., & Rich, S. (1988). Personality similarity in twins reared apart and together. *Journal of Personality and Social Psychology, 54,* 1031–1039.

Thomas, A., & Chess, S. (1977). *Temperament and development.* New York: Brunner-Mazel.

Tupes, E. C., & Christal, R. E. (1961). *Recurrent personality factors based on trait ratings* (USAF ASD Tech. Rep. No. 61–97).

Tupes, E. C., & Christal, R. E. (1992). Recurrent personality factors based on trait ratings. *Journal of Personality, 60,* 225–251.

White, R. W. (1976). *The enterprise of living: A view of personal growth.* New York: Holt, Rinehart & Winston.

Wiggins, J. S. (1980). Circumplex models of interpersonal behavior. In L. Wheeler (Ed.), *Review of Personality and Social Psychology* (pp. 256–294). Beverly Hills, CA: Sage.

Wiggins, J. S., & Trapnell, P. D. (1991). Personality structure: The return of the Big Five. In S. R. Briggs, R. Hogan, & W. H. Jones (Eds.), *Handbook of personality psychology.* Orlando, FL: Academic Press.

Young, P. T. (1936). *Motivation of behavior.* New York: Wiley.

Zwick, W. R., & Velicer, W. F. (1986). Comparison of five rules for determining the number of components to retain. *Psychological Bulletin, 99,* 432–442.

CHAPTER
17

THE DEVELOPMENT OF AGREEABLENESS AS A DIMENSION OF PERSONALITY

William G. Graziano
Texas A & M University

In any scientific enterprise, it is necessary to set priorities. In an emerging consensus, personality psychologists are assigning a top priority to the establishment of a language for describing the basic units of personality (Digman, 1990; Digman & Inouye, 1986; Goldberg, 1981; Hogan, 1983; John, 1990; McCrae & Costa, 1985). This consensus is derived from convergence in empirical work pointing toward a five-factor model (e.g., Digman, 1990; Digman & Takemoto-Chock, 1981; McCrae & Costa, 1987; McCrae & John, 1992) and from theoretical analyses offering explanations for the empirical regularities (e.g., Buss, 1991; Goldberg, 1981; Hogan, 1983; John, 1990; Wiggins & Trapnell, in press).

With few exceptions, empirical work on the five-factor model (or Big Five) is based on description of individual differences in adults by adult perceivers. Beyond the problem of empirical generality, there are conceptual problems associated with the restricted samples. The evidence supporting the five-factor model is pervasive but developmentally shallow. That is, the Big Five work is built largely on the phenomenology of adult natural language use, mostly in English or closely related languages (but see Church & Katigbak, 1989). The value of the five-factor model would be enhanced if it could be shown that Big Five dimensions in adults have developmental antecedents, or are linked to previous life adaptations. Whether these antecedents are linked to genetic differences (Bergeman et al., 1993), temperament (Digman, chap. 16 in this vol.), socialization (e.g., Halverson & Wampler, in press), or even quasi-unique nonshared family events (e.g., Dunn & Plomin, 1990), is less important than specifying some mechanisms that produce differences in personality (Buss, 1991; Connell & Furman, 1984; West & Graziano,

1989). If theoretically meaningful antecedents could be identified, we could have more confidence that the Big Five model offers a general structural representation of a set of adaptive solutions (Buss, 1991; Tooby & Cosmides, 1990).

The identification of antecedents is a difficult problem in developmental psychology (e.g., Emde & Harmon, 1984). Still, at least part of the problem lies at the adult personality end of the developmental continuum. When personality psychologists could not agree among themselves on the basic dimensions of adult personality structure, it was difficult for personality development researchers to establish a focus for the most productive developmental targets for framing their own research. In this regard, work on the Big Five dimensions can help researchers reexamine their perspectives on adult targets toward which personality development might be expected to proceed.

The purpose of this chapter is to examine one of the Big Five dimensions, Agreeableness, from a developmental perspective. There are several reasons why Agreeableness deserves such attention. First, an agreeablenesslike dimension seems to be pervasive in social perception and cognition. As we noted elsewhere (Graziano & Eisenberg, in press), previous research has been biased against the "discovery" of an agreeableness dimension, and the dimension still emerges. In fact, when Digman and Takemoto-Chock (1981) reanalyzed data from six major, large-scale studies, the first factor to emerge was labeled "friendly compliance vs. hostile non-compliance." The dimension is almost certainly not an artifact of population sampling: "Regardless of whether teachers rate children, officer candidates rate one another, college students rate one another, or clinical staff members rate graduate trainees, the results are pretty much the same" (Digman & Takemoto-Chock, 1981, p. 165). To this, we add that agreeableness may be even more salient as a personality dimension to persons reared in collectivist societies (e.g., Chinese) than to North Americans or Australians (Bond & Forgas, 1984).

Second, an agreeablenesslike dimension has special theoretical status in many different accounts of personality structure. Names and labels may differ across the diverse theoretical accounts, but conceptual similarities are apparent (see Graziano & Eisenberg, in press). For example, Wiggins (1990) marshaled evidence that two major (and apparently orthogonal) motivational systems, agency and communion, underlie interpersonal behavior. Communion, the striving for intimacy, union, and solidarity with others, can be mapped onto the Big Five dimension of Agreeableness. Digman and Takemoto-Chock (1981) explicitly linked this dimension to theorizing about the tensions between individual motives of selfishness and a societal concern for altruism.

In a similar vein, Hogan (1983) argued that humans needed to evolve characteristics that allowed them to capitalize on the advantages of group living. In particular, to survive and reproduce humans had to evolve procedures for cooperating, negotiating, and exchanging resources. Individuals who were unable or unwilling to make social adjustments may have been excluded from social groups, presumably to their personal and reproductive detriment.

Taking a different tack, Cosmides (1989) argued that establishing cooperative social exchanges is linked to reproductive competition, so the ability to form reciprocal alliances should have evolved as a major motive in humans. More specifically, Cosmides suggested that the human mind evolved with cognitive processes dedicated specifically to reasoning about social exchange. Similar conceptualizations of the social importance of an agreeableness-related dimension can be found in work by Buss (1991), Church and Katigbak (1989), and Low (1989).

If we add to this list theorizing about the genetic origins of altruism (e.g., Batson, 1983; Boorman & Levitt, 1980; Cunningham, 1985/1986; Eisenberg, Fabes, & Miller, in press; Hoffman, 1981; Simon, 1990), it is clear that an agreeableness-related dimension occupies an important theoretical niche in personality.

Third, agreeableness may be one of the most useful dimensions to examine from a developmental perspective, in that there appear to be early precursors of the dimension. One of the most widely used concepts in the childhood temperament literature is difficultness (Bates, 1986). This concept typically refers to a syndrome or collection of attributes in young children. At its core, the construct refers to frequent and intense expression of negative emotion. The term *difficult* refers to the interpersonal challenge this kind of child presents to parents and other caregivers. From a theoretical perspective, it would be valuable to uncover the origins of this aspect of early personality and to establish links, if any, to variations in agreeableness in older children and adults.

By way of foreshadowing, there are three complicating problems here. First, in the ordinary language descriptions of adults, Agreeableness may be perceived as a single dimension, but ultimately a multicomponent approach may yield greater predictive power. That is, Agreeableness may not be unidimensional, even within the sophisticated hierarchical-levels approach suggested by Digman (1990). Rather than placing disagreeable/hostile tendencies on one pole and agreeable/prosocial tendencies on the other pole, we might be better off exploring the possibility that such tendencies may not covary inversely (or even directly) with each other (see Victor, chap. 18 in this vol.).

Second, if Agreeableness in adults were composed of distinct components or domains, then the different components may be modularized (e.g., Cosmides, 1989), selectively activated, and may have different developmental antecedents. For example, Buss and Plomin (1986) suggested that Emotionality and Sociability may fuse with development into one large factor in adults, which they labeled Shyness. For another example, the hostile, aggressive module of Agreeableness may have its origins in the temperament of Emotionality, or in disruptions in attachment, whereas the prosocial module may have its origins in Sociability. These components might be relatively independent in infancy, but become more closely related to each other with development due to a variety of factors, including socialization experiences (Chess & Thomas, 1984; R. M. Lerner & J. Lerner, 1983).

Third, there appears to be a major link in adults between Agreeableness (Factor II) and Extraversion (Factor I) (see Digman, 1990, p. 421). Put differently, Agreeableness and Extraversion may be obliquely related, with overlapping characteristics and facets. Part of the developmental process may involve the evolution of links at some level between these two factors (cf. A. Buss & Plomin, 1986, p. 71).

THE DEVELOPMENT OF AGREEABLENESS: SOME POSSIBILITIES

There are several ways of approaching the development of Agreeableness. The concept of development is commonly associated with ordered structural change (Mahr, 1982). Within this general framework, there is room for alternatives. Unless stated otherwise, the working assumption is that Agreeableness is a single dimension, with a positive pole and a negative pole. We will, however, discuss attributes associated with the two poles separately when processes seem different. First, we focus on the biological underpinnings of Agreeableness. We consider the hypothesis that Agreeableness is a stable genetic disposition showing little apparent ordered change across the life span. Second, we consider Agreeableness in terms of stable individual differences interacting with transitional events in the interpersonal environment. Finally, we examine conceptual problems for future research.

Agreeableness as a Heritable Disposition

After reviewing some of the theoretical accounts of the origins of personality structure, especially the evolutionary accounts, a naive reader might be left with the impression that human personality structure is a fairly direct genetic manifestation of events in the Pleistocene era (cf. Oyama, 1985). In the interest of avoiding complicating but largely tangential issues (e.g., frequency-dependent selection), this section considers only the most direct issue: heritability of individual differences in agreeableness-related behaviors. For a more detailed analyses of social cross-pressures in the evolution of alternative strategies, see Graziano and Eisenberg (in press).

Contrary to some published opinions, the evidence on the differential heritability of an agreeableness-related dimension is not clear, at least as of this writing. According to the general consensus from twin data, approximately 40% to 50% of the variance in major, reliable personality dimensions is due primarily to genetic factors (Dunn & Plomin, 1990; Loehlin & Nichols, 1976; Plomin, DeFries, & McClearn, 1990). There is scant evidence to support strong claims about differential heritability of individual personality traits (cf. Buss & Plomin, 1986, pp. 71–72).

With this general trend in mind, we can examine the findings relevant to Agreeableness. There is suggestive evidence that Agreeableness seems to be more directly influenced by socialization processes than are the other four factors of the model. In their adoption/twin study, Bergeman et al. (1993) found shared rearing environment effects, but no evidence for genetic effects, on Agreeableness. This outcome stands in contrast to their findings for other dimensions, which showed substantial genetic influence. The Bergeman et al. result is consistent with findings that parental behavior in early childhood predicted empathic concern at adulthood (e.g., Koestner et al., 1990; Graziano & Eisenberg, in press; Halverson & Wampler, in press; Low, 1989; West & Graziano, 1989).

These results contrast with other results suggesting that some aspects of Agreeableness in adults may have heritable components. If altruism is accepted as a component of the Agreeableness dimension (Graziano & Eisenberg, in press), then additional evidence can be brought to bear on the issue of heritability. However, most of the research and theorizing on the role of genetics in altruism concerns the existence of a genetic basis of prosocial behavior in the entire human species, not the existence of biologically based mechanisms that might be the source of individual differences in altruism. Thus, the sociobiologists and psychologists interested in the genetic basis of altruism have done little work bearing directly on the issue of personality differences, much less personality development, in altruism.

An exception to these trends is a study by Rushton, Fulker, Neale, Nias, and H. J. Eysenck (1986), who reported analyses on questionnaire data from 573 adult twins. The questionnaires measured empathy, altruism, nurturance, aggressiveness, and assertiveness. Using maximum-likelihood model fitting, these authors suggested that approximately 50% of the variance on each of these measures was associated with genetic effects (vs. 0% associated with shared twin environment).

Most of the limited work on inherited differences in prosocial tendencies concerns the construct of empathy. Stimulated by sociobiological ideas, Batson (1983) and Hoffman (1981) proposed that the capacity for empathy is the biological substrate upon which human altruism is built. Empathy (and sympathy) has been linked empirically (Eisenberg & Fabes, 1991) as well as conceptually (Batson, 1987; Bierhoff, Klein, & Kramp, 1991; Blum, 1980; Feshbach, 1978; Hoffman, 1984; Staub, 1978) with prosocial behavior (including altruism). Therefore, if Hoffman and Batson were correct, genetically based individual differences in vicarious emotional responsivity to others could account for individual differences in altruism.

Consistent with the perspective that dispositional differences in both empathy and altruism have a biological basis, several groups of investigators have obtained high estimates of heritability (from .44 to .72) in studies of twins' self-reported empathy and prosocial behavior (Loehlin & Nichols, 1976; Matthews, Batson, Horn, & Rosenman, 1981; Rushton et al., 1986). These data must be interpreted with caution, however, because investigators frequently find higher relations between scores of identical twins than between scores of fraternal twins when self-report indices are used to measure aspects of personality (Plomin, 1986). Thus, the higher concordance for identical than fraternal twins' self-reported empathy and prosocial behavior could be due to the influence of genetically based personality traits (such as the need to appear in a socially desirable manner to others or oneself) that affect how individuals respond to self-report questionnaires.

If we turn to the negative side of Agreeableness, we see a somewhat different pattern. At the very least, there is evidence for the long-term stability of disagreeable behavior across the life span. Ill-tempered boys become men who are described as undercontrolled, irritable, and moody (Caspi, Bem, & Elder, 1989). These findings must be interpreted cautiously for the development of Agreeableness, however, given some reports of limited continuity between difficult infant temperament and adjustment in adulthood (e.g., Chess & Thomas, 1984).

In discussing their temperamental dimension of emotionality, Buss and Plomin (1984) suggested that in comparison with unemotional people, emotional people become distressed when confronted with emotional stimuli, and they react with higher levels of emotional arousal. As a consequence, they may be harder to soothe when stressed. Rowe and Plomin (1977) found a correlation of $-.42$ between ratings of children's emotionality and their soothability.

In one especially unpleasant form of disagreeableness, childhood aggression, chronic differences in emotional responding may play a key role. D. G. Perry and L. C. Perry (1974) found that chronically aggressive children react more aggressively when provoked, and "require" more suffering from their victims before ending an attack, than do nonaggressive children. Apparently, chronically aggressive children are not easy to placate or to soothe.

BIOLOGICAL DISPOSITIONS AND AGREEABLENESS

As a result of certain biological predispositions, individuals may follow a particular developmental trajectory leading to more or less Agreeableness (for an excellent general review of the biological bases of temperament, see Rothbart, 1989). At this juncture, it is not clear how such mechanisms might operate, but there are several speculative candidates.

Self-Regulation of Excitation

First, individual differences in Agreeableness may emerge as part of the ontogeny of systems of excitation and inhibition. If we can assume that Agreeableness is associated with the inhibition of negative affect, then models linking brain lateralization and inhibition are relevant to this discussion (cf. Rothbart, 1991).

Kinsbourne and Bemporad (1984) suggested a multiaxial, ontogenic model that explains the development of self-regulatory processes. In this model, the left frontotemporal cortex controls action over external change, including the planning and sequencing of acts (the "go" system). The right frontotemporal cortex controls internal emotional arousal (the "no go" system). The two systems operate synergistically, using information provided by posterior centers. Damage to the right orbital frontal cortex is associated with emotional disinhibition. A parallel line of thinking can be seen in Luria's (1966) work; the modulation of social behavior in accordance with the context is associated with the right frontal lobes. Damage to the left dorsolateral frontal area is associated with inaction and apathy. Overall, the normative evidence suggests that the right hemisphere develops sooner than the left.

Furthermore, Fox and Davidson (1984) suggested that there are differences in hemispheric specialization for affect. The left hemisphere is associated with positive affect and approach, whereas the right hemisphere is associated with negative affect and avoidance. Toward the end of the first year of life, development of commissural transfer permits left hemisphere inhibition of right hemisphere function. Two consequences are the inhibition of negative affect and the possibility of behavioral alternations between approach and avoidance.

The two models outlined previously were normative-developmental in focus, and described a supposedly universal pattern of neurological ontogeny. If there were individual differences, however, in the timing or completeness of any of these lateralization processes (as there surely must be), then there would be implications for origins of Agreeableness. That is, during ontogeny, individuals may differ in the strength or timing of their left hemispheric connections. With these differences, there would be corresponding differences in emotional expression, and in the inhibition of negative affect. Differences in expression in turn would lead to different socialization experiences. From a developmental perspective, even if the delayed ontogeny of inhibition were temporary, there could be long-term consequences.

Biochemical Differences and Agreeableness

A second speculative mechanism for explaining Agreeableness differences involves neuroregulatory amines (Panskepp, 1986). These neurochemical systems apparently operate globally to influence shifts in vigilance and tendencies to act. For present purposes, work by Cloninger is most relevant. Specifically, Cloninger (1987) speculated that norepinephrine functioning is related to reward dependence, which includes such behavior as being emotionally dependent (vs. coolly detached), warmly sympathetic (vs. tough-minded), sentimental, and sensitive to social cues. The bulk of the research on neuroregulatory amines has focused on psychiatric disorders, with relatively little work on normal adult personality processes.

Agreeableness in Interaction With Social Context

This section must be speculative because little is known about the ecological significance of personality for children's adaptations to their social environments (Graziano, 1987; Graziano & Waschull, in press; cf. Van Heck, 1989). If Agreeableness is generally important, then it is possible that its adaptive influence could be seen in relatively early social interaction.

The task of finding connections between the development of Agreeableness and context is complicated, however, by two additional factors. First, the confounding of personality and social learning histories of agreeable–disagreeable children may enhance dispositional tendencies, making authentic *developmental* processes harder to detect. In a passive genotype-environment (GE) correlation, agreeable–disagreeable children may share heredity as well as environmental influences with members of their families, and thus passively inherit environments correlated with their genetic dispositions. In a reactive GE correlation, agreeable–disagreeable children may systematically elicit different reactions from others. In an active GE correlation, agreeable–disagreeable children may actively select or create environments consistent with their own predispositions (i.e., "niche picking"). These correlations may provide clues as to how genotypes transact with environments during development (e.g., Plomin, DeFries, & McClearn, 1990, pp. 251–252; Scarr & McCartney, 1983).

Second, as children age, they live in different subcultures with different adaptation requirements (Higgins & Parsons, 1983; Lerner & Tubman, 1989; Simmons & Blythe, 1987). Personality attributes desirable in one childhood ecology may be less desirable in another (e.g., sociability). It is not implausible that Agreeableness differences could also interact with the social ecology. In this regard, it might be valuable to focus on periods of transition from one kind of ecology/subculture into another (e.g., home to school).

Modern attachment theorists (e.g., Main, Kaplan, & Cassidy, 1985) suggest that the early relationship between an infant and a caregiver provides a critical context for personality development. Some of this theorizing is relevant to the development of individual differences in Agreeableness. Main et al. suggested that early caregiver–child relationships induce the child to build a cognitive representation or "working model" of relationships in general. Sensitive, responsive caregiving leads to a positive model of relationships, whereas inconsistent, inept caregiving leads to a negative model. These working models are largely nonconscious, but influence the way subsequent relationship-relevant information is encoded and processed.

Further, parents of children who had been classified as securely attached seemed at ease and balanced in describing their own attachment-related experiences. Parents of children who had been classified as avoidant dismissed the value of attachment, and had difficulty recalling their own attachment-related experiences. Parents of children who had been classified as ambivalent seemed preoccupied, and had difficulty presenting a coherent account of their own attachment related experiences. (Incidentally, this may be an illustration of genotype–environment correlation.)

Kobak and Sceery (1988) classified college students into one of three adult attachment categories: Dismissing of Attachment, Secure, or Preoccupied. These classifications were then related to peer Q-sort ratings of ego resiliency, ego undercontrol, hostility, anxiety, and self-report measures of distress, perceived competence, and social support. The Secure group was rated as more ego resilient, less anxious, and less hostile by peers, and reported less distress and higher levels of social support, relative to the other two adult attachment groups. Presumably, these personality differences mediate the individual's "strategies" in initiating subsequent romantic and conjugal/natal relationships (Belsky, Steinberg, & Draper, 1991; Draper & Belsky, 1990; Draper & Harpending, 1982).

Modern attachment theory and its associated research results raise a host of issues for subsequent research on Agreeableness. First, this theory asserts that attachment processes early in life exert strong influences on later personality development. Within these analyses, however, it is not clear that attachment experiences in childhood, per se, are responsible for adult personality organization. How do we partition variance in personality between macro-ecological and social-organizational variables (e.g., Meehl, 1970)? Furthermore, why must we assume that social organizational variables like wife–husband relations cause personality development? The causal arrow could plausibly go the other way, through selective mating, and GE correlations.

Beyond these issues, attachment theory raises important questions about plasticity and sensitive periods in personality development. Still, modern attachment theory may be alone in suggesting mechanisms that justify a single-dimension approach to Agreeableness (for a somewhat different perspective, see Cairns, 1979, pp. 186–192; Cairns, 1986).

One of the most complex life ecologies surrounds the transition from childhood to adolescence. In this phase of the life cycle, physiological changes associated with puberty occur, relations with parents and peers are changing, and school structure and academic requirements are altered (Simmons & Blythe, 1987). There is evidence that during early adolescence the self-concept is reorganized, and personality may be undergoing rapid transition (Eccles et al., 1989). In this age group and social ecology, Agreeableness differences may be especially apparent.

Some data relevant to these speculations come from Digman and Inouye (1986), who asked classroom teachers in Hawaii to describe their own sixth-grade students. They conducted factor analyses and found clear evidence for the Big Five dimensions. Digman (1989) reported moderate stability across a 4-year period from childhood into early adolescence on Big Five dimensions.

Given that Big Five dimensions appear to be observable in adolescents by adult observers who know them reasonably well, Agreeableness differences in adolescents might be conceptually related to adaptation or "adjustment" within the school context. In their analysis of the components of adolescent self-concept, Eccles et al. (1989) reported that four domains appear to be especially important to adolescent self-evaluation. For both males and females, the most important domain was social competence. Social competence is, of course, a molar construct, but it does include components that overlap with Agreeableness, such as cooperation and positive social interaction. Given the premium adolescents place on competence in peer relations, it is plausible that Agreeableness (and possibly the so-called super-factors of Extraversion and Neuroticism) should be associated with adjustment.

Graziano and Ward (1992) probed the link among Big Five personality differences, self-reported personality differences, and adjustment to school among young adolescents. They used a multimethod converging analysis, with three sources of data: adolescent self-report on standardized personality inventories, classroom teacher trait ratings and evaluations of adjustment, and school guidance counselor evaluations of adjustment.

Participants were 91 adolescent students attending public schools in a nonurban school district in north Georgia (USA). They ranged from 11 to 14 years of age ($M = 12.12$ years). All student were sixth and seventh graders. Of these students, 32 were African Americans, and 1 was Hispanic. Each of these 91 participants provide self-evaluations, and were evaluated by at least one teacher and one school guidance counselor.

Results showed that teachers and counselors do perceive differences in Agreeableness among the students, and attribute these differences to adjustment and social life. Most interesting perhaps are the correlations associated with teachers' professional evaluation of adolescent adjustment to school (aggregated across two time periods). Teachers' ratings of Agreeableness were significantly correlated with evaluations of adjustment (.41, $p < .01$). Victor (chap. 18 in this vol.) found similar results in that Agreeableness was strongly negatively correlated with behavior problems. [Consistent with Digman & Inouye, the school-related dimension of Conscientiousness had a strong relation to teachers' evaluations of student adjustment (.72). For comparison, other significant relations were found for Neuroticism (–.46), and Extraversion (.31).]

Teachers completed a more focused evaluation of adolescent self-esteem and competence across five domains using the Harter (1983) scales. These evaluations were correlated with the Big Five trait ratings. Agreeableness was significantly related to self-evaluation in the domains of academics (.41), appearance (.21), and conduct (.43), but not social life (.19) or athletics (.13).

The correlation between teacher and counselor evaluation of adjustment was .44 ($p < .001$). Other correlations, however, suggested that the teachers and counselors seemed to be sensitive to different attributes in the adolescent student. For teachers, the best single Big Five predictor of adolescent adjustment was the teacher's own rating of Conscientiousness ($r = .72$). For counselors, however,

Agreeableness loomed almost as large as the school-work-related dimension of Conscientiousness. Counselors' evaluation of school adjustment was correlated with teachers' rating of the adolescents' Conscientiousness (.46), followed closely by Agreeableness (.39), and Neuroticism (−.34).

It is possible to classify adolescents as adjusted or not based on a joint median split of adult ratings. Specifically, Group 1 was students who both teachers and counselors rated as adjusted (i.e., above the sample median on the adjustment measure); Group 2 was students who both teachers and counselors said were not adjusted (i.e., below the sample median); Group 3 was students who counselors said were adjusted but teachers said were not adjusted; and Group 4 was students who counselors said were not adjusted, but teachers said were adjusted.

Groups 1 and 2 were the largest due to the significant correlation between teacher and counselor ratings of adjustment. Nonetheless, the rough four-fold classification allowed us to probe the dynamics of adult judgments of adjustment. Once students are classified into one of four categories, discriminant functions can be used to probe for Big Five differences among the categories.

Results indicated that Groups 1 and 2 could be significantly separated using the Big Five dimensions. In decreasing order of structural Rs, the dimensions were Conscientiousness (.73), Agreeableness (.52), Neuroticism (−.39), Openness to Experience, and Extraversion (both .24). None of the self-report measures exceeded .22.

CONCEPTUAL PROBLEMS FOR FUTURE RESEARCH

The literature outlined here suggests that the five-factor model in general, and Agreeableness in particular, may offer useful descriptions of "developmental targets" toward which personality development research could be aimed. There are several conceptual problems, however, that should be addressed. The first problem involves the conceptualization of the Agreeableness dimension. The immediate question involves the bipolar definition of the dimension. It is not clear whether hostile, unfriendly behavior should be regarded as the bipolar counterpart to friendly, altruistic behavior. For personality development researchers, this is an important issue because it concerns the specification of developmental targets, and ultimately developmental processes and mechanisms (e.g., Cairns, 1979, 1986).

An alternative to the bipolar approach is to treat the two poles as separate systems, and to assess whether there are different processes and developmental antecedents. The potential advantage of this alternative is greater specificity and predictive power. The potential disadvantage is a loss of a bigger explanatory picture. For example, if it could be demonstrated, with prospective longitudinal data (Halverson, 1988), that disruptions in parental attachment reliably produced anxious, hostile, unfriendly behavior, whereas secure attachments reliably produced relaxed, friendly, prosocial behavior, then a unified Agreeableness dimension would be better justified. To date, no such demonstration is available (cf. Cairns, 1979, 1986; Kobak & Sceery, 1988; Renken, Egeland, Marvinney, Manglesdorf, & Sroufe, 1989).

The second conceptual problem is related to the first. Without conceptual agreement on the personality dimensions, or on processes presumed to justify a single continuum (e.g., attachment), it is harder to specify the developmental mechanisms responsible for the structural transformation of persons across the life span. Is Agreeableness the adult fusion of genetic differences, expressed in childhood as Emotionality and Sociability? Buss and Plomin (1986) labeled this fusion Shyness, but research suggests that in adults, Extraversion and Agreeableness are linked. The main component of Extraversion appears to be Sociability. Conceptually, it would be valuable to have stronger hypotheses about how these attributes are interconnected before we attempt to specify the mechanisms that link them in development.

A third problem is related to the second, but involves processes of personality development itself. In its simplest form, the question is this: What is personality development the development of? Do age-related changes in Agreeableness reflect any structural transformation of the person, or are we seeing changes in behavioral manifestations of largely unchanging latent variables? The changes might reflect little more than accumulating life experience or changed demands from different ecologies or subcultures, which challenge the behavioral repertoire available to persons of different ages. Even within modern attachment theory (e.g., Main, Kaplan, & Cassidy, 1985), it is not clear what develops, or what developmental processes, if any, occur as the child builds "working models" of relationships. Are individual differences in adult Agreeableness manifestations in personality development of the structural transformation of the cognitive working model (e.g., Kobak & Sceery, 1988)? These questions beg for research.

These are daunting problems, but the literature reviewed in this chapter suggests some promising leads. In particular, a consensus is emerging on developmental targets. This is no small first step toward a greater understanding of personality structure and its development.

ACKNOWLEDGMENTS

Portions of this chapter were presented at a conference in Wassenaar, The Netherlands, on June 17–20, 1991. The conference, sponsored by Netherlands Institute for Advanced Study in the Humanities and Social Sciences, was entitled "The Development of the Structure of Temperament and Personality from Infancy to Adulthood."

REFERENCES

Bates, J. E. (1986). The measurement of temperament. In R. Plomin & J. Dunn (Eds.), *The study of temperament: Changes, continuities and challenges* (pp. 1–12). Hillsdale, NJ: Lawrence Erlbaum Associates.

Batson, C. D. (1983). Sociobiology and the role of religion in promoting prosocial behavior: An alternative view. *Journal of Personality and Social Psychology, 45*, 1380–1385.

Batson, C. D. (1987). Prosocial motivation: Is it ever truly altruistic? In L. Berkowitz (Ed.), *Advances in experimental social psychology* (pp. 65–122). New York: Academic Press.

Belsky, J., Steinberg, L., & Draper, P. (1991). Childhood experience, interpersonal development, and reproductive strategy: An evolutionary theory of socialization. *Child Development, 62*, 647–670.

Bergeman, C. S., Chipuer, H., Plomin, R., Pedersen, N. L., McClearn, G. E., Nesselroade, J. R., Costa, P. T., & McCrae, R. R. (1993). Genetic and environmental effects on openness to experience, agreeableness, and conscientiousness: An adoption/twin study. *Journal of Personality, 61*, 159–180.

Bierhoff, H. W., Klein, R., & Kramp, P. (1991). Evidence for the altruistic personality from data on accident research. *Journal of Personality, 59*, 263–280.

Blum, L. A. (1980). *Friendship, altruism and morality.* London: Routledge & Kegan Paul.

Bond, M. H., & Forgas, J. P. (1984). Linking person perception to behavior intentions across cultures: The role of cultural collectivism. *Journal of Cross-Cultural Psychology, 15*, 337–352.

Boorman, S. A., & Levitt, P. R. (1980). *The genetics of altruism.* New York: Academic Press.

Buss, A. H., & Plomin, R. (1984). *A temperament theory of personality development* (2nd ed.). New York: Wiley.

Buss, A. H., & Plomin, R. (1986). The EAS approach to temperament. In R. Plomin & J. Dunn (Eds.), *The study of temperament: Changes, continuities and challenges* (pp. 67–80). Hillsdale, NJ: Lawrence Erlbaum Associates.

Buss, D. M. (1991). Evolutionary personality psychology. In M. R. Rosenzweig & L. W. Porter (Eds.), *Annual Review of Psychology, 42*, 459–491.

Cairns, R. B. (1979). *Social development: The origins and plasticity of interchanges.* San Francisco: Freeman.

Cairns, R. B. (1986). An evolutionary and developmental perspective on aggression patterns. In C. Zahn Waxler, E. M. Cummings, & R. Iannoti (Eds.), *Altruism and aggression* (pp. 58–87). New York: Cambridge University Press.

Caspi, A., Bem, D., & Elder, G. H., Jr. (1989). Continuities and consequences of interactional styles across the life course. *Journal of Personality, 57*, 375–406.

Chess, S., & Thomas, A. (1984). *Origins and evolution of behavior disorders: Infancy to early adult life.* New York: Brunner/Mazel.

Church, A. T., & Katigbak, M. S. (1989). Internal, external, and self-reward structure of personality in non-Western culture: An investigation of cross-language and cross-cultural generalizability. *Journal of Personality & Social Psychology, 57*, 857–872.

Cloninger, C. R. (1987). Neurogetic adaptive mechanisms in alcoholism. *Science, 236*, 410–416.

Connell, J. P., & Furman, W. C. (1984). The study of transitions: Conceptual and methodological issues. In R. N. Emde & R. J. Harmon (Eds.), *Continuities and discontinuities in development* (pp. 153–174). New York: Plenum.

Cosmides, L. (1989). The logic of social exchange: Has natural selection shaped how humans reason? Studies with the Wason selection task. *Cognition, 31*, 187–276.

Cunningham, M. R. (1985/1986). Levites and brother's keepers: A sociobiological perspective on prosocial behavior. *Humboldt Journal of Social Relations, 13*, 35–67.

Digman, J. M. (1989). Five robust trait dimensions: Development, stability, and utility. *Journal of Personality, 57*, 195–214.

Digman, J. M. (1990). Personality structure: The emergence of the five-factor model. In M. R. Rosenzweig & L. W. Porter (Eds.), *Annual Review of Psychology, 41*, 417–440.

Digman, J. M., & Inouye, J. (1986). Further specification of the five robust factors of personality. *Journal of Personality & Social Psychology, 50*, 116–123.

Digman, J. M., & Takemoto-Chock, N. K. (1981). Factors in the natural language of personality: Re-analysis, comparison, and interpretation of six major studies. *Multivariate Behavioral Research, 16*, 149–170.

Draper, P., & Belsky, J. (1990). Personality development in evolutionary perspective. *Journal of Personality, 58*, 141–162.

Draper, P., & Harpending, H. (1982). Father absence and reproductive strategy: An evolutionary perspective. *Journal of Anthropological Research, 38*, 255–273.

Dunn, J., & Plomin, R. (1990). *Separate lives*. New York: Basic Books.

Eccles, J. S., Wigfield, A., Flanagan, C., Miller, C., Reuman, D., & Yee, D. (1989). Self-concepts, domain values, and self-esteem: Relations and changes at early adolescence. *Journal of Personality, 57*, 283–310.

Eisenberg, N. H., & Fabes, R. A. (1991). Prosocial behavior and empathy: A multimethod developmental perspective. In M. S. Clark (Ed.), *Prosocial behavior* (pp. 34–61). Newbury Park, CA: Sage.

Eisenberg, N. H., Fabes, R. A., & Miller, P. (in press). The evolutionary and neurological roots of prosocial behavior. In L. Ellis & H. Hoffman (Eds.), *Evolution, the brain, and criminal behavior: Explorations in biosocial criminology*.

Emde, R. N., & Harmon, R. J. (Eds.). (1984). *Continuities and discontinuities in development*. New York: Plenum.

Feshbach, N. D. (1978). Studies of empathic behavior in children. In B. A. Maher (Ed.), *Progress in experimental personality research* (Vol. 8, pp. 1–47). New York: Academic Press.

Fox, N. A., & Davidson, R. J. (1984). Hemispheric substrates of affect: A developmental model. In N. A. Fox & R. J. Davidson (Eds.), *The psychology of affective development* (pp. 353–382). Hillsdale, NJ: Lawrence Erlbaum Associates.

Goldberg, L. R. (1981). Language and individual differences: The search for universals in personality lexicons. In L. Wheeler (Ed.), *Review of personality and social psychology* (Vol. 2, pp. 141–165). Beverly Hills, CA: Sage.

Graziano, W. G. (1987). Lost in thought at the choice point: Cognition, context, and equity. In J. C. Masters & W. P. Smith (Eds.), *Social comparison, social justice and relative deprivation: Theoretical, empirical, and policy perspectives* (pp. 265–294). Hillsdale, NJ: Lawrence Erlbaum Associates.

Graziano, W. G., & Eisenberg, N. H. (in press). Agreeableness: A dimension of personality. In R. Hogan, J. Johnson, & S. Briggs (Eds.), *Handbook of personality psychology*. Orlando, FL: Academic Press.

Graziano, W. G., & Ward, D. (1992). Probing the Big Five in adolescence: Personality and adjustment during a developmental transition. *Journal of Personality, 60*, 425–439.

Graziano, W. G., & Waschull, S. (in press). Social development and self-monitoring. In N. Eisenberg (Ed.), *Review of Personality and Social Psychology* (Special Issue: Social Development). Thousand Oaks, CA: Sage.

Halverson, C. F. (1988). Remembering your parents: Reflections on the retrospective method. *Journal of Personality, 56*, 435–445.

Halverson, C. F., & Wampler, K. (in press). Family influences on personality development. In R. Hogan, J. Johnson, & S. Briggs (Eds.), *Handbook of personality psychology*. Orlando, FL: Academic Press.

Harter, S. (1983). Developmental perspectives on the self-system. In P. Mussen (Ed.), *Handbook of Child Psychology* (4th ed.) (Vol. 4, pp. 275–386). New York: Wiley.

Higgins, E. T., & Parsons, J. (1983). Social cognition and the social life of the child: Stages as subcultures. In E. T. Higgins, D. N. Ruble, & W. W. Hartup (Eds.), *Social cognition and social development: A sociocultural perspective* (pp. 15–62). New York: Cambridge University Press.

Hoffman, M. L. (1981). Is altruism part of human nature? *Journal of Personality and Social Psychology, 40,* 121–137.

Hoffman, M. L. (1984). Interaction of affect and cognition in empathy. In C. E. Izard, J. Kagan, & R. B. Zajonc (Eds.), *Emotions, cognition, and behavior* (pp. 103–131). Cambridge, MA: Cambridge University Press.

Hogan, R. T. (1983). A socioanalytic theory of personality. In M. Page (Ed.), *Nebraska symposium on motivation: Personality-current theory and research* (pp. 58–89). Lincoln, NE: University of Nebraska Press.

John, O. P. (1990). The Big Five-factor taxonomy: Dimensions of personality in the natural language and in questionnaires. In L. A. Pervin (Ed.), *Handbook of personality theory and research* (pp. 66–100). New York: Guilford.

Kinsbourne, M., & Bemporad, B. (1984). Lateralization of emotion: A model and the evidence. In N. A. Fox & R. J. Davidson (Eds.), *The psychology of affective development* (pp. 259–292). Hillsdale, NJ: Lawrence Erlbaum Associates.

Kobak, R. R., & Sceery, A. (1988). Attachment in late adolescence: Working models, affect regulation, and representations of self and others. *Child Development, 59,* 135–146.

Koestner, R., Franz, C., & Weinberger, J. (1990). The family origins of empathic concerns: A 26-year longitudinal study. *Journal of Personality and Social Psychology, 58,* 709–717.

Lerner, R. M., & Lerner, J. (1983). Temperament and adaptation across life: Theoretical and empirical issues. In P. B. Baltes & O. G. Brim (Eds.), *Life-span development and behavior* (Vol. 5, pp. 197–231). New York: Academic Press.

Lerner, R. M., & Tubman, J. G. (1989). Conceptual issues in studying continuity and discontinuity in personality development across life. *Journal of Personality, 57,* 343–373.

Loehlin, J. C., & Nichols, R. C. (1976). *Heredity, environment and personality.* Austin: University of Texas Press.

Low, B. S. (1989). Cross-cultural patterns in the training of children: An evolutionary perspective. *Journal of Comparative Psychology, 103,* 311–319.

Luria, A. R. (1966). *Higher cortical functions in man.* New York: Basic Books.

Mahr, E. (1982). *The growth of biological thought: Diversity, evolution, and inheritance.* Cambridge, MA: Bellknap.

Main, M., Kaplan, N., & Cassidy, J. (1985). Security in infancy, childhood, and adulthood: A move to the level of representation. In I. Bretherton & E. Waters (Eds.), *Growing points of attachment theory and research* (SRCD Monographs Serial No. 209, pp. 66–104). Chicago: University of Chicago Press.

Matthews, K. A., Batson, C. D., Horn, J., & Rosenman, R. H. (1981). "Principles in his nature which interest him in the fortune of others . . .": The heritability of empathic concern for others. *Journal of Personality, 49,* 237–247.

McCrae, R. R., & Costa, P. T. (1985). Updating Norman's "Adequate taxonomy": Intelligence and personality dimensions in the natural language and in questionnaires. *Journal of Personality and Social Psychology, 49,* 710–721.

McCrae, R. R., & Costa, P. T., Jr. (1987). Validation of the five-factor model of personality across instruments and observers. *Journal of Personality & Social Psychology, 52,* 81–90.

McCrae, R. R., & John, O. J. (1992). The five-factor model of personality structure: An introduction. *Journal of Personality, 60,* 175–215.

Meehl, P. E. (1970). Nuisance variables and the ex post facto design. In M. Radner & S. Winokur (Eds.), *Minnesota studies in the philosophy of science: Vol. 4. Analysis of theories and methods of physics and psychology* (pp. 373–402). Minneapolis: University of Minnesota Press.

Oyama, S. (1985). *The ontogeny of information: Developmental systems and evolution.* New York: Cambridge University Press.

Panskepp, J. (1986). The neurochemistry of behavior. In M. R. Rosenzweig & L. W. Porter (Eds.), *Annual Review of Psychology, 37,* 77–107.

Perry, D. G., & Perry, L. C. (1974). Denial of suffering in the victim as a stimulus to violence in aggressive boys. *Child Development, 45*, 55–62.
Plomin, R. (1986). *Development, genetics, and psychology.* Hillsdale, NJ: Lawrence Erlbaum Associates.
Plomin, R., DeFries, J. C., & McClearn, G. E. (1990). *Behavioral genetics: A primer* (2nd ed.). New York: Freeman.
Renken, B., Egeland, B., Marvinney, D., Manglesdorf, S., & Sroufe, A. (1989). Early childhood antecedents of aggression and passive-withdrawal in early elementary school. *Journal of Personality, 57*, 257–282.
Rothbart, M. K. (1989). Biological processes in temperament. In G. A. Kornstamm, J. Bates, & M. K. Rothbart (Eds.), *Temperament in childhood* (pp. 77–110). Chichester: Wiley.
Rothbart, M. K. (1991). Temperament: A developmental framework. In J. Strelau & A. Angleitner (Eds.), *Explorations in temperament: International perspectives on theory and measurement* (pp. 61–74). New York: Plenum.
Rowe, D., & Plomin, R. (1977). Temperament in early childhood. *Journal of Personality Assessment, 41*, 150–156.
Rushton, J. P., Fulker, D. W., Neal, M. C., Nias, D. K. B., & Eysenck, H. J. (1986). Altruism and aggression: The heritability of individual differences. *Journal of Personality and Social Psychology, 50*, 1192–1198.
Scarr, S., & McCartney, K. (1983). How people make their own environments: A theory of genotype–environment effects. *Child Development, 54*, 424–435.
Simmons, R. G., & Blythe, D. (1987). *Moving into adolescence: The impact of pubertal change and school context.* Hawthorn, NY: Aldine de Gruyler.
Simon, H. A. (1990). A mechanism for social selection and successful altruism. *Science, 250*, 1665–1668.
Staub, E. (1974). Helping a distressed person: Social, personality, and stimulus determinants. In L. Berkowitz (Ed.), *Advances in experimental social psychology* (Vol. 7, pp. 293–341). New York: Academic Press.
Tooby, J., & Cosmides, L. (1990). On the universality of human nature and the uniqueness of the individual: The role of genetics and adaptation. *Journal of Personality, 58*, 17–68.
Van Heck, G. (1989). Situational concepts: Definitions and classification. In P. J. Hettema (Ed.), *Personality and environment: Assessment of human adaptation* (pp. 53–69, 241–259). Chichester, England: Wiley.
West, S. G., & Graziano, W. G. (1989). Long-term stability and change in personality: An introduction. *Journal of Personality, 57*, 175–194.
Wiggins, J. S. (1990). Agency and communion as conceptual coordinates for the understanding and measurement of interpersonal behavior. In D. Cicchetti & W. Grove (Eds.), *Thinking critically in psychology: Essays in honor of Paul E. Meehl* (pp. 89–113). Minneapolis: University of Minnesota Press.
Wiggins, J. S., & Trapnell, P. (in press). Personality structures: The return of the Big Five. In S. R. Briggs, R. Hogan, & W. H. Jones (Eds.), *Handbook of personality psychology.* Orlando, FL: Academic Press.

CHAPTER

18

THE FIVE-FACTOR MODEL APPLIED TO INDIVIDUAL DIFFERENCES IN SCHOOL BEHAVIOR

James B. Victor
Hampton University

The resurgence of research interest in personality traits has led to findings that consistently produce five factors of personality. Most of the earlier studies that have shown the five-factor model, now often referred to as the Big Five, have come from peer ratings of adults in college or other educational settings (Norman, 1963; Tupes & Christal, 1961). Exceptions include the studies by Costa and McCrae (1980; McCrae & Costa, 1985), whose subjects were mature adults and data obtained included questionnaire data as well as ratings. In a recent review, Digman (1990) showed that consensus about the validity and usefulness of this approach has been steadily increasing. A variety of recent studies have revealed the presence of the Big Five dimensions in different languages (Angleitner, Ostendorf, & John, 1990; Hofstee, Brokken, & Land, 1981), internal judgments (Peabody & Goldberg, 1989), across methods of analysis (Goldberg, 1990), and in Belgian teachers' descriptions of children using "personal" constructs based on Kelly's (1955) work (Mervielde, chap. 20 in this vol.).

THE SCHOOL-AGE BIG FIVE

An important departure from adult ratings is the series of studies conducted by Digman and his colleagues (Digman, 1989; Digman & Inouye, 1986; Digman & Takemoto-Chock, 1981). These studies used teacher's ratings of young school age children for analysis. It is now clear that whether teachers rated children or college students rated each other, or officer candidates rated each other, or staff members rated their charges, the results were remarkably similar.

Although the names of the factors have varied a great deal from study to study, the names used in the McCrae and Costa studies (1985) are fairly representative of those used more recently in adult samples: Introversion/Extraversion, Conscientiousness, Agreeableness, Neuroticism, and Openness (also, often referred to as Culture). Repeated samples of studies of teachers' ratings of children, however, have led Digman (1989) to suggest slightly different labels. For example, slight factor structure differences of adjective loadings, with the strong negative end suggesting psychopathology, have led Digman to rename the Agreeableness factor as Friendly Compliance versus Hostile Noncompliance.

Similarly, because Conscientiousness consistently has shared variance with the Agreeableness factor (Friendly Compliance) and Achievement (school grades), Digman now prefers the construct label Will to Achieve. Finally, Digman (1989) suggested that the factor of Openness/Culture is best conceptualized as the broad domain of Intellect. For clarity, the more traditional names of Introversion/Extraversion, Neuroticism, Conscientiousness, Openness to Experience, and Agreeableness will be used here to refer to these Big Five constructs.

MODELS OF CHILD PSYCHOPATHOLOGY

An area that has been studied separately from the factor analytic approach to personality is the factor analytic approach to child psychopathology. Quay and Peterson (1967) proposed a factor analytically derived model based on symptoms and behavior statements commonly used by child and adolescent treatment workers in a variety of clinical settings. The original checklist and its updated version (Quay & Peterson, 1987) have been widely used and was the basis for much of our earlier work (Halverson & Victor, 1976; Victor & Halverson, 1975, 1976, 1980; Victor, Halverson, Inoff, & Buczkowski, 1973). The Revised Behavior Problem Checklist (RBPC; Quay & Peterson, 1967, 1987) has consistently produced four factors (Socialized Aggression, Attention Problems-Immaturity, Anxiety-Withdrawal, and Conduct Disorders). Two other factors have been reproduced in clinical populations, Psychotic Behavior and Motor Tension Excess. The dominant dimensions from the RBPC based on normal samples of children have been Conduct Disorders (more characteristic of male behavior), and to a lesser extent Anxiety-Withdrawal (more characteristic of female behavior).

A more recent approach to assessing child psychopathology has become increasingly popular, the Child Behavior Checklist (CBCL; Achenbach & Edlebrock, 1983); I view the approach by Quay and Peterson (1967, 1987) as more consistent with our own past research approach and the Big Five model.

What would be the advantage of viewing child behavior disorders through a broader model of the dimensions of personality? First, developmentalists have long been concerned, as have many child-care professionals and students of child psychopathology, of the negative "halo" effect when rating behavior disorders in children. Most methods of assessing behavior problems in children, including the most frequently used approaches (e.g., Achenbach & Edlebrock, 1983; Quay & Peterson, 1987), use only problem behaviors or symptoms when assessing children. There is no opportunity for the rater to give a fuller description of the child, thus disallowing a view of the child's relative strengths. Work is now underway to develop individual profiles across the Big Five dimensions for adults (de Raad, Hendriks, & Hofstee, chap. 5 in this vol.), and for children (Mervielde, chap. 20 in this vol.). If psychopathological behavior ratings on the RBPC and CBCC are largely subsumed under the Big Five model, it would then be possible to develop individual profiles across the five personality dimensions and get a fuller picture of the child's personality or behavior patterns.

Second, because child personality models are less well developed than adult models and have typically remained at the single construct level (e.g., Reflection-Impulsivity), it is much more difficult to study how personality changes (develops) over the developmental period. It has now been shown that the Big Five dimensions are essentially the same as for adults when teachers rate children from ages 4 to 12 (Digman, chap. 16 in this vol.; Mervielde, chap. 20 in this vol.). If, as I believe, behavior problems in children can largely be understood in terms of the Big Five personality model, then developmental change and related issues can be studied with this approach using a unified perspective from early childhood to adulthood.

Much of the variance in behavior problems in normal school populations can be explained by the Big Five model. More specifically, the dominant dimension in the school years, Conduct Disorders, can be described largely by the Big Five model of personality. In addition, the relations among these constructs can best be understood by including in the data set measures of academic achievement. More specifically, the Big Five model will account for much of the variance in academic achievement. The present study was a direct test of the commonality between personality, behavior problems, and school achievement.

METHOD

Research Participants

The sample consisted of 179 fifth- and sixth-grade children for whom measures were obtained on teacher-rated personality traits, standardized academic achievement, and teacher-rated school behavior problems. The school district is in a rural county on the Chesapeake Bay, Virginia. Families were predominantly working-class and 39 (22%) are African American.

Data Collection Procedures and Instruments

In the middle-school arrangement, each fifth- and sixth-grade level consisted of a team of four teachers. Each teacher was responsible for certain subjects to all of the students in the grade cohort. The data were collected over a 3-month period in the Spring and all teachers expressed comfort in rating all children.

Personality. Each homeroom teacher completed the Hawaii Scales for Judging Behavior (Digman & Inouye, 1986) on the class. The Hawaii Scales for Judging Child Behavior ask teachers to rate the students in their class on 43 adjectives, such as curious, jealous, fearful, considerate, and so on. Each teacher followed printed instructions that involved scaling all children in the class on *each* adjective (i.e., from those children who most closely represent the adjective to those that least represent the adjective). The outcome yields numerical values assigned as 1 for the lowest to 9 for the highest. This procedure resulted in distributions that were quasi-normal and symmetrical with very similar means and standard deviations across items.

Development of Big Five Dimensions. A principal-components analysis was performed and five factors were extracted. The factors were rotated using a normalized varimax method. The five factors were similar to those produced by Digman and his colleagues (Digman, 1989; Digman & Inouye, 1986; Digman & Takemoto-Chock, 1981). Table 18.1 summarizes the factor loadings for the five factors in the present study (Study V) as compared to the loading obtained by Digman and Inouye (Study D). The factors have been arranged in the order that they emerged for Digman and Inouye (1986). The five-factor model accounted for 66% of the variance in the present data set and the order determined by amount of variance accounted for each factor is discussed later.

The first factor was clearly the Extraversion factor found in most Big Five studies. The high loading adjectives that defined the factor for Digman and Inouye (1986) had similar high loadings in the present analysis. The present factor had a number of additional adjectives (jealous, spiteful, mannerly, conscientious, fickle, and nervous) that also had loadings not revealed in the Digman and Inouye (1986) study. This factor also emerged first in our analysis and accounted for 26% of the variance.

The second factor was Agreeableness (Goldberg, 1981; McCrae & Costa, 1987; Norman, 1963; Tupes & Christal, 1961). Digman argued that the negative end of the factor has a strong suggestion of psychopathology. Indeed, the present factor had strong negative loadings on spiteful, jealous, and touchy. The adjectives that loaded on this factor resembled those produced in the Digman studies. The factor was strongly bipolar. Digman preferred the label Friendly Compliance versus Hostile Noncompliance. It is referred to here with the more common label of Agreeableness. In the present analysis, however, it emerged third and accounted for 6.7% of the variance.

The third factor in both the present and in Digman's earlier studies was a good representation of the factor most often called Conscientiousness in adult studies (Costa & McCrae, 1988; Goldberg , 1981; McCrae & Costa, 1987). The factor has variously been labeled Superego Strength (Digman, 1963), Industriousness (Digman, 1972), and Will to Achieve (Digman, 1986) in samples of children. The factor was characterized here by typical positive loadings on neat, careful, persevering,

TABLE 18.1
Factor Loadings on the Hawaii Scales in the Present Study
Compared to Digman & Inouye (1986)

Scale	I Extraversion		II Agreeableness		III Conscientiousness		IV Neuroticism		V Openness to Experience	
	V*	D	V	D	V	D	V	D	V	D
Energetic	79	73	—	—	—	—	—	—	—	—
Restless	79	—	—	—	—	—	—	—	—	—
Gregarious	75	85	—	—	—	—	—	—	—	—
Tense	75	—	—	—	—	—	—	—	—	—
Impulsive	68	—	—	—	—	—	—	—	—	—
Outspoken	65	51	—	—	—	—	—	—	—	—
Fickle	65	—	—	—	—	—	—	—	—	—
Verbally fluent	60	43	—	—	—	—	—	—	—	—
Socially confident	58	44	—	—	—	—	−42	—	—	—
Assertive	55	53	−58	−57	—	—	—	—	—	—
Happy	41	63	—	—	—	—	—	—	—	—
Lethargic	−39	−50	—	—	—	—	—	—	−43	−42
Self-minimizing	−62	−46	45	41	—	—	—	—	—	—
Seclusive	−76	−77	—	—	—	—	—	—	—	—
Considerate	—	—	74	65	—	—	—	—	—	—
Conscientious	—	—	69	—	—	—	—	—	—	—
Mannerly	—	—	55	41	43	45	—	—	40	—
Complains	—	—	−50	−49	47	—	—	—	—	—
Touchy	—	—	−58	−74	—	—	51	—	—	—
Rude	—	—	−62	−65	—	—	—	—	—	—
Jealous	—	—	−70	77	—	—	—	—	—	—
Spiteful	—	—	−80	−70	—	—	—	—	—	—
Careful (work)	—	—	—	—	75	79	—	—	—	—
Neat	—	—	—	—	72	97	—	—	—	—
Persevering	—	—	—	—	52	72	—	—	58	—
Planful	—	—	—	—	50	65	—	—	63	—
Eccentric	—	—	—	—	−34	−74	—	—	—	—
Careless (property)	—	—	—	—	−62	−70	—	—	—	—
Irresponsible	—	—	—	—	−64	−78	—	—	—	—
Fearful	—	—	—	—	—	—	78	51	—	—
Rigid	—	—	—	—	—	—	65	—	—	—
Nervous	—	—	—	—	—	—	64	52	—	—
Concerned	—	—	—	—	—	—	58	58	—	—
Sensible	—	—	—	—	—	—	−41	—	57	50
Adaptable	—	—	—	—	—	—	−74	—	—	—
Knowledgeable	—	—	—	—	—	—	—	—	88	89
Imaginative	—	—	—	—	—	—	—	—	84	86
Verbal	—	—	—	—	—	—	—	—	84	84
Perceptive	—	—	—	—	—	—	—	—	83	87
Original	—	—	—	—	—	—	—	—	82	83
Curious	40	—	—	—	—	—	—	—	71	78
Esthetically Sensitive	—	—	—	—	—	—	—	—	53	34

Note: V* = Present study, D = Digman & Inouye (1986).
Decimals omitted; all values < .40 omitted; N = 179

planful, mannerly, and conscientiousness. The typical negative loadings were careless, irresponsible, eccentric, and impulsive. Conscientiousness emerged fifth in the present analysis and accounted for 3.4% of the variance.

The fourth factor was called Neuroticism and showed the least correspondence to the comparable Digman and Inouye (1986) factor. The Digman and Inouye factor, however, was rather weak, with only moderate loadings on adjectives of fearful, nervous, concerned, tense, and impulsive. The factor from the present analysis also had loadings on these same adjectives; the present analysis, however, had strong positive loadings on fearful, nervous, and rigid, along with negative loadings on adaptable, sensible, and socially confident. Thus this appears to be a stronger Neuroticism factor than the one described by Digman and Inouye (1986). This factor had been earlier called Anxiety by Digman (1989) and more frequently has been labeled Neuroticism by most students of the adult Big Five (Costa & McCrae, 1988; Eysenck, 1970; Goldberg, 1981). Here the present factor is labeled Neuroticism, so it cannot be confused with the Behavior Problem dimension of Anxiety-Withdrawal. In the present analysis this factor emerged fourth and accounted for 5% of the variance.

The fifth factor was labeled Openness to Experience. In the past, this factor has been called Culture (Norman, 1963; Tupes & Christal, 1961), Openness (Costa & McCrae, 1988), and Intellect (Digman & Inouye, 1986). The present factor five showed good correspondence to the loadings of the previous studies by Digman and his colleagues. In this analysis, the factor emerged second and accounted for 24.5% of the variance.

Factor scores were calculated using the regression method and these scores were used to analyze the relations between the Big Five dimensions, Behavior Problems, and Achievement scores.

Behavior Problems. A different teacher from the teacher that rated the Hawaii Scales completed the RBPC for each child (Quay & Peterson, 1987). The RBPC consisted of teacher's rating the 89 problem behaviors for each child. The RBPC is a common behavior problem scale used for school-age children. Scores were developed according to the manual for Conduct Disorder (CD), Socialized Aggression (SA), Attention Problems-Immaturity (AP), Anxiety-Withdrawal (AW), Psychotic Behavior (PB), and Motor Excess (ME). Psychotic Behavior was not used in the current analysis because only 14 children (8%) were rated on one item or more.

Results

To summarize the relations among the dimensions, a principal-components analysis with varimax rotation was performed on the five RBPC dimensions, the Big Five Personality Dimensions and the Composite Achievement score from the Iowa Tests of Basic Skills (ITBS; 1986). Five factors were extracted, using the eigenvalue of one rule. These five factors account for 76% of the variance. The factor loadings have been summarized in Table 18.2.

The first factor had strong loadings for the Big Five dimension of Openness to Experience (.89), Standardized Achievement (.83), and moderate loadings for Attention Problems (−.45) and Anxiety-Withdrawal (−.46). The correlation between Achievement and Openness to Experience, as can be seen from Table 18.3, is .63, $p < .001$. We have labeled this factor Openness to Experience and it accounts for 29% of the variance.

The second factor loaded with the Big Five dimension of Agreeableness (.86), Conduct Disorder (−.75), Socialized Aggression (−.60), and Motor Excess (−.44). The correlation, as seen in Table 18.3 between Agreeableness and Conduct Disorder is −.47, Socialized Aggression −.26, and Motor Tension Excess −.24, $p < .001$. This factor is interpreted as Agreeableness and accounts for 15.7% of the variance.

The third factor was characterized by a strong positive loading on Conscientiousness (.93) and a negative loading for Attention Problems (−.59). The correlation between Conscientiousness and Attention Problems from Table 18.3 is −.41, $p < .001$. This factor is labeled Conscientiousness and accounts for 11.6% of the variance.

The fourth factor loaded on Neuroticism (.85), the dimension of Anxiety-Withdrawal (.52), and Motor Tension Excess (.52). Recall that the positive pole of Neuroticism was composed of Fearful, Rigid, and Nervous clusters. This factor is reminiscent of Achenbach and Edlebrock's broad-band dimension of Internal-

TABLE 18.2
Factor Loadings of the Big Five Personality Dimensions,
Behavior Problem Factors, and Achievement Combined

Dimension	Factor				
	1	2	3	4	5
Openness to Experience (B5)	89	–	–	–	–
Achievement	83	–	–	–	–
Agreeableness (B5)[a]	–	86	–	–	–
Socialized Aggression (BP)	–	−60	–	–	–
Conduct disorder (BP)	–	−75	–	–	–
Conscientiousness (B5)[a]	–	–	93	–	–
Attention Problems (BP)	−45	–	−59	–	–
Neuroticism (B5)	–	–	–	85	–
Anxiety-Withdrawal (BP)	−46	–	–	52	−46
Motor Excess (BP)	–	−44	–	52	44
Extraversion (B5)	–	–	–	–	91

Note: Decimals omitted; all values < .40 omitted; $N = 179$. School Behavior Constructs were named as follows: 1 = Openness to Experience, 2 = Agreeableness, 3 = Conscientiousness, 4 = Neuroticism, 5 = Extraversion.

[a]Factor loading reflected.

TABLE 18.3
Summary of Correlations with Big Five Factors

	Factor				
	1	2	3	4	5
Achievement					
Composite Score	−15	−07	23*	−04	63**
Behavior Problems					
Conduct Disorder	33**	−47**	21*	−15	−13
Socialized Aggression	17*	−26**	−17*	09	−27**
Attention Problems	10	−13	−41**	15	−32**
Anxiety-Withdrawal	−24**	−03	−05	23**	−27**
Motor Excess	35**	−24**	−15	25**	−10**

Note: Factor 1 = Extraversion-Introversion, Factor 2 = Agreeableness, Factor 3 = Conscientiousness, Factor 4 = Neuroticism, Factor 5 = Openness to Experience.
*$p < .01$ and **$p < .001$, decimals omitted; $N = 179$.

izing behavior. The term *Neuroticism* is used for this dimension. The Neuroticism factor accounts for 9.9% of the variance.

The fifth factor loaded on the Big Five dimension of Extraversion (.91), the Behavior Problems dimension of Motor Excess (.44), and Anxiety-Withdrawal (−.46). The correlation between Extraversion and Conduct Disorder, as can be seen from Table 18.3, is .33, Motor Tension Excess .35, and Anxiety-Withdrawal −.24, all $p < .001$. This factor is reminiscent of the Achenbach and Edlebrock (1983) broad-band dimension of Externalizing Behavior and we have labeled this factor Extraversion.

Stepwise multiple regression was used to determine the amount of common variance between the Big Five model and Conduct Problems and Standardized Academic Achievement. Table 18.4 contains the stepwise multiple regression summary for Behavior Problems (Conduct Disorder). The full model accounted for nearly 40% of the variance (adjusted R) for Conduct Disorder. Agreeableness entered first and accounted for 22.7% of the variance, Extraversion was entered next and increased the variance accounted for by 10.3%. These were followed by Conscientiousness (4.1%), Openness to Experience (1.9%), and Neuroticism ($\approx 1\%$).

A stepwise regression was performed for the standardized achievement scores (the composite score from the ITBS) with the Big Five factor scores and the Behavior Problem scores. These results are shown in Table 18.5. The full model accounted for 49.4% of the variance for academic achievement. Openness to Experience was entered first and accounted for 39.1% of the variance. Attention problems was entered next and accounted for an additional 5.7%. These were followed by Conscientiousness, Extraversion, and Anxiety-Withdrawal, with each adding approximately 1%.

TABLE 18.4
Stepwise Multiple Regression Summary for Behavior Problems
with the Big Five Factors

Variable	R	R^2	δR^2	df	F
Agreeableness	47	22	—	1/177	50.29
Extraversion	57	32	10	2/176	42.84
Conscientiousness	61	36	04	3/175	34.57
Neuroticism	63	38	02	4/174	28.24
Openness to Experience	64	39	01	5/173	24.14

Note: Decimals omitted; R^2 = adjusted R^2; δR^2 = increase in R^2; all F's significant at $p < .0001$.

DISCUSSION

The purpose of this chapter is to bring together in the same data set measures from personality, behavior problems, and school achievement. The Big Five factors were consistent with previous studies of children as evidenced by the factor loadings. A few more adjectives showed low-level loadings on factors different from those presented by Digman & Inouye (1986).

All of the Behavior Problem dimensions produced reasonable levels of internal consistency. It should be noted that in an ostensibly normal sample, as here, high percentages of children receive zero scores on dimensions of the RBPC. For example, roughly 50% of the sample received a score of zero on the Conduct Disorder (22-item) dimension.

Factor analysis was used to summarize the underlying relations among the personality, behavior problem, and achievement variables. Two of the results support our hypotheses, namely, that the Big Five model would predict behavior problems and academic achievement. The present analysis, however, illustrated a much clearer pattern across the dimensions than anticipated. Five clear factors were present in the data set across the Big Five model, behavior problems, and

TABLE 18.5
Stepwise Multiple Regression Summary for Standard Achievement Scores
with the Big Five Factors and Behavior Problem Dimensions

Variable	R	R^2	δR^2	df	F
Openness to Experience	63	39	—	1/177	115.56
Attention Problems	68	46	06	2/176	75.60
Conscientiousness	69	47	01	3/175	53.64
Extraversion	70	48	01	4/174	42.56
Anxiety-Withdrawal	71	49	01	5/173	35.72

Note: Variables in the full model that were not entered were Conduct Disorder, Socialized Aggression, Motor Excess, Agreeableness and Neuroticism, decimals omitted; R^2 = adjusted R^2; δR^2 = increase in R^2; all F's significant at $p < .0001$.

academic achievement. The Big Five factors were the dominant markers of each dimension and subsumed the behavior problem and achievement variables.

Digman and his colleagues (1986) reported significant relations between Conscientiousness (Will to Achieve) with grade point average. It seems reasonable that Conscientiousness would be more related to obtaining grades with adjectives loading that emphasize responsibility, planning, careful work, and so on. Consistent with this idea, in our data, Openness to Experience, as opposed to Conscientiousness, was related to the measure of standardized achievement. It is also not surprising that Openness to Experience related to standardized achievement with the consistent loadings on adjectives such as verbal (vocabulary) and knowledge. Standardized achievement shares much common variance with intelligence, but grades are also known to be affected by nonintellectual aspects (motivation, organization, planning, conformity, etc.). I propose that standardized achievement will turn out to be, as here, consistently related to the Openness construct, whereas grade point average will be more related to the Conscientiousness construct, as in the Digman studies.

As noted earlier, the fifth construct, with Extraversion as a strong marker, was reminiscent of Achenbach and Edlebrock's (1983) broad-band dimension of Externalizing behavior. Conduct Disorders showed moderate loading on this factor. Agreeableness also showed strong loadings for Conduct Disorders. Our data showed Conduct Disorders to have two facets, one with Extraversion and one with Agreeableness. Recall that Digman (1989) argued that the negative pole of Agreeableness has a strong suggestion of psychopathology and noncompliance. Presumably, the negative pole may also be the more clearly pathological dimension due to the loading of Socialized Aggression. Children scoring high on either Extraversion or low on Agreeableness, however, would undoubtedly be difficult to manage in the classroom.

The dimension labeled Conscientiousness was made up of the strong personality marker, Conscientiousness, and the negative loaded behavior problem dimension, Attention Problems-Immaturity. Attention Problems-Immaturity was shown in these data to contain two facets; one in which the lack of Attention Problems-Immaturity contributed to Conscientiousness; and one in which it contributed modestly to Openness to Experience. I believe that Conscientiousness will turn out to be an important factor to study in school populations, in particular when the focus is gender differences. For example, Conscientiousness was the only Big Five dimension in these data to show a significant sex difference, with the girls scoring higher than boys, $t = 5.42, p < .001$.

The Big Five factor of Neuroticism subsumed the behavior problem dimensions of Anxiety-Withdrawal and Motor Tension Excess. As noted earlier, this construct seems reminiscent of Achenbach and Edlebrock's (1983) broadband factor of Internalizing behavior. Anxiety-Withdrawal loads positively on this construct as would be expected. Like Conduct Disorders, Anxiety-Withdrawal performed in a multifaceted fashion by contributing negatively to both Extraversion and Openness to Experience in the expected direction. In a similar manner, Motor Tension Excess showed multifaceted loadings; as a facet of Extraversion, Neuroticism, and negative of Agreeableness. All five of the behavior problem dimensions shared variance with more than one of the Big Five model factors.

It is clear from these data that the Big Five model accounted for much of the variance in both behavior disorders and achievement. Further, upon replication, the dimensions of the Big Five model, Behavior Problems, and Academic Achievement can be combined into new constructs that should be useful in school-based research. In addition, as a taxonomy of the Big Five is further developed (e.g., after Mervielde, chap. 20 in this vol.) the Big Five model profiles should have many clinical and school-based applications.

REFERENCES

Achenbach, T. M., & Edlebrock, C. (1983). *Manual for the Child Behavior Checklist.* Burlington, VT: University of Vermont, Department of Psychiatry.

Angleitner, A., Ostendorf, F., & John, O. (1990). Towards a taxonomy of personality descriptors in German: A psycholexical study. *European Journal of Personality, 4,* 89–118.

Costa, P. T., Jr., & McCrae, R. R. (1980). Still stable after all these years: Personality as a key to some issues in adulthood and old age. In P. Baltes & O. G. Brim, Jr. (Eds.), *Life span development and behavior* (Vol. 3, pp. 65–102). New York: Academic Press.

Costa, P. T., & McCrae, R. R. (1988). Personality in adulthood: A 6-year longitudinal study of self-reports and spouse ratings on the NED Personality Inventory. *Journal of Personality and Social Psychology, 54,* 853–863.

Digman, J. M. (1963). Principal dimensions of child personality as inferred from teachers' judgments. *Child Development, 34,* 43–60.

Digman, J. M. (1972). The structure of child personality as seen in behavioral ratings. In R. M. Dreger (Ed.), *Multivariate personality research* (pp. 587–611). Baton Rouge, LA: Claitor's Publishing.

Digman, J. M. (1989). Five robust trait dimensions: Development, stability, and utility. *Journal of Personality, 57,* 195–214.

Digman, J. M., & Inouye, J. (1986). Further specifications of the five robust factors of personality. *Journal of Personality and Social Psychology, 50,* 116–123.

Digman, J. M., & Takemoto-Chock, N. K. (1981). Factors in the natural language of personality: Re-analysis, comparison, and interpretation of six major studies. *Multivariate Behavioral Research, 16,* 149–170.

Eysenck, H. J. (1970). *The structure of human personality.* London: Methuen.

Goldberg, L. R. (1981). Language and individual differences: The search for universals in personality lexicons. In L. Wheeler (Ed.), *Review of personality and social psychology* (Vol. 2, pp. 141–165). Beverly Hills, CA: Sage.

Goldberg, L. R. (1990). An alternative "description of personality": The Big Five factor structure. *Journal of Personality and Social Psychology, 59,* 1216–1229.

Halverson, C. F., Jr., & Victor, J. B. (1976). Minor physical anomalies and problem behavior in elementary school children. *Child Development, 47,* 281–285.

Hofstee, W. K. B., Brokken, F. B., & Land, H. (1981). Constructie van een Standaard-Persoonlijkheids-Eigenschappen-lijst [Standard personality trait adjectives list] (SPEL). *Nederlands Tijdschrift voor Psychologie, 36,* 443–452.

Iowa Tests of Basic Skills (1986). Chicago, IL: Riverside Publishing Co.

Kelly, G. (1955). *The psychology of personal constructs.* New York: Norton.

McCrae, R. R., & Costa, P. T., Jr. (1985). Updating Norman's "Adequate Taxonomy": Intelligence and personality dimensions in natural language and in questionnaires. *Journal of Personality and Social Psychology, 49,* 710–721.

McCrae, R. R., & Costa, P. T., Jr. (1987). Validation of the five-factor model of personality across instruments and observers. *Journal of Personality, 52,* 81–90.

Norman, W. T. (1963). Toward an adequate taxonomy of personality attributes. *Journal of Personality and Social Psychology, 66,* 574–583.

Peabody, D., & Goldberg, L. R. (1989). Some determinants of factor structures from personality-trait descriptors. *Journal of Personality and Social Psychology, 57,* 552–567.

Quay, H. C., & Peterson, D. R. (1967). *Manual for the Behavior Problem Checklist.* Unpublished manuscript, University of Illinois.

Quay, H. C., & Peterson, D. R. (1987). *The Revised Behavior Problem Checklist.* Coral Gables, FL.

Tupes, E. C., & Christal, R. E. (1961). Recurrent personality factors based on trait ratings. (USAF AFD Tech. Rep., pp. 61–97). Lackland Air Force Base, TX.

Victor, J. B., Halverson, C. F., Jr., Inoff, G., & Buczkowski, H. (1973). Objective measures of first and second grade boys' free play and teachers' ratings on a behavior problems checklist. *Psychology in the Schools, 10,* 339–443.

Victor, J. B., & Halverson, C. F., Jr. (1975). Distractibility and hypersensitivity: Two behavioral factors in elementary school children. *Journal of Abnormal Child Psychology, 3,* 83–94.

Victor, J. B., & Halverson, C. F., Jr. (1976). Behavior problems in elementary school children: A follow-up study. *Journal of Abnormal Child Psychology, 4,* 17–29.

Victor, J. B., & Halverson, C. F., Jr. (1980). Children's friendship choices: Effects of school behavior. *Psychology in the Schools, 17,* 409–414.

PART

V

A Research Agenda for the Study of Personality and Temperament in Childhood Based on Free Description

This section represents the initial steps in a research agenda based on the lexical view of personality structure. Such a lexical view has been summarized best by Goldberg (1981):

> The most promising of the empirical approaches to systematizing personality differences have been based on one critical assumption: *Those individual differences that are of the most significance in the daily transactions of persons with each other will eventually become encoded in their language.* . . . Moreover, this fundamental axiom has a highly significant corollary: *The more important is an individual difference in human transactions, the more languages will have a term for it.* (pp. 141–142)

Obviously, to assess what people think are the important individual differences in children requires an analysis of the language people use to describe children. Unlike the lexical approach as applied to adults—in which researchers have analyzed the lexicon in dictionaries—developmental researchers must turn to free descriptions of children of different ages to find out if there is any consensus about what adults think is important to discuss when describing children. There is no "dictionary" to turn to.

It is interesting to note that there really is no consensus about which individual differences are important in childhood, much less what sort of structure those differences might be organized into. An analysis of the chapters devoted to "personality" in current introductory texts on child development or developmental psychology reveals almost no interest in "personality," "individual differences," or "personality structure." Except for the often cursory summary of temperament based on the nine-dimensional structure proposed by Thomas and Chess (1977), the developing structure of personality is neglected entirely. For example, Parke and Asher (1983) in a discussion of personality development neglected personality structure entirely. The editors of this volume believe that for child development and developmental psychology, individual differences in personality and personality structure are "empty sets," a *most* curious void given the intense interest in those issues in the literature on adults.

Chess and Thomas' dimensional scheme has been the basis for many questionnaires, but when individual items were factored, resulting factor structures failed to conform to a nine-dimensional structure (see Martin et al., chap. 8 in this vol.). It is not known whether some important personality dimensions were not obtained because Thomas and Chess were not interested in them, or whether dimensions were obtained because they wrote many items to measure what they believed to be important. Note that these analyses begin with a top-down, theory-driven set of items. As the research on the structure of temperament has progressed, it is clear that many constructs are possible in the analyses of top-down, theory-driven instruments (see Presley & Martin, in press; Strelau, 1991).

This discrepancy between top-down, theory-driven tests (like virtually *all* tests describing individual differences in children) and bottom-up, language frequency-based tests reflects the "etic-emic" distinctions used by cross-cultural researchers (Church & Katigbak, 1989; John, 1990). Cross-national work may be compromised and relatively uninformative because the investigator supplies the constructs to be rated. In this context, many researchers prefer the "emic" (culturally specific information-based) approach to instrument construction. Also, when we depend on a scheme like that of Thomas and Chess, we will get out of analyses what we put into it (even if they aren't the original nine "factors"), because parents will rate what is given to them—even if they would never use such terms in describing their own children.

We believe there is a distinct need to analyze child temperament and personality descriptors used in the natural languages of different cultures. It is clear that a dictionary-based approach to get an exhaustive collection of all relevant descriptors would be an awkward, roundabout way to develop the structure of individual differences in childhood. Other collections of terms could be made, notably from all the questionnaires, Q-sorts, and other instruments used to assess individual differences in childhood. Still, such psychology- and psychiatry-based collections would likely have less ecological validity than collections based on a large number of natural, free descriptions of children worded in the current language that people actually use to describe them. For young children these descriptions would not be self descriptions, but both parents and teachers could do the job.

In this section, the first pilot studies using such free descriptions of children are presented: one using Dutch parents (Treffers, Goedhart, & Kohnstamm), another using Belgian teachers (Mervielde), and the third using American parents and teachers (Havill, Allen, Halverson, & Kohnstamm).

Each of these chapters demonstrates the utility and fertility of the free-language approach to the structure of individual differences in childhood. Havill et al. show how most of the parental descriptions of American middle-class children can be easily coded in Big Five terminology, then analyzed by age and gender of rater and child, and finally compared to similar data from Holland and Belgium. Clearly for these languages at least, we have new information that a five- or six-dimension structure may evolve from parental natural language that is very much like the adult Big Five, and unlike existing analyses of temperament-based instruments. Mervielde also provides data indicating the usefulness of a free-description approach with teachers. Those data encourage the speculation that a new generation of instruments based on teacher-free descriptions may also be useful and needed.

The second part of the research strategy is yet to be carried out. Using the frequencies of these free-description categories, we need to begin to develop item pools to be rated by adults, then factored, clustered, and worked in instruments with good psychometric properties based on what adults think is important to describe in their children. The structure and content may be new and much more like adult versions based on lexical analyses. Data from the first and last chapters in this section also point to the possibilities of developing new item checklists and rating scales based on what parents find problematic when giving open-ended description of normal children (Havill et al.), or descriptions of children brought to a clinic for behavior problems (Goedhart, Treffers, & Kohnstamm). Taxonomies derived from such descriptors may yield a new generation of instruments describing behavior problems or dimensions that separate normal and clinically referred children.

We are hopeful that the free-description, lexical approach, when applied to the developing structure of temperament and personality, will provide new insights into important dimensions, how they change over time, and how they are linked with adult personality and structure. Such dimensions may also give us new and important information on how these childhood dimensions are related to important adaptive and maladaptive strategies over the life span.

REFERENCES

Church, A. T., & Katigbak, M. S. (1989). Internal, external and self reward structure of personality in non-Western culture: An investigation of cross-language and cross-cultural generalizability. *Journal of Personality and Social Psychology, 57*, 857–872.

Goldberg, L. R. (1981). Language and individual differences: The search for universals in personality lexicons. In L. Wheeler (Ed.), *Review of personality and social psychology* (Vol. 2, pp. 141–165) Beverly Hills, CA: Sage.

John, O. P. (1990). The "Big Five" factor taxonomy: Dimensions of personality in the natural language and in questionnaires. In L. A. Pervin (Ed.), *Handbook of personality: Theory and research* (pp. 66–100). New York: Guilford.

Parke, R. D., & Asher, S. R. (1983). Social and personality development. *Annual Reviews of Psychology, 34*, 465–509.

Presley, R., & Martin, R. (in press). Toward a macro-structure of childhood temperament. *Journal of Personality*.

Strelau, J. (1991). Renaissance in research in temperament: Where to? In J. Strelau & A. Angleitner (Eds.), *Explorations in temperament: International perspectives on theory and measurement* (pp. 337–358). New York: Plenum.

Thomas, A., & Chess, S. (1977). *Temperament and development*. New York: Brunner/Mazel.

CHAPTER

19

PARENTS' USE OF BIG FIVE CATEGORIES IN THEIR NATURAL LANGUAGE DESCRIPTIONS OF CHILDREN

Valerie L. Havill
Kathryn Allen
Charles F. Halverson
University of Georgia

Geldolph A. Kohnstamm
Leiden University

As the other chapters in this book attest, the five-factor model is pervasive in the adult personality literature (see also Digman, 1990; Digman & Takemoto-Chock, 1981; Goldberg, 1990; John, 1990). These five factors (or the Big Five) are usually labeled as (I) Extraversion, (II) Agreeableness, (III) Conscientiousness, (IV) Emotional Instability, and (V) Intellect, Culture, or Openness to Experience. They have emerged repeatedly across instruments, data sources, and languages in studies using adult samples, yet the developmental antecedents of the model remain largely unstudied.

In surveying the literature, we found little or no consensus on the main dimensions of personality in childhood. Instead, there is a confusing array of partially overlapping constructs described by different investigators. For example, Strelau (1991) reported that temperament researchers have identified, or are currently investigating over 80 traits or factors. This expanding number of traits goes hand in hand with the proliferation of diagnostic tools and techniques used to measure individual differences in children.

We undertook the analysis of the free descriptions of children's personalities by parents and teachers first because we were impressed by the lack of consensus of what constitutes personality structure in childhood (see Kohnstamm, Halverson, Havill, & Mervielde, in press) and second, because of our belief that parents and teachers may give us important information on the salient descriptors of individual differences in children of different ages. Parents are often asked to give personality descriptions of their children. These descriptions are most often collected in the form of standardized questionnaires, checklists, or Q-sorts. If we consider the "etic-emic" distinction used in anthropology (Church & Katigback, 1989), the use of such descriptions clearly is "etic." The measures are constructed based on what the theorist ("etic") thinks is important rather than on what informants use as important descriptors ("emic").

Most temperament studies of individual difference in children have used either the original Thomas and Chess (1977) items or adaptations and translations of the original items. It is possible that some personality dimensions were obtained because Thomas and Chess wrote many items to measure what they believed to be important, and conversely, that some dimensions were excluded or overlooked because they were not interested in them.

There is an instructive example of the limiting nature of etic studies of differences coming from the self-concept literature. W. J. McGuire and C. V. McGuire (1984) found that most studies on self-concept used investigator-provided constructs (what they termed "reactive studies" or etic by our definition). Such reactive responses do not provide information about how salient or important a dimension is to the participant. The McGuire and McGuire review of the self-concept literature revealed that 90% of the reactive research had focused on the evaluation aspects of self (self-esteem). In contrast, when children's free-response self descriptions (spontaneous self-concept) are used, they found only 7% of the responses to be evaluative. The McGuires argued that the spontaneous self-concept provides important information on what descriptors are salient for the individual.

In this study we preferred the "emic" (cultural-specific-informant-based) approach to instrument construction based on the lexical hypothesis. According to the basic premise of the lexical approach, language will encode individual differences or personality traits that are significant in daily social interaction. The more important a certain characteristic is, the more words there will be to describe it and the more it will be talked about. Klages (as cited in John, Angleitner, & Ostendorf, 1988) was the first to articulate the underlying assumption of the lexical hypothesis. His work was later followed by the research of Allport (1937), Cattell (1946), Norman (1963), and then Goldberg (1981, 1982).

Evidence supporting the lexical hypothesis can be seen in the anthropological literature. The universality of basic color terms and their order of emergence has been documented by Berlin and Kay (1969). Brown (1977, 1979) documented universal lexical order of emergence for folk botanical and zoological life-forms. Brown's studies included 105 very diverse languages, including North, South, and Central American Indian languages; African; Asian; and European languages. Goldberg (1981) predicted that there is a universal order of emergence of individual differences in personality descriptors encoded into the world's languages. The more important the individual difference is, the more languages that will have a term for it. Just as some colors can be identified as focal across cultures, some personality characteristics may emerge as focal across cultures and perhaps within age groups.

Naturally occurring descriptors from the personality lexicon would seem to provide more information about how individuals or cultures assess others, than does an analysis of all terms found in a dictionary. Whereas content analyses of dictionaries from a variety of languages might provide evidence for five universal factors, they would yield no information about what characteristics of children are truly the most salient to parents and teachers, nor would they provide any information on either qualitative or quantitative developmental changes in the structure of personality as revealed by the frequency of different descriptors at different ages.

PRELIMINARY STUDY

Participants

Fathers ($N = 90$) and mothers ($N = 95$), in separate interviews, were asked to describe their child(ren). One hundred and fifty-eight children were described (males = 88, females = 70). The mean age of the children in this sample was 80 months (range = 4.1 to 11.8 years); the sample was then split into older children and younger children for analyses comparing age differences (M age = 108 months for the older group and M age = 52 months for the younger group). The families contacted were involved in the ongoing Georgia Longitudinal Study.

Procedure

The parents of children in 96 families were asked simply to "tell us about your child." A total of 316 free-response protocols were obtained. The parents described their children in a videotaped interview. Parents provided 5,616 descriptions. The descriptions were then transcribed and coded.

Coding Procedures

The *Coding Manual for the English Lexicon of Personality Descriptions* (Havill, Halverson, & Allen, 1992) includes every unique word or phrase used by the parents. In collaboration with Elphick and Slotboom, instructions for coding free-language personality descriptions were developed to detail the coding process and to aid in the training of new coders. Coding guidelines include instructions regarding units of analysis, division of phrases, repetitions, and synonymity.

For our purposes, a unit of analysis was defined as an adjective, verb, noun, or phrase referring to a description of behavior, personality characteristic, or ability. Phrases referring to situational causes of behavior or to physical attributes were not coded. Because a unit of analysis could be a phrase, it was sometimes helpful to split the phrases into easily codable, simpler parts. Adjacent words or phrases could be divided and coded separately as two individual units if the meaning of each part was understood when considered independently. If a coder judged that meaning or context is lost by splitting the phrase, then the unit was coded as one single description. For example the phrase, "She likes to play outdoors and play with neighbor kids" can be separated into two distinct parts: (a) "she likes to play outdoors" and (b) "play with neighbor kids." The first phrase would be coded as referring to physical activity level and the second phrase would be coded as indicating extraversion or sociability. The phrase "she's so quick, her head works very, very fast" would be coded as a single unit because breaking the description into two parts could conceivably lead the coder to misinterpret "she's so quick" as referring to physical activity instead of cognitive proficiency.

When words or phrases were repeated verbatim or if phrases expressing the exact same literal meaning were used more than once in a single interview, these units were recorded and coded as repetitions, but were not included in frequency analyses more than once.

In free-language interviews, respondents often elaborate on a single characteristic by mentioning concrete, situation-specific behaviors to illustrate the personality characteristic. In such cases, the elaborative phrase or phrases were taken with the personality descriptive word or phrase and were coded as one unit of analysis. Respondents may also mention a descriptive characteristic in the past tense and contrast this with a similar descriptive characteristic in the present tense to illustrate how a child is now with respect to a younger age. In this case, the past-tense phrase was not coded separately, but was included in one unity with the present-tense phrase. The part of the phrase in the present tense was the subject of analysis. The past-tense word or phrase, however, may help the coder to assess the meaning or importance of the unity as a whole.

Words and phrases that were not coded as descriptive phrases included those referring to a person other than the target child or to children in general. These were considered nonrelevant phrases and were therefore not coded. Phrases offering collateral information was also excluded. These were phrases including information connected to the main issue, but so remote as to have no immediate relevance to the target child (e.g., "her parents are friends of mine," or "You have a lot of temper tantrums and things with all kids, you know, that is not specific to Susie, but that is something that would bother me about her"). If there was any reasonable doubt as to whether a respondent was referring to the target child directly, then the word or phrase was not be coded. Following the guidelines in the *English Coding Manual* (Havill et al., 1992), high interrater reliabilities were established in this study. All coding discrepancies or uncertainties were discussed and then coded consensually.

The goal in the creation of the *English Coding Manual* was to group together as many similar words and phrases as the parents could freely generate. The groupings were created to provide a guide for researchers who will code English descriptions or who need a model for the development of a personality lexicon other languages.

The descriptions were coded based on a system inspired by the Big Five framework, with several subcategories in each of the five dimensions. The *English Coding Manual* also includes an additional eight categories used by Kohnstamm, Slotboom, and Elphick (1993) in their coding of Dutch parents' natural language descriptions of children. The additional eight categories are: independence; maturity; health; rhythmicity; gender appropriate/attractiveness; school performance; desire to be cuddled; and relations with siblings and parents. (See Table 19.1.) The additional categories were created to accommodate all the child characteristics mentioned by parents in Holland.[1] Although this coding system partly follows the Five-Factor Model, the possibility that we will discover other dimensions has in no way been precluded. The goal of a free-description protocol is to select words or expressions from any category with a sufficient number of elements. (For further rationale see Kohnstamm et al., in press.)

Preliminary Findings

Parents in this study provided 5,616 descriptions of their children. Of those descriptions 4,751 (80%) were coded within the Big Five dimensions. Only 320 phrases, or 5.7% of all the descriptors gathered, could not be coded in any of the categories. Category XIV was created to contain all descriptions that could not be coded. Often the description was out of context, or too ambiguous to code (e.g., natural), or was not pertinent to personality (e.g., big ears). Table 19.2 shows the percentage of descriptors used by mothers and fathers that were coded in each of the Big Five dimensions and subcategories. We found more descriptors could be assigned to Dimension I (extraversion) than were coded in any other category. This finding differs from dictionary-based studies. The original Norman Big Five list (from Goldberg, 1990) showed more Factor II words (those pertaining to Agreeableness) available in the English lexicon than words referring to Extraversion/Introversion. Peabody and Goldberg (1989) found that when a representative selection of trait descriptors were factored, Agreeableness (II) tends to be the largest, whereas Emotional Stability (IV) and Openness to Experience (V) tended to be the smallest.

Table 19.3 shows frequencies of U.S., Dutch, and Flemish parents' descriptors compared to the Norman–Goldberg clusters. It is important to note that parents described their children with proportionally more friendly words, fewer conscientiousness and neuroticism words, and more openness to experience words than are proportionally available in the English language. Frequency of free-language

---

[1]Many of the overall coding categories were subdivided into smaller units termed "facets" (see Costa & McCrae, 1985). We have divided the Extraversion dimension into three subcategories: Sociability (IA), Leadership/Dominance (IB), and Activity (IC). Each subcategory is further divided into descriptors that are high (or positive) on the scale, or low (or negative). For example, the descriptor "couch potato" was coded as IC–. The coding indicates that the descriptor is low in extraversion, specifically in the activity subcategory.

TABLE 19.1
Summary of the English Lexicon Manual for Coding Personality
Descriptions of Children

Dimension 1: EXTRAVERSION
    Cluster 1A+: High Sociability
        Facet 1A+1: Enthusiasm
        Facet 1A+2: Likes to be with others
        Facet 1A+3: Fun to be with
    Cluster 1A−: Low Sociability
        Facet 1A−1: Aloof/Inhibited
        Facet 1A−2: Shy/Plays alone
    Cluster 1B+: Dominance/Leadership
    Cluster 1B−: Passivity/Lack of leadership
    Cluster 1C+: Activity/Pace/Tempo
        Facet 1C+1: High energy level
        Facet 1C+2: Unrestraint
    Cluster 1C−: Low Activity/Low Energy
Dimension 2: AGREEABLENESS
    Cluster 2A+: Helpful, sweet child
    Cluster 2A−: Uncooperative
    Cluster 2B+: Manageability
    Cluster 2B−: Unmanageability
        Facet 2B−1: Argumentative
        Facet 2B−2: Stubborn
        Facet 2B−3: Insists on own way
        Facet 2B−4: Difficult
    Cluster 2C+: Honesty/Sincerity
    Cluster 2C−: Insincere/Lying
Dimension 3: CONSCIENTIOUSNESS
    Cluster 3A: Carefulness
    Cluster 3B: Dependability
    Cluster 3C: Industriousness
Dimension 4: NEUROTICISM
    Cluster 4A+: Emotional reactivity
    Cluster 4A−: Emotional stability
    Cluster 4B: Self-confidence
    Cluster 4C: Anxiety/Fearfulness
Dimension 5: OPENNESS TO EXPERIENCE
    Cluster 5A: Open/Adventurous
    Cluster 5B: Interests/Hobbies
    Cluster 5C: Intelligence
Dimension 6: INDEPENDENCE
Dimension 7: MATURITY
Dimension 8: ILLNESS/HANDICAPS/HEALTH
Dimension 9: RHYTHMICITY
Dimension 10: GENDER APPROPRIATENESS/PHYSICAL CHARACTERISTICS
Dimension 11: SCHOOL PERFORMANCE/BEHAVIOR
Dimension 12: SEEKING CONTACT COMFORT
Dimension 13: FAMILY RELATIONSHIPS
Dimension 14: AMBIGUOUS/NOT CODABLE IN ABOVE CATEGORIES

TABLE 19.2
Summary Percentages by Informant

Dimension	Mothers	Fathers
EXTRAVERSION		
1A Sociability	15.7	17.1
1B Dominance/Leadership	2.6	2.4
1C Activity/Pace	8.7	10.1
TOTAL	27.0	29.6
AGREEABLENESS		
2A Helpful, sweet child	16.6	14.6
2B Manageability	7.5	7.5
2C Honesty/Sincerity	1.1	1.1
TOTAL	25.2	23.2
CONSCIENTIOUSNESS		
3A Carefulness	3.4	3.6
3B Dependability	0.4	0.5
3C Diligence	4.2	4.4
TOTAL	8.0	8.5
NEUROTICISM		
4A Emotional reactivity/Stability	5.8	4.8
4B Self-confidence	1.5	1.5
4C Anxious/Fearful	0.3	0.2
TOTAL	7.6	6.5
OPENNESS TO EXPERIENCE		
5A Open/Adventurous	4.1	5.1
5C Intelligence	6.7	7.2
TOTAL	10.8	12.3

Note: $n = 151$ for children described by mothers, $n = 150$ for children described by fathers.

TABLE 19.3
Proportions of Descriptors Sorted Over Categories
in English, Dutch, and Flemish

	Georgia, USA (%)	Holland (%)	Flemish (%)	Norman/Goldberg Clusters (%)
1. EXTRAVERSION	29.49	27.7	26.9	23.5
2. AGREEABLENESS	24.63	19.7	19.4	29.8
3. CONSCIENTIOUSNESS	8.32	6.6	7.4	23.0
4. EMOTIONAL REACTIVITY	7.05	10.3	8.7	14.5
5. OPENNESS TO EXPERIENCE	11.74	12.4	12.0	9.2
TOTAL 1 thru 5	81.23	76.7	74.4	100.0
6. INDEPENDENCE	1.14	3.9	3.8	
7. MATURITY	1.34	3.1	3.0	
8. ILLNESS/HEALTH	0.07	0.8	0.8	
9. RHYTHMICITY	0.13	1.0	1.5	
10. GENDER APPROPRIATE/ PHYSICAL ATTRACTIVENESS	1.34	1.4	1.1	
11. SCHOOL PERFORMANCE	2.21	3.1	3.3	
12. CONTACT COMFORT	0.40	1.2	1.9	
13. FAMILY RELATIONSHIPS	3.08	3.4	4.9	
14. AMBIGUOUS	5.77	5.3	5.3	
TOTAL (No. of descriptors)	5,616	4,957	5,498	

descriptors may reflect more than just availability and probably does index the underlying constructs' importance to parents. It is most interesting that the frequencies we have found in U.S. parents' free-language descriptors have also been obtained by Kohnstamm, Slotboom, and Elphick (1993) in a parallel study of Dutch parents. This cross-language replication suggests that Dutch and U.S. parents focus on similar domains of personality traits when they describe their children. Further international collaboration will allow for the investigation of cultural influence on attributions.

Martin (1992) coded teachers' natural language descriptions of students. He coded descriptors of 290 elementary students in a variety of educational settings. Although the frequencies he obtained cannot be directly compared with our data due to slightly different ways of parsing the descriptions, 89% of these teacher descriptors were coded in the Big Five dimensions. We believe this provides evidence to support the ecological validity of the Five-Factor Model. The natural personality lexicon allows for the examination of differences in the salience of the different dimensions of personality by the informant in different contexts and roles, yet the structure of personality remains much the same across informants, roles, and contexts.

Subgroup Differences in Descriptors

Although the primary goal of this study was to determine what characteristics parents ascribe to their children, we also compared the frequency of category useage for several subgroups to see how they might vary by age, gender of child, and by which parent, mother or father, provided the descriptions. Our analyses determined that descriptions of boys and girls were similar, but there were significant differences between the two groups in frequency of some categories. Girls were described by significantly more phrases denoting sociability—such as outgoing, talkative, adaptable, and enthusiastic (IA +)—whereas boys were described by more phrases like sullen, withdrawn, shy, reserved, and emotionally inexpressive (IA −).[2] Boys were also described as being more active than girls (IC +). Gender differences were also found in Factor V. A significantly higher percentage of phrases referring to openness to experience and adventurousness (VA) were used to describe boys than girls. Yet, there was no significant difference in the percentage of high VA descriptors or low VA descriptors used to describe sons and daughters. Boys, however, were described by significantly more positive phrases in category VC. Specifically, boys were described by more phrases such as intelligent, quick, bright, smart, and clever than were girls. It

---

[2] Martin (1992) analyzed teacher free-language descriptions of children and found that girls were described more often as shy (IA −) than were boys. A somewhat different procedure for selecting descriptive phrases was used in the study so the results are not directly comparable to our findings. Martin did, however, find that boys were described by teachers as highly active (IC +) and bright and intelligent (5C +) more often than were girls.

TABLE 19.4
Parents' Descriptions of Children by Gender

	Sons		Daughters	
	M	%	M	%
1. Extraversion	4.42	31.43	4.08	33.05
1A	1.81	16.88	2.61	21.01
1B	0.30	2.14	0.31	2.34
1C	1.68	12.41	1.16	9.61
2. Agreeableness	3.27	24.07	3.19	24.61
2A	2.02	14.64	2.20	16.68
2B	1.08	8.06	0.86	6.93
2C	0.18	1.24	0.14	1.01
3. Conscientiousness	1.20	8.15	1.22	8.91
3A	0.59	3.73	0.46	3.39
3B	0.02	0.09	0.14	0.89
3C	0.63	4.33	0.63	4.64
4. Emotional Reactivity	0.86	5.89	1.00	7.56
4A	0.66	4.45	0.74	5.58
4B	0.19	1.31	0.23	1.79
4C	0.02	0.14	0.03	0.20
5. Openness to Experience	1.94	14.09	1.44	11.15
5A	0.88	6.30	0.57	4.35
5C	1.07	7.79	0.87	6.81
Mean total number of descriptors given	13.75		12.87	

Note: $n = 110$ for sons, $n = 99$ for daughters. Percentage is the mean number of descriptors in a given category over the total number of descriptors given for that sample.

should be noted that the Big Five *domains* were strongly replicated in descriptions of mothers and fathers of boys and girls.

Table 19.5 shows the correlations between mothers' and fathers' description of children by category. Dimensions describing Extraversion, Agreeableness, and Neuroticism showed modest levels of parental agreement. These correlations indicated some low levels of consensus in parental free description although they are lower than agreement scores generally obtained with objective questionnaires. As measures of individual differences, proportion scores are rather unreliable and skewed, so the low levels and lack of correspondence are not too surprising.

Follow-up Study

To investigate the developmental changes within the structure of the Big Five, an additional 53 mothers were asked to describe their infants and toddlers. Mothers were interviewed when they were entering or leaving one of three preschools or child-care centers. This youngest group (males $N = 23$, females $N = 30$) had a mean age of 22.8 months.

TABLE 19.5
Correlations between Mother's and Father's Descriptions of Children

Dimension	r	p
1. Extraversion		
1A Sociability	.40	.00
1B Dominance/Leadership	.20	.01
1C Activity/Pace	.35	.00
2. Agreeableness		
2A Sweet, helpful child	.20	.01
2B Manageability	.22	.01
2C Sincerity/Honesty	−.06	ns
3. Conscientiousness		
3A Carefulness	.07	ns
3B Dependability	.09	ns
3C Diligence	.14	ns
4. Neuroticism		
4A Emotional Reactivity	.35	.00
4B Self-confidence	.17	.04
4C Anxiety/Fearfulness	.18	.03
5. Openness to Experience		
5A Openness to experience	.08	ns
5C Intelligence	.20	.01

Note: $n = 147$.

As shown in Table 19.6, our most interesting finding was that there were age differences between our youngest group (less than 3 years of age) and the two older groups on four of the Big Five dimensions. These differences indicate that mothers found some of the Big Five dimensions less appropriate for younger than for older children. The Big Five taxonomy, however, can still be considered useful for the youngest sample as it still accounts for 75.6% of all descriptors given in reference to infants and toddlers (as compared to 77% and 80% in older children, see Fig. 19.1).

The most provocative finding was that free-language responses provided by mothers of infants and toddlers indicated that very young children were not described with many words and phrases that could be coded in the dimensions of conscientiousness. Apparently, it is difficult to conceptualize toddlers as diligent or meticulous. The infrequent use of Conscientiousness (III) words may be puzzling initially. To explain these developmental trends, we propose the following explanation. Low conscientiousness words could be said to describe infants and toddlers as a group. Parents probably expect all infants to be irresponsible and inefficient. Words connoting lack of responsibility and efficiency, thus, do not distinguish very young children from their peers and therefore are not spontaneously used. They are not salient for social comparisons. We have a phrase in English for this obviousness that we have borrowed from the French: "It goes without saying."

TABLE 19.6
Mothers' Free Response Descriptions of Their Children by Age

	Age in Months		
Dimension	< 36 months M%	37–96 months M%	> 96 months M%
1. Extraversion	37.91[a]	25.98[b]	27.36[b]
2. Agreeableness	22.13[a]	25.48[b]	25.57[b]
3. Conscientiousness	1.53[a]	6.96[b]	10.19[c]
4. Emotional Reactivity	3.31[a]	8.57[b]	7.03[b]
5. Openness to Experience	10.68	10.73	10.14

Note: $n = 53$ for < 36 months; $n = 88$ for 37–96 months; $n = 63$ for > 96 months. In rows, percentages with different superscripts are significantly different.

We also found that parents use relatively few words to describe their infants and toddlers in terms of emotional stability/instability. Consistent with the previous explanation, it might be that older children can be more easily distinguished in terms or traits like these than infants and toddlers. A 12-year-old who cries easily or a 10-year-old who throws things when enraged can be seen and described as demonstrating very distinctive behaviors (i.e., an individual difference), whereas such behavior in a 2-year-old is not so distinctive.

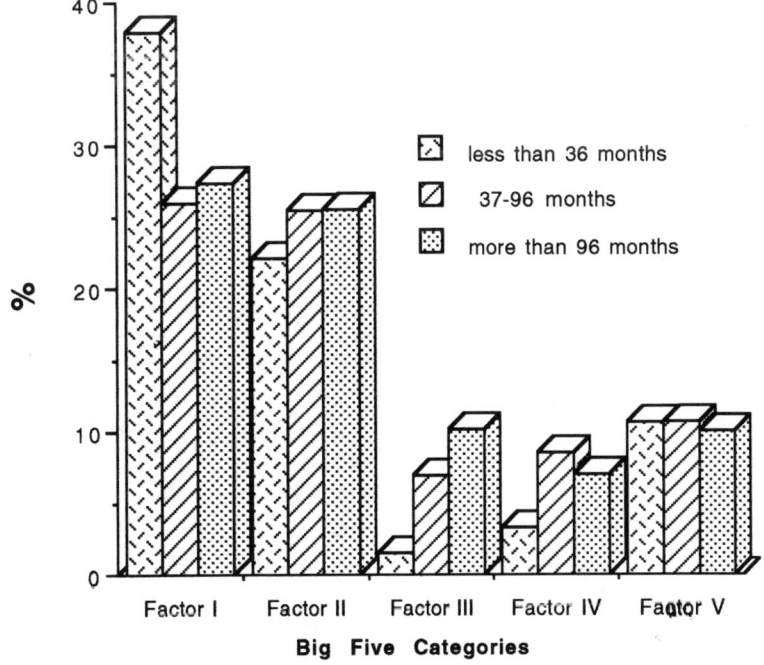

FIG. 19.1. Mothers' free response descriptions by dimension.

ADVANTAGES OF FREE RESPONSE DATA

Parents' free-response descriptions of their children are expected to reflect temperament and personality characteristics that are salient to the parent. Through such free descriptions, an extensive list of temperament and personality characteristics can be created, which then may be regarded as typical for parent perceptions of children of specific ages. A major advantage of the collection of parents' free descriptions is the ability to compile such normative data on characteristics or traits used by parents. When a frequency count is prepared, one then also knows how often a specific characteristic is mentioned. This frequency may also be a good index of the salience of that characteristic for the persons providing such descriptions.

Such a saliency analysis has revealed a discrepancy between theorists and parents on the importance of one of the major temperament dimensions in childhood, namely Rhythmicity. Whereas Rhythmicity is an important temperament dimension in the Thomas and Chess framework and in related instruments such as the Dimensions of Temperament Survey–Revised (DOTS–R) (Windle & Lerner, 1986), Rhythmicity (the regularity of behavior patterns) was seldom, if ever, mentioned by parents in either our study or in the Dutch studies employing free descriptions of children. Evidently, biological regularity (e.g., in sleep, eating, and elimination) is not a salient behavioral characteristic of young children beyond infancy for parents in these studies and irregularity of behavior does not constitute a problem.

This kind of selective perception and communication cannot be addressed with questionnaires because questionnaires require a respondent to answer all items in a questionnaire and only those items—even if a respondent has never thought about and would never communicate about certain items (like Rhythmicity).

Use of Natural Language to Identify Behavior Problems

To ascertain what "problems" parents in the United States found salient and freely talked about at various developmental ages we coded the free-language responses in terms of problems as well. The adjectives and phrases coded as problems were characteristics that the parents were dissatisfied with or would like to change. We found that the behavior problem descriptions were easily and reliably coded from the lexicon and could be described as a percentage of the total lexicon. Examples of behavior problem phrases in each of the coding clusters are shown in Table 19.7. Of all the descriptors gathered, 17.59% were coded as "problems." Figure 19.2 shows the percentages obtained for our sample of children older than age 3. It can be seen that the distribution of "problem" descriptors was fairly evenly divided among four of the Big Five dimensions; Dimension V (Openness to Experience) contained less than .5% of the problem descriptors. Parents' free-response descriptions for boys contained significantly more problems in Dimension I and Dimen-

TABLE 19.7
Examples of Behavior Problem Descriptors

Dimension	Problem Descriptors
1. Extraversion	
1A Sociability	sullen, withdrawn, lonely, too shy, aggressive, easily intimidated, cannot sit still, reckless
1B Dominance	
1C Activity/Pace	
2. Agreeableness	
2A Helpful, sweet child	selfish, violent, mean, impatient, stubborn, lies, argumentative, rebellious, defiant, sneaky, manipulative
2B Manageability	
2C Honesty/Sincerity	
3. Conscientiousness	
3A Carefulness	distractible, will not pay attention, careless, lazy, messy, lacks motivation
3B Dependability	
3C Diligence	
4. Neuroticism	
4A Emotional Reactivity	cries a lot, whiny, pouts, has a bad temper, mopes, too emotional, insecure, worried and anxious, lacks self-confidence
4B Self-confidence	
4C Anxious/Fearful	
5. Openness to Experience	afraid to try new things, slow to learn
5A Open/Adventurous	
5C Intelligence	

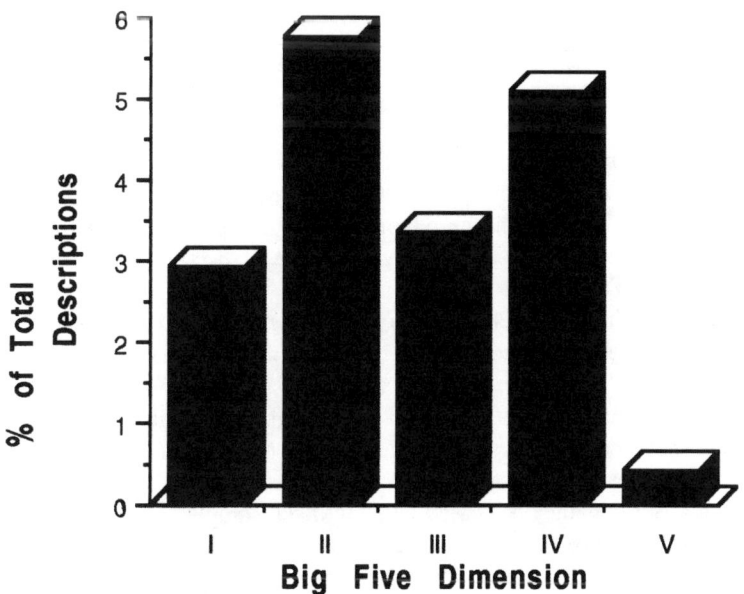

FIG. 19.2. Parents' behavior problem descriptions of children by dimension.

TABLE 19.8
Parents' Behavior Problem Descriptions of Children by Gender

	Sons		Daughters	
Dimension	M	%	M	%
1. Extraversion	.49	3.60	.29	2.17
1A	.18	1.40	.12	.97
1B	.17	1.15	.15	1.00
1C	.14	1.04	.03	.15
2. Agreeableness	.94	7.03	.60	5.11
2A	.18	1.24	.15	1.12
2B	.72	5.55	.43	3.72
2C	.04	.25	.03	.28
3. Conscientiousness	.48	3.16	.48	3.46
3A	.32	2.08	.19	1.42
3B	.00	.00	.04	.37
3C	.17	1.09	.25	1.68
4. Emotional Reactivity	.64	4.33	.72	5.11
4A	.46	3.16	.57	4.12
4B	.15	.97	.13	.83
4C	.03	.20	.03	.15
5. Openness to Experience	.05	.32	.07	1.00
5A	.03	.23	.06	.33
5C	.02	.09	.02	.17
Mean total number of descriptors given		13.75		12.87

Note: $n = 110$ for sons, $n = 99$ for daughters. Percentage is the mean number of problem descriptors in a given category over the total number of descriptors given for that sample.

sion II than descriptions of girls. Specifically, boys were described as having more problems in cluster IC (Activity) and cluster IIB (Manageability). Typical descriptions in cluster IC were "can't keep him still," "reckless," "won't stay seated at the dinner table," and in cluster IIB, "always argues," "irrationally stubborn," and "defiant." (See Table 19.8.)

Continuing this line of study, we can investigate behavior problems that are salient to parents across ages and across cultures. We can explore how and why age, birth order, gender of child, and gender of parents affect the frequency of behavior problem descriptors provided by teachers and parents. We will be able to identify what area of behavior (or which aspects of children's personalities) may create the greatest number of problems for parents. Findings such as these will be especially useful as they are based on nonclinical samples of children. Knowing what characteristics parents typically use in free descriptions of children at different ages also allows us to detect atypical parental descriptions. Such atypical free descriptions may suggest deviant parent–child relationships. These descriptions could possibly be developed into new diagnostic tools about parent–child relationships.

SUMMARY

The exploration of personality structure in childhood guided by natural language is exciting as it will allow us to align constructs in early childhood and adult personality domains. We conclude from the analyses reported previously that the Big Five dimensions account for a large proportion of adults' descriptions of children; making their absence in the children's literature on individual differences all the more remarkable. Adults find Big Five words and phrases as the basic language of personality but many temperament theorists do not.

We hope to remedy this discrepancy by working toward measurement models that recognize the importance that adults accord to these dimensions. Providing instruments that assess Big Five constructs in children would open an avenue where we might link child and adult literatures, both based on the lexicon of individual difference descriptions used by adult perceivers. We believe this model holds considerable promise for understanding personality in the life-span context.

The model also holds considerable promise for cross-cultural and cross-language research. Many theorists (see, for example, Digman, 1990, 1991; John, 1990) have proposed that the Five-Factor Model may be universal, based as it is on the human information-processing routines inherent in human language. Our methodology can be useful in assessing both those aspects of universality and those aspects that are culturally unique regarding the personality language of the development of individual differences. Such prospects are exciting and await inquiry.

REFERENCES

Allport, G. W. (1937). *Personality: A psychological interpretation*. New York: Holt.
Berlin, B., & Kay, P. (1969). *Basic color terms: Their universality and evolution*. Berkeley: University of California Press.
Brown, C. H. (1977). Folk botanical life-forms: Their universality and growth. *American Anthropologist, 79*, 317–342.
Brown, C. H. (1979). Folk zoological life-forms: Their universality and growth. *American Anthropologist, 81*, 791–817.
Cattell, R. B. (1946). *Description and measurement of personality*. New York: Worldbook.
Church, A. T., & Katigbak, M. S. (1989). Internal, external and self-reward structure of personality in non-Western culture: An investigation of cross-language and cross-cultural generalizability. *Journal of Personality and Social Psychology, 57*, 857–872.
Costa, P. T., & McCrae, R. R. (1985). *The NEO Personality Inventory manual*. Odessa, FL: Psychological Assessment Resources.
Digman, J. M. (1990). Personality structure: Emergence of the five-factor model. *Annual Review of Psychology, 41*, 417–440.
Digman, J. M. (1991). Personality structure: Emergence of the five factor model. *Current Sociology, 39*, 417–441.
Digman, J. M., & Takemoto-Chock, N. K. (1981). Factors in the natural language of personality: Re-analysis and recomparison of six major studies. *Multivariate Behavior Research, 16*, 149–170.

Goldberg, L. R. (1981). Language and individual differences: The search for universals in personality lexicons. In L. Wheeler (Ed.), *Review of personality and social psychology* (Vol. 2, pp. 141–165). Beverly Hills, CA: Sage.

Goldberg, L. R. (1982). From ace to zombie: Some explorations in the language of personality. In C. D. Spielberger & J. N. Butcher (Eds.), *Advances in Personality Assessment* (Vol. 1, pp. 203–234). Hillsdale, NJ: Lawrence Erlbaum Associates.

Goldberg, L. R. (1990). An Alternative "description of personality": The Big-Five factor structure. *Journal of Personality and Social Psychology, 59*, 1216–1229.

Havill, V. L., Halverson, C. F., & Allen, K. (1992). *The Coding Manual for the English Lexicon of Personality Descriptions*. Athens, GA: Georgia Longitudinal Study, Dept. of Child and Family Development, University of Georgia.

John, O. P. (1990). The "Big Five" factor taxonomy: Dimensions of personality in the natural language and in questionnaires. In L. A. Peruin (Ed.), *Handbook of personality: Theory and research* (pp. 66–100). New York: Guilford.

John, O. P., Angleitner, A., & Ostendorf, F. (1988). The lexical approach to personality: A historical review of trait taxonomic research. *European Journal of Personality, 2*, 171–203.

Kohnstamm, G. A., Halverson, C. F., Havill, V. L., & Mervielde, I. (in press). Parents' free descriptions of child characteristics: A cross-cultural search for the roots of the Big Five. In S. Harkness & C. Super (Eds.), *Parents' cultural belief systems: Cultural origins and developmental consequences*. New York: Guilford.

Kohnstamm, G. A., Slotboom, A., & Elphick, E. (1993). Dutch parents' free descriptions of child characteristics: A search for the onset of the five factor structure in adult perceptions. Unpublished manuscript.

Martin, R. P. (1992, September). Teachers' free descriptions of children. Paper presented at the fifth European child development conference, Seville, Spain.

McGuire, W. J., & McGuire, C. V. (1984). The spontaneous self-concept as affected by personal distinctiveness. In M. D. Lynch, A. Norem-Hebeisen, & K. Gergen (Eds.), *Self-concept: Advance in theory and research* (pp. 119–132). Cambridge, MA: Ballinger.

Norman, W. T. (1963). Toward an adequate taxonomy of personality attributes: Replicated factor structure in peer nomination personality ratings. *Journal of Abnormal and Social Psychology, 66*, 574–583.

Peabody, D., & Goldberg, L. R. (1989). Some determinants of factor structures from personality-trait descriptors. *Journal of Personality and Social Psychology, 57*, 552–568.

Strelau, J. (1991). Renaissance in research on temperament: Where to? In J. Strelau & A. Angleitner (Eds.), *Explorations in temperament: International perspectives on theory and measurement* (pp. 337–358). New York: Plenum.

Thomas, A., & Chess, S. (1977). *Temperament and development*. New York: Brunner/Mazel.

Windle, M., & Lerner, R. M. (1986). Reassessing the dimensions of temperamental individuality across the life-span: The Revised Dimensions of Temperament Survey (DOTS-R). *Journal of Adolescent Research, 1*, 213–230.

CHAPTER

20

A FIVE-FACTOR MODEL CLASSIFICATION OF TEACHERS' CONSTRUCTS ON INDIVIDUAL DIFFERENCES AMONG CHILDREN AGES 4 TO 12

Ivan Mervielde
University of Ghent

A recent review about the emergence of the five-factor model for personality (Digman, 1990) shows that the consensus about the validity and usefulness of this model is steadily increasing. A variety of studies illustrates the presence of the Big Five dimensions in different languages (Angleitner, Ostendorf, & John, 1990; Brokken, 1978; Hofstee, Brokken, & Land, 1981), questionnaires (Hogan, 1986; McCrae & Costa, 1987), internal judgments (Peabody & Goldberg, 1989) and across methods of analysis (Goldberg, 1990, 1992).

Skeptics might argue that the common denominator in studies of the five-factor model is a set of rating scales that are consistently used by different researchers and therefore tend to produce a similar factorial structure. Although this criticism may have been more valid in the early stages of this research, recent studies (Angleitner et al., 1990; Brokken, 1978; Hofstee et al., 1981; John, Angleitner, & Ostendorf, 1988; Mervielde, 1992; Ostendorf, 1990) show that the five-factor structure emerges in different cultures and language communities. Still, given the problems with translation of terms from one language to another (Hofstee, 1990; Mervielde, 1977), the equivalence of those five-factor solutions is difficult to establish.

It remains an open question whether the same structure would emerge when the raters, instead of the researchers, select the relevant features to describe self or others. Kelly (1955) introduced personal construct psychology, emphasizing the important role of the person's own conceptual system for understanding behavior. Personal constructs, as conceived by Kelly, are not restricted to personality descriptors but personality traits are a major subcategory of personal constructs. Kelly's theory postulates that persons utilize a specific set of concepts to organize their experiences. The emphasis in personal construct theory is thus on the individual differences in personal construct systems.

If the five-factor model embodies the major categories for observing individual differences then they should be present in a reasonable sample of personal constructs as well. If each person acquires at least some useful constructs to delineate individual differences, then it is reasonable to expect that the concepts of a group of persons may even be more adequate to portray the range of perceived individual differences.

The main database for research on the five-factor model has not been the language as used by the *modal* language user, but the language as compiled in dictionaries. The rationale for taking the dictionary as the definitive database is that the importance of a trait is considered to be proportional to the number of terms the language provides to encode it. Most language speakers use a limited set of the traits listed in the dictionary. Our passive vocabulary is considerably larger than the active one. Nevertheless, passive vocabulary terms can and will be used if the task requires it, but they may be less suitable as cues for the retrieval of information because they play a minor role in encoding experiences. The case of the generality of the five-factor model could indeed be strengthened if research shows that the Big Five are equally prominent in the active, spontaneous vocabulary of the language user.

The purpose of the present study was to assess the value of the five-factor model as a paradigm for teachers' personal constructs about individual differences among children. The major reason to elicit information on perceived childhood differences from teachers is that they continually interact with and observe groups of same-age children. Moreover, teachers are supposedly less emotionally involved with the children than the parents and therefore are expected to be more objective. Over the years, teachers observe many children and presumably acquire reliable knowledge about individual differences. Observing children in school settings limits the range of observable behaviors but the same proviso can be made for parents providing observations on children in home settings.

METHOD

Subjects

One hundred and thirteen, third-year psychology students from the University of Ghent interviewed 226 kindergarten or primary school teachers. This assignment was part of the requirements for the course in personality psychology. Each student made an appointment with two teachers, usually from the school where they received their own kindergarten or primary education. Almost all Belgian children go to school at the age of 3 and have 2 or 3 years of preschool education. There were two samples with kindergarten teachers: one with 28 second-year kindergarten teachers (children age 4–5 years) and another with 28 third-year kindergarten teachers (children age 5–6 years). The primary school teachers were drawn from each of the six primary school grades. The number of teachers in the six samples is 29 (age 6–7), 29 (age 7–8), 30 (age 8–9), 30 (age 9–10), 26 (age 10–11), and 26 (age 11–12).

Elicitation of Constructs

Kelly's personal construct psychology was explained to students as part of the lectures on personality psychology. The students received written instructions about how to elicit constructs reflecting the teachers' conception of individual differences. They asked teachers to think about the pupils in their current class and to list several characteristics illustrating differences among pupils. The students emphasized that elicited constructs should reflect differences in temperament and personality and be formulated as traits or adjectives. They recorded the elicited constructs on an answer sheet providing space for maximum 18 entries.

Abridged Big Five Circumplex (AB5C) Classification

The constructs elicited from the teachers were classified according to the Dutch version of the Abridged Big Five Circumplex (AB5C) taxonomy, developed by Hofstee and De Raad (1991) (see also chap. 5 in this vol.). This model integrates the five-dimensional simple-structure and the circumplex models of personality. It contains the 10 circumplexes that can be formed by pitting all five factors against each other. Each circumplex is further partitioned into 12 segments of 30° by inserting additional factors at angles of 30° and 60° with the base factors. Each trait is characterized by its loading on a subset of two out of the five factors. The 12 segments of each circumplex are labeled as combinations of the two circumplex factors. To illustrate this, the clockwise order for the A-E (Agreeableness-Extraversion) circumplex, starting at the top, is as follows: A+A+, A+E+, E+A+, E+E+, A–E+, A–A–, A–E–, E–A–, E–E–, E–A+, A+E–.

The complete AB5C-model has 45 bipolar factors, 5 "pure" factors and 40 factors resulting from pair wise combinations of the five factors. Hofstee and De Raad (1991) classified 551 Dutch traits according to this AB5C algorithm. Constructs elicited from the sample of teachers were looked up in the table with 551 AB5C terms and assigned their AB5C classification.

RESULTS

AB5C Classification

The 226 kindergarten and primary school teachers listed a total of 3,265 constructs. The average number of constructs listed per teacher is 14.45 and the range extended from 7 to 18. The complete sample of teachers produced 768 different constructs. A computerized procedure checked the AB5C classification for all elicited constructs. Table 20.1 lists the number and percentage of "missing" constructs for each age level. Forty-two percent of the teachers' constructs were not part of the AB5C taxonomy. The retrieval rate ranged from 54% for teachers of 4- to 5-year-old children, to 64% for those teaching classes with 10- to 11-year-old children. Inspection of the list with all "missing" terms showed several reasons for unsuccessful classification. The most important category "missing terms" were adjectives that were not part of the AB5C taxonomy, such as "slordig" (shoddy) and "aandachtig" (attentive). Some of these can be linked to differences between "Dutch" and "Flemish." Another category had constructs expressed by combining adjectives such as "gesloten-introvert" (uncommunicative-introvert). A third group of classification failures had constructs formulated as nouns, adverbs, and even as verbs, such as "agressiviteit" (aggressiveness), "sociaal voelend" (socially sensitive), "actief meewerken" (cooperate actively). Matching these missing constructs to AB5C terms would increase the retrieval rate. It was calculated that matching the 80 most frequently missing constructs to AB5C terms would reduce the missing rate to 20%. This strategy was not adopted because related terms do no necessarily have a similar AB5C classification. Moreover, given the variety of missing terms, it was unlikely that the present sample of retrieved constructs was substantially biased.

Frequently Listed Constructs

The percentage of teachers listing each different construct was computed. Table 20.2 lists constructs elicited from more than 10% of the teachers as well as their AB5C factor pole classification and loading. The English translation (between brackets) is only illustrative. Inspection of the U.S. version of the AB5C (Hofstee, De Raad, & Goldberg, 1992) indicated that translated terms may be assigned to a different factor pole. Table 20.2 shows that the top four constructs contain three terms classified as A+E+. The seven most frequently listed constructs included five terms with a primary loading on each of the Big Five. Inspection of Table 20.2

TABLE 20.1
Number of Teachers' Constructs Missing From AB5C List

Sample (year)	Number of Teachers	Missing Terms	Total Number	% Missing
4–5	28	183	395	46.33
5–6	28	164	402	40.88
6–7	29	182	437	41.65
7–8	29	180	424	42.45
8–9	30	209	451	46.34
9–10	30	184	430	42.79
10–11	26	134	367	36.51
11–12	26	136	359	37.88
Total	226	1,372	3,265	42.02

TABLE 20.2
Most Frequently Listed Constructs

Construct	Factor Pole	AB5C Loading	% of Teachers
Behulpzaam (helpful)	A+E+	0.474	28.32
Spontaan (spontaneous)	E+E+	0.562	27.79
Sociaal (social)	A+E+	0.466	26.11
Vriendelijk (friendly)	A+E+	0.491	25.22
Zelfstandig (independent)	S+I+	0.494	25.22
Creatief (creative)	I+A+	0.306	25.22
Leergierig (studious)	C+I+	0.293	21.68
Slordig (shoddy)			21.24
Agressief (aggressive)	A−I+	0.444	20.80
Aandachtig (attentive)			19.91
Zenuwachtig (nervous)	S−E−	−0.595	19.91
Rustig (calm)	A+S+	0.513	19.03
Eerlijk (honest)	A+C+	0.407	17.26
Zelfverzekerd (self-confident)	S+E+	0.663	16.81
Bedeesd (timid)	I−E−	−0.452	16.81
Intelligent (intelligent)	I+S+	0.291	16.37
Verstandig (sensible)	S+C+	0.420	16.37
Lui (lazy)	C−E+	−0.427	16.37
Nauwkeurig (accurate)			15.49
Stil (silent)			15.04
Open (open)	E+E+	0.535	15.04
Beleefd (polite)			14.60
Aanhankelijk (attached)	S−A+	−0.409	14.16
Actief (active)	E+I+	0.411	13.27
Geinteresseerd (interested)			12.38
Lief (kind)			12.83
Speels (playful)	E+I+	0.377	12.39
Koppig (obstinate)	A−I+	0.395	12.39
Ijverig (industrious)	C+C+	0.572	11.95
Verstrooid (absent-minded)	C−E−	−0.375	11.50
Gevoelig (sensitive)	S−A+	−0.457	11.06
Verlegen (shy)	E−S−	−0.468	10.62
Gesloten (uncommunicative)	E−E−	−0.649	10.18
Opvliegend (short-tempered)	A−S−	−0.507	10.18

Note: A = Agreeableness, C = Conscientiousness, E = Extraversion, I = Intellect, S = Stability.

demonstrated that the five factors were clearly present among the most popular constructs listed by the teachers. Agreeableness was the most prominent factor, with eight primary loadings. Intellect had only three primary loadings, but the second largest number of secondary loadings. The most popular construct missing in the AB5C taxonomy is "slordig" (shoddy, sloppy). Notice that the number of missing constructs increases with decreasing popularity. Eighty-five percent of the constructs (listed by only one teacher) could not be retrieved from the AB5C taxonomy.

Classification by AB5C Factor Pole

The top of the distribution of the teachers' personal constructs over AB5C factor poles is reported in Table 20.3. The 551 terms classified according to the AB5C algorithm were distributed over 88 factor poles. Classification of all the teachers' constructs showed that 68 (77%) AB5C factor poles were present in the sample of teachers' constructs. Three quarter of the constructs, listed by the teachers, were allocated to one of these "popular" factor poles. Among the 24 most-allotted AB5C factor poles, each of the Big Five factors was clearly present. Agreeableness, Extraversion, and Conscientiousness were each represented by 5 factor poles with a primary A, E, or C loading. Emotional Stability had 6 factor poles in the top of the distribution. Intellect was the primary part of 3 factor poles and the secondary for 5 of the 24.

Comparison of the distribution of percentage of terms across all factor poles for both the AB5C taxonomy and the teachers' constructs showed a moderate degree of correspondence. The correlation between AB5C and teacher percentages over factor poles was .51 ($p < .001$).

TABLE 20.3
Most Frequently Allocated AB5C Factor Poles

Factor Pole	AB5C terms		Teachers	
	Frequency	%	Frequency	%
A+E+	28	5.08	194	10.25
E+E+	3	0.54	104	5.49
S−E−	10	1.81	103	5.44
A−I+	16	2.90	89	4.70
E+I+	12	2.18	88	4.65
C+C+	9	1.63	86	4.54
S+I+	12	2.18	70	3.70
I+S+	7	1.27	64	3.38
S−A+	6	1.09	60	3.17
I+A+	5	0.91	56	2.96
A+S+	5	0.91	51	2.69
C+I+	2	0.36	50	2.64
I−E−	12	2.18	47	2.48
E−E−	6	1.09	46	2.43
A+C+	13	2.36	46	2.43
S+C+	9	1.63	44	2.32
C−E−	9	1.63	43	2.27
E+A+	21	3.81	40	2.11
S+E+	5	0.91	38	2.01
C−E+	5	0.91	37	1.95
A−S−	4	0.73	28	1.48
C+I−	7	1.27	28	1.48
E−S−	15	2.72	26	1.37
S+A+	6	1.09	25	1.32

Note: A = Agreeableness, C = Conscientiousness, E = Extraversion, I = Intellect, S = Stability.

The top of Table 20.3 shows that the most frequently allocated factor pole was A+E+. This pole had the highest percentage of concepts for both the AB5C taxonomy and for the teachers' constructs. The second most popular factor pole for the teachers was E+E+. The AB5C taxonomy included only three terms—"spontaan" (spontaneous), "open" (open) and "uitbundi" (exuberant)—but they were highly popular among teachers as constructs for delineating individual differences. The percentage of teachers listing the three terms was 27.79 (spontaan), 15.04 (open), and 3.10 (uitbundig). Such examples illustrate that, at least at the factor pole level, popularity of constructs among teachers may not correspond to the number of terms in the AB5C taxonomy. Twenty AB5C factor poles were not represented in the sample of constructs listed by the teachers. The most important "missing" factor pole was C−A− (14 terms in the AB5C taxonomy). It contains highly undesirable traits such as "sadistisch" (sadistic), "narcistisch" (narcistic), "immoreel" (immoral), "destructief" (destructive), "excentriek" (eccentric), "verdorven" (perverted), "schaamteloos" (shameless). The pole S+E− (AB5C frequency = 5) may be missing for a similar reason. Five bipolar factors, all with a low AB5C frequency, were not present among the teachers' concepts: A−C+/A+C−, E+C+/E−C−, E−I+/E+I−, C+S−/C−S+, I+S−/I−S+. The missing factors had their primary loading on four of the five factors, suggesting no systematic pattern for missing factors. The remaining eight missing factor poles were A+E−, S+S+, S+E−, C+E−, I+E−, S+C−, S+I−, I+C+, and C−I+.

The Five-Factor Model Classification

Aggregating the percentage of AB5C terms and personal constructs with primary loadings on each of the Big Five generated the distribution of concepts over the five factors, summarized in Table 20.4. Inspection of the bold figures in this table demonstrates a remarkable correspondence between both distributions. For Conscientiousness, Extraversion, and Agreeableness the differences were less or slightly more than 1%. For the two remaining factors, Stability and Intellect, the difference was around 2%. The correlation between both distributions was .93.

There can be little doubt that, at the five-factor level, the distribution of personal constructs elicited from teachers was very similar to the AB5C taxonomy.[1] It should be stressed that no rating scales or features were supplied to the teachers. They were

---

[1] The similarity was slightly less when "missing" constructs were replaced by or linked to synonym terms that are part of the 551 terms classified according to the AB5C algorithm. Replacing the 80 most frequent "missing" constructs by synonyms increased the retrieval rate to 80.43%. The selection of synonyms was based on a recently published Dutch synonym dictionary. The main difference with the distribution reported in Table 20.4 was a decrease in the percentage of Agreeableness terms to 23.80% and an increase in Conscientiousness terms to 21.88%. Teachers seemed to use a variety of Conscientiousness terms that are not part of the 551 classified by Hofstee and DeRaad. This difference probably resulted from disparities between Flemish and Dutch and from the distinctive construct system of teachers.

TABLE 20.4
Summed Frequencies for Five-Factor Model Classification

AB5C-Factor	AB5C		Teachers	
	Frequency	%	Frequency	%
Extraversion	**108**	**19.60**	**392**	**20.71**
E+	54	9.80	276	14.58
E−	54	9.80	116	6.13
Agreeableness	**160**	**29.04**	**528**	**27.89**
A+	71	12.89	337	17.80
A−	89	16.15	191	10.09
Conscientiousness	**87**	**15.79**	**286**	**15.11**
C+	38	6.90	188	9.93
C−	49	8.89	98	5.18
Stability	**106**	**19.24**	**420**	**22.19**
S+	53	9.62	182	9.61
S−	53	9.62	238	12.57
Intellect	**90**	**16.33**	**267**	**14.10**
I+	39	7.08	159	8.40
I−	51	9.26	108	5.71

completely free to choose the relevant concepts. Although no structure was imposed, they collectively produced a distribution that was almost a replica of the AB5C distribution.

Splitting the five-factor distributions into positive and negative poles illustrated a bias for positive constructs. This tendency was most prominent for Extraversion and Agreeableness and somewhat less pronounced for Conscientiousness and Intellect. Teachers formulated individual differences in Stability primarily with constructs located at the negative pole. The bias toward positive factor pole terms corresponds to the preference for social desirable constructs observed in previous research (Mervielde, 1991). The positive poles of the Big Five contain the more desirable traits. The reverse effect for stability could be traced to the use of constructs such as "zenuwachtig" (nervous), "impulsief" (impulsive), "gevoelig" (sensitive), "jaloers" (jealous), and "wispelturig" (volatile).

Five-Factor Model Classification by Age Level

The 226 teachers had classes with children ranging from 4 to 12 years. The stability of the construct distribution over age levels is portrayed in Fig. 20.1. Inspection of this figure illustrates very little systematic change across age levels. Agreeableness was the most important factor for all age levels. Extraversion and Stability remained close to each other except for the oldest children. Finally, Intellect and Conscientiousness attracted the lowest percentage of constructs for all age levels, except for Conscientiousness at age level 11–12.

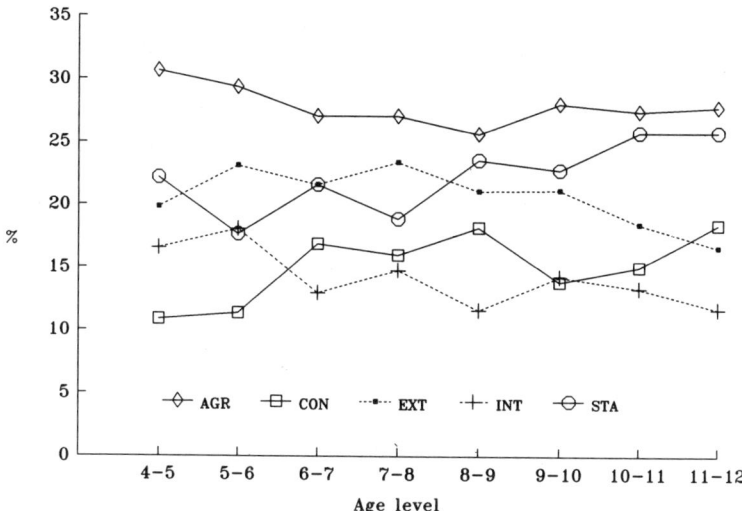

FIG. 20.1. Percent of constructs by age level and main AB5C factor.

The overall similarity between the teachers' and the AB5C distribution, across a range of age levels, provides more evidence for the value of the five-factor structure as a model for teachers' construction of individual differences.

DISCUSSION

The similarity of the distribution of constructs elicited form teachers to the distribution of terms in the AB5C taxonomy confirms the value of the five-factor paradigm as a model for the way teachers construct individual differences among children age 4 to 12 years. Teachers have first-hand, daily experience with children of the same age group and their acquired knowledge about individual differences should not be easily dismissed. Moreover, many child personality and temperament studies rely on judgments by teachers (Kohnstamm, Bates, & Rothbart, 1989) and thus indirectly corroborate the value of their knowledge and expertise.

Skepticism about the impact of imposed rating scales on the outcome of five-factor model research may be less warranted, given the clear emergence of the five-factor structure in the present study. The presence of the five factors in a sample of constructs, elicited from teachers, corroborates the assumption that the number of synonyms reflects the importance of a trait. The distribution of teachers' constructs was primarily shaped by the popularity of the constructs and to a lesser extent by the number of synonyms. The AB5C distribution, on the other hand, depends solely on the number of synonyms. The high degree of similarity between both distributions, at least at the five-factor level, provides evidence for a significant relation between number of synonyms and popularity or usage frequency of traits and trait categories.

Besides the remarkable correspondence at the five-factor level, the study also demonstrated moderate similarity of the teachers' constructs to the AB5C taxonomy at the factor pole level. But, even at the level of single constructs, it was demonstrated that the five factors were represented among the seven most popular constructs elicited from the teachers.

The correspondence between the distribution of constructs in the AB5C taxonomy and the constructs elicited from the teachers extends the five-factor model research in several ways. It showed that the five-factors emerged even when the researcher did not impose a predefined set of categories or rating scales to structure the ratings. Teachers construed individual differences among children with concepts, similar in distribution, to those surfacing from large-scale studies of self-ratings on adjectives, culled from dictionaries. Finally, the study showed that the construct distribution was fairly stable across samples of kindergarten and primary school teachers.

ACKNOWLEDGMENTS

This research was supported by grant 01173391 from the Research Council of the University of Ghent.

The author is indebted to Wim Hofstee and Boele DeRaad for providing an unpublished version of the AB5C-taxonomy.

REFERENCES

Angleitner, A., Ostendorf, F., & John, O. (1990). Towards a taxonomy of personality descriptors in German: A psycho-lexical study. *European Journal of Personality, 4*, 89–118.

Brokken, F. B. (1978). *The language of personality.* Unpublished doctoral dissertation, University of Groningen, The Netherlands.

Digman, J. M. (1990). Personality structure: Emergence of the five-factor model. *Annual Review of Psychology, 41*, 417–440.

Goldberg, L. R. (1990). An alternative "description of personality": The Big Five factor structure. *Journal of Personality and Social Psychology, 59*, 1216–1229.

Goldberg, L. R. (1992). The development of markers for the Big-Five factor structure. *Psychological Assessment, 4*, 26–42.

Hofstee, W. K. B. (1990). The use of everyday language for scientific purposes. *European Journal of Personality, 4*, 77–88.

Hofstee, W. K. B., Brokken, F. B., & Land, H. (1981). Constructie van een Standaard-Persoonlijkheids-Eigenschappen-lijst [Construction of a Standard personality trait list] (SPEL). *Nederlands Tijdschrift voor Psychologie, 36*, 443–452.

Hofstee, W. K. B., & DeRaad, B. (1991). Persoonlijkheids-structuur: De AB5C-taxonomie van Nederlandse eigenschapstermen [Personality structure: The AB5C-taxonomy of Dutch trait terms]. *Nederlands Tijdschrift voor Psychologie, 46*, 262–274.

Hofstee, W. K. B., de Raad, B., & Goldberg, L. R. (1992). Integration of the Big Five and circumplex approaches to trait structure. *Journal of Personality and Social Psychology, 63*, 146–163.

Hogan, R. (1986). *Hogan Personality Inventory manual.* Minneapolis, MN: National Computer Systems.

John, O. P., Angleitner, A., & Ostendorf, F. (1988). The lexical approach to personality: A historical review of trait taxonomic research. *European Journal of Personality, 2*, 171–203.

Kelly, G. A. (1955). *The psychology of personal constructs* (2 Vols.). New York: Norton.

Kohnstamm, G. A., Bates, J. E., & Rothbart, M. K. (1989). (Eds.). *Temperament in childhood.* Chichester, England: Wiley.

McCrae, R. R., & Costa, P. T., Jr. (1987). Validation of the five-factor model of personality across instruments and observers. *Journal of Personality and Social Psychology, 52*, 81–90.

Mervielde, I. (1977). Ratings for likableness and subjective frequency of personality traits and interpersonal behaviors. *Psychologica Belgica, 17*, 143–156.

Mervielde, I. (1991). *Which personality language: A comparison of judgments with personal and general personality traits* (Reports in Psychology No. 1991-2). Belgium: University of Ghent.

Mervielde, I. (1992). The B5BBS-25: A Flemish set of bipolar markers for the "Big Five" personality factors. *Psychologica Belgica, 23*, 195–210.

Ostendorf, F. (1990). *Sprache und Persönlichkeitsstruktur: Zur Validität des Fünffaktoren-Modells der Persönlichkeit.* [Language and personality structure: On the validity of the five-factor model of personality structure]. Regensburg, Germany: Roderer Verlag.

Peabody, D., & Goldberg, L. R. (1989). Some determinants of factor structures from personality-trait descriptors. *Journal of Personality and Social Psychology, 57*, 552–567.

CHAPTER

21

THE FIVE-FACTOR MODEL IN CHILD PSYCHIATRY: PARENTS' FREE PERSONALITY DESCRIPTIONS OF THEIR CHILDREN

A. W. Goedhart
Ph. D. A. Treffers
Geldolph A. Kohnstamm
University of Leiden

In child and adolescent diagnostic psychiatry a large amount of information on the referred child is gathered in interviews with the parents. This information is not only factual; a judgment is also obtained from the parents about aspects such as the developmental progress, current functioning, and current problems of the child. Practically all parents have an opinion on these matters, which has been formed in part from discussions with each other and other individuals. For the diagnostic process, it is important to know what sort of picture parents have of their child. Information about this can be obtained by asking parents to complete a standardized questionnaire, as well as by means of free personality descriptions.

This study addresses the question of the extent to which parents' free descriptions of their child can be judged and analyzed and the extent to which the outcome of such an analysis can be related to diagnostic data, in this case to the diagnostic classification.

The five-factor model originated in personality descriptions expressed in everyday language. In the majority of research studies, though, the descriptions are in terms of adjectives, which subjects are required to use in making judgments about themselves or others. The five-factor model is based predominantly on empirically established systematic variation between adjective descriptors. But it does not necessarily follow that the model can be applied to free descriptions. Free descriptions—for example by parents of their children—comprise not only adjectives, but nouns and verbs as well (for example, "is a dare-devil" and "cries easily"). A direct test of the applicability of the five-factor model to a content analysis of free descriptions is not feasible. But it is possible, in a context where personality descriptions come routinely to the fore—for example, in a diagnostic setting—to determine the extent to which the model can be used, and, if usable, its value.

In order to analyze a free description, the description must first be split up into units. Because of the variety of units, their categorization has to depend on more or less subjective judgments. An indication of the utility of the classificatory system can be gained by determining the interjudge reliability, and the number of units that, according to the judges, are classifiable in terms of the five factors (the "cover"). This study investigates the utility of the model and considers the value of such a content analysis for child psychiatric diagnostics.

To our knowledge, this methodology has not been used to date in child and adolescent psychiatry. Our primary concern, as is the case with all new diagnostic methods, is with the external validity of the method. We therefore focus on differences between descriptions of children registered at a child and adolescent psychiatric outpatients' clinic and descriptions of children in a comparison group comprised of schoolchildren. We then examine the type of differences existing between the descriptions of children in a number of diagnostic groups and the descriptions of children in the comparison group. We would like to emphasize that in this article we refer consistently to Factors I to V; this does not mean we have empirically demonstrated that the categorization system we used is identical to the five-factor model, nor does it mean that the factors were established by factor analysis. We assume, rather, that the five categories, which we set up on the basis of the relevant literature, bear a close relationship to the factors of the five-factor model, and also that our assigning of units to the five categories is consistent with the five-factor model.

METHOD

Subjects

Descriptions were obtained from the parents of 207 children from age 4 to 12 years. In the case where both parents were present at an interview they drew up the description together. The children had all undergone a complete psychiatric investigation at the outpatients' clinic of the Academic Center for Child and Adolescent Psychiatry, Curium, from 1989 to 1990. This group of children is referred to as the "research group." Descriptions were also obtained from the parents of 136 primary school children (91 parents cooperated; in case they had more children attending the school they gave separate descriptions of each child; at the time of the study there were 244 children attending the school). This group is referred to as the "comparison group." Table 21.1 shows the distribution of age and sex for the two groups. It appears that the research group contains relatively fewer girls, $\chi^2(1, N = 343$, after Yates' correction$) = 8.1, p < .005$, as well as relatively fewer children from the younger age group, and more children

TABLE 21.1
Age and Sex of Children in the Research Group and the Comparison Group

Group	Age					
	4–6 years		7–9 years		10–12 years	
	Boy	Girl	Boy	Girl	Boy	Girl
Research group (Curium)	36	14	48	33	54	22
Comparison group (primary school)	17	27	32	27	20	13

from the older age group, $\chi^2(2, N = 343) = 6.4, p < .05$. In comparisons of the two groups, the difference in composition are taken into account.

Procedure

During the initial interview, which is conducted with the parents of all children referred to the Curium, the following question is routinely asked: "How would you describe (name of child)?" The reaction to this question is transcribed as literally as possible, and is otherwise noted down using the key words used by the parents. There is no limit on the number of descriptive terms. The responses are stored anonymously in a computer file, together with other routinely collected diagnostic data (See Treffers, Goedhart, Waltz, & Koudijs, 1990). All the data on the research group originates in this database.

For the collection of information on the comparison group, we received the co-operation of a primary school in an average-size town. In a letter circulated by the school, we requested parents for permission to ask via the telephone a question relating to their child(ren). Telephone contact was then made with parents who had given permission. Christian name, age, and sex of each child were first noted, and then the following question asked: "Could you describe what (name of child) is like?" Answers and requests for more information were transcribed verbatim.

Scoring Method

The descriptions were spilt up into units, where each unit contained one characteristic of the child. A unit can consist of a single adjective or part of the sentence. Thus, for example, the description "a difficult child requiring constant attention, can be sweet," was split up into the following three units, each of which could be independently judged: "difficult," "child requiring constant attention," and "can be sweet." For the coding of the descriptions, a manual was developed, giving an overview of terms that have been categorized under the five factors by Dutch-,

English-, and German-speaking researchers (Brokken, 1978; John, 1989; McCrae & Costa, 1985; Ostendorf, 1990; Peabody & Goldberg, 1989). This manual was a precursor of the manual used by Havill et al., chapter 19, this volume; see also Kohnstamm, Halverson, Havill, and Mervielde (in press).

To distinguish between the two poles of a factor, the first-named pole is regarded as "positive" and the second-named as "negative." Poles regarded as positive are Extraversion (Factor I), Agreeableness (Factor II), Conscientiousness (Factor III), Emotional stability (Factor IV), and Openness/Intellect (Factor V). Poles regarded as negative are Introversion (Factor I), Disagreeableness (Factor II), Unconscientiousness (Factor III), Neuroticism (Factor IV), and Unimaginative (Factor V). For the coding of a unit, the following four categories were used on each of the five factors:

0: The unit cannot be classified under this factor.
1: The unit can be classified under the positive pole of the factor.
2: The unit can be classified under this factor, but it is not clear under which pole.
3: The unit can be classified under the negative pole of the factor.

From the coded scores of individual units, the entire description of each child was summarized by computing the following two indices for each of the five factors:

1. *Intensity of use*: the proportion of units assigned a coded score of 1, 2, or 3 on the relevant factor, in comparison with the total number of units comprising the description. The intensity of use of a factor is nil when *no* units could be scored on the factor, and is one when all the units could be scored on the factor. The intensity of use provides an indication of the relevance of a particular factor in a description's classification.

2. *Valency*: the predominant tendency in the coding of the units. A valency h(high) indicates that the units classified under the relevant factor refer more often to the positive pole of the factor than to the negative pole; a valency n(neutral) indicates that it is not clear which pole the units refer to; and a valency l(low) indicates that the units refer more often to the negative pole of the factor than to the positive pole.

The valency of a factor was calculated as follows: If every unit in the description had a coded score of 0, then a valency score of n was assigned to the factor; for the remaining cases, the mean of the coded scores was calculated over the units having coded scored of 1, 2, or 3. From the resulting means of the coded scores, the valency scores were derived as follows: valency score (h), mean between 1.00 and 1.70; valency score (n), mean between 1.71 and 2.29; valency score (l), mean between 2.30 and 3.00.

In order to illustrate the coding at unit level, and the calculation of the intensity of use and the valency score for each factor, the analysis of the description "She is likeable, but can be quite rude. She is a very creative child, but is awfully messy," is shown in Table 21.2.

From the intensity of use scores it can be seen that Factor II is highly relevant in the classification of this description. The valency scores indicate that for Factor I, for example, the description points toward "Extravert," but that for Factor II it is not clear to which pole the description refers.

The descriptions of three sets of 10 children from the research group were independently coded by three judges. After each set was coded the results were discussed. Then the results of all the remaining children in the study were coded by two judges. In this way, each of the three judges coded two thirds of the remaining descriptions.

RESULTS

Interjudge Reliability

Cohen's kappa was used as the measure of agreement between judges in the coding of the units (Popping, 1989). The mean values of kappa for each of the five factors (over the three combinations of two out of three judges) were .74 (I), .69 (II), .61 (III), .75 (IV), .78 (V). If we take into account the fact that there are four categories under consideration here, and that the distribution of the marginals departs strongly from the rectangular distribution, then the level of agreement may be regarded as satisfactory to good. Agreement between the judges appeared to be slightly better for the research group, but the differences

TABLE 21.2
Coding of an Example of a Description

Units	Factor				
	I Extraversion	II Agreeableness	III Conscientiousness	IV Emotional Stability	V Openness/ Intellect
1. likeable	0	1	0	0	0
2. can be quite rude	1	3	0	0	0
3. very creative	0	0	0	0	1
4. awfully messy	0	0	3	0	0
Intensity of use[a]	.25	.50	.25	.00	.25
Valency score	h	n	l	n	h

[a]The sum over the five factors of the intensity of use can be greater than 1, due to the possibility that a unit can be scored on more than one factor.

here were too small to warrant further consideration. For the rest of the study, the coded scores assigned to each unit (by two and three judges respectively) were combined as follows: A coded score of 0, 1, or 3 was assigned when at least two judges coded the unit as 0, 1, or 3, respectively, on the relevant factor. And a coded score of 2 was assigned in the remaining cases. These coded scores were used in the calculations of intensity of use and valency.

Cover of the Five-Factor Model

The descriptions of the children attending the psychiatric outpatients' clinic contain an average of 4.7 units. The descriptions of the comparison group contain an average of 8.7 units. This difference is significant [$t(339) = 10.55, p < .0001$]. The percentage of units classifiable under the five-factor model is 93.6% for the research group and 85.5% for the comparison group.

To gain an impression of the content of the units that could not be classified under the five-factor model, the following supplementary categories were formulated (Bohlmann & Kleingeld, 1991; Schutter & Fernhout, 1990): not clearly pejorative (e.g., unusual); details about the child's development (e.g., childish); physical characteristics (e.g., too fat); statements about the child's health (e.g., asthmatic); and motor skills (e.g., fond of sport). When a unit could not be classified under any of the five factors, that is, when it received a coded score of zero five times, then it was judged in terms of the supplementary categories. It appeared that in more than 80% of these cases one of the supplementary categories was applicable. Thus, with this extended form of the five-factor model it was possible to achieve almost full cover. The coding of the units under the supplementary categories is not further discussed.

Differences Between the Two Groups

Because the distributions of both age and sex for the two groups differ (see Table 21.1), hierarchical log-linear analyses were used to determine whether these two variables could be omitted from the analyses of differences between the groups with respect to intensity of use and valency score (referred to as dependent variables). In accordance with the recommendations of Bishop, Fienberg, and Holland (1975), the model chosen was always the simplest one with a satisfactory fit (criterion $p > .05$), unless a more complex model did give a significant better explanation of the relations. The simplest model consists of the interactions Group × Age and Group × Sex. When this model (in which a Group × Dependent Variable interaction is absent) is chosen, there are no other differences between the two groups.

In the second model is the interaction Group × Dependent Variable. When this model is chosen, the variables Age and Sex can be omitted from the analysis of the differences between the two groups.

In the third and fourth models, the second model is extended with the interactions Dependent Variable × Age and Dependent Variable × Sex. In the fifth and sixth models, the first-order interaction Group × Dependent Variable is extended to a third-order interaction with the variables age and sex. Finally, in the seventh model, the second model is extended with the interaction Dependent Variable × Age × Sex.

The first, simplest model held for *intensity of use* on Factor III; that is, there are differences on age and sex on this factor, but no differences between the two groups. For the *valency scores* on Factor I, the seventh model applied. This means a comparison of the two groups as a whole is of little value. Further analysis revealed an age effect for boys: Boys older than 9 years often described as introverted compared with boys younger than 9 years. For girls, there was a Group × Age interaction, which is most clearly manifested in the finding that for the 7 to 12 year age group girls in the comparison group were far more often described as extraverted than were girls in the research group (60% vs. 20%). Because the focus of this study is on differences between the two groups, the data relating to the valency scores on Factor I are not considered further.

In the eight remaining cases, the second model was applicable.

Differences in Intensity of Use for Factors I, II, IV, and V

Table 21.3 shows *intensity of use* for the five factors for the research and comparison groups. It can be seen, for example, that for the research group practically all the descriptions (100% − 9% = 91%) contain at least one unit that relates to the second factor (agreeable–disagreeable behavior); for 50% of the descriptions, more than half of all the units fall under this factor. For the comparison group, this factor is used less frequently. As stated earlier, Factor III is used fairly equally for the two groups. The three remaining factors (I, IV, and V) are used less in the research group, partly because of the more intensive use of terms (units) falling under Factor II.

When a significant difference in the distribution of intensity of use was found between the groups (Test A in Table 21.3), then a more precise determination of the differences in the use of the factor was made. For this, two types of difference were distinguished: First, differences in the frequency with which a factor was used (Scores 1, 2, or 3) or not used (Score 0) (Test B); and second, differences in the frequencies of the Scores 1, 2, and 3, that is, focusing on differences in the intensity of use scores in the cases when the relevant factor was used (Test C). These additional comparisons are mutually independent. The chi-quadrate of the overall comparison is roughly split into two components. The relative magnitude of the chi-quadrate values obtained from Tests B and C, then gives a good indication of the nature of the overall difference (see Everitt, 1976).

It may be concluded from Table 21.3 that the differences between the two groups on Factor I and V are mainly due to the fact that these factors fail to be

TABLE 21.3
Intensity of Use of the Five Factors

Group	Relative Number of Units Classified Under Factor				Test of Differences Between Groups[c]
	(0) 0 zero units	(1) .01– .33 ≤ one-third	(2) .34– .50 ≤ half	(3) .51– 1.00 > half	
Factor I: Extraversion					
Research[a]	30%	27%	20%	23%	A: $\chi^2 = 28.1$, $p < .0001$
Comparison[b]	9%	48%	18%	26%	B: $\chi^2 = 20.4$, $p < .0001$
					C: $\chi^2 = 6.2$, $p < .05$
Factor II: Agreeableness					
Research	9%	20%	20%	50%	A: $\chi^2 = 42.5$, $p < .0001$
Comparison	15%	43%	25%	17%	B: nonsignificant
					C: $\chi^2 = 40.6$, $p < .001$
Factor III: Conscientiousness					
Research	48%	37%	9%	6%	A: nonsignificant
Comparison	49%	40%	8%	3%	B:
					C:
Factor IV: Emotional Stability					
Research	45%	29%	12%	14%	A: $\chi^2 = 21.0$, $p < .0001$
Comparison	32%	49%	15%	5%	B: $\chi^2 = 5.9$, $p < .05$
					C: $\chi^2 = 14.0$, $p < .001$
Factor V: Openness/Intellect					
Research	78%	19%	3%	1%	A: $\chi^2 = 71.5$, $p < .0001$
Comparison	33%	47%	17%	3%	B: $\chi^2 = 66.5$, $p < .0001$
					C: nonsignificant

[a] $N = 207$.
[b] $N = 136$.
[c] Using the chi-quadrate test, the distributions of the two groups were first compared (A, $df = 3$). If the distributions differed, the difference between the groups was tested with regard to the contrast used/not used (B, $df = 1$, χ^2 after Yates' correction), and also with regard to differences in the frequency distributions over the scores 1, 2, and 3 (C, $df = 2$).

used by the research group more often than by the comparison group. In contrast, the differences on Factors II and IV are related mainly to frequency differences in the Scores 1, 2, and 3. The relevance of these factors in the representation of a description appears to be greater in the research group.

Differences in Valency Scores for Factors I, II, IV, and V

Valency scores for Factors II to V were analyzed in the same way as intensity of use. As explained previously, a comparison of valency scores on Factor I is not feasible because of the interaction of differences between the groups with age and with sex.

In Table 21.4 the valency-score distributions for the remaining four factors are presented separately for the two groups. The statistical tests indicate that the frequency distributions of these scores differ significantly for the two groups on all four factors. These differences were analyzed more precisely using the method used in Table 21.3. In this case, the distinction was between differences in the frequency with which a pole of the factor was applicable (Score 1 or 3) or not applicable (Score 2) (Test B), and differences in the frequencies of the Scores 1 and 3, that is, differences in the frequency of the high and the low valency scores (Test C).

Because the focus of this study is mainly on the direction of differences between the groups, the proportion of positive valency scores to negative valency scores was also calculated. These proportions are also reported in Table 21.4.

The difference in the distribution of Factor V between the two groups appears almost wholly due to a relatively pronounced absence of this factor or to an ambivalent use of it in the descriptions of children in the research group. This also holds, though to a lesser extent, for Factor IV.

Differences in the valency-score distributions for Factors II and III appear to be mainly due to a difference in direction: The descriptions of the children in the research group point more often to disagreeableness and to unconscientiousness. Again, this also holds to a lesser extent for Factor IV.

Comparing these proportions with the results of a study of teachers' free descriptions of Flemish schoolchildren (Mervielde, 1991a, chapter 20, this volume), there appears to be good agreement between Mervielde's results and the results for the comparison group on Factors III and IV. The percentages obtained for the Flemish teachers on Factor II are consistent with the proportions found for the research group. In contrast to Dutch parents, Flemish teachers make use of the negative pole of Factor V (unimaginative), namely, in 40% of the cases.

Descriptions of Children in Different Diagnostic Groups

Lastly, we investigated differences between specific diagnostic groups that were part of the research group, and matched comparison groups that were part of the total comparison group. For the diagnostic groups we selected children who had been assigned one of the *Diagnostic and Statistical Manual of Mental Disorders*

TABLE 21.4
Distribution of Valency Scores and the Proportion of Positive to
Negative Valencies for the Factors II, III, IV, and V

	Valency scores			Test of Differences Between Groups[c]
	(h) high	(n) neutral	(l) low	
Factor II: Agreeableness				
Percentages:				
Res. group[a]	41%	37%	22%	A: $\chi^2 = 6.1, p < .05$
Comp. group[b]	46%	42%	12%	B: nonsignificant
Proportion h/l:				C: $\chi^2 = 4.7, p < .05$
Res. group	.65		.35	
Comp. group	.80		.20	
Factor III: Conscientiousness				
Percentages:				
Res. group	10%	74%	16%	A: $\chi^2 = 17.1, p < .0005$
Comp. group	27%	61%	12%	B: $\chi^2 = 6.2, p < .05$
Proportion h/l:				C: $\chi^2 = 4.7, p < .05$
Res. group	.40		.60	
Comp. group	.70		.30	
Factor IV: Emotional Stability				
Percentages:				
Res. group	6%	65%	30%	A: $\chi^2 = 9.1, p < .01$
Comp. group	15%	53%	32%	B: $\chi^2 = 4.3, p < .05$
Proportion h/l:				C: nonsignificant
Res. group	.16		.84	
Comp. group	.31		.69	
Factor V: Openness/Intellect				
Percentages:				
Res. group	15%	85%	1%	A: $\chi^2 = 66.1, p < .0001$
Comp. group	54%	43%	4%	B: $\chi^2 = 64.2, p < .0001$
Proportion h/l:				C: nonsignificant
Res. group	.94		.06	
Comp. group	.94		.06	

[a] $N = 207$.
[b] $N = 136$.
[c] Using the chi-quadrate test, the distributions of the two groups were first compared (A, $df = 2$). If the distributions differed, then the difference between the groups was tested with regard to the frequency distributions of the valency scores applicable (h, l) versus not applicable (n) (B, $df = 1$, χ^2 after Yates' correction), and with regard to the frequency distributions of the valency scores positive (h) versus negative (l) (C, $df = 1$, χ^2 after Yates' correction).

DSM–III–R diagnoses belonging to the cluster of depressive disorders and children with the DSM–III–R diagnosis oppositional defiant disorder. Because these classifications are related to age and sex, age and sex were taken into account in the subject selection. Two subgroups of the research group were selected, namely, all children age 7 to 12 years in whom a *depressive disorder* had been diagnosed ($n = 64$; in the research group the classification depressive disorder occurred rarely in children younger than 7 years); and all boys in whom *oppositional disorder* had been diagnosed ($n = 27$; this diagnosis was made only rarely with girls).

The two groups were compared with their age- and/or sex-matched controls from the comparison group on valency score for each of the five factors, for example, the same sort of comparison as described in Table 21.4(C). The results of the comparisons between depressive children and their age-equivalents from the comparison group are presented here. The number appearing in brackets is the (varying) number of children for whom the valency score on the relevant dimension is 1 or 3:

Factor I: Comparatively more depressive children ($N = 30$) than their age-matched controls ($N = 62$) were described as introvert: 43% versus 18%, χ^2 (1 df, after Yates' correction) = 5.6, $p < .05$.

Factor II: Comparatively more depressive children ($n = 43$) than their age-matched controls ($N = 53$) were described as disagreeable: 45% versus 23%, χ^2 (1 df, after Yates' correction) = 7.3, $p < .01$.

Factor III: Comparatively more depressive children ($N = 14$) than their age-matched controls ($N = 33$) were described as careless: 71% versus 24%, χ^2 (1 df, after Yates' correction) = 7.4, $p < .01$.

Factors IV and V: There were no differences.

Because of the limited number of both positive and negative coded scores falling on Factors III, IV, and V for oppositional boys, comparisons between oppositional boys and sex-matched controls were made only on Factors I and II. There appeared to be virtually no difference on Factor I. On Factor II, oppositional boys were more often described in terms of disagreeableness (50% of the 18 cases versus 23% of their 43 controls); however, as this difference failed to reach significance, it can only be regarded as a trend, χ^2 (1 df, after Yates' correction) = 3.1, $p < .08$.

DISCUSSION

The use of the five factor model in the analysis of parents' free descriptions of their children has produced some important findings. After a short training period, satisfactory to good agreement between judges was obtained on the coding of the units into which the descriptions were split. It must be noted that an alternative to unit coding proved not to be feasible. Having coded all the units of a description, the judges evaluated the entire description on each of the five factors. For this they were required to judge the number of times that a particular pole (Code 1 or 3) was used. But they also judged the force of the terms used (which is not taken into account in the coding of the units), as well as the general effect of the description. The interjudge reliability, however, of these global scores was unsatisfactory. A more nuanced method of coding the descriptions as a whole appeared to be too strongly influenced by idiosyncratic opinions of the judges.

A high percentage of the units could be classified under one or more factors of the five-factor model: In particular, the percentage cover for the research group (93.6%) may be regarded as high.

In comparing the data of the children with psychiatric problems with that of the children in the comparison group, we should exercise restraint, because the method of data collection for the two groups differed in a number of ways. The parents of the children in the comparison group were, on the initiative of the researchers, voluntary participants. These parents were requested as part of scientific research, to give a description of the child. Many of the parents indicated that they enjoyed the challenge of the unusual telephone contact. They gave personal and detailed descriptions. The parents in the research group gave their descriptions in an interview taking place in the context of child psychiatric help. In the course of this interview they had already provided a lot of information about the child. This probably explains why the total number of descriptions from parents in the comparison group was so much higher.

In this study, the findings relating to two factors stand out immediately. First, it is apparent that for children in the research group a large proportion of the descriptions relate to Factor II, and these descriptions point only slightly more often in the direction of disagreeable. Further analysis indicated that the parents of referred children more often combine both negative and positive terms. The background to this is probably that during the intake interview at a child psychiatric clinic, parents often describe their child in terms of "difficult." Apparently in order to "compensate" for this, they also emphasize that the child is "likeable." The notion that this factor is a possible "psychopathology" factor, as suggested by Digman (1989), is therefore not acceptable, at least when parents are the source of the information. It is conceivable that information from teachers regarding difficult children would point more unequivocally in a negative direction.

The second notable finding is that the children from the research group are only seldom described in terms of "(lack of) openness/intellect/imagination." An explanation for this could be that the parents of the children in the comparison group were approached through the school. Another explanation could be that for children with psychiatric problems, the parents' attention is, in most cases, not primarily focused on the child's intellectual functioning. Also, the parents may not expect the therapist to be particularly interested in this area.

It was somewhat surprising that a significantly higher percentage of children in the comparison group were described in terms relating to the fourth factor (Emotional Stability-Neuroticism). Insofar as this factor applied to the descriptions of children in the research group, it appeared to have a high relevance (that is its intensity of use was greater than .33). With regard to the third factor, the differences are limited to the valency scores. The children with psychiatric problems are described by their parents relatively more often in negative terms. A number of the differences found between the research and comparison groups appear to become more pronounced when the comparison is confined to depressive children age 7 to 12 years. Depressive children were more often described as introvert, and on the third factor were (even) more often described in terms relating to the negative pole, for example, careless, aimless, and lazy. Depressive children also appear to be described more often as disagreeable; this difference was also found, though to a less extent, in the comparison of the two complete groups. These findings are consistent with the clinical picture of depressive children, who are often passive and dysphoric.

Because of their limited number, boys with oppositional behavior could only be investigated with regard to differences on the first two factors. These boys tended to be more often described as disagreeable than were their sex-matched controls. This finding is noteworthy because the study was concerned only with the description of a child, and not with "symptoms"; the latter being enquired into independently.

The findings presented here provide ground for further study into the categorization of parents' free descriptions of their children using the five-factor model. A follow-up study will investigate how the data can be related to a personality inventory completed by the children, as well as to teacher ratings of the children's behavior.

In addition, attention will be focused on target symptoms, as formulated independently by the parents; these are the symptoms given by the parents as the most important reason for a psychiatric investigation of their child. An initial analysis has revealed that the target symptoms can be only partially classified under the five factors. Classification appeared impossible for many symptoms (e.g., enuresis and physical complaints). This could be because such symptoms do not reflect or imply (stable) personality traits. But it seems expedient that in the practical application of a category system for free personality descriptions, personality and behavior characteristics falling outside the five-factor model be placed in a limited number of extra categories.

ACKNOWLEDGMENTS

Thanks to C. F. M. van Lieshout for suggestions for improvements to the text.

REFERENCES

Bishop, Y. M. M., Fienberg, S. E., & Holland, P. W. (1975). *Discrete multivariate analysis.* Cambridge, MA: MIT Press.

Bohlmann, A., & Kleingeld, K. (1991). *Persoonskenmerken van kinderen genoemd door ouders en het vijffactorenmodel ("Big Five") uit de persoonlijkheidspsychologie* [Personality attributes of children given by their parents and the five-factor model ("Big Five") of personality]. Afstudeerproject Kinder- en Jeugdpsychiatrie. Leiden: Faculteit Geneeskunde.

Brokken, F. B. (1978). *The language of personality.* Groningen: Dissertatie.

Digman, J. M. (1989). Five robust trait dimensions: Development, stability, and utility. *Journal of Personality, 57,* 195–214.

Everitt, B. S. (1976). *The analysis of contingency tables.* London: Chapman & Hall.

John, O. P. (1989). Towards a taxonomy of personality descriptors. In D. M. Buss & N. Cantor (Eds.), *Personality psychology: Recent trends and emerging directions* (pp. 261–271). New York: Springer.

Kohnstamm, G. A., Halverson, C. F., Havill, V. L., & Mervielde, I. (in press). Parents' free descriptions of child characteristics: A cross-cultural search for the roots of the Big Five. In C. Super & S. Harkness (Eds.), *Parents' cultural belief systems: Cultural origins and developmental consequences.* New York: Guilford Press.

McCrae, R. R., & Costa, P. T. (1985). Updating Norman's adequate taxonomy: Intelligence and personality dimensions in natural language and in questionnaires. *Journal of Personality and Social Psychology, 49,* 710–721.

Mervielde, I. (1991). *The Big Five in parents' versus teachers' constructs.* Paper presented at the conference "The Development of the Structure of Temperament and Personality from Infancy to Adulthood." Wassenaar, Netherlands Institute for Advanced Studies (NIAS).

Ostendorf, F. (1991). *Sprache und Persönlichkeitsstruktur: zur Validität des Fünf-Faktoren-Modells der Persönlichkeit* [Language and personality structure: The validity of the five-factor model of personality]. Regensburg: Roderer.

Peabody, D., & Goldberg, L. R. (1989). Some determinants of factor structures from personality-trait descriptors. *Journal of Personality and Social Psychology, 57,* 552–567.

Popping, R. (1989). *AGREE. Computing agreement on nominal data (version 5.0).* Groningen: ProGAMMA.

Schutter, N., & Fernhout, H. (1990). *De beschrijving door ouders van de ontwikkeling en de persoonlijkheid van kinderen op een polikliniek kinderpsychiatrie.* [Parents' free descriptions of the development and the personality of children attending an outpatient clinic for child and adolescent psychiatry]. Afstudeerproject Kinder- en Jeugdpsychiatrie. Leiden: Faculteit Geneeskunde, 1990.

Treffers, Ph. D. A., Goedhart, A. W., Waltz, J., & Koudijs, E. (1990). The systematic collection of patient data in a centre for child and adolescent psychiatry. *British Journal of Psychiatry, 157,* 744–748.

AUTHOR INDEX

A

Achenbach, T. M., 181, *184*, 319, *322*, 356, 357, 364, *365*
Acredolo, C., 174, *184*, 214, *218*
Aesberg, M., 44, *49*, *50*
Ahadi, S. A., 153, *155*, 192, 199, 203, *205*, *207*
Allen, K., 373, 374, *386*
Allen, L., 181, 182, *185*
Allport, G. W., 8, *34*, 91, 92, *106*, 203, *205*, 241, *262*, 324, 335, *336*, 372, *385*
Alpert, R., 180, *185*
Altemeyer, B., 18, *34*
Anderson, J., 130, *135*
Andreas, D., 251, 259, 262, *264*
Angleitner, A., 64, 70, 74, 78, 84, *90*, 92, 106, *107*, *108*, 293, *317*, 323, *337*, 355, *365*, 372, *386*, 387, *396*, *397*
Arenberg, D., 55, *67*, 146, 148, *149*, 181, *184*
Arrindell, W. A., 81, *88*
Asberg, M., 66, *68*
Asendorpf, J. B., 294, *316*
Asher, S. R., 368, *370*

B

Babcock, J. C., 43, *47*
Baker, E. H., 160, 162, 163, 165, 169, *171*
Bandura, A., 247, *262*
Bank, L., 117, *135*
Bantelman, J., 70, 74, 78, 84, *90*
Barefoot, J. C., 145, *150*
Barnes, B., 37, *47*
Barratt, E. S., 66, *67*
Barrett, K. C., 190, *205*
Barrett, P. T., 60, *67*, 81, *88*, 199, *206*
Barrick, M. R., 106, *107*
Barten, S., 174, *184*
Baruch, I., 45, *47*
Bates, J. E., 157, *172*, 201, *205*, 215, 216, *218*, 227–229, 231, 238, *239*, *240*, 242, 250, 261, *263*, 341, *351*, 395, *397*
Bathurst, K., 214, *218*
Batson, C. D., 341, 343, *351*, *353*
Bayles, K., 238, *239*, 261, *263*
Baylis, G. C., 44, *47*, *50*
Beckman, H., 42, *49*
Beech, A., 44, *47*
Behar, L., 229, 231, *239*
Bell, R., 212, 217, *218*
Belsky, J., 247, *263*, 347, *351*, 352
Bem, D. J., 210, 211, 214, *218*, 282, *290*, 294, *316*, 344, *351*
Bemporad, B., 345, *353*

Bentler, P. M., 122, 129, 130, *135*, *136*
Bergeman, C. S., 339, 343, *351*
Berlin, B., 372, *385*
Bernieri, F., 247, *264*
Bierhoff, H. W., 343, *351*
Birch, H. G., 151, *155*, 158, *172*, 229, 230, *240*
Birchall, P. M. A., 45, *48*
Birenbaum, M., 72, *88*
Birns, B., 174, *184*
Bishop, Y. M. M., 404, *412*
Block, J., 9, *34*, 116, 134, *135*, 175, *184*, 222, 225, 231, *239*, 249, *263*, 268, 271, 273, 274, *289*, *290*, 293, 294, 296, *317*
Block, J. H., 175, *184*, 222, 225, 231, *239*, 249, *263*, 268, 273, *289*, *290*, 293, 294, 296, *317*
Blum, L. A., 343, *351*
Blunden, D., 181, *186*
Blythe, D., 346, 347, *354*
Bohlin, G., 159, 162, 163, 164, 167, *171*, *172*, 228–231, *239*, *239*, *240*
Bohlmann, A., 404, *412*
Bolasco, S., 134, *136*
Bollen, K. A., 130, *135*
Bond, M. H., 323, *336*, 340, *351*
Boone, L., 180, *186*
Boorman, S. A., 341, *351*
Borgatta, E. F., 18, *34*
Borge, A., 43, *50*
Borkenau, P., 73, 74, 78, 84, *88*, 118, *135*, 323, 324, *336*
Bornstein, M. H., 242, *263*
Bosch, R. van den, 42, *47*
Bouchard, T. J., Jr., 258, *265*, 325, 335, *336*, *338*
Boylan, A., 204, *207*
Bradshaw, D. L., 248, *263*
Brand, C. R., 92, *107*
Breckler, S. J., 132, *135*
Bridger, W., 174, *184*
Briggs, S. R., 7, *34*, 92, *107*, 118, 134, *135*, *136*, 189, *205*
Brokken, F. B., 92, 95, 96, *107*, *108*, 293, *317*, 355, *366*, 387, *396*, 402, *412*
Broks, P., 43, 44, *47*, *48*
Bronson, W. C., 282, *290*
Brophy, C., 181, *185*
Broughton, R., 94, *109*
Brown, C. H., 372, *385*
Browne, M. W., 117, 120–122, 124, *135*
Brunnquell, D., 247, *263*

Buchsbaum, M. S., 42, 44, *47*, *50*, 66, *68*, 181, *186*
Buckhout, R., 198, *206*
Buczkowski, H. J., 181, *187*, 356, *366*
Burk, E., 320, *322*
Busch, C. M., 2, *5*, 223, *225*, 271, 272, 278, *291*, 293, 295, *317*
Buss, A. H., 60, 66, *67*, 70, 72, 73, 74, 78, 84, 85, 87, *88*, 152, *155*, 157, 168, *171*, 174, *184*, *185*, 190, *205*, 209, 212, 213, 217, *218*, 222, 225–233, 234, 238, *239*, 242, *263*, *264*, 282, *290*, 325, 331, 332, 335, *336*, 341, 342, 344, 350, *351*
Buss, D. M., 2, *4*, 106, *107*, 175, *184*, 339, 340, 341, *351*
Butcher, J. E., 175, *184*

C

Cadwell, J., 169, *172*
Cairns, R. B., 347, 349, 350, *351*
Camac, C., 38, *51*, 56, *68*, 72, *90*, 177, *187*, 201, *207*
Campbell, D. T., 114, 115, 120, 127, *136*
Campbell, B. A., 180, *184*
Campbell, D., 180, *184*, *186*
Campos, J. J., 190, *205*, 241, 242, 248–250, 258, 260, *263*, *264*
Carey, G., 249, 258, *263*, *265*
Carey, W. B., 151, *155*, 158, *171*, *172*, 228, *239*
Carlier, M., 72, *88*
Carr, S., *239*, *240*
Carver, C. S., 190, *205*
Caspi, A., 210–212, 214, *218*, 268, 269, 271, 272, 276, 278, 282, *290*, *291*, 344, *351*
Cassidy, J., 346, 350, *353*
Cattell, R. B., 8, *34*, 40, 48, 53, *67*, 81, 84, 89, 91, *107*, 122, *136*, 189, *205*, 283, *290*, 326, 327, *336*, 372, *385*
Chapman, M., 212, 217, *218*
Chappa, H. J., 45, *48*
Checkley, S. A., 44, *48*
Chess, S., 66, *68*, 88, *90*, 151, *155*, 158, 166, *172*, 174, *185*, *186*, 190, *207*, 228–230, *240*, 242, 247, *263*, *264*, *265*, 320, *322*, 325, 331, *338*, 341, 344, *351*, 368, *370*, 372, *386*
Chipuer, H., 339, *351*

AUTHOR INDEX

Christal, R. E., 8, *35*, 323, *338*, 355, 358, 360, *366*
Christianson, S. A., 198, *205*
Chugani, H. T., 204, *205*
Church, A. T., 339, 341, *351*, 368, *369*, 372, *385*
Cillessen, A. H. N., 294, 296, 297, *317*, *318*
Claridge, G. S., 41, 43–45, *47*, *48*, *50*
Clark, L. A., 195, *207*, 249, *265*
Clark, M. C., 260, *265*
Clark, C. M., 142, *150*
Clarke-Stewart, K. A., 180, *184*
Cloninger, C. R., 345, *351*
Coan, R. A., 326, *336*
Cohen, D. J., 180, *184*
Collins, L. M., 134, *136*
Comrey, A. L., 177, *184*
Conley, J. J., 176, *184*
Connell, J. P., 339, *351*
Coppi, R., 134, *136*
Corsini, R. J., 18, *34*
Corulla, W. J., 71, 86, *89*
Cosmides, L., 340, 341, *351*, *354*
Costa, P. T., 1, 2, *4*, *5*, 7, 16, 18, 19, 21, 24, *34*, 38, *48*, *50*, 54, 55, 60, 64, *67*, 69, 73, 74, 75, 77, 78, 82, 84, 86, 87, *89*, 92, 93, 105, 106, *107*, *108*, 118, 122, 123, 128, *136*, *137*, 140, 142, 143–147, 148, *148*, *149*, *150*, 169, 170, 171, *172*, 176, *186*, 190, *205*, 223, *225*, 243, 244, *263*, 267, 271, 272, 276, 278, 280, 282, *290*, *291*, 293, 295, *317*, 323, 324, *336*, *337*, 339, *351*, *353*, 355, 356, 358, 360, *365*, *366*, 375, *385*, 387, *397*, 402, *412*
Coursey, R. D., 42, 44, *50*
Cranston, G. C., 44, *50*
Craske, B., 43, *49*
Crichton, L., 247, *263*
Crockenberg, S., 174, *184*, 212, 214, *218*
Cronbach, L. J., 46, *48*
Crook, G., 210, *219*
Crow, T. J., 41, *48*
Crowne, D. P., 199, *205*
Cudeck, R., 122, *136*
Cunningham, M. R., 341, *351*

D

Daniels, D., 214, *218*
Davidson, R. J., 200, *207*, 345, *352*
Davis, A. L., 242, *264*
Dawkins, R., 65, *67*
Dawson, D. V., 142, *150*
DeFries, J. C., 214, *219*, 243, 258, 260, *263*, *265*, 342, *354*
DeFruyt, F., 224, *225*
Dembroski, T. M., 2, *4*
DeRaad, B., 7, *34*, 40, *48*, 92, 94, 95, 96, 105, 106, *107*, *108*, 118, *136*, 280, 287, *290*, 293, 298, 303, 314, *317*, 389, 390, *397*
Derryberry, D., 190, 191, 192, 196, 198, 204, *205*, *207*, 213, *219*, 242, *265*, 324, *338*
DeRubeis, R., 242, *264*
Dibble, E., 180, *184*
Diener, E., 199, *205*
Digman, J. M., 1, *4*, 7, 8, *34*, 69, 70, *89*, 91, 92, 106, *107*, 112, 116, *136*, 140, *149*, 152, *155*, 157, *172*, 176, *184*, 201, 202, *205*, 210, 216, *218*, 227, 228, 231, 232, 238, 239, *239*, 267, 268, 276, 278, 280, *290*, 293, 295, *317*, 323, 324, 326, 327, 331, 334, *336*, 339, 340, 341, 342, 347, *351*, *352*, 355, 356, 358, 359, 360, 363, 364, *365*, 371, 385, *385*, 387, *396*, 410, *412*
Dishion, T., 117, *135*
Diskin, S. D., 247, *264*
Dobroth, K. M., 294, *317*
Dommel, N., 115, *137*
Douglas, K., 148, *149*, 181, *184*
Downs, A. C., 180, *185*
Draper, P., 347, *351*, *352*
Dunlap, D. N., 183, *185*
Dunn, J., 339, 342, *352*
Dureski, C., 174, *184*
Dye, D. A., 140, 143, *149*

E

Earl, N. L., 142, *150*
Earls, F. J., 157, *172*
Eason, R. G., 43, *48*
Eaton, W. O., 174, 175, 180, *184*, *186*, 209, *219*
Eaves, L. J., 247, *263*
Ebbesen, E. B., 294, *317*
Eber, H. W., 40, *48*, 283, *290*
Eccles, J. S., 347, 348, *352*
Eckerman, C. O., 180, *186*
Edlebrock, C., 181, *184*, 356, 357, 364, *365*
Edman, G., 44, *49*, *50*, 66, *68*

Egan, V., 92, *107*
Egeland, B., 247, *263*, 350, *354*
Eisenberg, N. H., 118, *136*, 340–343, *352*
Elder, G. H., Jr., 210, 211, 214, *218*, 344, *351*
Elliott, T. K., 249, *264*
Elphick, E., 375, 378, *386*
Emde, R. N., 340, *352*
Endler, N. S., 55, *68*
Erikson, E. H., 142, *149*, 334, *336*
Escalona, S. K., 152, *155*
Escofier, B., 122, *136*
Eugenio, P., 198, *206*
Everett, J. E., 327, *336*
Everitt, B. S., 405, *412*
Ewald, R., 42, *49*
Eysenck, H. J., 19, *34*, 37, 38, 41, 42, 43, 45–47, *48*, *49*, 53–55, 60, 64, 66, *67*, 72, *89*, *90*, 91, 92, 105, 106, *107*, 140, *149*, 190, 191, 194, 199, *206*, 209, 211, *218*, 232, *239*, 247, *263*, 275, *290*, 325, 331, 335, *336*, *337*, *338*, 343, *354*, 360, *365*
Eysenck, M. W., 37, *49*, 53, 64, 66, *67*, 190, 191, *206*, 325, *337*
Eysenck, S. B. G., 38, *49*, 53, 55, 60, *67*, 72, *89*, *90*, 140, *149*, 199, *206*

F

Fabes, R. A., 341, 343, *352*
Fales, E., 180, *185*
Farrington, D., 268, *291*
Feldman, S. S., 247, *263*
Ferguson, L. R., 180, *185*
Fernhout, H., 402, *412*
Feshbach, N. D., 343, *352*
Field, T., 260, *263*
Field, D., 146, 148, *149*
Fienberg, S. E., 404, *412*
Fillenbaum, G. G., 142, *150*
Finch, M. D., 143, *150*
Finn, S. E., 145, *149*
Fiske, D. W., 112, 114, 115, 120, 127, *136*, 323, *337*
Flanagan, C., 347, 348, *352*
Flor-Henry, P., 43, *49*
Foa, U. G., 104, *107*
Foa, E. B., 104, *107*
Forgas, J. P., 340, *351*
Fox, N. A., 345, *352*
Frankel, K. A., 201, *205*, 229, *239*

Franz, C., 343, *353*
Freeland, C. A., 201, *205*, 261, *263*
Freeman, F. N., 335, *337*
Freud, S., 334, *337*
Fries, M. E., 152, *155*
Frith, C. D., 44, *49*
Fry, D, 212, *218*
Fujita, F., 199, *205*
Fulker, D. W., 214, *219*, 243, 260, *263*, *265*, 335, *338*, 343, *354*
Fullard, W., 158, *172*
Funder, D. C., 112, 116, 133, 134, *136*, 250, *263*, 273, *290*, 294, *316*, *317*
Furman, W. C., 339, *351*

G

Garber, J., 294, *318*
Garcia-Coll, C. T., 239, *240*
Garino, E., 159, 162–164, *172*
Garrison, W. T., 157, *172*
Garvey, C. R., 180, *185*
Gatewood, M. C., 180, *185*
Gattaz, W. F., 42, *49*
Gaughran, J. M., 242, *263*
Gerbing, D. W., 130, *135*
Gershenhorn, S., 214, *219*
Gewirtz, J., 45, *50*
Gibbons, J., 262, *264*
Gillner, A., 44, *49*
Given, K., 247, *264*
Gjerde, P. F., 249, *263*, 274, 289, *289*, *290*, 294, *317*, *318*
Goedhart, A. W., 401, *412*
Goldberg, L. R., 1, *4*, *5*, 7–9, 16, 18, 23, *34*, 35, 38, *49*, 54, *67*, *68*, 70, 86, *89*, 92, 104, 106, *107*, *108*, 118, 123, *136*, 140, *149*, 176, *185*, 189, 200, *206*, 242–244, *263*, 267, 280, 287, 288, *290*, 293, 298, 303, 311, 314, *317*, *318*, 323, 326, 329, *337*, 339, *352*, 355, 358, 360, *365*, *366*, 367, *369*, 371, 372, 375, *386*, 387, 390, *396*, *397*, 402, *412*
Goldsmith, H. H., 134, *136*, 174, *185*, 190, *205*, 209, 211, 213, *218*, 241, 242, 247, 248, 249, 250, 256, 258, 259, 260, *263*, *264*
Goldstein, I. B., 43, *49*
Goldstein, S., 260, *263*
Goodenough, F. L., 180, *185*

Gornal, M., 294, *318*
Gorsuch, R. L., 81, *89*, 177, *186*
Gottfried, A., 214, *218*
Gottlieb, G., 211, *219*
Gough, H. G., 72, *89*, 144, 147, *149*
Grawe, J. M., 180, *184*
Gray, J. A., 45, *47*, 190–192, 194, 198, *206*
Graziano, W. G., 46, *49*, 115, 118, *136*, *138*, 140, *149*, 268, 276, *290*, 339, 340, 342, 343, 346, 348, *352*, *354*
Greenberg, L. M., 181, *186*
Grinsted, A. D., 181, *185*
Groos, K., 334, *337*
Gruzelier, J., 43, *49*
Gudjonsson, G. H., 46, *49*
Guerin, D., 214, *218*
Guilford, J. P., 53, *68*, 146, *149*, 325, 326, *337*
Guilford, J. S., 146, *149*
Gunnar, M., 251, 259, 262, *264*

H

Haan, N., 144–146, *149*
Hagekull, B., 159, 162–164, 167, *171*, *172*, 210, *219*, 228–231, 239, *239*, *240*
Haier, R. J., 42, *50*
Hakstian, A. R., 122, *136*
Hall, C. S., 37, *49*
Hall, G., 45, *50*
Hall, C. A., 249, *264*
Halverson, C. F., 181, *187*, 324, *337*, 339, 343, 349, *352*, 356, *365*, *366*, 371, 373, 374, *386*, 402, *412*
Hampson, S. E., 92, *108*, 329, *337*
Hare, R. D., 43, *49*
Harkness, S., 212, *220*
Harman, H. H., 75, *89*, 298, *317*
Harmon, C., 204, *206*
Harmon, R. J., 340, *352*
Harpending, H., 347, *352*
Harris, C. W., 134, *136*
Harris, M. J., 247, *264*
Harter, S., 348, *352*
Hartka, E., 144, *149*
Haselager, G., 294, *317*
Hatfield, J. S., 180, *185*
Havill, V. L., 371, 373, 374, *386*, 402, *412*
Hawkins, H. L., 199, *206*
Hegvik, R. L., 158, 159, 162–164, *172*
Heilbrun, A. B., Jr., 147, *149*

Heinicke, C., 247, *264*
Helson, R., 145, 148, *149*
Hemsley, D. R., 45, *47*
Herbener, E. S., 212, *218*, 276, *290*
Hershey, K., 192, *207*
Hertzig, M., 158, *172*, 229, 230, *240*
Hetherington, E. M., 180, *186*
Heymans, G., 152, *155*
Higgins, E. T., 190, *206*, 346, *352*
Hinde, R. A., 174, *185*, 242, *264*
Hinton, J., 43, *49*
Ho, D. Y. F., 197, 198, *206*
Hobson, L., 214, *218*
Hocevar, D., 118, 128, *137*
Hoffman, H., 198, *205*
Hoffman, M. L., 341, 343, *353*
Hofstee, W. K. B., 2, *5*, 7, *34*, 66, *68*, 91–95, 105, 106, *107*, *108*, 118, *136*, 280, 287, *290*, 298, 303, 314, *317*, 355, *366*, 387, 389, 390, *396*, *397*
Hogan, R. T., 2, *5*, 55, *68*, 70, *89*, 339, 340, *353*, 387, *397*
Holland, P. W., 404, *412*
Holstein, R. B., 180, *186*
Holzinger, K. J., 335, *337*
Holzman, P. E., 42, *50*
Homel, P., 242, *263*
Honzik, M. P., 181, 182, *185*
Horn, J. L., 77, 84, *89*, 122, 134, *136*, 209, *219*, 343, *353*
Horney, K., 334, *337*
Horowitz, F., 211, *219*
Hoskens, M., 105, *107*
Howarth, E., 91, *108*, 177, *185*
Howell, C. T., 319, *322*
Hoyle, F., 40, *49*
Huba, G. J., 118, 122, *136*, *137*
Hubert, N., 212, *219*
Humphreys, L. G., 327, *337*
Hundal, P. S., 122, *136*
Hutchinson, C. A., 180, *185*
Huttenlocher, P. R., 204, *206*
Huttunen, M. O., 162–165, *172*
Hyler, S. E., 128, *136*

I

Iacono, W. G., 42, *49*
Ingberg-Sacks, V., 45, *50*
Inoff, G., 181, *187*, 356, *366*

Inouye, J., 7, *34*, 70, *89*, 92, *107*, 140, *149*, 152, *155*, 176, *184*, 202, *205*, 278, *290*, 293, 295, *317*, 323, 327, *336*, 347, *352*, 355, 358–360, 363, *365*
Irwin, O. C., 180, *185*

J

Jacklin, C. N., 214, *209*, 295, *317*
Jackson, D. N., 72, *89*, 106, *109*
Jaco, K. L., 249, *264*
Jacobs, A., 183, *185*
Jansen, I. I., 294, *317*
Janssen, A. W. H., 294, 296, 297, *318*
Jessor, R., 144, 145, *149*
John, O. P., 1, 2, *5*, 8, *34*, 38, *49*, 69, 70, 73, 87, *89*, 92, 105, *108*, 112, 113, *136*, *137*, 157, *172*, 201, *206*, 231, *240*, 267, 268, 269, 271, 272, 274, 277, 278, *291*, 293, *317*, 323, *337*, 339, *353*, 355, *365*, 368, *370*, 371, 372, 385, *386*, 387, *396*, *397*, 402, *412*
Johnson, M., 180, *186*
Johnson, M. H., 204, *206*
Johnson, J. A., 93, 105, *108*
Joireman, J., 60–63
Jones, E. E., 116, *136*
Joseph, M., 210, *219*
Julia, H. L., 180, *186*
Jung, C. G., 142, *149*
Jutai, J. W., 42, *49*

K

Kagan, J., 148, *149*, 180, *185*, 210, 213, *219*, 254, 262, *264*
Kaiser, H. F., 75, *90*
Kaplan, E. B., 142, *150*
Kaplan, N., 346, 350, *353*
Kaprio, J., 214, *219*
Kashy, D. A., 115, 118, 127–129, *136*
Katigbak, M. S., 339, 341, *351*, 368, *369*, 372, *385*
Katkin, W., 42, *50*
Kay, P., 372, *385*
Keele, S. W., 199, *206*
Kelly, G. A., 355, *366*, 387, *397*
Kendall, P. C., 181, *185*
Kennenburg, M., 297, *318*
Kenny, D. A., 112, 115, 118, 127–129, *136*

Keogh, B. K., 169, *172*
Kessen, W., 180, *185*
Kestenbaum, R., 251, 259, 262, *264*
Kiers, H., 56, *68*, 72, *90*, 106, *108*
Kinsbourne, M., 345, *353*
Klein, R., 343, *351*
Kleingeld, K., 404, *412*
Kline, P., 81, *88*
Klinteberg, B., 44, *49*
Kloosterman, K., 95, *107*
Klopp, B., 268, *290*
Kobak, R. R., 347, 350, *353*
Koch, H. L., 180, *185*
Kochanska, G., 242, *264*
Koestner, R., 343, *353*
Kohnstamm, G. A., 153, *155*, 157, *172*, 324, 325, *337*, 371, 375, 378, 395, *397*, 402, *412*
Kojima, H., 122, *136*
Koot, J. M., 294, 296, 297, *318*
Koperski, J. A., 180, *185*
Korn, S., 158, *172*, 229, 230, *240*
Korner, A. F., 180, *185*
Koskenvuo, M., 214, *219*
Koudijs, E., 401, *412*
Kraemer, H. C., 180, *185*
Kraft, M., 60–63
Kramer, T. H., 198, *206*
Kramp, P., 343, *351*
Kuhlman, D. M., 38, *51*, 56, 57, 59, 60, 61–63, *68*, 72, *90*, 177, *187*, 201, *207*
Kuhn, T. S., 37, *49*
Kumka, D., 143, *150*
Kuyek, J., 180, *184*

L

Lachman, M. E., 248, *265*
Lamb, M. E., 190, *205*, 214, *220*
Lambemon, M. W. E., 297, *318*
Lambert, N. M., 159, 162, 164, 167, 169, *172*
Land, H., 95, *108*, 355, *366*, 387, *396*
Lang, S., 251, 259, 262, *264*
Lang, E., 180, *184*, *186*
Langinvainio, H., 214, *219*
Langlois, J. H., 180, *185*
LaPouse, R., 181, *185*
Larsen, R. J., 199, *206*
Lasley, J. F., 334, *337*
Launay, G., 42, *49*
Lazarus, R. S., 190, *206*

LeDoux, J. E., 204, *206*
Lee, C. L., 229, 231, *240*
Lerner, R. M., 70, 74, 78, 84, 85, *90*, 134, *136*, 158, 160, *172*, 213, 214, *219*, 247, *264*, 341, 346, *353*, 382, *386*
Lerner, J. V., 213, 214, *219*, 341, *353*, 247, *264*
Levin, H., 247, *265*
Levin, S., 42, *50*
Levitt, M. J., 260, *265*
Levitt, P. R., 341, *351*
Levy, D. L., 42, *50*
Lidberg, L, 44, *49*
Lindhagen, K., 162–164, 167, *171*, *172*, 230, 239, *239*, *240*
Lindzey, G., 37, *49*
Lipton, R. B., 42, *50*
Loeber, R., 268, *291*
Loehlin, J. C., 209, *219*, 242, 244, 247, *264*, 335, *337*, 342, 343, 346, *353*
Loftus, G. R., 198, *205*
Loftus, E. F., 198, *205*
Lorys, A., 162–165, *172*
Lounsbury, M. L., 201, *205*, 261, *263*
Low, B. S., 341, 343, *353*
Lubow, R. E., 45, 47, *50*
Ludlow, C., 181, *186*
Lumry, A., 42, *49*
Luria, A. R., 345, *353*
Lykken, D. T., 42, *49*, 242, 258, *264*, *265*, 325, *338*
Lynam D., 268, *290*
Lyon, M., 256, 260, *264*
Lytton, H., 180, *185*

M

Mabry, P. D., 180, *184*
MacCallum, R. C., 127, *137*
Maccoby, E. E., 214, *219*, 247, *265*, 295, *317*
MacFarlane, J. W., 181, 182, *185*
Macintosh, N. J., 45, *50*
MacLeod, C., 199, *206*
Magnusson, D., 55, *68*, 72, *89*
Mahr, E., 342, *353*
Main, M., 346, 350, *353*
Malmo, R., 43, *50*
Mangelsdorf, S., 251, 259, 262, *264*, 350, *354*
Manwell, E. M., 180, *185*
Marlow, D. A., 199, *205*
Marsh, H. W., 118, 128, *137*
Martin, P., 228, *240*

Martin, R. P., 153, *155*, 158, 159, 160, 162–165, 167–169, *172*, 175, 176, *185*, 320, 321, *322*, 368, *370*, 378, *386*
Martin, N. G., 247, *263*
Marvinney, D., 350, *354*
Maslin, C. A., 201, *205*, 229, *239*
Maslow, A. H., 331, *337*
Matheny, A. P., 174–176, 182, *185*, *186*, 239, *240*
Mathews, A., 199, *206*, 209, 214, *219*
Matthews, G., 38, *50*, 91, *108*
Matthews, K. A., 343, *353*
Mauro, J. A., 190, 201, *207*, 281, *291*
Mazziotta, J. C., 204, *205*
McAdams, D. P., 92, *108*
McCall, R. B., 174, *185*, 242, *264*
McCartney, K., 247, *264*, 346, *354*
McClearn, G. E., 339, 342, *351*, *354*
McClowry, S. G., 159, 162, 163, *172*
McClusky, K., 212, *218*
McConaughy, S. H., 319, *322*
McCrae, R. R., 1, 2, *4*, *5*, 7, 8, 16, 18, 19, 21, 24, *34*, 38, *48*, *50*, 54, 55, 60, 64, *67*, 69, 73–75, 77, 78, 82, 84, 86, 87, *89*, 92, 93, 104–106, *108*, 112, 113, 118, 122, 123, 124, 128, *136*, *137*, 140, 142–147, 148, *148*, *149*, *150*, 159, 162, 163, 164, 169, 170, 171, *172*, 176, *186*, 190, *205*, 223, *225*, 243, 244, *263*, 267, 269, 271, 272, 276, 278, 280, 282, *290*, *291*, 293, 295, *317*, 323, 324, *336*, *337*, 339, *351*, *353*, 355, 356, 358, 360, *365*, *366*, 375, *385*, 387, *397*, 402, *412*
McDevitt, S. C., 158, *172*, 228, *240*
McGhee, Z., 181, *186*
McGue, M., 242, *264*, 335, *336*
McGuffin, P., 42, *50*
McGuire, W. J., 372, *386*
McGuire, C. V., 372, *386*
McKeen, N. A., 174, *186*
McKenzie, J., 38, *50*
McPherson, L. M., 43, *49*
McWilliam, J., 44, *47*
Meehl, P. E., 347, *353*
Mengert, I. G., 180, *185*
Mershon, B., 177, *186*
Mervielde, I., 224, *225*, 371, *386*, 387, 394, *397*, 402, 407, *412*
Mey, J. Th. H., 294, 296, 297, *318*
Mikkelsen, E. J., 181, *186*
Milar, C. R., 180, *186*

Miller, P., 341, *352*
Miller, C., 347, 348, *352*
Millsap, R. E., 144, 146, 148, *149*
Mischel, W., 53, *68*, 153, *155*, 196, 200, *207*, 294, *317*
Mitchell, B. C., 335, *337*
Moane, G., 145, *149*
Modin, I., 44, *49*
Moffitt, T. E., 268, 269, 271, 272, 278, *290*, *291*
Monk, M. A., 181, *185*
Montag, I., 71, *88*
Montanelli, R. G., 327, *337*
Morrow, J., 210, 212, *220*
Mortimer, J. T., 143, 145, *150*
Moss, H. A., 148, *149*
Mosteller, F., 122, *137*
Mount, M. K., 106, *107*
Mulder, E., 95, *107*
Murphy, D. L., 42, 44, *50*, 66, *68*
Mushak, P., 180, *186*

N

Nakazato, H. S., 323, *336*
Nash S. C., 247, *263*
Neal, M. C., 260, *264*, 335, *338*, 343, *354*
Necowitz, L. B., 127, *137*
Nesselroade, J. R., 158, *172*, 339, *351*
Netter, P., 209, *219*
Newcomb, M. D., 122, *136*
Nias, D. K. B., 335, *338*, 343, *354*
Nichols, R. C., 342, 343, *353*
Nicholson, J. N., 176, *186*
Nisbett, R. E., 116, *136*
Nitz, K., 213, 214, *219*
Norman, W. T., 8, *35*, 54, *68*, 140, *150*, 189, *206*, 293, *317*, 323, *337*, 355, 358, 360, *366*, 372, *386*
Nunnally, J. C., 81, *90*, 327, *337*
Nuss, S. M., 239, *240*

O

O'Boyle, C. G., 198, *207*
O'Tauma, L. A., 180, 181, *186*
Oberklaid, F., 159, 162–164, *172*
Odbert, H. S., 8, *34*, 91, 92, *106*, 203, *205*
Ohyabu, Y., 180, *186*
Olweus, D., 274, *291*
Oreland, L., 44, *49*
Ostendorf, F., 2, *5*, 64, 69, 73, 74, 78, 84, *88*, *90*, 92, 93, 105, 106, *107*, *108*, 118, *135*, 323, 324, *336*, *337*, 355, *365*, 372, *386*, 387, *396*, *397*, 402, *412*
Owens, N. W., 180, *186*
Oyama, S., 211, *219*, 342, *353*
Ozer, D. J., 276, *290*, 294, 298, *317*, *318*

P

Padan-Belkin, E. 180, *186*
Pages, J., 122, *136*
Palermo, M., 158, *172*
Panskepp., J., 345, *353*
Panter, A. T., 118, 122, *137*
Parke, R., 273, *290*, 368, *370*
Parsons, J., 346, *352*
Partington, M. W., 180, *184*, *186*
Passini, F. T., 140, *150*
Patterson, G. R., 117, *135*
Patton, J. H., 66, *67*
Paulsen, K., 180, *186*
Peabody, D., 7, *35*, 104, 106, *108*, 293, *318*, 355, *366*, 375, *386*, 387, *397*, 402, *412*
Peake, P. K., 153, *155*, 196, 200, *207*
Pearce, J. M., 45, *50*
Pedersen, N. L., 339, *351*
Peidmont, R. L., 144, *150*
Peloquin, L. J., 42, *49*
Perry, D. G., 344, *354*
Perry, L. C., 344, *354*
Peterson, S. E., 196, 204, *206*
Peterson, D. R., 322, *322*, 356, 357, 360, *366*
Phelps, M. E., 204, *205*
Pincus, A. L., 8, *35*, 130, 132, *138*
Plomin, R., 60, 66, *67*, 70, 72, 73, 74, 78, 84, 85, 87, *88*, 152, *155*, 157, 168, *171*, 174, *184*, *185*, 190, *205*, 209, 211, 212, 213, 214, 217, *218*, *219*, 220, 222, 225, 227–234, 238, *239*, 247, 256, 258, 260, *263*, *264*, *265*, 282, 288, *291*, 325, 331, 332, *336*, 339, 341, 342, 344, 346, 350, *351*, *352*, *354*
Popping, R., 403, *412*
Posner, M. I., 195, 196, 204, *206*, *207*
Powell, T., 44, *47*
Powell, A., 113, *137*
Power, M., 210, *219*
Power, T., 214, *219*
Presley, R., 158–160, 162–165, 167, *172*, 320, 321, *322*, 368, *370*

Pressé, M. C., 175, *184*
Prior, M., 159, 162–164, *172*, 210, *219*
Pullis, M. E., 169, *172*

Q

Quay, H. C., 322, *322*, 356, 357, 360, *366*

R

Radke-Yarrow, M., 274, *291*
Ramsey-Klee, D. M., 247, *264*
Rapoport, J. L., 181, *186*
Rawlings, D., 43, *47*, *50*
Reed, J. D., 182, *186*
Rende, R., 209, *219*, 335, *336*
Renken, B., 350, *354*
Resnick, S., 210, 213, *219*
Reuman, D., 347, 348, *352*
Revelle, W., 116, *137*
Reznick, J. S., 262, *264*
Rheingold, H. L., 180, *186*
Rich, S., 258, *265*, 325, *338*
Richards, T. W., 180, *186*
Rieder, R. O., 128, *136*
Rieser-Danner, L. A., 134, *136*
Riksen-Walraven, J. M. A., 294, 296, 297, *318*
Robins, R. W., 267–269, 271, 272, 274, 277, 278, 289, *290*, *291*
Robinson, D. L., 45, *48*
Roeffen, J. T. W. M., 294, *318*
Rogers, C. R., 331, *337*
Romer, D., 116, *137*
Roosen, M. A., 294, *318*
Rose, B., 214, *219*
Rosenberg, M., 18, *35*
Rosenman, R. H., 343, *353*
Rosolack, T., 38, *49*
Rothbart, M. K., 152, 153, *155*, 157, 169, *172*, 174, *185*, *186*, 189–192, 194–198, 200, 203, 204, *205*, *206*, *207*, 210, 213, 216, *219*, 228, *240*, 242, 249, 250, 251, 259, *264*, *265*, 281, *291*, 324, 325, 326, 331, 332, *337*, *338*, 344, *354*, 395, *397*
Rothstein, M., 106, *108*
Routh, D. K., 180, 181, *186*
Rowe, D., 344, *354*
Royce, J. R., 66, *68*, 113, *137*
Roznowski, M., 127, *137*

Ruch, W., 70, 73, 74, 78, 80, 84, 86, *90*
Rudinger, G., 115, *137*
Rusalov, V. M., 66, *68*, 70, *90*
Rushton, J. P., 335, *338*, 343, *354*

S

Saccuzzo, D. P., 43, *50*
Salonen, R., 162–165, *172*
Sander, L. W., 180, *186*
Sanson, A., 159, 162–164, *172*
Sarna, S., 214, *219*
Saucier, G., 7, *35*, 104, *109*
Saudino, K. J., 174, 175, *184*, *186*, 209, *219*
Scafidi, F., 260, *263*
Scarr, S., 212, 214, *219*, 346, *354*
Sceery, A., 347, 350, *353*
Schalling, D., 44, *49*, *50*, 66, *68*
Scheier, M. F., 190, *205*
Schneider, P. A., 180, *185*
Schoggen, P., 217, *219*
Schroeder, S. R., 180, *186*
Schroeder, C. S., 180, 181, *186*
Schubert, D. L., 43, *50*
Schutter, N., 402, *412*
Schwartz, G. E., 200, *207*
Schwarzer, R., 113, *137*
Sears, R. R., 247, *265*
Segal, E. L., 258, *265*, 325, *338*
Seitz, M., 42, *49*
Serlin, R. C., 75, *90*
Sewell, J., 159, 162–164, *172*
Shagass, C., 43, *50*
Shiraishi, D., 324, *336*
Shoda, Y., 153, *155*, 196, 200, *207*
Siebenheller, E., 297, *318*
Siebenheller, F. A., 294, 296, 297, *318*
Siegler, I. C., 142, 145, *150*
Siever, L. J., 42, *50*
Simmons, R. G., 346, 347, *354*
Simon, H. A., 341, *354*
Simons, R. F., 42, *50*
Sirignano, S. W., 248, *265*
Skeels, H. M., 335, *338*
Skinner, M., 117, *135*
Skodak, M., 335, *338*
Slabach, E., 210, 212, *220*
Slade, P. D., 42, *49*, *50*
Slotboom, A., 375, 378, *386*
Smith, G. A., 43, *47*
Smith, A. A., 43, *50*

Smithson, P., 44, *47*
Sneath, P., 38, 40, *50*
Snidman, N., 210, 213, *219*, 254, *264*
Snow, M., 214, *219*
Sokal, R., 38, 40, *50*
Sortek, A. J., *50*
Spring, C., 181, *186*
Sprio, A., 158, *172*
Sroufe, L. A., 229, *240*, 350, *354*
Stafford, D., 214, *219*
Staub, E., 343, *354*
Steinberg, L., 347, *351*
Stenberg, C., 190, *205*
Stevenson, J., 260, *264*
Stevenson-Hinde, J., 242, *265*
Stouthamer-Loeber, M., 268, 269, 271, 272, 278, *290*, *291*
Strauman, T. J., 122, *137*
Streit, H., 180, *185*
Strelau, J., 66, *68*, 69, 70, 72, 73, 74, 78, 84, *90*, 209, *220*, 368, *370*, 371, *386*
Stringfield, S., 229, 231, *239*
Stripp, A., 210, *219*
Super, C., 212, *220*

T

Takemoto-Chock, N. K., 69, *89*, 91, *107*, 202, *205*, 280, *290*, 323, 326, 327, *336*, 339, 340, *352*, 355, 358, *365*, 371, *385*
Talwar, 213, 214, *219*
Tanaka, J. S., 118, 122, 130, *137*
Tanskanen, A., 162, 163, 164, 165, *172*
Tatsuoka, M. M., 40, *48*, 283, *290*
Teglasi, H., 159, 163, 164, *172*
Tellegen, A., 191, 195, 200, *207*, 242, 248, 249, 251, 258, *264*, *265*, 325, 335, *338*
Teta, P., 60, 61, 62, 63
Tett, R. P., 106, *109*
Thobin, A., 214, *219*
Thomas, A., 66, *68*, 88, *90*, 151, *155*, 157, 166, *172*, 174, *185*, *186*, 190, *207*, 228, 229, 230, *240*, 247, *263*, *264*, *265*, 320, *322*, 325, 331, *338*, 341, 344, *351*, 368, *370*, 372, *386*
Thompson, R., 214, *220*
Thorndike, R. M., 122, *137*
Thornquist, M., 56, *68*, 72, *90*
Thurstone, T. G., 121, *137*
Thurstone, L. L., 118, 121, *137*
Tipper, S. P., 44, *50*

Tomlinson-Keasey, C., 273, *290*
Toner, I. J., 180, *186*
Tooby, J., 340, *354*
Trapnell, P. D., 1, 2, 3, *5*, 7, 8, *35*, 93, *109*, 128, *137*, 231, *240*, 323, *338*, 339, *354*
Treffers, Ph. D. A., 401, *412*
Trull, T. J., 118, *138*
Tsoi, M. M., 176, *186*
Tuason, V. B., 42, *49*
Tubman, J. G., 346, *353*
Tucker, J. R., 44, *49*, 117, 118, 120, 121, 133, *137*
Tukey, J. W., 122, *137*
Tupes, E. C., 8, *35*, 323, *338*, 355, 358, 360, *366*
Turnure, C., 180, *186*

U

Unterweger, E., 74, *90*

V

Vaillant, G. E., 142, 145, *150*
Valentine, B. H., 42, *49*
van Aken, M. A. G., 294, 297, *316*, *317*, *318*
van Brink, P. W. M., 294, 296, 297, *318*
van Busschbach, A., 297, *318*
Van der Ende, J., 81, *88*
Van der Kamp, L., 153, *155*
van der Veer, R., 297, *318*
Van Heck, G. L., 2, *5*, 346, *354*
Van Huss, W. D., 181, *187*
Van IJzendoorn, M. H., 294, 297, *318*
Van Kammen, W., 268, *291*
van Lieshout, C. F. M., 294, 296, 297, *318*
van Seyen, E. T. J., 294, *318*
van Vliet-visser, S., 297, *318*
Vaucouleurs, G. de, 40, *50*
Vaughn, B. E., 294, *318*
Vega-Lahr, N., 260, *263*
Velicer, W. F., 77, 84, *90*, 160, 162, 163, 165, 169, *171*, 327, *338*
Venables, P., 43, 45, *50*, *51*
Victor, J. B., 181, *187*, 356, *365*, *366*
Von Eye, A., 134, *137*

AUTHOR INDEX

W

Wachs, T. D., 210–212, 214, 215, 217, *219*, 220
Wainer, H., 177, *187*
Walker, R. N., 181, *187*
Waller, N. G., 200, *207*, 249, 251, *265*
Walton, M. D., 180, *186*
Waltz, J., 401, *412*
Wampler, K., 339, 343, *352*
Ward, D., 140, *149*, 268, 276, *290*, 348, *352*
Waschull, S., 346, *352*
Waterman, A. S., 142, 145, *150*
Waters, E., 229, 231, *240*, 294, *318*
Watson, D., 191, 195, *207*, 249, *265*
Weber, R. A., 260, *265*
Weinberger, J., 343, *353*
Weinberger, D. A., 199, 200, *207*
Weiner, I., 45, *51*
Weingartner, H., 181, *186*
Weiss, D. J., 122, *137*
Weiss, A. P., 180, *185*
Welsh, K. A., 142, *150*
Werner, H., 282, *291*
Wessel, J. A., 181, *187*
West, S. G., 116, *136*, *138*, 339, 343, *354*
Westerman, M. A., 122, *137*
Wetzler, S., 122, *137*
Whitbourne, S. K., 142, 145, *150*
White, R. W., 332, 334, *338*
White, C. T., 43, *48*
Widaman, K. F., 118, *138*, 273, *290*
Widiger, T. A., 118, *138*
Wiersma, E., 152, *155*
Wigfield, A., 347, 348, *352*
Wiggins, J. S., 1, 2, 3, *5*, 7, 8, *35*, 54, *68*, 93, 94, 106, *109*, 128, 130, 132, *137*, *138*, 223, *225*, 231, *240*, 287, *291*, 323, 334, *338*, 339, 340, *354*
Wilcox, K. J., 258, *265*, 325, *338*
Willerman, L, 209, *219*

Williams, R. B., 145, *150*
Williams, J. P., 180, *185*
Williams, E. J., 180, *185*
Wilson, R. S., 214, *219*, 239, *240*
Wilson, G. D., 46, *51*
Winborne, W. C., 118, 122, *137*
Windle, M., 70, 74, 78, 84, 85, *90*, 134, *138*, 160–163, 165, 167, 168, *172*, 382, *386*
Windmiller, M., 159, 162–164, 167, 169, *172*
Winer, B. J., 114, *138*
Wink, P., 145, 148, *149*
Wippman, J., 229, *240*
Wisenbaker, J., 162–165, *172*
Wolk, S., 239, *240*
Woolf, P., 152, *155*

Y

Yasamy, M. T., 42, *51*
Ye, R. M., 153, *155*, 192, *205*
Yee, D., 347, 348, *352*
Yellin, A. M., 181, *186*
Young, P. T., 332, *338*

Z

Zahn, T. P., 181, *186*
Zalstein, N., 45, *50*
Zeanah, C. H., 239, *240*
Zhang, Y., 153, *155*
Ziaie, H., 198, *207*
Zimmerman, W. S., 53, *68*, 146, *149*, 325, *337*
Zonderman, A. B., 145, *150*
Zuckerman, M., 38, 44, 46, *51*, 54–66, *68*, 72, 74, 79, 84–87, *90*, 92, 105, *109*, 177, *187*, 191, 201, *207*
Zwan-Woudstra, H., 297, *318*
Zwick, W. R., 77, *90*, 327, *338*

SUBJECT INDEX

A

Achievement measurement in childhood
    Iowa Tests of Basic Skills, 360
Activity level, 161–165
    developmental trajectory, 177–182
    in infancy, 169–170, 174–175
    in adulthood, 176–177
    relation to
        Big 5, 169–170
        extraversion, 176
        social behavior, 175
Adaptability, 166–167
    relation to big 5, 170
Age
    effects on big 5, 380–381, 394–395, 404–405
    factor generality across, 310–311
    relation to natural language descriptions of teachers, 394–395
Agreeableness
    biological dispositions
        self-regulation of excitation, 344–345
        neuroregulatory amines, 345
    development of, 342–349
    importance of, 340–341
    problems for future research, 349–350
    social interaction, 346–349

    attachment, 346–347
Anxiety systems, *see* Neuroticism
Attention, 198–199
    related to
        conscientiousness, 200
        psychoticism, 43–44

B

Behavior Problem Measures in Childhood
    Preschool Behavior Questionnaire, 229
    Revised Behavior Problem Checklist, 356, 357, 360
    Child Behavior Checklist, 356, 357
Big 5
    alternative models of, 55–59
    AB5C circumplex model, 94–104
    dimensions of, *see* Structure
    generality of, 7
    higher order factors of, 329–331
    history of, 8, 91–92, 323–324, 355–356, 387
    in childhood, 326–329, 355–357
    measurement in adolescence, *see* California Child Q-Set
    measurement in adulthood, *see* Personality measurement, adult

Big 5 *(cont.)*
    measurement in childhood, *see* Hawaii
        Scales for Judging Behavior
    relation to
        adolescent school performance, 275–276
        adolescent delinquent behavior, 276
        adolescent IQ, 276
        age, 380–381, 394–395, 404–405
        childhood achievement, 360–364
        childhood behavior problems, 360–365,
            403–409
        childhood diagnosis, 407–409
        childhood temperament, 244–246
        ego control/resilience, 273–275
        factors of California Child Q-Set, 298–303
        natural language descriptors, 375–378
        race, 276
        SES, 276
        teacher-based description, 392–395
        temperament, 169–170
    structure, 1–4, 8–12, 31–33, 53–54, 123–127,
            231–232, 267–268, 339–350, 356, 371
        compared with Eysenck's PEN model,
            12–24, 31–33, 38, 92
            Cattell's 16PF, 25–27
            Tellegen's Pos/Neg Affect, 28–31
            Zuckerman model, 55–64
        external analysis of, 112
        internal analysis of, 111–113
Biological Rhythmicity, 168–169
    relation to Big 5, 170

C

Canonical analysis, 121

E

Effortful control, 194–197
    relation to
        agreeableness, 200–202
        anxiety, 198–200
        approach, 197–198
        personality development, 197–202
        self-regulation, 195
Ego
    control/resilience, 273–275
Etic-Emic distinction in personality
    measurement, 368, 372

Extraversion, 191–194

F

Factor analysis
    interbattery analysis, 120–127
    invariance of structure, 117–133, 140–142
    modeling personality structure, 113–114
    multiple measurement designs, 115
    representative crossed designs, 114–115
Free-response data, *see* Natural language based
    measurement

G

Gender
    differences in natural language descriptors,
        378–379, 404–405
    factor generality across, 310
Genetics
    relation to parent-child resemblance, 247,
        257–259
    relation to personality, 243–244
    relation to temperament, 335, 342–344
Goldberg's synonym clusters, 9–12
    relation to
        Eysenck's PEN model, 12–24
        Cattell's Model, 25–27
        Tellegen's MPQ factors, 28–30

I

Impulsive Unsocialized Sensation Seeking
    (ImpUSS), 56–57
Inhibition, 167–168
    relation to big 5, 170

N

Natural language based measurement,
        368–369, 388
    advantages of, 382
    coding of, 373–385, 389, 401–403
        AB5C classification, 389–396
    descriptions of problem behaviors, 382–384,
        400–412

SUBJECT INDEX

diagnosis, used in, 407–409
  teacher based, 388–396
  parent based, 400–411
Negative Emotionality, 165
  relation to Big 5, 170
NEO-PI
  comparison to Goldberg's Big 5 model, 123–127
  origins, 55
  stability in
    young adults, 140–147
    older adults, 147–148
  structure of, 76–84, 123–133
Neuroticism, 194–195

P

PEN model of adult personality, 38–41
  relation to
    Goldberg's synonym clusters, 12–16
    McCrae and Costa NEO-PI, 16
    Big 5, 12–24
Personality
  dimensions of in childhood, 371
Personality measurement, adolescent, 268–273
Personality measurement, adult, 242–243
  Goldberg's Inventory, 242–243
  Neo-Personality Inventory, 243
  Tellegen's Multidimensional Personality Questionnaire, 248
  Zuckerman-Kulhman Personality Questionnaire, 59–64
Personality measurement, child
  California Child Q-Set, 268–269
    factor structure of, 278–282, 296–316
    error variance of, 283–289
  Dutch version (Nijmegen California Child Q-Set), 293, 296
  Hawaii Scales for Judging Behavior, 358–359
Personality, twin similarity, 243–244
Pittsburgh Youth Study, 268
Psychopathology, child
  models of, 356–357
Psychoticism
  nomothetic network, 39–48
  relation to
    agreeableness and conscientiousness, 41–42

HLA B27, 42
hallucination, 42
eyetracking, 42
attentional processes, 43–44
latent inhibition, 45–47

S

Sex, *see* Gender
Source of ratings
  factorial generality across, 311–313, 326
Surgency, *see* Extraversion

T

Task persistence, 166
  relation to big 5, 170
Teacher ratings of personality
  factor comparison to parent ratings, 304–310, 311–313, 319
  factor structure of, 326–329
  validity of, 320
Temperament, adult
  relation to Big 5, 73–74
  factor structure, 75–88
Temperament, childhood
  prediction of, 233–235
  dimensions (*see* structure of)
Temperament, defined, 227, 241–242, 324–325
  compared with personality, 69–70, 86–88
Temperament, infant (see activity level, adaptability, agreeableness, biological rhythmicity, inhibition, negative emotionality), 228, 230
  dimensions (*see* structure of)
  relation to
    childhood temperament, 232–234
    ego strength/effectance, 235
    behavior problems, 235
    big 5, 170, 209–218, 235–238, 244–248, 331–334
    parental personality, 250–259
Temperament measurement
  Baby Behavior Questionnaire, 228–230
  Dimensions of Temperament Scale-Revised, 76–80
  EASI-III Temperament Survey, 76–80, 229–230

reliability, 76
Rothbart Infant Behavior Questionnaire, 249
Rothbart Children's Behavior Questionnaire, 192–194, 244–245
stability of, 210–211
Strelau Temperament Inventory, 76–80
Toddler Behavior Questionnaire, 228–230
Uppsala Longitudinal Study, 228–231
Temperament structure (see activity level, adaptability, biological rhythmicity, inhibition, negative emotionality, task persistence), 70–71, 77–79, 81–82, 157–169, 229–231
compared to personality structure, 71–73, 215–218

Z

Zygosity, measurement, 242